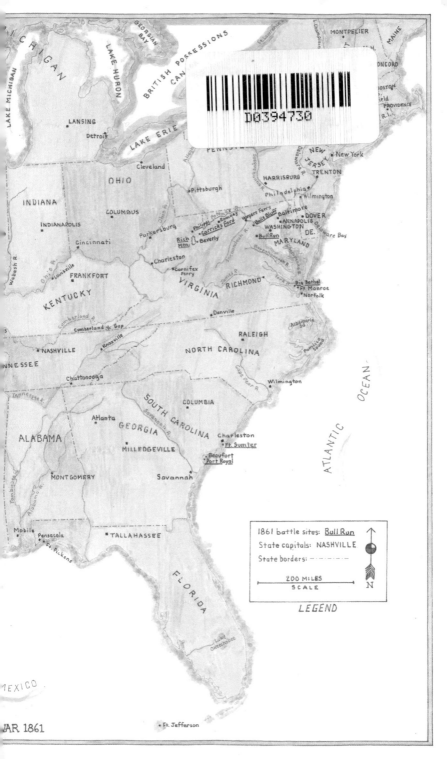

THE CIVIL WAR

THE FIRST YEAR

# THE CIVIL WAR

## THE FIRST YEAR TOLD
## BY THOSE WHO LIVED IT

*Edited by*
*Brooks D. Simpson*
*Stephen W. Sears*
*Aaron Sheehan-Dean*

THE LIBRARY OF AMERICA

The paper used in this publication meets the
minimum requirements of the American National Standard for
Information Sciences–Permanence of Paper for Printed
Library Materials, ANSI Z39.48–1984.

Distributed to the trade in the United States
by Penguin Group (USA) Inc.
and in Canada by Penguin Books Canada Ltd.

Library of Congress Control Number: 2010931718
ISBN 978-1-59853-088-9

———

First Printing
The Library of America—212

Manufactured in the United States of America

*The Civil War:*
*The First Year Told by Those Who Lived It*
is published with support from

# THE ANDREW W. MELLON FOUNDATION

and

# THE NATIONAL ENDOWMENT
# FOR THE HUMANITIES

# Contents

# Preface

"Has there ever been another historical crisis of the magnitude of 1861–65 in which so many people were so articulate?"
—Edmund Wilson

This Library of America volume is the first in a four-volume series bringing together memorable and significant writing by participants in the American Civil War. Each volume in the series covers approximately one year of the conflict, from the election of Abraham Lincoln in November 1860 to the end of the war in the spring of 1865, and presents a chronological selection of documents from the broadest possible range of authoritative sources—diaries, letters, speeches, military reports, newspaper articles, memoirs, poems, and public papers. Drawing upon an immense and unique body of American writing, the series offers a narrative of the war years that encompasses military and political events and their social and personal reverberations. Created by persons of every class and condition, the writing included here captures the American nation and the American language in the crucial period of their modern formation. Selections have been chosen for their historical significance, their literary quality, and their narrative energy, and are printed from the best available sources. The goal has been to shape a narrative that is both broad and balanced in scope, while at the same time doing justice to the number and diversity of voices and perspectives preserved for us in the writing of the era.

# Introduction

As Abraham Lincoln looked out from the East Portico of the United States Capitol on March 4, 1865, he saw assembled before him a throng of Americans, each of whom had been marked in some way by nearly four long years of war. It had been precisely four years since he had stood in the same place and expressed his hope that somehow war could be avoided. Now he recalled that moment as he delivered his Second Inaugural Address. "All dreaded it—all sought to avert it," he declared. Yet that had not been enough. "Both parties deprecated war; but one of them would *make* war rather than let the nation survive; and the other would *accept* war rather than let it perish. And the war came."

The letters, diaries, speeches, poems, memoirs, and other documents collected in this volume help us understand how and why that war came, and how Americans, North and South, white and black, male and female, experienced secession and armed conflict as it moved across the land. Few of them doubted that slavery was, as Lincoln said in his Second Inaugural, "somehow, the cause of the war." Yet, as the President also recalled, no one "expected for the war, the magnitude, or the duration, which it has already attained." Most Americans "looked for an easier triumph, and a result less fundamental and astounding" than what eventually happened, including the destruction of slavery. It is often difficult for readers today to grasp just how revolutionary and astonishing the Civil War was to those who experienced it, and how events that we may believe to have been practically inevitable were at best barely conceivable to many Americans at the time. By reading what people wrote as history unfolded before them, we can gain a better appreciation for what people thought was at stake, and for what the war was all about.

In the same address Lincoln spoke of "the bond-man's two hundred and fifty years of unrequited toil." The origins of the Civil War can indeed be traced back to 1619 and the beginnings of African slavery in Virginia, and then forward through the compromises regarding slavery adopted by the Constitutional Convention, the spread of cotton cultivation throughout the Deep South, the Missouri Compromise of 1820 that prohibited slavery in most of the Louisiana Purchase territory, and the emergence of the abolitionist movement in the 1830s. With the outbreak of the U.S.-Mexican War in 1846, the pace of events quickened, as the prospect of acquiring new territory revived the sectional controversy over the expansion of slavery. An attempt by Henry Clay—the seventy-three-year-old Kentucky Whig celebrated for his role in passing the Missouri Compromise—to fashion a new compromise in 1850 faltered when his "Omnibus Bill" failed to win Senate approval. It fell to a younger man, the ambitious Illinois Democrat Stephen A. Douglas, to forge two different sectionally-based coalitions, one to pass antislavery measures—the admission of California as a free state, the abolition of the slave trade in the District of Columbia—and another to adopt proslavery ones—a new, stronger fugitive slave law, the organization of New Mexico and Utah as territories where slavery would be permitted. None of these measures were supported by a majority of both Northern and Southern senators and representatives, and what became known as the "Compromise of 1850" was more of an uneasy truce.

In 1854 Stephen A. Douglas ended the truce he had helped fashion four years earlier. Hoping to win Southern support for the construction of a transcontinental railroad along a northern route, Douglas won passage of the Kansas-Nebraska Act, which repealed the Missouri Compromise and allowed the question of whether slavery would be permitted in the two newly-organized territories to be decided by their voters. Over the next two years, the passage of the act led to armed conflict in Kansas, the bloody caning of Charles Sumner on the Senate floor, the formation of the Republican Party, and the resurgence of the political career of Abraham Lincoln.

Any expectation that the sectional controversy would be resolved by the Supreme Court ended with the furor aroused in 1857 by the *Dred Scott* decision, which held that the basic principle of the Republican Party—that Congress could exclude slavery from the territories—was unconstitutional. An attempt later in the year to fraudulently impose a proslavery state constitution on Kansas caused Douglas to break with the Southern wing of his party. By 1859 many Southern Democrats were demanding the adoption of a federal slave code, calling for the reopening of the African slave trade, and contemplating secession if a "Black Republican" won the presidency in 1860. The movement toward disunion was hastened by John Brown's failed raid on the federal armory at Harpers Ferry, Virginia, in October 1859. In the immediate aftermath of the incident, white Southerners were fearful that antislavery agitation would soon lead to even bloodier acts of rebellion. Their fear turned to anger when many prominent Northerners praised Brown—Ralph Waldo Emerson declared that he would "make the gallows as glorious as the cross"—and mourned his execution.

It is hardly surprising that this convulsive political atmosphere produced a presidential campaign with four candidates. The Democrats met in April in Charleston, South Carolina, but became hopelessly deadlocked because of Southern opposition to the candidacy of Stephen A. Douglas. After adjourning for six weeks, they reconvened in Baltimore and split along sectional lines, with Northern delegates nominating Douglas and Southerners choosing Vice President John Breckinridge of Kentucky as their candidate. In May the Constitutional Union Party, founded mainly by conservative Whigs from the border states, met in Baltimore and nominated John Bell, a Unionist slaveholder from Tennessee. Later that month the Republicans gathered in Chicago, where Senator William H. Seward of New York, the presumed front-runner for the nomination, was defeated on the third ballot by Abraham Lincoln, in part because many delegates believed Lincoln would have greater appeal to voters in Pennsylvania and the lower Midwest. While Douglas broke with tradition and actively campaigned throughout the country, Lincoln stayed close to Springfield and made no formal speeches.

The election results on November 6 starkly demonstrated the extent of the sectional divide. Breckinridge carried all of the slave states except for Virginia, Kentucky, and Tennessee, which went for Bell, and Missouri, which was won by Douglas. With the exception of New Jersey, whose electoral votes were split between Lincoln and Douglas, Lincoln carried all of the free states. In the end he won a majority of 180 out of 303 electoral votes while receiving 40 percent of the popular vote. For the first time the United States had elected an openly antislavery president from an avowedly antislavery party.

As news of the Republican victory spread across the land, Americans began wondering what would happen next. Would South Carolina secede, and if it did, would the other states from the Deep South immediately follow, or wait for Lincoln's inauguration? Was another compromise, or truce, still possible? How would the North respond to disunion? By February 1861 seven Southern states had seceded and formed the Confederate States of America. Their actions raised new questions and new uncertainties. What would the border states and the upper South do? Would the new Lincoln administration attempt to resupply Fort Sumter, one of the few federal military installations that had not fallen into the hands of the secessionists? Once the Confederate bombardment of Sumter brought war to the sundered nation, people throughout the land asked how long would the war last, how would it end, and what would be its consequences?

We can recapture the uncertainties and the expectations of the period by reading what people thought and said as they witnessed what was happening around them. Few observers anticipated a long or bloody conflict, although one West Point graduate, who had since fallen on hard times and was now clerking in his father's general store, predicted "the doom of Slavery." At the time he penned those words in April 1861, Ulysses S. Grant had no idea that he might be instrumental in the demise of the "peculiar institution." The first nine months of the war would see relatively few battles compared to the years that followed. Some were Confederate victories—First Manassas, Wilson's Creek, Ball's Bluff—and some were Union ones—Rich Mountain, Belmont, Port Royal. Contrary to many predictions, the war would not be suddenly decided by one or two battles. Both sides needed time to raise, organize, and train troops, and to find regimental officers and generals capable of leading them. By January 1862 the Union had kept the crucial border states of Maryland, Kentucky, and Missouri from joining the Confederacy, but was still searching for a strategy that would successfully carry the war into the South. No one knew how much longer the conflict would last, and given that so few people had expected ever to see what had already happened since the election of November 1860, it would have been foolhardy for anyone to have tried to predict what would happen next.

# Charleston Mercury: What Shall the South Carolina Legislature Do?

## November 3, 1860

Three days before the 1860 presidential election, this editorial appeared in the *Charleston Mercury*, a newspaper owned by Robert Barnwell Rhett and edited by his son, Robert Barnwell Rhett Jr. The elder Rhett had advocated secession during the 1850 sectional crisis, and in a speech delivered on July 4, 1859 declared that the South should secede if a Republican president was elected in 1860. In its editorial anticipating a Republican victory, the *Mercury* addressed a question that divided many secessionists in 1860: should the slaveholding states secede individually by "separate action," or first hold a general convention and then secede together by "co-operative action." Circumstances favored immediate action in South Carolina, where the legislature would meet on November 5 to choose presidential electors (in 1860 South Carolina was the only state that chose electors by this method). After learning of Lincoln's victory, the legislature called for the election of a state convention that would meet on January 15, 1861.

---

THE ISSUE before the country is the extinction of slavery. No man of common sense, who has observed the progress of events, and who is not prepared to surrender the institution, with the safety and independence of the South, can doubt that the time for action has come—now or never. The Southern States are now in the crisis of their fate; and, if we read aright the signs of the times, nothing is needed for our deliverance, but that the ball of revolution be set in motion. There is sufficient readiness among the people to make it entirely successful. Co-operation will follow the action of any State. The example of a forward movement only is requisite to unite Southern States in a common cause. Under these circumstances, the Legislature of South Carolina is about to meet. It happens to assemble in advance of the Legislature of any other State. Being in session at this momentous juncture—the Legislature of that State which is most united in the policy of freeing the South from Black Republican domination—the eyes of the whole country, and most especially of the resistance party of the Southern States, is intently turned upon the conduct of this body. We have innumerable assurances that the men of action in each and all of the Southern States, earnestly desire South Carolina to exhibit promptitude and decision in this conjuncture. Other States are torn and divided, to a greater or less extent, by old party issues. South Carolina alone is not. Any practical move would enable the people of other States to rise above their past divisions, and lock shields on the broad ground of Southern security. The course of our Legislature will either greatly stimulate and strengthen, or unnerve the resistance elements of the whole South. A Convention is the point to which their attention will be chiefly directed.

The question of calling a Convention by our Legislature, does not necessarily involve the question of separate or co-operative action. That is a question for the Convention when it assembles, under the circumstances which shall exist when it assembles. All desire the action of as many Southern States as possible, for the formation of a Southern Confederacy. But each should not delay and wait on the other. As these States are separate sovereignties, each must act separately; and whether one or the other acts first or last, we suppose is of no sort of consequence. What is really essential is this—that by the action of one or more States, there shall be the *reasonable probability* that a Southern Confederacy will be formed. We say *probability*,—because there is no certainty in the future of human affairs; and in the position in which the South will be placed by the election of an Abolitionist white man as President of the United States, and an Abolitionist colored man as Vice-President of the United States, we should not hesitate, somewhat to venture. The existence of slavery is at stake. The evils of submission are too terrible for us to risk them, from vague fears of failure, or a jealous distrust of our sister Cotton States. We think, therefore, that the approaching Legislature should provide for the assembling of a Convention of the people of South Carolina, as soon as it is ascertained that

Messrs. LINCOLN and HAMLIN will have a majority in the Electoral Colleges for President and Vice-President of the United States. The only point of difficulty is as *to the time when the Convention shall assemble.* In our judgment, it should assemble *at the earliest possible time* consistent with the opportunity for co-operative action of other Southern States, which may, like ourselves, be determined not to submit to Black Republican domination at Washington. Delay is fatal; while our move will retard no willing State from co-operation. South Carolina, as a sovereign State, is bound to protect her people, but she should so act as to give the other Southern States the opportunity of joining in this policy. The Governors of Alabama, Mississippi and Georgia can act simultaneously. With this qualification, *the earliest time is the best*, for the following reasons:

1. Our great agricultural staples are going to market. The sooner we act, the more of these staples we will have on hand, to control the conduct of the people of the North and of foreign nations, to secure a peaceful result for our deliverance. Thousands at the North, and millions in Europe, need our Cotton to keep their looms in operation. Let us act, before we have parted with our agricultural productions for the season.

2. The commercial and financial interests of the South require that we should act speedily in settling our relations towards the North. Suspense is embarrassment and loss. Decision, with separation, will speedily open new sources of wealth and prosperity, and relieve the finances of the South through the establishment of new channels. In all changes of Government, respect should be had to all classes of the people, and the least possible loss be inflicted on any.

3. The moral effect of promptitude will be immense. Delay will dispirit our friends, and inspire confidence in our enemies. The evils against which we are to provide are not the growth of yesterday. They have been gathering head for thirty years. We have tried, again and again, to avert them by compromise and submission. Submission has failed to avert them; and wise, prompt and resolute action is our last and only course for safety.

4. Black Republican rule at Washington will not commence until the 4th of March next—four short months. Before that time all that South Carolina or the other Southern States

intend to do, should be done. The settlement of our relations towards the General Government, in consequence of our measures of protection, should be completed during the existing Administration.

5. It is exceedingly important, also, that our measures should be laid as soon as possible before *the present Congress.* The secession of one or more States from the Union must be communicated to the President of the United States. He has done all he could to arrest the sectional madness of the North. He knows that we are wronged and endangered by Black Republican ascendancy, and he will not, we have a right to suppose, lend himself to carry out their bloody policy.

6. By communication from the President of the United States, as well as by the withdrawal from Congress of the members of the seceding States, the question of the right of a State to secede from the Union, with the question of a Force Bill, must arise in Congress for action. The Representatives from the other Southern States will most probably be forced either to continue members of a body which orders the sword to be drawn against the seceding States, or they must leave it. They will most probably leave it; and thus the South will be brought together by action in Congress, even though they fail to co-operate at once by their State authorities. It will not be wise to pretermit either of these instrumentalities for the union and co-action of the Southern States; but, it is our opinion, that Congress is the best place to unite them. By prompt action, and through the question of secession in Congress, the agitations which must ensue, will not only tend to unite the Southern members of Congress, but to unite and stimulate State action in the States they represent.

We conclude, therefore, by urging the Legislature about to assemble, to provide for the calling a Convention, as soon as it is ascertained that Messrs. LINCOLN and HAMLIN have the majority in the Electoral Colleges for President and Vice-President of the United States; and that this Convention shall assemble at the earliest day practicable, consistent with the knowledge of our course by our sister Southern States. To this end we would respectfully suggest Nov. 22d and 23d as the day of election, and December 15th as the time of assembling the Convention of the people of South Carolina.

# John G. Nicolay: Memoranda Regarding Abraham Lincoln

November 5-6, 1860

The day before the election, Abraham Lincoln met in Springfield, Illinois, with Henry S. Sanford, a Northern diplomat and businessman who sought to warn Lincoln about the growing agitation in the South. Their conversation was recorded in a memorandum written by John G. Nicolay, a former journalist and state government clerk who had become Lincoln's personal secretary earlier in the year. Nicolay also wrote a memorandum describing Lincoln's visit to the polls on election day.

---

SANFORD Called to see—if the alarms of many persons might not by some means be relieved—the alarms from the South are seriously affecting our work—am myself largely interested—get no orders from the South—

—reassure the men honestly alarmed

—Lincoln—"There are no such men." have thought much about it—it is the trick by which the South breaks down every Northern man—I would go to Washington without the support of the men who supported me and were my friends before election. I would be as powerless as a block of buckeye wood—

(The man still insisted.)

L.—The honest man (you are talking of honest men) will look at our platform and what I have said—there they will find everything I could now say or which they would ask me to say. —all I could say would be but repetition. Having told them all these things ten times already would they believe the eleventh declaration?

Let us be practical—there are many general terms afloat such as 'conservatism'—'enforcement of the irrepressible conflict at the point of the bayonet'—'hostility to the South &c'—all of which mean nothing without definition. What then could I say to allay their fears, if they will not define what particular act or acts they fear from me or my friends?

(gentleman hands him letters)

"recognize them as a sett of liars and knaves who signed that statement about Seward last year."

(gentleman insists there are other names on the list.) (Mr. L. although he had talked quite good-naturedly before evidently betrayed a little feeling at this part of the conversation.)

(after reading the letter) "Well after reading it, it is about what I expected to find it. (laughing)

"it annoyed me a little to hear that gang of men called respectable. their conduct a year ago was a disgrace to any civilized man."

(the gentleman suggested that the south were making armed preparations, &c.)

L. The North does not fear invasion from the Sl S— and we of the North certainly have no desire and never had to invade the South.

I am rather pleased at the idea that the South is making some 'preparation.' They have talked about a Black Republican Victory until the——

Gen. Have we backed this time?

L. "That is what I am pressed to do now."

"If I shall begin to yield to these threats—If I begin dallying with them, the men who have elected me, if I shall be elected, would give me up before my inauguration—and the South seeing it, would deliberately kick me out."—

If (my friends) should desire me to repeat anything I have before said, I should have no objection to do so. If they required me to say something I had not yet said, I should either do so *or get out of the way.*

If I should be elected the first duty to the Country would be to stand by the men who elected me.

*November 5, 1860*

———

It is Election day—and Hon. A Lincoln has just been over to vote. The Court House steps, (in which building the polls were held,) were thronged with People, who welcomed him with immense cheering, and followed him in dense numbers along the hall and up stairs into the Court room, which was also crowded. Here the applause became absolutely deafening, and from the time he entered the room and until he cast his vote and again left it, there was wild huzzaing, waving of hats, and all sorts of demonstrations of applause,—rendering all other noises insignificant & futile.

*November 6, 1860*

# New-York Daily Tribune: Going to Go

November 9, 1860

The *Tribune*, founded and edited by Horace Greeley, was one of the most widely read and influential Republican newspapers in the country. Greeley wrote this editorial responding to the possibility of secession and published it three days after the election. It appeared at a time when many Northerners were uncertain as to whether the states in the lower South would actually leave the Union, or were merely using the threat of secession to extract new concessions regarding slavery. Greeley's apparent willingness to allow the Cotton States to "go in peace" drew criticism from those who found the prospect of disunion unacceptable.

––––––––––

THE PEOPLE of the United States have indicated, according to the forms prescribed by the Constitution, their desire that Abraham Lincoln of Illinois shall be their next President, and Hannibal Hamlin of Maine their Vice-President. A very large plurality of the popular vote has been cast for them, and a decided majority of Electors chosen who will undoubtedly vote for and elect them on the first Wednesday in December next. The electoral votes will be formally sealed up and forwarded to Washington, there to be opened and counted, on a given day in February next, in the presence of both Houses of Congress; and it will then be the duty of Mr. John C. Breckinridge, as President of the Senate, to declare Lincoln and Hamlin duly elected President and Vice-President of these United States.

Some people do not like this, as is very natural. Dogberry discovered, a good while ago, that "When two ride a horse, one must ride behind." That is not generally deemed the preferable seat; but the rule remains unaffected by that circumstance. We know how to sympathize with the defeated; for we remember how *we* felt when Adams was defeated; and Clay; and Scott; and Fremont. It is decidedly pleasanter to be on the

8

winning side, especially when—as now—it happens also to be the right side.

We sympathize with the afflicted; but we cannot recommend them to do anything desperate. What is the use? They are beaten now; they may triumph next time: in fact, they have generally had their own way: had they been subjected to the discipline of adversity as often as we have, they would probably bear it with more philosophy, and deport themselves more befittingly. We live to learn: and one of the most difficult acquirements is that of meeting reverses with graceful fortitude.

The telegraph informs us that most of the Cotton States are meditating a withdrawal from the Union because of Lincoln's election. Very well: they have a right to meditate, and meditation is a profitable employment of leisure. We have a chronic, invincible disbelief in Disunion as a remedy for either Northern or Southern grievances. We cannot perceive any necessary relation between the alleged disease and this ultra-heroic remedy: still, we say, if anybody sees fit to meditate Disunion, let them do so unmolested. That was a base and hypocritic row that the House once raised, at Southern dictation, about the ears of John Quincy Adams, because he presented a petition for the dissolution of the Union. The petitioner had a right to make the request; it was the Member's duty to present it. And now, if the Cotton States consider the value of the Union debatable, we maintain their perfect right to discuss it. Nay: we hold with Jefferson to the inalienable right of communities to alter or abolish forms of government that have become oppressive or injurious; and if the Cotton States shall become satisfied that they can do better out of the Union than in it, we insist on letting them go in peace. The right to secede may be a revolutionary one, but it exists nevertheless; and we do not see how one party can have a right to do what another party has a right to prevent. We must ever resist the asserted right of any State to remain in the Union and nullify or defy the laws thereof; to withdraw from the Union is quite another matter. And whenever a considerable section of our Union shall deliberately resolve to go out, we shall resist all coercive measures designed to keep it in. We hope never to live in a republic whereof one section is pinned to the residue by bayonets.

But while we thus uphold the practical liberty if not the

abstract right of secession, we must insist that the step be taken, if it ever shall be, with the deliberation and gravity befitting so momentous an issue. Let ample time be given for reflection; let the subject be fully canvassed before the people; and let a popular vote be taken in every case before secession is decreed. Let the people be told just why they are urged to break up the confederation; let them have both sides of the question fully presented; let them reflect, deliberate, then vote; and let the act of secession be the echo of an unmistakable popular fiat. A judgment thus rendered, a demand for separation so backed, would either be acquiesced in without the effusion of blood, or those who rushed upon carnage to defy and defeat it would place themselves clearly in the wrong.

The measures now being inaugurated in the Cotton States with a view (apparently) to Secession, seem to us destitute of gravity and legitimate force. They bear the unmistakable impress of haste—of passion—of distrust of the popular judgment. They seem clearly intended to precipitate the South into rebellion before the baselessness of the clamors which have misled and excited her can be ascertained by the great body of her people. We trust that they will be confronted with calmness, with dignity, and with unwavering trust in the inherent strength of the Union and the loyalty of the American People.

# Jefferson Davis to Robert Barnwell Rhett Jr.

In a private letter to the editor of the *Charleston Mercury*, Senator Jefferson Davis of Mississippi expressed caution about the prospects for secession by separate state action. On November 10, the day Davis wrote to Rhett, the South Carolina legislature advanced the meeting of its state convention to December 17. This action, taken in response to reports of growing support for secession in Georgia, Alabama, and Mississippi, would affect the course of events throughout the South.

---

WARREN COUNTY, Missi., Nov. 10, 1860.
DEAR SIR:—I had the honor to receive, last night, yours of the 27th ulto., and hasten to reply to the inquiries propounded. Reports of the election leave little doubt that the event you anticipated has occurred, that electors have been chosen securing the election of Lincoln, and I will answer on that supposition.

My home is so isolated that I have had no intercourse with those who might have aided me in forming an opinion as to the effect produced on the mind of our people by the result of the recent election, and the impressions which I communicate are founded upon antecedent expressions.

1. I doubt not that the Gov'r of Missi. has convoked the Legislature to assemble within the present month, to decide upon the course which the State should adopt in the present emergency. Whether the Legislature will direct the call of a convention, of the State, or appoint delegates to a convention of such Southern States as may be willing to consult together for the adoption of a Southern plan of action, is doubtful.

2. If a convention, of the State, were assembled, the proposition to secede from the Union, independently of support from neighboring States, would probably fail.

3. If South Carolina should first secede, and she alone should take such action, the position of Missi. would not

probably be changed by that fact. A powerful obstacle to the separate action of Missi. is the want of a port; from which follows the consequence that her trade being still conducted through the ports of the Union, her revenue would be diverted from her own support to that of a foreign government; and being geographically unconnected with South Carolina, an alliance with her would not vary that state of case.

4. The propriety of separate secession by So. Ca. depends so much upon collateral questions that I find it difficult to respond to your last enquiry, for the want of knowledge which would enable me to estimate the value of the elements involved in the issue, though exterior to your state. Georgia is necessary to connect you with Alabama and thus to make effectual the coöperation of Missi. If Georgia would be lost by immediate action, but could be gained by delay, it seems clear to me that you should wait. If the secession of So. Ca. should be followed by an attempt to coerce her back into the Union, that act of usurpation, folly and wickedness would enlist every true Southern man for her defence. If it were attempted to blockade her ports and destroy her trade, a like result would be produced, and the commercial world would probably be added to her allies. It is therefore probable that neither of those measures would be adopted by any administration, but that federal ships would be sent to collect the duties on imports outside of the bar; that the commercial nations would feel little interest in that; and the Southern States would have little power to counteract it.

The planting states have a common interest of such magnitude, that their union, sooner or later, for the protection of that interest is certain. United they will have ample power for their own protection, and their exports will make for them allies of all commercial and manufacturing powers.

The new states have a heterogeneous population, and will be slower and less unanimous than those in which there is less of the northern element in the body politic, but interest controls the policy of states, and finally all the planting communities must reach the same conclusion. My opinion is, therefore, as it has been, in favor of seeking to bring those states into cooperation before asking for a popular decision upon a new policy and relation to the nations of the earth. If So. Ca.

should resolve to secede before that cooperation can be ob
tained, to go out leaving Georgia and Alabama and Louisiana
in the Union, and without any reason to suppose they will follow her; there appears to me to be no advantage in waiting
until the govt. has passed into hostile hands and men have
become familiarized to that injurious and offensive perversion
of the general government from the ends for which it was established. I have written with the freedom and carelessness of
private correspondence, and regret that I could not give more
precise information. Very respectfully, Yrs, etc..

JEFFN DAVIS.

DEBATING SECESSION:
GEORGIA, NOVEMBER 1860

# Benjamin Hill: Speech at Milledgeville

November 15, 1860

Several prominent Georgians, including Senator Robert Toombs and former congressman Alexander H. Stephens, gave speeches at the state capital in November 1860 while the legislature debated whether to call a convention to consider secession. A successful lawyer active in Georgia politics, Benjamin Hill was a former Whig who had joined the nativist American (Know Nothing) Party during the 1850s. Like many southern Whig-Americans alarmed by the prospect of secession, Hill had supported John Bell, the Constitutional Union candidate, in the 1860 presidential election. (Bell, who ran on a pledge to *"recognize* no political principle other than *the Constitution of the Country, the Union of the States, and the Enforcement of the Laws,"* carried Virginia, Kentucky, and Tennessee, but lost in the remainder of the South to John C. Breckinridge.) Hill would vote against secession at the Georgia convention in January 1861; he then went on to serve in the Provisional Confederate Congress and in the Confederate Senate. His refusal in November 1860 to commit himself to either unconditional unionism or to immediate secession was shared by many southern "conditional unionists" and "conditional secessionists" in 1860–61.

----

*Ladies and Friends:* While I am speaking to you to-night I earnestly beg for perfect quietness and order. It seems to be a general idea that public speakers feel highly complimented when their opinions are received with boisterous applause. I do not so feel on any occasion, and certainly would not so regard such a demonstration now. The occasion is a solemn and serious one, and let us treat it in no light or trivial manner. One more request. I have invoked good order. I yet more earnestly invoke your kind and considerate attention. No people ever assembled to deliberate a graver issue. The government is the result of much toil, much blood, much anxiety, and much treasure. For nearly a century we have been accustomed to speak and boast of it as the best on earth. Wrapped up in it are the lives, the happiness, the interests, and the peace of thirty millions of freemen now living, and of unnumbered millions in the future.

Whether we shall now destroy that government or make another effort to preserve it and reform its abuses, is the question before us. Is that question not entitled to all the wisdom, the moderation, and the prudence we can command? Were you ever at sea in a storm? Then you know the sailor often finds it necessary, to enable him to keep his ship above the wave, to throw overboard his freight, even his treasure. But with his chart and his compass he never parts. However dark the heavens or furious the winds, with these he can still point the polar star, and find the port of his safety. Would not that sailor be mad who should throw these overboard?

We are at sea, my friends. The skies are fearfully darkened. The billows roll threateningly. Dangers are on every side. Let us throw overboard our passions, our prejudices, and our party feelings, however long or highly valued. But let us hold on — hold on to reason and moderation. These, and these alone, point always to the fixed star of truth, by whose guidance we may yet safely come to shore.

We must agree. We do agree if we but knew it. Our people must be united to meet this crisis. Divisions now would not only be unfortunate, but exceedingly disastrous. If divisions arise they cannot be based on our interests or our purposes, for these are and must be the same. Divisions must find their origin in our suspicions and jealousies. Let us give these suspicions and jealousies to the winds. Let us assume as the basis of every argument that we are all equally honest, and equally desirous in our various ways of securing one end—our equality and rights. There must be one way better than all others. Let our ambition be to find that way, and unite our people in the advocacy of that way.

I have listened with earnest attention to the eloquent speeches made by all sides, and I believe a common ground of agreement can be found, if not for universal, at least for very general agreement. Those who hold that the Constitution is wrong, and the Union bad *per se*, of course will agree to nothing but immediate disunion, and such I shall not be able to affect.

In the first place what are our grievances. All the speakers, thus far, even the most ultra, have admitted that the mere Constitutional election of any man is no ground for resistance. The mere election of Mr. Lincoln is on all sides admitted not to be grievance. Our State would not be thrown on a false issue on this point.

We complain, in general terms, that the anti-slavery sentiment at the North has been made an element of political power.

In proof of this we make the following specifications:

1. That a large political party has been organized in the Northern States, the great common idea of which is to prohibit the extension of slavery by Congress, and hostility to slavery generally.

2. That this party has succeeded in getting the control of many of the Northern State Legislatures and have procured the passage of acts nullifying the fugitive slave law, encouraging the rescue of fugitives, and seeking to punish as felons citizens of our Southern States who pursue their slaves in the assertion of a plain Constitutional right.

3. That this party has elected governors in Northern States who refuse, some openly and others under frivolous pretexts, to do their plain Constitutional duties, when these involve the recognition of property in slaves.

4. That Northern courts, chosen by the same party, have assumed to declare the fugitive slave law unconstitutional in the teeth of the decisions of the United States courts, and of every department of the United States Government.

5. We complain that the Northern States, thus controlled, are seeking to repudiate every Constitutional duty or provision, in favor or in recognition of slavery—to work the extinction of slavery, and to secure to the negro social and political equality with the white race; and, as far as possible, they disregard and nullify even the laws of the Southern States on these subjects. In proof of this complaint, we show that Northern governors have actually refused to deliver up fugitives from

justice, when the crime charged against such fugitives recognized under State law property in slaves.

Thus, a Northern man married a Southern lady having a separate estate in slaves. He deceived the lady, stole her negroes, sold them, and pocketed the money, and fled to a Northern State. He was charged with larceny under the laws of the State in which the crime was committed. A true bill was obtained and a demand was properly made for his return, and the Governor of the State to which he fled refused to deliver him up on the ground that to commit larceny a man must steal property, and as slaves were not property according to the laws of the Northern State, it could not be property according to the laws of the Southern State; that therefore the Southern court, jury, and governor were all wrong in obeying the laws of their own State, instead of the laws of the Northern State; that the defendant was not guilty and could not be guilty, and should not be delivered up.

The same principle was involved to shield several of the conspirators in the John Brown raid.

The inexorable logic of this party, on such a premise, must array them against the whole Constitution of the United States; because that instrument, in its very frame-work, is a recognition of property in slaves. It was made by slaveholding States. Accordingly we find this party a disunion party, and its leaders—those of them who follow their logic to its practical consequences—disunionists *per se*. I would not quote from the low and the ignorant of that party, but I will quote from the learned and the honored.

One of the most learned disciples of this party, says:

The Constitution is the cause of every division which this vexed question of slavery has ever occasioned in this country. If (the Constitution) has been the fountain and father of our troubles, by attempting to hold together, as reconciled, two opposing principles, which will not harmonize nor agree, the only hope of the slave is over the ruins of the government. The dissolution of the Union is the abolition of slavery.

One of the ablest, and oldest, and long honored senators of that party—a senator even before the existence of the Republican party—said to the nominating convention of that party:

I believe that this is not so much a convention to change the administration of the government, as to say whether there shall be any government to be administered. You have assembled, not to say whether this Union shall be preserved, but to say whether it shall be a blessing or a scorn and hissing among the nations.

I could quote all night, my friends, to show that the tendency of the Republican party is to disunion. That to be a Republican is to be logically and practically against the Constitution and the Union. And we complain that this party is warring upon us, and at the same time, and in the same way, and by a necessary consequence, warring upon the Constitution and the Union.

6. We complain, in the last place, that this party, having thus acquired the control of every department of government—legislative, executive, and judicial—in several of the Northern States, and having thus used every department of the State government so acquired, in violation of the Constitution of the United States, in disregard of the laws of the Southern States, and in utter denial of the property and even liberty of the citizens of the Southern States—this party, I say, with these principles, and this history, has at last secured the executive department of the Federal Government, and are seeking to secure the other two departments—the legislative and the judicial.

Here, then, is a party seeking to administer the government on principles which must destroy the government—proposing to preserve the Union upon a basis on which the Union, in the very nature of things, cannot stand; and offering peace on terms which must produce civil war.

Now, my friends, the next question is, shall these grievances be resisted? I know of no man who says they ought not to be resisted. For myself, I say, and say with emphasis, they ought to be resisted—resisted effectively and at all hazards.

What lessons have we here? We have seen differences running high—even apparent bitterness engendered. Passion gets up, debates become jeers and gibes and defiance. One man says he will not resist Lincoln. His adversary pronounces that treason to the South and the man a black Republican. Another man says he will resist Lincoln and demand immediate secession. His adversary pronounces that treason to the Constitution and the man a disunionist.

What do you mean by Lincoln? Stop and define. The first means by Lincoln the man elected, the second means by Lincoln the issue on which he is elected. Neither will resist the first, both will resist the latter, and so they agree and did agree all the time they were disputing!

These grievances are our real complaint. They have advanced to a point which makes a crisis: and that point is the election of Lincoln. We dare not, we will not let this crisis pass without a settlement. That settlement must wipe out existing grievances, and arrest threatened ones. We owe it to our Constitution, to our country, to our peace, to our posterity, to our dignity, to our self-respect as Union men and Southern men, to have a cessation of these aggressions and an end to these disturbances. I do not think we should wait for any further violation of the Constitution. The Constitution has already been violated and even defied. These violations are repeated every day. We must resist, and to attempt to resist and not do so effectively—even to the full extent of the evil—will be to bring shame on ourselves, and our State, and our cause.

Having agreed on our complaints, and discovered that all our suspicions of each other are unfounded, and that our disputes on this point had their origin in hasty conclusions and thoughtless mistakes, let us, with an encouraged charity and forbearance, advance to the next step in this argument.

Who shall inaugurate this resistance? Who shall determine the mode, the measure, and the time of this resistance?

My reply is: The people through their delegate convention duly assembled.

It is not necessary for me now to urge this point. Here again we have had disputes without differences.

I have the pleasure of announcing to-night that the prominent leaders, of all shades of opinion on this subject, came together this day, and agreed that it was the right and privilege of the people in convention to pass on these questions. On this point we have disputed for a week, and to-day, acting as Georgians should act, we came together in a spirit of kindness, and in fifteen minutes our hearts were all made glad by the discovery that our differences or disputes were founded on groundless suspicions, and *we are agreed*. We are all for resistance, and we are all for the people in convention to say how and where and by what means we shall resist.

I never beheld a scene which made my heart rejoice more sincerely. Oh, that I could see the same spirit of concord on the only remaining question of difference. With my heart full of kindness I beg you, my friends, accompany me now to question. I do believe we can agree again. My solemn conviction is that we differ as little on this as we did on the other point, in every material view. At least, nearly all the quarrels of the world in all ages have been founded more in form than substance.

Some men are honest, wise, and prudent. Others are equally honest and intelligent, but rash and impetuous. The latter are often to be loved and encouraged; but the first alone are to be relied on in emergencies.

We often appeal to the history of our fathers to urge men to indignation and resentment of wrongs. Let us study all that history. Let me show you from that history, an example of metal and over-confidence on the one hand, and of coolness and wisdom on the other.

During our colonial history, the English government sent General Braddock to America to dislodge and drive back the French and Indians. The general, in arranging the company, assigned to his own command the duty of recovering the Ohio Valley and the great Northwest. It was necessary to capture Fort Duquesne. He never thought of any difficulties in the way of success. He promised Newcastle to be beyond the mountains in a very short period. Duquesne he thought would stop him only three or four days, and there was no obstruction to his march to Niagara. He declared the Indians might frighten the raw American militia, but could make no impression on the British regulars. This was Braddock.

One of that raw American militia who had joined Braddock's command, was the young Washington, then only about twenty-three years old. He became one of Braddock's aids. Hearing his general's boasts, and seeing his thoughtless courage, Washington quietly said to him, "We shall have more to do than to go up the hills and come down." Speaking of

Braddock to another, Washington said, "He was incapable of arguing without warmth, or giving up any point he had asserted, be it ever so incompatible with reason or common sense."

Braddock was considered on all hands to be a brave, gallant, and fearless officer.

Here, then, are two men, both brave, noble, and intelligent, engaged together to accomplish a common enterprise for the good of their country. The one was rash, thoughtless, never calculating difficulties, nor looking forward to and providing against obstructions.

He arranged his express and sent forward the news of his victory beforehand. But the other was cool, calculating, cautious, wise, and moderate. He was a man who thought before he acted and then he acted the hero.

Now, for results: Braddock was surprised before he reached the fort. His British regulars fled before the yelling Indians, and the raw American militia were slain by them. Braddock himself fought bravely and he was borne from the field of his shame, leaving more than half his little army dead, and himself senseless with a mortal wound. After the lapse of a day he came to himself, and his first exclamation was, "Who would have thought it!" Again he roused up and said, "We shall better know how to deal with them another time." Poor general, it was too late, for with that sentence he died! For more than a century he has slept near Fort Necessity, and his only history might be written for his epitaph: "He was brave but rash, gallant but thoughtless, noble but bigoted. He fought hastily, died early, and here he lies."

The young Washington was also brave, and in the thickest of the fight. Horse after horse fell from under him. The bullets of the Indians whistled around him and through his clothes, but Providence spared him. Even the Indians declared some God protected him. So cool, so brave, so wise and thoughtful was the conduct of this young officer, before, during, and after the battle that even then a distinguished man "points him out as a youth raised up by Providence for some noble work." Who does not know the history of Washington; yet who can tell it? Our glorious revolution, that wise Constitution, this happy, widespread, and ever spreading country—struggling millions fired on by the example of his success, are some of the chapters already written in that history. Long chapters of yet unrealized glory, and power, and happiness shall be endlessly added, if the wisdom of him who redeemed our country can be continued to those who inherit it. The last hour of constitutional liberty, perpetuated to the glory of the end, or cut short in the frenzy of anarchy, shall wind up the history of Washington. Behold here the sudden destructon of the rash man and his followers, and the still unfolding success of the cool and thoughtful man, and then let us go to work to meet this crisis that is upon us.

Though there are various modifications of opinions, there are really but two modes of resistance proposed. One method is to make no further effort in the Union, but to assume that the Union either cannot or ought not to be preserved, and secede at once and throw ourselves upon the consequences. The other method is to exhaust certain remedies for these grievances in the Union, with the view of preserving our rights and the Union with them, if possible; looking, however, to and preparing for secession as an ultimate resort, certainly to be had, if those grievances cannot be remedied and completely remedied and ended in the Union.

Irreconcilable as these differences at first view seem to be, I maintain a point of complete reconciliation can be reached.

Now, let us look to the reason urged by the advocates of these two modes of redress.

The advocates of the first mode declare that these grievances are the fruits of an original, innate anti-slavery fanaticism. That the history of the world will show that such fanaticism is never convinced, is never satisfied, never reasons, and never ends but in victory or blood. That accordingly this fanaticism in the Northern States has been constantly progressive, always getting stronger and more impudent, defiant, and aggressive; and that it will never cease except in our subjugation unless we tear loose from it by dissolving the Union. These advocates say they have no faith in any resistance in the Union, because, in the nature of the evil, none can be effectual.

The advocates of the second mode of resistance, of whom I am humbly one, reason after another fashion: We say, in the first place, that while it is true that this anti-slavery sentiment has become fanatical with many, yet it is not necessarily so in its nature, nor was it so in its origin. Slavery has always existed in some form. It is an original institution. Besides, we say the agitation now upon us did not originate in fanaticism or philanthropy but in cupidity.

England owned the West Indies and there she had some slaves. She had possessions in East India which she believed were adapted to the growth of cotton, and which article of produce she desired to monopolize.

The Southern States were her only dangerous competitors. She desired to cripple or break down the cultivation of the cotton plant in the South. The South could not use her own soil and climate in the successful production of cotton without the African slave. England therefore must manage to set free the slave and turn the South over to some inadequate peasantry system, something like the coolie system. To this end England raised a great cry of philanthropy in behalf of the poor negro. As a show of sincerity she abolished slavery in the West Indies near us, thinking thereby to affect the same institutions in her Southern neighbor. She taught her lessons of false philanthropy to our Northern pulpits and Northern papers, and thus to our Northern people.

At this time the Northern politicians saw in this inflammable subject fine material for political agitation, party success, and self-promotion. They leaped upon the wave and rode on it. The Southern politicians raised the counter cry, leaped on the counter wave, and met the Northern politicians—in office. As long as the people answered the politicians called, and the result is what we now see. The subject is interminable in politics, because utterly illegitimate as a political issue. Thus it has never approached, but receded from a political solution, and increasing in excitement as it has progressed; all statesmanship, North and South, is dwarfed to a mere wrangling about African slavery. Slavery will survive, but the Constitution, the Union, and peace may not. The Southern States will continue to raise cotton, but the hoping subject of tyranny in the earth may not continue to point to the beautiful success of the experiment of self-government in America.

While the storm which England raised in America has been going on, England has been trying to raise cotton in India. She has failed. Her factories are at home, but her cotton can't come from India. She must have cotton. Four millions of her people can't live without it. The English throne can't stand without it. It must come from the Southern States. It can't be raised in the South without slave labor. And England has become the defender of slavery in the South.

I will frankly state that this revolution in English sentiment and policy has not yet reached the Northern people. The same causes must slowly produce it.

But while the anti-slavery sentiment has spread in the North, the pro-slavery sentiment has also strengthened in America. In our early history the Southern statesmen were anti-slavery in feeling. So were Washington, Jefferson, Madison, Randolph, and many of that day, who had never studied the argument of the cotton gin, nor heard the eloquent productions of the great Mississippi Valley. Now our people not only see the justice of slavery, but its providence too. The world can never give up slavery until it is ready to give up clothing and food. The South is a magnificent exemplification of the highest Christian excellence. She is feeding the hungry, clothing the naked, blessing them that curse her, and doing good to them that despitefully use and persecute her.

We say again that even the history of the slavery agitation in this country does not justify the very conclusion that Abolitionism has been always progressive. Whenever popular sentiment in politics has condemned the agitation, Abolitionism has declined. Many instances could be given. In 1848 the Abolition candidate for the Presidency received about 300,000 votes. At the end of Mr. Fillmore's administration in 1852, the candidate of that party received about half that vote, and a fugitive slave could be recovered almost without opposition in any Northern State. Even the act of Massachusetts, nullifying the fugitive slave law of 1793, had not been applied to the new fugitive slave law of 1850, and was not so applied until 1855, after the agitation had been revived.

These, and many other similar reasons, we urge for believing that all the enumerated grievances—the results of slavery agitation—are curable by remedies within the Union.

But suppose our reasoning all wrong! How shall we be convinced? Only by the experiment; for in the nature of the case, nothing but a trial can test the virtue of the remedies proposed. Let us try these remedies, and if we fail, this failure will establish the truth of the positions of the advocates of immediate secession, and we shall all join in that remedy.

For let it be understood, we are all agreed that these grievances shall be resisted—shall be remedied—most effectively remedied; and if this cannot be done in the Union, then the Union must go. And we must not let this crisis pass without forever solving this doubt. If the Union and the peace of slavery cannot exist together, then the Union must go; for slavery can never go, the necessities of man and the laws of Heaven will never let it go, and it must have peace. And it has been tantalized and meddled with as long as our self-respect can permit.

But what remedies in the Union do we propose? I will answer:

The grievances enumerated are of two kinds—existing and threatened. The existing actual grievances are all violations of the Federal Constitution and Federal laws, either by Northern citizens or Northern States. Now, what does good statesmanship, good logic, and common sense naturally suggest? Why, that the Federal Government shall enforce its laws. No State can enforce, or punish, for the violation of a Federal law. The power offended must adequately punish the offender. The punishment must be such as to redress the past, and by certainty and terror secure the future. The Federal law is offended. The Northern States and people are the offenders. The South is damaged by the offense. This gives her the right to demand the redress at the hands of the Federal Government, and if that government, for want of will or power, shall not grant the redress, then that government is a demonstrated failure. And when government ends, self-defense begins. We can then take redress in our own way, and to our entire satisfaction.

Let the Georgia Convention meet. Let her not simply demand but command that this war on slavery shall cease—that these unconstitutional acts and proceedings shall be repealed and abandoned by the States, or repudiated and redressed by the Federal Government. Let her invite all the States to join in this demand. If no others will come to their duty and meet with us, let the fifteen Southern States join in this demand, and let the penalty of refusal, even to the demand of one State, be the abandonment of the Union, and any other, even harsher remedy, each State may think her rights and honor require.

We have an instance before us, made by the North. When, in 1833, South Carolina was refusing to obey a Federal law, in the execution of which the Northern States had an interest, Congress passed a force bill, and put it in the hands of a Southern President for enforcement, even with the army and the navy and the militia—if needed.

Let us turn this battery against Northern rebels. The constitutionality of the act which South Carolina resisted was doubted. A Southern State never nullified, nor refused to obey, a plain constitutional law. But here are the Northern States, and people nullifying and setting at defiance the plainest Constitutional provisions, and laws passed in pursuance thereof; and, instead of demanding of the Federal Government the enforcement of its laws for the protection of our rights, we are spending our breath and wasting our strength, in vain boastings of wrath and hurtful divisions of our own people.

Some of our wisest Southern statesmen think we have laws already sufficient for this crisis, if enforced. We have an act in 1795, and one in 1807, and perhaps others, to execute the laws, to suppress insurrections, and repel invasions. If these and other enactments are sufficient, let us have them enforced.

*A Voice.*—The presidents we have already had won't enforce that law.

*Mr. Hill.*—Then you ought to have dissolved long ago. If the grievance has been by men of our own choosing, why have we not complained before. Let us begin now. Let us begin with Mr. Buchanan. A few days ago, and perhaps now, a fugitive is standing protected by a Northern mob in a Northern State, in defiance of the United State Marshal. Let us demand now that Mr. Buchanan enforce the law against that rebel and against that State which protects him, or suffers him to be protected on her soil. Let us have out the army and navy, and if they are not sufficient let there be a call for volunteers. Many of us say we are ready to fight, anxious to fight. Here is a chance. Let us tender our services.

If the laws now existing are not sufficient, let us have them sufficient. It is our right. We are entitled to a force bill for every clause in the Constitution necessary to our rights. What have our statesmen been after that these laws are not sufficient? Some of these nullifying grievances have existed since 1843, and is it possible that our statesmen have been all asleep, or lost or forgetful in wrangling about slavery? Let us begin now and perfect our laws for the enforcement of every Constitutional right, and against every rebel enemy. Let the convention add to the contingencies of disruption in the Georgia platform. Let the refusal to enforce the laws granted for our protection and defense be one contingency, and the refusal to grant the laws needed for that protection and defense be another contingency.

*A Voice.*—How long will you wait?

*Mr. Hill.*—Until the experiment is tried and both the demands enumerated may be tested and the contingencies may transpire before the fourth of March next. If they do not, if a larger time shall be needed, Mr. Lincoln cannot do us damage. As you heard last night, he cannot even form his Cabinet unless he make it acceptable to a Democratic Senate. And I go further and say that he cannot get even his salary—not a dime to pay for his breakfast—without the consent of Congress.

Nor would I have the Southern States, nor even Georgia, to hesitate to demand the enforcement of those laws at the hands of Mr. Lincoln, if we cannot test it before. The North demanded of a Southern President the execution of the law against a Southern State in 1833. Now let the South compel a Northern President to execute the laws against a Northern people; yea, the very rebels that elected him.

*A Voice.*—Do you believe Lincoln would issue his proclamation?

*Mr. Hill.*—We can make him do it. It is his oath. He will be a traitor to refuse, and we shall have the right to hang him. He dare not refuse. He would be on Southern territory, and for his life he dare not refuse.

*A Voice.*—The "Wide Awakes" will be there.

*Mr. Hill.*—Very well, if we are afraid of the "Wide Awakes" we had better surrender without further debate. The "Wide Awakes" will be there if we secede, and if they are to be dreaded, our only remedy is to hide. No, my friends, we are not afraid of anybody. Arm us with the laws of our country and the Constitution of our fathers, and we fear no enemy. Let us make war upon that Constitution and against those laws and we will be afraid of every noise in the bushes. He who feels and knows he is right, is afraid of nothing; and he who feels and knows he is wrong, is afraid of nothing, too.

We were told the other night by a gentleman urging immediate secession that we had never had a member in Congress but who was afraid to demand the laws for the enforcement of these Constitutional rights. And this is true, but whose fault is that? Shame upon us that we have been afraid to demand our rights at the hands of our own government, administered to this hour by men of our own choice, and yet insist on our courage to sustain us in seceding from that government in defiance of its power. No, we have a right to go out, but let us know we *must* exercise that right before we go, and how can we know it unless we ask first? The Declaration of Independence, which you invoke for an example, says, a decent respect to the opinions of mankind requires us to declare the causes which impel us to the separation. When we separate and allege our grievances as our causes, and mankind shall ask us if we attempted, even demanded a redress of those grievances and causes before we went out, shall we hang our heads and say no? A people who are afraid to demand respect for their rights, can have no rights worthy to be respected. Our fathers demanded, yea petitioned, warned, and conjured, and not until the government was deaf to the voice of justice and consanguinity, did they acquiesce in the necessity which announced their separation. It is not the cowardice of fear, but the courage of right and duty, to demand redress at the hands of our government.

I confess I am anxious to see the strength of this government now tested. The crisis is on us; not of our seeking, but in spite of our opposition, and now let us meet it.

I believe we can make Lincoln enforce the laws. If fifteen Southern States will take that Constitution and the laws and his oath, and shake them in the face of the President, and demand their observance and enforcement, he cannot refuse. Better make *him* do it than any one else. It will be a magnificent vindication of the power and the majesty of the law, to make the President enforce the law, even to hanging, against the very rebels who have chosen him to trample upon it. It will be a vindication that will strike terror to the hearts of the evil-doers for a century to come. Why, Lincoln is not a monarch. He has no power outside of the law, and none inside of the law except to enforce it. The law is our king over all. From the President to the humblest citizen we are the equal subjects of this only ruler. We have no cause for fear except when we offend this only sovereign of the Republican citizen, and have no occasion for despair until his protection is denied us.

I am also willing, as you heard last night, that our Convention or State should demand of the nullifying States the repeal of their obnoxious laws. I know this idea has been characterized as ridiculous. I cannot see wherein. You would make such demands of any foreign power interfering with your rights, and why do less toward a confederate State?

But in my opinion, the wisest policy, the most natural remedy, and the surest way to vindicate our honor and self-respect, is to demand the unconditional observance of the Constitution by every State and people, and to enforce that demand. And if it be necessary, call out for this purpose the whole power of the government even to war on the rebellious State. And when a State shall allow a fugitive to be rescued in her jurisdiction and carried beyond the reach of the owner, require her to indemnify the owner, and make the government compel that indemnity, even to the seizure of the property of the offending State and her people. One such rigid enforcement of the law will secure universal obedience. Let the law be executed though the heavens fall, for there can be no government without law, and law is but sand, if not enforced. If need be, let the State continuing in rebellion against the Constitution be driven from the Union. Is this Union a good? If so, why should we surrender its blessings because Massachusetts violates the laws of that Union? Punish the guilty. Drive Massachusetts to the duties of the Constitution or from its benefits. Make the general government do this, and abandon the government when it shall take sides with the criminal. It would be a trophy to fanaticism, above all her insolence, to drive the dutiful out of the Union with impunity on its part. Let us defend the Union against its enemies, until that Union shall take sides with the enemy, and then let us defend ourselves against both.

In the next place let us consider the benefits of this policy. First, let us consider its benefits if we succeed; and then its benefits if we fail.

If we succeed we shall have brought about a triumph of law over the fell spirit of mobocracy, never surpassed in the world's history, and the reward of that triumph will be the glorious vindication of our equality and honor, and at the same time the establishment of the Union in its integrity forever. And I tell you, my friends, we owe it to our history, ourselves, and our posterity, yea, to constitutional liberty itself, to make this trial. Can it be possible that we are living under a government that has no power to enforce its laws? We have boasted of our form of government. We have almost canonized its authors as saints, for their patriotism and wisdom. They have reputations world-wide. They have been, for nearly a century, lauded as far above all antiquity, and all previous statesmen. Their faces and their forms have been perpetuated in brass and marble for the admiring gaze of many generations made happy in the enjoyment of their labors. In verse and song, in history and philosophy, in light literature and graver learning, their names are eulogized, and their deeds commemorated, and their wisdom ennobled. The painter has given us the very faces and positions of the great counselors, as they sat together deliberating in the formation of this Constitution. The pulpit has placed their virtues next to the purity and inspiration of the early apostles. The Senate Chamber has invoked their sayings as the test of good policy. The fireside has held up to its juvenile circle their manners as the models of good breeding. The demagogue on the hustings has falsely caught at their mantles to hide his own shame.

All this, because we have been accustomed to believe that they succeeded in framing the best Constitution and in organizing the best government the world ever saw. Is that government, after all, a failure? Who shall give us a better, and how shall we commemorate the worth of such wiser benefactors? But if this government cannot enforce its laws, then it is a failure.

We have professed to feel and realize its blessings. Eloquence has portrayed in magic power its progress in all the elements of power, wealth, greatness, and happiness. Not a people on earth, since we achieved our independence, has shown symptoms of a desire to be free, that we have not encouraged by our sympathies, and as the sufficient evidence of all success in self-government, we have pointed them to our example. There is not a people on earth who do not point to America and sigh for a government like that of the United States. Shall we now say to all these: Stop, you are mistaken. Our reputation is not deserved. Be content with your harsher rule. The people are not capable of self-government. This very government, which you admire, and which we have thought was a model, is unable to protect our own people from the robber, the thief, the murderer, and the fanatic!

Fellow-citizens, before we settle down in such a conclusion, let us make the effort and put this government to the test.

Another advantage to be derived from success is, that we shall thus end the agitation of slavery forever. Its agitation in politics was wrong from the beginning. Debate its morality and justice as much as you please. It will stand the argument. But don't drag it down into a party political issue. Show me the man who agitates slavery as a political party question and I will show you the true enemy of slavery and the Union, I care not whether he lives North or South. The safety and peace of the slaveholder and the Union demand that this agitation should not longer be allowed

But, in the second place, if we fail, we cannot be damaged, but great benefits will result from the effort.

In the next place we shall have time to get ready for secession. If we secede now, in what condition are we? Our secession will either be peaceable or otherwise. If peaceable, we have no ships to take off our produce. We could not get and would not have those of the government from which we had just seceded. We have no treaties, commercial or otherwise, with any other power. We have no postal system among our own people. Nor are we prepared to meet any one of the hundred inconveniences that must follow, and all of which can be avoided by taking time.

But suppose our secession be not peaceable. In what condition are we for war? No navy, no forts, no arsenals, no arms but bird guns for low trees. Yet a scattered people, with nothing dividing us from our enemy but an imaginary line, and a long sea and gulf coast extending from the Potomac to Galveston Bay, if all should secede. In what condition are we to meet the thousand ills that would beset us, and every one of which can be avoided by taking time. "We have more to do than to go up the hills and come down." Secession is no holiday work.

While we are seeking to redress our wrongs in the Union, we can go forward, making all necessary preparations to go out if it should become necessary. We can have a government system perfect, and prepared, ready for the emergency, when the necessity for separation shall come.

Again, if we fail to get redress in the Union, that very failure will unite the people of our State. The only real ground of difference now is: some of us think we can get redress in the Union, and others think we cannot. Let those of us who still have faith make that effort which has never been made, and if we fail, then we are ready to join you. If you will not help us make that effort, at least do not try to prevent. Let us have a fair trial. Keep cool and keep still. If we cannot save our equality, and rights, and honor in the Union, we shall join you and save them out of it.

*Voice.*—When you fail to save your rights in the Union, if you refuse to go with us then, what will you do?

*Mr. Hill.*—But we will go. We allow not *if* to our conduct in that connection. If, when we come to join you, you get stubborn and refuse to go, then we shall go without you.

Now, my secession friends, I have all confidence in your zeal and patriotism, but simply let us take time and get ready. Let us work for the best, and prepare for the worst. Until an experiment is made, I shall always believe that the Constitution has strength enough to conquer all its enemies—even the Northern fanatic. If it proves to have not that strength, I will not trust it another hour.

A third benefit to be derived from the failure of an honest effort to redress our grievances in the Union, is the Union of all the Southern States. Some of the States will not secede now. Some of the States who suffer most from the grievances we have enumerated will not secede now. Because they think these grievances can be redressed in the Union. If this idea be a dream, let us wake up to the reality by an actual experiment.

A further benefit to be desired is, that if all the Southern States get ready and secede together, we shall be allowed to do so peaceably. Certainly, it is our right to go peaceably any way. The government, though having the right to enforce its laws against all the world, has no right to coerce back a seceding State. But the attempt might be made and the peace broken, if only one State should secede, or even a few. But let all the Southern States get ready and go together, and no earthly power would interfere or molest. My own opinion is that every Western and Northwestern State, and the Middle States, and perhaps all but the New England States, would go with us. And the glorious result at last might be that we should hold the government with all its power, and thrust off only those who have been faithless to it.

But the Southern States alone, with the territory naturally falling into our hands, would form the greatest government then on earth. The world must have our products; and after peace was once secured to us, the world would furnish our navies and our army, without the expense to us of a ship or a soldier.

Finally, my friends, we shall have secured, by this policy, the good opinion of all mankind and of ourselves. We shall have done our duty to history, to our children, and to Constitutional liberty, the great experiment of self-government. We shall have also discerned the defects in our present government, and will be prepared to guard against them in another. Above all we shall have found good consciences, and secured that, either in the Union or out of it, which is dearer to us than any Union, and more to be desired than all constitutions however venerated—that which is the end of all our efforts, and the desire of all our hearts, our equality as States, our rights as citizens, and our honor as men.

# New York Daily News:
## The Right of States to Secede

November 16, 1860

The *New York Daily News* was a conservative newspaper that had supported John C. Breckinridge, the proslavery Southern Democratic candidate, in the 1860 election. Despite its stated opposition to the principle of secession, in subsequent editorials the *Daily News* would consistently oppose attempts to "coerce" the seceding states, and in June 1861 it would denounce the Lincoln administration's war measures as illegal and unconstitutional.

———————

THE PEOPLE often act without reflection. Statesmen and politicians, either contracting the sentiment of the populace or influenced by ambitious motives, encourage the action of the people upon an erroneous and often fatal idea. The present agitation at the South is of this nature. If it is not quieted it will bring evils upon this Confederacy, the number and extent of which it is painful to think of, and the termination of which it is impossible to foretell. The Herald and The Tribune both tell us that a State has a right to secede; but can we believe them? Let the reflecting men study the formation of this Government, the only true source of information, and learn for themselves whether a State has such a right or not.

On the Fourth day of July, 1776, thirteen American colonies declared themselves free and independent States. Throwing off their allegiance to the British Crown and the Governments, which at that time consisted of the Provincial, Proprietary and Charter Governments, they established one of their own. In 1774 the first Congress passed the Bill of Rights, which is as dear to us as the Bill of Rights passed during the reign of Charles the First is to Englishmen. The affairs of the Government were conducted by Congress until near the close of the Revolution, without any substantial form of government.

In March, 1781, the last State acceded to the Articles of Confederation, and the Thirteen Independent States became a confederacy called The United States of America. The object of the States in establishing a confederacy under the Articles of Confederation was to form *a permanent union* for the mutual support and protection of each other. The intention of parties in forming a contract should always be considered. Knowing the intention of our forefathers, can we violate their contract? Each State, in accepting the Articles of Confederation, was bound by them. It was a contract and was binding. Secessionists ask who would enforce it? We answer, the majority. The Articles commenced thus: "Articles of Confederation and PERPETUAL UNION, between the States of," &c. Then came the articles defining the powers granted by the States to Congress, and the rights reserved to themselves. In Article 13 it says: "And the Articles of this Confederation shall be *inviolably* observed by *every* State, and the Union shall be *perpetual.*" At the close of the last Section in the same Article and immediately preceding the signing of the Articles—that there might be no mistake in the duration of the Union—the language is nearly repeated, viz.: "And that the Articles thereof shall be inviolably observed by the States we respectively represent, and that the Union shall be *perpetual.*"

One of the main arguments used by persons believing that States have a right to secede is this, that there is no *definite* time fixed for the duration of the Confederacy. Can anything be more plain than the language used that it is to be *perpetual*, to *endure forever*? They will say to this that under the Constitution, which is substituted for the Articles of Confederation, no such language is used. Not until they had signed the Articles of Confederation did they become United States, and in that contract they declared themselves to be United States, and to remain united forever. They, as United States, adopted the Constitution. It reads thus: "Constitution of the United States of America. We, the people of the United States, in order to form a *more perfect Union*, &c." Not to limit the Union, but to make it more perfect! They became United States, and *forever* under the Articles of Confederation, and neither was abrogated or annulled by the Constitution! In the words of the preamble, both were affirmed. Where does the power lie to alter the compact? In the highest power of the land. In the States themselves and with the Government, as with all corporate bodies, the majority must rule. No decree of a Court can dissolve the States as it can a Corporation. The only power is with the States themselves, and a State once a member of the Confederacy cannot secede without the consent of the others —the majority must rule. If there was any other power to decree the dissolution of the Union, it should be left to that power; but there is none. The General Government cannot coerce a Territory to become a member of the Confederacy. But once having signed the compact and become a member of the Union, it cannot withdraw without the consent of the other members.

If one State has a right to withdraw, all may withdraw; and we should have loss of name, loss of national existence, civil war, servile war, loss of liberty, and, ultimately, the subjugation and overthrow of the most glorious Republic which ever existed. Could Pennsylvania withdraw from the Union if Congress did not impose a high protective tariff on iron, what would be the result? She would have to support a Government at great expense; maintain an army and navy; the tariff she might impose would not benefit her at all; on the contrary, it would prove a detriment; there being no greater comity between her and other countries, the other States would purchase iron where they could buy the cheapest. Bankruptcy of the State would follow, and, consequently, poverty of her citizens. The same rule would apply, in a greater or less degree, to every other State. The whole country, and every individual, would necessarily feel the effects of secession; but it would be most injurious to the seceding States. History tells us that States cannot exist disunited. The compact of these States is binding upon all, and the man who attempts to violate it will be responsible to future generations for the misery which his acts may produce.

"I AM FOR THE UNION AS IT IS":
TEXAS, NOVEMBER 1860

## Sam Houston to H. M. Watkins and Others

As the post-election crisis continued, sixty-four Texas citizens sent Governor Sam Houston a public letter from Huntsville requesting his opinion on "the best course to pursue" at a time when "too hasty action may prove deleterious, and to prolong too much an expression of opinion may prove fatal to our best interests." Houston wrote this reply as part of his ultimately unsuccessful campaign to keep Texas from leaving the Union. By refusing to call a special session of the legislature, Houston hoped to prevent the meeting of a state convention, but in January 1861 secessionists held extralegal elections for convention delegates, and on February 1 the convention voted 166–8 to secede. The secession ordinance was then submitted to a popular vote and approved by a 3-to-1 margin on February 23. When Houston refused to swear allegiance to the new Confederate States of America, the hero of Texas independence was removed from office on March 16, 1861.

---

Austin, Texas, November 20, 1860.
Messrs. H. M. Watkins, P. W. Kittrell, Sanford Gibbs, R. P. Archer, James L. Smither, G. M. Baker, and Others.

Gentlemen: Your letter of the 14th inst., asking my views respecting the present crisis in our political affairs, is at hand. I can reply but briefly; and I shall therefore do so the more frankly, feeling that this is a time when the plain truth should be spoken by every lover of his country.

I recognize among you the names of men of all parties. Some of you are my old and tried friends, and patriotic citizens of Texas. To such, especially, I look with confidence now, when the country is agitated and revolution threatened. In all the troubles of the Republic I found you to be the friends of Constitutional liberty. Having seen the throes of one Revolution, having shared in its vicissitudes, and having borne a part in bringing Texas into the Union, I trust that you, in common

with patriots of those times, will ask some more weighty reason for overthrowing the Government, than rash enthusiasts
yet have given; and that while others are carried away by the
impulse of the moment, the men of experience will be calm
and decided.

I had hoped that an opportunity would have been afforded
me to rejoice in the triumph of some one of the conservative
candidates for the Presidency. Had the candidates for whom
the voice of Texas was declared, been elected, I should have
had an additional cause of gratification; but such is not the
case. On the contrary, I must regret and deplore the election
of men whose only claims to the confidence and support of the
whole country, must be the official character with which the
Constitution invests them.

In remembering the many evidences which a portion of
the Northern people have presented of their willingness to disregard their constitutional obligations and infringe upon the
rights of their Southern brethren, I am not in the least surprised at the indignant responses now uttered by Southern
men. It shows that if the time should come when we can no
longer trust to the Constitution for our rights, the people will
not hesitate to maintain them. It will be well if those States,
which have yielded to a fanatical sentiment, so far as to interpose between the Federal authority and the Constitutional
rights of a whole section of the Union, will now, inspired by a
spirit of patriotism and nationality, retrace that step. Upon a
citizen of their own section and one of their own party, they
have now placed a responsibility which he cannot avoid. As the
Chief Executive of the nation, he will be sworn to support the
Constitution and execute the Laws. His oath will bring him in
conflict with the unconstitutional statutes, created by his party
in many of the States. Elected by that party, it is but natural
that the conservatism of the nation will watch his course with
jealous care, and demand at his hands a rigid enforcement of
the Federal laws. Should he meet the same resistance, which
other Executives have met, it will be his duty to call to his aid
the conservative masses of the country, and they will respond
to the call.—Should he falter or fail, and by allowing the laws
to be subverted, aid in oppressing the people of the South, he
must be hurled from power. From the moment of his inaugu-

ration, there will commence an "irrepressible conflict" different from that which the party of Mr. Lincoln is based upon. It will be an "irrepressible conflict" between The Constitution, which he has sworn to support, and the unconstitutional enactments and aims of the party which has placed him in power. He had declared that the Fugitive Slave Law is Constitutional. In its enforcement, the conflict is with the North alone. I need not assure you that whenever the time shall come, when we must choose between a loss of our Constitutional rights and revolution, I shall choose the latter; but if I, who have led the people of Texas in stormy times of danger, hesitate to plunge into revolution now, it is not because I am ready to submit to the Black Republican rule, but because I regard the Constitution of my country, and am determined to stand by it. Mr. Lincoln has been constitutionally elected and, much as I deprecate his success, no alternative is left me but to yield to the Constitution. The moment that instrument is violated by him, I will be foremost in demanding redress and the last to abandon my ground.

When I contemplate the horrors of civil war, such as a dissolution of the Union will ultimately force upon me, I cannot believe that the people will rashly take a step fraught with these consequences. They will consider well the blessings of the government we have, and it will only be when the grievances we suffer are of a nature that, as freemen, we can no longer bear them, that we will raise the standard of revolution. Then the civilized world, our own consciences, and posterity, will justify us. If that time should come, then will be the day and hour. If it has not—if our rights are yet secure, we cannot be justified Has the time come? If it has, the people who have to bear the burthens of revolution must themselves effect the work.

Those who reside in cities and towns, where masses are carried in crowds and influenced by passionate appeals, may be ready for hasty action, but the working men and farmers, whose all is identified with the prosperity and peace of the country, will ask time to reflect.

As all will be alike involved in the horrors which will come after dissolution all have the right to consider whether dissolution shall come. The liberties and securities of all are at stake. It is not a question for politicians to tamper with. The masses must settle it for themselves. They are to consider whether with Congress and the Supreme Court largely in favor of the Constitution, revolution will be justified, because the President, who is constitutionally elected, is inimical to them. It must come to this.

With all these checks and guarantees in our favor, it is urged that we should no longer wait, but at once let go the Constitution. Passion is rash—wisdom considers well her way. When the bone and sinew of the country, after calmly considering the issue in all its bearings, shall feel that a yoke of oppression is upon them, they will rise to shake it off. Then, when their now peaceful homes are the scene of desolation, they will feel no pang of regret. Moved by a common feeling of resistance, they will not ask for the forms of law to justify their action. Nor will they follow the noisy demagogue who will flee at the first show of danger. Men of the people will come forth to lead them, who will be ready to risk the consequences of revolution.

If the Union be dissolved now, will we have additional security for slavery? Will we have our rights better secured? After enduring civil war for years, will there be any promise of a better state of things than we now enjoy? Texas, especially, has these things to consider. Our Treasury is nearly empty. We have near half a million of dollars in the Treasury of the United States. A million of our school fund is invested in U. S. Bonds. We have an extensive frontier to defend. Pecuniary or personal considerations ought to weigh nothing when tyranny is in the scale; but are we justified in sacrificing these, when we have yet the Constitution to protect us and our rights are secured.

Let us not embrace the higher law principle of our enemies and overthrow the Constitution; but when we have to resist, let it be in the name of the Constitution and to uphold it.

Why this military display and call to arms in Texas. Have we enemies at home or is an enemy marching upon us? When was there the time, when the citizens of the country were not ready to flock to its standard in its defense? Are the people to deliberate on this question with a military despotism in their midst, ready to coerce them? We want sober thought and calm reason, not furious harrangues or the argument of bayonets.

If this government is to fall, wisdom must furnish another and a better one, and if patriots yield now to the rash and reck-

less, who only aspire to military glory, or for anarchy and rapine, they may find that in the wreck of one free government,
they have lost the power to rear another.

I trust the gloom which now hangs over the land will soon
be dispelled. Now is the time for the patriot to come forth and
consider what is to be gained by a change. We are called upon
to desert the gallant thousands who for years have been fighting our battles against fanaticism in the North. Heretofore
they have aided us to conquer and we have been willing to
abide with them. Now, after a struggle more glorious than any
yet have been made, they have been driven back. They still
offer us the guarantees of the Constitution and are ready to
battle with us in its defense. Let true men all over Texas and
the South see to it, that we leave them not without a cause.

I cannot believe that we can find at present more safety out
of the Union than in it. Yet I believe it due to the people that
they should know where they stand. Mr. Lincoln has been
elected upon a sectional issue. If he expects to maintain that
sectional issue, during his administration, it is well we should
know it. If he intends to administer the government with
equality and fairness, we should know that. Let us wait and
see.

I have left upon record my position, should the rights of
Texas be sacrificed by the Federal Government. In reply to Mr.
Seward, in the Senate, I used these words; and I pray my
friends to consider them calmly, as they were uttered:

"Whenever one section of this country presumes upon its
strength for the oppression of the other, then will our Constitution be a mockery, and it would matter not how soon it were
severed into a thousand atoms and scattered to the four winds.
If the principles are disregarded upon which the annexation of
Texas was consummated, there will be for her neither honor
nor interest in the Union; if the mighty in the face of written
law, can place with impunity an iron yoke upon the neck of the
weak, Texas will be at no loss how to act, or where to go
before the blow aimed at her vitals is inflicted. In a spirit of
good faith she entered the federal fold. By that spirit she will
continue to be influenced until it is attempted to make her the
victim of federal wrong.

"And she will violate no federal rights, so will she submit to no violation of her rights by federal authority. The covenant she entered into with the Government must be observed, or it will be annulled. Louisiana, was a purchase, California, New Mexico, and Utah a conquest, but Texas was a voluntary annexation. If the condition of her admission is not complied with on the one part, it is not binding on the other. If I know Texas, she will not submit to the threatened degradation foreshadowed in the recent speech of the Senator from New York. She would prefer restoration to that independence which she once enjoyed, to the ignominy ensuing from sectional dictation. Sorrowing for the mistake which she had committed in sacrificing her independence at the altar of her patriotism, she would unfurl again the banner of the "Lone Star" to the breeze, and re-enter upon a national career, where, if no glory awaited her, she would, at least, be free from subjection by might, to wrong and shame."

Here, I take my stand! So long as the Constitution is maintained by the "Federal authority," and Texas is not made the victim of "federal wrong" I am for the Union as it is.

I am now an aged man. My locks have become white in toiling, as I believe, for the liberties of mankind. Were I young, that I might look forward to the future, feeling that whatever danger might come my strong arm would be at hand to defend my family, I should feel less anxiety than I do at present. The years that I will have to endure the misfortunes of civil war, will be but few. If I could feel that with the close of my career would end the miseries of my race, I could share its misfortunes with patience; but to feel that the perils of revolution must continue; that war with its attendant horrors of bloodshed, rapine, and devastation must still be visited upon it, would embitter my last moments, and after living to witness the dissolution of the best government that ever existed, I would sink to the grave without a hope that freedom would be regenerated or our posterity ever enjoy again the blessings with which we have parted. Let us pause and ponder well before we take action outside of the Constitution! Truly thy friend

Sam Houston.

## George Templeton Strong: Diary, November 20, November 26–December 1, 1860

George Templeton Strong was a successful lawyer in New York City who served as a trustee of Columbia College and as a vestryman of Trinity Church. A former Whig turned Republican, Strong recorded his reaction to the growing secessionist movement in the diary he had been keeping for 25 years.

*November 20.*   Wall Street was a shade less disconsolate this morning. Stocks rallied at the First Board but began to waver and fall again at the Second. The banks cannot bring about a decisive reaction; the disease is too deep-seated.

The revolutionary movement in South Carolina and the Gulf States seems, on the whole, to be gaining strength and consistency. No signs yet of any "sober second thought." Conservatism and common-sense (if any be left in the Cotton States), are still intimidated and silent. Probably the Border States, led by Virginia, will try to mediate and pacify. Dissolution of the Union and re-opening of the slave trade would be disastrous to them, so they naturally desire to make peace. But their mediation will probably be upon the basis of recognition by the North of the extremest Southern exactions (slave trade excepted). The North must consent that slavery be introduced into the territories; Massachusetts, Vermont, Wisconsin, and other states must repeal their "personal liberty" laws that interfere with the Fugitive Slave Law. That plan will not work. Those state laws ought to be repealed, but the South has no right to demand their repeal and make their enactment an excuse for treason, because they are utterly unconstitutional and mere nullities, and no one doubts the United States Supreme Court would so adjudge them.

If these traitors succeed in dismembering the country, they

will have a front place in the Historical Gallery of Celebrated Criminals. No political crime was ever committed as disastrous to mankind and with so little to provoke or excuse the wrong as that which these infamous disunionists are conspiring to perpetrate. . . .

---

*November 26.* Today's newspapers indicate no new symptom in our sore national sickness. The tide is still rising, I think, in all the Cotton States. Reaction and ebb are sure to follow, but they may come too late. This growing excitement may do irreparable mischief before it dies out and reaction sets in. The country may be overwhelmed by a flood of disaster and disgrace before the tide begins to fall.

*November 27.* Nothing new in Wall Street, except that stocks are all down again. Secession certainly gains favor at the South, and grows more threatening every day. But there are symptoms of backing down at the North. There are demonstrations toward repeal of the obnoxious "personal liberty bills" of certain Northern states. It seems likely that Republican leaders and wire-pullers have concluded on a policy of concession and conciliation. I hope it may be in time to prevent terrible mischief.

These "personal liberty laws" are unconstitutional and void. They are mere nullities, and do no harm to the South. What one nigger has South Carolina lost by the legislation of Vermont or Wisconsin? The clamor about them is a palpable humbug. Still they ought to be repealed, being wrong in spirit and interest.

*November 28.* No political news of importance. The progress of events has startled and staggered some of our notables, who were laughing secession to scorn a fortnight ago. John C. Green, for one, "never dreamed these Southerners would go so far." I think, from all indications, that the Republican leaders are frightened and ready to concede everything, to restore the Missouri Compromise line and satisfy the fugitive slave remedies of the South. A movement that way has certainly begun. But it may be too soon for the North and too late for the South. Suppose it prevail. How will it be received in Massachusetts and Western New York? Will Republicans feel that they have been sold by their leaders, and recalcitrate into more intense anti-Southern feeling? I think they will and that many Republicans will enroll themselves as Abolitionists. But if this crisis pass over without disruption and ruin, if our national life endure another year, I think a strong Union party will come into being and control extremists, South and North both.

*November 29.* Thanksgiving Day. No political news today. Congress meets Monday. Mr. Ruggles's friend, Senator Dixon, is in town on his way to Washington. Horribly frightened. Connecticut expects him to do something in the Senate, and he is anxiously enquiring, "What shall I do to be saved from the humiliation of admitting that I'm unequal to my high place?"

Tom Corwin was in town Tuesday night with the draft of some "Bill of Rights" which he means to propose, affirming the rights which the South pretends to believe endangered.

There's a bad prospect for both sections of the country. Southern ruffianism and brutality are very bad, but the selfishness, baseness, and corruption of the North are not good at all. Universal suffrage has been acquiesced in for many years. It is no longer debated. But it's at the root of our troubles. What we want is a strong government, instead of a "government of opinion." If there be disunion, a strong government will be demanded and will come into being somehow, both North and South. Democracy and equality and various other phantasms will be dispersed and dissipated and will disappear forever when two hostile families of states stand side by side, and a great civil war becomes inevitable. To which party will God give a great general, when that crisis is upon us?

*December 1.* Sorry to learn that the Vermont legislature refuses to repeal its personal liberty bill.

A money indemnity for run-away niggers might satisfy the South (if it wanted to be satisfied), but I fear no such arrangement is practicable. Every worthless Cuffee and superannuated Dinah south of the Potomac would be somehow exported into the free states within a year and would have to be paid for.

One hears queer talk in these days of excitement. That white-cravatted, conservative, old, quiet Dutchman, Edward Bancker, thinks every man ought to be hanged that voted for Lincoln, and "means to go South and shoulder a musket." So he tells me, but I think fear for the future of his bank stocks and real estate has slightly deranged his mind, for he is said to have experienced some slight aberrations a few years since, when he had a fierce quarrel with a neighbor about a right of way on Staten Island. Willy Cutting talks mysteriously of an organization to revolutionize the city immediately upon the secession of the South. New York and Brooklyn are to be a free port, and with one or two adjoining counties, Westchester and Kings, I suppose, to constitute an independent principality. Mayor and Common Council to be kicked out, if not hanged, and suffrage to be confined to owners of $5,000 worth of property. A promising prospect.

Why *do* the people so furiously rage together just now? What has created our present unquestionable irritation against the South? What has created the Republican party?

Its nucleus was the abolition handful that has been vaporing for thirty years, and which, till about 1850, was among the more insignificant of our *isms*. Our feeling at the North till that time was not hostility to slavery, but indifference to it, and reluctance to discuss it. It was a disagreeable subject with which we had nothing to do. The battles in Congress about the right of petition, and the Giddings business, made little impression on us. But the clamor of the South about the admission of California ten years ago introduced the question of slavery to the North as one in which it had an interest adverse to the South. That controversy taught us that the two systems could not co-exist in the same territory. It opened our eyes to the fact that there were two hostile elements in the country, and that if we allowed slaves to enter any territorial acquisition, our own free labor must be excluded from it. The question was unfortunate for our peace. But we might have forgotten it had not S. A. Douglas undertaken to get Southern votes by repealing the Missouri Compromise. That was the fatal blow. Then came the atrocious effort to force slavery on Kansas by fraud and violence, with the full support of old Buchanan and his Southern counselors, the brutal beating of the eloquent and erudite Sumner with the cordial approbation and applause of the South, the project to revive the slave trade, and (a little earlier) a sentimental romance, *Uncle Tom's Cabin*, that set all Northern women crying and sobbing over the sorrows of

Sambo. The Fugitive Slave Law stimulated sectional feeling by making slavery visible in our own communities, and above all, the intolerable brag and bluster and indecent arrogance of the South has driven us into protest against their pretensions, and into a determination to assert our own rights in spite of their swagger.

# Edward Bates: Diary, November 22, 1860

A successful lawyer and former congressman from St. Louis, Missouri, Edward Bates was a candidate for the Republican presidential nomination in 1860, receiving 48 out of 466 votes on the first ballot. Bates recorded his appraisal of the movement toward secession in his diary.

———————

*Wednesday night. Nov 22.*

The news from *the South*, as to secession, does not improve. The leaders of the movement, in Alabama, Georgia, and especially S. Carolina, are more urgent than ever, taking every means to get their followers pledged to extreme measures, and to draw in and commit the timid and the doubtful, without allowing time to look to the consequences and reflect upon the bottomless pit that lies before them.

Still I think that (except with a few demented fanatics) it is all brag and bluster, hoping thus to make a better compromise with the timid patriotism of their opponents. In playing this dangerous game, they may go farther than they now intend, and actually commit their states to open rebellion and civil war. If they *will* push it to that dread extremity, the Government, having been as mild and forbearing as possible, up to that point, will no doubt, find it wise policy to make the war as sharp and prompt as possible, in order to shorten it, and prevent its running into social and servile war, and chronic anarchy, such as prevails in Mexico.

The letters and telegrams from *the South*, bear plain evidence of exaggeration, and make a false shewing of the unanimity of the people, in support of the traitorous design. A very little time will show.

If we must have civil war, perhaps it is better now, than at a future day.

# William G. Brownlow to R. H. Appleton

A Methodist minister and the editor of the *Knoxville Whig*, William G. Brownlow was a leading Unionist in eastern Tennessee. Brownlow wrote this letter in response to a note, dated November 23 from Greenwood, South Carolina, in which R. H. Appleton cancelled his subscription to the *Whig*, proclaiming: "Secession now and forever! So say the Methodists of South Carolina." Brownlow printed his letter to Appleton in his newspaper on December 8 and continued to argue against secession. In a referendum held on February 9, 1861, Tennessee voters rejected holding a state convention by 69,387 to 57,798, with opposition to secession especially strong in eastern Tennessee, a mountainous region where, as in western Virginia, there were relatively few slaveholders. After the outbreak of the war the Tennessee legislature declared its independence from the United States, and on June 8 a second referendum endorsed its decision by 104,913 to 47,238, although 70 percent of the voters in eastern Tennessee continued to oppose secession. Brownlow refused to swear allegiance to the Confederacy and maintained the *Whig* as a Unionist newspaper until its suppression on October 24. Arrested for treason on December 6, the defiant editor was imprisoned without trial and then sent across the lines into Union territory in March 1862.

---

KNOXVILLE, Nov. 29, 1860.

MR. APPLETON:—

Your note, calling for account and ordering a discontinuance, is before me. You are not indebted to me for subscription, but, on the contrary, there are fifteen weeks of subscription due you. I take no offence whatever at your discontinuance, as *that* is every man's right in this free country. But, before parting with you, you must allow me to give you my views upon your favorite doctrine of "Secession." I am equally opposed to the wicked spirit of *Sectionalism* at the North and of *Secession* at the South. Your motto is, "Secession now and forever!" I offset this with the following patriotic sentiments from General JACKSON'S Message of 1833:—

"THE CONSTITUTION AND THE LAW IS SUPREME, AND THE UNION IS INDISSOLUBLE."

Sir, the political journals, North and South, are discussing the right of a State to secede from the Union. For my part, I deny the right of secession altogether, though I admit the right of *revolution* when circumstances justify it. It must be an *extreme* case of oppression on the part of Government, and of *continued* oppression, that will justify revolution. Such a case was presented when the American Colonies revolted; and in that case revolution was called for and was successful.

But the idea of one of these States at its pleasure claiming and exercising the right to secede from this Union, is a more monstrous and absurd doctrine than has ever been put forth in any republic. If the doctrine be true that the right exists, our Government is a mere rope of sand. Concede the truth of this dogma, and Cuba, after we may have paid *two hundred millions* for her purchase to Old Spain, may take offence, and, as a State, may at once secede, and leave the United States Treasury to whistle! We now have a case in point. Texas speaks of going out of the Union with Carolina, and I presume will do so. Less than twenty years ago, she was admitted into the Union upon her own solicitation, our Government paying millions to discharge her debts, and other millions to go into her coffers. Is she now at liberty to secede with all this booty, and array herself against this Government in all time to come? Certainly not. For, if she is, Louisiana, and all the States carved out of that purchase, for which we paid FIFTEEN MILLIONS, may do likewise, and carry with them the mouth of the Mississippi River, transferring it to any European Power.

So, too, States in which large amounts of Government property may be situated may at any time secede with that property, —just as South Carolina, Georgia, Florida, and Alabama, with their Government fortifications, arsenals, custom-houses, navy-yards, and other property, strung along the coasts from Charleston to Mobile, may at any time do. Construct a Pacific Railroad at an expense of millions paid from the common treasure, and the two or three States through which it passes, and which it so enriches, may take offence at something Maine and

New Hampshire are doing, and decamp with the whole road, its stationary, running stock, and guarantees, taking all the property with them, and forming an alliance with some Government hostile to the very nation which built the road. Now, are Maryland, Virginia, Tennessee, Kentucky, and other States remaining loyal to the Union, to look quietly on, and even approve the exodus of those which have been thus enriched at their expense, and recognize the right of each of them to secede and take the common property of all the remaining States with them? I say most emphatically not!

This question of the right of secession is upon us, and we have to look it in the face, and meet it as it becomes men. Therefore let us reason together upon the subject, divesting ourselves of passion and prejudice. The right of secession, if it exist at all, is an *absolute* one, and a State has as much right to exercise it at one time as another. The Secessionists will concede the correctness of this position. If she may secede at will, she may do so in anticipation of a bloody and protracted war with a foreign Power, so as to avoid any draft upon her for men or money. If she can secede when she chooses, she owes no allegiance to the Government one hour after she decides to secede, but will then be just as independent of the Government as she is of France or England. In the midst of a violent and protracted foreign war, then, it will be the right of any one of the States of this Union, not only to desert our own Government, but at the same time to ally herself to the enemy the remaining States are fighting! Our Government, under such principles, if recognized, could not exist twenty-four hours. Other nations, and our own citizens, could have no faith in the permanence of such a Government. It would lack the vital principle of existence, because it would lack every thing like credit. No capitalist with a thimbleful of sense would lend it a dollar; for no man could feel assured that such a Government would last long enough to pay a six months' loan, to say nothing of loans for a term of years. All who deal with Governments repose upon their *public faith*; and where this is destroyed they feel that all is lacking. Business must be destroyed; for men of sense and means would not embark either their industry or capital, unless it were under the shelter of laws and institutions not liable to change. In support of this, I need only call attention to the great fall in the price of State bonds, negroes, and all other property in the South, in *antici-pation* of the rupture with which we are threatened. Things are bad enough with us in the South, and they are even worse at the North, because of what seems to be inevitable. And yet they are to grow worse each day we live in this state of uncertainty. And your good State of South Carolina, Mr. Appleton, is more to blame for these evils which affect the country than any one State in the Union.

I have, myself, no sympathy or respect for the anti-slavery men of the North, who are agitating this question, and enacting their "Personal Liberty Laws," with a view to defeat the operations of the "Fugitive Slave Law." I am a native of Virginia, as also were my parents before me, but for thirty years I have been a citizen of Tennessee, and I expect to end my days within her borders. My wife and children are natives of Tennessee, and all I have is here. I am a Union man in the fullest acceptation of that term, and I shall stand by the ship of state, as long as the storm is howling overhead, and the breakers are roaring on the lee-shore, though we have neither sun, moon, nor stars to light the way! And pardon me, sir, when I ask you, who but cowards would seek to desert the ship? Who but madmen would seek for safety out of it? Who but crazy mutineers would refuse to come to the rescue of the ship, passengers, and crew? South Carolina, at this trying moment, refuses to do duty. The storm affrights her. Her Senators and Representatives in Congress resign their seats, instead of remaining at their posts, and fighting the battle on the floor of Congress, where it ought to be fought and must be lost or won. Their hearts fail before the Northern Abolition *Simoon*, and seeing only death, as they apprehend, staring them in the face, if they abide on board, they take to the boats, abandon the vessel in which we have all sailed together, through many a gale, these eighty years past, and intend, with *poles* and *paddles*, to *scuttle* through their cypress-swamps!

I admit the danger that menaces you all on board; but do you not multiply the peril tenfold by desertion? An overwhelming majority of the people of the Southern States have decided at the ballot-box in favor of the Union, voting for

BELL and DOUGLAS. I regard the Abolitionists as the "mutineers;" and I ask you, I ask all South Carolina, is it manly, is it magnanimous, is it just, to throw yourselves into the sea, and leave these border States to destruction? No, Mr. Appleton, it is not magnanimous, it is not just! I tell you, and your Methodist brethren, in the language of the good Book they so much revere, that "Except ye abide in the ship, ye cannot be saved."

I am sorry to hear you say that the Methodists of South Carolina are now and forever the advocates of Secession! To appeal to them in behalf of the Union, is but beating the air, and wasting one's breath; but I say to them, through you, that I will stand to the Stars and Stripes—I shall cling to the Union! I say to them, however, as a heroic Christian apostle said to an equally panic-stricken generation of bolters, "Except ye abide in the ship, ye cannot be saved." You may leave the vessel,—you may go out in the rickety boats of your little State, and hoist your miserable *cabbage-leaf* of a Palmetto flag; but, depend upon it, men and brethren, you will be dashed to pieces on the rocks!

But the clergy,—the ministers of God, the followers on earth of the Prince of Peace,—at this threatening crisis, are going likewise! I know there are among that class of citizens, in South Carolina, some of the best men, as well as the most fearless and self-sacrificing men, of which the American people can boast. Why, oh, why are these men on the side of civil war, bloodshed, and revolution? They have offered up prayers and supplication, and made appeals to Heaven, but, alas! they have been—not for the preservation but for the destruction of the Union. I hear of no Paul among them, seeking to calm the minds of his companions, and to declare to them, "Except ye abide in the ship, ye cannot be saved." The venerable Dr. PIERCE, of Georgia, is an exception to this rule, and has spoken out like an American citizen and a Christian philosopher. To my mind it is clear that the clergy of South Carolina are wanting in *courage* to do what their "consciences dictate to be done." If they possessed the courage of their Master, they would from a Christian stand-point speak out in thunder tones! Jesus of Nazareth walked the earth thirty odd years, in the midst of millions of Roman Empire slaves, and dared to counsel them against rebellion and insurrection, and to exhort them to be *obedient to their masters*. Here was a courage worthy of God! Would that my South Carolina Methodist brethren would endeavor, humbly and courageously, to follow His example!

I believe the Union is in danger, and in regard to the consequences of its dissolution I shall not lengthen out this epistle in an attempt to portray the consequences. What I have to say to your ministers and church-going people is, that the importance of the times demands the grave and serious reflection and prayerful deliberation of every individual and State, before they proceed to take any action. One false step, such as contemplated by South Carolina, may plunge the people of the United States into unutterable woe! We now need the cool deliberation, the conservatism, and the wisdom of the nation, to "pour oil upon the troubled waters,"—to calm the storm now raging in the political elements, and to save this Union. And to no class of men living have we greater cause to look for help in this good work, than to the ministers and members of the Methodist Church, whose Discipline and Constitution, as well as their Bible, require loyalty to the civil Government, obedience to rulers, and a devotion to a country that forbids their assenting to its overthrow, directly or indirectly! The South should resist unlawful aggressions, but she should do it *in* the Union, *under* the Constitution, and with a scrupulous regard to the *forms* of law. Secession is no remedy for any evils in our Government, real or imaginary, past, present, or to come.

I will go further, if you please, and affirm that the Constitution has, in the clearest terms, recognized the right of property in slaves. That sacred instrument prohibits any State into which a slave may have fled, from passing any law to discharge him from bondage, and declares that he shall be surrendered to his lawful owner by the authorities of any State within whose limits he may be found. More than this, sir, the Constitution makes the existence of slavery our foundation of political power, by giving to the Slave States representatives in Congress not only in proportion to the whole number of free negroes, but also in proportion to the *three-fifths of the number of slaves.* The Northern States, by their "Personal Liberty Laws," have placed themselves in a state of revolution, and unless they repeal these laws, the revolution—a thing that never goes backward—must go on, until these rebellious States are declared out of the Union, and the truly conservative States take the Union in charge!

I have, my dear sir, defined my position, and in such terms as not to be misunderstood. I have already extended my remarks beyond what I intended in the outset. I will therefore close with brief extracts from the pens of three distinguished men, and I ask your attention to what they have said. The two first assisted in framing the Constitution. Mr. JEFFERSON remarked, in a letter to John Taylor, dated June 1, 1798,

> "If on the temporary superiority of the one party the other is to resort to a scission of the Union, no Federal Government can ever exist.
>
> "Who can say what would be the evils of a scission, and when and where they would end? Better keep together as we are; haul off from Europe as soon as we can, and from attachments to all portions; and, if they show their power just sufficiently to hoop us together, it will be the happiest situation in which we can exist. If the game were sometimes against us at home, we must have patience till luck turns, and then we shall have opportunity to win back the principles we have lost."

Mr. MADISON, in a paper he drew up a short time before his death, gives us this advice:—

> "The advice nearest my heart and deepest in my conviction is, that the Union of the States be cherished and perpetuated. Let the open enemy to it be regarded as a Pandora with her box opened, and the disguised one as the serpent creeping with his deadly wiles into Paradise."

Gen. JACKSON, in his message to Congress, January 7, 1833, thus disposes of the question of Secession:—

> "The right of the people of a single State to absolve themselves at will, and without the consent of the other States, from their most solemn obligations, and hazard the liberties and happiness of the millions composing this Union, cannot be acknowledged. Such authority is believed utterly repugnant both to the principles upon which

the General Government is constituted, and to the objects which it was expressly formed to attain."

To these sentiments I subscribe as heartily and as unswervingly as I do to those I have preceded them with.

Very respectfully, &c.,

W. G. Brownlow.

# Frederick Douglass: The Late Election

## December 1860

In the spring of 1860 Frederick Douglass returned to his home in Rochester, New York, from a lecture tour of Britain. Writing in June in his abolitionist journal *Douglass' Monthly*, he described the recently nominated Abraham Lincoln as "a man of unblemished private character; a lawyer, standing near the front rank at the bar of his own State, has a cool, well balanced head; great firmness of will; is perseveringly industrious; and one of the most frank, honest men in political life." Although Douglass wished the Republican platform had called for "'Death to Slavery,' instead of 'No more Slave States,'" he expressed his hopes for Lincoln's election. (Douglass would himself vote for his longtime friend Gerrit Smith, the Radical Abolition candidate, on whose ticket he served as an elector in New York State.) Following the election he reassessed Lincoln and the Republican Party in an article in the December *Douglass' Monthly*.

---

OUR LAST monthly paper announced the probable election of Abraham Lincoln and Hannibal Hamlin, the Republican candidates for President and Vice President of the U. S. What was then only speculation and probability, is now an accomplished fact. Pennsylvania, in her State election of October, it is true, had made this result, to a degree, certain; but there were efforts and appliances resorted to by the enemies of the Republican party, which could not fail to cause doubt and anxiety in the minds of the most sanguine.—The deed is, however, now done, and a new order of events connected with the great question of slavery, is now fairly opening upon the country, the end whereof the most sagacious and far-sighted are unable to see and declare. No preceding election resembles this in its issues and parties, and none resembles it in the effects it has already produced, and is still likely to produce. It was a contest between sections, North and South, as to what shall be the

57

principles and policy of the national Government in respect to the slave system of the fifteen Southern States. The broadest assertion of a right of property in man, holding such property equally innocent, sacred and legal under the Constitution, as property in houses, lands, horses, sheep, and horned cattle, and like the latter entitled to Congressional protection in all the Territories, and by parity of reasoning, in all the States of the American Union. The Southern candidate for the Presidency, Mr. Breckinridge, fully represented this broad assertion of what Lord Mansfield well declared to be so opposed to nature, that nothing short of positive law could support it, and Brougham denounced as the "wild and guilty fantasy" of property in man. Mr. Lincoln, the Northern Republican candidate, while admitting the right to hold men as slaves in the States already existing, regards such property as peculiar, exceptional, local, generally an evil, and not to be extended beyond the limits of the States where it is established by what is called positive law. We thus simply state the issue, more for the benefit of our trans-Atlantic friends and readers, than for those at home, who have heard and read little else during the last three or four months. The clamor now raised by the slaveholders about "Northern aggression," "sectional warfare," as a pretext of dissolving the Union, has this basis only: The Northern people have elected, against the opposition of the slaveholding South, a man for President who declared his opposition to the further extension of slavery over the soil belonging to the United States. Such is the head and front, and the full extent of the offense, for which "minute men" are forming, drums are beating, flags are flying, people are arming, "banks are closing," "stocks are falling," and the South generally taking on dreadfully.

By referring to another part of our present monthly, our respected readers will find a few samples of the spirit of the Southern press on the subject. They are full of intrigue, smell of brimstone, and betoken a terrific explosion. Unquestionably, "secession," "disunion," "Southern Confederacy," and the like phrases, are the most popular political watch words of the cotton-growing States of the Union. Nor is this sentiment to be entirely despised. If Mr. Lincoln were really an Abolition President, which he is not; if he were a friend to the Abolition movement, instead of being, as he is, its most powerful enemy, the dissolution of the Union might be the only effective mode of perpetuating slavery in the Southern States—since if it could succeed, it would place slavery beyond the power of the President and his Government. But the South has now no such cause for disunion. The present alarm and perturbation will cease; the Southern fire-eaters will be appeased and will retrace their steps.—There is no sufficient cause for the dissolution of the Union. Whoever lives through the next four years will see Mr. Lincoln and his Administration attacked more bitterly for their pro-slavery truckling, than for doing any anti-slavery work. He and his party will become the best protectors of slavery where it now is, and just such protectors as slave-holders will most need. In order to defeat him, the slave-holders took advantage of the ignorance and stupidity of the masses, and assured them that Lincoln is an Abolitionist. This, Mr. Lincoln and his party will lose no time in scattering to the winds as false and groundless. With the single exception of the question of slavery extension, Mr. Lincoln proposes no measure which can bring him into antagonistic collision with the traffickers in human flesh, either in the States or in the District of Columbia. The Union will, therefore, be saved simply because there is no cause in the election of Mr. Lincoln for its dissolution. Slavery will be as safe, and safer, in the Union under such a President, than it can be under any President of a Southern Confederacy. This is our impression, and we deeply regret the facts from which it is derived.

With an Abolition President we should consider a successful separation of the slave from the free States a calamity, greatly damaging to the prospects of our long enslaved, bruised and mutilated people; but under what may be expected of the Republican party, with its pledges to put down the slaves should they attempt to rise, and to hunt them should they run away, a dissolution of the Union would be highly beneficial to the cause of liberty.—The South would then be a Sicily, and the North a Sardinia. Mr. Lincoln would then be entirely absolved from his slave-hunting, slave-catching and slave-killing pledges, and the South would have to defend slavery with her own guns, and hunt her Negroes with her own dogs. In truth, we really wish those brave, fire-eating, cotton-growing States would just now go at once outside the Union and set up for themselves, where they could be got at without disturbing other people, and got away from without encountering other people. Such a consummation was "one devoutly to be wished." But no, cunning dogs, they will smother their rage, and after all the dust they can raise, they will retire within the Union and claim its advantages.

What, then, has been gained to the anti-slavery cause by the election of Mr. Lincoln? Not much, in itself considered, but very much when viewed in the light of its relations and bearings. For fifty years the country has taken the law from the lips of an exacting, haughty and imperious slave oligarchy. The masters of slaves have been masters of the Republic. Their authority was almost undisputed, and their power irresistible. They were the President makers of the Republic, and no aspirant dared to hope for success against their frown. Lincoln's election has vitiated their authority, and broken their power. It has taught the North its strength, and shown the South its weakness. More important still, it has demonstrated the possibility of electing, if not an Abolitionist, at least an *anti-slavery reputation* to the Presidency of the United States. The years are few since it was thought possible that the Northern people could be wrought up to the exercise of such startling courage. Hitherto the threat of disunion has been as potent over the politicians of the North, as the cat-o'-nine-tails is over the backs of the slaves. Mr. Lincoln's election breaks this enchantment, dispels this terrible nightmare, and awakes the nation to the consciousness of new powers, and the possibility of a higher destiny than the perpetual bondage to an ignoble fear.

Another probable effect will be to extinguish the reviving fires of the accursed foreign slave trade, which for a year or two have been kindled all along the Southern coast of the Union. The Republican party is under no necessity to pass laws on this subject. It has only to enforce and execute the laws already on the statute book. The moral influence of such prompt, complete and unflinching execution of the laws, will be great, not only in arresting the specific evil, but in arresting the tide of popular demoralization with which the successful prosecution of the horrid trade in naked men and women was overspreading the country. To this duty the Republican party will be prompted, not only by the conscience of the North, but by what perhaps will be more controlling party interests.

It may also be conceded that the election of Lincoln and Hamlin, notwithstanding the admission of the former that the South is entitled to an efficient Fugitive Slave Law, will render the practice of recapturing and returning to slavery persons who have heroically succeeded, or may hereafter succeed in reaching the free States, more unpopular and odious than it would have been had either Douglas, Bell or Breckinridge been elected. Slaves may yet be hunted, caught and carried back to slavery, but the number will be greatly diminished, because of the popular disinclination to execute the cruel and merciless Fugitive Slave Law. Had Lincoln been defeated, the fact would have been construed by slave-holders, and their guilty minions of the country, as strong evidence of the soundness of the North in respect to the alleged duty of hounding down and handing over the panting fugitive to the vengeance of his infuriated master. No argument is needed to prove this gain to the side of freedom.

But chief among the benefits of the election, has been the canvass itself. Notwithstanding the many cowardly disclaimers, and miserable concessions to popular prejudice against the colored people, which Republican orators have felt themselves required, by an intense and greedy desire of success, to make, they have been compelled also to recur to first principles of human liberty, expose the baseless claim of property in man, exhibit the hideous features of slavery, and to unveil, for popular execration, the brutal manners and morals of the guilty slave-masters.—The canvass has sent all over the North most learned and eloquent men to utter the great truths which Abolitionists have for twenty years been earnestly, but unsuccessfully endeavoring to get before the public mind and conscience. We may rejoice in the dissemination of the truth by whomsoever proclaimed, for the truth will bear its own weight, and bring forth its own fruit.

Nevertheless, this very victory threatens and may be the death of the modern Abolition movement, and finally bring back the country to the same, or a worse state, than Benj. Lundy and Wm. Lloyd Garrison found it thirty years ago. The Republican party does not propose to abolish slavery anywhere, and is decidedly opposed to Abolition agitation. It is not even, by the confession of its President elect, in favor of the repeal of that thrice-accursed and flagrantly unconstitutional Fugitive Slave Bill of 1850. It is plain to see, that once in power, the policy of the party will be only to seem a little less yielding to the demands of slavery than the Democratic or Fusion party, and thus render ineffective and pointless the whole Abolition movement of the North. The safety of our movement will be found only by a return to all the agencies and appliances, such as writing, publishing, organizing, lecturing, holding meetings, with the earnest aim not to prevent the extension of slavery, but to abolish the system altogether. Congress should be at once memorialized for the abolition of slavery in the District of Columbia, and the slave trade between the States. The same zeal, activity, energy and earnestness should be displayed in circulating petitions, as in the earlier stages of the movement. We have the pen, voice and influence of only one man, and that man of the most limited class; but with few or many, in whatever vicissitudes which may surround the cause, now or hereafter, we shall join in no cry, and unite in no demand less than the complete and universal *abolition* of the whole slave system. Slavery shall be destroyed.

# William T. Sherman to Thomas Ewing Sr. and to John Sherman

William T. Sherman, an 1840 graduate of West Point, had resigned from the army as a captain in 1853 and worked as a banker in San Francisco before accepting a position in 1859 as superintendent of the new State Seminary and Military Academy at Alexandria, Louisiana. Sherman described the political situation in the state after the 1860 election in letters to his father-in-law, Thomas Ewing Sr., and to his brother John, who was then serving as a Republican congressman from Ohio. When the Louisiana convention voted 113–17 in favor of secession on January 26, 1861, Sherman would resign his position and rejoin his wife and children in Lancaster, Ohio.

---

Louisiana State Seminary of Learning
and Military Academy
Alexandria, Decr. 1, 1860

Hon. Thos. Ewing
Dear Sir

Since I last wrote you I have observed a marked change in public opinion here—I was in town all day yesterday, with a Dr. Smith, Senator in the State Legislature, who is the Vice President of our Board of Supervisors and who is just from New Orleans—He is originally from Kentucky, but was an active supporter of Breckinridge in this state. He tells me he was surprised at the tone of feeling in New Orleans, which he described, and which I find corroborated by the Editorials of all the leading City papers. All go to the effect that secession is a sure thing, the only questions being the times when and how. Immediate Secession, unqualified and unconditional is the prevailing sentiment, the Bell party going even further than the Breckinridge adherents. Dr. Smith will attend the Session of the Legislature next week, the 10th inst, and says the calling of a convention will be the first and inevitable step—this will be he says unanimous—next the arming of the state, and putting herself in an attitude of defense—to this he says there will be no opposition. The convention will meet in January and the Questions submitted to them will be immediate Secession, or a General convention of all southern states, Louisiana to instruct her Delegates, to demand that the Northern States shall repeal the Laws adverse to slavery, and give pledges of future good behavior—Dr. S. thinks it will be all the Conservative men of this state will attempt, to carry this latter alternative against the adherents of the immediate secession: but I told him that for the South to demand of the North such conditions would be idle. The machinery of a Democratic Government is too slow, to bring about such pledges under a pressure when public feeling cannot be moulded by men—It occurs to me that Texas might withdraw from the Confederation, resuming her status as before the Treaty—It might be that S. Carolina, Georgia Alabama and Florida might also fall out, & arrange by Treaty for the break of our Commercial Sea bond, but the moment Mississipi Arkansas, & Louisiana declare an independence, sovereign & complete, with a right to control, interrupt or tax the Commerce of the Mississipi, justly and fairly a storm would arise in those states bordering on the Territories, that would be fearful as compared with anything heretofore known on this Continent. They argue, however as their policy will be free trade, no possible interruption can occur to the usual navigation: but however they may start, some tax and obstruction will result, and then of course retaliation & war.

Now for myself I have told the Governor & all in Authority that as long as Louisiana is a part of the United States I will serve here in my present sphere, and moreover in case of domestic insurrection or molestation from without, I will head the Cadets under my Command, but that I will do no act inconsistent with my allegiance to the General Government: that as long as the form of Govt. indicated by the Constitution of the U.S. is in existence, that I will stand by it—As I have no other means of existence now save this, I will stay here till the Convention meets and does some act of Treason. Then I shall quit—but when to go is a question I cannot solve, and must trust to the confusion that must result from the dissolution of this Govt. I must therefore change my whole plan, and leave

Ellen where she is, till this storm either subsides, or passes away, or until I can do something else: If I leave here suddenly & unexpectedly, I will fetch up at St. Louis—Clay has been very sick, is so still, but I begin to have hopes. Give Ellen the benefit of your advice as to probabilities &c—I am in good health but must have continuous and active employment. as ever with respect,

W. T. Sherman

Louisiana State Seminary of Learning
and Military Academy.
Alexandria, Decr. 1, 1860.

Dear Brother,

When I last wrote you I had observed what I thought a general quiet, and determination to submit as heretofore to the General Election of Lincoln, and as the House which has been under construction for me was drawing to a completion I gave Ellen notice to hold herself ready to start about the 15 instant with all the family, so as to get out of Ohio before the close of the River, and to take advantage of the present condition of Red River. But the whole case has changed. The quiet which I thought the usual acquiescence of the People was merely the prelude to the storm of opinion that now seems irresistable—Politicians have by hearing the prejudices of the people, and moving with the current have succeeded in destroying the Government—It cannot be stopped now I fear—I was in Alexandria all day yesterday, and had a full and unreserved conversation with Dr. S. A. Smith, State Senator, who is a man of education, property, influence and qualified to Judge—He was during the canvas a Breckinridge man, but though a Southern in opinion is really opposed to a dissolution of our Government. He has returned from New Orleans where he says he was amazed to See evidences of Public sentiment which could not be mistaken—The Legislature meets Dec. 10—at Baton Rouge—the calling a Convention forthwith is to be unanimous—the Bill for arming the State ditto—The Convention will meet in January, and only two questions will be agitated—Immediate dissolution, a declaration of State Independence, a General Convention of Southern States with instructions to demand of the Northern States to repeal all laws hostile to Slavery, and pledges of future good behavior.

Of course this latter demand cannot from the nature of an anarchical Democratic Government ever be entertained & therefore if these things be so, and all the Public prints of New Orleans confirm these views of Dr. Smith, Uncle Sam is already a Sick old man—whether the South or North be benefitted is a question that no man can solve—If Texas would draw off, no great harm would follow—Even if S. Carolina, Georgia, Alabama & Florida would cut away, it might be the rest could get along, but I think the secession of Mississipi, Louisiana and Arkansas will bring war—for though they now say that Free trade is their Policy yet it wont be long before steamboats will be taxed and molested all the way down. Therefore when the Convention meets in January, as they will assuredly do, and resolve to secede, or to elect members to a General Convention with instructions inconsistent with the nature of things I must quit this place for it is neither right for me to Stay nor would the Governor be justified in placing me in this position of Trust for the moment Louisiana assumes a position of hostility then this becomes an arsenal & fort. I wont move however until the last moment for I am at a loss what else to do. I will watch the proceedings of Congress with deep interest, and catch at the first chance of reconciliation —Let me hear the moment you think dissolution is inevitable. What Mississipi and Georgia do, this State will do likewise. Affectionately,

W. T. S.

# *James Buchanan: from the Annual Message to Congress*

President James Buchanan met with his cabinet on November 9 to discuss the situation in the South and particularly in South Carolina. Buchanan proposed a general convention of the states to address the sectional crisis and on November 10 presented the cabinet with a draft document condemning the doctrine of secession. The draft drew praise from the four Unionist members of the cabinet, but was criticized by its three Southerners—Secretary of the Treasury Howell Cobb, Secretary of War John Floyd, and Secretary of the Interior Jacob Thompson—all of whom would later join the Confederacy. In preparing his annual message to Congress, the President drew upon a legal opinion regarding the constitutionality of secession and coercion submitted by Attorney General Jeremiah Black. Despite his hope that it would reduce sectional tensions, Buchanan's message was criticized by many Southerners for denying the constitutionality of secession, and by many Northerners for concluding that the federal government could not prevent states from seceding.

---

WASHINGTON CITY, *December 3, 1860.*
*Fellow-Citizens of the Senate and House of Representatives:*

Throughout the year since our last meeting the country has been eminently prosperous in all its material interests. The general health has been excellent, our harvests have been abundant, and plenty smiles throughout the land. Our commerce and manufactures have been prosecuted with energy and industry, and have yielded fair and ample returns. In short, no nation in the tide of time has ever presented a spectacle of greater material prosperity than we have done until within a very recent period.

Why is it, then, that discontent now so extensively prevails, and the Union of the States, which is the source of all these blessings, is threatened with destruction?

The long-continued and intemperate interference of the

Northern people with the question of slavery in the Southern States has at length produced its natural effects. The different sections of the Union are now arrayed against each other, and the time has arrived, so much dreaded by the Father of his Country, when hostile geographical parties have been formed.

I have long foreseen and often forewarned my countrymen of the now impending danger. This does not proceed solely from the claim on the part of Congress or the Territorial legislatures to exclude slavery from the Territories, nor from the efforts of different States to defeat the execution of the fugitive-slave law. All or any of these evils might have been endured by the South without danger to the Union (as others have been) in the hope that time and reflection might apply the remedy. The immediate peril arises not so much from these causes as from the fact that the incessant and violent agitation of the slavery question throughout the North for the last quarter of a century has at length produced its malign influence on the slaves and inspired them with vague notions of freedom. Hence a sense of security no longer exists around the family altar. This feeling of peace at home has given place to apprehensions of servile insurrections. Many a matron throughout the South retires at night in dread of what may befall herself and children before the morning. Should this apprehension of domestic danger, whether real or imaginary, extend and intensify itself until it shall pervade the masses of the Southern people, then disunion will become inevitable. Self-preservation is the first law of nature, and has been implanted in the heart of man by his Creator for the wisest purpose; and no political union, however fraught with blessings and benefits in all other respects, can long continue if the necessary consequence be to render the homes and the firesides of nearly half the parties to it habitually and hopelessly insecure. Sooner or later the bonds of such a union must be severed. It is my conviction that this fatal period has not yet arrived, and my prayer to God is that He would preserve the Constitution and the Union throughout all generations.

But let us take warning in time and remove the cause of danger. It can not be denied that for five and twenty years the agitation at the North against slavery has been incessant. In 1835 pictorial handbills and inflammatory appeals were circulated extensively throughout the South of a character to excite the passions of the slaves, and, in the language of General Jackson, "to stimulate them to insurrection and produce all the horrors of a servile war." This agitation has ever since been continued by the public press, by the proceedings of State and county conventions and by abolition sermons and lectures. The time of Congress has been occupied in violent speeches on this never-ending subject, and appeals, in pamphlet and other forms, indorsed by distinguished names, have been sent forth from this central point and spread broadcast over the Union.

How easy would it be for the American people to settle the slavery question forever and to restore peace and harmony to this distracted country! They, and they alone, can do it. All that is necessary to accomplish the object, and all for which the slave States have ever contended, is to be let alone and permitted to manage their domestic institutions in their own way. As sovereign States, they, and they alone, are responsible before God and the world for the slavery existing among them. For this the people of the North are not more responsible and have no more right to interfere than with similar institutions in Russia or in Brazil.

Upon their good sense and patriotic forbearance I confess I still greatly rely. Without their aid it is beyond the power of any President, no matter what may be his own political proclivities, to restore peace and harmony among the States. Wisely limited and restrained as is his power under our Constitution and laws, he alone can accomplish but little for good or for evil on such a momentous question.

And this brings me to observe that the election of any one of our fellow-citizens to the office of President does not of itself afford just cause for dissolving the Union. This is more especially true if his election has been effected by a mere plurality, and not a majority of the people, and has resulted from transient and temporary causes, which may probably never again occur. In order to justify a resort to revolutionary resistance, the Federal Government must be guilty of "a deliberate, palpable, and dangerous exercise" of powers not granted by the Constitution. The late Presidential election, however, has been held in strict conformity with its express provisions. How, then, can the result justify a revolution to destroy this very Constitution? Reason, justice, a regard for the Constitution, all require that we shall wait for some overt and dangerous act on the part of the President elect before resorting to such a remedy. It is said, however, that the antecedents of the President elect have been sufficient to justify the fears of the South that he will attempt to invade their constitutional rights. But are such apprehensions of contingent danger in the future sufficient to justify the immediate destruction of the noblest system of government ever devised by mortals? From the very nature of his office and its high responsibilities he must necessarily be conservative. The stern duty of administering the vast and complicated concerns of this Government affords in itself a guaranty that he will not attempt any violation of a clear constitutional right.

After all, he is no more than the chief executive officer of the Government. His province is not to make but to execute the laws. And it is a remarkable fact in our history that, notwithstanding the repeated efforts of the antislavery party, no single act has ever passed Congress, unless we may possibly except the Missouri compromise, impairing in the slightest degree the rights of the South to their property in slaves; and it may also be observed, judging from present indications, that no probability exists of the passage of such an act by a majority of both Houses, either in the present or the next Congress. Surely under these circumstances we ought to be restrained from present action by the precept of Him who spake as man never spoke, that "sufficient unto the day is the evil thereof." The day of evil may never come unless we shall rashly bring it upon ourselves.

It is alleged as one cause for immediate secession that the Southern States are denied equal rights with the other States in the common Territories. But by what authority are these denied? Not by Congress, which has never passed, and I believe never will pass, any act to exclude slavery from these Territories; and certainly not by the Supreme Court, which has solemnly decided that slaves are property, and, like all other property, their owners have a right to take them into the common Territories and hold them there under the protection of the Constitution.

So far then, as Congress is concerned, the objection is not to anything they have already done, but to what they may do hereafter. It will surely be admitted that this apprehension of future danger is no good reason for an immediate dissolution of the Union. It is true that the Territorial legislature of Kansas, on the 23d February, 1860, passed in great haste an act over the veto of the governor declaring that slavery "is and shall be forever prohibited in this Territory." Such an act, however, plainly violating the rights of property secured by the Constitution, will surely be declared void by the judiciary whenever it shall be presented in a legal form.

Only three days after my inauguration the Supreme Court of the United States solemnly adjudged that this power did not exist in a Territorial legislature. Yet such has been the factious temper of the times that the correctness of this decision has been extensively impugned before the people, and the question has given rise to angry political conflicts throughout the country. Those who have appealed from this judgment of our highest constitutional tribunal to popular assemblies would, if they could, invest a Territorial legislature with power to annul the sacred rights of property. This power Congress is expressly forbidden by the Federal Constitution to exercise. Every State legislature in the Union is forbidden by its own constitution to exercise it. It can not be exercised in any State except by the people in their highest sovereign capacity, when framing or amending their State constitution. In like manner it can only be exercised by the people of a Territory represented in a convention of delegates for the purpose of framing a constitution preparatory to admission as a State into the Union. Then, and not until then, are they invested with power to decide the question whether slavery shall or shall not exist within their limits. This is an act of sovereign authority, and not of subordinate Territorial legislation. Were it otherwise, then indeed would the equality of the States in the Territories be destroyed, and the rights of property in slaves would depend not upon the guaranties of the Constitution, but upon the shifting majorities of an irresponsible Territorial legislature. Such a doctrine, from its intrinsic unsoundness, can not long influence any considerable portion of our people, much less can it afford a good reason for a dissolution of the Union.

The most palpable violations of constitutional duty which have yet been committed consist in the acts of different State legislatures to defeat the execution of the fugitive-slave law. It ought to be remembered, however, that for these acts neither Congress nor any President can justly be held responsible. Having been passed in violation of the Federal Constitution, they are therefore null and void. All the courts, both State and national, before whom the question has arisen have from the beginning declared the fugitive-slave law to be constitutional. The single exception is that of a State court in Wisconsin, and this has not only been reversed by the proper appellate tribunal, but has met with such universal reprobation that there can be no danger from it as a precedent. The validity of this law has been established over and over again by the Supreme Court of the United States with perfect unanimity. It is founded upon an express provision of the Constitution, requiring that fugitive slaves who escape from service in one State to another shall be "delivered up" to their masters. Without this provision it is a well-known historical fact that the Constitution itself could never have been adopted by the Convention. In one form or other, under the acts of 1793 and 1850, both being substantially the same, the fugitive-slave law has been the law of the land from the days of Washington until the present moment. Here, then, a clear case is presented in which it will be the duty of the next President, as it has been my own, to act with vigor in executing this supreme law against the conflicting enactments of State legislatures. Should he fail in the performance of this high duty, he will then have manifested a disregard of the Constitution and laws, to the great injury of the people of nearly one-half of the States of the Union. But are we to presume in advance that he will thus violate his duty? This would be at war with every principle of justice and of Christian charity. Let us wait for the overt act. The fugitive-slave law has been carried into execution in every contested case since the commencement of the present Administration, though often, it is to be regretted, with great loss and inconvenience to the master and with considerable expense to the Government. Let us trust that the State legislatures will repeal their unconstitutional and obnoxious enactments. Unless this shall be done without unnecessary delay, it is impossible for any human power to save the Union.

The Southern States, standing on the basis of the Constitution, have a right to demand this act of justice from the States of the North. Should it be refused, then the Constitution, to which all the States are parties, will have been willfully violated by one portion of them in a provision essential to the domestic security and happiness of the remainder. In that event the injured States, after having first used all peaceful and constitutional means to obtain redress, would be justified in revolutionary resistance to the Government of the Union.

I have purposely confined my remarks to revolutionary resistance, because it has been claimed within the last few years that any State, whenever this shall be its sovereign will and pleasure, may secede from the Union in accordance with the Constitution and without any violation of the constitutional rights of the other members of the Confederacy; that as each became parties to the Union by the vote of its own people assembled in convention, so any one of them may retire from the Union in a similar manner by the vote of such a convention.

In order to justify secession as a constitutional remedy, it must be on the principle that the Federal Government is a mere voluntary association of States, to be dissolved at pleasure by any one of the contracting parties. If this be so, the Confederacy is a rope of sand, to be penetrated and dissolved by the first adverse wave of public opinion in any of the States. In this manner our thirty-three States may resolve themselves into as many petty, jarring, and hostile republics, each one retiring from the Union without responsibility whenever any sudden excitement might impel them to such a course. By this process a Union might be entirely broken into fragments in a few weeks which cost our forefathers many years of toil, privation, and blood to establish.

Such a principle is wholly inconsistent with the history as well as the character of the Federal Constitution. After it was framed with the greatest deliberation and care it was submitted to conventions of the people of the several States for ratification. Its provisions were discussed at length in these bodies, composed of the first men of the country. Its opponents contended that it conferred powers upon the Federal Government dangerous to the rights of the States, whilst its advocates maintained that under a fair construction of the instrument there was no foundation for such apprehensions. In that mighty struggle between the first intellects of this or any other country it never occurred to any individual, either among its opponents or advocates, to assert or even to intimate that their efforts were all vain labor, because the moment that any State felt herself aggrieved she might secede from the Union. What a crushing argument would this have proved against those who dreaded that the rights of the States would be endangered by the Constitution! The truth is that it was not until many years after the origin of the Federal Government that such a proposition was first advanced. It was then met and refuted by the conclusive arguments of General Jackson, who in his message of the 16th of January, 1833, transmitting the nullifying ordinance of South Carolina to Congress, employs the following language:

The right of the people of a single State to absolve themselves at will and without the consent of the other States from their most solemn obligations, and hazard the liberties and happiness of the millions composing this Union, can not be acknowledged. Such authority is believed to be utterly repugnant both to the principles upon which the General Government is constituted and to the objects which it is expressly formed to attain.

It is not pretended that any clause in the Constitution gives countenance to such a theory. It is altogether founded upon inference; not from any language contained in the instrument itself, but from the sovereign character of the several States by which it was ratified. But is it beyond the power of a State, like an individual, to yield a portion of its sovereign rights to secure the remainder? In the language of Mr. Madison, who has been called the father of the Constitution—

It was formed by the States; that is, by the people in each of the States acting in their highest sovereign capacity, and formed, consequently, by the same authority which formed the State constitutions. * * * Nor is the Government of the United States, created by the Constitution, less a government, in the strict sense of the term, within the sphere of its powers than the governments created by the constitutions of the States are within their several spheres. It is, like them, organized into legislative, executive, and judiciary departments. It operates, like them, directly on persons and things, and, like them, it has at command a physical force for executing the powers committed to it.

It was intended to be perpetual, and not to be annulled at the pleasure of any one of the contracting parties. The old Articles of Confederation were entitled "Articles of Confederation and Perpetual Union between the States," and by the thirteenth article it is expressly declared that "the articles of this Confederation shall be inviolably observed by every State, and the Union shall be perpetual." The preamble to the Constitution of the United States, having express reference to the Articles of Confederation, recites that it was established "in order to form a more perfect union." And yet it is contended that this "more perfect union" does not include the essential attribute of perpetuity.

But that the Union was designed to be perpetual appears conclusively from the nature and extent of the powers conferred by the Constitution on the Federal Government. These powers embrace the very highest attributes of national sovereignty. They place both the sword and the purse under its control. Congress has power to make war and to make peace, to raise and support armies and navies, and to conclude treaties with foreign governments. It is invested with the power to coin money and to regulate the value thereof, and to regulate commerce with foreign nations and among the several States. It is not necessary to enumerate the other high powers which have been conferred upon the Federal Government. In order to carry the enumerated powers into effect, Congress possesses the exclusive right to lay and collect duties on imports, and, in common with the States, to lay and collect all other taxes.

But the Constitution has not only conferred these high powers upon Congress, but it has adopted effectual means to restrain the States from interfering with their exercise. For that purpose it has in strong prohibitory language expressly declared that—

No State shall enter into any treaty, alliance, or confederation; grant letters of marque and reprisal; coin money; emit bills of credit;

make anything but gold and silver coin a tender in payment of debts; pass any bill of attainder, ex post facto law, or law impairing the obligation of contracts.

Moreover—

No State shall without the consent of the Congress lay any imposts or duties on imports or exports, except what may be absolutely necessary for executing its inspection laws.

And if they exceed this amount the excess shall belong to the United States. And—

No State shall without the consent of Congress lay any duty of tonnage, keep troops or ships of war in time of peace, enter into any agreement or compact with another State or with a foreign power, or engage in war, unless actually invaded or in such imminent danger as will not admit of delay.

In order still further to secure the uninterrupted exercise of these high powers against State interposition, it is provided that—

This Constitution and the laws of the United States which shall be made in pursuance thereof, and all treaties made or which shall be made under the authority of the United States, shall be the supreme law of the land, and the judges in every State shall be bound thereby, anything in the constitution or laws of any State to the contrary notwithstanding.

The solemn sanction of religion has been superadded to the obligations of official duty, and all Senators and Representatives of the United States, all members of State legislatures, and all executive and judicial officers, "both of the United States and of the several States, shall be bound by oath or affirmation to support this Constitution."

In order to carry into effect these powers, the Constitution has established a perfect Government in all its forms—legislative, executive, and judicial; and this Government to the extent of its powers acts directly upon the individual citizens of every State, and executes its own decrees by the agency of its own officers. In this respect it differs entirely from the Government under the old Confederation, which was confined to making requisitions on the States in their sovereign character. This left it in the discretion of each whether to obey or to refuse, and they often declined to comply with such requisitions. It thus became necessary for the purpose of removing this barrier and "in order to form a more perfect union" to establish a Government which could act directly upon the people and execute its own laws without the intermediate agency of the States. This has been accomplished by the Constitution of the United States. In short, the Government created by the Constitution, and deriving its authority from the sovereign people of each of the several States, has precisely the same right to exercise its power over the people of all these States in the enumerated cases that each one of them possesses over subjects not delegated to the United States, but "reserved to the States respectively or to the people."

To the extent of the delegated powers the Constitution of the United States is as much a part of the constitution of each State and is as binding upon its people as though it had been textually inserted therein.

This Government, therefore, is a great and powerful Government, invested with all the attributes of sovereignty over the special subjects to which its authority extends. Its framers never intended to implant in its bosom the seeds of its own destruction, nor were they at its creation guilty of the absurdity of providing for its own dissolution. It was not intended by its framers to be the baseless fabric of a vision, which at the touch of the enchanter would vanish into thin air, but a substantial and mighty fabric, capable of resisting the slow decay of time and of defying the storms of ages. Indeed, well may the jealous patriots of that day have indulged fears that a Government of such high powers might violate the reserved rights of the States, and wisely did they adopt the rule of a strict construction of these powers to prevent the danger. But they did not fear, nor had they any reason to imagine, that the Constitution would ever be so interpreted as to enable any State by her own act, and without the consent of her sister States, to discharge her people from all or any of their federal obligations.

It may be asked, then, Are the people of the States without redress against the tyranny and oppression of the Federal Government? By no means. The right of resistance on the part of the governed against the oppression of their governments can

not be denied. It exists independently of all constitutions, and
has been exercised at all periods of the world's history. Under
it old governments have been destroyed and new ones have
taken their place. It is embodied in strong and express language in our own Declaration of Independence. But the distinction must ever be observed that this is revolution against
an established government, and not a voluntary secession from
it by virtue of an inherent constitutional right. In short, let us
look the danger fairly in the face. Secession is neither more nor
less than revolution. It may or it may not be a justifiable revolution, but still it is revolution.

What, in the meantime, is the responsibility and true position of the Executive? He is bound by solemn oath, before
God and the country, "to take care that the laws be faithfully
executed," and from this obligation he can not be absolved by
any human power. But what if the performance of this duty, in
whole or in part, has been rendered impracticable by events
over which he could have exercised no control? Such at the
present moment is the case throughout the State of South
Carolina so far as the laws of the United States to secure the
administration of justice by means of the Federal judiciary are
concerned. All the Federal officers within its limits through
whose agency alone these laws can be carried into execution
have already resigned. We no longer have a district judge, a
district attorney, or a marshal in South Carolina. In fact, the
whole machinery of the Federal Government necessary for the
distribution of remedial justice among the people has been demolished, and it would be difficult, if not impossible, to replace it.

The only acts of Congress on the statute book bearing
upon this subject are those of February 28, 1795, and March 3,
1807. These authorize the President, after he shall have ascertained that the marshal, with his *posse comitatus*, is unable to
execute civil or criminal process in any particular case, to call
forth the militia and employ the Army and Navy to aid him in
performing this service, having first by proclamation commanded the insurgents "to disperse and retire peaceably to
their respective abodes within a limited time." This duty can
not by possibility be performed in a State where no judicial authority exists to issue process, and where there is no marshal to

execute it, and where, even if there were such an officer, the entire population would constitute one solid combination to resist him.

The bare enumeration of these provisions proves how inadequate they are without further legislation to overcome a united opposition in a single State, not to speak of other States who may place themselves in a similar attitude. Congress alone has power to decide whether the present laws can or can not be amended so as to carry out more effectually the objects of the Constitution.

The same insuperable obstacles do not lie in the way of executing the laws for the collection of the customs. The revenue still continues to be collected as heretofore at the customhouse in Charleston, and should the collector unfortunately resign a successor may be appointed to perform this duty.

Then, in regard to the property of the United States in South Carolina. This has been purchased for a fair equivalent, "by the consent of the legislature of the State," "for the erection of forts, magazines, arsenals," etc., and over these the authority "to exercise exclusive legislation" has been expressly granted by the Constitution to Congress. It is not believed that any attempt will be made to expel the United States from this property by force; but if in this I should prove to be mistaken, the officer in command of the forts has received orders to act strictly on the defensive. In such a contingency the responsibility for consequences would rightfully rest upon the heads of the assailants.

Apart from the execution of the laws, so far as this may be practicable, the Executive has no authority to decide what shall be the relations between the Federal Government and South Carolina. He has been invested with no such discretion. He possesses no power to change the relations heretofore existing between them, much less to acknowledge the independence of that State. This would be to invest a mere executive officer with the power of recognizing the dissolution of the confederacy among our thirty-three sovereign States. It bears no resemblance to the recognition of a foreign *de facto* government, involving no such responsibility. Any attempt to do this would, on his part, be a naked act of usurpation. It is therefore my duty to submit to Congress the whole question in all its bearings.

The course of events is so rapidly hastening forward that the emergency may soon arise when you may be called upon to decide the momentous question whether you possess the power by force of arms to compel a State to remain in the Union. I should feel myself recreant to my duty were I not to express an opinion on this important subject.

The question fairly stated is, Has the Constitution delegated to Congress the power to coerce a State into submission which is attempting to withdraw or has actually withdrawn from the Confederacy? If answered in the affirmative, it must be on the principle that the power has been conferred upon Congress to declare and to make war against a State. After much serious reflection I have arrived at the conclusion that no such power has been delegated to Congress or to any other department of the Federal Government. It is manifest upon an inspection of the Constitution that this is not among the specific and enumerated powers granted to Congress, and it is equally apparent that its exercise is not "necessary and proper for carrying into execution" any one of these powers. So far from this power having been delegated to Congress, it was expressly refused by the Convention which framed the Constitution.

It appears from the proceedings of that body that on the 31st May, 1787, the clause "*authorizing an exertion of the force of the whole against a delinquent State*" came up for consideration. Mr. Madison opposed it in a brief but powerful speech, from which I shall extract but a single sentence. He observed:

> The use of force against a State would look more like a declaration of war than an infliction of punishment, and would probably be considered by the party attacked as a dissolution of all previous compacts by which it might be bound.

Upon his motion the clause was unanimously postponed, and was never, I believe, again presented. Soon afterwards, on the 8th June, 1787, when incidentally adverting to the subject, he said: "Any government for the United States formed on the supposed practicability of using force against the unconstitutional proceedings of the States would prove as visionary and fallacious as the government of Congress," evidently meaning the then existing Congress of the old Confederation.

Without descending to particulars, it may be safely asserted that the power to make war against a State is at variance with the whole spirit and intent of the Constitution. Suppose such a war should result in the conquest of a State; how are we to govern it afterwards? Shall we hold it as a province and govern it by despotic power? In the nature of things, we could not by physical force control the will of the people and compel them to elect Senators and Representatives to Congress and to perform all the other duties depending upon their own volition and required from the free citizens of a free State as a constituent member of the Confederacy.

But if we possessed this power, would it be wise to exercise it under existing circumstances? The object would doubtless be to preserve the Union. War would not only present the most effectual means of destroying it, but would vanish all hope of its peaceable reconstruction. Besides, in the fraternal conflict a vast amount of blood and treasure would be expended, rendering future reconciliation between the States impossible. In the meantime, who can foretell what would be the sufferings and privations of the people during its existence?

The fact is that our Union rests upon public opinion, and can never be cemented by the blood of its citizens shed in civil war. If it can not live in the affections of the people, it must one day perish. Congress possesses many means of preserving it by conciliation, but the sword was not placed in their hand to preserve it by force.

But may I be permitted solemnly to invoke my countrymen to pause and deliberate before they determine to destroy this the grandest temple which has ever been dedicated to human freedom since the world began? It has been consecrated by the blood of our fathers, by the glories of the past, and by the hopes of the future. The Union has already made us the most prosperous, and ere long will, if preserved, render us the most powerful, nation on the face of the earth. In every foreign region of the globe the title of American citizen is held in the highest respect, and when pronounced in a foreign land it causes the hearts of our countrymen to swell with honest pride. Surely when we reach the brink of the yawning abyss we shall recoil with horror from the last fatal plunge.

By such a dread catastrophe the hopes of the friends of freedom throughout the world would be destroyed, and a long night of leaden despotism would enshroud the nations. Our example for more than eighty years would not only be lost, but it would be quoted as a conclusive proof that man is unfit for self-government.

It is not every wrong—nay, it is not every grievous wrong— which can justify a resort to such a fearful alternative. This ought to be the last desperate remedy of a despairing people, after every other constitutional means of conciliation had been exhausted. We should reflect that under this free Government there is an incessant ebb and flow in public opinion. The slavery question, like everything human, will have its day. I firmly believe that it has reached and passed the culminating point. But if in the midst of the existing excitement the Union shall perish, the evil may then become irreparable.

Congress can contribute much to avert it by proposing and recommending to the legislatures of the several States the remedy for existing evils which the Constitution has itself provided for its own preservation. This has been tried at different critical periods of our history, and always with eminent success. It is to be found in the fifth article, providing for its own amendment. Under this article amendments have been proposed by two-thirds of both Houses of Congress, and have been "ratified by the legislatures of three-fourths of the several States," and have consequently become parts of the Constitution. To this process the country is indebted for the clause prohibiting Congress from passing any law respecting an establishment of religion or abridging the freedom of speech or of the press or of the right of petition. To this we are also indebted for the bill of rights which secures the people against any abuse of power by the Federal Government. Such were the apprehensions justly entertained by the friends of State rights at that period as to have rendered it extremely doubtful whether the Constitution could have long survived without those amendments.

Again the Constitution was amended by the same process, after the election of President Jefferson by the House of Representatives, in February, 1803. This amendment was rendered necessary to prevent a recurrence of the dangers which had seriously threatened the existence of the Government during the pendency of that election. The article for its own amendment was intended to secure the amicable adjustment of conflicting constitutional questions like the present which might arise between the governments of the States and that of the United States. This appears from contemporaneous history. In this connection I shall merely call attention to a few sentences in Mr. Madison's justly celebrated report, in 1799, to the legislature of Virginia. In this he ably and conclusively defended the resolutions of the preceding legislature against the strictures of several other State legislatures. These were mainly founded upon the protest of the Virginia legislature against the "alien and sedition acts," as "palpable and alarming infractions of the Constitution." In pointing out the peaceful and constitutional remedies—and he referred to none other—to which the States were authorized to resort on such occasions, he concludes by saying that—

The legislatures of the States might have made a direct representation to Congress with a view to obtain a rescinding of the two offensive acts, or they might have represented to their respective Senators in Congress their wish that two-thirds thereof would propose an explanatory amendment to the Constitution; or two-thirds of themselves, if such had been their option, might by an application to Congress have obtained a convention for the same object.

This is the very course which I earnestly recommend in order to obtain an "explanatory amendment" of the Constitution on the subject of slavery. This might originate with Congress or the State legislatures, as may be deemed most advisable to attain the object. The explanatory amendment might be confined to the final settlement of the true construction of the Constitution on three special points:

1. An express recognition of the right of property in slaves in the States where it now exists or may hereafter exist.

2. The duty of protecting this right in all the common Territories throughout their Territorial existence, and until they shall be admitted as States into the Union, with or without slavery, as their constitutions may prescribe.

3. A like recognition of the right of the master to have his slave who has escaped from one State to another restored and "delivered up" to him, and of the validity of the fugitive-slave law enacted for this purpose, together with a declaration that all State laws impairing or defeating this right are violations of

the Constitution, and are consequently null and void. It may be objected that this construction of the Constitution has already been settled by the Supreme Court of the United States, and what more ought to be required? The answer is that a very large proportion of the people of the United States still contest the correctness of this decision, and never will cease from agitation and admit its binding force until clearly established by the people of the several States in their sovereign character. Such an explanatory amendment would, it is believed, forever terminate the existing dissensions, and restore peace and harmony among the States.

It ought not to be doubted that such an appeal to the arbitrament established by the Constitution itself would be received with favor by all the States of the Confederacy. In any event, it ought to be tried in a spirit of conciliation before any of these States shall separate themselves from the Union.

# *J.D.B. DeBow:*
# *The Non-Slaveholders of the South*

In *The Impending Crisis of the South: How to Meet It* (1857) Hinton Rowan Helper of North Carolina had argued that slavery harmed the interests of nonslaveholding whites. Describing slaveholders as "arrant demagogues," Helper wrote that slavery lay "at the root of all the shame, poverty, ignorance, tyranny, and imbecility of the South." *The Impending Crisis* was widely distributed in abridged form in the North, while its circulation was banned in several southern states. James D. B. DeBow, the secessionist editor of the influential Southern monthly *DeBow's Review*, sought to refute Helper's argument in an article that first appeared as part of a series of pro-secession pamphlets published in Charleston, South Carolina, by Robert Gourdin.

---

NASHVILLE, Dec. 5, 1860.

*My dear Sir.*—Whilst in Charleston recently, I adverted, in conversation with you, to some considerations affecting the question of slavery in its application to the several classes of population at the South and especially to the non-slaveholding class, who, I maintained, were even more deeply interested than any other in the maintainance of our institutions, and in the success of the movement now inaugurated, for the entire social, industrial and political independence of the South. At your request, I promised to elaborate and commit to writing the points of that conversation, which I now proceed to do, in the hope that I may thus be enabled to give some feeble aid to a cause which is worthy of the Sydneys, Hampdens and Patrick Henrys, of earlier times.

When in charge of the national census office, several years since, I found that it had been stated by an abolition Senator from his seat, that the number of slaveholders at the South did not exceed 150,000. Convinced that it was a gross misrepresentation of the facts, I caused a careful examination of the returns to be made, which fixed the actual number at 347,255, and communicated the information, by note, to Senator Cass, who read it in the Senate. I first called attention to the fact that the number embraced slaveholding families, and that to arrive at the actual number of slaveholders, it would be necessary to multiply by the proportion of persons, which the census showed to a family. When this was done, the number was swelled to about 2,000,000.

Since these results were made public, I have had reason to think, that the separation of the schedules of the slave and the free, was calculated to lead to omissions of the single properties, and that on this account it would be safe to put the number of families at 375,000, and the number of actual slaveholders at about two million and a quarter.

Assuming the published returns, however, to be correct, it will appear that one-half of the population of South Carolina, Mississippi, and Louisiana, excluding the cities, are slaveholders, and that one-third of the population of the entire South are similarly circumstanced. The average number of slaves is nine to each slave-holding family, and one-half of the whole number of such holders are in possession of less than five slaves.

It will thus appear that the slaveholders of the South, so far from constituting numerically an insignificant portion of its people, as has been malignantly alleged, make up an aggregate, greater in relative proportion than the holders of any other species of property whatever, in any part of the world; and that of no other property can it be said, with equal truthfulness, that it is an interest of the whole community. Whilst every other family in the States I have specially referred to, are slaveholders, but one family in every three and a half families in Maine, New Hampshire, Massachusetts and Connecticut, are holders of agricultural land; and, in European States, the proportion is almost indefinitely less. The proportion which the slaveholders of the South, bear to the entire population is greater than that of the owners of land or houses, agricultural stock, State, bank, or other corporation securities anywhere else. No political economist will deny this. Nor is that all. Even in the States which are among the largest slaveholding, South Carolina, Georgia and Tennessee, the land proprietors outnumber nearly two to one, in relative proportion, the owners of the same property in Maine, Massachusetts and Connecticut, and if the average number of slaves held by each family throughout the South be but nine, and if one-half of the whole number of slaveholders own under five slaves, it will be seen how preposterous is the allegation of our enemies, that the slaveholding class is an organized wealthy aristocracy. *The poor men of the South are the holders of one to five slaves, and it would be equally consistent with truth and justice, to say that they represent, in reality, its slaveholding interest.*

The fact being conceded that there is a very large class of persons in the slaveholding States, who have no direct ownership in slaves; it may be well asked, upon what principle a greater antagonism can be presumed between them and their fellow-citizens, than exists among the larger class of non-landholders in the free States and the landed interest there? If a conflict of interest exists in one instance, it does in the other, and if patriotism and public spirit are to be measured upon so low a standard, the social fabric at the North is in far greater danger of dissolution than it is here.

Though I protest against the false and degrading standard, to which Northern orators and statesmen have reduced the measure of patriotism, which is to be expected from a free and enlightened people, and in the name of the non-slaveholders of the South, fling back the insolent charge that they are only bound to their country by its "loaves and fishes," and would be found derelict in honor and principle and public virtue in proportion as they are needy in circumstances; I think it but easy to show that the interest of the poorest non-slaveholder among us, is to make common cause with, and die in the last trenches in defence of, the slave property of his more favored neighbor.

The non-slaveholders of the South may be classed as either such as desire and are incapable of purchasing slaves, or such as have the means to purchase and do not because of the absence of the motive, preferring to hire or employ cheaper white labor. A class conscientiously objecting to the ownership of slave-property, does not exist at the South, for all such scruples have long since been silenced by the profound and unanswerable arguments to which Yankee controversy has driven our statesmen, popular orators and clergy. Upon the sure testimony of God's Holy Book, and upon the principles of universal polity, they have defended and justified the institution. The exceptions which embrace recent importations into Virginia, and into some of the Southern cities from the free States of the North, and some of the crazy, socialistic Germans in Texas, are too unimportant to affect the truth of the proposition.

The non-slaveholders are either urban or rural, including among the former the merchants, traders, mechanics, laborers and other classes in the towns and cities; and among the latter, the tillers of the soil in sections where slave property either could, or could not be profitably employed.

As the *competition of free labor with slave labor* is the gist of the argument used by the opponents of slavery, and as it is upon this that they rely in support of a future social *conflict* in our midst, it is clear that in cases where the competition cannot possibly exist, the argument, whatever weight it might otherwise have, must fall to the ground.

Now, from what can such competition be argued in our cities? Are not all the interests of the merchant and those whom he employs of necessity upon the side of the slaveholder? The products which he buys, the commodities which he sells, the profits which he realizes, the hopes of future fortune which sustain him; all spring from this source, and from no other. The cities, towns and villages of the South, are but so many agencies for converting the products of slave labor into the products of other labor obtained from abroad, and as in every other agency the interest of the agent is, that the principal shall have as much as possible to sell, and be enabled as much as possible to buy. In the absence of every other source of wealth at the South, its mercantile interests are so interwoven with those of slave labor as to be almost identical. What is true of the merchant is true of the clerk, the drayman, or the laborer whom he employs—the mechanic who builds his houses, the lawyer who argues his causes, the physician who heals, the teacher, the preacher, etc., etc. If the poor mechanic could have ever complained of the competition, in the cities, of slave labor with his, that cause of complaint in the enormous increase of value of slave property has failed, since such increase has been exhausting the cities and towns of slave labor, or making it so valuable that he can work in competition with it and receive a rate of remuneration greatly higher than in any of the non-slaveholding towns or cities at the North. In proof of this, it is only necessary to advert to the example of the City of Charleston, which has a larger proportion of slaves than any other at the South, where the first flag of Southern independence was unfurled, and where the entire people, with one voice, rich and poor, merchant, mechanic and laborer, stand nobly together. Another illustration may be found in the city of New York, almost as dependent upon Southern slavery as Charleston itself, which records a majority of nearly thirty thousand votes against the further progress of abolitionism.

As the competition does not exist in the cities it is equally certain that it does not exist in those sections of the South, which are employed upon the cultivation of commodities, in which slave labor could not be used, and that there exists no conflict there except in the before stated cases of Virginia and Texas, and some of the counties of Missouri, Maryland and Kentucky. These exceptions are, however, too unimportant to affect the great question of slavery in fifteen States of the South, and are so kept in check as to be incapable of effecting any mischief even in the communities referred to. It would be the baldest absurdity to suppose that the poor farmers of South Carolina, North Carolina and Tennessee, who grow corn, wheat, bacon and hogs and horses, are brought into any sort of competition with the slaves of these or other States, who, while they consume these commodities, produce but little or none of them.

The competition and conflict, if such exist at the South, between slave labor and free labor, is reduced to the single case of such labor being employed side by side, in the production of the same commodities and could be felt only in the cane, cotton, tobacco and rice fields, where almost the entire agricultural slave labor is exhausted. Now, any one cognizant of the actual facts, will admit that the free labor which is employed upon these crops, disconnected from and in actual independence of the slave-holder, is a very insignificant item in the account, and whether in accord or in conflict would affect nothing the permanency and security of the institution. It is a competition from which the non-slaveholder cheerfully retires when the occasion offers, his physical organization refusing to endure that exposure to tropical suns and fatal miasmas which alone are the condition of profitable culture and any attempt to reverse the laws which God has ordained, is attended with disease and death. Of this the poor white foreign laborer upon our river swamps and in our southern cities, especially in Mobile and New Orleans, and upon the public works of the South, is a daily witness.

Having then followed out, step by step, and seen to what amounts the so much paraded competition and conflict between the non-slaveholding and slaveholding interests of the South; I will proceed to present several general considerations which must be found powerful enough to influence the non-slaveholders, if the claims of patriotism were inadequate, to resist any attempt to overthrow the institutions and industry of the section to which they belong.

1. *The non-slaveholder of the South is assured that the remuneration afforded by his labor, over and above the expense of living, is larger than that which is afforded by the same labor in the free States.* To be convinced of this he has only to compare the value of labor in the Southern cities with those of the North, and to take note annually of the large number of laborers who are represented to be out of employment there, and who migrate to our shores, as well as to other sections. No white laborer in return has been forced to leave our midst or remain without employment. Such as have left, have immigrated from States where slavery was less productive. Those who come among us are enabled soon to retire to their homes with a handsome competency. The statement is nearly as true for the agricultural as for other interests, as the statistics will show.

The following table was recently compiled by Senator Johnson, of Tennessee, from information received in reply to a circular letter sent to the points indicated.

Daily wages in New Orleans, Charleston and Nashville:

| Bricklayers. | Carpenters. | Laborers |
|---|---|---|
| $2½ to 3½ | $2¼ to 2¾ | $1 to 1½. |

Daily wages in Chicago, Pittsburg and Lowell, Mass.:

| Bricklayers. | Carpenters. | Laborers. |
|---|---|---|
| $1½ to $2 | $1½ to 1¾ | 75¢ to $1. |

The rates of board weekly for laborers as given in the census of 1850, were in Louisiana $2 70, South Carolina $1 75, Tennessee $1 32, in Illinois $1 49, Pennsylvania $1 72, Massachusctts $2 12. The wages of the agricultural classes as given in Parliamentary reports are in France $20 to $30 per annum with board. In Italy $12 to $20 per annum. In the United States agricultural labor is highest in the Southwest, and lowest in the Northwest, the South and North differing very little, by the official returns.

2. *The non-slaveholders, as a class, are not reduced by the necessity of our condition, as is the case in the free States, to find employment in crowded cities and come into competition in close and sickly workshops and factories, with remorseless and untiring machinery.* They have but to compare their condition in this particular with the mining and manufacturing operatives of the North and Europe, to be thankful that God has reserved them for a better fate. Tender women, aged men, delicate children, toil and labor there from early dawn until after candle light, from one year to another, for a miserable pittance, scarcely above the starvation point and without hope of amelioration. The records of British free labor have long exhibited this and those of our own manufacturing States are rapidly reaching it and would have reached it long ago, but for the excessive bounties which in the way of tariffs have been paid to it, without an equivalent by the slaveholding and non-slaveholding laborer of the South. Let this tariff cease to be paid for a single year and the truth of what is stated will be abundantly shown.

3. *The non-slaveholder is not subjected to that competition with foreign pauper labor, which has degraded the free labor of the North and demoralized it to an extent which perhaps can never be estimated.* From whatever cause, it has happened, whether from climate, the nature of our products or of our labor, the South has been enabled to maintain a more homogeneous population and show a less admixture of races than the North. This the statistics show.

RATIO OF FOREIGN TO NATIVE POPULATION.

Eastern States . . . . . . . . . . . . . . . . . . . . . . . . . . . . . 12.65 in every 100
Middle States . . . . . . . . . . . . . . . . . . . . . . . . . . . 19.84  "        "
Southern States . . . . . . . . . . . . . . . . . . . . . . . . . 1.86  "        "
South-western States . . . . . . . . . . . . . . . . . . . . . 5.34  "        "
North-western States . . . . . . . . . . . . . . . . . . . . . 12.75  "        "

Our people partake of the true American character, and are mainly the descendants of those who fought the battles of the Revolution, and who understand and appreciate the nature and inestimable value of the liberty which it brought. Adhering to the simple truths of the Gospel and the faith of their fathers, they have not run hither and thither in search of all the absurd and degrading isms which have sprung up in the rank soil of infidelity. They are not Mormons or Spiritualists, they are not Owenites, Fourierites, Agrarians, Socialists, Free-lovers or Millerites. They are not for breaking down all the forms of society and of religion and re-constructing them; but prefer law, order and existing institutions to the chaos which radicalism involves. The competition between native and foreign labor in the Northern States, has already begotten rivalry and heart-burning, and riots; and lead to the formation of political parties there which have been marked by a degree of hostility and proscription to which the present age has not afforded another parallel. At the South we have known none of this, except in two or three of the larger cities, where the relations of slavery and freedom scarcely exist at all. The foreigners that are among us at the South are of a select class, and from education and example approximate very nearly to the native standard.

4. *The non-slaveholder of the South preserves the status of the white man, and is not regarded as an inferior or a dependant.* He is not told that the Declaration of Independence, when it says that all men are born free and equal, refers to the negro equally with himself. It is not proposed to him that the free negro's vote shall weigh equally with his own at the ballot-box, and that the little children of both colors shall be mixed in the classes and benches of the school-house, and embrace each other filially in its outside sports. It never occurs to him, that a white man could be degraded enough to boast in a public assembly, as was recently done in New York, of having actually slept with a negro. And his patriotic ire would crush with a blow the free negro who would dare, in his presence, as is done in the free States, to characterize the father of the country as a "scoundrel." No white man at the South serves another as a body servant, to clean his boots, wait on his table, and perform the menial services of his household. His blood

revolts against this, and his necessities never drive him to it. He is a companion and an equal. When in the employ of the slave-holder, or in intercourse with him, he enters his hall, and has a seat at his table. If a distinction exists, it is only that which ed-ucation and refinement may give, and this is so courteously ex-hibited as scarcely to strike attention. The poor white laborer at the North is at the bottom of the social ladder, whilst his brother here has ascended several steps and can look down upon those who are beneath him, at an infinite remove.

5. *The non-slaveholder knows that as soon as his savings will admit, he can become a slaveholder, and thus relieve his wife from the necessities of the kitchen and the laundry, and his chil-dren from the labors of the field.* This, with ordinary frugality, can, in general, be accomplished in a few years, and is a process continually going on. Perhaps twice the number of poor men at the South own a slave to what owned a slave ten years ago. The universal disposition is to purchase. It is the first use for savings, and the negro purchased is the last possession to be parted with. If a woman, her children become heir-looms and make the nucleus of an estate. It is within my knowledge, that a plantation of fifty or sixty persons has been established, from the descendants of a single female, in the course of the lifetime of the original purchaser.

6. *The large slaveholders and proprietors of the South begin life in great part as non-slaveholders.* It is the nature of property to change hands. Luxury, liberality, extravagance, depreciated land, low prices, debt, distribution among children, are con-tinually breaking up estates. All over the new States of the Southwest enormous estates are in the hands of men who began life as overseers or city clerks, traders or merchants. Often the overseer marries the widow. Cheap lands, abundant harvests, high prices, give the poor man soon a negro. His ten bales of cotton bring him another, a second crop increases his pur-chases, and so he goes on opening land and adding labor until in a few years his draft for $20,000 upon his merchant becomes a very marketable commodity.

7. *But should such fortune not be in reserve for the non-slaveholder, he will understand that by honesty and industry it may be realized to his children.* More than one generation of poverty in a family is scarcely to be expected at the South, and

is against the general experience. It is more unusual here for poverty than wealth to be preserved through several generations in the same family.

8. *The sons of the non-slaveholder are and have always been among the leading and ruling spirits of the South; in industry as well as in politics.* Every man's experience in his own neighborhood will evince this. He has but to task his memory. In this class are the McDuffies, Langdon Cheves, Andrew Jacksons, Henry Clays, and Rusks, of the past; the Hammonds, Yanceys, Orrs, Memmingers, Benjamins, Stephens, Soules, Browns of Mississippi, Simms, Porters, Magraths, Aikens, Maunsel Whites, and an innumerable host of the present; and what is to be noted, these men have not been made demagogues for that reason, as in other quarters, but are among the most conservative among us. Nowhere else in the world have intelligence and virtue disconnected from ancestral estates, the same opportunities for advancement, and nowhere else is their triumph more speedy and signal.

9. *Without the institution of slavery, the great staple products of the South would cease to be grown, and the immense annual results, which are distributed among every class of the community, and which give life to every branch of industry, would cease.* The world furnishes no instances of these products being grown upon a large scale by free labor. The English now acknowledge their failure in the East Indies. Brazil, whose slave population nearly equals our own, is the only South American State which has prospered. Cuba, by her slave labor, showers wealth upon old Spain, whilst the British West India Colonies have now ceased to be a source of revenue, and from opulence have been, by emancipation, reduced to beggary. St. Domingo shared the same fate, and the poor whites have been massacred equally with the rich.

EXPORTS.

|  | 1789. | 1860. |
|---|---|---|
| HAYTI, . . . . . . . . . . . . . . . . . . . . | $27,829,000 | $5 to 6,000,000 |

Sugar is no longer exported, and the quantity of Coffee scarcely exceeds one-third, and of Cotton one-tenth, of the exports of 1789. This I give upon Northern authority.

| JAMAICA. | 1805. | 1857. |
|---|---|---|
| Sugar | 150,352 hhds. | 30,459 hhds. |
| Rum | 93,950 " | 15,991 " |
| Coffee | 24,137,393 lbs. | 7,095,623 lbs. |

The value of the present slave production of the South is thus given:

*United States Exports for 1859.*

| Of Southern Origin— | 1859. |
|---|---|
| Cotton | $161,434,923 |
| Tobacco | 21,074,038 |
| Rice | 2,207,048 |
| Naval Stores | 3,694,474 |
| Sugar | 196,735 |
| Molasses | 75,699 |
| Hemp | 9,227 |
| Total | 188,693,496 |
| Other from South | 8,108,632 |
| Cotton Manufactures | 4,989,733 |
| Total from South | 198,389,351 |
| From the North | 78,217,202 |
| Total Merchandise | 278,392,080 |
| Specie | 57,502,305 |

To the Southern credit, however, must be given:

| | |
|---|---|
| 60 per cent. of the cotton manufactured, being, for raw materials | $3,669,106 |
| Breadstuffs (the North having received from the South a value as large in these as the whole foreign export) | 40,047,000 |
| | 43,716,106 |
| Add | 198,389,351 |
| Southern | 242,105,457 |
| Northern contributions | 34,501,008 |

10. *If emancipation be brought about as will undoubtedly be the case, unless the encroachments of the fanatical majorities of the North are resisted now the slaveholders, in the main, will escape the degrading equality which must result, by emigration, for which they would have the means, by disposing of their personal*

*chattels: whilst the non-slaveholders, without these resources, would be compelled to remain and endure the degradation.* This is a startling consideration. In Northern communities, where the free negro is one in a hundred of the total population, he is recognized and acknowledged often as a pest, and in many cases even his presence is prohibited by law. What would be the case in many of our States, where every other inhabitant is a negro, or in many of our communities, as for example the parishes around and about Charleston, and in the vicinity of New Orleans where there are from twenty to one hundred negroes to each white inhabitant? Low as would this class of people sink by emancipation in idleness, superstition and vice, the white man compelled to live among them, would by the power exerted over him, sink even lower, unless as is to be supposed he would prefer to suffer death instead.

In conclusion, my dear sir, I must apologize to the non-slaveholders of the South, of which class, I was myself until very recently a member, for having deigned to notice at all the infamous libels which the common enemies of the South have circulated against them, and which our every-day experience refutes; but the occasion seemed a fitting one to place them truly and rightly before the world. This I have endeavored faithfully to do. They fully understand the momentous questions which now agitate the land in all their relations. They perceive the inevitable drift of Northern aggression, and know that if necessity impel to it, as I verily believe it does at this moment, the establishment of a Southern confederation will be a sure refuge from the storm. *In such a confederation our rights and possessions would be secure, and the wealth being retained at home, to build up our towns and cities, to extend our railroads, and increase our shipping, which now goes in tariffs or other involuntary or voluntary tributes,* \* *to other sections; opu-*

---

\*The annual drain in profits which is going on from the South to the North is thus set down by Mr. Kettell, of New York:

Bounties to fisheries, per annum . . . . . . . . . . . . . . . . . . . . . . . . .$1,500,000
Customs, per annum, disbursed at the North . . . . . . . . . . . . . .40,000,000
Profits of manufacturers . . . . . . . . . . . . . . . . . . . . . . . . . . . . .30,000,000
Profits of importers . . . . . . . . . . . . . . . . . . . . . . . . . . . . . . . . .16,000,000
Profits of shipping, imports and exports . . . . . . . . . . . . . . . . . .40,000,000
Profits of travellers . . . . . . . . . . . . . . . . . . . . . . . . . . . . . . . . . .60,000,000

*lence would be diffused throughout all classes, and we should become the freest, the happiest and the most prosperous and powerful nation upon earth.*

Your obedient servant,

J. D. B. DeBOW.

Robert N. Gourdin, Esq., Charleston, S. C.

---

Profits of teachers and others at the South, sent North  . . . . . . . . 5,000,000
Profits of agents, brokers, commissions, etc.  . . . . . . . . . . . . . . .10,000,000
Profits of capital drawn from the South . . . . . . . . . . . . . . . . . .30,000,000

Total from these sources . . . . . . . . . . . . . . . . . . . . . . . .$231,500,000

This, from the beginning of the Government, making all proper deduction from year to year, has given to the North over $2,500,000,000 of Southern wealth. Are her accumulations, then, surprising, and can one be surprised if accumulation should appear to be less in the South!

# Joseph E. Brown to Alfred H. Colquitt and Others

December 7, 1860

Joseph E. Brown had defeated Benjamin Hill in 1857 to become governor of Georgia. In this public letter in support of secession, Brown argued that the poor whites of the Georgia mountains had a vital interest in preserving slavery. On January 19, 1861, the state convention voted, 164–133, not to delay action until after Lincoln took office, and then approved, 208–89, an ordinance of secession.

---

*Gentlemen:* Your letter requesting me to give to the people of Georgia my views upon the issues involved in the election of delegates to the State Convention, which is to assemble in January next, has been received.

Such is the extent of my official labors at present, that I can devote but little time to the preparation of a reply. If, however, any importance is attached to my opinions, in the present perilous times, I cheerfully give them to my fellow citizens. I propose to discuss briefly three propositions.

1st. Is the election of Mr. Lincoln to the Presidency, sufficient cause to justify Georgia and the other Southern States in seceding from the Union?

2d. What will be the results to the institution of slavery which will follow submission to the inauguration and administration of Mr. Lincoln as the President of one section of the Union?

3d. What will be the effect which the abolition of Slavery will have upon the interests and the social position of the large class of nonslaveholders and poor white laborers, who are in the South?

First, is the election of Mr. Lincoln sufficient cause to justify the secession of the Southern States from the Union? In my opinion the election of Mr. Lincoln, viewed only in the light of the triumph of a successful candidate, is not sufficient cause for a dissolution of the Union. This, however, is a very contracted and narrow view of the question. Mr. Lincoln is a mere mote in the great political atmosphere of the country, which, as it floats, only shows the direction in which the wind blows. He is the mere representative of a fanatical abolition sentiment—the mere instrument of a great triumphant political party, the principles of which are deadly hostile to the institution of Slavery, and openly at war with the fundamental doctrines of the Constitution of the United States. The rights of the South, and the institution of slavery, are not endangered by the triumph of Mr. Lincoln, as a man; but they are in imminent danger from the triumph of the powerful party which he represents, and of the fanatical abolition sentiment which brought him into power, as the candidate of the Northern section of the Union, over the united opposition of the Southern section against him. The party embracing that sentiment, has constantly denied, and still denies, our equality in the Union, and our right to hold our slaves as property; and avows its purpose to take from us our property, so soon as it has the power. Its ability to elect Mr. Lincoln as its candidate, shows it now has the power to control the Executive branch of the Government. As the President, with the advice and consent of the Senate, appoints the Judges of the Supreme Court of the United States, when vacancies occur, its control of the Executive power will, in a few years, give it the control of the Judicial Department; while the constant increase of abolition sentiment, in the Northern States, now largely in the majority in Congress, together with the admission of other free States, will very soon, give it the power in the Legislative Department. The whole Government will then be in the hands of our enemies. The election of Mr Lincoln is the first great step in this programme. It is the triumph of the Northern over the Southern section of the Union: of Northern fanaticism over Southern equality and Southern rights. While, therefore, the election of Mr. Lincoln, as a man, is no sufficient cause to justify secession, the triumph of the Northern section of the Union over the Southern section, upon a platform of avowed hostility to our rights, does, in my opinion, afford ample cause to justify the South in withdrawing from a confederacy where her equality, her honor, and the rights of her people, can no longer be protected.

Second, What will be the result to the institution of slavery, which will follow submission to the inauguration and administration of Mr. Lincoln as the President of one section of the Union? My candid opinion is, that it will be the total abolition of slavery, and the utter ruin of the South, in less than twenty-five years. If we submit now, we satisfy the Northern people that, come what may, we will never resist. If Mr. Lincoln places among us his Judges, District Attorneys, Marshals, Post Masters, Custom House officers, etc., etc., by the end of his administration, with the control of these men, and the distribution of public patronage, he will have succeeded in dividing us to an extent that will destroy all our moral powers, and prepare us to tolerate the running of a Republican ticket, in most of the States of the South, in 1864. If this ticket only secured five or ten thousand votes in each of the Southern States, it would be as large as the abolition party was in the North a few years since. It would hold a balance of power between any two political parties into which the people of the South may hereafter be divided. This would soon give it the control of our elections. We would then be powerless, and the abolitionists would press forward, with a steady step, to the accomplishment of their object. They would refuse to admit any other slave States to the Union. They would abolish slavery in the District of Columbia, and at the Forts, Arsenals and Dock Yards, within the Southern States, which belong to the United States. They would then abolish the internal slave trade between the States, and prohibit a slave owner in Georgia from carrying his slaves into Alabama or South Carolina, and there selling them. These steps would be taken one at a time, cautiously, and our people would submit. Finally, when we were sufficiently humiliated, and sufficiently in their power, they would abolish slavery in the States. It will not be many years before enough of free States may be formed out of the present territories of the United States, and admitted into the Union, to give them sufficient strength to change the Constitution, and remove all Constitutional barriers which now deny to Congress this power. I do not doubt, therefore, that sub-

mission to the administration of Mr. Lincoln will result in the
final abolition of slavery. If we fail to resist now, we will never
again have the strength to resist.

3rd, What effect will the abolition of slavery have upon the
interest and social position of the large class of nonslaveholders
and poor white laborers in the South? Here would be the
scene of the most misery and ruin. Probably no one is so unjust as to say that it would be right to take from the slaveholder
his property without paying him for it. What would it cost to
do this? There are, in round numbers, 4,500,000 slaves in the
Southern States. They are worth, at a low estimate, 500 dollars
each. All will agree to this. Multiply the 4,500,000 by 500 and
you have twenty-two hundred and fifty millions of dollars,
which these slaves are worth. No one would agree that it is
right to rob the Southern slaveholders of this vast sum of
money without compensation. The Northern States would
not agree to pay their proportion of the money, and the people
of the South must be taxed to raise the money. If Georgia were
only an average Southern State, she would have to pay one
fifteenth part of this sum, which would be $150,000,000.
Georgia is much more than an average State, and she must
therefore pay a larger sum. Her people now pay less than half a
million of dollars a year, of tax. Suppose we had ten years
within which to raise the $150,000,000, we should then have
to raise, in addition to our present tax, $15,000,000 per an-
num, or over thirty times as much as we now pay.—The poor
man, who now pays one dollar, would then have to pay
$30.00. But suppose the Northern States agreed to help pay
for these slaves, (who believes they would do it?) the share of
Georgia would then be about one thirtieth of the twenty-two
hundred and fifty millions of dollars, or over seventy-five millions; which, if raised in ten years, would be over fifteen times
as much as our present tax. In this calculation, I have counted
the slave-holder as taxed upon his own slaves to raise money to
pay him for them. This would be great injustice to him. If the
sum is to be raised by the tax upon others, the nonslaveholders
and poor white men of the South, would have to pay nearly
the whole of this enormous sum, out of their labor. This
would load them and their children with grievous indebted-
ness and heavy taxes for a long time to come. But suppose we

were rid of this difficulty, what shall be done with these 4,500,000 negroes, when set free? Some of the Northern States have already passed laws prohibiting free negroes from coming into their limits. They will help to harbor our runaway slaves, but will not receive among them our free negroes. They would not permit them to go there and live with them. Then what? One may say, send them to Africa. To such a proposition I might reply, send them to the moon. You may say that is not practicable. It is quite as much so as it is for us to pay for and send this vast number of negroes to Africa, with the means at our command.

No one would be so inhuman as to propose to send them to Africa and set them down upon a wild, naked sea coast, without provisions for at least one year. What will it cost to take them from their present home to Africa, and carry provisions there to keep them a single year? (if left with only one year's supply, many of them would starve to death.) It cannot be done for $250.00 each. At that sum it would amount to eleven hundred and twenty-five millions of dollars. Where will we get the money? Our people must be taxed to raise it. This would be half as large a sum as the above estimate of the value of the negroes. If the Southern States had it to raise Georgia's part would be over $75,000,000, which added to the part of the amount to be paid to owners for the negroes, would amount to $225,000,000; which must be raised by taxing the people, or loading them with a debt which would virtually enslave our whole people for generations to come. It must be remembered that we own no territory in Africa large enough to colonize 4,500,000 people. This too must be bought at a very heavy cost. The Northern people would not consent to be taxed to raise these enormous sums, either to pay for the negroes, or to pay for sending them to Africa, or to pay for land upon which to colonize them; as they do not wish to do either. They wish to take them from their owners without pay, and set them free, and let them remain among us. Many people at the North, say that negroes are our fit associates; that they shall be set free, and remain among us—intermarrying with our children, and enjoying equal privileges with us. But suppose we were over the difficulty of paying the owners for the negroes, and they were taken from their masters without pay, and set free and left among us, (which is the ultimate aim of the Black Republicans,) what would be the effect upon our society? We should still have rich men and poor men. But few of our slave owners have invested all they have in negroes. Take their negroes from them unjustly, and they will many of them still be more wealthy than their neighbors. If all were left for a time with equal wealth, every person who has noticed man and society knows that, in a few years, some would grow rich and others poor. This has always been the case, and always will be. If we had no negroes, the rich would still be in a better condition to take care of themselves than the poor. They would still seek the most profitable and secure investment for their capital. What would this be? The answer suggests itself to every mind: it would be land. The wealthy would soon buy all the lands of the South worth cultivating. Then what? The poor would all become tenants, as they are in England, the New England States, and all old countries where slavery does not exist. But I must not lose sight of the 4,500,000 free negroes to be turned loose among us. They, too, must become tenants, with the poor white people for they would not be able to own lands. A large proportion of them would spend their time in idleness and vice, and would live by stealing, robbing and plundering. Probably one fourth of the whole number would have to be maintained in our penitentiary, prisons, and poor houses. Our people, poor and rich, must be taxed to pay the expense of imprisoning and punishing them for crime. This would be a very heavy burden. But suppose three fourths of the whole number would work for a living. They would have to begin the world miserably poor, with neither land, money nor provisions. They must therefore become day laborers for their old masters, or such others as would employ them. In this capacity they would at once come in competition with the poor white laborers. Men of capital would see this, and fix the price of labor accordingly. The negro has only been accustomed to receive his victuals and clothes for his labor. Few of them, if free, would expect anything more. It would therefore be easy to employ them at a sum sufficient to supply only the actual necessaries of life. The poor white man would then go to the wealthy landowner and say, I wish employment. Hire me to work. I have a wife and children who must have bread. The land-owner would offer probably twenty cents per day. The laborer would say, I cannot support my family on that sum. The landlord replies, That is not my business. I am sorry for you, but I must look to my own interest. The black man who lives on my land has as strong an arm, and as heavy muscles as you have, and can do as much labor. He works for me at that rate, you must work for the same price, or I cannot employ you. The negro comes into competition with the white man and fixes the price of his labor, and he must take it or get no employment.

Again, the poor white man wishes to rent land from the wealthy landlord—this landlord asks him half the crop of common upland or two thirds or even three fourths, for the best bottom land. The poor man says this seems very hard. I cannot make a decent support for my family at these rates. The landlord replies, here are negroes all around me anxious to take it at these rates; I can let you have it for no less. The negro therefore, comes into competition with the poor white man, when he seeks to rent land on which to make his bread, or a shelter to protect his wife and his little ones, from the cold and from the rain; and when he seeks employment as a day laborer. In every such case if the negro will do the work the cheapest, he must be preferred. It is sickening to contemplate the miseries of our poor white people under these circumstances. They now get higher wages for their labor than the poor of any other country on the globe. Most of them are land owners, and they are now respected. They are in no sense placed down upon a level with the negro. They are a superior race, and they feel and know it. Abolish slavery, and you make the negroes their equals, legally and socially (not naturally, for no human law can change God's law) and you very soon make them all tenants, and reduce their wages for daily labor to the smallest pittance that will sustain life. Then the negro and the white man, and their families, must labor in the field together as equals. Their children must go to the same poor school together, if they are educated at all. They must go to church as equals; enter the Courts of justice as equals, sue and be sued as equals, sit on juries together as equals, have the right to give evidence in Court as equals, stand side by side in our military corps as equals, enter each others' houses in social intercourse as equals; and very soon their children must marry together as equals. May our kind Heavenly Father avert the evil, and deliver the poor from such a fate. So soon as the slaves were at liberty, thousands of them would leave the cotton and rice fields in the lower parts of our State, and make their way to the healthier climate in the mountain region. We should have them plundering and stealing, robbing and killing, in all the lovely vallies of the mountains. This I can never consent to see. The mountains contain the place of my nativity, the home of my manhood, and the theatre of most of the acts of my life; and I can never forget the condition and interest of the people who reside there. It is true, the people there are generally poor; but they are brave, honest, patriotic, and pure hearted. Some who do not know them, have doubted their capacity to understand these questions, and their patriotism and valor to defend their rights when invaded. I know them well, and I know that no greater mistake could be made. They love the Union of our fathers, and would never consent to dissolve it so long as the constitution is not violated, and so long as it protects their rights; but they love liberty and justice more; and they will never consent to submit to abolition rule, and permit the evils to come upon them, which must result from a continuance in the Union when the government is in the hands of our enemies, who will use all its power for our destruction. When it becomes necessary to defend our rights against so foul a domination, I would call upon the mountain boys as well as the people of the lowlands, and they would come down like an avalanche and swarm around the flag of Georgia with a resolution that would strike terror into the ranks of the abolition cohorts of the North. Wealth is timid, and wealthy men may cry for peace, and submit to wrong for fear they may lose their money: but the poor, honest laborers of Georgia, can never consent to see slavery abolished, and submit to all the taxation, vassalage, low wages and downright degradation, which must follow. They will never take the negro's place; God forbid.

I know that some contemptible demagogues have attempted to deceive them by appealing to their prejudices, and asking them what interest they have in maintaining the rights of the wealthy slaveholder. They cannot be deceived in this way. They know that the government of our State protects their lives, their families and their property; and that every dollar the wealthy slaveholder has, may be taken by the government of the State, if need be, to protect the rights and liberties of all. One man, in a large neighborhood, has a mill. Not one in fifty has a mill. What would be thought of the public speaker who would appeal to the fifty, and ask them what interest they have in defending their neighbor's mill, if an abolition mob were trying to burn it down? Another has a store. Not one in fifty has a store. Who would say the fifty should not help the one if an invader is about to burn his store? Another has a blacksmith shop. Not one in fifty has a blacksmith shop. Shall the shop be destroyed by the common enemy and no one protect the owner because no one near, has the same peculiar kind of property? It may be that I have no horse, and you have a horse; or that I have a cow, and you have no cow. In such case, if our rights of property are assailed by a common enemy, shall we not help each other? Or I have a wife and children, and a house, and another has neither wife and children, nor house. Will he, therefore, stand by and see my house burned and my wife and children butchered, because he has none? The slaveholder has honestly invested the money, which it has cost him years of toil to make, in slaves, which are guaranteed to him by the laws of our State. The common enemy of the South seeks to take the property from him. Shall all who do not own slaves, stand by and permit it to be done? If so, they have no right to call on the slaveholder, by taxation, or otherwise, to help protect their property or their liberties. Such a doctrine is monstrous; and he who would advance it, deserves to be rode upon the sharpest edge of one of Lincoln's rails. The doctrine strikes at the very foundation of society, and if carried out, would destroy all property, and all protection to life, liberty and happiness.

The present is a critical time with the people of the South. We all, poor and rich, have a common interest, a common destiny. It is no time to be wrangling about old party strifes. Our common enemy, the Black Republican party, is united and triumphant. Let us all unite. If we cannot all see alike, let us have charity enough towards each other, to admit that all are equally patriotic in their efforts to advance the common cause. My honest convictions are, that we can never again live in peace with the Northern abolitionists, unless we can have new constitutional guarantees, which will secure our equal rights in the Territories, and effectually stop the discussion of the slavery question in Congress, and secure the rendition of fugitive slaves. These guarantees I do not believe the people of the Northern States will ever give, while we remain together in the Union. Their opinion is, that we will always compromise away a portion of our rights, and submit, for the sake of peace. If the Cotton States would all secede from the Union before the inauguration of Mr. Lincoln, this might possibly lead to a Convention of all the States, which might terminate in a reunion with the new constitutional guarantees necessary for our protection. If the Northern States then failed to give these guarantees, there can be no doubt that Virginia, Maryland, North Carolina, Delaware, Kentucky, Missouri, and Tennessee would unite with the Cotton States in a Southern Confederacy and we should form a Republic in which, under the old Constitution of our fathers, our people could live in security and peace. I know that many of our people honestly believe that it would be best to wait for these border slave States to go out with us. If we wait for this, we shall *submit*; for some of those States will not consent to go, and the North will then consent to give us no new guarantees of peace. They will say that we have again blustered and submitted, as we always do.

In my late message to the General Assembly, I recommended the enactment of retaliatory laws against these Northern States which have nullified the fugitive slave law. I think those laws should still be enacted. They would have been equally applicable had either of the other candidates for the Presidency been successful. Now that Mr. Lincoln is successful, they should be upon our statute book, so long as we remain in the Union. There can no longer be a reasonable doubt, that the gallant State of South Carolina will secede from the Union very soon after her Convention meets. The States of Florida, Alabama and Mississippi will follow in quick succession. While our Convention is in session, we shall probably be surrounded on every side but one, with free and independent States out of the Union. With these States, we have a common interest. Thus surrounded, shall Georgia remain under abolition rule, and refuse to unite with her sister States around her? I trust not. If so, we forfeit all claim to our proud title of

Empire State of the South. Why remain? Will the Northern States repeal their personal liberty bills and do us justice? No. The Legislature of one of the nullifying States (Vermont) has just adjourned. A bill has been introduced for the repeal of those unconstitutional and offensive laws. The question has been discussed, and it is reported that the House in which the bill was introduced, has refused to pass the repealing law, by a vote of over two-thirds. This action has been had with full knowledge of the state of things now existing in the South, and shows a deliberate determination not to do us justice. Is further notice to Vermont necessary? I am aware that the fears of some have been appealed to, and they have been told that if we secede, the United States Government will attempt to coerce us back into the Union, and we shall have war.

The President in his late message, while he denies our Constitutional right to secede, admits that the General Government has no Constitutional right to coerce us back into the Union, if we do secede. Secession is not likely, therefore, to involve us in war. Submission may. When the other States around us secede, if we remain in the Union, thousands of our people will leave our State, and it is feared that the standard of revolution and rebellion may be raised among us, which would at once involve us in civil war among ourselves. If we must fight, in the name of all that is sacred, let us fight our common enemy, and not fight each other.

In my opinion, our people should send their wisest and best men to the Convention, without regard to party distinctions, and should intrust much to their good judgment and sound discretion, when they meet. They may, then, have new lights before them, which we do not now have; and they should be left free to act upon them.

My fervent prayer is, that the God of our fathers may inspire the Convention with wisdom, and so direct their counsels as to protect our rights and preserve our liberties to the latest generation.

> I am, gentlemen, with great respect,
> Your fellow citizen,
> JOSEPH E. BROWN

# *Abraham Lincoln to John A. Gilmer*

Abraham Lincoln remained in Springfield after the election, where he met with Republican leaders, considered cabinet appointments, and was beset by office-seekers. John A. Gilmer, an American (Know Nothing) congressman from North Carolina, wrote to Lincoln from Washington on December 10. Warning that the "present perilous condition of the Country" threatened the "destruction of the Union," Gilmer asked the president-elect to publicly answer a series of questions regarding his positions on slavery in the hope that a "clear and definite exposition of your views" might "go far to quiet, if not satisfy all reasonable minds." Lincoln replied on December 15.

———————

Strictly confidential.

Hon. John A. Gilmer:          Springfield, Ill. Dec 15, 1860.

My dear Sir—Yours of the 10th is received. I am greatly disinclined to write a letter on the subject embraced in yours; and I would not do so, even privately as I do, were it not that I fear you might misconstrue my silence. Is it desired that I shall shift the ground upon which I have been elected? I can not do it. You need only to acquaint yourself with that ground, and press it on the attention of the South. It is all in print and easy of access. May I be pardoned if I ask whether even you have ever attempted to procure the reading of the Republican platform, or my speeches, by the Southern people? If not, what reason have I to expect that any additional production of mine would meet a better fate? It would make me appear as if I repented for the crime of having been elected, and was anxious to apologize and beg forgiveness. To so represent me, would be the principal use made of any letter I might now thrust upon the public. My old record cannot be so used; and that is precisely the reason that some new declaration is so much sought.

Now, my dear sir, be assured, that I am not questioning *your* candor; I am only pointing out, that, while a new letter would hurt the cause which I think a just one, you can quite as well effect every patriotic object with the old record. Carefully read pages 18, 19, 74, 75, 88, 89, & 267 of the volume of Joint Debates between Senator Douglas and myself, with the Republican Platform adopted at Chicago, and all your questions will be substantially answered. I have no thought of recommending the abolition of slavery in the District of Columbia, nor the slave trade among the slave states, even on the conditions indicated; and if I were to make such recommendation, it is quite clear Congress would not follow it.

As to employing slaves in Arsenals and Dockyards, it is a thing I never thought of in my life, to my recollection, till I saw your letter; and I may say of it, precisely as I have said of the two points above.

As to the use of patronage in the slave states, where there are few or no Republicans, I do not expect to inquire for the politics of the appointee, or whether he does or not own slaves. I intend in that matter to accommodate the people in the several localities, if they themselves will allow me to accommodate them. In one word, I never have been, am not now, and probably never shall be, in a mood of harassing the people, either North or South.

On the territorial question, I am inflexible, as you see my position in the book. On that, there is a difference between you and us; and it is the only substantial difference. You think slavery is right and ought to be extended; we think it is wrong and ought to be restricted. For this, neither has any just occasion to be angry with the other.

As to the state laws, mentioned in your sixth question, I really know very little of them. I never have read one. If any of them are in conflict with the fugitive slave clause, or any other part of the constitution, I certainly should be glad of their repeal; but I could hardly be justified, as a citizen of Illinois, or as President of the United States, to recommend the repeal of a statute of Vermont, or South Carolina.

With the assurance of my highest regards I subscribe myself Your obt. Servt.,                                    A. LINCOLN

P.S. The documents referred to, I suppose you will readily find in Washington.                                    A. L.

# New-York Daily Tribune:
# The Right of Secession

December 17, 1860

Thurlow Weed, the editor of the *Albany Evening Journal* and a powerful figure in the New York Republican party, had criticized Horace Greeley's stance on secession. Greeley responded to his journalistic and political rival in an editorial.

———————

*The Albany Evening Journal* courteously controverts our views on the subject of Secession. Here is the gist of its argument:

"Seven or eight States" *have* "pretty unanimously made up their minds" to leave the Union. Mr. Buchanan, in reply, says that "ours is a Government of popular opinion," and hence, if States rebel, there is no power residing either with the Executive or in Congress, to resist or punish. Why, then, is not this the end of the controversy? Those "seven or eight States" are going out. The Government remonstrates, but acquiesces. And THE TRIBUNE regards it "*unwise to undertake to resist such Secession by Federal force.*"

If an individual, or "a single State," commits Treason, the same act in two or more individuals, or two or more States, is alike treasonable. And how is Treason against the Federal Government to be resisted, except by "Federal force?"

Precisely the same question was involved in the South Carolina Secession of 1833. But neither President Jackson, nor Congress, nor the People, took this view of it. The President issued a Proclamation declaring Secession Treason. Congress passed a Force Law; and South Carolina, instead of "madly shooting from its sphere," returned, if not to her senses, back into line.

—Does *The Journal* mean to say that if *all* the States and their People should become tired of the Union, it would be treason on their part to seek its dissolution?

—We have repeatedly asked those who dissent from our view of this matter to tell us frankly whether they do or do not assent to Mr. Jefferson's statement in the Declaration of Independence that governments "derive their *just* powers from *the consent of the governed*; and that, whenever any form of government becomes destructive of these ends, *it is the right of the people to alter or abolish it*, and to institute a new government," &c., &c. We *do* heartily accept this doctrine, believing it intrinsically sound, beneficent, and one that, universally accepted, is calculated to prevent the shedding of seas of human blood. And, if it justified the secession from the British Empire of Three Millions of colonists in 1776, we do not see why it would not justify the secession of Five Millions of Southrons from the Federal Union in 1861. If we are mistaken on this point, why does not some one attempt to show wherein and why? For our own part, while we deny the right of slaveholders to hold slaves against the will of the latter, we cannot see how Twenty Millions of people can rightfully hold Ten or even Five in a detested union with them, by military force.

Of course, we understand that the principle of Jefferson, like any other broad generalization, may be pushed to extreme and baleful consequences. We can see why Governor's Island should not be at liberty to secede from the State and Nation and allow herself to be covered with French or British batteries commanding and threatening our City. There is hardly a great principle which may not be thus "run into the ground." But if seven or eight contiguous States shall present themselves authentically at Washington, saying, "We hate the Federal Union; we have withdrawn from it; we give you the choice between acquiescing in our secession and arranging amicably all incidental questions on the one hand, and attempting to subdue us on the other"—we could not stand up for coercion, for subjugation, for we do not think it would be just. We hold the right of Self-Government sacred, even when invoked in behalf of those who deny it to others. So much for the question of Principle.

Now as to the matter of Policy:

South Carolina will certainly secede. Several other Cotton States will probably follow her example. The Border States are evidently reluctant to do likewise. South Carolina has grossly insulted them by her dictatorial, reckless course. What she expects and desires is a clash of arms with the Federal Government, which will at once commend her to the sympathy and coöperation of every Slave State, and to the sympathy (at least) of the Pro-Slavery minority in the Free States. It is not difficult to see that this would speedily work a political revolution, which would restore to Slavery all, and more than all, it has lost by the canvass of 1860. We want to obviate this. We would expose the seceders to odium as disunionists, not commend them to pity as the gallant though mistaken upholders of the rights of their section in an unequal military conflict.

We fully realize that the dilemma of the incoming Administration will be a critical one. It must endeavor to uphold and enforce the laws, as well against rebellious slaveholders as fugitive slaves. The new President must fulfill the obligations assumed in his inauguration oath, no matter how shamefully his predecessor may have defied them. We fear that Southern madness may precipitate a bloody collision that all must deplore. But if ever "seven or eight States" send agents to Washington to say "We want to get out of the Union," we shall feel constrained by our devotion to Human Liberty to say, Let them go! And we do not see how we could take the other side without coming in direct conflict with those Rights of Man which we hold paramount to all political arrangements, however convenient and advantageous.

# Benjamin F. Wade:
## Remarks in the U.S. Senate

### December 17, 1860

Benjamin Wade of Ohio entered the Senate as a Whig in 1851 and was subsequently elected as a Republican. He made these remarks during a debate over whether the Senate should appoint a special committee to address the sectional crisis. After engaging in an extended exchange with several Southern senators over the enforcement of the fugitive slave law, Wade spoke in defense of the platform adopted by the 1860 Republican convention.

---

BUT, SIR, I wish to inquire whether the southern people are injured by, or have any just right to complain of, that platform of principles that we put out, and on which we have elected a President and Vice President. I have no concealments to make, and I shall talk to you, my southern friends, precisely as I would talk upon the stump on the subject. I tell you that in that platform we did lay it down that we would, if we had the power, prohibit slavery from another inch of free territory under this Government. I stand on that position to-day. I have argued it probably to half a million people. They stand there, and have commissioned and enjoined me to stand there forever; and, so help me God, I will. I say to you frankly, gentlemen, that while we hold this doctrine, there is no Republican, there is no convention of Republicans, there is no paper that speaks for them, there is no orator that sets forth their doctrines, who ever pretends that they have any right in your States to interfere with your peculiar institution; but, on the other hand, our authoritative platform repudiates the idea that we have any right or any intention ever to invade your peculiar institution in your own States.

Now, what do you complain of? You are going to break up

said on the other point to which he called my attention a little while ago. Here it is:

"Nor do we suppose that there will be any overt acts upon the part of Mr. Lincoln. For one, I do not dread these overt acts. I do not propose to wait for them. Why, sir, the power of this Federal Government could be so exercised against the institution of slavery in the southern States, as that, without an overt act, the institution would not last ten years. We know that, sir; and seeing the storm which is approaching, although it may be seemingly in the distance, we are determined to seek our own safety and security before it shall burst upon us and overwhelm us with its fury, when we are not in a situation to defend ourselves."

That is what the Senator said.

Mr. IVERSON. Yes; that is what I said.

Mr. WADE. Well, then, you did not expect that Mr. Lincoln would commit any overt act against the Constitution—that was not it—you were not going to wait for that, but were going to proceed on your supposition that probably he might; and that is the sense of what I said before.

Well, Mr. President, I have disavowed all intention on the part of the Republican party to harm a hair of your heads anywhere. We hold to no doctrine that can possibly work you an inconvenience. We have been faithful to the execution of all the laws in which you have any interest, as stands confessed on this floor by your own party, and as is known to me without their confessions. It is not, then, that Mr. Lincoln is expected to do any overt act by which you may be injured; you will not wait for any; but anticipating that the Government may work an injury, you say you will put an end to it, which means simply, that you intend either to rule or ruin this Government. That is what your complaint comes to; nothing else. We do not like your institution, you say. Well, we never liked it any better than we do now. You might as well have dissolved the Union at any other period as now, on that account, for we stand in relation to it precisely as we have ever stood: that is, repudiating it among ourselves as a matter of policy and morals, but nevertheless admitting that where it is out of our jurisdiction, we have no hold upon it, and no designs upon it.

Then, sir, as there is nothing in the platform on which Mr.

Lincoln was elected of which you complain, I ask, is there anything in the character of the President elect of which you
ought to complain? Has he not lived a blameless life? Did he
ever transgress any law? Has he ever committed any violation
of duty of which the most scrupulous can complain? Why,
then, your suspicions that he will? I have shown that you have
had the Government all the time until, by some misfortune or
maladministration, you brought it to the very verge of destruction, and the wisdom of the people had discovered that it
was high time that the scepter should depart from you, and be
placed in more competent hands; I say that this being so, you
have no constitutional right to complain; especially when we
disavow any intention so to make use of the victory we have
won as to injure you at all.

This brings me, sir, to the question of compromises. On the
first day of this session, a Senator rose in his place and offered
a resolution for the appointment of a committee to inquire
into the evils that exist between the different sections, and to
ascertain what can be done to settle this great difficulty! That
is the proposition, substantially. I tell the Senator that I know
of no difficulty; and as to compromises, I had supposed that
we were all agreed that the day of compromises was at an end.
The most solemn compromises we have ever made have been
violated without a whereas. Since I have had a seat in this
body, one of considerable antiquity, that had stood for more
than thirty years, was swept away from your statute-books.
When I stood here in the minority arguing against it; when I
asked you to withhold your hand; when I told you it was a sacred compromise between the sections, and that when it was
removed we should be brought face to face with all that sectional bitterness that has intervened; when I told you that it
was a sacred compromise which no man should touch with
his finger, what was your reply? That it was a mere act of
Congress—nothing more, nothing less—and that it could be
swept away by the same majority that passed it. That was true
in point of fact, and true in point of law; but it showed the
weakness of compromises. Now, sir, I only speak for myself;
and I say that, in view of the manner in which other compromises have been heretofore treated, I should hardly think any
two of the Democratic party would look each other in the face

and say "compromise" without a smile. [Laughter.] A compromise to be brought about by act of Congress, after the experience we have had, is absolutely ridiculous.

But what have we to compromise? Sir, I am one of those who went forth with zeal to maintain the principles of the great Republican party. In a constitutional way we met, as you met. We nominated our candidates for President and Vice President, and you did the same for yourselves. The issue was made up; and we went to the people upon it. Although we have been usually in the minority; although we have been generally beaten, yet, this time, the justice of our principles, and the maladministration of the Government in your hands, convinced the people that a change ought to be wrought; and after you had tried your utmost, and we had tried our utmost, we beat you; and we beat you upon the plainest and most palpable issue that ever was presented to the American people, and one that they understood the best. There is no mistaking it; and now, when we come to the Capitol, I tell you that our President and our Vice President must be inaugurated, and administer the Government as all their predecessors have done. Sir, it would be humiliating and dishonorable to us if we were to listen to a compromise by which he who has the verdict of the people in his pocket, should make his way to the presidential chair. When it comes to that, you have no Government; anarchy intervenes; civil war may follow it; all the evils that may come to the human imagination may be consequent upon such a course as that. The moment the American people cut loose from the sheet anchor of free government and liberty—that is, whenever it is denied in this Government that a majority fairly given shall rule—the people are unworthy of free government. Sir, I know not what others may do; but I tell you that, with the verdict of the people given in favor of the platform upon which our candidates have been elected, so far as I am concerned, I would suffer anything to come before I would compromise that away. I regard it as a case where I have no right to extend comity or generosity. A right, an absolute right, the most sacred that a free people can ever bestow on any man, is their undisguised, fair verdict, that gives him a title to the office that he is chosen to fill; and he is recreant to the principle of free government who will ask a question beyond the fact whether a man has the verdict of the people, or if he will entertain for a moment a proposition in addition to that. It is all I want. If we cannot stand there, we cannot stand anywhere. Any other principle than that would be as fatal to you, my friends, as to us. On any other principle, anarchy must immediately ensue.

You say that he comes from a particular section of the country. What of that? If he is an honest man, bound by his constitutional duties, has he not as good a right to come from one side as the other? Here, gentlemen, we ought to understand each other's duties a little. I appeal to every candid man upon the other side, and I put this question: if you had elected your candidate, Mr. Breckinridge, although we should have been a good deal disheartened, as everybody is that loses his choice in such a matter as this; although it would have been an overthrow that we should have deplored very much, as we have had occasion almost always to deplore the result of national elections, still do you believe that we would have raised a hand against the Constitution of our country because we were fairly beaten in an election? Sir, I do not believe there is a man on the other side who will not do us more credit than to suppose that if the case were reversed, there would be any complaint on our side. There never has been any from us under similar circumstances, and there would not be now. Sir, I think we have patriotism enough to overcome the pride and the prejudice of the canvass, and submit gracefully to the unmistakable verdict of the people; and as I have shown that you have nothing else to complain of, I take it that this is your complaint. Some of you have said that the election of Mr. Lincoln showed hostility to you and your institution. Sir, it is the common fate of parties to differ, and one does not intend to follow exactly the course of policy of the other; but when you talk of constitutional rights and duties, honest men will observe them alike, no matter to what party they belong.

I say, then, that so far as I am concerned, I will yield to no compromise. I do not come here begging, either. It would be an indignity to the people that I represent if I were to stand here parleying as to the rights of the party to which I belong. We have won our right to the Chief Magistracy of this nation in the way that you have always won your predominance; and if you are as willing to do justice to others as to exact it from them, you would never raise an inquiry as to a committee for compromises. Here I beg, barely for myself, to say one thing more. Many of you stand in an attitude hostile to this Government; that is to say, you occupy an attitude where you threaten that, unless we do so and so, you will go out of this Union and destroy the Government. I say to you, for myself, that, in my private capacity, I never yielded to anything by way of threat, and in my public capacity I have no right to yield to any such thing; and therefore I would not entertain a proposition for any compromise; for, in my judgment, this long, chronic controversy that has existed between us must be met, and met upon the principles of the Constitution and laws, and met now. I hope it may be adjusted to the satisfaction of all; and I know no other way to adjust it, except that way which is laid down by the Constitution of the United States. Whenever we go astray from that, we are sure to plunge ourselves into difficulties. The old Constitution of the United States, although commonly and frequently in direct opposition to what I could wish, nevertheless, in my judgment, is the wisest and best Constitution that ever yet organized a free Government; and by its provisions I am willing, and intend, to stand or fall. Like the Senator from Mississippi, I ask nothing more. I ask no ingrafting upon it. I ask nothing to be taken away from it. Under its provisions a nation has grown faster than any other in the history of the world ever did before in prosperity, in power, and in all that makes a nation great and glorious. It has ministered to the advantages of this people; and now I am unwilling to add or take away anything till I can see much clearer than I can now that it wants either any addition or lopping off.

There is one other subject about which I ought to say something. On that side of the Chamber, you claim the constitutional right, if I understand you, to secede from the Government at pleasure, and set up an adverse Government of your own; that one State, or any number of States, have a perfect constitutional right to do it. Sir, I can find no warrant in the Constitution for any doctrine like that. In my judgment, it would be subversive of all constitutional obligation. If this is so, we really have not now, and never have had, a Government; for that certainly is no Government of which a State can do just as it pleases, any more than it would be of an individual. How can a man be said to be governed by law, if he will obey the law or not just as he sees fit? It puts you out of the pale of Government, and reduces this Union of ours, of which we have all boasted so much, to a mere conglomeration of States, to be held at the will of any capricious member of it. As to South Carolina, I will say that she is a small State; and probably, if she were sunk by an earthquake to-day, we would hardly ever find it out, except by the unwonted harmony that might prevail in this Chamber. [Laughter.] But I think she is unwise. I would be willing that she should go her own gait, provided we could do it without an example fatal to all government; but standing here in the highest council of the nation, my own wishes, if I had any, must be under the control of my constitutional duty.

I do not see how any man can contend that a State can go out of this Union at pleasure, though I do not propose now to argue that question, because that has been done by men infinitely more able to argue it than I am. When it was raised some thirty years ago, and challenged the investigation of the best minds of this nation of all parties, it received a verdict that I supposed had put it at rest forever. General Jackson, with all the eminent men that surrounded him in his Cabinet, and in the councils of the nation, with hardly any exception, except Mr. Calhoun, held that the doctrine was a delusion, not to be found in the Constitution of the United States; and not only so, but utterly destructive of all Governments. Mr. Calhoun held the contrary. Mr. Webster, in his great controversy with Mr. Hayne upon that subject, was supposed to have overthrown him, even upon nullification, so utterly, that it was believed at the time that the doctrine could never arise or sprout up again. But here it is today in full bloom and glory: a State has a right to secede. Mr. Calhoun did not hold so. He held that a State had a right to nullify a law of Congress that they believed to be unconstitutional. He took that distinction between the power of a State to nullify a law of Congress and secession. Grounding herself upon the resolutions of 1798–99, he held that a State, in her sovereign capacity, judging in the last resort as to whether a law was warranted by the Constitution or not, must be the sole judge of the infraction of the

Constitution by the enactment of a law, and also of the mode of remedy. In that, he hardly had a second at that period. But when you come to the doctrine of secession, he himself says that that is not a constitutional remedy. He did not treat it as such. Nay, sir, he goes much further than the President of the United States has gone in his message, in which he declares that the United States has no power to make war upon a seceding State. Mr. Calhoun says we undoubtedly have that power. One remedy he calls peaceable and constitutional, and the other not. I have not the book with me; I intended to have brought it, but forgot it; but you will find this doctrine laid down in his famous letter to Governor Hamilton, taking and working out the distinction between peaceable nullification and secession, that puts an end to all the relationship between the General Government and the State, and enables the General Government, if they see fit, to declare war upon such a State. Therefore I take it that a State has no constitutional right to go out of this Government.

I acknowledge, to the fullest extent, the right of revolution, if you may call it a right, and the destruction of the Government under which we live, if we are discontented with it, and on its ruins to erect another more in accordance with our wishes. I believe nobody at this day denies the right; but they that undertake it, undertake it with this hazard: if they are successful, then all is right, and they are heroes; if they are defeated, they are rebels. That is the character of all revolution: if successful, of course it is well; if unsuccessful, then the Government from which they have rebelled treats them as traitors.

I do not say this because I apprehend that any party intends to make war upon a seceding State. I only assert their right from the nature of the act, if they see fit to do so; but I would not advise nor counsel it. I should be very tender of the rights of a people, if I had full power over them, who are about to destroy a Government which they deliberately come to the conclusion they cannot live under; but I am persuaded that the necessities of our position compel us to take a more austere ground, and hold that if a State secedes, although we will not make war upon her, we cannot recognize her right to be out of the Union, and she is not out until she gains the consent of the Union itself; and that the Chief Magistrate of the nation, be he who he may, will find under the Constitution of the United States that it is his sworn duty to execute the law in every part and parcel of this Government; that he cannot be released from that obligation; for there is nothing in the Constitution of the United States that would warrant him in saying that a single star has fallen from this galaxy of stars in the Confederacy. He is sworn not to know that a State has seceded, or pay the least respect to their resolutions that claim they have. What follows? Not that we would make war upon her, but we should have to exercise every Federal right over her if we had the power; and the most important of these would be the collection of the revenues. There are many rights that the Federal Government exercises over the States for the peculiar benefit of the people there, which, if they did not want, they could dispense with. If they did not want the mails carried there, the President might abolish the offices, and cease to carry their mails. They might forego any such duty peculiarly for the benefit of the people. They might not elect their officers and send them here. It is a privilege they have; but we cannot force them to do it. They have the right under the Constitution to be represented upon equal terms with any other State; but if they see fit to forego that right, and do not claim it, it is not incumbent upon the President to endeavor to force them to do an act of that kind.

But when you come to those duties which impose obligations upon them, in common with the other members of the Confederacy, he cannot be released from his duty. Therefore, it will be incumbent on the Chief Magistrate to proceed to collect the revenue of ships entering their ports, precisely in the same way and to the same extent that he does now in every other State of the Union. We cannot release him from that obligation. The Constitution, in thunder tones, demands that he shall do it alike in the ports of every State. What follows? Why, sir, if he shuts up the ports of entry so that a ship cannot discharge her cargo there or get papers for another voyage, then ships will cease to trade; or, if he undertakes to blockade her, and thus collect it, she has not gained her independence by secession. What must she do? If she is contented to live in this equivocal state all would be well, perhaps; but she could not live there. No people in the world could live in that condition.

What will they do? They must take the initiative and declare war upon the United States; and the moment that they levy war force must be met by force; and they must, therefore, hew out their independence by violence and war. There is no other way under the Constitution, that I know of, whereby a Chief Magistrate of any politics could be released from this duty. If this State, though seceding, should declare war against the United States, I do not suppose there is a lawyer in this body but what would say that the act of levying war is treason against the United States. That is where it results. We might just as well look the matter right in the face.

The Senator from Texas says—it is not exactly his language —we will force you to an ignominious treaty up in Faneuil Hall. Well, sir, you may. We know you are brave; we understand your prowess; we want no fight with you; but, nevertheless, if you drive us to that necessity, we must use all the powers of this Government to maintain it intact in its integrity. If we are overthrown, we but share the fate of a thousand other Governments that have been subverted. If you are the weakest, then you must go to the wall; and that is all there is about it. That is the condition in which we stand, provided a State sets herself up in opposition to the General Government.

I say that is the way it seems to me, as a lawyer. I see no power in the Constitution to release a Senator from this position. Sir, if there was any other, if there was an absolute right of secession in the Constitution of the United States when we stepped up there to take our oath of office, why was there not an exception in that oath? Why did it not run "that we would support the Constitution of the United States unless our State shall secede before our term was out?" Sir, there is no such immunity. There is no way by which this can be done that I can conceive of, except it is standing upon the Constitution of the United States, demanding equal justice for all, and vindicating the old flag of the Union. We must maintain it, unless we are cloven down by superior force.

Well, sir, it may happen that you can make your way out of the Union, and that, by levying war upon the Government, you may vindicate your right to independence. If you should do so, I have a policy in my mind. No man would regret more than myself that any portion of the people of these United

States should think themselves impelled, by grievances or any-thing else, to depart out of this Union, and raise a foreign flag and a hand against the General Government. If there was any just cause on God's earth that I could see that was within my reach, of honorable release from any such pretended griev-ance, they should have it; but they set forth none; I can see none. It is all a matter of prejudice, superinduced unfortu-nately, I believe, as I intimated before, more because you have listened to the enemies of the Republican party and what they said of us, while, from your intolerance, you have shut out all light as to what our real principles are. We have been called and branded in the North and in the South and everywhere else, as John Brown men, as men hostile to your institutions, as meditating an attack upon your institutions in your own States—a thing that no Republican ever dreamed of or ever thought of, but has protested against as often as the question has been up; but your people believe it. No doubt they believe it because of the terrible excitement and reign of terror that prevails there. No doubt they think so, but it arises from false information, or the want of information—that is all. Their prejudices have been appealed to until they have become un-controlled and uncontrollable.

Well, sir, if it shall be so; if that "glorious Union," as we all call it, under which the Government has so long lived and prospered, is now about to come to a final end, as perhaps it may, I have been looking around to see what policy we should adopt; and through that gloom which has been mentioned on the other side, if you will have it so, I still see a glorious future for those who stand by the old flag of the nation. There lie the fair fields of Mexico all before us. The people there are preju-diced against you. They fear you intend to overrun and enslave them. You are a slavery propaganda, and you are fillibusters. That has raised a violent antagonism between you and them. But, sir, if we were once released from all obligation to this in-stitution, in six months they would invite us to take a protec-torate over them. They owe England a large debt, and she has been coaxing and inviting us to take the protectorate of that nation. They will aid us in it; and I say to the commercial men of the North, if you go along with me, and adopt this policy, if we must come to this, you will be seven-fold indemnified by the trade and commerce of that country for what you lose by the secession. Talk about eating ice and granite in the North! Why, sir, Great Britain now carries on a commerce with Mexico to the amount of nearly a hundred million dollars. How much of it do we get? Only about eight million. Why so? Because, by our treatment of Mexico, we have led them to fear and to hate us; and they have been compelled, by our illiberal policy, to place themselves under the shadow of a stronger nation for their own protection.

The Senator from Illinois [Mr. DOUGLAS] and my colleague [Mr. PUGH] have said that we Black Republicans were advocates of negro equality, and that we wanted to build up a black government. Sir, it will be one of the most blessed ideas of the times, if it shall come to this, that we will make inducements for every free black among us to find his home in a more congenial climate in Central America or in Lower Mexico, and we will be divested of every one of them; and then, endowed with the splendid domain that we shall get, we will adopt a homestead policy, and we will invite the poor, the destitute, industrious white man from every clime under heaven, to come in there and make his fortune. So, sir, we will build up a nation, renovated by this process, of white laboring men. You may build yours up on compulsory servile labor, and the two will flourish side by side; and we shall very soon see whether your principles, or that state of society, or ours, is the most prosperous or vigorous. I might say, sir, that, divested of this institution, who doubts that the provinces of Canada would knock at our doors in a day? Therefore, my friends, we have all the elements for building up an empire—a Republic, founded on the great principles of the Declaration of Independence, that shall be more magnificent, more powerful, and more just than this world has ever seen at any other period. I do not know that I should have a single second for this policy; but it is a policy that occurs to me, and it reconciles me in some measure to the threatened loss or secession of these States.

But, sir, I am for maintaining the Union of these States. I will sacrifice everything but honor to maintain it. That glorious old flag of ours, by any act of mine, shall never cease to wave over the integrity of this Union as it is. But if they will not have it so, in this new, renovated Government of which I have spoken, the 4th of July, with all its glorious memories, will never be repealed. The old flag of 1776 will be in our hands, and shall float over this nation forever; and this Capitol, that some gentlemen said would be reserved for the southern republic, shall still be the Capitol. It was laid out by Washington; it was consecrated by him; and the old flag that he vindicated in the Revolution shall still float from the Capitol. [Applause in the galleries.]

The PRESIDING OFFICER. The Sergeant-at-Arms will take proper measures to preserve order in the gallery or clear it.

Mr. WADE. I say, sir, I stand by the Union of these States. Washington and his compatriots fought for that good old flag. It shall never be hauled down, but shall be the glory of the Government to which I belong, as long as my life shall continue. To maintain it, Washington and his compatriots fought for liberty and the rights of man. And here I will add that my own father, although but a humble soldier, fought in the same great cause, and went through hardships and privations sevenfold worse than death, in order to bequeath it to his children. It is my inheritance. It was my protector in infancy, and the pride and glory of my riper years; and, Mr. President, although it may be assailed by traitors on every side, by the grace of God, under its shadow I will die.

# John J. Crittenden:
# Remarks in the U.S. Senate

December 18, 1860

A former Whig who helped form the Constitutional Union party in 1860, Senator John J. Crittenden of Kentucky made these remarks while proposing a set of constitutional amendments and congressional resolutions regarding slavery that became known as the Crittenden Compromise. His proposals were referred to a special Committee of Thirteen, whose members included Crittenden, Benjamin Wade, William H. Seward, Stephen A. Douglas, Jefferson Davis, and Robert Toombs. The compromise failed to win committee approval when all five of its Republican members, along with Davis and Toombs, voted against the amendment regarding slavery in the territories. Crittenden brought his proposals before the full Senate in January 1861, but they were again blocked by determined Republican opposition. Lincoln helped defeat the Crittenden proposals by writing several private letters to Republican leaders urging that there be no compromises made on the question of extending slavery.

——————————

Mr. CRITTENDEN. I am gratified, Mr. President, to see in the various propositions which have been made, such a universal anxiety to save the country from the dangerous dissensions which now prevail; and I have, under a very serious view and without the least ambitious feeling whatever connected with it, prepared a series of constitutional amendments, which I desire to offer to the Senate, hoping that they may form, in part at least, some basis for measures that may settle the controverted questions which now so much agitate our country. Certainly, sir, I do not propose now any elaborate discussion of the subject. Before presenting these resolutions, however, to the Senate, I desire to make a few remarks explanatory of them, that the Senate may understand their general scope.

The questions of an alarming character are those which have

grown out of the controversy between the northern and southern sections of our country in relation to the rights of the slaveholding States in the Territories of the United States, and in relation to the rights of the citizens of the latter in their slaves. I have endeavored by these resolutions to meet all these questions and causes of discontent, and by amendments to the Constitution of the United States, so that the settlement, if we can happily agree on any, may be permanent, and leave no cause for future controversy. These resolutions propose, then, in the first place, in substance, the restoration of the Missouri compromise, extending the line throughout the Territories of the United States to the eastern border of California, recognizing slavery in all the territory south of that line, and prohibiting slavery in all the territory north of it; with a provision, however, that when any of those Territories, north or south, are formed into States, they shall then be at liberty to exclude or admit slavery as they please; and that, in the one case or the other, it shall be no objection to their admission into the Union. In this way, sir, I propose to settle the question, both as to territory and slavery, so far as it regards the Territories of the United States.

I propose, sir, also, that the Constitution shall be so amended as to declare that Congress shall have no power to abolish slavery in the District of Columbia so long as slavery exists in the States of Maryland and Virginia; and that they shall have no power to abolish slavery in any of the places under their special jurisdiction within the southern States.

These are the constitutional amendments which I propose, and embrace the whole of them in regard to the questions of territory and slavery. There are other propositions in relation to grievances, and in relation to controversies, which I suppose are within the jurisdiction of Congress, and may be removed by the action of Congress. I propose, in regard to legislative action, that the fugitive slave law, as it is commonly called, shall be declared by the Senate to be a constitutional act, in strict pursuance of the Constitution. I propose to declare, that it has been decided by the Supreme Court of the United States to be constitutional, and that the southern States are entitled to a faithful and complete execution of that law, and that no amendment shall be made hereafter to it which will impair its efficiency. But, thinking that it would not impair its efficiency, I have proposed amendments to it in two particulars. I have understood from gentlemen of the North that there is objection to the provision giving a different fee where the commissioner decides to deliver the slave to the claimant, from that which is given where he decides to discharge the alleged slave; the law declares that in the latter case he shall have but five dollars, while in the other he shall have ten dollars—twice the amount in one case than in the other. The reason for this is very obvious. In case he delivers the servant to his claimant, he is required to draw out a lengthy certificate, stating the principal and substantial grounds on which his decision rests, and to return him either to the marshal or to the claimant to remove him to the State from which he escaped. It was for that reason that a larger fee was given to the commissioner, where he had the largest service to perform. But, sir, the act being viewed unfavorably and with great prejudice, in a certain portion of our country, this was regarded as very obnoxious, because it seemed to give an inducement to the commissioner to return the slave to the master, as he thereby obtained the larger fee of ten dollars instead of the smaller one of five dollars. I have said, let the fee be the same in both cases.

I have understood, furthermore, sir, that inasmuch as the fifth section of that law was worded somewhat vaguely, its general terms had admitted of the construction in the northern States that all the citizens were required, upon the summons of the marshal, to go with him to hunt up, as they express it, and arrest the slave; and this is regarded as obnoxious. They have said, "in the southern States you make no such requisition on the citizen;" nor do we, sir. The section, construed according to the intention of the framers of it, I suppose, only intended that the marshal should have the same right in the execution of process for the arrest of a slave that he has in all other cases of process that he is required to execute—to call on the *posse comitatus* for assistance where he is resisted in the execution of his duty, or where, having executed his duty by the arrest, an attempt is made to rescue the slave. I propose such an amendment as will obviate this difficulty and limit the right of the master and the duty of the citizen to cases where, as in regard to all other process, persons may be called upon to assist in resisting opposition to the execution of the laws.

I have provided further, sir, that the amendments to the Constitution which I here propose, and certain other provisions of the Constitution itself, shall be unalterable, thereby forming a permanent and unchangeable basis for peace and tranquillity among the people. Among the provisions in the present Constitution, which I have by amendment proposed to render unalterable, is that provision in the first article of the Constitution which provides the rule for representation, including in the computation three fifths of the slaves. That is to be rendered unchangeable. Another is the provision for the delivery of fugitive slaves. That is to be rendered unchangeable.

And with these provisions, Mr. President, it seems to me we have a solid foundation upon which we may rest our hopes for the restoration of peace and good-will among all the States of this Union, and all the people. I propose, sir, to enter into no particular discussion. I have explained the general scope and object of my proposition. I have provided further, which I ought to mention, that, there having been some difficulties experienced in the courts of the United States in the South in carrying into execution the laws prohibiting the African slave trade, all additions and amendments which may be necessary to those laws to render them effectual should be immediately adopted by Congress, and especially the provisions of those laws which prohibit the importation of African slaves into the United States. I have further provided it as a recommendation to all the States of this Union, that whereas laws have been passed of an unconstitutional character, (and all laws are of that character which either conflict with the constitutional acts of Congress, or which in their operation hinder or delay the proper execution of the acts of Congress,) which laws are null and void, and yet, though null and void, they have been the source of mischief and discontent in the country, under the extraordinary circumstances in which we are placed; I have supposed that it would not be improper or unbecoming in Congress to recommend to the States, both North and South, the repeal of all such acts of theirs as were intended to control, or intended to obstruct the operation of the acts of Congress, or which in their operation and in their application have been made use of for the purpose of such hindrance and opposition, and that they will repeal these laws or make such explanations or corrections of them as to prevent their being used for any such mischievous purpose.

I have endeavored to look with impartiality from one end of our country to the other; I have endeavored to search up what appeared to me to be the causes of discontent pervading the land; and, as far as I am capable of doing so, I have endeavored to propose a remedy for them. I am far from believing that, in the shape in which I present these measures, they will meet with the acceptance of the Senate. It will be sufficiently gratifying if, with all the amendments that the superior knowledge of the Senate may make to them, they shall, to any effectual extent, quiet the country.

Mr. President, great dangers surround us. The Union of these States is dear to the people of the United States. The long experience of its blessings, the mighty hopes of the future, have made it dear to the hearts of the American people. Whatever politicians may say; whatever of dissension may, in the heat of party politics, be created among our people, when you come down to the question of the existence of the Constitution, that is a question beyond all party politics; that is a question of life and death. The Constitution and the Union are the life of this great people—yes, sir, the life of life. We all desire to preserve them, North and South; that is the universal desire. But some of the southern States, smarting under what they conceive to be aggressions of their northern brethren and of the northern States, are not contented to continue this Union, and are taking steps, formidable steps, towards a dissolution of the Union, and towards the anarchy and the bloodshed, I fear, that are to follow. I say, sir, we are in the presence of great events. We must elevate ourselves to the level of the great occasion. No party warfare about mere party questions or party measures ought now to engage our attention. They are left behind; they are as dust in the balance. The life, the existence of our country, of our Union, is the mighty question; and we must elevate ourselves to all those considerations which belong to this high subject.

I hope, therefore, gentlemen will be disposed to bring the

sincerest spirit of conciliation, the sincerest spirit and desire to adjust all these difficulties, and to think nothing of any little concessions of opinions that they may make, if thereby the Constitution and the country can be preserved.

The great difficulty here, sir—I know it; I recognize it as the difficult question, particularly with the gentlemen from the North—is the admission of this line of division for the territory, and the recognition of slavery on the one side, and the prohibition of it on the other. The recognition of slavery on the southern side of that line is the great difficulty, the great question with them. Now, I beseech them to think, and you, Mr. President, and all, to think whether, for such a comparative trifle as that, the Union of this country is to be sacrificed. Have we realized to ourselves the momentous consequences of such an event? When has the world seen such an event? This is a mighty empire. Its existence spreads its influence throughout the civilized world. Its overthrow will be the greatest shock that civilization and free government have received; more extensive in its consequences; more fatal to mankind and to the great principles upon which the liberty of mankind depends, than the French revolution with all its blood, and with all its war and violence. And all for what? Upon questions concerning this line of division between slavery and freedom? Why, Mr. President, suppose this day all the southern States, being refused this right; being refused this partition; being denied this privilege, were to separate from the northern States, and do it peacefully, and then were to come to you peacefully and say, "let there be no war between us; let us divide fairly the Territories of the United States:" could the northern section of the country refuse so just a demand? What would you then give them? What would be the fair proportion? If you allowed them their fair relative proportion, would you not give them as much as is now proposed to be assigned on the southern side of that line, and would they not be at liberty to carry their slaves there, if they pleased? You would give them the whole of that; and then what would be its fate?

Is it upon the general principle of humanity, then, that you [addressing Republican Senators] wish to put an end to slavery, or is it to be urged by you as a mere topic and point of party controversy to sustain party power? Surely I give you

credit for looking at it upon broader and more generous principles. Then, in the worst event, after you have encountered
disunion, that greatest of all political calamities to the people
of this country, and the disunionists come, the separating
States come, and demand or take their portion of the Territories, they can take, and will be entitled to take, all that will now
lie on the southern side of the line which I have proposed.
Then they will have a right to permit slavery to exist in it; and
what do you gain for the cause of anti-slavery? Nothing whatever. Suppose you should refuse their demand, and claim the
whole for yourselves: that would be a flagrant injustice which
you would not be willing that I should suppose would occur.
But if you did, what would be the consequence? A State north
and a State south, and all the States, north and south, would
be attempting to grasp at and seize this territory, and to get all
of it that they could. That would be the struggle, and you
would have war; and not only disunion, but all these fatal consequences would follow from your refusal now to permit slavery to exist, to recognize it as existing, on the southern side of
the proposed line, while you give to the people there the right
to exclude it when they come to form a State government, if
such should be their will and pleasure.

Now, gentlemen, in view of this subject, in view of the
mighty consequences, in view of the great events which are
present before you, and of the mighty consequences which are
just now to take effect, is it not better to settle the question
by a division upon the line of the Missouri compromise? For
thirty years we lived quietly and peacefully under it. Our
people, North and South, were accustomed to look at it as a
proper and just line. Can we not do so again? We did it then to
preserve the peace of the country. Now you see this Union in
the most imminent danger. I declare to you that it is my
solemn conviction that unless something be done, and something equivalent to this proposition, we shall be a separated
and divided people in six months from this time. That is my
firm conviction. There is no man here who deplores it more
than I do; but it is my sad and melancholy conviction that that
will be the consequence. I wish you to realize fully the danger.
I wish you to realize fully the consequences which are to follow. You can give increased stability to this Union; you can

give it an existence, a glorious existence, for great and glorious centuries to come, by now setting it upon a permanent basis, recognizing what the South considers as its rights; and this is the greatest of them all: it is that you should divide the territory by this line and allow the people south of it to have slavery when they are admitted into the Union as States, and to have it during the existence of the territorial government. That is all. Is it not the cheapest price at which such a blessing as this Union was ever purchased? You think, perhaps, or some of you, that there is no danger, that it will but thunder and pass away. Do not entertain such a fatal delusion. I tell you it is not so. I tell you that as sure as we stand here disunion will progress. I fear it may swallow up even old Kentucky in its vortex—as true a State to the Union as yet exists in the whole Confederacy—unless something be done; but that you will have disunion, that anarchy and war will follow it, that all this will take place in six months, I believe as confidently as I believe in your presence. I want to satisfy you of the fact.

Mr. President, I rise to suggest another consideration. I have been surprised to find, upon a little examination, that when the peace of 1783 was made, which recognized the independence of this country by Great Britain, the States north of Mason and Dixon's line had but a territory of one hundred and sixty-four thousand square miles, while the States south of Mason and Dixon's line had more than six hundred thousand square miles. It was so divided. Virginia shortly afterwards ceded to the United States all that noble territory northwest of the Ohio river, and excluded slavery from it. That changed the relative proportion of territory. After that, the North had four hundred and twenty-five thousand square miles, and the South three hundred and eighty-five thousand. Thus, at once, by the concession of Virginia, the North, from one hundred and sixty-four thousand, rose to four hundred and twenty-five thousand square miles, and the South fell from six hundred thousand to three hundred and eighty-five thousand square miles. By that cession the South became smaller in extent than the North. Well, let us look beyond. I intend to take up as little time as possible, and to avoid details; but take all your subsequent acquisitions of Florida, of Louisiana, of Oregon, of Texas, and the acquisitions made from Mexico. They have been so divided and so disposed of that the North has now two millions, two hundred thousand square miles of territory, and the South has less than one million.

Under these circumstances, when you have been so greatly magnified—I do not complain of it, I am stating facts—when your section has been made so mighty by these great acquisitions, and to a great extent with the perfect consent of the South, ought you to hesitate now upon adopting this line which will leave to you on the north side of it nine hundred and odd thousand square miles, and leave to the South only two hundred and eighty-five thousand? It will give you three times as much as it will give her. There is three times as much land in your portion as in hers. The South has already occupied some of it, and it is in States; but altogether the South gets by this division two hundred and eighty-five thousand square miles, and the North nine hundred thousand. The result of the whole of it is, that the North has two million two hundred thousand square miles and the South only one million.

I mention this as no reproach, as no upbraiding, as no complaint—none at all. I do not speak in that spirit; I do not address you in that temper. But these are the facts, and they ought, it seems to me, to have some weight; and when we come to make a peace-offering, are we to count it, are we to measure it nicely in golden scales? You get a price, and the dearest price, for all the concession asked to be made—you have the firmer establishment of your Union; you have the restoration of peace and tranquillity, and the hopes of a mighty future, all secured by this concession. How dearly must one individual, or two individuals, or many individuals, value their private opinions if they think them more important to the world than this mighty interest of the Union and Government of the United States!

Sir, it is a cheap sacrifice. It is a glorious sacrifice. This Union cost a great deal to establish it; it cost the yielding of much of public opinion and much of policy, besides the direct or indirect cost of it in all the war to establish the independence of this country. When it was done, General Washington himself said, Providence has helped us, or we could not have accomplished this thing. And this gift of our wisest men; this great work of their hands; this work in the foundation and the structure of which Providence himself, with his benignant hand, helped—are we to give it all up for such small considerations? The present exasperation; the present feeling of disunion, is the result of a long-continued controversy on the subject of slavery and of territory. I shall not attempt to trace that controversy; it is unnecessary to the occasion, and might be harmful. In relation to such controversies, I will say, though, that all the wrong is never on one side, or all the right on the other. Right and wrong, in this world, and in all such controversies, are mingled together. I forbear now any discussion or any reference to the right or wrong of the controversy, the mere party controversy; but in the progress of party, we now come to a point where party ceases to deserve consideration, and the preservation of the Union demands our highest and our greatest exertions. To preserve the Constitution of the country is the highest duty of the Senate, the highest duty of Congress—to preserve it and to perpetuate it, that we may hand down the glories which we have received to our children and to our posterity, and to generations far beyond us. We are, Senators, in positions where history is to take notice of the course we pursue.

History is to record us. Is it to record that when the destruction of the Union was imminent; when we saw it tottering to its fall; when we saw brothers arming their hands for hostility with one another, we stood quarreling about points of party politics; about questions which we attempted to sanctify and to consecrate by appealing to our conscience as the source of them? Are we to allow such fearful catastrophies to occur while we stand trifling away our time? While we stand thus, showing our inferiority to the great and mighty dead, showing our inferiority to the high positions which we occupy, the country may be destroyed and ruined; and to the amazement of all the world, the great Republic may fall prostrate and in ruins, carrying with it the very hope of that liberty which we have heretofore enjoyed; carrying with it, in place of the peace we have enjoyed, nothing but revolution and havoc and anarchy. Shall it be said that we have allowed all these evils to come upon our country, while we were engaged in the petty and small disputes and debates to which I have referred? Can it be that our name is to rest in history with this everlasting stigma and blot upon it?

Sir, I wish to God it was in my power to preserve this Union by renouncing or agreeing to give up every conscientious and other opinion. I might not be able to discard it from my mind; I am under no obligation to do that. I may retain the opinion, but if I can do so great a good as to preserve my country and give it peace, and its institutions and its Union stability, I will forego any action upon my opinions. Well now my friends, [addressing the Republican Senators,] that is all that is asked of you. Consider it well, and I do not distrust the result. As to the rest of this body, the gentlemen from the South, I would say to them, can you ask more than this? Are you bent on revolution, bent on disunion? God forbid it. I cannot believe that such madness possesses the American people. This gives reasonable satisfaction. I can speak with confidence only of my own State. Old Kentucky will be satisfied with it, and she will stand by the Union and die by the Union if this satisfaction be given. Nothing shall seduce her. The clamor of no revolution, the seductions and temptations of no revolution, will tempt her to move one step. She has stood always by the side of the Constitution; she has always been devoted to it, and is this day. Give her this satisfaction, and I believe all the States of the South that are not desirous of disunion as a better thing than the Union and the Constitution, will be satisfied and will adhere to the Union, and we shall go on again in our great career of national prosperity and national glory.

But, sir, it is not necessary for me to speak to you of the consequences that will follow disunion. Who of us is not proud of the greatness we have achieved? Disunion and separation destroy that greatness. Once disunited, we are no longer great. The nations of the earth who have looked upon you as a formidable Power, a mighty Power, and rising to untold and immeasurable greatness in the future, will scoff at you. Your flag, that now claims the respect of the world, that protects American property in every port and harbor of the world, that protects the rights of your citizens everywhere, what will become of it? What becomes of its glorious influence? It is gone; and with it the protection of American citizens and property. To say nothing of the national honor which it displayed to all the world, the protection of your rights, the protection of your property abroad is gone with that national flag, and we are hereafter to conjure and contrive different flags for our different republics according to the feverish fancies of revolutionary patriots and disturbers of the peace of the world. No, sir; I want to follow no such flag. I want to preserve the union of my country. We have it in our power to do so, and we are responsible if we do not do it.

I do not despair of the Republic. When I see before me Senators of so much intelligence and so much patriotism, who have been so honored by their country, sent here as the guardians of that very union which is now in question, sent here as the guardians of our national rights, and as guardians of that national flag, I cannot despair; I cannot despond. I cannot but believe that they will find some means of reconciling and adjusting the rights of all parties, by concessions, if necessary, so as to preserve and give more stability to the country and to its institutions.

Mr. President, I have occupied more time than I intended. My remarks were designed and contemplated only to reach to an explanation of this resolution.

The PRESIDENT OFFICER, (Mr. FITZPATRICK in the chair.) Does the Senator desire the resolution to be read?

Mr. CRITTENDEN. Yes, sir; I ask that it be read to the Senate.

Mr. GREEN. The hour has arrived for the consideration of the special order.

Mr. CRITTENDEN. I desire to present this resolution now to the Senate; and I ask that it may be read and printed.

The PRESIDENT OFFICER. The Secretary will report the resolution.

The Secretary read it, as follows:

A joint resolution (S. No. 50) proposing certain amendments to the Constitution of the United States.

Whereas serious and alarming dissensions have arisen between the northern and southern States, concerning the rights and security of the rights of the slaveholding States, and especially their rights in the common territory of the United States; and whereas it is eminently desirable and proper that these dissensions, which now threaten the very existence of this Union, should be permanently quieted and settled by constitutional provisions, which shall do equal justice to all sections, and thereby restore to the people that peace and good-will which ought to prevail between all the citizens of the United States: Therefore,

*Resolved by the Senate and House of Representatives of the United States of America in Congress assembled*, (two thirds of both Houses concurring,) That the following articles be, and are hereby, proposed and submitted as amendments to the Constitution of the United States, which shall be valid to all intents and purposes, as part of said Constitution, when ratified by conventions of three fourths of the several States:

ARTICLE 1. In all the territory of the United States now held, or hereafter acquired, situate north of latitude 36° 30′, slavery or involuntary servitude, except as a punishment for crime, is prohibited while such territory shall remain under territorial government. In all the territory south of said line of latitude, slavery of the African race is hereby recognized as existing, and shall not be interfered with by Congress, but shall be protected as property by all the departments of the territorial government during its continuance. And when any Territory, north or south of said line, within such boundaries as Congress may prescribe, shall contain the population requisite for a member of Congress according to the then Federal ratio of representation of the people of the United States, it shall, if its form of government be republican, be admitted into the Union, on an equal footing with the original States, with or without slavery, as the constitution of such new State may provide.

ART. 2. Congress shall have no power to abolish slavery in places under its exclusive jurisdiction, and situate within the limits of States that permit the holding of slaves.

ART. 3. Congress shall have no power to abolish slavery within the District of Columbia, so long as it exists in the adjoining States of Virginia and Maryland, or either, nor without the consent of the inhabitants, nor without just compensation first made to such owners of slaves as do not consent to such abolishment. Nor shall Congress at any time prohibit officers of the Federal Government, or members of Congress, whose duties require them to be in said District, from bringing with them their slaves, and holding them as such during the time their duties may require them to remain there, and afterwards taking them from the District.

ART. 4. Congress shall have no power to prohibit or hinder the transportation of slaves from one State to another, or to a Territory in which slaves are by law permitted to be held, whether that transportation be by land, navigable rivers, or by the sea.

ART. 5. That in addition to the provisions of the third paragraph of
the second section of the fourth article of the Constitution of the
United States, Congress shall have power to provide by law, and it
shall be its duty so to provide, that the United States shall pay to the
owner who shall apply for it, the full value of his fugitive slave in all
cases when the marshal or other officer whose duty it was to arrest
said fugitive was prevented from so doing by violence or intimidation,
or when, after arrest, said fugitive was rescued by force, and the
owner thereby prevented and obstructed in the pursuit of his remedy
for the recovery of his fugitive slave under the said clause of the Constitution and the laws made in pursuance thereof. And in all such
cases, when the United States shall pay for such fugitive, they shall
have the right, in their own name, to sue the county in which said violence, intimidation, or rescue was committed, and to recover from
it, with interest and damages, the amount paid by them for said fugitive slave. And the said county, after it has paid said amount to the
United States, may, for its indemnity, sue and recover from the wrong
doers or rescuers by whom the owner was prevented from the recovery of his fugitive slave, in like manner as the owner himself might
have sued and recovered.

ART. 6. No future amendment of the Constitution shall affect the
five preceding articles; nor the third paragraph of the second section
of the first article of the Constitution; nor the third paragraph of the
second section of the fourth article of said Constitution; and no
amendment shall be made to the Constitution which shall authorize
or give to Congress any power to abolish or interfere with slavery in
any of the States by whose laws it is, or may be, allowed or permitted.

And whereas, also, besides those causes of dissension embraced in
the foregoing amendments proposed to the Constitution of the
United States, there are others which come within the jurisdiction of
Congress, and may be remedied by its legislative power; and whereas
it is the desire of Congress, as far as its power will extend, to remove
all just cause for the popular discontent and agitation which now disturb the peace of the country, and threaten the stability of its institutions: Therefore,

1. *Resolved by the Senate and House of Representatives of the United
States of America in Congress assembled,* That the laws now in force
for the recovery of fugitive slaves are in strict pursuance of the plain
and mandatory provisions of the Constitution, and have been sanctioned as valid and constitutional by the judgment of the Supreme
Court of the United States; that the slaveholding States are entitled
to the faithful observance and execution of those laws, and that they

ought not to be repealed, or so modified or changed as to impair their efficiency; and that laws ought to be made for the punishment of those who attempt by rescue of the slave, or other illegal means, to hinder or defeat the due execution of said laws.

2. That all State laws which conflict with the fugitive slave acts of Congress, or any other constitutional acts of Congress, or which, in their operation, impede, hinder, or delay the free course and due execution of any of said acts, are null and void by the plain provisions of the Constitution of the United States; yet those State laws, void as they are, have given color to practices, and led to consequences, which have obstructed the due administration and execution of acts of Congress, and especially the acts for the delivery of fugitive slaves, and have thereby contributed much to the discord and commotion now prevailing. Congress, therefore, in the present perilous juncture, does not deem it improper, respectfully and earnestly to recommend the repeal of those laws to the several States which have enacted them, or such legislative corrections or explanations of them as may prevent their being used or perverted to such mischievous purposes.

3. That the act of the 18th of September, 1850, commonly called the fugitive slave law, ought to be so amended as to make the fee of the commissioner, mentioned in the eighth section of the act, equal in amount in the cases decided by him, whether his decision be in favor of or against the claimant. And to avoid misconstruction, the last clause of the fifth section of said act, which authorizes the person holding a warrant for the arrest or detention of a fugitive slave, to summon to his aid the *posse comitatus*, and which declares it to be the duty of all good citizens to assist him in its execution, ought to be so amended as to expressly limit the authority and duty to cases in which there shall be resistance or danger of resistance or rescue.

4. That the laws for the suppression of the African slave trade, and especially those prohibiting the importation of slaves in the United States, ought to be made effectual, and ought to be thoroughly executed; and all further enactments necessary to those ends ought to be promptly made.

# Henry Adams to Charles Francis Adams Jr.

Charles Francis Adams, the son of John Quincy Adams and the grandson of John Adams, was serving his first term as a Republican representative from Massachusetts when Congress reconvened in December 1860. Adams would play a prominent role on the special Committee of Thirty Three that was appointed on December 4 to consider proposals for sectional compromise. Five measures were reported from the committee in January 1861, only one of which would be adopted by both the House and Senate: a constitutional amendment forbidding Congress from abolishing or interfering with slavery in the states. The amendment was approved by the House, 133–65, on February 28 (with Adams voting in favor), and by the Senate, 24–12, on March 3, but was ratified by only two states. During the winter of 1860–61 Henry Adams, who had recently returned from two years of travel and study in Europe, served as his father's private secretary. He described events in Washington to his older brother, Charles Francis Adams Jr.

---

Tuesday. Dec. 18. 1860.

Dear Charles

I'm a confoundedly unenterprising beggar. It's an outrageous bore to make calls and as society is all at odds and ends here, I make no acquaintances except those of the family. Even political matters are slow. There are no fights. Everyone is good-natured except those who are naturally misanthropic and even those who are so frightened that they can't breathe in more than a whisper, still keep their temper.

This makes it almost slow work. Then we dine at five and after that I don't feel as if I wanted to run much, especially as there are no parties nor receptions. The President divides his time between crying and praying; the Cabinet has resigned or else is occupied in committing treason. Some of them have done both. The people of Washington are firmly convinced that there is to be an attack on Washington by the southerners

or else a slave insurrection, and in either case or in any contingency they feel sure of being ruined and murdered. There is
no money nor much prospect of any and all sources of income
are dry, so that no one can entertain. You see from this that
there's no great chance for any violent gaiety.

Every one takes to politics for an occupation, but do you
know, to me this whole matter is beginning to get stale. It
does not rise to the sublime at all. It is merely the last convulsion of the slave-power, and only makes me glad that the beast
is so near his end. I have no fear for the result at all. It must
come out right. But what a piece of meanness and rascality, of
braggadocio and nonsense the whole affair is. What insolence
in the South and what cowardice and vileness at the North.
The other day in that precious Committee of Thirty Three
where our good father is doing his best to do nothing, in
stalked the secessionists with Reuben Davis of Miss. at their
head, and flung down a paper which was to be their ultimatum. That was to be taken up at once or the South would secede. The Committee declined to take it up till they had
discussed the Fugitive Slave law. So out stalked the secessionists but not wholly away. They only seceded into the next
room where they sat in dignity, smoking and watching the remaining members through the folding doors, while Davis returned to say that he did not wish to be misunderstood; they
seceded only while the other proposition should be under discussion. Is that not a specimen of those men. Their whole
game is a bare bluff.

The heroism of this struggle is over. That belonged to us
when we were a minority; when Webster was pulled down and
afterwards in the Kansas battle and the Sumner troubles. But
now these men are struggling for power and they kick so hard
that our men hardly dare say they'll take the prize they've won.
In Massachusetts all are sound except Rice, but we've some
pretty tight screws on him and I think he'll hold. Thayer I
count out. Of course he's gone. But Pennsylvania is rotten to
the core just as she was in the revolution when John Adams
had such a battle with Dickinson. There is some sound principle in the western counties but Philadelphia is all about our
ears. Ohio is not all she should be, and Indiana is all she should
not be just as that mean state always was. Illinois is tolerably

well in some respects and Wisconsin is a new Vermont, but there's too low a tone everywhere. They don't seem to see their way.

Dec. 20.    Mr Appleton and Mr Amory have been on here the last four or five days engaged in saving the Union. Mr Appleton has buried himself among his southern friends so as not to encourage much any politeness on our side. After passing two whole days in the senate-chamber with Mason and his other attachments, he tapped Sumner on the shoulder and pretended to be very glad to see him. Sumner had not taken any notice of him of course till then, but on this notice, he turned round and they shook hands. The conversation however was not very brotherly, as Sumner in answer to some remark on the state of affairs, immediately began to haul the Boston Courier and Caleb Cushing over the coals as the great causes of the present misrepresentation, which Appleton of course couldn't quite agree in. However, it was all friendly enough I believe. Appleton called here when he knew that our father must be at the House, without asking for mamma, and never has called on Sumner at all.

Mr Amory dined here to-day. Mr Etheridge was invited to meet him but didn't come. Anthony of R.I. was also invited and did come. We had a very pleasant dinner. Mr Amory was amusing and told us his experiences in saving the country, which don't seem to have been very successful. He had talked with Douglas a long time and Douglas had been moral, demonstrating from the examples of Wellington and Peale, that a change of sentiments in cases of urgency was the duty of good citizens. Mr Amory seemed to think that Douglas was the very dirtiest beast he had yet met. He is, by the way, by his present course, destroying the power he has left. Pugh's speech to-day was disgusting. Those men are trying to build the Democratic party up again.

That blessed committee is still at work all the time and tomorrow a vote will be taken on the territorial question. Our father's course will be such as not to need much active support since Winter Davis is assuming the decided course of breaking with the south and he will bear the brunt of the battle. It seems likely that no minority report of any consequence will be needed. Tomorrow will decide and I have a letter all ready for next Monday's Advertiser in case the vote should go right. As to last Monday's letter which has not appeared, I am not sorry for it, as it was written when everything looked fishy. You can tell Hale this and mark what he says or looks, for I do much mistrust me that he suppressed that letter. One ought to have appeared this morning and I shall look with curiosity tomorrow to see.

I am not sorry that affairs have taken such a turn as to relieve our father. He will be strongly pushed for the Treasury and I don't care to have him expose himself now. Lincoln is all right. You can rely on that. He has exercised a strong influence through several sources on this committee and always right, but as yet there is no lisp of a Cabinet. Not even Seward had been consulted a week ago, though perhaps this visit of his to New York may have something to do with it.

As for my Advertiser letters, it will take a little time for me to make headway enough here to do much. But I do not wish to hurry matters. As yet there has been no great demand; that is, no active fighting, and I doubt if there will be. But these things will arrange themselves so soon as I begin to take a position here.

Johnson's speech yesterday was a great relief to us and it cut the secessionists dreadfully hard. Jeff. Davis was in a fever all through it and they all lost their temper. Sumner dined here yesterday and was grand as usual, full of the diplomatic corps. He told Alley a little while ago that of course if he went into the Cabinet it could be only as Sec. of State, and Alley recommended him to give up all idea of it. I think he'd better.

H.B.A.

# John G. Nicolay: Memorandum Regarding Abraham Lincoln

December 22, 1860

On December 20 South Carolina became the first state to break away from the Union when its convention approved an ordinance of secession, 169–0. The following day a report appeared in *The New York Times* claiming that President Buchanan had ordered Major Robert Anderson, the commander of the federal garrison at Fort Moultrie in Charleston harbor, to surrender if attacked. In fact, Secretary of War John Floyd had sent instructions to Anderson on December 21, ordering him to "exercise a sound military discretion" if his command came under attack, but to avoid "a vain and useless sacrifice" of life "upon a mere point of honor." Abraham Lincoln's response to the *Times* report was recorded in Springfield by his secretary John G. Nicolay.

———————

WHEN Mr. Lincoln came to the office this morning, after the usual salutations, he asked me what the news was. I asked him if he had seen the morning dispatches. He replied "no." "Then," said I, "there is an important rumor you have not seen. The Times correspondent telegraphs that Buchanan has sent instructions to Maj. Anderson to surrender Fort Moultrie if it is attacked."

"If that is true they ought to hang him!" said he with warmth.

After some further conversation he remarked—

"Among the letters you saw me mail yesterday was one to Washburne, (of Ill.) who had written me that he had just had a long conversation with Gen. Scott, and that the General felt considerably outraged that the President would not act as he wished him to in reinforcing the forts &c. I wrote to Washburne to tell Gen. Scott confidentially, that I wished him to be prepared, immediately after my inauguration to make arrangements at once to hold the forts, or if they have been taken, to take them back again."

Afterwards he repeated the substance of the above in another conversation with Wm H Herndon; adding at the close with much emphasis: "There can be no doubt that in *any* event that is good ground to live and to die by."

# South Carolina Declaration
# of the Causes of Secession

December 24, 1860

Four days after voting to secede, the South Carolina convention approved the declaration that follows, as well as an address calling for the formation of a "Confederacy of Slaveholding States."

---

## DECLARATION OF THE IMMEDIATE CAUSES WHICH INDUCE AND JUSTIFY THE SECESSION OF SOUTH CAROLINA FROM THE FEDERAL UNION.

The People of the State of South Carolina, in Convention assembled, on the 26th day of April, A. D., 1852, declared that the frequent violations of the Constitution of the United States, by the Federal Government, and its encroachments upon the reserved rights of the States, fully justified this State in then withdrawing from the Federal Union; but in deference to the opinions and wishes of the other slaveholding States, she forbore at that time to exercise this right. Since that time, these encroachments have continued to increase, and further forbearance ceases to be a virtue.

And now the State of South Carolina having resumed her separate and equal place among nations, deems it due to herself, to the remaining United States of America, and to the nations of the world, that she should declare the immediate causes which have led to this act.

In the year 1765, that portion of the British Empire embracing Great Britain, undertook to make laws for the government of that portion composed of the thirteen American Colonies. A struggle for the right of self-government ensued, which resulted, on the 4th of July, 1776, in a Declaration, by the Colonies, "that they are, and of right ought to be, FREE AND

INDEPENDENT STATES; and that, as free and independent States, they have full power to levy war, conclude peace, contract alliances, establish commerce, and to do all other acts and things which independent States may of right do."

They further solemnly declared that whenever any "form of government becomes destructive of the ends for which it was established, it is the right of the people to alter or abolish it, and to institute a new government." Deeming the Government of Great Britain to have become destructive of these ends, they declared that the Colonies "are absolved from all allegiance to the British Crown, and that all political connection between them and the State of Great Britain is, and ought to be, totally dissolved."

In pursuance of this Declaration of Independence, each of the thirteen States proceeded to exercise its separate sovereignty; adopted for itself a Constitution, and appointed officers for the administration of government in all its departments— Legislative, Executive and Judicial. For purposes of defence, they united their arms and their counsels; and, in 1778, they entered into a League known as the Articles of Confederation, whereby they agreed to entrust the administration of their external relations to a common agent, known as the Congress of the United States, expressly declaring, in the first Article "that each State retains its sovereignty, freedom and independence, and every power, jurisdiction and right which is not, by this Confederation, expressly delegated to the United States in Congress assembled."

Under this Confederation the war of the Revolution was carried on, and on the 8d September, 1783, the contest ended, and a definite Treaty was signed by Great Britain, in which she acknowledged the independence of the Colonies in the following terms:

"ARTICLE 1.—His Britannic Majesty acknowledges the said United States, viz: New Hampshire, Massachusetts Bay, Rhode Island and Providence Plantations, Connecticut, New York, New Jersey, Pennsylvania, Delaware, Maryland, Virginia, North Carolina, South Carolina and Georgia, to be FREE, SOVEREIGN AND INDEPENDENT STATES; that he treats with them as such; and for himself, his heirs and successors, relinquishes all claims to the government, propriety and territorial rights of the same and every part thereof."

Thus were established the two great principles asserted by the Colonies, namely: the right of a State to govern itself; and the right of a people to abolish a Government when it becomes destructive of the ends for which it was instituted. And concurrent with the establishment of these principles, was the fact, that each Colony became and was recognized by the mother Country as a FREE, SOVEREIGN AND INDEPENDENT STATE.

In 1787, Deputies were appointed by the States to revise the Articles of Confederation, and on 17th September, 1787, these Deputies recommended, for the adoption of the States, the Articles of Union, known as the Constitution of the United States.

The parties to whom this Constitution was submitted, were the several sovereign States; they were to agree or disagree, and when nine of them agreed the compact was to take effect among those concurring; and the General Government, as the common agent, was then to be invested with their authority.

If only nine of the thirteen States had concurred, the other four would have remained as they then were—separate, sovereign States, independent of any of the provisions of the Constitution. In fact, two of the States did not accede to the Constitution until long after it had gone into operation among the other eleven; and during that interval, they each exercised the functions of an independent nation.

By this Constitution, certain duties were imposed upon the several States, and the exercise of certain of their powers was restrained, which necessarily implied their continued existence as sovereign States. But to remove all doubt, an amendment was added, which declared that the powers not delegated to the United States by the Constitution, nor prohibited by it to the States, are reserved to the States, respectively, or to the people. On 23d May, 1788, South Carolina, by a Convention of her People, passed an Ordinance assenting to this Constitution, and afterwards altered her own Constitution, to conform herself to the obligations she had undertaken.

Thus was established, by compact between the States, a

Government, with defined objects and powers, limited to the express words of the grant. This limitation left the whole remaining mass of power subject to the clause reserving it to the States or to the people, and rendered unnecessary any specification of reserved rights.

We hold that the Government thus established is subject to the two great principles asserted in the Declaration of Independence; and we hold further, that the mode of its formation subjects it to a third fundamental principle, namely: the law of compact. We maintain that in every compact between two or more parties, the obligation is mutual; that the failure of one of the contracting parties to perform a material part of the agreement, entirely releases the obligation of the other; and that where no arbiter is provided, each party is remitted to his own judgment to determine the fact of failure, with all its consequences.

In the present case, that fact is established with certainty. We assert that fourteen of the States have deliberately refused, for years past, to fulfil their constitutional obligations, and we refer to their own Statutes for the proof.

The Constitution of the United States, in its fourth Article, provides as follows:

"No person held to service or labor in one State, under the laws thereof, escaping into another, shall, in consequence of any law or regulation therein, be discharged from such service or labor, but shall be delivered up, on claim of the party to whom such service or labor may be due."

This stipulation was so material to the compact, that without it that compact would not have been made. The great number of the contracting parties held slaves, and they had previously evinced their estimate of the value of such a stipulation by making it a condition in the Ordinance for the government of the territory ceded by Virginia, which now composes the States north of the Ohio River.

The same article of the Constitution stipulates also for rendition by the several States of fugitives from justice from the other States.

The General Government, as the common agent, passed laws to carry into effect these stipulations of the States. For many years these laws were executed. But an increasing hostility on the part of the non-slaveholding States to the institution of slavery, has led to a disregard of their obligations, and the laws of the General Government have ceased to effect the objects of the Constitution. The States of Maine, New Hampshire, Vermont, Massachusetts, Connecticut, Rhode Island, New York, Pennsylvania, Illinois, Indiana, Michigan, Wisconsin and Iowa, have enacted laws which either nullify the Acts of Congress or render useless any attempt to execute them. In many of these States the fugitive is discharged from the service or labor claimed, and in none of them has the State Government complied with the stipulation made in the Constitution. The State of New Jersey, at an early day, passed a law in conformity with her constitutional obligation; but the current of anti-slavery feeling has led her more recently to enact laws which render inoperative the remedies provided by her own law and by the laws of Congress. In the State of New York even the right of transit for a slave has been denied by her tribunals; and the States of Ohio and Iowa have refused to surrender to justice fugitives charged with murder, and with inciting servile insurrection in the State of Virginia. Thus the constituted compact has been deliberately broken and disregarded by the non-slaveholding States, and the consequence follows that South Carolina is released from her obligation.

The ends for which this Constitution was framed are declared by itself to be "to form a more perfect union, establish justice, insure domestic tranquillity, provide for the common defence, promote the general welfare, and secure the blessings of liberty to ourselves and our posterity."

These ends it endeavored to accomplish by a Federal Government, in which each State was recognized as an equal, and had separate control over its own institutions. The right of property in slaves was recognized by giving to free persons distinct political rights, by giving them the right to represent, and burthening them with direct taxes for three-fifths of their slaves; by authorizing the importation of slaves for twenty years; and by stipulating for the rendition of fugitives from labor.

We affirm that these ends for which this Government was instituted have been defeated, and the Government itself has been made destructive of them by the action of the non-slaveholding States. Those States have assumed the right of deciding upon the propriety of our domestic institutions; and have denied the rights of property established in fifteen of the States and recognized by the Constitution; they have denounced as sinful the institution of slavery; they have permitted the open establishment among them of societies, whose avowed object is to disturb the peace and to eloign the property of the citizens of other States. They have encouraged and assisted thousands of our slaves to leave their homes; and those who remain, have been incited by emissaries, books and pictures to servile insurrection.

For twenty-five years this agitation has been steadily increasing, until it has now secured to its aid the power of the common Government. Observing the *forms* of the Constitution, a sectional party has found within that Article establishing the Executive Department, the means of subverting the Constitution itself. A geographical line has been drawn across the Union, and all the States north of that line have united in the election of a man to the high office of President of the United States, whose opinions and purposes are hostile to slavery. He is to be entrusted with the administration of the common Government, because he has declared that that "Government cannot endure permanently half slave, half free," and that the public mind must rest in the belief that slavery is in the course of ultimate extinction.

This sectional combination for the submersion of the Constitution, has been aided in some of the States by elevating to citizenship, persons, who, by the supreme law of the land, are incapable of becoming citizens; and their votes have been used to inaugurate a new policy, hostile to the South, and destructive of its peace and safety.

On the 4th of March next, this party will take possession of the Government. It has announced that the South shall be excluded from the common territory, that the judicial tribunals shall be made sectional, and that a war must be waged against slavery until it shall cease throughout the United States.

The guaranties of the Constitution will then no longer exist; the equal rights of the States will be lost. The slaveholding States will no longer have the power of self-government, or self-protection, and the Federal Government will have become their enemy.

Sectional interest and animosity will deepen the irritation, and all hope of remedy is rendered vain, by the fact that public opinion at the North has invested a great political error with the sanctions of a more erroneous religious belief.

We, therefore, the People of South Carolina, by our delegates in Convention assembled, appealing to the Supreme Judge of the world for the rectitude of our intentions, have solemnly declared that the Union heretofore existing between this State and the other States of North America, is dissolved, and that the State of South Carolina has resumed her position among the nations of the world, as a separate and independent State; with full power to levy war, concluded peace, contract alliances, establish commerce, and to do all other acts and things which independent States may of right do.

# Abner Doubleday: from Reminiscences of Forts Sumter and Moultrie in 1860–'61

Captain Abner Doubleday, an 1842 graduate of West Point, had been assigned to Fort Moultrie in Charleston Harbor in 1858, and was commanding an artillery company there when the secession crisis began. In his 1876 memoir, Doubleday described Fort Sumter; Major Robert Anderson's assumption of command at Charleston on November 21, 1860; and Anderson's crucial decision to relocate the garrison from its highly vulnerable position at Fort Moultrie, where it was exposed to an overland attack, to a more secure one inside Fort Sumter.

---

THE FIRST thing that attracted the eye of the stranger, upon approaching Charleston from the sea, was Fort Sumter. It was built on an artificial island made of large blocks of stone. The walls were of dark brick, and designed for three tiers of guns. The whole structure, as it rose abruptly out of the water, had a gloomy, prison-like appearance. It was situated on the edge of the channel, in the narrowest part of the harbor, between Fort Moultrie and Cummings Point, distant about a mile from the former place, and twelve hundred yards from the latter. The year before, it had been used by us as a temporary place of confinement and security for some negroes that had been brought over from Africa in a slaver captured by one of our naval vessels. The inevitable conflict was very near breaking out at that time; for there was an eager desire on the part of all the people around us to seize these negroes, and distribute them among the plantations; and if the Government had not acted promptly in sending them back to Africa, I think an attempt would have been made to take them from us by force, on the ground that some of them had violated a State law by landing at Moultrieville.

---

It was now openly proclaimed in Charleston that declarations in favor of the Union would no longer be tolerated; that the time for deliberation had passed, and the time for action had come.

On the 21st our new commander arrived and assumed command. He felt as if he had a hereditary right to be there, for his father had distinguished himself in the Revolutionary War in defense of old Fort Moultrie against the British, and had been confined a long time as a prisoner in Charleston. We had long known Anderson as a gentleman; courteous, honest, intelligent, and thoroughly versed in his profession. He had been twice brevetted for gallantry—once for services against the Seminole Indians in Florida, and once for the battle of Molino del Rey in Mexico, where he was badly wounded. In politics he was a strong pro-slavery man. Nevertheless, he was opposed to secession and Southern extremists. He soon found himself in troubled waters, for the approaching battle of Fort Moultrie was talked of everywhere throughout the State, and the mob in Charleston could hardly be restrained from making an immediate assault. They were kept back once through the exertions of Colonel Benjamin Huger, of the Ordnance Department of the United States Army. As he belonged to one of the most distinguished families in Charleston, he had great influence there. It was said at the time that he threatened if we were attacked, or rather mobbed, in this way, he would join us, and fight by the side of his friend Anderson.* Colonel Memminger, afterward the Confederate Secretary of the Treasury, also exerted himself to prevent any irregular and unauthorized violence.

---

Anderson had been urged by several of us to remove his command to Fort Sumter, but he had invariably replied that he was specially assigned to Fort Moultrie, and had no right to vacate it without orders. Our affairs, however, were becoming

*He left the United States service soon after the attack on Fort Sumter, and joined the Confederates. He did so reluctantly, for he had gained great renown in our army for his gallantry in Mexico, and he knew he would soon have been promoted to the position of Chief of our Ordnance Department had he remained with us.

critical, and I thought it my duty to speak to him again on the subject. He still apparently adhered to his decision. Nevertheless, he had fully determined to make the change, and was now merely awaiting a favorable opportunity. To deceive the enemy, he still kept at work with unabated zeal on the defenses of Fort Moultrie. This exactly suited the purposes of the rebel leaders, for they knew we could make no effectual defense there, and our preparations would only increase the prestige of their victory. We were not authorized to commence hostilities by burning the adjacent houses, and yet, if they were not leveled, clouds of riflemen could occupy them, and prevent our men from serving the guns. Under any circumstances, it was plain that we must soon succumb from over-exertion and loss of sleep incident to repelling incessant attacks from a host of enemies. The fact that through the provident care of the Secretary of War the guns of Fort Sumter would also be turned upon us, enfilading two sides of Fort Moultrie, and taking another side in reverse, was quite decisive as to the impossibility of our making a lengthened defense.

Up to this time we had hoped, almost against hope, that, even if the Government were base enough to desert us, the loyal spirit of the patriotic North would manifest itself in our favor, inasmuch as our little force represented the supremacy of the Constitution and the laws; but all seemed doubt, apathy, and confusion there. Yancey was delivering lectures in the Northern States, as a representative of the Disunionists, not only without molestation, but with frequent and vociferous applause from the Democratic masses, who could not be made to believe there was any real danger.

In making his arrangements to cross over, Anderson acted with consummate prudence and ability. He only communicated his design to the staff-officers, whose co-operation was indispensable, and he waited until the moment of execution before he informed the others of his intention. No one, of course, would deliberately betray a secret of this kind, but it sometimes happens, under such circumstances, that officers give indications of what is about to take place by sending for their washing, packing their trunks, and making changes in their messing arrangements.

Without knowing positively that any movement had been

projected, two circumstances excited my suspicions. Once, while I was walking with the major on the parapet, he turned to me abruptly, and asked me what would be the best course to take to render the gun-carriages unserviceable. I told him there were several methods, but my plan would be to heap pitch-pine knots around them, and burn them up. The question was too suggestive to escape my attention.

On the day previous to our departure, I requested him to allow me to purchase a large quantity of wire, to make an entanglement in front of the part of the work I was assigned to defend. He said, with a quizzical look, "Certainly; you shall have a mile of wire, if you require it." When I proposed to send for it immediately, he smiled, and objected in such a peculiar way that I at once saw that he was no longer interested in our efforts to strengthen Fort Moultrie.

As a preliminary to the proposed movement, he directed the post quartermaster, Lieutenant Hall, to charter three schooners and some barges, for the ostensible purpose of transporting the soldiers' families to old Fort Johnson, on the opposite side of the harbor, where there were some dilapidated public buildings belonging to the United States. The danger of the approaching conflict was a good pretext for the removal of the non-combatants. All this seemed natural enough to the enemy, and no one offered any opposition. In reality, these vessels were loaded with supplies for all the troops, with reference to a prolonged residence in Fort Sumter. Hall was directed to land every thing there as soon as a signal-gun was fired. In the mean time he sailed for Fort Johnson, and lay off and on, waiting for the signal.

Anderson had broken up his own mess, and on the last evening of our stay (December 26th) I left my room to ask him in to take tea with us. The sun was just setting as I ascended the steps leading to the parapet and approached him. He was in the midst of a group of officers, each of whom seemed silent and distrait. As I passed our assistant-surgeon, I remarked, "It is a fine evening, Crawford." He replied in a hesitating and embarrassed manner, showing that his thoughts were elsewhere. I saw plainly that something unusual had occurred. Anderson approached me as I advanced, and said quietly, "I have determined to evacuate this post immediately, for the purpose of occupying Fort Sumter; I can only allow you twenty minutes to form your company and be in readiness to start." I was surprised at this announcement, and realized the gravity of the situation at a glance. We were watched by spies and vigilance-committees, who would undoubtedly open fire upon us as soon as they saw the object of the movement. I was naturally concerned, too, for the safety of my wife, who was the only lady in the fort at that time, and who would necessarily be exposed to considerable danger. Fortunately, I had little or no property to lose, as, in anticipation of a crisis, I had previously sent every thing of value to New York. Some of the other officers did not fare so well. The doctor, not expecting so sudden a *dénouement*, had necessarily left his medical stores unpacked. Foster, who had taken a house outside for his family, was wholly unprepared, and lost heavily.

I made good use of the twenty minutes allowed me. I first went to the barracks, formed my company, inspected it, and saw that each man was properly armed and equipped. This left me ten minutes to spare. I dashed over to my quarters; told my wife to get ready to leave immediately, and as the fighting would probably commence in a few minutes, I advised her to take refuge with some family outside, and get behind the sand-hills as soon as possible, to avoid the shot. She hastily threw her wearing-apparel into her trunks, and I called two men to put her baggage outside the main gate. I then accompanied her there, and we took a sad and hasty leave of each other, for neither knew when or where we would meet again. As soon as this was accomplished, I strapped on my revolver, tied a blanket across my shoulders, and reported to Major Anderson that my men were in readiness to move.

In the mean time Lieutenant Jefferson C. Davis, of my company, who had been detailed to command the rear guard, aimed the guns, which were already loaded, to bear upon the passage to Fort Sumter, and Captain Foster and Assistant-surgeon Crawford, with two sergeants and three privates, remained with him, and took post at five columbiads, in readiness to carry out Major Anderson's design, which was to sink the guard-boats, should they attempt to fire into us or run us down while *en route*. Certainly the major showed no lack of determination or energy on this occasion.

If we were successful in crossing, Davis was to follow with the remainder of the men. Foster and Mr. Moale agreed to remain behind until morning. They also volunteered to place themselves at the guns, and cover the retreat of the rear guard under Davis, in case an attempt was made to intercept them.

The chaplain, the Rev. Matthias Harris, being a noncombatant, and having his family in the village, was not notified. Neither was Surgeon Simons, of the army, who was living in a house adjoining the fort, and directly in line with our guns. When he saw the movement in progress, he hastened out with his family, to shelter them behind the sand-hills as soon as possible.

Every thing being in readiness, we passed out of the main gates, and silently made our way for about a quarter of a mile to a spot where the boats were hidden behind an irregular pile of rocks, which originally formed part of the sea-wall. There was not a single human being in sight as we marched to the rendezvous, and we had the extraordinary good luck to be wholly unobserved. We found several boats awaiting us, under charge of two engineer officers, Lieutenants Snyder and Meade. They and their crews were crouched down behind the rocks, to escape observation. In a low tone they pointed out to me the boats intended for my company, and then pushed out rapidly to return to the fort. Noticing that one of the guard-boats was approaching, they made a wide circuit to avoid it. I hoped there would be time for my party to cross before the steamer could overhaul us; but as among my men there were a number of unskilful oarsmen, we made but slow progress, and it soon became evident that we would be overtaken in mid-channel. It was after sunset, and the twilight had deepened, so that there was a fair chance for us to escape. While the steamer was yet afar off, I took off my cap, and threw open my coat to conceal the buttons. I also made the men take off their coats, and use them to cover up their muskets, which were lying alongside the rowlocks. I hoped in this way that we might pass for a party of laborers returning to the fort. The paddle-wheels stopped within about a hundred yards of us; but, to our great relief, after a slight scrutiny, the steamer kept on its way. In the mean time our men redoubled their efforts, and we soon arrived at our destination. As we ascended the steps of the wharf, crowds of workmen rushed out to meet us, most of them wearing secession emblems. One or two Union men among them cheered lustily, but the majority called out angrily, "What are these soldiers doing here?" I at once formed my men, charged bayonets, drove the tumultuous mass inside the fort, and seized the guard-room, which commanded the main entrance. I then placed sentinels to prevent the crowd from encroaching on us. As soon as we had disembarked, the boats were sent back for Seymour's company. The major landed soon after in one of the engineer boats, which had coasted along to avoid the steamer. Seymour's men arrived in safety, followed soon after by the remaining detachments, which had been left behind as a rear-guard. The latter, however, ran a good deal of risk, for in the dark it passed almost under the bow of the guard-boat *Niña*. The whole movement was successful beyond our most sanguine expectations, and we were highly elated. The signal-gun was fired, and Hall at once sailed over, and landed the soldiers' families and supplies. As soon as the schooners were unloaded, the disloyal workmen were placed on board and shipped off to the main-land. Only a few of the best and most reliable were retained.

Upon leaving me, my wife took refuge temporarily in the residence of Dan Sinclair, the sutler of the post, a most excellent man, and one to whom we were indebted for many kindnesses. Finding that the people of Moultrieville were not yet aware of the change that had taken place, and that every thing was tranquil, she ventured back to the fort, and finished the removal of all our effects. After this, in company with the chaplain's family, she walked up and down the beach the greater part of the night, looking anxiously toward Fort Sumter to see if there were any indications of trouble or disturbance there. In the morning she took up her residence at the chaplain's house. As for the other ladies, both Mrs. Simons and Mrs. Foster fled to the city at the first intimation of danger, and Mrs. Seymour was already there.

## Catherine Edmondston: Diary, December 26–27, 1860

Catherine Edmondston lived with her husband, Patrick, on their plantation in Halifax County, North Carolina. While visiting her parents in Aiken, South Carolina, she learned that Anderson had moved his garrison from Fort Moultrie to Fort Sumter. President Buchanan had told a delegation of South Carolina congressmen on December 10 that he did not intend to reinforce the garrison at Fort Moultrie. Many Southerners believed Buchanan had also promised not to change the military situation at Charleston in any way, and thus saw the occupation of Fort Sumter as the violation of his pledge.

---

DECEMBER 26, 1860

In the morning we had a terrible revulsion of feeling which seemed to plunge us at once from the most profound peace into almost War! Major Anderson, the U S Commander of Forts Moultrie, Sumter, & Pinckney, in the night suddenly evacuated Moultrie & Pinckney after spiking the Guns, burning the carriages, and cutting down the Flag staff, and retreated with his whole command into Sumter! Most remarkable conduct & well calculated to bring on the attack which he seems to dread, but of which, beyond a few idle threats there has as yet been no evidence. We heard it on the morning of the 26th, & it seemed to plunge us into a sea of care after basking in the sunshine of happiness.

DECEMBER 27, 1860

On the 27th the Government of SC took possession of the vacant forts Moultrie & Pinckney & hoisted the Palmetto Flag in defiance as it were to the US. Preparations were hastily made to put them in a defencible position. Troops were ordered from the interior, & batteries commenced on the channel with a view to prevent the re-inforcement of Sumter.

Thus has one ill advised act thrown down the gauntlet as it were, which SC is not slow to accept!

We had a delightful visit in Aiken disturbed only by exciting news from Charleston and the passage of Troops, which was so new to us that it excited the liveliest forebodings. The Ladies of SC displayed an enthusiasm & earnestness in their preparations for War that was almost sublime in its unity & self devotion. They spent their whole time scraping lint, making bandages, & even learned to make Cartridges. One lady in Aiken made 500 with her own hands. Never was known such unanimity of action amongst all classes.

South Carolina having seceeded from the US, amidst the jeers & laughter of the whole country calmly organized her own government & prepared for War singly and alone. It at first made one smile to see the news from Washington put under the head of "Foreign News," but all disposition to it was soon taken away by the sight of the terribly earnest way in which all looked at & spoke of it. I often thought, "Have we indeed come to this?" Pray God that Mr. Buchanan would quietly withdraw the troops from Sumter. Let SC peaceably go her own way. Perhaps after a little, when she sees that Mr Lincoln does not meddle with Slavery, she may return & this threatened dismemberment of our country may be prevented. But God ordained otherwise. Papa entered most keenly into it, regretted that he was not a son of her soil, & was as enthused about the attitude adopted by SC as the youngest man in the State.

On the 3d of Jan Georgia seized Fort Pulaski, & Alabama, the arsenal at Mt Vernon with 20,000 stand of arms.

# Stephen F. Hale to Beriah Magoffin

By the end of November 1860 secession conventions had been called in South Carolina, Georgia, Florida, Alabama, and Mississippi. Anticipating the secession of their states, the governors of Mississippi and Alabama sent commissioners to the other fourteen slaveholding states to encourage their secession and to promote the formation of a southern confederacy. (The state conventions of South Carolina, Georgia, and Louisiana would also appoint commissioners.) Stephen F. Hale, a lawyer and state legislator from Alabama who had been born and educated in Kentucky, returned to his native state in late December 1860. With the legislature not in session, he sent this letter to Beriah Magoffin, the state's governor. Magoffin summoned the legislature into session in January 1861, but it voted not to call a state convention.

---

FRANKFORT, *December 27, 1860*.

His Excellency B. MAGOFFIN,
*Governor of the Commonwealth of Kentucky:*

I have the honor of placing in your hands herewith a commission from the Governor of the State of Alabama, accrediting me as a commissioner from that State to the sovereign State of Kentucky, to consult in reference to the momentous issues now pending between the Northern and Southern States of this confederacy. Although each State, as a sovereign political community, must finally determine these grave issues for itself, yet the identity of interests, sympathy, and institutions, prevailing alike in all of the slave-holding States, in the opinion of Alabama renders it proper that there should be a frank and friendly consultation by each one with her sister Southern States touching their common grievances and the measures necessary to be adopted to protect the interest, honor, and safety of their citizens. I come, then, in a spirit of fraternity, as the commissioner on the part of the State of Alabama, to confer with the authorities of this Commonwealth in reference to the infraction of our constitutional rights, wrongs done and threatened to be done, as well as the mode and measure of redress proper to be adopted by the sovereign States aggrieved to preserve their sovereignty, vindicate their rights, and protect their citizens. In order to a clear understanding of the appropriate remedy, it may be proper to consider the rights and duties, both of the State and citizen, under the Federal compact, as well as the wrongs done and threatened. I therefore submit for the consideration of Your Excellency the following propositions, which I hope will command your assent and approval:

1. The people are the source of all political power, and the primary object of all good governments is to protect the citizen in the enjoyment of life, liberty, and property; and whenever any form of government becomes destructive of these ends, it is the inalienable right and the duty of the people to alter or abolish it.

2. The equality of all the States of this confederacy, as well as the equality of rights of all the citizens of the respective States under the Federal Constitution, is a fundamental principle in the scheme of the federal government. The union of these States under the Constitution was formed "to establish justice, insure domestic tranquillity, provide for the common defense, promote the general welfare, and secure the blessings of liberty to her citizens and their posterity;" and when it is perverted to the destruction of the equality of the States, or substantially fails to accomplish these ends, it fails to achieve the purposes of its creation, and ought to be dissolved.

3. The Federal Government results from a compact entered into between separate, sovereign, and independent States, called the Constitution of the United States, and amendments thereto, by which these sovereign States delegated certain specific powers to be used by that Government for the common defense and general welfare of all the States and their citizens; and when these powers are abused, or used for the destruction of the rights of any State or its citizens, each State has an equal right to judge for itself as well of the violations and infractions of that instrument as of the mode and measure of redress; and if the interest or safety of her citizens demands it, may resume

the powers she had delegated without let or hindrance from the Federal Government or any other power on earth.

4. Each State is bound in good faith to observe and keep on her part all the stipulations and covenants inserted for the benefit of other States in the constitutional compact (the only bond of union by which the several States are bound together), and when persistently violated by one party to the prejudice of her sister States, ceases to be obligatory on the States so aggrieved, and they may rightfully declare the compact broken, the union thereby formed dissolved, and stand upon their original rights as sovereign and independent political communities; and further, that each citizen owes his primary allegiance to the State in which he resides, and hence it is the imperative duty of the State to protect him in the enjoyment of all his constitutional rights, and see to it that they are not denied or withheld from him with impunity by any other State or government.

If the foregoing propositions correctly indicate the objects of this government, the rights and duties of the citizen, as well as the rights, powers, and duties of the State and Federal Governments under the Constitution, the next inquiry is, what rights have been denied, what wrongs have been done, or threatened to be done, of which the Southern States or the people of the Southern States can complain?

At the time of the adoption of the Federal Constitution African slavery existed in twelve of the thirteen States. Slaves are recognized both as property and as a basis of political power by the Federal compact, and special provisions are made by that instrument for their protection as property. Under the influences of climate and other causes, slavery has been banished from the Northern States; the slaves themselves have been sent to the Southern States and there sold, and their price gone into the pockets of their former owners at the North. And in the meantime African slavery has not only become one of the fixed domestic institutions of the Southern States, but forms an important element of their political power, and constitutes the most valuable species of their property, worth, according to recent estimates, not less than $4,000,000,000; forming, in fact, the basis upon which rests the prosperity and wealth of most of these States, and supplying the commerce of the world with its richest freights, and furnishing the manufactories of two continents with the raw material, and their operatives with bread. It is upon this gigantic interest, this peculiar institution of the South, that the Northern States and their people have been waging an unrelenting and fanatical war for the last quarter of a century; an institution with which is bound up not only the wealth and prosperity of the Southern people, but their very existence as a political community. This war has been waged in every way that human ingenuity, urged on by fanaticism, could suggest. They attack us through their literature, in their schools, from the hustings, in their legislative halls, through the public press, and even their courts of justice forget the purity of their judicial ermine to strike down the rights of the Southern slave-holder and override every barrier which the Constitution has erected for his protection; and the sacred desk is desecrated to this unholy crusade against our lives, our property, and the constitutional rights guaranteed to us by the compact of our fathers. During all this time the Southern States have freely conceded to the Northern States and the people of those States every right secured to them by the Constitution, and an equal interest in the common territories of the Government; protected the lives and property of their citizens of every kind, when brought within Southern jurisdiction; enforced through their courts, when necessary, every law of Congress passed for the protection of Northern property, and submitted ever since the foundation of the Government, with scarcely a murmur, to the protection of their shipping, manufacturing, and commercial interests, by odious bounties, discriminating tariffs, and unjust navigation laws, passed by the Federal Government to the prejudice and injury of their own citizens.

The law of Congress for the rendition of fugitive slaves, passed in pursuance of an express provision of the Constitution, remains almost a dead letter upon the statute book. A majority of the Northern States, through their legislative enactments, have openly nullified it, and impose heavy fines and penalties upon all persons who aid in enforcing this law, and some of those States declare the Southern slave-holder who goes within their jurisdiction to assert his legal rights under this Government; you are going to involve us in war and blood, from a mere suspicion that we shall justify that which we stand everywhere pledged not to do. Would you be justified in the eyes of the civilized world in taking so monstrous a position, and predicating it on a bare, groundless suspicion? We do not love slavery. Did you not know that before today? before this session commenced? Have you not a perfect confidence that the civilized world are against you on this subject of loving slavery or believing that it is the best institution in the world? Why, sir, everything remains precisely as it was a year ago. No great catastrophe has occurred. There is no recent occasion to accuse us of anything. But all at once, when we meet here, a kind of gloom pervades the whole community and the Senate Chamber. Gentlemen rise and tell us that they are on the eve of breaking up this Government, that seven or eight States are going to break off their connection with the Government, retire from the Union, and set up a hostile Government of their own, and they look imploringly over to us, and say to us "you can prevent it; we can do nothing to prevent; but it all lies with you." Well, sir, what can we do to prevent it? You have not even condescended to tell us what you want; but I think I see through the speeches that I have heard from gentlemen on the other side. If we would give up the verdict of the people, and take your platform, I do not know but you would be satisfied with it. I think the Senator from Texas rather intimated, and I think the Senator from Georgia more than intimated, that if we would take what is exactly the Charleston platform on which Mr. Breckinridge was placed, and give up that on which we won our victory, you would grumblingly and hesitatingly be satisfied.

Mr. IVERSON. I would prefer that the Senator would look over my remarks before quoting them so confidently. I made no such statement as that. I did not say that I would be satisfied with any such thing. I would not be satisfied with it.

Mr. WADE. I did not say that the Senator said so; but by construction I gathered that from his speech. I do not know that I was right in it.

Mr. IVERSON. The Senator is altogether wrong in his construction.

Mr. WADE. Well, sir, I have now found what the Senator

the Constitution guilty of a high crime, and affix imprison ment in the penitentiary as the penalty. The Federal officers who attempt to discharge their duties under the law, as well as the owner of the slave, are set upon by mobs, and are fortunate if they escape without serious injury to life or limb; and the State authorities, instead of aiding in the enforcement of this law, refuse the use of their jails, and by every means which unprincipled fanaticism can devise give countenance to the mob and aid the fugitive to escape. Thus there are annually large amounts of property actually stolen away from the Southern States, harbored and protected in Northern States and by their citizens; and when a requisition is made for the thief by the Governor of a Southern State upon the Executive of a Northern State, in pursuance of the express conditions of the Federal Constitution, he is insultingly told that the felon has committed no crime, and thus the criminal escapes, the property of the citizen is lost, the sovereignty of the State is insulted, and there is no redress, for the Federal courts have no jurisdiction to award a mandamus to the Governor of a sovereign State to compel him to do an official executive act, and Congress, if disposed, under the Constitution has no power to afford a remedy. These are wrongs under which the Southern people have long suffered, and to which they have patiently submitted, in the hope that a returning sense of justice would prompt the people of the Northern States to discharge their constitutional obligations and save our common country. Recent events, however, have not justified their hopes. The more daring and restless fanatics have banded themselves together, have put in practice the terrible lessons taught by the timid by making an armed incursion upon the sovereign State of Virginia, slaughtering her citizens, for the purpose of exciting a servile insurrection among her slave population, and arming them for the destruction of their own masters. During the past summer the abolition incendiary has lit up the prairies of Texas, fired the dwellings of the inhabitants, burned down whole towns, and laid poison for her citizens, thus literally executing the terrible denunciations of fanaticism against the slaveholder, "Alarm to their sleep, fire to their dwellings, and poison to their food."

The same fell spirit, like an unchained demon, has for years swept over the plains of Kansas, leaving death, desolation, and ruin in its track. Nor is this the mere ebullition of a few half-crazy fanatics, as is abundantly apparent from the sympathy manifested all over the North, where, in many places, the tragic death of John Brown, the leader of the raid upon Virginia, who died upon the gallows a condemned felon, is celebrated with public honors, and his name canonized as a martyr to liberty; and many, even of the more conservative papers of the Black Republican school, were accustomed to speak of his murderous attack upon the lives of the unsuspecting citizens of Virginia in a half-sneering and half-apologetic tone. And what has the Federal Government done in the meantime to protect slave property upon the common territories of the Union? Whilst a whole squadron of the American Navy is maintained on the coast of Africa at an enormous expense to enforce the execution of the laws against the slave-trade (and properly, too), and the whole Navy is kept afloat to protect the lives and property of American citizens upon the high seas, not a law has been passed by Congress or an arm raised by the Federal Government to protect the slave property of citizens from Southern States upon the soil of Kansas, the common territory and common property of the citizens of all the States, purchased alike by their common treasure, and held by the Federal Government, as declared by the Supreme Court of the United States, as the trustee for all their citizens; but, upon the contrary, a territorial government, created by Congress and supported out of the common treasury, under the influence and control of emigrant-aid societies and abolition emissaries, is permitted to pass laws excluding and destroying all that species of property within her limits, thus ignoring on the part of the Federal Government one of the fundamental principles of all good governments—the duty to protect the property of the citizen—and wholly refusing to maintain the equal rights of the States and the citizens of the States upon their common territories.

As the last and crowning act of insult and outrage upon the people of the South, the citizens of the Northern States, by overwhelming majorities, on the 6th day of November last, elected Abraham Lincoln and Hannibal Hamlin President and Vice-President of the United States. Whilst it may be admitted that the mere election of any man to the Presidency is not *per se* a sufficient cause for a dissolution of the Union, yet when the issues upon and circumstances under which he was elected are properly appreciated and understood, the question arises whether a due regard to the interest, honor, and safety of their citizens, in view of this and all the other antecedent wrongs and outrages, do not render it the imperative duty of the Southern States to resume the powers they have delegated to the Federal Government and interpose their sovereignty for the protection of their citizens.

What, then, are the circumstances under which and the issues upon which he was elected? His own declarations and the current history of the times but too plainly indicate he was elected by a Northern sectional vote, against the most solemn warnings and protestations of the whole South. He stands forth as the representative of the fanaticism of the North, which, for the last quarter of a century, has been making war upon the South, her property, her civilization, her institutions, and her interests; as the representative of that party which overrides all constitutional barriers, ignores the obligation of official oaths, and acknowledges allegiance to a higher law than the Constitution, striking down the sovereignty and equality of the States, and resting its claims to popular favor upon the one dogma—the equality of the races, white and black.

It was upon this acknowledgment of allegiance to a higher law that Mr. Seward rested his claims to the Presidency in a speech made by him in Boston before the election. He is the exponent, if not the author, of the doctrine of the irrepressible conflict between freedom and slavery, and proposes that the opponents of slavery shall arrest its further expansion, and by Congressional legislation exclude it from the common territories of the Federal Government, and place it where the public mind shall rest in the belief that it is in the course of ultimate extinction. He claims for free negroes the right of suffrage and an equal voice in the Government; in a word, all the rights of citizenship, although the Federal Constitution, as construed by the highest judicial tribunal in the world, does not recognize Africans imported into this country as slaves or their descendants—whether free or slaves—as citizens.

These were the issues presented in the last Presidential

canvass, and upon these the American people passed at the ballot box. Upon the principles then announced by Mr. Lincoln and his leading friends we are bound to expect his administration to be conducted. Hence it is that in high places among the Republican party the election of Mr. Lincoln is hailed not simply as a change of administration, but as the inauguration of new principles and a new theory of government, and even as the downfall of slavery. Therefore it is that the election of Mr. Lincoln cannot be regarded otherwise than a solemn declaration, on the part of a great majority of the Northern people, of hostility to the South, her property, and her institutions; nothing less than an open declaration of war, for the triumph of this new theory of government destroys the property of the South, lays waste her fields, and inaugurates all the horrors of a San Domingo servile insurrection, consigning her citizens to assassinations and her wives and daughters to pollution and violation to gratify the lust of half-civilized Africans. Especially is this true in the cotton-growing States, where, in many localities, the slave outnumbers the white population ten to one.

If the policy of the Republicans is carried out according to the programme indicated by the leaders of the party, and the South submits, degradation and ruin must overwhelm alike all classes of citizens in the Southern States. The slave-holder and non-slave-holder must ultimately share the same fate; all be degraded to a position of equality with free negroes, stand side by side with them at the polls, and fraternize in all the social relations of life, or else there will be an eternal war of races, desolating the land with blood, and utterly wasting and destroying all the resources of the country. Who can look upon such a picture without a shudder? What Southern man, be he slave-holder or non-slave-holder, can without indignation and horror contemplate the triumph of negro equality, and see his own sons and daughters in the not distant future associating with free negroes upon terms of political and social equality, and the white man stripped by the heaven-daring hand of fanaticism of that title to superiority over the black race which God himself has bestowed? In the Northern States, where free negroes are so few as to form no appreciable part of the community, in spite of all the legislation for their protection, they still remain a degraded caste, excluded by the ban of society from social association with all but the lowest and most degraded of the white race. But in the South, where in many places the African race largely predominates, and as a consequence the two races would be continually pressing together, amalgamation or the extermination of the one or the other would be inevitable. Can Southern men submit to such degradation and ruin? God forbid that they should.

But it is said there are many constitutional conservative men at the North who sympathize with and battle for us. That is true; but they are utterly powerless, as the late Presidential election unequivocally shows, to breast the tide of fanaticism that threatens to roll over and crush us. With them it is a question of principle, and we award to them all honor for their loyalty to the Constitution of our fathers; but their defeat is not their ruin. With us it is a question of self-preservation. Our lives, our property, the safety of our homes and our hearthstones, all that men hold dear on earth, is involved in the issue. If we triumph, vindicate our rights, and maintain our institutions, a bright and joyous future lies before us. We can clothe the world with our staple, give wings to her commerce, and supply with bread the starving operative in other lands, and at the same time preserve an institution that has done more to civilize and Christianize the heathen than all human agencies besides—an institution alike beneficial to both races, ameliorating the moral, physical, and intellectual condition of the one and giving wealth and happiness to the other. If we fail, the light of our civilization goes down in blood, our wives and our little ones will be driven from their homes by the light of our own dwellings, the dark pall of barbarism must soon gather over our sunny land, and the scenes of West India emancipation, with its attendant horrors and crimes (that monument of British fanaticism and folly), be re-enacted in their own land upon a more gigantic scale.

Then, is it not time we should be up and doing, like men who know their rights and dare maintain them? To whom shall the people of the Southern States look for the protection of their rights, interests, and honor? We answer, to their own sons and their respective States. To the States, as we have seen, under our system of government, is due the primary allegiance of the citizen, and the correlative obligation of protection devolves upon the respective States—a duty from which they cannot escape, and which they dare not neglect without a violation of all the bonds of fealty that hold together the citizen and the sovereign. The Northern States and their citizens have proved recreant to their obligations under the Federal Constitution. They have violated that compact and refused to perform their covenants in that behalf.

The Federal Government has failed to protect the rights and property of the citizens of the South, and is about to pass into the hands of a party pledged for the destruction not only of their rights and their property, but the equality of the States ordained by the Constitution, and the heaven-ordained superiority of the white over the black race. What remains, then, for the Southern States and the people of these States if they are loyal to the great principles of civil and religious liberty, sanctified by the sufferings of a seven-years' war and baptized with the blood of the Revolution? Can they permit the rights of their citizens to be denied and spurned, their property spirited away, their own sovereignty violated, and themselves degraded to the position of mere dependencies instead of sovereign States; or shall each for itself, judging of the infractions of the constitutional compact, as well as the mode and measure of redress, declare that the covenants of that sacred instrument in their behalf, and for the benefit of their citizens, have been willfully, deliberately, continuously, and persistently broken and violated by the other parties to the compact, and that they and their citizens are therefore absolved from all further obligations to keep and perform the covenants thereof; resume the powers delegated to the Federal Government, and, as sovereign States, form other relations for the protection of their citizens and the discharge of the great ends of government? The union of these States was one of fraternity as well as equality; but what fraternity now exists between the citizens of the two sections? Various religious associations, powerful in numbers and influence, have been broken asunder, and the sympathies that bound together the people of the several States at the time of the formation of the Constitution have ceased to exist, and feelings of bitterness and even hostility have sprung up in their place. How can this be reconciled and a spirit of fraternity established? Will the people of the North cease to make war upon the institution of slavery and award to it the protection guaranteed by the Constitution? The accumulated wrongs of many years, the late action of their members in Congress refusing every measure of justice to the South, as well as the experience of all the past, answers, No, never!

Will the South give up the institution of slavery and consent that her citizens be stripped of their property, her civilization destroyed, the whole land laid waste by fire and sword? It is impossible. She cannot; she will not. Then why attempt longer to hold together hostile States under the stipulations of a violated Constitution? It is impossible. Disunion is inevitable. Why, then, wait longer for the consummation of a result that must come? Why waste further time in expostulations and appeals to Northern States and their citizens, only to be met, as we have been for years past, by renewed insults and repeated injuries? Will the South be better prepared to meet the emergency when the North shall be strengthened by the admission of the new Territories of Kansas, Nebraska, Washington, Jefferson, Nevada, Idaho, Chippewa, and Arizona as non-slave-holding States, as we are warned from high sources will be done within the next four years, under the administration of Mr. Lincoln? Can the true men at the North ever make a more powerful or successful rally for the preservation of our rights and the Constitution than they did in the last Presidential contest? There is nothing to inspire a hope that they can.

Shall we wait until our enemies shall possess themselves of all the powers of the Government; until abolition judges are on the Supreme Court bench, abolition collectors at every port, and abolition postmasters in every town; secret mail agents traversing the whole land, and a subsidized press established in our midst to demoralize our people? Will we be stronger then or better prepared to meet the struggle, if a struggle must come? No, verily. When that time shall come, well may our adversaries laugh at our folly and deride our impotence. The deliberate judgment of Alabama, as indicated by the joint resolutions of her General Assembly, approved February 24, 1860, is that prudence, patriotism, and loyalty to all the great principles of civil liberty, incorporated in our Constitution and consecrated by the memories of the past, demand that all the Southern States should now resume their delegated powers, maintain the rights, interests, and honor of their citizens, and vindicate their own sovereignty. And she most earnestly but respectfully invites her sister sovereign State, Kentucky, who so gallantly vindicated the sovereignty of the States in 1798, to the consideration of these grave and vital questions, hoping she may concur with the State of Alabama in the conclusions to which she has been driven by the impending dangers that now surround the Southern States. But if, on mature deliberation, she dissents on any point from the conclusions to which the State of Alabama has arrived, on behalf of that State I most respectfully ask a declaration by this venerable Commonwealth of her conclusions and position on all the issues discussed in this communication; and Alabama most respectfully urges upon the people and authorities of Kentucky the startling truth that submission or acquiescence on the part of the Southern States at this perilous hour will enable Black Republicanism to redeem all its nefarious pledges and accomplish all its flagitious ends; and that hesitation or delay in their action will be misconceived and misconstrued by their adversaries and ascribed not to that elevated patriotism that would sacrifice all but their honor to save the Union of their fathers, but to division and dissension among themselves and their consequent weakness; that prompt, bold, and decided action is demanded alike by prudence, patriotism, and the safety of their citizens.

Permit me, in conclusion, on behalf of the State of Alabama, to express my high gratification at the cordial manner in which I have been received as her commissioner by the authorities of the State of Kentucky, as well as the profound personal gratification which, as a son of Kentucky, born and reared within her borders, I feel at the manner in which I, as the commissioner from the State of my adoption, have been received and treated by the authorities of the State of my birth. Please accept assurances of the high consideration and esteem of,

Your obedient servant, &c.,

S. F. HALE,
*Commissioner from the State of Alabama.*

# Herman Melville: Misgivings

Herman Melville published *Battle-Pieces and Aspects of the War*, his first book of poetry, in 1866. In his preface, Melville wrote that with "few exceptions, the Pieces in this volume originated in an impulse imparted by the fall of Richmond" in April 1865, and were "composed without reference to collective arrangement, but, being brought together in review, naturally fell into the order assumed." Melville placed "Misgivings" at the beginning of the volume, immediately following a poem about the execution of John Brown.

---

WHEN ocean-clouds over inland hills
    Sweep storming in late autumn brown,
And horror the sodden valley fills,
    And the spire falls crashing in the town,
I muse upon my country's ills—
The tempest bursting from the waste of Time
On the world's fairest hope linked with man's foulest crime.

Nature's dark side is heeded now—
    (Ah! optimist-cheer disheartened flown)—
A child may read the moody brow
    Of yon black mountain lone.
With shouts the torrents down the gorges go,
And storms are formed behind the storm we feel:
The hemlock shakes in the rafter, the oak in the driving keel.

# Mary Jones to Charles C. Jones Jr.

Mary Jones lived with her husband Charles, a Presbyterian clergyman, at Montevideo plantation in Liberty County, Georgia. Her eldest child, Charles Jr., was a lawyer in Savannah.

———————

Montevideo, *Thursday*, January 3rd, 1861

My dear Son,

Your affectionate favor was this day received, and from our heart of hearts we respond to your kind wishes—"A Happy New Year!"—although every moment seems fraught with the sad foreboding that it may be only one of trial and suffering. But "God is our refuge and strength, a very present help in trouble. Therefore will not we fear." Read Psalm 46. I trust the Lord of Hosts will be with us!

An indescribable sadness weighs down my soul as I think of our once glorious but now dissolving Union! Our children's children—what will constitute their national pride and glory? *We* have no alternative; and necessity demands that we now protect ourselves from entire destruction at the hands of those who have rent and torn and obliterated every national bond of union, of confidence and affection. When your brother and yourself were very little fellows, we took you into old Independence Hall; and at the foot of Washington's statue I pledged you both to support and defend the Union. *That Union* has passed away, and you are free from your mother's vow.

Your father thinks the occupation of Fort Pulaski will produce more effect than anything that has occurred. How can the South delay united and decided action? . . . The results may be awful unless we are united.

Did your father tell you old Montevideo gave forth her response on the night of the 26th in honor of Carolina and in sympathy with Savannah? Strange to say, as we walked out to view the illumination from the lawn, we discovered that there were thirteen windows on the front of the house, each of which had one brilliant light resembling a star; and without design one of them had been placed far in the ascendant—emblematic, as we hailed it, of the noble and gallant state which must ever be regarded as the polar star of our Southern confederacy.

And now, my dear son, we will look within the home circle. I trust you have regained your accustomed strength, and dear little Julia still improving. Your sister and Robert and the little ones have been with us for two weeks, and left us today. So did your uncle, who spent the day and night with us.

Enclosed I send your brother's letter, with the hope that you may yet help him to obtain the appointment. Would it be possible for you individually, or through Colonel Lawton or anyone else, to see *Governor Brown* whilst he is in Savannah, and if possible to secure the appointment for him? Poor boy, my heart sympathizes very deeply with his disappointments and perplexities. I know you will do all you can to aid him. I believe him worthy of and qualified for the trust, or I would not ask it even for my child.

Your dear father is very unwell from a severe cold. I want to write Ruth a few lines, and my paper is at an end. . . . With love from Father and myself to you both, and kisses for our little darling,

Your affectionate mother,
M. Jones.

# Henry Adams to Charles Francis Adams Jr.

Henry Adams wrote to his brother at a time when their father's attempts to frame a sectional compromise made him an increasingly controversial figure in their home state. In late December 1860 Charles Francis Adams sponsored a proposal in the Committee of Thirty-Three for the immediate admission of New Mexico, with the tacit understanding that it would enter the Union as a slave state. Adams hoped the measure would help draw the border states away from the secessionist Deep South, but his support for the proposal was criticized by many Massachusetts Republicans for abandoning the essential party principle of opposition to the expansion of slavery. Although the committee voted 13–11 in favor of admitting New Mexico, the measure was rejected by the House, 115–71, on March 1.

---

Washington. 8 Jan. 1861.

My dear Boy

Your story temporarily bluffs me, but I'll see if I can't find something to go it better. The account shall be settled immediately. If you see Ben Crowninshield I wish you would ask him whether he has received a letter I wrote him in answer to one of his, and why he has not answered it.

I think we do not feel so confident here as usual. Seward is evidently very low-spirited, though that is owing partly to the labor of preparing his speech. But I have noticed a marked change in the tone of our excellent father, consequent on information which he has received but has not confided in me. Until now he has steadily believed that the border-states would not go, and his measures were intended to influence them. But now I think he gives it up. His theory is that all depends on Virginia and that Virginia is lost. If this turns out to be the case, it increases our difficulties very badly. It makes war inevitable; war before the 4th of March.

God forbid that I should croak, or foresee what is not to

come. You and I, friend, are young enough to be sanguine
where others despair. For one, I intend to remain in this city. If
there is war I intend to take such part in it as is necessary or
useful. It would be a comfort if such times come, to know that
the Massachusetts regiments are ready, and if one can be
formed on the Cromwell type, I will enrol myself. Of course
we can not doubt the result; but I must confess that I had
hoped to avoid a real battle. If Virginia and Maryland secede,
they will strike at this city, and we shall have to give them such
an extermination that it were better we had not been borne. I
do not want to fight them. Is thy servant a South Carolinian
that he should do this thing. They are mad, mere maniacs, and
I want to lock them up till they become sane; not kill them. I
want to educate, humanize and refine them, not send fire and
sword among them. Let those that will, howl for war. I claim
to be sufficiently philanthropic to dread it, and sufficiently
Christian to wish to avoid it and to determine to avoid it, except in self-defence. Tell your warlike friends in Massachusetts
that we want no bloodthirsty men here. If the time comes
when men are wanted, it will be men who fight because there
is no other way; not because they are angry; men who will
come with their bibles as well as their rifles and who will pray
God to forgive them for every life they take.

I am confident that if an actual conflict could be kept off for
a few months, there could be none. The South are too weak to
sustain such a delay. There would be a reaction among themselves from mere starvation and ruin. But if Virginia goes out,
I do not see how it is to be avoided.

This is solemn, but I have enough self-respect to keep me
from joining with any body of men who act from mere passion
and the sense of wrong. Don't trust yourself to that set, for
they will desert you when you need their support. They don't
know what they're after. Support any honorable means of conciliation. Our position will be immensely strengthened by it.
We cannot be too much in the right. It is time for us, who
claim to lead this movement, to become cool and to do nothing without the fear of God before our eyes.

I passed this evening at the Bayards where I saw Florey for
the first time. I like the Bayards well. They're ladies, which is
more than I can say for most of the young women here. They

send all sorts of regards to you and John and Arthur and hope you will come on. Tomorrow evening I shall take tea there with some of their friends.

Loo is here and is amiable as possible. Since New Years day, I have been laid up by a violent cold which completely upset me, but now it's over. I don't hear much that is very novel. Seward dined here yesterday and was for him quite subdued.

My letters have, I think, done some good in sustaining papa at home and it was a relief to see the Advertiser of yesterday declare itself at last. I am convinced that his course is the only true and great one, and that it will ultimately meet the wishes of the whole North. You need not fear a compromise. The worst that is to be feared is, in my opinion a division in the party. No compromise would, I think, call back the South. We are beyond that stage where a compromise can prevent the struggle. Let them pass their measures if they can; the contest is on us and all the rotten twine that ever was spun, can't tie up this breach.

Yrs ever    H.B.A.

# Mississippi Declaration of the Causes of Secession

January 9, 1861

On January 9, 1861, Mississippi became the second state to break away from the Union when its convention voted, 85–15, to secede. It was quickly followed by Florida (January 10), Alabama (January 11), Georgia (January 19), Louisiana (January 26), and Texas (February 1). In Alabama the convention approved a secession ordinance that described the Republicans as "a sectional party avowedly hostile to the domestic institutions and to the peace and security of the people of the State," while the Georgia and Texas conventions adopted declarations of causes similar to the ones issued in South Carolina and Mississippi. The Georgia declaration denounced the "avowed purpose" of the Republican party "to subvert our society and subject us not only to the loss of our property but the destruction of ourselves, our wives, and our children, and the desolation of our homes, our altars, and our firesides." In Texas, the convention declared that the Republicans "demand the abolition of negro slavery throughout the confederacy, the recognition of political equality between the white and negro races, and avow their determination to press on their crusade against us, so long as a negro slave remains in these States."

---

## A DECLARATION OF THE IMMEDIATE CAUSES WHICH INDUCE AND JUSTIFY THE SECESSION OF THE STATE OF MISSISSIPPI FROM THE FEDERAL UNION.

In the momentous step which our State has taken of dissolving its connection with the government of which we so long formed a part, it is but just that we should declare the prominent reasons which have induced our course.

Our position is thoroughly identified with the institution of slavery—the greatest material interest of the world. Its labor supplies the product which constitutes by far the largest and most important portions of the commerce of the earth. These products are peculiar to the climate verging on the tropical regions, and by an imperious law of nature, none but the black race can bear exposure to the tropical sun. These products have become necessities of the world, and a blow at slavery is a blow at commerce and civilization. That blow has been long aimed at the institution, and was at the point of reaching its consummation. There was no choice left us but submission to the mandates of abolition, or a dissolution of the Union, whose principles had been subverted to work out our ruin.

That we do not overstate the dangers to our institution, a reference to a few unquestionable facts will sufficiently prove.

The hostility to this institution commenced before the adoption of the Constitution, and was manifested in the well-known Ordinance of 1787, in regard to the Northwestern Territory.

The feeling increased, until, in 1819–20, it deprived the South of more than half the vast territory acquired from France.

The same hostility dismembered Texas and seized upon all the territory acquired from Mexico.

It has grown until it denies the right of property in slaves, and refuses protection to that right on the high seas, in the Territories, and wherever the government of the United States had jurisdiction.

It refuses the admission of new slave States into the Union, and seeks to extinguish it by confining it within its present limits, denying the power of expansion.

It tramples the original equality of the South under foot.

It has nullified the Fugitive Slave Law in almost every free State in the Union, and has utterly broken the compact which our fathers pledged their faith to maintain.

It advocates negro equality, socially and politically, and promotes insurrection and incendiarism in our midst.

It has enlisted its press, its pulpit and its schools against us, until the whole popular mind of the North is excited and inflamed with prejudice.

It has made combinations and formed associations to carry out its schemes of emancipation in the States and wherever else slavery exists.

It seeks not to elevate or to support the slave, but to destroy his present condition without providing a better.

It has invaded a State, and invested with the honors of martyrdom the wretch whose purpose was to apply flames to our dwellings, and the weapons of destruction to our lives.

It has broken every compact into which it has entered for our security.

It has given indubitable evidence of its design to ruin our agriculture, to prostrate our industrial pursuits and to destroy our social system.

It knows no relenting or hesitation in its purposes; it stops not in its march of aggression, and leaves us no room to hope for cessation or for pause.

It has recently obtained control of the Government, by the prosecution of its unhallowed schemes, and destroyed the last expectation of living together in friendship and brotherhood.

Utter subjugation awaits us in the Union, if we should consent longer to remain in it. It is not a matter of choice, but of necessity. We must either submit to degradation, and to the loss of property worth four billions of money, or we must secede from the Union framed by our fathers, to secure this as well as every other species of property. For far less cause than this, our fathers separated from the Crown of England.

Our decision is made. We follow in their footsteps. We embrace the alternative of separation; and for the reasons here stated, we resolve to maintain our rights with the full consciousness of the justice of our course, and the undoubting belief of our ability to maintain it.

# Elizabeth Blair Lee to Samuel Phillips Lee

From the Maryland estate of her politically prominent family, Elizabeth Blair Lee wrote about unfolding events to her husband, an American naval officer on his way to join the East India squadron in the China Sea. Her father, Francis Preston Blair, was a former adviser to President Andrew Jackson who had joined the Republican party, her brother Montgomery would serve as postmaster general in the Lincoln administration, and her brother Frank was a Republican congressman from Missouri who would become a general in the Union army.

---

Silver Spring    December 25, 1860
Dear Phil   It might happen that currents winds & waves might prevent you from stopping at the Cape of Good Hope & on getting to Batavia you would want to know how even these 15 days have passed with us Well your pilot letter alone made me feel you had gone when for a time not even the perpetual talk of civil war around me here reconciled me— however I rally quickly & now I can feel thankful for all the mercies of God on this day of rejoicing— Tho I so miss you aching to share with me the exhuberance of Blair in Xmas gifts & joys

No political event has occurred except that South Carolina ordained herself on the 20th out of the Union whereupon the stocks rise. Patriotism is now above par. The Union Flag streams from nearly every house top— Father returned home from the City last night singing & happier about politics than Ive seen him since the election— Still he & all thinking men are sure that peaceable secession is a fallacy

Our party are in the labors of Cabinet Making & from all I hear it will hardly get through safely for the party— Bates has certainly got a place & L feels obliged to ask Seward & yet he dont want him to accept— but *he will*. so it hangs at present Our Maryland nominee has also got a promise in writing— but *all* are yet held under advisement— Things pecuniary are not any brighter in St Louis    Frank from necessity has gone to work at Law with Bay as a partner

*Jany 9th 1861*  I concluded to make this letter cover the first month of your absence & it has been a long weary one This year commences with a warlike aspect    Majr Anderson in command at Fort Moultrie denied reinforcement tho his importunate wife insulted the President when her entreaties failed to move him to send them— But Providence over rules even the most determined— An immense theft to the amount of several Millions of State Bonds lodged in the Interior Dept was discovered or confessed by a Mr. Bailey book keeper— Floyd was implicated in this fraud & he availed himself of Maj Andersons transfer of his forces to Fort Sumter to make a plea for resignation— These changes have produced a change of policy in the administration— Old Buck is now odius to the South because he has concluded not to act any longer in concert with Traitors and to execute the Laws & protect Govt property— Andersons movement was masterly & has made him now the Hero of the day. On yesterday there was nearly as many guns fired in his honor as that of Genl Jackson— whose spirit is now invoked daily for the protection of the Country. Mississippi is to secede to day & tomorrow King Jeff is to make his adieux to the Senate. He will take his wrath out of old Buck— But on this change of policy in the President    Stocks begin to rise again & there is a tone of firmness & hope in the community— that has given at least more fortitude to bear our troubles with—

*Jany 10th*  Mr Slidell and Mr. Davis were intense in the bitterness of their denunciations of the President around whom now the Republicans rally as it is a great onus off the Republican party that he devotes to the South & Democracy should begin the War— which I fear was commenced yesterday— A Steamer was sent to Maj Anderson by Scotts orders under Holt— now acting Secy of War with more men & provisions. She was fired at by the South Carolinians from Fort Moultrie & a light house battery when she put back— Anderson sent an officer to Govr Pickens— they say with a threat to destroy Charleston if that attack on the Steamer was repeated to day. Her owners are telegraphed today that she safely unloading at Fort Sumter— it looks like a back down in S.C. & it will be no misfortune to the Country to prove she is unequal to any of

her threats    Anderson says he could hold his position in defiance of the whole South— I see to day that Hartstene has resigned— he is the highest on the list who have done so & there are very few resignations— Comre Shubrick went to Charleston & has returned saying they are all stark mad— *save men of large estates* & it is evident they are to be fleeced The Jews have already quit— The monied men north will not take the U State Loan— whilst the Treasury Department is in the hands of a Secessionist— Our Party are in great distress at the idea of having Cameron in the Treasury it is said to day he declines but that tis thought a ruse— to quiet the protest now being made against this appointment— Even the Sun— the hotest Secession paper in Maryland gives up that Maryland will go out— there is no disunion or secession in the State— Our neighbors are all civil & even when there was talk of attacking Washn we were to be protected. But the Presidents change of front has quieted all *that talk* for it never amounted to anything else— The North rallies unitedly to the Union & for the execution of the Laws & a maintenance of the Constitution— in letter & spirit— Thus your people are on the strongest & safest side of the Contest— Missouri is to go thro the ferment of her democratic Legislature— but she is considered safe & so is Kentucky— North Carolina & Tennesse— but Virginia is shaky— but it will go back to the people there & that will give time— & confidently hoped a happy result
Thompson resigned when reinforcements were sent to Majr Anderson who is a kinsman of Mary Blair & a Kentuckian were at the Brevort with the Jesups this fall

Our home routine has been unaltered & so far this winter we have good health— Blair is rarely kept indoors all day— The winter is very wet so far & tho frequent snow— no ice yet to put up for summer— Mary & Betty in town    I do less reading than ever before. They have got used to doing without me & want to keep the habit— but so far my home here is comfortable— Our boy is sturdy & well & everybodys pet & particularly his Grand Pa's— who is of late struck with his abiding loyal love to my Papa— it was only yesterday he ordered Becky to Pack his clothing— "I am going to Sea to talk to Papa— he would not take either Becky or I with "Papa will take care of me" Yours ever Lizzie

# Catherine Edmondston:
## Diary, January 9–13, 1861

On December 28, 1860, three commissioners from South Carolina met with President Buchanan and demanded the evacuation of Fort Sumter. At the insistence of Jeremiah Black, who had replaced Lewis Cass as secretary of state earlier in the month, the President rejected their demands in a strongly worded reply drafted by Black and Edwin Stanton, the new attorney general. Buchanan then approved a plan to supply and reinforce the fort, and on January 5, 1861, the chartered steamer *Star of the West* sailed from New York with two hundred soldiers on board. The ship reached Charleston on January 9 but safely retreated after being fired upon. Lacking instructions, Major Anderson did not order the guns at Fort Sumter to open fire. Catherine Edmondston and her husband were visiting his brother Lawrence at his house overlooking Charleston harbor when the *Star of the West* arrived.

---

JANUARY 9, 1861

On the morning of the 9th as we were dressing we suddenly heard the report of a heavy gun! followed by another! and another! A few moments sufficed to collect us all out in the front of the house where we had a fine view of Sumter, Moultrie & the Channel, and there sad to relate, steaming up the channel was a vessel with the US Flag flying at her peak! The expected re-inforcements for Sumter doubtless! Boom! Another cannon from the shore Batteries on Morris Island. "Is she struck?" No! On she comes! Another! and another, whilst Sumter opens her Port Holes and slowly runs out her cannon, prepared for instant action. Now a heavy gun from Fort Moultrie! Will Sumter respond? No! Not yet! Another from Moultrie! How with Sumter now? Still silent! The vessel turns slowly. Is she struck? No one can tell, but slowly, reluctantly as it were, almost with a baffled look, the Steamer retreats down the channel.

Thank God! Every one ejaculates! But what think we of the treacherous Government who whilst pretending to treat, assuring its own Cabinet & the nation that no re-inforcements should be sent, deliberately breaks faith and attempts it? I blush for my country! Would that the North was not our exponent! Eleven guns in all were fired. Good God! Is this true? Is this the beginning of the Civil War of which we have heard so much, was the thought which sprung into my mind. And as I afterwards sat at Lawrence's breakfast table and looked from the luxurious & peaceful family scene in doors, across the still smooth water smiling in the beauty of the crisp morning air, to Sumter, standing stern, silent, sullen, defiant as it were, bristling with cannon, whilst a light smoke stealing up from her Battlements told that they were heating shot, ready for instant action, & thought how in an instant it could all be changed, that horror & ruin might take the place of peace and comfort, never did I feel so vividly the full force & beauty of the Collect for Peace in our Prayer book. Never did I utter it so fervently, never desire it so earnestly!

The same day we went back to the city & found it full of flying rumours. Men in Uniform filling the streets, singly and in squads, all wending their way to East Bay where steamers were firing up & leaving with re-inforcements, munitions of War & supplies for Pinckney, Moultrie & the Batteries below on Morris Island. Left on the same day for Raleigh.

JANUARY 10, 1861

Arrived on the morning of the 10th carrying with us the news of the repulse of the "Star of the West"—for so was the steamer called—& Mr Buchanan's treachery. Every where it was received with surprised dismay, the feeling almost universally being to leave SC to herself, give her her Fort if she required it, but deny her all the benefits of the Government, refuse her all Postal intercourse etc. Predictions were freely made that in that event, in a year at most she would if Mr Lincoln's government should be an impartial one, petition to return into the Union. She met but few sympathizers, but Mr Miller is the only man whom I have yet seen who upholds the action of the Government. Margaret's exclamation when she heard it was "Why Kate, you have been seeing History!"

Found Annie D at home, her Mother having become uneasy at last begged her father to go for her. I am glad of it, as a grave cause of uneasiness is thus removed from their minds. Frank Coffin and John Devereux struck up a friendship to which David's & Jonathan's was but a joke. The other children all well and already inflamed against the Yankees & "old Lincoln." The North is sowing the wind; see that ere the next generation she does not reap the Whirlwind!

JANUARY 13, 1861

Got home safely to Looking Glass on Sunday the 13th. My cough much better, from a practice reccommended me by Dr Coffin of "swabbing out" my throat with a spunge and a weak solution of Caustic. Saw Mrs Mills at Mt Pleasant—told me she had been cured of her Asthma by Iodide of Potassa. Made a note for Dolly's benefit.

Found Father much excited against SC—cannot say enough of the folly of her conduct. It almost frightened me to hear him. I hope he will not say so much to Mr Edmondston. I do not think he does her full justice. For instance he thinks it beneath their pretentions to chivalry, ungenerous & unhandsome in fact, that they fired one shot at the Star of the West after she turned to retreat! I do not agree with him, & tho' this "Gentlemen of the English Guards fire . . . we never fire first!" may be very grand—yet it is too high strung for me! I never before heard of an action in which the firing ceased until the Flag was hauled down.

We went on as usual all the month of Jan. Killed Hogs, attended to house hold matters, Planted garden seed, Rode, walked, went to Hascosea, wrote letters, Read my new books —in short enjoyed ourselves in our usual way, the only draw back being the difference of feeling on Political matters between ourselves & father. As for Mama & Susan they are really bitter in their expressions, & Susan talked more nonsense about her "devotion to the Flag" than I ever thought I should hear a sensible woman like her utter! Altogether it was rather uncomfortable at times being with them.

Brother had a hearty laugh on me. He declared that he thought that the war would begin then & there between Mama & myself, because when I said that SC & Va had both a right to their Forts Sumter & Monro, & that when they re-claimed them the Government ought to restore them, she be-came personal, called me "Catherine Edmondston!" told me that I had been brought up by honest people, & that she was surprised that I should be guilty of uttering such dishon-ourable & dishonest sentiments, & more to the same purpose. I made some retort & was going on when fortunately I re-membered my Mother's last injunction & checked myself. But I was very indignant! What a pity that politics will intrude into private life!

# Jefferson Davis: Farewell Address in the U.S. Senate

January 21, 1861

On the morning of January 21, 1861, five southern senators—David Yulee and Stephen Mallory of Florida, Clement Clay and Benjamin Fitzpatrick of Alabama, and Jefferson Davis of Mississippi—announced on the Senate floor that they were "withdrawing" as a result of the secession of their respective states. (James Hammond and James Chesnut of South Carolina did not return to Washington when Congress reconvened in December 1860, and Robert Toombs of Georgia and Albert Brown of Mississippi had left the Senate earlier in January; Alfred Iverson of Georgia would withdraw on January 28, followed by Judah Benjamin and John Slidell of Louisiana on February 4.) During its special session in March 1861, the Republican-controlled Senate of the new 37th Congress approved a resolution declaring the seats of Mallory, Clay, Davis, Brown, Toombs, and Benjamin to be vacant. (The resolution did not address the seats formerly held by Yulee, Fitzpatrick, Hammond, Iverson, and Slidell, all of whose terms had expired with the end of the 36th Congress.) When the Senate reconvened in July 1861, it expelled nine senators from Arkansas, North Carolina, Tennessee, Texas, and Virginia who had joined the Confederacy, as well as James Chesnut of South Carolina (who had never formally withdrawn), leaving the unionist Andrew Johnson of Tennessee as the sole remaining senator from the eleven Confederate states.

---

I RISE, Mr. President, for the purpose of announcing to the Senate that I have satisfactory evidence that the State of Mississippi, by a solemn ordinance of her people in convention assembled, has declared her separation from the United States. Under these circumstances, of course my functions are terminated here. It has seemed to me proper, however, that I should appear in the Senate to announce that fact to my associates, and I will say but very little more. The occasion does not invite me to go into argument; and my physical condition would not permit me to do so if it were otherwise; and yet it seems to become me to say something on the part of the State I here represent, on an occasion so solemn as this.

It is known to Senators who have served with me here, that I have for many years advocated, as an essential attribute of State sovereignty, the right of a State to secede from the Union. Therefore, if I had not believed there was justifiable cause; if I had thought that Mississippi was acting without sufficient provocation, or without an existing necessity, I should still, under my theory of the Government, because of my allegiance to the State of which I am a citizen, have been bound by her action. I, however, may be permitted to say that I do think she has justifiable cause, and I approve of her act. I conferred with her people before that act was taken, counseled them then that if the state of things which they apprehended should exist when the convention met, they should take the action which they have now adopted.

I hope none who hear me will confound this expression of mine with the advocacy of the right of a State to remain in the Union, and to disregard its constitutional obligations by the nullification of the law. Such is not my theory. Nullification and secession, so often confounded, are indeed antagonistic principles. Nullification is a remedy which it is sought to apply within the Union, and against the agent of the States. It is only to be justified when the agent has violated his constitutional obligation, and a State, assuming to judge for itself, denies the right of the agent thus to act, and appeals to the other States of the Union for a decision; but when the States themselves, and when the people of the States, have so acted as to convince us that they will not regard our constitutional rights, then, and then for the first time, arises the doctrine of secession in its practical application.

A great man who now reposes with his fathers, and who has been often arraigned for a want of fealty to the Union, advocated the doctrine of nullification, because it preserved the Union. It was because of his deep-seated attachment to the Union, his determination to find some remedy for existing ills short of a severance of the ties which bound South Carolina to the other States, that Mr. Calhoun advocated the doctrine of nullification, which he proclaimed to be peaceful, to be within the limits of State power, not to disturb the Union, but only to be a means of bringing the agent before the tribunal of the States for their judgment.

Secession belongs to a different class of remedies. It is to be justified upon the basis that the States are sovereign. There was a time when none denied it. I hope the time may come again, when a better comprehension of the theory of our Government, and the inalienable rights of the people of the States, will prevent any one from denying that each State is a sovereign, and thus may reclaim the grants which it has made to any agent whomsoever.

I therefore say I concur in the action of the people of Mississippi, believing it to be necessary and proper, and should have been bound by their action if my belief had been otherwise; and this brings me to the important point which I wish on this last occasion to present to the Senate. It is by this confounding of nullification and secession that the name of a great man, whose ashes now mingle with his mother earth, has been invoked to justify coercion against a seceded State. The phrase "to execute the laws," was an expression which General Jackson applied to the case of a State refusing to obey the laws while yet a member of the Union. That is not the case which is now presented. The laws are to be executed over the United States, and upon the people of the United States. They have no relation to any foreign country. It is a perversion of terms, at least it is a great misapprehension of the case, which cites that expression for application to a State which has withdrawn from the Union. You may make war on a foreign State. If it be the purpose of gentlemen, they may make war against a State which has withdrawn from the Union; but there are no laws of the United States to be executed within the limits of a seceded State. A State finding herself in the condition in which Mississippi has judged she is, in which her safety requires that she should provide for the maintenance of her rights out of the Union, surrenders all the benefits, (and they are known to be many,) deprives herself of the advantages, (they are known to be great,) severs all the ties of affection, (and they are close and enduring,) which have bound her to the Union; and thus divesting herself of every benefit, taking upon herself every burden, she claims to be exempt from any power to execute the laws of the United States within her limits.

I well remember an occasion when Massachusetts was arraigned before the bar of the Senate, and when then the doctrine of coercion was rife and to be applied against her because of the rescue of a fugitive slave in Boston. My opinion then was the same that it is now. Not in a spirit of egotism, but to show that I am not influenced in my opinion because the case is my own, I refer to that time and that occasion as containing the opinion which I then entertained, and on which my present conduct is based. I then said, if Massachusetts, following her through a stated line of conduct, chooses to take the last step which separates her from the Union, it is her right to go, and I will neither vote one dollar nor one man to coerce her back; but will say to her, God speed, in memory of the kind associations which once existed between her and the other States.

It has been a conviction of pressing necessity, it has been a belief that we are to be deprived in the Union of the rights which our fathers bequeathed to us, which has brought Mississippi into her present decision. She has heard proclaimed the theory that all men are created free and equal, and this made the basis of an attack upon her social institutions; and the sacred Declaration of Independence has been invoked to maintain the position of the equality of the races. That Declaration of Independence is to be construed by the circumstances and purposes for which it was made. The communities were declaring their independence; the people of those communities were asserting that no man was born—to use the language of Mr. Jefferson—booted and spurred to ride over the rest of mankind; that men were created equal—meaning the men of the political community; that there was no divine right to rule; that no man inherited the right to govern; that there were no classes by which power and place descended to families, but that all stations were equally within the grasp of each member of the body-politic. These were the great principles they announced; these were the purposes for which they made their declaration; these were the ends to which their enunciation was directed. They have no reference to the slave; else, how happened it that among the items of arraignment made against

George III was that he endeavored to do just what the North has been endeavoring of late to do—to stir up insurrection among our slaves? Had the Declaration announced that the negroes were free and equal, how was the Prince to be arraigned for stirring up insurrection among them? And how was this to be enumerated among the high crimes which caused the colonies to sever their connection with the mother country? When our Constitution was formed, the same idea was rendered more palpable, for there we find provision made for that very class of persons as property; they were not put upon the footing of equality with white men—not even upon that of paupers and convicts; but, so far as representation was concerned, were discriminated against as a lower caste, only to be represented in the numerical proportion of three fifths.

Then, Senators, we recur to the compact which binds us together; we recur to the principles upon which our Government was founded; and when you deny them, and when you deny to us the right to withdraw from a Government which thus perverted threatens to be destructive of our rights, we but tread in the path of our fathers when we proclaim our independence, and take the hazard. This is done not in hostility to others, not to injure any section of the country, not even for our own pecuniary benefit; but from the high and solemn motive of defending and protecting the rights we inherited, and which it is our sacred duty to transmit unshorn to our children.

I find in myself, perhaps, a type of the general feeling of my constituents towards yours. I am sure I feel no hostility to you, Senators from the North. I am sure there is not one of you, whatever sharp discussion there may have been between us, to whom I cannot now say, in the presence of my God, I wish you well; and such, I am sure, is the feeling of the people whom I represent towards those whom you represent. I therefore feel that I but express their desire when I say I hope, and they hope, for peaceful relations with you, though we must part. They may be mutually beneficial to us in the future, as they have been in the past, if you so will it. The reverse may bring disaster on every portion of the country; and if you will have it thus, we will invoke the God of our fathers, who delivered them from the power of the lion, to protect us from the ravages of the bear; and thus, putting our trust in God and in our own firm hearts and strong arms, we will vindicate the right as best we may.

In the course of my service here, associated at different times with a great variety of Senators, I see now around me some with whom I have served long; there have been points of collision; but whatever of offense there has been to me, I leave here; I carry with me no hostile remembrance. Whatever offense I have given which has not been redressed, or for which satisfaction has not been demanded, I have, Senators, in this hour of our parting, to offer you my apology for any pain which, in heat of discussion, I have inflicted. I go hence unencumbered of the remembrance of any injury received, and having discharged the duty of making the only reparation in my power for any injury offered.

Mr. President, and Senators, having made the announcement which the occasion seemed to me to require, it only remains to me to bid you a final adieu.

## Robert E. Lee to
## George Washington Custis Lee

An 1829 graduate of West Point who had distinguished himself in the U.S.-Mexican War, Lieutenant Colonel Robert E. Lee wrote to his eldest son while serving as the acting commander of the Department of Texas. Lee would return to Washington on March 1 and resign his commission in the U.S. Army on April 20, three days after Virginia voted to secede.

———————

FORT MASON, TEXAS, January 23, 1861.

I received Everett's "Life of Washington" which you sent me, and enjoyed its perusal. How his spirit would be grieved could he see the wreck of his mighty labors! I will not, however, permit myself to believe, until all ground of hope is gone, that the fruit of his noble deeds will be destroyed, and that his precious advice and virtuous example will so soon be forgotten by his countrymen. As far as I can judge by the papers, we are between a state of anarchy and civil war. May God avert both of these evils from us! I fear that mankind will not for years be sufficiently Christianized to bear the absence of restraint and force. I see that four States have declared themselves out of the Union; four more will apparently follow their example. Then, if the Border States are brought into the gulf of revolution, one-half of the country will be arrayed against the other. I must try and be patient and await the end, for I can do nothing to hasten or retard it.

The South, in my opinion, has been aggrieved by the acts of the North, as you say. I feel the aggression, and am willing to take every proper step for redress. It is the principle I contend for, not individual or private benefit. As an American citizen, I take great pride in my country, her prosperity and institutions, and would defend any State if her rights were invaded.

But I can anticipate no greater calamity for the country than a dissolution of the Union. It would be an accumulation of all the evils we complain of, and I am willing to sacrifice everything but honor for its preservation. I hope, therefore, that all constitutional means will be exhausted before there is a resort to force. Secession is nothing but revolution. The framers of our Constitution never exhausted so much labor, wisdom, and forbearance in its formation, and surrounded it with so many guards and securities, if it was intended to be broken by every member of the Confederacy at will. It was intended for "perpetual union," so expressed in the preamble, and for the establishment of a government, not a compact, which can only be dissolved by revolution, or the consent of all the people in convention assembled. It is idle to talk of secession. Anarchy would have been established, and not a government, by Washington, Hamilton, Jefferson, Madison, and the other patriots of the Revolution. . . . . Still, a Union that can only be maintained by swords and bayonets, and in which strife and civil war are to take the place of brotherly love and kindness, has no charm for me. I shall mourn for my country and for the welfare and progress of mankind. If the Union is dissolved, and the Government disrupted, I shall return to my native State and share the miseries of my people, and save in defense will draw my sword on none.

# Jefferson Davis: Inaugural Address

### February 18, 1861

Delegates from South Carolina, Georgia, Florida, Alabama, Mississippi, and Louisiana met on February 4, 1861, in Montgomery, where they were later joined by representatives from Texas. The delegates adopted a provisional constitution for the Confederate States of America, and on February 9 voted by state delegations for a provisional president and vice-president. Although he had not sought the position, Jefferson Davis received the votes of all six states. A West Point graduate, Davis had commanded a Mississippi volunteer regiment in Mexico and later served as secretary of war in the Pierce administration. He was favored by the delegates because of his military background, and because of reports that his election would be favorably received in Virginia. Davis arrived in Montgomery on February 16 and delivered his inaugural address two days later.

———————

*Gentlemen of the Congress of the Confederate States of America, Friends, and Fellow-citizens:* Called to the difficult and responsible station of Chief Magistrate of the Provisional Government which you have instituted, I approach the discharge of the duties assigned to me with humble distrust of my abilities, but with a sustaining confidence in the wisdom of those who are to guide and aid me in the administration of public affairs, and an abiding faith in the virtue and patriotism of the people. Looking forward to the speedy establishment of a permanent government to take the place of this, which by its greater moral and physical power will be better able to combat with many difficulties that arise from the conflicting interests of separate nations, I enter upon the duties of the office to which I have been chosen with the hope that the beginning of our career, as a Confederacy, may not be obstructed by hostile opposition to our enjoyment of the separate existence and independence we have asserted, and which, with the blessing of Providence, we intend to maintain.

Our present political position has been achieved in a manner unprecedented in the history of nations. It illustrates the American idea that governments rest on the consent of the governed, and that it is the right of the people to alter or abolish them at will whenever they become destructive of the ends for which they were established. The declared purpose of the compact of the Union from which we have withdrawn was to "establish justice, insure domestic tranquillity, provide for the common defense, promote the general welfare, and secure the blessings of liberty to ourselves and our posterity;" and when, in the judgment of the sovereign States composing this Confederacy, it has been perverted from the purposes for which it was ordained, and ceased to answer the ends for which it was established, a peaceful appeal to the ballot box declared that, so far as they are concerned, the Government created by that compact should cease to exist. In this they merely asserted the right which the Declaration of Independence of July 4, 1776, defined to be "inalienable." Of the time and occasion of its exercise they as sovereigns were the final judges, each for itself. The impartial and enlightened verdict of mankind will vindicate the rectitude of our conduct; and He who knows the hearts of men will judge of the sincerity with which we have labored to preserve the Government of our fathers in its spirit.

The right solemnly proclaimed at the birth of the United States, and which has been solemnly affirmed and reaffirmed in the Bills of Rights of the States subsequently admitted into the Union of 1789, undeniably recognizes in the people the power to resume the authority delegated for the purposes of government. Thus the sovereign States here represented have proceeded to form this Confederacy; and it is by abuse of language that their act has been denominated a revolution. They formed a new alliance, but within each State its government has remained; so that the rights of person and property have not been disturbed. The agent through which they communicated with foreign nations is changed, but this does not necessarily interrupt their international relations. Sustained by the consciousness that the transition from the former Union to the present Confederacy has not proceeded from a disregard on our part of just obligations, or any failure to perform every constitutional duty, moved by no interest or passion to invade the rights of others, anxious to cultivate peace and commerce with all nations, if we may not hope to avoid war, we may at least expect that posterity will acquit us of having needlessly engaged in it. Doubly justified by the absence of wrong on our part, and by wanton aggression on the part of others, there can be no cause to doubt that the courage and patriotism of the people of the Confederate States will be found equal to any measure of defense which their honor and security may require.

An agricultural people, whose chief interest is the export of commodities required in every manufacturing country, our true policy is peace, and the freest trade which our necessities will permit. It is alike our interest and that of all those to whom we would sell, and from whom we would buy, that there should be the fewest practicable restrictions upon the interchange of these commodities. There can, however, be but little rivalry between ours and any manufacturing or navigating community, such as the Northeastern States of the American Union. It must follow, therefore, that mutual interest will invite to good will and kind offices on both parts. If, however, passion or lust of dominion should cloud the judgment or inflame the ambition of those States, we must prepare to meet the emergency and maintain, by the final arbitrament of the sword, the position which we have assumed among the nations of the earth.

We have entered upon the career of independence, and it must be inflexibly pursued. Through many years of controversy with our late associates of the Northern States, we have vainly endeavored to secure tranquillity and obtain respect for the rights to which we were entitled. As a necessity, not a choice, we have resorted to the remedy of separation, and henceforth our energies must be directed to the conduct of our own affairs, and the perpetuity of the Confederacy which we have formed. If a just perception of mutual interest shall permit us peaceably to pursue our separate political career, my most earnest desire will have been fulfilled. But if this be denied to us, and the integrity of our territory and jurisdiction be assailed, it will but remain for us with firm resolve to appeal to arms and invoke the blessing of Providence on a just cause.

As a consequence of our new condition and relations, and with a view to meet anticipated wants, it will be necessary to provide for the speedy and efficient organization of branches of the Executive department having special charge of foreign intercourse, finance, military affairs, and the postal service. For purposes of defense, the Confederate States may, under ordinary circumstances, rely mainly upon the militia; but it is deemed advisable, in the present condition of affairs, that there should be a well-instructed and disciplined army, more numerous than would usually be required on a peace establishment. I also suggest that, for the protection of our harbors and commerce on the high seas, a navy adapted to those objects will be required. But this, as well as other subjects appropriate to our necessities, have doubtless engaged the attention of Congress.

With a Constitution differing only from that of our fathers in so far as it is explanatory of their well-known intent, freed from sectional conflicts, which have interfered with the pursuit of the general welfare, it is not unreasonable to expect that States from which we have recently parted may seek to unite their fortunes to ours under the Government which we have instituted. For this your Constitution makes adequate provision; but beyond this, if I mistake not the judgment and will of the people, a reunion with the States from which we have separated is neither practicable nor desirable. To increase the power, develop the resources, and promote the happiness of the Confederacy, it is requisite that there should be so much of homogeneity that the welfare of every portion shall be the aim of the whole. When this does not exist, antagonisms are engendered which must and should result in separation.

Actuated solely by the desire to preserve our own rights, and promote our own welfare, the separation by the Confederate States has been marked by no aggression upon others, and followed by no domestic convulsion. Our industrial pursuits have received no check, the cultivation of our fields has progressed as heretofore, and, even should we be involved in war, there would be no considerable diminution in the production of the staples which have constituted our exports, and in which the commercial world has an interest scarcely less than our own. This common interest of the producer and consumer can only be interrupted by exterior force which would obstruct the transmission of our staples to foreign markets—a course of conduct which would be as unjust, as it would be detrimental, to manufacturing and commercial interests abroad.

Should reason guide the action of the Government from which we have separated, a policy so detrimental to the civilized world, the Northern States included, could not be dictated by even the strongest desire to inflict injury upon us; but, if the contrary should prove true, a terrible responsibility will rest upon it, and the suffering of millions will bear testimony to the folly and wickedness of our aggressors. In the meantime there will remain to us, besides the ordinary means before suggested, the well-known resources for retaliation upon the commerce of an enemy.

Experience in public stations, of subordinate grade to this which your kindness has conferred, has taught me that toil and care and disappointment are the price of official elevation. You will see many errors to forgive, many deficiencies to tolerate; but you shall not find in me either want of zeal or fidelity to the cause that is to me the highest in hope, and of most enduring affection. Your generosity has bestowed upon me an undeserved distinction, one which I neither sought nor desired. Upon the continuance of that sentiment, and upon your wisdom and patriotism, I rely to direct and support me in the performance of the duties required at my hands.

We have changed the constituent parts, but not the system of government. The Constitution framed by our fathers is that of these Confederate States. In their exposition of it, and in the judicial construction it has received, we have a light which reveals its true meaning.

Thus instructed as to the true meaning and just interpretation of that instrument, and ever remembering that all offices are but trusts held for the people, and that powers delegated are to be strictly construed, I will hope by due diligence in the performance of my duties, though I may disappoint your expectations, yet to retain, when retiring, something of the good will and confidence which welcome my entrance into office.

It is joyous in the midst of perilous times to look around upon a people united in heart, where one purpose of high resolve animates and actuates the whole; where the sacrifices to be made are not weighed in the balance against honor and right and liberty and equality. Obstacles may retard, but they cannot long prevent, the progress of a movement sanctified by its justice and sustained by a virtuous people. Reverently let us invoke the God of our fathers to guide and protect us in our efforts to perpetuate the principles which by his blessing they were able to vindicate, establish, and transmit to their posterity. With the continuance of his favor ever gratefully acknowledged, we may hopefully look forward to success, to peace, and to prosperity.

# Frederick Douglass: The New President

### March 1861

On the eve of Lincoln's inauguration, Douglass used his *Monthly* to praise the president-elect for refusing to endorse compromise proposals that would have permitted the extension of slavery.

---

OF ONE satisfaction, one ray of hope amid the darkness of the passing hour, and the reign of doubt and distraction, we may now safely begin to assure ourselves. Before we can again speak to our respected readers through this channel, the long desired 4th of March will have come, Lincoln will be inaugurated at Washington, and his policy declared. Whatever that policy may be towards the seceded and confederated States; whatever it may be towards Slavery, the ruling cause of our nation's troubles, it will at least be a great relief to know it, to rejoice in and defend it, if right, and to make war upon it if wrong. To know what it is, is now the main thing. If he is going to abandon the principles upon which he was elected, compliment the South for being wrong, and censure himself and friends for being right, court treason and curse loyalty, desert his friends and cleave to his enemies, turn his back on the cause of Freedom and give new guarantees to the system of Slavery—whatever policy, whether of peace or war, or neither, it will be a vast gain at least to know what it is. Much of the present trouble is owing to the doubt and suspense caused by the shuffling, do-nothing policy of Mr. Buchanan.— No man has been able to tell an hour before hand what to expect from that source. However well disposed he may have been, the slaveholding thieves and traitors about him have had him under their thumb from the beginning until now. Every man who wishes well to the country will rejoice at his outgoing, and feel that though he leaves the body politic weakened, and the nation's Constitution shattered, his out going, like the subsidence of some pestilence walking in darkness, is a cause for devout thanksgiving. A month longer in power, and perhaps, the epitaph of the American Republic might, if it may not now, be written, and its death consigned to the mouldy tombs of once great, but now extinct, nations.

While not at all too confident of the incorruptible purity of the new President, (for we remember the atmosphere of Washington, and the subtle devices of the enemies of Liberty, among whom he has now gone,) still we hope something from him. His stately silence during these last tumultuous and stormy three months, his stern refusal thus far to commit himself to any of the much advocated schemes of compromise, his refusal to have concessions extorted from him under the terror instituted by thievish conspirators and traitors, the cool and circumspect character of his replies to the various speeches, some delicate, appropriate, and sensible, and some rudely curious and prying, made to him during his circuitous route to Washington, the modesty with which he has pushed aside the various compliments bestowed upon him, all prove that he has not won deceitfully the title of Honest Old Abe. True, indeed, he has made no immoderate promises to the cause of freedom. His party has made none. But what were small in Chicago, will be found large at Washington, and what were moderate in the canvass, have become much augmented by the frowning difficulties since flung in the way of their accomplishment by the movement for disunion. It was a small thing six months ago to say, as the Republican party did say, that the Union shall be preserved, but events have now transpired, which make this a very solemn matter to reduce to practice. Most things are easier said than done, and this thing belongs to the general rule. That declaration in the Chicago platform implied that those who uttered it, believed that this Government possesses ample power for its own preservation, and that those powers should be in their hands, faithfully wielded for that purpose. This, then, is the first question: Will Mr. Lincoln boldly grapple with the monster of Disunion, and bring down his proud looks?

Will he call upon the haughty slave masters, who have risen

in arms, to break up the Government, to lay down those arms, and return to loyalty, or meet the doom of traitors and rebels? He must do this, or do worse.—He must do this, or consent to be the despised representative of a defied and humbled Government. He must do this, or own that party platforms are the merest devices of scheming politicians to cheat the people, and to enable them to crawl up to place and power. He must do this, or compromise the fundamental principle upon which he was elected, to wit, the right and duty of Congress to prohibit the farther extension of Slavery. Will he compromise? Time and events will soon answer this question. For the present, there is much reason to believe that he will not consent to any compromise which will violate the principle upon which he was elected; and since none which does not utterly trample upon that principle can be accepted by the South, we have a double assurance that there will be no compromise, and that the contest must now be decided, and decided forever, which of the two, Freedom or Slavery, shall give law to this Republic. Let the conflict come, and God speed the Right, must be the wish of every true-hearted American, as well as of that of an onlooking world.

# Abraham Lincoln: First Inaugural Address

### March 4, 1861

Lincoln began drafting his inaugural address in Springfield in January 1861 and completed it after his arrival in Washington on February 23. The final version incorporated revisions suggested by his Illinois friend, Orville H. Browning, and by William H. Seward (some of these changes are presented in the Notes in this volume).

———————

FELLOW CITIZENS of the United States:

In compliance with a custom as old as the government itself, I appear before you to address you briefly, and to take, in your presence, the oath prescribed by the Constitution of the United States, to be taken by the President "before he enters on the execution of his office."

I do not consider it necessary, at present, for me to discuss those matters of administration about which there is no special anxiety, or excitement.

Apprehension seems to exist among the people of the Southern States, that by the accession of a Republican Administration, their property, and their peace, and personal security, are to be endangered. There has never been any reasonable cause for such apprehension. Indeed, the most ample evidence to the contrary has all the while existed, and been open to their inspection. It is found in nearly all the published speeches of him who now addresses you. I do but quote from one of those speeches when I declare that "I have no purpose, directly or indirectly, to interfere with the institution of slavery in the States where it exists. I believe I have no lawful right to do so, and I have no inclination to do so." Those who nominated and elected me did so with full knowledge that I had made this, and many similar declarations, and had never recanted them. And more than this, they placed in the platform, for my acceptance, and as a law to themselves, and to me, the clear and emphatic resolution which I now read:

"*Resolved*, That the maintenance inviolate of the rights of the States, and especially the right of each State to order and control its own domestic institutions according to its own judgment exclusively, is essential to that balance of power on which the perfection and endurance of our political fabric depend; and we denounce the lawless invasion by armed force of the soil of any State or Territory, no matter under what pretext, as among the gravest of crimes."

I now reiterate these sentiments: and in doing so, I only press upon the public attention the most conclusive evidence of which the case is susceptible, that the property, peace and security of no section are to be in anywise endangered by the now incoming Administration. I add too, that all the protection which, consistently with the Constitution and the laws, can be given, will be cheerfully given to all the States when lawfully demanded, for whatever cause—as cheerfully to one section, as to another.

There is much controversy about the delivering up of fugitives from service or labor. The clause I now read is as plainly written in the Constitution as any other of its provisions:

"No person held to service or labor in one State, under the laws thereof, escaping into another, shall, in consequence of any law or regulation therein, be discharged from such service or labor, but shall be delivered up on claim of the party to whom such service or labor may be due."

It is scarcely questioned that this provision was intended by those who made it, for the reclaiming of what we call fugitive slaves; and the intention of the law-giver is the law. All members of Congress swear their support to the whole Constitution—to this provision as much as to any other. To the proposition, then, that slaves whose cases come within the terms of this clause, "shall be delivered up," their oaths are unanimous. Now, if they would make the effort in good temper, could they not, with nearly equal unanimity, frame and pass a law, by means of which to keep good that unanimous oath?

There is some difference of opinion whether this clause should be enforced by national or by state authority; but surely that difference is not a very material one. If the slave is to be surrendered, it can be of but little consequence to him, or to others, by which authority it is done. And should any one, in any case, be content that his oath shall go unkept, on a merely unsubstantial controversy as to *how* it shall be kept?

Again, in any law upon this subject, ought not all the safeguards of liberty known in civilized and humane jurisprudence to be introduced, so that a free man be not, in any case, surrendered as a slave? And might it not be well, at the same time, to provide by law for the enforcement of that clause in the Constitution which guarranties that "The citizens of each State shall be entitled to all previleges and immunities of citizens in the several States?"

I take the official oath to-day, with no mental reservations, and with no purpose to construe the Constitution or laws, by any hypercritical rules. And while I do not choose now to specify particular acts of Congress as proper to be enforced, I do suggest, that it will be much safer for all, both in official and private stations, to conform to, and abide by, all those acts which stand unrepealed, than to violate any of them, trusting to find impunity in having them held to be unconstitutional.

It is seventy-two years since the first inauguration of a President under our national Constitution. During that period fifteen different and greatly distinguished citizens, have, in succession, administered the executive branch of the government. They have conducted it through many perils; and, generally, with great success. Yet, with all this scope for precedent, I now enter upon the same task for the brief constitutional term of four years, under great and peculiar difficulty. A disruption of the Federal Union heretofore only menaced, is now formidably attempted.

I hold, that in contemplation of universal law, and of the Constitution, the Union of these States is perpetual. Perpetuity is implied, if not expressed, in the fundamental law of all national governments. It is safe to assert that no government proper, ever had a provision in its organic law for its own termination. Continue to execute all the express provisions of our national Constitution, and the Union will endure forever—it being impossible to destroy it, except by some action not provided for in the instrument itself.

Again, if the United States be not a government proper, but

an association of States in the nature of contract merely, can it, as a contract, be peaceably unmade, by less than all the parties who made it? One party to a contract may violate it—break it, so to speak; but does it not require all to lawfully rescind it?

Descending from these general principles, we find the proposition that, in legal contemplation, the Union is perpetual, confirmed by the history of the Union itself. The Union is much older than the Constitution. It was formed in fact, by the Articles of Association in 1774. It was matured and continued by the Declaration of Independence in 1776. It was further matured and the faith of all the then thirteen States expressly plighted and engaged that it should be perpetual, by the Articles of Confederation in 1778. And finally, in 1787, one of the declared objects for ordaining and establishing the Constitution, was "*to form a more perfect union.*"

But if destruction of the Union, by one, or by a part only, of the States, be lawfully possible, the Union is *less* perfect than before the Constitution, having lost the vital element of perpetuity.

It follows from these views that no State, upon its own mere motion, can lawfully get out of the Union,—that *resolves* and *ordinances* to that effect are legally void; and that acts of violence, within any State or States, against the authority of the United States, are insurrectionary or revolutionary, according to circumstances.

I therefore consider that, in view of the Constitution and the laws, the Union is unbroken; and, to the extent of my ability, I shall take care, as the Constitution itself expressly enjoins upon me, that the laws of the Union be faithfully executed in all the States. Doing this I deem to be only a simple duty on my part; and I shall perform it, so far as practicable, unless my rightful masters, the American people, shall withhold the requisite means, or, in some authoritative manner, direct the contrary. I trust this will not be regarded as a menace, but only as the declared purpose of the Union that it *will* constitutionally defend, and maintain itself.

In doing this there needs to be no bloodshed or violence; and there shall be none, unless it be forced upon the national authority. The power confided to me, will be used to hold, occupy, and possess the property, and places belonging to the government, and to collect the duties and imposts; but beyond what may be necessary for these objects, there will be no invasion—no using of force against, or among the people anywhere. Where hostility to the United States, in any interior locality, shall be so great and so universal, as to prevent competent resident citizens from holding the Federal offices, there will be no attempt to force obnoxious strangers among the people for that object. While the strict legal right may exist in the government to enforce the exercise of these offices, the attempt to do so would be so irritating, and so nearly impracticable with all, that I deem it better to forego, for the time, the uses of such offices.

The mails, unless repelled, will continue to be furnished in all parts of the Union. So far as possible, the people everywhere shall have that sense of perfect security which is most favorable to calm thought and reflection. The course here indicated will be followed, unless current events, and experience, shall show a modification, or change, to be proper; and in every case and exigency, my best discretion will be exercised, according to circumstances actually existing, and with a view and a hope of a peaceful solution of the national troubles, and the restoration of fraternal sympathies and affections.

That there are persons in one section, or another who seek to destroy the Union at all events, and are glad of any pretext to do it, I will neither affirm or deny; but if there be such, I need address no word to them. To those, however, who really love the Union, may I not speak?

Before entering upon so grave a matter as the destruction of our national fabric, with all its benefits, its memories, and its hopes, would it not be wise to ascertain precisely why we do it? Will you hazard so desperate a step, while there is any possibility that any portion of the ills you fly from, have no real existence? Will you, while the certain ills you fly to, are greater than all the real ones you fly from? Will you risk the commission of so fearful a mistake?

All profess to be content in the Union, if all constitutional rights can be maintained. Is it true, then, that any right, plainly written in the Constitution, has been denied? I think not. Happily the human mind is so constituted, that no party can reach to the audacity of doing this. Think, if you can, of a sin-

gle instance in which a plainly written provision of the Constitution has ever been denied. If, by the mere force of numbers,
a majority should deprive a minority of any clearly written constitutional right, it might, in a moral point of view, justify revolution—certainly would, if such right were a vital one. But
such is not our case. All the vital rights of minorities, and of individuals, are so plainly assured to them, by affirmations and
negations, guarranties and prohibitions, in the Constitution,
that controversies never arise concerning them. But no organic
law can ever be framed with a provision specifically applicable
to every question which may occur in practical administration.
No foresight can anticipate, nor any document of reasonable
length contain express provisions for all possible questions.
Shall fugitives from labor be surrendered by national or by
State authority? The Constitution does not expressly say. *May*
Congress prohibit slavery in the territories? The Constitution
does not expressly say. *Must* Congress protect slavery in the
territories? The Constitution does not expressly say.

From questions of this class spring all our constitutional
controversies, and we divide upon them into majorities and
minorities. If the minority will not acquiesce, the majority
must, or the government must cease. There is no other alternative; for continuing the government, is acquiescence on one
side or the other. If a minority, in such case, will secede rather
than acquiesce, they make a precedent which, in turn, will divide and ruin them; for a minority of their own will secede
from them, whenever a majority refuses to be controlled by
such minority. For instance, why may not any portion of a new
confederacy, a year or two hence, arbitrarily secede again, precisely as portions of the present Union now claim to secede
from it. All who cherish disunion sentiments, are now being
educated to the exact temper of doing this. Is there such perfect identity of interests among the States to compose a new
Union, as to produce harmony only, and prevent renewed
secession?

Plainly, the central idea of secession, is the essence of anarchy. A majority, held in restraint by constitutional checks, and
limitations, and always changing easily, with deliberate changes
of popular opinions and sentiments, is the only true sovereign
of a free people. Whoever rejects it, does, of necessity, fly to

anarchy or to despotism. Unanimity is impossible; the rule of a minority, as a permanent arrangement, is wholly inadmissable; so that, rejecting the majority principle, anarchy, or despotism in some form, is all that is left.

I do not forget the position assumed by some, that constitutional questions are to be decided by the Supreme Court; nor do I deny that such decisions must be binding in any case, upon the parties to a suit, as to the object of that suit, while they are also entitled to very high respect and consideration, in all paralel cases, by all other departments of the government. And while it is obviously possible that such decision may be erroneous in any given case, still the evil effect following it, being limited to that particular case, with the chance that it may be over-ruled, and never become a precedent for other cases, can better be borne than could the evils of a different practice. At the same time the candid citizen must confess that if the policy of the government, upon vital questions, affecting the whole people, is to be irrevocably fixed by decisions of the Supreme Court, the instant they are made, in ordinary litigation between parties, in personal actions, the people will have ceased, to be their own rulers, having, to that extent, practically resigned their government, into the hands of that eminent tribunal. Nor is there, in this view, any assault upon the court, or the judges. It is a duty, from which they may not shrink, to decide cases properly brought before them; and it is no fault of theirs, if others seek to turn their decisions to political purposes.

One section of our country believes slavery is *right*, and ought to be extended, while the other believes it is *wrong*, and ought not to be extended. This is the only substantial dispute. The fugitive slave clause of the Constitution, and the law for the suppression of the foreign slave trade, are each as well enforced, perhaps, as any law can ever be in a community where the moral sense of the people imperfectly supports the law itself. The great body of the people abide by the dry legal obligation in both cases, and a few break over in each. This, I think, cannot be perfectly cured; and it would be worse in both cases *after* the separation of the sections, than before. The foreign slave trade, now imperfectly suppressed, would be ultimately revived without restriction, in one section; while fugitive slaves, now only partially surrendered, would not be surrendered at all, by the other.

Physically speaking, we cannot separate. We cannot remove our respective sections from each other, nor build an impassable wall between them. A husband and wife may be divorced, and go out of the presence, and beyond the reach of each other; but the different parts of our country cannot do this. They cannot but remain face to face; and intercourse, either amicable or hostile, must continue between them. Is it possible then to make that intercourse more advantageous, or more satisfactory, *after* separation than *before*? Can aliens make treaties easier than friends can make laws? Can treaties be more faithfully enforced between aliens, than laws can among friends? Suppose you go to war, you cannot fight always; and when, after much loss on both sides, and no gain on either, you cease fighting, the identical old questions, as to terms of intercourse, are again upon you.

This country, with its institutions, belongs to the people who inhabit it. Whenever they shall grow weary of the existing government, they can exercise their *constitutional* right of amending it, or their *revolutionary* right to dismember, or overthrow it. I can not be ignorant of the fact that many worthy, and patriotic citizens are desirous of having the national constitution amended. While I make no recommendation of amendments, I fully recognize the rightful authority of the people over the whole subject, to be exercised in either of the modes prescribed in the instrument itself; and I should, under existing circumstances, favor, rather than oppose, a fair oppertunity being afforded the people to act upon it.

I will venture to add that, to me, the convention mode seems preferable, in that it allows amendments to originate with the people themselves, instead of only permitting them to take, or reject, propositions, originated by others, not especially chosen for the purpose, and which might not be precisely such, as they would wish to either accept or refuse. I understand a proposed amendment to the Constitution— which amendment, however, I have not seen, has passed Congress, to the effect that the federal government, shall never interfere with the domestic institutions of the States, including that of persons held to service. To avoid misconstruction of what I have said, I depart from my purpose not to speak of particular amendments, so far as to say that, holding such a provision to now be implied constitutional law, I have no objection to its being made express, and irrevocable.

The Chief Magistrate derives all his authority from the people, and they have conferred none upon him to fix terms for the separation of the States. The people themselves can do this also if they choose; but the executive, as such, has nothing to do with it. His duty is to administer the present government, as it came to his hands, and to transmit it, unimpaired by him, to his successor.

Why should there not be a patient confidence in the ultimate justice of the people? Is there any better, or equal hope, in the world? In our present differences, is either party without faith of being in the right? If the Almighty Ruler of nations, with his eternal truth and justice, be on your side of the North, or on yours of the South, that truth, and that justice, will surely prevail, by the judgment of this great tribunal, the American people.

By the frame of the government under which we live, this same people have wisely given their public servants but little power for mischief; and have, with equal wisdom, provided for the return of that little to their own hands at very short intervals.

While the people retain their virtue, and vigilence, no administration, by any extreme of wickedness or folly, can very seriously injure the government, in the short space of four years.

My countrymen, one and all, think calmly and *well*, upon this whole subject. Nothing valuable can be lost by taking time. If there be an object to *hurry* any of you, in hot haste, to a step which you would never take *deliberately*, that object will be frustrated by taking time; but no good object can be frustrated by it. Such of you as are now dissatisfied, still have the old Constitution unimpaired, and, on the sensitive point, the laws of your own framing under it; while the new administration will have no immediate power, if it would, to change either. If it were admitted that you who are dissatisfied, hold the right side in the dispute, there still is no single good reason for precipitate action. Intelligence, patriotism, Christianity, and a firm reliance on Him, who has never yet forsaken this favored land, are still competent to adjust, in the best way, all our present difficulty.

In *your* hands, my dissatisfied fellow countrymen, and not in *mine*, is the momentous issue of civil war. The government will not assail *you*. You can have no conflict, without being yourselves the aggressors. *You* have no oath registered in Heaven to destroy the government, while *I* shall have the most solemn one to "preserve, protect and defend" it.

I am loth to close. We are not enemies, but friends. We must not be enemies. Though passion may have strained, it must not break our bonds of affection. The mystic chords of memory, streching from every battle-field, and patriot grave, to every living heart and hearthstone, all over this broad land, will yet swell the chorus of the Union, when again touched, as surely they will be, by the better angels of our nature.

# Catherine Edmondston: Diary, March 4, 1861

On the day of President Lincoln's inauguration Catherine Edmondston was at her home in Halifax County, North Carolina. In her diary she alludes to Lincoln's secret railroad trip from Philadelphia to Washington on the night of February 22–23 after he was warned of a plot to assassinate him in Baltimore. The incident was ridiculed in the opposition press, which claimed (falsely) that Lincoln had disguised himself with a Scottish plaid cap.

---

MARCH 4, 1861

Today was inaugrated that wretch Abraham Lincoln President of the US. We are told not to speak evil of Dignities, but it is hard to realize he is a Dignity. Ah! would that Jefferson Davis was our President. He is a man to whom a gentleman could look at without mortification as cheif of his nation. "How glorious was the" President elect on his tour, asking at Railway Stations for impudent girls who had written him about his whiskers & rewarding their impudence with a kiss! Faugh! Sweet Republican simplicity how charming thou art, when the future head of a great nation, a man upon whom all eyes are bent measures his august person inch by inch with a visitor whom he fears is taller than himself & chuckles to find himself mistaken. But then Saul was a head & shoulders higher than the multitude—why should not Abraham rest his importance on his stature? How dignified was his entrance in disguise into his future Capital. How grateful should we be to the long cloak & Scotch Cap which saved him from the bloody designs of his Southern enemies. Well, we have a Rail Splitter and a tall man at the head of our affairs! Ned Bartley is both & perhaps excels Mr Lincoln in one or both points, but then he is not of Anglo Saxon blood. Neither is the Vice President Mr Hannibal Hamlin. Gentlemen we can match you on all points to a nicety. Ah my country! God keep you when such hands hold the helm!

# Alexander H. Stephens: "Corner-Stone" Speech

## March 21, 1861

A former congressman who had opposed immediate secession in the Georgia convention, Stephens was unanimously elected as the provisional vice-president of the Confederacy in February 1861. The text of his speech at the Savannah Atheneum first appeared in the *Savannah Republican* and was accompanied by a reporter's note stating that it was not "a perfect report, but only such a sketch of the address" that embraced the most important points. Stephens would claim after the war that the printed text of his Savannah speech contained "several glaring errors" and exaggerated the importance of his use of the "corner-stone" image to describe the role of slavery in the Confederacy. In a speech delivered in Atlanta nine days before he spoke at Savannah, Stephens had employed the same metaphor, asserting that the founders of the Confederacy had "solemnly discarded the pestilent heresy of fancy politicians, that all men, all races, were equal, and we had made African *inequality* and subordination, and the *equality* of white men, the chief corner stone of the Southern Republic."

---

MR. MAYOR, AND GENTLEMEN OF THE COMMITTEE, AND FELLOW CITIZENS:—For this reception you will please accept most profound and sincere thanks. The compliment is doubtless intended as much, or more, perhaps, in honor of the occasion, and my public position, in connection with the great events now crowding upon us, than to me personally and individually. It is however none the less appreciated by me on that account. We are in the midst of one of the greatest epochs in our history. The last ninety days will mark one of the most memorable eras in the history of modern civilization.

[There was a general call from the outside of the building for the speaker to go out, that there were more outside than in.]

The Mayor rose and requested silence at the doors, that Mr.

Stephens' health would not permit him to speak in the open air.

Mr. STEPHENS said he would leave it to the audience whether he should proceed indoors or out. There was a general cry indoors, as the ladies, a large number of whom were present, could not hear outside.

Mr. STEPHENS said that the accommodation of the ladies would determine the question, and he would proceed where he was.

[At this point the uproar and clamor outside was greater still for the speaker to go out on the steps. This was quieted by Col. Lawton, Col. Freeman, Judge Jackson, and Mr. J. W. Owens going out and stating the facts of the case to the dense mass of men, women, and children who were outside, and entertaining them in brief speeches—Mr. Stephens all this while quietly sitting down until the furor subsided.]

Mr. STEPHENS rose and said: When perfect quiet is restored, I shall proceed. I cannot speak so long as there is any noise or confusion. I shall take my time—I feel quite prepared to spend the night with you if necessary. [Loud applause.] I very much regret that every one who desires cannot hear what I have to say. Not that I have any display to make, or any thing very entertaining to present, but such views as I have to give, I wish *all*, not only in this city, but in this State, and throughout our Confederate Republic, could hear, who have a desire to hear them.

I was remarking, that we are passing through one of the greatest revolutions in the annals of the world. Seven States have within the last three months thrown off an old government and formed a new. This revolution has been signally marked, up to this time, by the fact of its having been accomplished without the loss of a single drop of blood. [Applause.]

This new constitution, or form of government, constitutes the subject to which your attention will be partly invited. In reference to it, I make this first general remark. It amply secures all our ancient rights, franchises, and liberties. All the great principles of Magna Charta are retained in it. No citizen is deprived of life, liberty, or property, but by the judgment of his peers under the laws of the land. The great principle of religious liberty, which was the honor and pride of the old constitution, is still maintained and secured. All the essentials of the old constitution, which have endeared it to the hearts of the American people, have been preserved and perpetuated. [Applause.] Some changes have been made. Of these I shall speak presently. Some of these I should have preferred not to have seen made; but these, perhaps, meet the cordial approbation of a majority of this audience, if not an overwhelming majority of the people of the Confederacy. Of them, therefore, I will not speak. But other important changes do meet my cordial approbation. They form great improvements upon the old constitution. So, taking the whole new constitution, I have no hesitancy in giving it as my judgment that it is decidedly better than the old. [Applause.]

Allow me briefly to allude to some of these improvements. The question of building up class interests, or fostering one branch of industry to the prejudice of another under the exercise of the revenue power, which gave us so much trouble under the old constitution, is put at rest forever under the new. We allow the imposition of no duty with a view of giving advantage to one class of persons, in any trade or business, over those of another. All, under our system, stand upon the same broad principles of perfect equality. Honest labor and enterprise are left free and unrestricted in whatever pursuit they may be engaged. This subject came well nigh causing a rupture of the old Union, under the lead of the gallant Palmetto State, which lies on our border, in 1833. This old thorn of the tariff, which was the cause of so much irritation in the old body politic, is removed forever from the new. [Applause.]

Again, the subject of internal improvements, under the power of Congress to regulate commerce, is put at rest under our system. The power claimed by construction under the old constitution, was at least a doubtful one—it rested solely upon construction. We of the South, generally apart from considerations of constitutional principles, opposed its exercise upon grounds of its inexpediency and injustice. Notwithstanding this opposition, millions of money, from the common treasury had been drawn for such purposes. Our opposition sprang from no hostility to commerce, or all necessary aids for facilitating it. With us it was simply a question, upon *whom* the burden should fall. In Georgia, for instance, we have done as

much for the cause of internal improvements as any other portion of the country according to population and means. We
have stretched out lines of railroads from the seaboard to the
mountains; dug down the hills, and filled up the valleys at a
cost of not less than twenty-five millions of dollars. All this was
done to open an outlet for our products of the interior, and
those to the west of us, to reach the marts of the world. No
State was in greater need of such facilities than Georgia, but
we did not ask that these works should be made by appropriations out of the common treasury. The cost of the grading, the
superstructure, and equipments of our roads, was borne by
those who entered on the enterprise. Nay, more—not only the
cost of the iron, no small item in the aggregate cost, was borne
in the same way—but we were compelled to pay into the common treasury several millions of dollars for the privilege of
importing the iron, after the price was paid for it abroad.
What justice was there in taking this money, which our people
paid into the common treasury on the importation of our
iron, and applying it to the improvement of rivers and harbors
elsewhere?

The true principle is to subject the commerce of every
locality, to whatever burdens may be necessary to facilitate it.
If Charleston harbor needs improvement, let the commerce of
Charleston bear the burden. If the mouth of the Savannah
river has to be cleared out, let the sea-going navigation which
is benefitted by it, bear the burden. So with the mouths of the
Alabama and Mississippi river. Just as the products of the interior, our cotton, wheat, corn, and other articles, have to bear
the necessary rates of freight over our railroads to reach the
seas. This is again the broad principle of perfect equality and
justice. [Applause.] And it is especially set forth and established in our new constitution.

Another feature to which I will allude, is that the new constitution provides that cabinet ministers and heads of departments may have the privilege of seats upon the floor of the
Senate and House of Representatives—may have the right to
participate in the debates and discussions upon the various
subjects of administration. I should have preferred that this
provision should have gone further, and required the President to select his constitutional advisers from the Senate and

House of Representatives. That would have conformed entirely to the practice in the British Parliament, which, in my judgment, is one of the wisest provisions in the British constitution. It is the only feature that saves that government. It is that which gives it stability in its facility to change its administration. Ours, as it is, is a great approximation to the right principle.

Under the old constitution, a secretary of the treasury for instance, had no opportunity, save by his annual reports, of presenting any scheme or plan of finance or other matter. He had no opportunity of explaining, expounding, inforcing, or defending his views of policy; his only resort was through the medium of an organ. In the British parliament, the premier brings in his budget and stands before the nation responsible for its every item. If it is indefensible, he falls before the attacks upon it, as he ought to. This will now be the case to a limited extent under our system. In the new constitution, provision has been made by which our heads of departments can speak for themselves and the administration, in behalf of its entire policy, without resorting to the indirect and highly objectionable medium of a newspaper. It is to be greatly hoped that under our system we shall never have what is known as a government organ. [Rapturous applause.]

[A noise again arose from the clamor of the crowd outside, who wished to hear Mr. Stephens, and for some moments interrupted him. The mayor rose and called on the police to preserve order. Quiet being restored, Mr. S. proceeded.]

Another change in the constitution relates to the length of the tenure of the presidential office. In the new constitution it is six years instead of four, and the President rendered ineligible for a re-election. This is certainly a decidedly conservative change. It will remove from the incumbent all temptation to use his office or exert the powers confided to him for any objects of personal ambition. The only incentive to that higher ambition which should move and actuate one holding such high trusts in his hands, will be the good of the people, the advancement, prosperity, happiness, safety, honor, and true glory of the confederacy. [Applause.]

But not to be tedious in enumerating the numerous changes for the better, allow me to allude to one other—though last, not least. The new constitution has put at rest, *forever*, all the agitating questions relating to our peculiar institution—African slavery as it exists amongst us—the proper *status* of the negro in our form of civilization. This was the immediate cause of the late rupture and present revolution. Jefferson in his forecast, had anticipated this, as the "rock upon which the old Union would split." He was right. What was conjecture with him, is now a realized fact. But whether he fully comprehended the great truth upon which that rock *stood* and *stands*, may be doubted. The prevailing ideas entertained by him and most of the leading statesmen at the time of the formation of the old constitution, were that the enslavement of the African was in violation of the laws of nature; that it was wrong in *principle*, socially, morally, and politically. It was an evil they knew not well how to deal with, but the general opinion of the men of that day was that, somehow or other in the order of Providence, the institution would be evanescent and pass away. This idea, though not incorporated in the constitution, was the prevailing idea at that time. The constitution, it is true, secured every essential guarantee to the institution while it should last, and hence no argument can be justly urged against the constitutional guarantees thus secured, because of the common sentiment of the day. Those ideas, however, were fundamentally wrong. They rested upon the assumption of the equality of races. This was an error. It was a sandy foundation, and the government built upon it fell when the "storm came and the wind blew."

Our new government is founded upon exactly the opposite idea; its foundations are laid, its corner-stone rests upon the great truth, that the negro is not equal to the white man; that slavery—subordination to the superior race—is his natural and normal condition. [Applause.]

This, our new government, is the first, in the history of the world, based upon this great physical, philosophical, and moral truth. This truth has been slow in the process of its development, like all other truths in the various departments of science. It has been so even amongst us. Many who hear me, perhaps, can recollect well, that this truth was not generally admitted, even within their day. The errors of the past generation still clung to many as late as twenty years ago. Those at the North, who still cling to these errors, with a zeal above knowledge, we justly denominate fanatics. All fanaticism springs from an aberration of the mind—from a defect in reasoning. It is a species of insanity. One of the most striking characteristics of insanity, in many instances, is forming correct conclusions from fancied or erroneous premises; so with the anti-slavery fanatics; their conclusions are right if their premises were. They assume that the negro is equal, and hence conclude that he is entitled to equal privileges and rights with the white man. If their premises were correct, their conclusions would be logical and just—but their premise being wrong, their whole argument fails. I recollect once of having heard a gentleman from one of the northern States, of great power and ability, announce in the House of Representatives, with imposing effect, that we of the South would be compelled, ultimately, to yield upon this subject of slavery, that it was as impossible to war successfully against a principle in politics, as it was in physics or mechanics. That the principle would ultimately prevail. That we, in maintaining slavery as it exists with us, were warring against a principle, a principle founded in nature, the principle of the equality of men. The reply I made to him was, that upon his own grounds, we should, ultimately, succeed, and that he and his associates, in this crusade against our institutions, would ultimately fail. The truth announced, that it was as impossible to war successfully against a principle in politics as it was in physics and mechanics, I admitted; but told him that it was he, and those acting with him, who were warring against a principle. They were attempting to make things equal which the Creator had made unequal.

In the conflict thus far, success has been on our side, complete throughout the length and breadth of the Confederate States. It is upon this, as I have stated, our social fabric is firmly planted; and I cannot permit myself to doubt the ultimate success of a full recognition of this principle throughout the civilized and enlightened world.

As I have stated, the truth of this principle may be slow in development, as all truths are and ever have been, in the various branches of science. It was so with the principles announced by Galileo—it was so with Adam Smith and his principles of political economy. It was so with Harvey, and his theory of the circulation of the blood. It is stated that not a single one of the medical profession, living at the time of the announcement of the truths made by him, admitted them. Now, they are universally acknowledged. May we not, therefore, look with confidence to the ultimate universal acknowledgment of the truths upon which our system rests? It is the first government ever instituted upon the principles in strict conformity to nature, and the ordination of Providence, in furnishing the materials of human society. Many governments have been founded upon the principle of the subordination and serfdom of certain classes of the same race; such were and are in violation of the laws of nature. Our system commits no such violation of nature's laws. With us, all of the white race, however high or low, rich or poor, are equal in the eye of the law. Not so with the negro. Subordination is his place. He, by nature, or by the curse against Canaan, is fitted for that condition which he occupies in our system. The architect, in the construction of buildings, lays the foundation with the proper material—the granite; then comes the brick or the marble. The substratum of our society is made of the material fitted by nature for it, and by experience we know that it is best, not only for the superior, but for the inferior race, that it should be so. It is, indeed, in conformity with the ordinance of the Creator. It is not for us to inquire into the wisdom of his ordinances, or to question them. For his own purposes, he has made one race to differ from another, as he has made "one star to differ from another star in glory."

The great objects of humanity are best attained when there is conformity to his laws and decrees, in the formation of governments as well as in all things else. Our confederacy is founded upon principles in strict conformity with these laws. This stone which was rejected by the first builders "is become the chief of the corner"—the real "corner-stone"—in our new edifice. [Applause.]

I have been asked, what of the future? It has been apprehended by some that we would have arrayed against us the civilized world. I care not who or how many they may be against us, when we stand upon the eternal principles of truth, *if we are true to ourselves and the principles for which we contend*, we are obliged to, and must triumph. [Immense applause.]

Thousands of people who begin to understand these truths are not yet completely out of the shell; they do not see them in their length and breadth. We hear much of the civilization and christianization of the barbarous tribes of Africa. In my judgment, those ends will never be attained, but by first teaching them the lesson taught to Adam, that "in the sweat of his brow he should eat his bread," [applause,] and teaching them to work, and feed, and clothe themselves.

But to pass on: Some have propounded the inquiry whether it is practicable for us to go on with the confederacy without further accessions? Have we the means and ability to maintain nationality among the powers of the earth? On this point I would barely say, that as anxiously as we all have been, and are, for the border States, with institutions similar to ours, to join us, still we are abundantly able to maintain our position, even if they should ultimately make up their minds not to cast their destiny with us. That they ultimately will join us—be compelled to do it—is my confident belief; but we can get on very well without them, even if they should not.

We have all the essential elements of a high national career. The idea has been given out at the North, and even in the border States, that we are too small and too weak to maintain a separate nationality. This is a great mistake. In extent of territory we embrace five hundred and sixty-four thousand square miles and upward. This is upward of two hundred thousand square miles more than was included within the limits of the original thirteen States. It is an area of country more than double the territory of France or the Austrian empire. France, in round numbers, has but two hundred and twelve thousand square miles. Austria, in round numbers, has two hundred and forty-eight thousand square miles. Ours is greater than both combined. It is greater than all France, Spain, Portugal, and Great Britain, including England, Ireland, and Scotland, together. In population we have upward of five millions, according to the census of 1860; this includes white and black. The entire population, including white and black, of the original thirteen States, was less than four millions in 1790, and still less in '76, when the independence of our fathers was achieved.

If they, with a less population, dared maintain their independence against the greatest power on earth, shall we have any apprehension of maintaining ours now?

In point of material wealth and resources, we are greatly in advance of them. The taxable property of the Confederate States cannot be less than twenty-two hundred millions of dollars! This, I think I venture but little in saying, may be considered as five times more than the colonies possessed at the time they achieved their independence. Georgia, alone, possessed last year, according to the report of our comptroller-general, six hundred and seventy-two millions of taxable property. The debts of the seven confederate States sum up in the aggregate less than eighteen millions, while the existing debts of the other of the late United States sum up in the aggregate the enormous amount of one hundred and seventy-four millions of dollars. This is without taking into the account the heavy city debts, corporation debts, and railroad debts, which press, and will continue to press, as a heavy incubus upon the resources of those States. These debts, added to others, make a sum total not much under five hundred millions of dollars. With such an area of territory as we have—with such an amount of population—with a climate and soil unsurpassed by any on the face of the earth—with such resources already at our command—with productions which control the commerce of the world—who can entertain any apprehensions as to our ability to succeed, whether others join us or not?

It is true, I believe I state but the common sentiment, when I declare my earnest desire that the border States should join us. The differences of opinion that existed among us anterior to secession, related more to the policy in securing that result by co-operation than from any difference upon the ultimate security we all looked to in common.

These differences of opinion were more in reference to policy than principle, and as Mr. Jefferson said in his inaugural, in 1801, after the heated contest preceding his election, there might be differences of opinion without differences on principle, and that all, to some extent, had been federalists and all republicans; so it may now be said of us, that whatever differences of opinion as to the best policy in having a co-operation with our border sister slave States, if the worst came to the worst, that as we were all co-operationists, we are now all for independence, whether they come or not. [Continued applause.]

In this connection I take this occasion to state, that I was not without grave and serious apprehensions, that if the worst came to the worst, and cutting loose from the old government should be the only remedy for our safety and security, it would be attended with much more serious ills than it has been as yet. Thus far we have seen none of those incidents which usually attend revolutions. No such material as such convulsions usually throw up has been seen. Wisdom, prudence, and patriotism, have marked every step of our progress thus far. This augurs well for the future, and it is a matter of sincere gratification to me, that I am enabled to make the declaration. Of the men I met in the Congress at Montgomery, I may be pardoned for saying this, an abler, wiser, a more conservative, deliberate, determined, resolute, and patriotic body of men, I never met in my life. [Great applause.] Their works speak for them; the provisional government speaks for them; the constitution of the permanent government will be a lasting monument of their worth, merit, and statesmanship. [Applause.]

But to return to the question of the future. What is to be the result of this revolution?

Will every thing, commenced so well, continue as it has begun? In reply to this anxious inquiry, I can only say it all depends upon ourselves. A young man starting out in life on his majority, with health, talent, and ability, under a favoring Providence, may be said to be the architect of his own fortunes. His destinies are in his own hands. He may make for himself a name, of honor or dishonor, according to his own acts. If he plants himself upon truth, integrity, honor and uprightness, with industry, patience and energy, he cannot fail of success. So it is with us. We are a young republic, just entering upon the arena of nations; we will be the architects of our own fortunes. Our destiny, under Providence, is in our own hands. With wisdom, prudence, and statesmanship on the part of our public men, and intelligence, virtue and patriotism on the part of the people, success, to the full measures of our most sanguine hopes, may be looked for. But if unwise counsels prevail—if we become divided—if schisms arise—if dissensions spring up—if factions are engendered—if party spirit, nourished by unholy personal ambition shall rear its hydra head, I have no good to prophesy for you. Without intelligence, virtue, integrity, and patriotism on the part of the people, no republic or representative government can be durable or stable.

We have intelligence, and virtue, and patriotism. All that is required is to cultivate and perpetuate these. Intelligence will not do without virtue. France was a nation of philosophers. These philosophers became Jacobins. They lacked that virtue, that devotion to moral principle, and that patriotism which is essential to good government. Organized upon principles of perfect justice and right—seeking amity and friendship with all other powers—I see no obstacle in the way of our upward and onward progress. Our growth, by accessions from other States, will depend greatly upon whether we present to the world, as I trust we shall, a better government than that to which neighboring States belong. If we do this, North Carolina, Tennessee, and Arkansas cannot hesitate long; neither can Virginia, Kentucky, and Missouri. They will necessarily gravitate to us by an imperious law. We made ample provision in our constitution for the admission of other States; it is more guarded, and wisely so, I think, than the old constitution on the same subject, but not too guarded to receive them as fast as it may be proper. Looking to the distant future, and, perhaps, not very far distant either, it is not beyond the range of possibility, and even probability, that all the great States of the north-west will gravitate this way, as well as Tennessee, Kentucky, Missouri, Arkansas, etc. Should they do so, our doors are wide enough to receive them, but not until they are ready to assimilate with us in principle.

The process of disintegration in the old Union may be expected to go on with almost absolute certainty if we pursue the right course. We are now the nucleus of a growing power which, if we are true to ourselves, our destiny, and high mission, will become the controlling power on this continent. To what extent accessions will go on in the process of time, or where it will end, the future will determine. So far as it con-

cerns States of the old Union, this process will be upon no
such principles of *reconstruction* as now spoken of, but upon
*reorganization* and new assimilation. [Loud applause.] Such
are some of the glimpses of the future as I catch them.

But at first we must necessarily meet with the inconveniences and difficulties and embarrassments incident to all
changes of government. These will be felt in our postal affairs
and changes in the channel of trade. These inconveniences, it
is to be hoped, will be but temporary, and must be borne with
patience and forbearance.

As to whether we shall have war with our late confederates,
or whether all matters of differences between us shall be amicably settled, I can only say that the prospect for a peaceful adjustment is better, so far as I am informed, than it has been.

The prospect of war is, at least, not so threatening as it has
been. The idea of coercion, shadowed forth in President Lincoln's inaugural, seems not to be followed up thus far so vigorously as was expected. Fort Sumter, it is believed, will soon
be evacuated. What course will be pursued toward Fort Pickens, and the other forts on the gulf, is not so well understood.
It is to be greatly desired that all of them should be surrendered. Our object is *peace*, not only with the North, but with
the world. All matters relating to the public property, public li-
abilities of the Union when we were members of it, we are
ready and willing to adjust and settle upon the principles of
right, equity, and good faith. War can be of no more benefit to
the North than to us. Whether the intention of evacuating
Fort Sumter is to be received as an evidence of a desire for a
peaceful solution of our difficulties with the United States, or
the result of necessity, I will not undertake to say. I would fain
hope the former. Rumors are afloat, however, that it is the result of necessity. All I can say to you, therefore, on that point
is, keep your armor bright and your powder dry. [Enthusiastic
cheering.]

The surest way to secure peace, is to show your ability to
maintain your rights. The principles and position of the present administration of the United States—the republican party
—present some puzzling questions. While it is a fixed principle
with them never to allow the increase of a foot of slave territory,

they seem to be equally determined not to part with an inch "of the accursed soil." Notwithstanding their clamor against the institution, they seemed to be equally opposed to getting more, or letting go what they have got. They were ready to fight on the accession of Texas, and are equally ready to fight now on her secession. Why is this? How can this strange paradox be accounted for? There seems to be but one rational solution—and that is, notwithstanding their professions of humanity, they are disinclined to give up the benefits they derive from slave labor. Their philanthropy yields to their interest. The idea of enforcing the laws, has but one object, and that is a collection of the taxes, raised by slave labor to swell the fund, necessary to meet their heavy appropriations. The spoils is what they are after—though they come from the labor of the slave. [Continued applause.]

Mr. Stephens reviewed at some length, the extravagance and profligacy of appropriations by the Congress of the United States for several years past, and in this connection took occasion to allude to another one of the great improvements in our new constitution, which is a clause prohibiting Congress from appropriating any money from the treasury, except by a two-third vote, unless it be for some object which the executive may say is necessary to carry on the government.

When it is thus asked for, and estimated for, he continued, the majority may appropriate. This was a new feature.

Our fathers had guarded the assessment of taxes by insisting that representation and taxation should go together. This was inherited from the mother country, England. It was one of the principles upon which the revolution had been fought. Our fathers also provided in the old constitution, that all appropriation bills should originate in the representative branch of Congress, but our new constitution went a step further, and guarded not only the pockets of the people, but also the public money, after it was taken from their pockets.

He alluded to the difficulties and embarrassments which seemed to surround the question of a peaceful solution of the controversy with the old government. How can it be done? is perplexing many minds. The President seems to think that he cannot recognize our independence, nor can he, with and by the advice of the Senate, do so. The constitution makes no such provision. A general convention of all the States has been suggested by some.

Without proposing to solve the difficulty, he barely made the following suggestion:

"That as the admission of States by Congress under the constitution was an act of legislation, and in the nature of a contract or compact between the States admitted and the others admitting, why should not this contract or compact be regarded as of like character with all other civil contracts— liable to be rescinded by mutual agreement of both parties? The seceding States have rescinded it on their part, they have resumed their sovereignty. Why cannot the whole question be settled, if the north desire peace, simply by the Congress, in both branches, with the concurrence of the President, giving their consent to the separation, and a recognition of our independence?" This he merely offered as a suggestion, as one of the ways in which it might be done with much less violence by constructions to the constitution than many other acts of that government. [Applause.] The difficulty has to be solved in some way or other—this may be regarded as a fixed fact.

Several other points were alluded to by Mr. Stephens, particularly as to the policy of the new government toward foreign nations, and our commercial relations with them. Free trade, as far as practicable, would be the policy of this government. No higher duties would be imposed on foreign importations than would be necessary to support the government upon the strictest economy.

In olden times the olive branch was considered the emblem of peace; we will send to the nations of the earth another and far more potential emblem of the same, the cotton plant. The present duties were levied with a view of meeting the present necessities and exigencies, in preparation for war, if need be; but if we have peace, and he hoped we might, and trade should resume its proper course, a duty of ten per cent. upon foreign importations it was thought might be sufficient to meet the expenditures of the government. If some articles should be left on the free list, as they now are, such as breadstuffs, etc., then, of course, duties upon others would have to be higher—but in no event to an extent to embarrass trade and commerce. He concluded in an earnest appeal for union and harmony, on part of all the people in support of the common cause, in which we were all enlisted, and upon the issues of which such great consequences depend.

If, said he, we are true to ourselves, true to our cause, true to our destiny, true to our high mission, in presenting to the world the highest type of civilization ever exhibited by man—there will be found in our lexicon no such word as fail.

Mr. Stephens took his seat, amid a burst of enthusiasm and applause, such as the Athenæum has never had displayed within its walls, within "the recollection of the oldest inhabitant."

# Edward Bates: Diary, March 9–April 8, 1861

On the day after his inauguration President Lincoln was told that the garrison at Fort Sumter would run out of supplies within six weeks. As the new cabinet debated whether to evacuate the fort or attempt to resupply it, their deliberations were recorded by Edward Bates, who had been appointed attorney general by Lincoln.

---

*Mar 9. Saturday night.* A Cabinet Council upon the State of the Country. I was astonished to be informed that Fort Sumter, in Charleston harbor *must* be evacuated, and that General Scott, Genl. Totten and Major Anderson concur in opinion, that, as the place has but 28 days provision, it must be relieved, if at all, in that time; and that it will take a force of 20,000 men at least, and a bloody battle, to relieve it!

&lt;For several days after this, consultations were held as to the feasibility of relieving Fort Sumter, at which were present, explaining and aiding, Gen Scott, Gen Totten, Comodore Stringham, and Mr. Fox who seems to be *au fait* in both nautical and military matters. The *army* officers and *navy* officers differ widely about the degree of danger to rapid moving vessels passing under the fire of land batteries—The *army* officers think destruction almost inevitable, where the *navy* officers think the danger but slight. The one believes that Sumter cannot be relieved—not even provisioned—without an army of 20.000 men and a bloody battle: The other (the naval) believes that with light, rapid vessels, they can cross *the bar* at high tide of a dark night, run the enemy's forts (Moultrie and Cummings' Point) and reach Sumter with little risk. They say that the greatest danger will be in landing at Sumter, upon which point there may be a concentrated fire. They do not doubt that the place *can* be and *ought* to be relieved. Mr. Fox is anxious to risk his life in leading the relief, and Comodore Stringham seems equally confident of success.

The naval men have convinced me fully that the thing can be done, and yet, as the doing of it would be almost certain to *begin the war*, and as Charleston is of little importance, as compared with the chief points in the Gulf, I am willing to yield to the *military* counsel. and evacuate Fort Sumter, at the same time strengthening the Forts in the Gulf, so as to *look down* opposition, and guarding the coast, with all our naval power, if need be, so as to close any port at pleasure.

And to this effect, I gave the President my written opinion, on the 16th. of March.>

*March 16.* The President of the United States has required my opinion, in writing, upon the following question

"Assuming it to be possible to now provision Fort Sumter, under all the circumstances, is it wise to attempt it?"

This is not a question of lawful right nor physical power, but of prudence and patriotism only. The right is in my mind unquestionable, and I have no doubt at all that the Government has the power and means, not only to provision the fort, but also, if the exigency required, to man it, with its war complement of 650 men, so as to make it impregnable to any local force that could be brought against it. Assuming all this we come back to the question "Under all the circumstances is it wise *now* to provision the fort?"

The wisdom of the act must be tested by the value of the object to be gained, and by the hazard to be encountered in the enterprise. The object to be gained by the supply of provision, is not to strengthen the fortress, so as to command the harbor and enforce the laws, but only to prolong the labors and privations of the brave little garrison that has so long held it, with patient courage. The possession of the fort as we now hold it, does not enable us to collect the revenue or enforce the laws of commerce and navigation. It may indeed involve a point of honor or a point of pride, but I do not see any great national interest involved in the bare fact of holding the fort, as we now hold it— and to hold it at all we must supply it with provisions. And it seems to me that we may in humanity and patriotism, safely waive the point of pride, in the consciousness that we have the power and lack nothing but the will, to hold

Fort Sumter in such condition as to command the harbor of Charleston, cut off all its commerce, and even lay the City in ashes.

The hazards to be met are many and obvious. If the attempt be made in rapid boats light enough to pass the bar in safety, still they must pass under the fire of Fort Moultrie and the batteries on Morris Island. They might possibly escape that danger, but they cannot hope to escape the armed guard boats which ply all night from the Fort to the outer edge of the bar These armed guard boats would be sure to take or destroy our unarmed tugs, unless repelled by force, either from our ships outside the bar, or from Fort Sumter within; and that is war. True, war already exists by the act of South Carolina; but this Government has thus far, magnanimously forborne to retort the outrage. And I am willing to forbear yet longer, in the hope of a peaceful solution of our present difficulties. I am most unwilling to strike—I will not say the first blow, for South Carolina has already struck that—but I am unwilling "*under all the circumstances*" at this moment to do any act which may have the semblance, before the world of beginning a civil war, the terrible consequences of which would, I think, find no parallel in modern times. For I am convinced that flagrant Civil war in the Southern States would soon become a social war, and that could hardly fail to bring on a servile war, the horrors of which need not be dwelt upon. To avoid these evils I would make great sacrifices, and fort Sumter is one; but if war be forced upon us by causeless and pertinacious rebellion, I am for resisting it with all the might of the nation.

I am persuaded moreover, that, in several of the misguided States of the South, a large portion of the people are really lovers of the Union, and anxious to be safely back, under the protection of its flag. A reaction has already begun, and, if encouraged by wise, moderate and firm measures on the part of this government, I persuade myself that the nation will be restored to its integrity without the effusion of blood.

For these reasons, I am willing to evacuate fort Sumter, rather than be an active party in the beginning of civil war. The port of Charleston is comparatively, a small thing. If the present difficulties should continue and grow, I am convinced that the real struggle will be at the Mississippi for it is not politically possible for any foreign power to hold the mouth of that river, against the people of the middle and upper valley.

If fort Sumter must be evacuated, then it is my decided opinion that the more Southern forts Pickens, Key West &c should, with out delay, be put in condition of easy defense against all assailants; and that the whole coast, from South Carolina to Texas, should be as well guarded as the power of the navy will enable us.

Upon the whole, I do not think it *wise now* to attempt to provision Fort Sumter.

On the 29th. of March, in Cabinet Council on these subjects, I suggested that, in the desultory conversations by which we had usually conducted our consultations, it was hard to arrive at definite conclusions, and therefore I proposed that the President should state his questions, and require our opinions *seriatim*. This being agreed to, I immediately wrote and read the following memorandum—

"It is my decided opinion that Fort Pickens and Key West ought to be re inforced and supplied so as to *look down* opposition, at all hazards—And this, whether fort Sumter be or be not evacuated."

"It is also my opinion that there ought to be a *naval* force kept upon the Southern coast, sufficient to *command it*, and, if need be *actually close* any port that, practically, ought to be closed, whatever other Station is left unoccupied."

"It is also my opinion that there ought to be immediately established, a line of light, fast-running vessels, to pass, as rapidly as possible, between N. Y. or Norfolk at the North, and Key West or other point in the gulf at the South."

"As to fort Sumter, I think the time is come when it ought to be either evacuated or relieved."

The President was pleased with this mode of proceeding, and requested the other ministers to do the like—which was done—Mr. Seward gave his advice for the immediate evacuation of fort Sumter.

*April 8.   Monday.*   To preserve continuity on this important subject, I skip over several days—

This Admn. has kept its own counsel pretty well, yet, its

general purpose to preserve its authority as far as possible, in the South, seems to be known by the press, though its particular means are still only guessed at. For some days, the public is much excited with rumors of military expeditions to various points, tho' most of the guesses point rather to the Gulf than to Charleston.

In fact, at this moment, the matter stands thus—An expedition to *provision* fort Sumter, well appointed, consisting of light-draft, rapid steamers (drawing only 5 or 6 feet, so as to pass Charleston bar) commanded by Mr. Fox, leaves N. York to day or tomorrow, and will reach Charleston on the 11th., or 12th. at farthest. If Maj: Anderson hold out till then, one of two things will happen—either the fort will be well provisioned, the Southrons forbearing to assail the boats, or a fierce contest will ensue, the result of which cannot be foreseen— The fort may be demolished or the City burned—In either case there will be much slaughter.

The President has sent a private messenger to Govr. Pickens, notifying him that *provisions* only, and not men, arms or ammunition, will be landed, and that no attempt will be made to reinforce the fort, unless the provisions or the fort be fired upon.

From the first, I have insisted that it was a capital error to allow batteries to be built around fort Sumter—the erection of those batteries being an *assault*, equal to the throwing of shells. In answer to my direct question today, the Sec.y. of War (Genl. Cameron) told me that the erection of batteries to assail fort Pickens wd. not be allowed—if attempted the Fort would prevent it with shot and shell.

A large naval force is ordered to the southern coast, and, in 3 or 4 days, either there will be some sharp fighting, or the prestige of the Government will be quietly reëstablished.

# Gideon Welles: Memoir of Events, March 1861

Secretary of State William Seward sought to establish himself as the dominant figure in the new administration during the debate over Fort Sumter. Secretary of the Navy Gideon Welles would recall Seward's role in the deliberations in a short memoir written several years after the war.

———————————

MR. SEWARD, who from the first had viewed with no favor any attempt to relieve Sumter, soon became a very decisive and emphatic opponent of any proposition that was made; said he had entertained doubts, and the opinions and arguments of Major Anderson and his officers, confirmed by the distinguished military officers who were consulted, had fully convinced him that it would be abortive and useless. It was a duty to defer to these military gentlemen, whose profession and study made them experts, who had by long and faithful service justly acquired the positions they held, and who possessed the confidence of the country. It was, he was satisfied, impossible to relieve and reinforce the garrison; the attempt would provoke immediate hostilities, and if hostilities could not be avoided, he deemed it important that the Administration should not strike the first blow.

The President, though much distressed with the conclusions of the military officers, and the decisive concurrence of the Secretary of State in those conclusions, appeared to acquiesce in what seemed to be a military necessity, but was not disposed to yield until the last moment, and when there was no hope of accomplishing the work if attempted. In the mean time, he sent Mr. Lamon, his late law-partner, to Charleston and others also to make inquiries, among them Mr. Fox, who, like Commander Ward, had been a volunteer under the late administration to relieve Sumter and who never abandoned the idea of its practicability.

Commander Ward was so fully convinced by the arguments of General Scott and General Totten and the opinions of the officers of the garrison, so dissuaded by the opposition of Mr. Seward and the general current of views which prevailed, that he wholly abandoned the project, stating, however, that he held himself in readiness to obey orders and take charge of an expedition, if the Government should at any time deem it expedient that an effort should be made. On the 11th of March he left Washington, and returned to New York.

A strange state of things existed at that time in Washington. The atmosphere was thick with treason. Party spirit and old party differences prevailed, however, amidst these accumulating dangers. Secession was considered by most persons as a political party question, not as rebellion. Democrats to a large extent sympathized with the Rebels more than with the Administration, which they opposed, not that they wished secession to be successful and the Union divided, but they hoped that President Lincoln and the Republicans would, overwhelmed by obstacles and embarrassments, prove failures. The Republicans, on the other hand, were scarcely less partisan and unreasonable. Crowds of them at this period, when the storm of civil war was about bursting on the country, thronged the anterooms of the President and Secretaries, clamorous for the removal of all Democrats, indiscriminately, from office. Patriotism was with them no test, no shield from party malevolence. They demanded the proscription and exclusion of such Democrats as opposed the Rebel movements and clung to the Union, with the same vehemence that they demanded the removal of the worst Rebels who advocated a dissolution of the Union.

Neither party appeared to be apprehensive of or to realize the gathering storm. There was a general belief, indulged in by most persons, that an adjustment would in some way be brought about, without any extensive resort to extreme measures. It seemed probable there might be some outbreak in South Carolina, and perhaps in one or two other places, but such would, it was believed, be soon and easily suppressed. The threatened violence which the nullifiers had thundered for thirty years in the ears of the people had caused their threats to be considered as the harmless ebullitions of excited demagogues throughout the North, while at the South those utterances had so trained the Southern mind, and fired the Southern heart, as to cause them to be received as truthful. The South were, therefore, more united and earnest at this crisis, more determined on seceding, than either the Democrats or Republicans supposed. But, while the great body of the people and most of their leaders in the Northern States, listening to the ninety-day prophecies of Mr. Seward, were incredulous as to any extensive, serious disturbance, there were not a few whose forebodings were grave and sad. All the calamities which soon befell the country these men anticipated. Yet such as were in positions of responsibility would not permit themselves to despond, or despair of the Republic. Mr. Seward possessed a hopeful and buoyant spirit which did not fail him in that dark period, and at no time were his party feelings more decided than during the spring of 1861. Old Whig associates he clung to and strove to retain. All Democrats he distrusted, unless they became identified with the Republican Party. He had probably overestimated his own power and ability to allay the rising storm, and had not the personal influence he supposed. He had prophesied during the winter peace and harmony, within a very brief period after the change of administration was to be effected. These unfortunate prophecies, which became a matter of mirth with many of his friends and of ridicule among his opponents, were not entirely vain imaginings or without some foundation. In the confident belief that he could, if once in place and power, effect conciliation and peace, it had been an object with him to tide the difficulties past the 4th of March. He therefore had operated to that end, and so had Mr. Buchanan, though for different reasons.

Through Mr. Stanton, after that gentleman entered Mr. Buchanan's Cabinet, Mr. Seward and others were secretly advised in regard to the important measures of the Buchanan Administration, and in the course of the winter Mr. Seward came to an understanding, as was alleged and as events and circumstances indicated, with certain of the leading Secessionists. Among other things it was asserted that an agreement had been entered into that no assault should be made on Fort Sumter, provided the garrison should not be reinforced. Mr. Buchanan was to observe the status thus understood during the short remaining period of his administration, and Mr. Seward, as the coming premier, was, on the change of administration, to carry forward the policy of non-reinforcement of Sumter. If not supplied or reinforced, famine would certainly effect the downfall of the fortress without bloodshed on either side. Until blood was spilled, there was hope of conciliation. In fulfillment of this arrangement, Mr. Seward opposed any and every scheme to reinforce Sumter, and General Scott, who was old and much under his influence, if not a party to the understanding, seconded or took a leading part in that opposition.

On the 5th of March commissioners from the Rebel Government arrived in Washington and soon put themselves in communication with the Secretary of State, but the specific object which they had in view, and the negotiations or understanding between him and the parties were not immediately detailed to the Cabinet. They undoubtedly influenced the mind and course of Mr. Seward, who did not relinquish the hope of a peaceful adjustment of difficulties, and he in conversation continued to allure his friends with the belief that he should be able to effect a reconciliation.

In the many, almost daily, discussions which for a time were held in regard to Sumter, the opposition to forwarding supplies gathered strength. Commodore Stringham, as well as Commander Ward, on a final application which I made to him, by request of the President, and finally by the President himself, said he was compelled to advise against it. The time had gone by. It was too late. The military gentlemen had satisfied him it was impossible, that nothing could be gained by it, were the attempt made, that it would be attended with a useless sacrifice of blood and treasure, and he felt constrained to state his belief of the inability of the Navy to give relief.

Postmaster-General Blair, who had been a close and near observer of what had taken place through the winter and spring, took an opposite view from Mr. Seward and General Scott. To some extent he was aware of the understanding which Mr. Seward had with the members of Buchanan's Administration, or was suspicious of it, and his indignation that any idea of abandoning Sumter should be entertained or thought of was unbounded. With the exception of Mr. Seward, all his colleagues concurred with Mr. Blair at the commencement, but as the subject was discussed, and the impossibility and inutility of the scheme was urged, with assurance from the first military men in the country, whose advice was sought and given, that it was a military necessity to leave Sumter to its fate, the opinions of men changed, or they began at least to waver. Mr. Blair saw these misgivings, in which he did not at all participate, and finally, observing that the President, with the acquiescence of the Cabinet, was about adopting the Seward and Scott policy, he wrote his resignation, determined not to continue in the Cabinet if no attempt were made to relieve Fort Sumter. Before handing in his resignation, a delay was made at the request of his father. The elder Blair sought an interview with the President, to whom he entered his protest against non-action, which he denounced as the offspring of intrigue. His earnestness and indignation aroused and electrified the President; and when, in his zeal, Blair warned the President that the abandonment of Sumter would be justly considered by the people, by the world, by history, as treason to the country, he touched a chord that responded to his invocation. The President decided from that moment that an attempt should be made to convey supplies to Major Anderson, and that he would reinforce Sumter. This determination he communicated to the members of the Cabinet as he saw them, without a general announcement in Cabinet-meeting. The resolve inspired all the members with hope and courage, except Mr. Seward, who was evidently disappointed. He said it was of vastly more importance to turn our attention to Fort Pickens. I told him this had been done and how; that we had a considerable naval force there, almost the whole of the Home Squadron, and we had sent, a fortnight before, orders to land the troops under Captain Vogdes from the Brooklyn. He said that still more should, in his opinion, be done; that it was practicable to save Fort Pickens, but it was confessedly impossible to retain Sumter. One would be a waste of effort and energy and life, would extinguish all hope of peace, and compel the Government to take the initiative in hostile demonstrations, while the other would be an effective and peaceable movement. Although, as already mentioned, stated Cabinet-meetings were not then established, the members were in those early days of the Administration frequently together, and the President had every day more or less interviews with them, individually or collectively. The Secretary of State spent much of each day at the Executive Mansion and was vigilant to possess himself of every act, move, and intention of the President and of each of his associates. Perhaps there was an equal desire on their part to be informed of the proceedings of the Administration in full, but less was known of the transactions of the State Department than of any other.

# William H. Seward:
# Memorandum for the President

Seward's attempts to assume the dominant role in the administration culminated in this memorandum. As part of his recommendations for domestic policy, Seward advocated the defense and reinforcement of "all the Forts in the Gulf." By April 1, 1861, the federal government retained only three posts in the Gulf of Mexico: Fort Taylor on Key West, Fort Jefferson in the Dry Tortugas, and Fort Pickens on Santa Rosa Island at the entrance to Pensacola Bay, all of which would remain in Union hands throughout the war.

———————

SOME THOUGHTS for the President's consideration

April 1. 1861.

1st. We are at the end of a month's administration and yet without a policy either domestic or foreign.

2d This, however, is not culpable, and it has been unavoidable. The presence of the Senate, with the need to meet applications for patronage have prevented attention to other and more grave matters.

3d. But further delay to adopt and prosecute our policies for both domestic and foreign affairs would not only bring scandal on the Administration, but danger upon the country.

4th. To do this we must dismiss the applicants for office. But how? I suggest that we make the local appointments forthwith, leaving foreign or general ones for ulterior and occasional action.

5th. The policy—at home. I am aware that my views are singular, and perhaps not sufficiently explained. My system is built upon this *idea* as a ruling one, namely that we must

*Change the question before the Public from one upon Slavery, or about Slavery*

248

for a question upon *Union or Disunion*.

In other words, from what would be regarded as a Party question to one of *Patriotism* or *Union*

The occupation or evacuation of Fort Sumter, although not in fact a slavery, or a party question is so *regarded*. Witness, the temper manifested by the Republicans in the Free States, and even by Union men in the South.

I would therefore terminate it as a safe means for changing the issue. I deem it fortunate that the last Administration created the necessity.

For the rest. I would simultaneously defend and reinforce all the Forts in the Gulf, and have the Navy recalled from foreign stations to be prepared for a blockade. Put the Island of Key West under Martial Law

This will raise distinctly the question of *Union* or *Disunion*. I would maintain every fort and possession in the South.

For *Foreign Nations.*

I would demand explanations from *Spain* and France, categorically, at once.

I would seek explanations from Great Britain and Russia, and send agents into *Canada*, *Mexico* and *Central America*, to rouse a vigorous continental *spirit of independence* on this continent against European intervention.

And if satisfactory explanations are not received from Spain and France,

Would convene Congress and declare war against them

But whatever policy we adopt, there must be an energetic prosecution of it.

For this purpose it must be somebody's business to pursue and direct it incessantly.

Either the President must do it himself, and be all the while active in it; or

Devolve it on some member of his Cabinet. Once adopted, debates on it must end, and all agree and abide.

It is not in my especial province.

But I neither seek to evade nor assume responsibility

# Abraham Lincoln to William H. Seward

It is likely this letter was never sent and that Lincoln instead responded to Seward's memorandum in a private conversation.

---

Hon: W. H. Seward:    Executive Mansion April 1, 1861

My dear Sir: Since parting with you I have been considering your paper dated this day, and entitled "Some thoughts for the President's consideration." The first proposition in it is, "1st. We are at the end of a month's administration, and yet without a policy, either domestic or foreign."

At the *beginning* of that month, in the inaugeral, I said "The power confided to me will be used to hold, occupy and possess the property and places belonging to the government, and to collect the duties, and imposts." This had your distinct approval at the time; and, taken in connection with the order I immediately gave General Scott, directing him to employ every means in his power to strengthen and hold the forts, comprises the exact domestic policy you now urge, with the single exception, that it does not propose to abandon Fort Sumpter.

Again, I do not perceive how the re-inforcement of Fort Sumpter would be done on a slavery, or party issue, while that of Fort Pickens would be on a more national, and patriotic one.

The news received yesterday in regard to St. Domingo, certainly brings a new item within the range of our foreign policy; but up to that time we have been preparing circulars, and instructions to ministers, and the like, all in perfect harmony, without even a suggestion that we had no foreign policy.

Upon your closing propositions, that "whatever policy we adopt, there must be an energetic prossecution of it"

"For this purpose it must be somebody's business to pursue and direct it incessantly"

"Either the President must do it himself, and be all the while active in it, or"

"Devolve it on some member of his cabinet"

"Once adopted, debates on it must end, and all agree and abide" I remark that if this must be done, *I* must do it. When a general line of policy is adopted, I apprehend there is no danger of its being changed without good reason, or continuing to be a subject of unnecessary debate; still, upon points arising in its progress, I wish, and suppose I am entitled to have the advice of all the cabinet. Your Obt. Servt.     A. LINCOLN

# Mary Chesnut, Diary, April 7–15, 1861

On April 6 President Lincoln sent a message to the governor of South Carolina, informing him that an expedition would be sent to supply Fort Sumter "with provisions only; and that, if such attempt be not resisted, no effort to throw in men, arms, ammunition, will be made, without further notice, or in case of an attack on the fort." In response, Jefferson Davis and his cabinet ordered the fort captured before the relief expedition arrived. The outbreak of the war at Charleston was witnessed and later described by Mary Chesnut. Her husband, James Chesnut, helped draft the South Carolina ordinance of secession after leaving the U.S. Senate. A member of the Provisional Confederate Congress, James Chesnut served as an aide to General Pierre G. T. Beauregard during the siege of Fort Sumter. (Mary Chesnut kept a journal during the 1860s that she extensively revised and expanded between 1881 and 1884. Selections from her 1880s manuscript were published posthumously in 1905 as *A Diary from Dixie*, and in a new edition using the same title in 1949. The text presented in this volume is taken from *Mary Chesnut's Civil War* [1981], edited by C. Vann Woodward, which prints the text of the 1880s manuscript, but also includes significant passages from the 1860s journal that Chesnut omitted in her revised version.)

———————

*April 7, 1861.* Yesterday Mrs. Wigfall and I made a few visits. At the first house they wanted Mrs. Wigfall to settle a dispute. "Was she indeed fifty-five?" Fancy her face—more than ten years bestowed upon her so freely.

Then Mrs. Gibbes asked me if I had ever been in Charleston before.

Says Charlotte Wigfall (to pay me for my snigger when that false fifty was flung in her teeth), "And she thinks this is her native heath and her name is MacGregor."

She said it all came upon us for breaking the Sabbath, for indeed it was Sunday.

Allen Green came up to speak to me at dinner in all of his soldier's toggery. It sent a shiver through me.

Tried to read Margaret Fuller Ossoli. But could not.

The air is too full of war news. And we are all so restless. News so warlike I quake. My husband speaks of joining the artillery. . . . [     ] last night I find he is my all, and I would go mad without him. Mr. Manning read me a letter from his wife last night—very complimentary."

Went to see Miss Pinckney—one of the last of the 18th century Pinckneys. She inquired particularly about a portrait of her father, Charles Cotesworth Pinckney —which she said had been sent by him to my husband's grandfather. I gave a good account of it. It hangs in the place of honor in the drawing room at Mulberry. She wanted to see my husband, for "his grandfather, my father's friend, was one of the handsomest men of his day."

We came home, and soon Mr. Robert Gourdin and Mr. Miles called.

Governor Manning walked in, bowed gravely, and seated himself by me.

Again he bowed low, in mock heroic style and, with a grand wave of his hand, said, "Madame, your country is invaded."

When I had breath to speak, I asked, "What does he mean?"

"He means this. There are six men-of-war outside of the bar. Talbot and Chew have come to say that hostilities are to begin. Governor Pickens and Beauregard are holding a council of war."

Mr. Chesnut then came in. He confirmed the story.

Wigfall next entered in boisterous spirits. He said, "There was a sound of revelry by night, &c&c&c."

In any stir or confusion, my heart is apt to beat so painfully. Now the agony was so stifling—I could hardly see or hear. The men went off almost immediately. And I crept silently to my room, where I sat down to a good cry.

Mrs. Wigfall came in, and we had it out on the subject of civil war. We solaced ourselves with dwelling on all its known horrors, and then we added what we had a right to expect, with Yankees in front and negroes in the rear.

"The slave-owners must expect a servile insurrection, of course," said Mrs. Wigfall, to make sure that we were unhappy enough.

Suddenly loud shouting was heard. We ran out. Cannon

after cannon roared. We met Mrs. Allen Green in the passage-way, with blanched cheeks and streaming eyes.

Governor Means rushed out of his room in his dressing gown and begged us to be calm.

"Governor Pickens has ordered, in the plenitude of his wisdom, seven cannon to be fired as a signal to the Seventh Regiment. Anderson will hear as well as the Seventh Regiment. Now you go back and be quiet: fighting in the streets has not begun yet."

So we retired. Dr. Gibbes calls Mrs. Allen Green "Dame Placid." There was no placidity today. Cannons bursting and Allen on the island.

No sleep for anybody last night. The streets were alive with soldiers, men shouting, marching, singing.

Wigfall, the Stormy Petrel, in his glory. The only thoroughly happy person I see.

Today things seem to have settled down a little.

One can but hope still. Lincoln or Seward have made such silly advances and then far sillier drawings back. There may be a chance for peace, after all.

Things are happening so fast.

My husband has been made an aide-de-camp of General Beauregard.

Three hours ago we were quietly packing to go home. The convention has adjourned.

Now he tells me the attack upon Fort Sumter may begin tonight. Depends upon Anderson and the fleet outside. The *Herald* says that this show of war outside of the bar is intended for Texas.

John Manning came in with his sword and red sash. Pleased as a boy to be on Beauregard's staff while the row goes on. He has gone with Wigfall to Captain Hartstene with instructions.

Mr. Chesnut is finishing a report he had to make to the convention.

Mrs. Hayne called. She had, she said, "but one feeling, pity for those who are not here."

Jack Preston, Willie Alston—"the take-life-easys," as they are called—with John Green, "the big brave," have gone down to the island—volunteered as privates.

Seven hundred men were sent over. Ammunition wagons rumbling along the streets all night. Anderson burning blue lights—signs and signals for the fleet outside, I suppose.

Today at dinner there was no allusion to things as they stand in Charleston Harbor. There was an undercurrent of intense excitement. There could not have been a more brilliant circle. In addition to our usual quartet (Judge Withers, Langdon Cheves, and Trescot) our two governors dined with us, Means and Manning.

These men all talked so delightfully. For once in my life I listened.

That over, business began. In earnest, Governor Means rummaged a sword and red sash from somewhere and brought it for Colonel Chesnut, who has gone to demand the surrender of Fort Sumter.

---

And now, patience—we must wait.

---

Why did that green goose Anderson go into Fort Sumter? Then everything began to go wrong.

Now they have intercepted a letter from him, urging them to let him surrender. He paints the horrors likely to ensue if they will not.

He ought to have thought of all that before he put his head in the hole.

*April 12, 1861.*    Anderson will not capitulate.

---

Yesterday was the merriest, maddest dinner we have had yet. Men were more audaciously wise and witty. We had an unspoken foreboding it was to be our last pleasant meeting. Mr. Miles dined with us today. Mrs. Henry King rushed in: "The news, I come for the latest news—all of the men of the King family are on the island"—of which fact she seemed proud.

While she was here, our peace negotiator—or envoy—came in. That is, Mr. Chestnut returned—his interview with

Colonel Anderson had been deeply interesting—but was not inclined to be communicative, wanted his dinner. Felt for Anderson. Had telegraphed to President Davis for instructions.

What answer to give Anderson, &c&c. He has gone back to Fort Sumter, with additional instructions.

When they were about to leave the wharf, A. H. Boykin sprang into the boat, in great excitement; thought himself ill-used. A likelihood of fighting—and he to be left behind!

———————

I do not pretend to go to sleep. How can I? If Anderson does not accept terms—at four—the orders are—he shall be fired upon.

I count four—St. Michael chimes. I begin to hope. At half-past four, the heavy booming of a cannon.

I sprang out of bed. And on my knees—prostrate—I prayed as I never prayed before.

There was a sound of stir all over the house—pattering of feet in the corridor—all seemed hurrying one way. I put on my double gown and a shawl and went, too. It was to the housetop.

The shells were bursting. In the dark I heard a man say "waste of ammunition."

I knew my husband was rowing about in a boat somewhere in that dark bay. And that the shells were roofing it over—bursting toward the fort. If Anderson was obstinate—he was to order the forts on our side to open fire. Certainly fire had begun. The regular roar of the cannon—there it was. And who could tell what each volley accomplished of death and destruction.

The women were wild, there on the housetop. Prayers from the women and imprecations from the men, and then a shell would light up the scene. Tonight, they say, the forces are to attempt to land.

The *Harriet Lane* had her wheelhouse smashed and put back to sea.

———————

We watched up there—everybody wondered. Fort Sumter did not fire a shot.

Today Miles and Manning, colonels now—aides to Beauregard—dined with us. The latter hoped I would keep the peace. I give him only good words, for he was to be under fire all day and night, in the bay carrying orders, &c.

Last night—or this morning truly—up on the housetop I was so weak and weary I sat down on something that looked like a black stool.

"Get up, you foolish woman—your dress is on fire," cried a man. And he put me out. It was a chimney, and the sparks caught my clothes. Susan Preston and Mr. Venable then came up. But my fire had been extinguished before it broke out into a regular blaze.

Do you know, after all that noise and our tears and prayers, nobody has been hurt. Sound and fury, signifying nothing. A delusion and a snare.

Louisa Hamilton comes here now. This is a sort of news center. Jack Hamilton, her handsome young husband, has all the credit of a famous battery which is made of RR iron. Mr. Petigru calls it the boomerang because it throws the balls back the way they came—so Lou Hamilton tells us. She had no children during her first marriage. Hence the value of this lately achieved baby. To divert Louisa from the glories of "the battery," of which she raves, we asked if the baby could talk yet.

"No—not exactly—but he imitates the big gun. When he hears that, he claps his hands and cries 'Boom boom.'" Her mind is distinctly occupied by three things—Lieutenant Hamilton, whom she calls Randolph, the baby, and "the big gun"—and it refuses to hold more.

Pryor of Virginia spoke from the piazza of the Charleston Hotel.

I asked what he said, irreverent woman. "Oh, they all say the same thing, but he made great play with that long hair of his, which he is always tossing aside."

———————

Somebody came in just now and reported Colonel Chesnut asleep on the sofa in General Beauregard's room. After two such nights he must be so tired as to be able to sleep anywhere.

———————

Just bade farewell to Langdon Cheves. He is forced to go home, to leave this interesting place. Says he feels like the man who was not killed at Thermopylae. I think he said that unfortunate had to hang himself when he got home for very shame. Maybe fell on his sword, which was a strictly classic way of ending matters.

———————

I do not wonder at Louisa Hamilton's baby. We hear nothing, can listen to nothing. Boom, boom, goes the cannon—all the time. The nervous strain is awful, alone in this darkened room.

"Richmond and Washington ablaze," say the papers. Blazing with excitement. Why not? To us these last days' events seem frightfully great.

We were all in that iron balcony. Women—men we only see at a distance now. Stark Means, marching under the piazza at the head of his regiment, held his cap in his hand all the time he was in sight.

Mrs. Means leaning over, looking with tearful eyes.

"Why did he take his hat off?" said an unknown creature. Mrs. Means stood straight up.

"He did that in honor of his mother—he saw me." She is a proud mother—and at the same time most unhappy. Her lovely daughter Emma is dying in there, before her eyes—consumption. At that moment I am sure Mrs. Means had a spasm of the heart. At least, she looked as I feel sometimes. She took my arm, and we came in.

———————

*April 13, 1861.*   Nobody hurt, after all. How gay we were last night.

Reaction after the dread of all the slaughter we thought those dreadful cannons were making such a noise in doing.

Not even a battery the worse for wear.

Fort Sumter has been on fire. He has not yet silenced any of our guns. So the aides—still with swords and red sashes by way of uniform—tell us.

But the sound of those guns makes regular meals impossible. None of us go to table. But tea trays pervade the corridors, going everywhere.

Some of the anxious hearts lie on their beds and moan in solitary misery. Mrs. Wigfall and I solace ourselves with tea in my room.

These women have all a satisfying faith. "God is on our side," they cry. When we are shut in, we (Mrs. Wigfall and I) ask, "Why?" We are told: "Of course He hates the Yankees."

"You'll think that well of Him."

Not by one word or look can we detect any change in the demeanor of these negro servants. Laurence sits at our door, as sleepy and as respectful and as profoundly indifferent. So are they all. They carry it too far. You could not tell that they hear even the awful row that is going on in the bay, though it is dinning in their ears night and day. And people talk before them as if they were chairs and tables. And they make no sign. Are they stolidly stupid or wiser than we are, silent and strong, biding their time?

So tea and toast come. Also came Colonel Manning, A.D.C. —red sash and sword— to announce that he has been under fire and didn't mind. He said gaily, "It is one of those things— a fellow never knows how he will come out of it until he is tried. Now I know. I am a worthy descendant of my old Irish hero of an ancestor who held the British officer before him as a shield in the Revolution. And backed out of danger gracefully." Everybody laughs at John Manning's brag. We talked of *St. Valentine's Eve; or, The Maid of Perth* and the drop of the white doe's blood that sometimes spoiled all.

---

The war steamers are still there, outside the bar. And there were people who thought the Charleston bar "no good" to

Charleston. The bar is our silent partner, sleeping partner, and yet in this fray he is doing us yeoman service.

*April 15, 1861.*   I did not know that one could live such days of excitement.

They called, "Come out—there is a crowd coming."

A mob indeed, but it was headed by Colonels Chesnut and Manning.

The crowd was shouting and showing these two as messengers of good news. They were escorted to Beauregard's headquarters. Fort Sumter had surrendered.

Those up on the housetop shouted to us, "The fort is on fire." That had been the story once or twice before.

---

When we had calmed down, Colonel Chesnut, who had taken it all quietly enough—if anything, more unruffled than usual in his serenity—told us how the surrender came about.

Wigfall was with them on Morris Island when he saw the fire in the fort, jumped in a little boat and, with his handkerchief as a white flag, rowed over to Fort Sumter. Wigfall went in through a porthole.

When Colonel Chesnut arrived shortly after and was received by the regular entrance, Colonel Anderson told him he had need to pick his way warily, for it was all mined.

As far as I can make out, the fort surrendered to Wigfall.

But it is all confusion. Our flag is flying there. Fire engines have been sent to put out the fire.

Everybody tells you half of something and then rushes off to tell something else or to hear the last news. Manning, Wigfall, John Preston, &c, men without limit, beset us at night.

In the afternoon, Mrs. Preston, Mrs. Joe Heyward, and I drove round the Battery. We were in an open carriage. What a changed scene. The very liveliest crowd I think I ever saw. Everybody talking at once. All glasses still turned on the grim old fort.

## *Abner Doubleday: from* Reminiscences of Forts Sumter and Moultrie in 1860–'61

In his 1876 memoir, Abner Doubleday described the bombardment of Fort Sumter and the negotiations leading to its surrender on April 14, 1861.

---

As soon as the outline of our fort could be distinguished, the enemy carried out their programme. It had been arranged, as a special compliment to the venerable Edmund Ruffin, who might almost be called the father of secession, that he should fire the first shot against us, from the Stevens battery on Cummings Point, and I think in all the histories it is stated that he did so; but it is attested by Dr. Crawford and others who were on the parapet at the time, that the first shot really came from the mortar battery at Fort Johnson.* Almost immediately afterward a ball from Cummings Point lodged in the magazine wall, and by the sound seemed to bury itself in the masonry about a foot from my head, in very unpleasant proximity to my right ear. This is the one that probably came with Mr. Ruffin's compliments. In a moment the firing burst forth in one continuous roar, and large patches of both the exterior and interior masonry began to crumble and fall in all directions. The place where I was had been used for the manufacture of cartridges, and there was still a good deal of powder there, some packed and some loose. A shell soon struck near the ventilator, and a puff of dense smoke entered the room, giving me a strong impression that there would be an immediate explosion. Fortunately, no sparks had penetrated inside.

Nineteen batteries were now hammering at us, and the balls

---

*I have since learned that the shell from Fort Johnson was not a hostile shot, but was simply intended as a signal for the firing to commence.

and shells from the ten-inch columbiads, accompanied by shells from the thirteen-inch mortars which constantly bombarded us, made us feel as if the war had commenced in earnest.

When it was broad daylight, I went down to breakfast. I found the officers already assembled at one of the long tables in the mess-hall. Our party were calm, and even somewhat merry. We had retained one colored man to wait on us. He was a spruce-looking mulatto from Charleston, very active and efficient on ordinary occasions, but now completely demoralized by the thunder of the guns and crashing of the shot around us. He leaned back against the wall, almost white with fear, his eyes closed, and his whole expression one of perfect despair.* Our meal was not very sumptuous. It consisted of pork and water, but Dr. Crawford triumphantly brought forth a little farina, which he had found in a corner of the hospital.

When this frugal repast was over, my company was told off in three details for firing purposes, to be relieved afterward by Seymour's company. As I was the ranking officer, I took the first detachment, and marched them to the casemates, which looked out upon the powerful iron-clad battery of Cummings Point.

In aiming the first gun fired against the rebellion I had no feeling of self-reproach, for I fully believed that the contest was inevitable, and was not of our seeking. The United States was called upon not only to defend its sovereignty, but its right to exist as a nation. The only alternative was to submit to a powerful oligarchy who were determined to make freedom forever subordinate to slavery. To me it was simply a contest, politically speaking, as to whether virtue or vice should rule.

My first shot bounded off from the sloping roof of the battery opposite without producing any apparent effect. It seemed useless to attempt to silence the guns there; for our metal was not heavy enough to batter the work down, and every ball glanced harmlessly off, except one, which appeared

---

*In this he was an exception to most negroes. Those I have seen in the colored regiments in Texas have shown themselves to be among the best and most reliable men in the service for operations against the Indians. It was a line of negroes that charged over the torpedoes at Mobile.

to enter an embrasure and twist the iron shutter, so as to stop the firing of that particular gun.

I observed that a group of the enemy had ventured out from their intrenchments to watch the effect of their fire, but I sent them flying back to their shelter by the aid of a forty-two-pounder ball, which appeared to strike right in among them.

---

The firing continued all day, without any special incident of importance, and without our making much impression on the enemy's works. They had a great advantage over us, as their fire was concentrated on the fort, which was in the centre of the circle, while ours was diffused over the circumference. Their missiles were exceedingly destructive to the upper exposed portion of the work, but no essential injury was done to the lower casemates which sheltered us.

Some of these shells, however, set the officers' quarters on fire three times; but the flames were promptly extinguished once or twice through the exertions of Peter Hart, whose activity and gallantry were very conspicuous.

The night was an anxious one for us, for we thought it probable that the launches, filled with armed men from the fleet, might take advantage of the darkness to come in with provisions and supplies. Then, too, it was possible that the enemy might attempt a night attack. We were on the alert, therefore, with men stationed at all the embrasures; but nothing unusual occurred. The batteries fired upon us at stated intervals all night long. We did not return the fire, having no ammunition to waste.

On the morning of the 13th, we took our breakfast—or, rather, our pork and water—at the usual hour, and marched the men to the guns when the meal was over.

From 4 to 6 1/2 A.M. the enemy's fire was very spirited. From 7 to 8 A.M. a rain-storm came on, and there was a lull in the cannonading. About 8 A.M. the officers' quarters were ignited by one of Ripley's incendiary shells, or by shot heated in the furnaces at Fort Moultrie. The fire was put out; but at 10 A.M. a mortar shell passed through the roof, and lodged in the flooring of the second story, where it burst, and started the flames afresh. This, too, was extinguished; but the hot shot soon followed each other so rapidly that it was impossible for us to contend with them any longer. It became evident that the entire block, being built with wooden partitions, floors, and roofing, must be consumed, and that the magazine, containing three hundred barrels of powder, would be endangered; for, even after closing the metallic door, sparks might penetrate through the ventilator. The floor was covered with loose powder, where a detail of men had been at work manufacturing cartridge-bags out of old shirts, woolen blankets, etc.

While the officers exerted themselves with axes to tear down and cut away all the wood-work in the vicinity, the soldiers were rolling barrels of powder out to more sheltered spots, and were covering them with wet blankets. The labor was accelerated by the shells which were bursting around us; for Ripley had redoubled his activity at the first signs of a conflagration. We only succeeded in getting out some ninety-six barrels of powder, and then we were obliged to close the massive copper door, and await the result. A shot soon after passed through the intervening shield, struck the door, and bent the lock in such a way that it could not be opened again. We were thus cut off from our supply of ammunition, but still had some piled up in the vicinity of the guns. Anderson officially reported only four barrels and three cartridges as on hand when we left.

By 11 A.M. the conflagration was terrible and disastrous. One-fifth of the fort was on fire, and the wind drove the smoke in dense masses into the angle where we had all taken refuge. It seemed impossible to escape suffocation. Some lay down close to the ground, with handkerchiefs over their mouths, and others posted themselves near the embrasures, where the smoke was somewhat lessened by the draught of air. Every one suffered severely. I crawled out of one of these openings, and sat on the outer edge; but Ripley made it lively for me there with his case-shot, which spattered all around. Had not a slight change of wind taken place, the result might have been fatal to most of us.

Our firing having ceased, and the enemy being very jubilant, I thought it would be as well to show them that we were not all dead yet, and ordered the gunners to fire a few rounds more. I heard afterward that the enemy loudly cheered Anderson for his persistency under such adverse circumstances.

The scene at this time was really terrific. The roaring and crackling of the flames, the dense masses of whirling smoke, the bursting of the enemy's shells, and our own which were exploding in the burning rooms, the crashing of the shot, and the sound of masonry falling in every direction, made the fort a pandemonium. When at last nothing was left of the building but the blackened walls and smoldering embers, it became painfully evident that an immense amount of damage had been done. There was a tower at each angle of the fort. One of these, containing great quantities of shells, upon which we had relied, was almost completely shattered by successive explosions. The massive wooden gates, studded with iron nails, were burned, and the wall built behind them was now a mere heap of débris, so that the main entrance was wide open for an assaulting party. The sally-ports were in a similar condition, and the numerous windows on the gorge side, which had been planked up, had now become all open entrances.

About 12.48 P.M. the end of the flag-staff was shot down, and the flag fell.* It had been previously hanging by one halliard, the other having been cut by a piece of shell. The exultation of the enemy, however, was short-lived. Peter Hart found a spar in the fort, which answered very well as a temporary flag-staff. He nailed the flag to this, and raised it triumphantly by nailing and tying the pole firmly to a pile of gun-carriages on the parapet. This was gallantly done, without undue haste, under Seymour's supervision, although the enemy concentrated all their fire upon the spot to prevent Hart from carrying out his intention. From the beginning, the rebel gunners had been very ambitious to shoot the flag down, and had wasted an immense number of shots in the attempt.

---

About 2 P.M., Senator Wigfall, in company with W. Gourdin Young, of Charleston, unexpectedly made his appearance at one of the embrasures, having crossed over from Morris Island in a small boat, rowed by negroes. He had seen the flag come down, and supposed that we had surrendered in consequence

*It is claimed that this shot was fired by Lieutenant W. C. Preston, of South Carolina.

of the burning of the quarters. This visit was sanctioned by the commander of Morris Island, Brigadier-general James W. Simons. An artillery-man, serving his gun, was very much astonished to see a man's face at the entrance, and asked him what he was doing there. Wigfall replied that he wished to see Major Anderson. The man, however, refused to allow him to enter until he had surrendered himself as a prisoner, and given up his sword. This done, another artillery-man was sent to bring an officer. Lieutenant Davis came almost immediately, but it took some time to find Anderson, who was out examining the condition of the main gates. I was not present during this scene, or at the interview that ensued, as I was engaged in trying to save some shells in the upper story from the effects of the fire. Wigfall, in Beauregard's name, offered Anderson his own terms, which were, the evacuation of the fort, with permission to salute our flag, and to march out with the honors of war, with our arms and private baggage, leaving all other war material behind. As soon as this matter was arranged, Wigfall returned to Cummings Point.

In the mean time, Beauregard having noticed the white flag, sent a boat containing Colonel James Chestnut, and Captain Lee, Colonel Roger A. Pryor, and Colonel William Porcher Miles, to ascertain the meaning of the signal. A second boat soon followed, containing Major D. K. Jones, who was Beauregard's adjutant-general, Ex-Governor J. L. Manning, and Colonel Charles Alston.

Miles and Pryor were exceedingly astonished when they heard that Wigfall had been carrying on negotiations in Beauregard's name, and stated that, to their certain knowledge, he had had no communication with Beauregard. They spoke of the matter with great delicacy, for Wigfall was a parlous man, and quick to settle disputed points with the pistol. Anderson replied with spirit that, under the circumstances, he would run up his flag again, and resume the firing. They begged him, however, not to take action until they had had an opportunity to lay the whole subject before General Beauregard; and Anderson agreed to wait a reasonable time for that purpose. The boat then returned to the city. In due time another boat arrived, containing Colonels Chestnut and Chisholm, and Captain Stephen D. Lee, all aids of Beauregard. They came to notify Major Anderson that the latter was willing to treat with him on the basis proposed. Colonel Charles Alston soon came over with Major Jones (who was chief-of-staff to Beauregard, and adjutant-general of the Provisional Army), to settle the details of the evacuation. There was some difficulty about permitting us to salute our flag; but that, too, was finally conceded. In case we held out for another day, the rebels had made arrangements to storm the fort that night.

All of the preliminaries having been duly adjusted, it was decided that the evacuation should take place the next morning. Our arrangements were few and simple, but the rebels made extensive preparations for the event, in order to give it the greatest *éclat*, and gain from it as much prestige as possible. The population of the surrounding country poured into Charleston in vast multitudes, to witness the humiliation of the United States flag. We slept soundly that night for the first time, after all the fatigue and excitement of the two preceding days.

The next morning, Sunday, the 14th, we were up early, packing our baggage in readiness to go on board the transport. The time having arrived, I made preparations, by order of Major Anderson, to fire a national salute to the flag. It was a dangerous thing to attempt, as sparks of fire were floating around everywhere, and there was no safe place to deposit the ammunition. In that portion of the line commanded by Lieutenant Hall, a pile of cartridges lay under the muzzle of one of the guns. Some fire had probably lodged inside the piece, which the sponging did not extinguish, for, in loading it, it went off prematurely, and blew off the right arm of the gunner, Daniel Hough, who was an excellent soldier. His death was almost instantaneous. He was the first man who lost his life on our side in the war for the Union. The damage did not end here, for some of the fire from the muzzle dropped on the pile of cartridges below, and exploded them all. Several men in the vicinity were blown into the air, and seriously injured. Their names were George Fielding, John Irwin, George Pinchard, and Edwin Galway, and, I think, James Hayes. The first-named being very badly hurt, was left behind, to be cared for by the rebels.

He was sent over to Charleston, where he was well treated, finally cured, and forwarded to us without being exchanged.

The salute being over, the Confederate troops marched in to occupy the fort. The Palmetto Guard, Captain Cuthbert's company, detailed by Colonel De Saussure, and Captain Hollinquist's Company B, of the regulars, detailed by Colonel Ripley, constituted the new garrison under Ripley.* Anderson directed me to form the men on the parade-ground, assume command, and march them on board the transport. I told him I should prefer to leave the fort with the flag flying, and the drums beating Yankee Doodle, and he authorized me to do so. As soon as our tattered flag came down, and the silken banner made by the ladies of Charleston was run up, tremendous shouts of applause were heard from the vast multitude of spectators; and all the vessels and steamers, with one accord, made for the fort. Corporal Bringhurst came running to tell me that many of the approaching crowd were shouting my name, and making threatening demonstrations. The disorder, however, was immediately quelled by the appearance of Hartstein, an ex-officer of our navy, who threw out sentinels in all directions, and prevented the mob from landing.

*Edmund Ruffin entered the fort as a volunteer ensign of the Palmetto Guard; Captain Samuel Ferguson received the keys of Fort Sumter, and raised the Confederate flag over the ramparts; Lieutenant-colonel F. J. Moses raised the State flag. Moses has since figured as the Republican governor of South Carolina.

# George Templeton Strong:
# Diary, April 13–16, 1861

On April 15, the day after Fort Sumter surrendered, President Lincoln issued a proclamation calling forth 75,000 militia and summoning Congress to meet on July 4 in special session. George Templeton Strong recorded the reaction in New York City to the beginning of hostilities.

---

*April 13.*    Here begins a new chapter of my journal, entitled WAR—EXSURGAT DEUS *et dissipentere inimici ejus, et fugerunt qui oderunt eum a facie ejus. Amen!*

This morning's papers confirmed last night's news; viz., that the rebels opened fire at Sumter yesterday morning. During the day came successive despatches, *all one way*, of course, for the Charleston telegraphs are under Charleston control, and in addition to the local taste for brag and lying, there are obvious motives for a high-colored picture of damage done the fort. It tends to prevent reinforcement by any supplementary expedition that might be extemporized if the parties appeared to be at all equally matched.

In substance, the despatches say that firing ceased at six P.M. yesterday, but shells continued to be thrown into the fort all night at intervals of twenty minutes. Cannonade resumed this morning with brilliant success. The fort on fire. "Flames bursting from the embrasures." Raft outside and men passing up water. Great havoc among them. Two explosions in the fort. Major Anderson "believed to be gradually (!) blowing it up." Nobody hurt in the rebel batteries. No impression made on that formidable battle-scow "the Floating Battery." Major Anderson has ceased firing. Then came a fourth edition of the *Evening Post*, with a despatch that he has surrendered. This was while I was at the New York Club. On coming home, I find Ellie in possession of a still later *Herald* extra. The ships are engaged with the batteries; (this we had earlier). Two are sunk. The rest are shelling the city, which is on fire. I take this last item to be invented for the sake of stimulating wrath and fury in the Border States.

To shell Charleston, the ships must have worked their way into the harbor and passed Sumter. If so, they must have silenced the batteries and been able to throw supplies into the fort, which is hardly to be hoped. Had they done so, the object of the expedition would have been accomplished. And I doubt whether they would have fired on the city under any circumstances. But that damnable little hornet's nest of treason deserves to be shelled. It's a political Sodom. . . .

So Civil War is inaugurated at last. God defend the Right.

The Northern backbone is much stiffened already. Many who stood up for "Southern rights" and complained of wrongs done the South now say that, since the South has fired the first gun, they are ready to go all lengths in supporting the government. The New York *Herald* is noncommittal this morning. It may well be upholding the Administration and denouncing the Democratic party within a week. It takes naturally to eating dirt and its own words (the same thing). Would I were in Sumter tonight, even with the chance of being forced to surrender (seventy men against seven thousand) and of being lynched thereafter by the Chivalry of Charleston. The seventy will be as memorable as the "four hundred" of the Light Brigade at Balaklava, whatever be their fate.

It is said the President will assume the right to call for volunteers, whether the law give it or not. If he does, there will soon be a new element in the fray; viz., the stern anti-slavery Puritanism that survives in New England and in the Northwest. Ossawattomie John Brown would be worth his weight in gold just now. What a pity he precipitated matters and got himself prematurely hanged!

*April 14*, SUNDAY. Fine day. Morning *Herald* announces *Surrender of Fort Sumter* and great jubilation in Charleston. To Trinity Church with Ellie and Miss Rosalie and Johnny. On our way back, I made a detour to the *Tribune* office. The whole story discredited there. Lots of private despatches quoted, inconsistent with surrender, and tending to show there had been no serious fight.

Mr. Ruggles dined with us. This evening Dr. Rae and his pretty wife were here by appointment, with their two young friends from England. . . . There is no doubt that Fort Sumter has surrendered. Despatches received by Mrs. Anderson, Cottenet, and others settle that point. But no reliable details of the transactions have reached us. If it be true, as Charleston telegrams assert, that after forty hours' firing "no one is hurt," *Punch* and the *Charivari* have an inviting topic for jokes at our expense. . . .

From all I can learn, the effect of this on Democrats, heretofore Southern and quasi-treasonable in their talk, has fully justified the sacrifice. I hear of F. B. Cutting and Walter Cutting, Hewitt, Lewis Rutherfurd, Judge Vanderpoel, and others of that type denouncing rebellion and declaring themselves ready to go all lengths in upholding government. If this class of men has been secured and converted to loyalty, the gain to the country is worth ten Sumters. CAM, heretofore strongly Southern in his talk, was declaring his readiness this evening to shoulder a musket in defence of Washington. That is the next point to be thought of. "He is the true Pope who lives in the Vatican." It must be defended at any cost.

At Trinity Church today, Vinton read the prayer, "In time of war and tumults," and the Amen of the white-robed choir boys was emphasized by a suggestive trumpet-stop coloring from the organ.

*April 15.* Events multiply. The President is out with a proclamation calling for 75,000 volunteers and an extra session of Congress July 4. It is said 200,000 more will be called within a few days. Every man of them will be wanted before this game is lost and won. Change in public feeling marked, and a thing to thank God for. We begin to look like a United North. Willy Duncan (!) says it may be necessary to hang Lincoln and Seward and Greeley hereafter, but our present duty is to sustain Government and Law, and give the South a lesson. The New York *Herald* is *in equilibrio* today, just at the turning point. Tomorrow it will denounce Jefferson Davis as it denounced Lincoln a week ago. The *Express* is half traitorous and half in favor of energetic action against traitors. The *Journal of Commerce* and the little *Day-Book* show no signs of reformation yet, but though they are contemptible and without material influence for evil, the growing excitement against their treasonable talk will soon make them more cautious in its utterance. The *Herald* office has already been threatened with an attack.

Mayor Wood out with a "proclamation." He must still be talking. It is brief and commonplace, but winds up with a recommendation to everybody to obey the laws of the land. This is significant. The cunning scoundrel sees which way the cat is jumping and puts himself right on the record in a vague general way, giving the least possible offence to his allies of the Southern Democracy. The *Courier* of this morning devotes its leading article to a ferocious assault on Major Anderson as a traitor beyond Twiggs, and declares that he has been in collusion with the Charleston people all the time. This is wrong and bad. It is premature, at least. . . .

Expedition to Governor's Island this morning; Ellie and I, Charley Strong and wife, Dan Messenger, Christie, Miss Kate Fearing, Tom Meyer, and one or two more. Officer of the day was Lieutenant Webb of Maine, whose guests we were. He treated us most hospitably, and had out the band, playing an hour or two for our delectation. Its programme included that jolliest of tunes, "Dixie Land," and "Hail Columbia." We took off our hats while the latter was played. Everybody's patriotism is rampant and demonstrative now. About three hundred recruits on the Island, mostly quite raw. I discoursed with one of them, an honest-looking, simple-minded boy from somewhere near Rochester, probably some small farmer's son. "He had voted for Abe Lincoln, and as there was going to be trouble, he might as well *fight* for Abe Lincoln," so he enlisted two weeks ago. "Guessed they were going to get some hard knocks when they went down South, but then he had always kind o' wanted to see the world—that was one reason why he 'listed."

Great activity on the Island. Guns and all manner of warlike munitions and apparatus are being shipped, generally for Pensacola.

*April 16.* A fine storm of wind and rain all day. The conversion of the New York *Herald* is complete. It rejoices that rebellion is to be put down and is delighted with Civil War, because it will so stimulate the business of New York, and all this is what "we" (the *Herald*, to wit) have been vainly preaching for months. This impudence of old J. G. Bennett's is too vast to be appreciated at once. You must look at it and meditate over it for some time (as at Niagara and St. Peter's) before you can take in its immensity. His capitulation is a set-off against the loss of Sumter. He's a discreditable ally for the North, but when you see a rat leaving the enemy's ship for your own, you overlook the offensiveness of the vermin for the sake of what its movement indicates. This brazen old scoundrel was hooted up Fulton Street yesterday afternoon by a mob, and the police interfered to prevent it from sacking his printing office. Though converted, one can hardly call him penitent. St. Paul did not call himself the Chief of the Apostles and brag of having been a Christian from the first.

This and other papers say the new war policy will strangle secession in the Border States. But it seems to me that every indication from Virginia, North Carolina, and elsewhere points the other way. No news from Slave-ownia today, but most gladdening reports from North, West, and East of unanimity and resolution and earnestness. We are aroused at last, and I trust we shall not soon relapse into apathy. Ellie indisposed again. I begin to be seriously uneasy about the constantly recurring attacks of slight illness—headache and the like—that have visited her of late.

Trinity Church Vestry tonight; special meeting on St. George's Chapel and a very long debate. The appropriation required is large ($6,000 per annum, at least), and in moving it, I premised that the whole question turned on the ability of the vestry to spend that sum. If they have it to spare, the Chapel can be maintained, otherwise not; and a smaller appropriation just keeping up the establishment in its present dead-alive condition would do no good and be simply throwing away so much money, besides bringing a certain amount of discredit on Trinity Church. A smaller appropriation was moved as a substitute and carried by a large majority, Swift and I voting in the negative, with three or four others. . . .

Thence to New York Club. Our talk was of war. Subscribed to a fund for equipment of the Twelfth Regiment and put down my name for a projected Rifle Corps, but I fear my nearsightedness is a grave objection to my adopting that arm. I hear that Major Burnside has surrendered his treasurership of the Illinois Central Railroad and posted down to Rhode Island to assume command of volunteers from that state. Telegram that 2,500 Massachusetts volunteers are quartered in Faneuil Hall, awaiting orders.

GOD SAVE THE UNION, AND CONFOUND ITS ENEMIES. AMEN.

# The New York Times:
# The People and the Issue

April 15, 1861

A former assistant to Horace Greeley, Henry Raymond founded *The New York Times* in 1851. Originally a Free Soil Whig, Raymond became a Republican, and had supported Lincoln in the 1860 election.

———————

THE REVERBERATIONS from Charleston harbor have brought about what months of logic would have been impotent to effect—the rapid condensation of public sentiment in the Free States. The North is now a unit. Party lines have shriveled, as landmarks disappear before the outpouring of volcanic lava. The crucial test of this is New York City—the spot most tainted by the Southern poison. Not the thick insulation which the commercial spirit puts between the conscience and duty—not the obliquity engendered by long years of the most perverse political education—have been able to withstand the electric fire of loyal indignation evoked by the assassin-stroke aimed at the heart of the Republic. There are now no such ardent supporters of the Government as those who have been life-long Democrats. It is a fact full of omen, and one which persons imperfectly acquainted with the impulses that lie at the bottom of the popular heart could never have anticipated, that the very roughs of the City are aroused, and bring their passionate devotion to the cause of their country. One intense, inspiring sentiment of patriotism has fused all other passions in its fiery heat. Let the Administration now know that twenty millions of loyal freemen approve its act, and imperiously demand the vindication of the integrity and majesty of the Republic.

Viewed in the light of these events, the lull that for so many weeks reigned in the public spirit becomes very intelligible. A suspense—a long, dumb, unconscious waiting, very pathetic in its character—held the people's mind. Treason so vile paralyzed thought and will. The way was not clear what to do. It could not at first be believed that the country really held men so insane, so suicidal, as to attempt to transform such threats as theirs into deeds. The sheer demonism which marked the programme of social construction put forth by the Slave Power, caused it rather to assume the aspect of a terrific species of irony. And then, when the designs of the rebels became only too apparent, and it was evident that naught but the exercise of sovereign Might could avail to check those frenzied men, there was honest hesitancy in resorting to the force of arms. Civil war runs counter to the theory of the Republic. The framers of our Government made such provisions as would forever render rebellion unnecessary. All experience has shown how easily this Government can be induced to change its rulers, if any good reason for doing so was presented, and earnestly and persistently forced upon public opinion. Besides this, there was a doubt in many minds as to the degree to which the theory of Democracy allowed of opposition to the avowed and deliberate will of sovereign States. On the whole, it presented itself as a painful, perplexing problem. That problem has at length been solved by the public conscience, and the solution sweeps away forever the sophistries as to State Rights and coercion which entangled the subject. The lull is over—and an equinoctial storm of popular indignation has ensued.

In entering upon this struggle, the great community of Free States does so, prepared to bring to bear on the vindication of its national honor inexhaustible material resources. Her census shows returns which, under other circumstances, would have been the wonder of the world. It has, indeed, been industriously declared by timid croakers that "war is national ruin." There is no more absurd chimera. The Free States are richer and more populous than England was under PITT, when she fought the long fight with NAPOLEON, and vastly stronger than France when she battled triumphantly against all the Continental powers.

As to moral force, it panoplies the Republic as with a wall of fire. She enters the contest with that triple arming which justice gives to a cause. The moral conscience of the world is on her side. It is true that the rebels, lured by the support of that European element whose sympathies are contingent with the rate of duties levied on imported goods by the United States, have hoped for the recognition of the European Powers. That delusion is doomed to be rudely dispelled. The rulers of England and France do not dare to recognize that League. The unmaking of Ministries would hang on the decision, and they know it.

The Administration is not brought face to face with a *Revolution*. This is not the attitude. It has to deal with a plot, a conspiracy. There will be no "fraternal blood" shed, unless it be the blood of men who are willfully and persistently in the position of traitors. The right of revolution is not denied;—changes, prompted by causes material or moral, and effected through legal and constitutional means, are contemplated with calmness. But that Treason should be claimed as a right—that anarchy should rule—it is this which thrills with indignant amazement. How profound has been the humiliation, how hot the indignation, are shown in the tumultuous surgings of passion that are now baptising with one common sentiment of constitutional unity and patriotic devotion every loyal American heart.

# Pittsburgh Post: The War Begun—The Duty of American Citizens

April 15, 1861

The *Pittsburgh Post* was a Democratic newspaper that had supported Stephen A. Douglas, the Northern Democratic candidate, in 1860.

---

FOR TWO days the country has been in a condition of the most intense excitement.

The awful catastrophe so long anticipated has at last fallen upon us.

The die is cast. The choice between compromise and battles has been made. Civil war is upon us. "Unto the end of the war desolations are determined."

For two days business has been almost suspended in our streets, and every one, old and young, men and women, have been asking, "What of the battle?"

The telegraph first announced the brief fact that the battle had commenced. Then came statement after statement—contradictory, inconsistent, almost incredible. Fort Sumter was on fire. Its magazines had exploded. Its walls were crumbling. The U. S. vessels were in the offing, not firing a gun. The white flag, the Federal flag, the flag of the Confederate States, were each in turn reported as floating from Fort Sumter. People scarce knew what to believe.

The despatches which we publish this morning leave no doubt that Fort Sumter has unconditionally surrendered to the forces of the Confederate States; that Major Anderson has been driven out by fire within the walls of the fort; that a brisk cannonading from the Charleston batteries has seriously damaged the fort; that Major Anderson and his command have been compelled to yield; that the United States vessels in the harbor of Charleston looked calmly on and made no effort to reinforce or assist the fort, and, most singular of all, that after two thousand balls had been fired the battle had resulted without the loss of a single man on either side.

Thus much for the facts which may be found in this morning's paper.

The war has begun. The first blow has been struck. The aspect of the question is now wholly changed from what it has hitherto been. Before it was a political one, and all the conservative men deprecating the horrors of a civil war, have earnestly urged a fair compromise granting to the South her just rights under the Constitution. But the South has determined not to wait for the adjustment of the difficulty lawfully and Constitutionally, but has decided upon an armed revolution against the Government. The South has struck the first blow, a successful blow, but one which will unite the North as one man for the Union. The authority of the Government of our country must be maintained and supported by every loyal American citizen. The wrongs of the South are now a matter of minor consideration. The integrity of the Government and the authority of those who hold its power, is now the great object of national consideration.

A civil war has actually commenced between the sections of this once glorious Union. The heart of every patriot bleeds at this solemn truth. The true men of the country have now a great duty to perform. The preliminaries are over—revolution has taken arms and proceeded to the last extremity—and now every man who reveres the memory of Washington, must use his efforts and devote his wealth, his personal services and his life if necessary, in defending the integrity of the Government which the patriots of the revolution handed down as a PERPETUAL BLESSING to their posterity.

However much we may deprecate the political causes which have driven the South to this insane madness—this fratricidal war—the time is past for crimination and recrimination as to what might have been done, and what ought to have been done. The Flag of Our Country—the glorious Stars and Stripes must be supported and defended by every American. The fight has now begun. An appeal has been made to the

God of Battles. The past must answer for itself. Those who have caused the war must answer to their country and their God for what they have done.

The American flag—the flag of our Union—and the honored banner of a government which is bound to protect the interests of the whole country, the North as well as the South —has been fired into by American citizens, disloyal to the government of the country. We have appreciated their wrongs— we have advocated the restoration of their rights—we have not spared their enemies.

But now, they have fired upon the flag of their country, and of ours. No American of true heart and brave soul will stand this. No American ought to stand it.

The integrity of a great government must be maintained. Its power to punish, as well as to protect its children must be used. Political partizanship must now cease to govern men on this issue. Pennsylvania and Pennsylvanians are for the Union. The government which the people have appointed, and which is responsible to the people for its every act, would be derelict of its duty as a government, if it did not protect its property, its citizens, its flag, and its granted rights against all usurpers, all rebels, all traitors—external or internal foes, of whatever character.

We were born and bred under the stars and stripes. We have been taught to regard the anniversary of American Independence as a sacred day. For our whole life we have looked upon our national emblems as tokens of safety and prosperity to us and to our children, and no matter what may have been the wrongs of the South, in the Union, we would have resisted them to the extent of our ability; but when the South becomes an enemy to the American system of government; takes an attitude of hostility to it, and fires upon the flag, which she, as well as we, are bound to protect, our influence goes for that flag, no matter whether a Republican or a Democrat holds it, and we will sustain any administration, no matter how distasteful its policy may be to us personally, in proving to the world, that the American eagle,—the proud bird of our banner—fears not to brave the wrath of foreign foes, or the mad rebellion of its own fostered children.

## *William Howard Russell:*
## *from* My Diary North and South

An Anglo-Irish correspondent for *The Times* of London, William Howard Russell had become famous for his war reporting from the Crimea and India. He landed at New York on March 16, 1861, to observe the secession crisis firsthand, and would remain in America until April 9, 1862. In *My Diary North and South* (1863), he described his visit to Charleston on April 17, three days after the surrender of Fort Sumter.

---

*April 17th.*—The streets of Charleston present some such aspect as those of Paris in the last revolution. Crowds of armed men singing and promenading the streets. The battle-blood running through their veins—that hot oxygen which is called "the flush of victory" on the cheek; restaurants full, revelling in bar rooms, club-rooms crowded, orgies and carousings in tavern or private house, in tap-room, from cabaret—down narrow alleys, in the broad highway. Sumter has set them distraught; never was such a victory; never such brave lads; never such a fight. There are pamphlets already full of the incident. It is a bloodless Waterloo or Solferino.

After breakfast I went down to the quay, with a party of the General's staff, to visit Fort Sumter. The senators and governors turned soldiers wore blue military caps, with "palmetto" trees embroidered thereon; blue frockcoats, with upright collars, and shoulder-straps edged with lace, and marked with two silver bars, to designate their rank of captain; gilt buttons, with the palmetto in relief; blue trowsers, with a gold-lace cord, and brass spurs—no straps. The day was sweltering, but a strong breeze blew in the harbour, and puffed the dust of Charleston, coating our clothes, and filling our eyes with powder. The streets were crowded with lanky lads, clanking spurs, and

sabres, with awkward squads marching to and fro, with drum-
mers beating calls, and ruffles, and points of war; around them
groups of grinning negroes delighted with the glare and glit-
ter, a holiday, and a new idea for them—secession flags waving
out of all the windows—little Irish boys shouting out, "Battle
of Fort Sumter! New edishun!"—As we walked down towards
the quay, where the steamer was lying, numerous traces of the
unsettled state of men's minds broke out in the hurried conversations of the various friends who stopped to speak for a few
moments. "Well, governor, the old Union is gone at last!"
"Have you heard what Abe is going to do?" "I don't think
Beauregard will have much more fighting for it. What do you
think?" And so on. Our little Creole friend, by the bye, is popular beyond description. There are all kinds of doggerel
rhymes in his honour—one with a refrain—

> "With cannon and musket, with shell and petard,
>   We salute the North with our Beau-regard"—

is much in favour.

We passed through the market, where the stalls are kept by
fat negresses and old "unkeys." There is a sort of vulture or
buzzard here, much encouraged as scavengers, and—but all
the world has heard of the Charleston vultures—so we will
leave them to their garbage. Near the quay, where the steamer
was lying, there is a very fine building in white marble, which
attracted our notice. It was unfinished, and immense blocks of
the glistening stone destined for its completion, lay on the
ground. "What is that?" I inquired. "Why, it's a custom-house
Uncle Sam was building for our benefit, but I don't think he'll
ever raise a cent for his treasury out of it." "Will you complete
it?" "I should think not. We'll lay on few duties; and what we
want is free-trade, and no duties at all, except for public purposes. The Yankees have plundered us with their custom-
houses and duties long enough." An old gentleman here
stopped us. "You will do me the greatest favour," he said to
one of our party who knew him, "if you will get me something
to do for our glorious cause. Old as I am, I can carry a musket
—not far, to be sure, but I can kill a Yankee if he comes near."
When he had gone, my friend told me the speaker was a man
of fortune, two of whose sons were in camp at Morris' Island,

but that he was suspected of Union sentiments, as he had a Northern wife, and hence his extreme vehemence and devotion.

There was a large crowd around the pier staring at the men in uniform on the boat, which was filled with bales of goods, commissariat stores, trusses of hay, and hampers, supplies for the volunteer army on Morris' Island. I was amused by the names of the various corps, "Tigers," "Lions," "Scorpions," "Palmetto Eagles," "Guards," of Pickens, Sumter, Marion, and of various other denominations, painted on the boxes. The original formation of these volunteers is in companies, and they know nothing of battalions or regiments. The tendency in volunteer outbursts is sometimes to gratify the greatest vanity of the greatest number. These companies do not muster more than fifty or sixty strong. Some were "dandies," and "swells," and affected to look down on their neighbours and comrades. Major Whiting told me there was difficulty in getting them to obey orders at first, as each man had an idea that he was as good an engineer as any body else, "and a good deal better, if it came to that." It was easy to perceive it was the old story of volunteer and regular in this little army.

As we got on deck, the major saw a number of rough, long-haired-looking fellows in coarse gray tunics, with pewter buttons and worsted braid lying on the hay-bales smoking their cigars. "Gentlemen," quoth he, very courteously, "You'll oblige me by not smoking over the hay. There's powder below." "I don't believe we're going to burn the hay this time, kernel," was the reply, "and anyway, we'll put it out afore it reaches the 'bustibles," and they went on smoking. The major grumbled, and worse, and drew off.

Among the passengers were some brethren of mine belonging to the New York and local papers. I saw a short time afterwards a description of the trip by one of these gentlemen, in which he described it as an affair got up specially for himself, probably in order to avenge himself on his military persecutors, for he had complained to me the evening before, that the chief of General Beauregard's staff told him to go to ——, when he applied at head-quarters for some information. I found from the tone and looks of my friends, that these literary gentlemen were received with great disfavour, and Major Whiting, who is a bibliomaniac, and has a very great liking for the best English writers, could not conceal his repugnance and antipathy to my unfortunate confrères. "If I had my way, I would fling them into the water; but the General has given them orders to come on board. It is these fellows who have brought all this trouble on our country."

The traces of dislike of the freedom of the press, which I, to my astonishment, discovered in the North, are broader and deeper in the South, and they are not accompanied by the signs of dread of its power which exist in New York, where men speak of the chiefs of the most notorious journals very much as people in Italian cities of past time might have talked of the most infamous bravo or the chief of some band of assassins. Whiting comforted himself by the reflection that they would soon have their fingers in a vice, and then pulling out a ragged little sheet, turned suddenly on the representative thereof, and proceeded to give the most unqualified contradiction to most of the statements contained in "the full and accurate particulars of the Bombardment and Fall of Fort Sumter," in the said journal, which the person in question listened to with becoming meekness and contrition. "If I knew who wrote it," said the major, "I'd make him eat it."

I was presented to many judges, colonels, and others of the mass of society on board, and, "after compliments," as the Orientals say, I was generally asked, in the first place, what I thought of the capture of Sumter, and in the second, what England would do when the news reached the other side. Already the Carolinians regard the Northern States as an alien and detested enemy, and entertain, or profess, an immense affection for Great Britain.

When we had shipped all our passengers, nine-tenths of them in uniform, and a larger proportion engaged in chewing, the whistle blew, and the steamer sidled off from the quay into the yellowish muddy water of the Ashley River, which is a creek from the sea, with a streamlet running into the head waters some distance up.

The shore opposite Charleston is more than a mile distant, and is low and sandy, covered here and there with patches of brilliant vegetation, and long lines of trees. It is cut up with creeks, which divide it into islands, so that passages out to sea exist between some of them for light craft, though the navigation is perplexed and difficult. The city lies on a spur or promontory between the Ashley and the Cooper rivers, and the land behind it is divided in the same manner by similar creeks, and is sandy and light, bearing, nevertheless, very fine crops, and trees of magnificent vegetation. The steeples, the domes of public buildings, the rows of massive warehouses and cotton stores on the wharfs, and the bright colours of the houses, render the appearance of Charleston, as seen from the river front, rather imposing, From the mastheads of the few large vessels in harbour floated the Confederate flag. Looking to our right, the same standard was visible, waving on the low, white parapets of the earthworks which had been engaged in reducing Sumter.

That much-talked-of fortress lay some two miles ahead of us now, rising up out of the water near the middle of the passage out to sea between James' Island and Sullivan's Island. It struck me at first as being like one of the smaller forts off Cronstadt, but a closer inspection very much diminished its importance; the material is brick, not stone, and the size of the place is exaggerated by the low back ground, and by contrast with the sea-line. The land contracts on both sides opposite the fort, a projection of Morris' Island, called "Cumming's point," running out on the left. There is a similar promontory from Sullivan's Island, on which is erected Fort Moultrie, on the right from the sea entrance. Castle Pinckney, which stands on a small island at the exit of the Cooper River, is a place of no importance, and it was too far from Sumter to take any in the bombardment: the same remarks apply to Fort Johnson on James' Island, on the right bank of the Ashley River below Charleston. The works which did the mischief were the batteries of sand on Morris' Island, at Cumming's Point, and Fort Moultrie. The floating battery, covered with railroad-iron, lay a long way off, and could not have contributed much to the result.

As we approached Morris' Island, which is an accumulation of sand covered with mounds of the same material, on which there is a scanty vegetation alternating with salt-water marshes, we could perceive a few tents in the distance among the sand-hills. The sand-bag batteries, and an ugly black parapet, with guns peering through port-holes as if from a ship's side, lay before us. Around them men were swarming like ants, and a crowd in uniform were gathered on the beach to receive us as we landed from the boat of the steamer, all eager for news, and provisions, and newspapers, of which an immense flight immediately fell upon them. A guard with bayonets crossed in a very odd sort of manner, prevented any unauthorised persons from landing. They wore the universal coarse gray jacket and trousers, with worsted braid and yellow facings, uncouth caps, lead buttons stamped with the palmetto-tree. Their unbronzed fire-locks were covered with rust. The soldiers lounging about were mostly tall, well-grown men, young and old, some with the air of gentlemen; others coarse, long-haired fellows, without any semblance of military bearing, but full of fight, and burning with enthusiasm, not unaided, in some instances, by coarser stimulus.

The day was exceedingly warm and unpleasant, the hot wind blew the fine white sand into our faces, and wafted it in minute clouds inside eyelids, nostrils, and clothing; but it was necessary to visit the batteries, so on we trudged into one and out of another, walked up parapets, examined profiles, looked along guns, and did everything that could be required of us. The result of the examination was to establish in my mind the conviction, that if the commander of Sumter had been allowed to open his guns on the island, the first time he saw an indication of throwing up a battery against him, he could have saved his fort. Moultrie, in its original state, on the opposite side, could have been readily demolished by Sumter. The design of the works was better than their execution—the sand-bags were rotten, the sand not properly revetted or banked up, and the traverses imperfectly constructed. The barbette guns of the fort looked into many of the embrasures, and commanded them.

The whole of the island was full of life and excitement. Officers were galloping about as if on a field-day or in action. Commissariat carts were toiling to and fro between the beach and the camps, and sounds of laughter and revelling came from the tents. These were pitched without order, and were of all shapes, hues, and sizes, many being disfigured by rude charcoal drawings outside, and inscriptions such as "The Live Tigers," "Rattlesnake's-hole," "Yankee Smashers," &c. The vicinity of the camps was in an intolerable state, and on calling the attention of the medical officer who was with me, to the danger arising from such a condition of things, he said with a sigh, "I know it all. But we can do nothing. Remember they're all volunteers, and do just as they please."

In every tent was hospitality, and a hearty welcome to all comers. Cases of champagne and claret, French pâtés, and the like, were piled outside the canvas walls, when there was no room for them inside. In the middle of these excited gatherings I felt like a man in the full possession of his senses coming in late to a wine party. "Won't you drink with me, sir, to the— (something awful)—of Lincoln and all Yankees?" "No! if you'll be good enough to excuse me." "Well, I think you're the only Englishman who won't." Our Carolinians are very fine fellows, but a little given to the Bobadil style—hectoring after a cavalier fashion, which they fondly believe to be theirs by hereditary right. They assume that the British crown rests on a cotton bale, as the Lord Chancellor sits on a pack of wool.

In one long tent there was a party of roystering young men, opening claret, and mixing "cup" in large buckets; whilst others were helping the servants to set out a table for a banquet to one of their generals. Such heat, tobacco-smoke, clamour, toasts, drinking, hand-shaking, vows of friendship! Many were the excuses made for the more demonstrative of the Edonian youths by their friends. "Tom is a little cut, sir; but he's a splendid fellow—he's worth half-a-million of dollars." This reference to a money standard of value was not unusual or perhaps unnatural, but it was made repeatedly; and I was told wonderful tales of the riches of men who were lounging round, dressed as privates, some of whom at that season, in years gone by, were looked for at the watering places as the great lions of American fashion. But Secession is the fashion here. Young ladies sing for it; old ladies pray for it; young men are dying to fight for it; old men are ready to demonstrate it. The founder of the school was St. Calhoun. Here his pupils carry out their teaching in thunder and fire. States' Rights are displayed after its legitimate teaching, and the Palmetto flag and the red bars of the Confederacy are its exposition. The utter contempt and loathing for the venerated Stars and Stripes, the abhorrence of the very words United States, the intense hatred of the Yankee on the part of these people, cannot be conceived by anyone who has not seen them. I am more satisfied than ever that the Union can never be restored as it was, and that it has gone to pieces, never to be put together again, in the old shape, at all events by any power on earth.

After a long and tiresome promenade in the dust, heat, and fine sand, through the tents, our party returned to the beach, where we took boat, and pushed off for Fort Sumter. The Confederate flag rose above the walls. On near approach the marks of the shot against the *pain coupé*, and the embrasures near the salient were visible enough; but the damage done to the hard brickwork was trifling, except at the angles: the edges of the parapets were ragged and pock-marked, and the quay wall was rifted here and there by shot; but no injury of a kind to render the work untenable could be made out. The greatest damage inflicted was, no doubt, the burning of the barracks, which were culpably erected inside the fort, close to the flank wall facing Cumming's Point.

As the boat touched the quay of the fort, a tall, powerful-looking man came through the shattered gateway, and with uneven steps strode over the rubbish towards a skiff which was waiting to receive him, and into which he jumped and rowed off. Recognising one of my companions as he passed our boat, he suddenly stood up, and with a leap and a scramble tumbled in among us, to the imminent danger of upsetting the party. Our new friend was dressed in the blue frockcoat of a civilian, round which he had tied a red silk sash—his waistbelt supported a straight sword, something like those worn with Court dress. His muscular neck was surrounded with a loosely-fastened silk handkerchief; and wild masses of black hair, tinged with grey, fell from under a civilian's hat over his collar; his unstrapped trousers were gathered up high on his legs, displaying ample boots, garnished with formidable brass spurs. But his face was one not to be forgotten—a straight, broad brow, from which the hair rose up like the vegetation on a river bank, beetling black eyebrows—a mouth coarse and grim, yet full of power, a square jaw—a thick argumentative nose—a new growth of scrubby beard and moustache—these were relieved by eyes of wonderful depth and light, such as I never saw before but in the head of a wild beast. If you look some day when the sun is not too bright into the eye of the Bengal tiger, in the Regent's Park, as the keeper is coming round, you will form some notion of the expression I mean. It was flashing, fierce, yet calm—with a well of fire burning behind and spouting through it, an eye pitiless in anger, which now and then sought to conceal its expression beneath half-closed lids, and then burst out with an angry glare, as if disdaining concealment.

This was none other than Louis T. Wigfall, Colonel (then of his own creation) in the Confederate army, and Senator from Texas in the United States—a good type of the men whom the institutions of the country produce or throw off—a remarkable man, noted for his ready, natural eloquence; his exceeding ability as a quick, bitter debater; the acerbity of his taunts; and his readiness for personal encounter. To the last he stood in his place in the Senate at Washington, when nearly every other Southernman had seceded, lashing with a venomous and instant tongue, and covering with insults, ridicule, and abuse, such men as Mr. Chandler, of Michigan, and other Republicans: never missing a sitting of the House, and seeking out adversaries in the bar rooms or the gambling tables. The other day, when the fire against Sumter was at its height, and the fort, in flames, was reduced almost to silence, a small boat put off from the shore, and steered through the shot and the splashing waters right for the walls. It bore the colonel and a negro oarsman. Holding up a white handkerchief on the end of his sword, Wigfall landed on the quay, clambered through an embrasure, and presented himself before the astonished Federals with a proposal to surrender, quite unauthorised, and "on his own hook," which led to the final capitulation of Major Anderson.

I am sorry to say, our distinguished friend had just been paying his respects *sans bornes* to Bacchus or Bourbon, for he was decidedly unsteady in his gait and thick in speech; but his head was quite clear, and he was determined I should know all about his exploit. Major Whiting desired to show me round the work, but he had no chance. "Here is where I got in," quoth Colonel Wigfall. "I found a Yankee standing here by the traverse, out of the way of our shot. He was pretty well scared when he saw me, but I told him not to be alarmed, but to take me to the officers. There they were, huddled up in that corner behind the brickwork, for our shells were tumbling into the yard, and bursting like,"—&c. (The Colonel used strong illustrations and strange expletives in narrative.) Major Whiting shook his military head, and said something uncivil to me, in private, in reference to volunteer colonels and the like, which gave him relief; whilst the martial Senator—I forgot to say that he has the name, particularly in the North, of having killed more than half a dozen men in duels—(I had an escape of being another)—conducted me through the casemates with uneven steps, stopping at every traverse to expatiate on some phase of his personal experiences, with his sword dangling between his legs, and spurs involved in rubbish and soldiers' blankets.

In my letter I described the real extent of the damage inflicted, and the state of the fort as I found it. At first the batteries thrown up by the Carolinians were so poor, that the United States' officers in the fort were mightily amused at them, and anticipated easy work in enfilading, ricocheting, and battering them to pieces, if they ever dared to open fire. One morning, however, Capt. Foster, to whom really belongs the credit of putting Sumter into a tolerable condition of defence with the most limited means, was unpleasantly surprised by seeing through his glass a new work in the best possible situation for attacking the place, growing up under the strenuous labours of a band of negroes. "I knew at once," he said, "the rascals had got an engineer at last." In fact, the Carolinians were actually talking of an escalade when the officers of the regular army, who had "seceded," came down and took the direction of affairs, which otherwise might have had very different results.

There was a working party of Volunteers clearing away the rubbish in the place. It was evident they were not accustomed to labour. And on asking why negroes were not employed, I was informed: "The niggers would blow us all up, they're so stupid; and the State would have to pay the owners for any of them who were killed and injured." "In one respect, then, white men are not so valuable as negroes?" "Yes, sir,—that's a fact."

Very few shell craters were visible in the terreplein; the military mischief, such as it was, showed most conspicuously on the parapet platforms, over which shells had been burst as heavily as could be, to prevent the manning of the barbette guns. A very small affair, indeed, that shelling of Fort Sumter. And yet who can tell what may arise from it? "Well, sir," exclaimed one of my companions, "I thank God for it, if it's only because we are beginning to have a history for Europe. The universal Yankee nation swallowed us up."

Never did men plunge into unknown depth of peril and trouble more recklessly than these Carolinians. They fling themselves against the grim, black future, as the cavaliers under Rupert may have rushed against the grim, black Ironsides. Will they carry the image farther? Well! The exploration of Sumter was finished at last, not till we had visited the officers of the garrison, who lived in a windowless, shattered room, reached by a crumbling staircase, and who produced whiskey and crackers, many pleasant stories and boundless welcome. One young fellow grumbled about pay. He said: "I have not received a cent. since I came to Charleston for this business." But Major Whiting, some days afterwards, told me he had not got a dollar on account of his pay, though on leaving the United States' army he had abandoned nearly all his means of subsistence. These gentlemen were quite satisfied it would all be right eventually; and no one questioned the power or inclination of the Government, which had just been inaugurated under such strange auspices, to perpetuate its principles and reward its servants.

After a time our party went down to the boats, in which we were rowed to the steamer that lay waiting for us at Morris' Island. The original intention of the officers was to carry us over to Fort Moultrie, on the opposite side of the Channel, and to examine it and the floating iron battery; but it was too late to do so when we got off, and the steamer only ran across and swept around homewards by the other shore. Below, in the cabin, there was spread a lunch or quasi dinner; and the party of Senators, past and present, aides-de-camp, journalists, and flaneurs, were not indisposed to join it. For me there was only one circumstance which marred the pleasure of that agreeable reunion. Colonel and Senator Wigfall, who had not sobered himself by drinking deeply, in the plenitude of his exultation alluded to the assault on Senator Sumner as a type of the manner in which the Southerners would deal with the Northerners generally, and cited it as a good exemplification of the fashion in which they would bear their "whipping." Thence, by a natural digression, he adverted to the inevitable consequences of the magnificent outburst of Southern indignation against the Yankees on all the nations of the world, and to the immediate action of England in the matter as soon as the news came. Suddenly reverting to Mr. Sumner, whose name he loaded with obloquy, he spoke of Lord Lyons in terms so coarse, that, forgetting the condition of the speaker, I resented the language applied to the English Minister, in a very unmistakeable manner; and then rose and left the cabin. In a moment I was followed on deck by Senator Wigfall: his manner much calmer, his hair brushed back, his eye sparkling. There was nothing left to be desired in his apologies, which were repeated and energetic. We were joined by Mr. Manning, Major Whiting, and Senator Chesnut, and others, to whom I expressed my complete contentment with Mr. Wigfall's explanations. And so we returned to Charleston. The Colonel and Senator, however, did not desist from his attentions to the good—or bad—things below. It was a strange scene—these men, hot and red-handed in rebellion, with their lives on the cast, trifling and jesting, and carousing as if they had no care on earth—all excepting the gentlemen of the local press, who were assiduous in note and food taking. It was near nightfall before we set foot on the quay of Charleston. The city was indicated by the blaze of lights, and by the continual roll of drums, and the noisy music, and the yelling cheers which rose above its streets. As I walked towards the hotel, the evening drove of negroes, male and female, shuffling through the streets in all haste, in order to escape the patrol and the last peal of the curfew bell, swept by me; and as I passed the guard-house of the police, one of my friends pointed out the armed sentries pacing up and down before the porch, and the gleam of arms in the room inside. Further on, a squad of mounted horsemen, heavily armed, turned up a bye-street, and with jingling spurs and sabres disappeared in the dust and darkness. That is the horse patrol. They scour the country around the city, and meet at certain places during the night to see if the niggers are all quiet. Ah, Fuscus! these are signs of trouble.

"Integer vitæ, scelerisque purus
Non eget Mauri jaculis neque arcu,
Nec venenatis gravidâ sagittis,
        Fusce, pharetrâ."

But Fuscus is going to his club; a kindly, pleasant, chatty, card-playing, cocktail-consuming place. He nods proudly to an old white-woolled negro steward or head-waiter—a slave—as a proof which I cannot accept, with the curfew tolling in my ears, of the excellencies of the domestic institution. The club was filled with officers; one of them, Mr. Ransome Calhoun,* asked me what was the object which most struck me at Morris' Island; I tell him—as was indeed the case—that it was a letter copying-machine, a case of official stationery, and a box of Red Tape, lying on the beach, just landed and ready to grow with the strength of the young independence.

But listen! There is a great tumult, as of many voices coming up the street, heralded by blasts of music. It is a speech-making from the front of the hotel. Such an agitated, lively multitude! How they cheer the pale, frantic man, limber and dark-haired, with uplifted arms and clenched fists, who is perorating on the balcony! "What did he say?" "Who is he?" "Why it's he again!" "That's Roger Pryor—he says that if them Yankee trash don't listen to reason, and stand from under, we'll march to the North and dictate the terms of peace in Faneuil Hall! Yes, sir—and so we will, certa-i-n su-re!" "No matter, for all that; we have shown we can whip the Yankees whenever we meet them—at Washington or down here." How much I heard of all this to-day—how much more this evening! The hotel as noisy as ever—more men in uniform arriving every few minutes, and the hall and passages crowded with tall, good-looking Carolinians.

*Since killed in a duel by Mr. Rhett.

# Charles C. Jones Sr. to Charles C. Jones Jr.

Educated at Andover and Princeton, Charles C. Jones was a Presbyterian clergyman and plantation owner in Liberty County, Georgia, known for his evangelical work among slaves. He wrote to his son, the mayor of Savannah, shortly after the outbreak of the war.

———————

Montevideo, *Saturday*, April 20th, 1861

My dear Son,

We are aware of your numerous engagements, and never think anything of your not writing as frequently as usual, for we know that you will always write us whenever you can. Your two last came last night with the papers.

A kind Providence seems to watch over our Confederacy. Whoever read or heard of so important and desperate a battle as that of Fort Sumter without the loss of a man on the side of the victors or on the side of the vanquished? And how remarkable that the only men killed were killed saluting their own flag as it was lowered in defeat! May this battle be an earnest of all others that shall be forced upon us in its merciful and glorious success. All honor to Carolina! I hope our state may emulate her bravery and patriotism—and *her self-sacrificing generosity*, in that she has borne out of her own treasury the entire expense of her army and fortifications and all matériel of war, and has not and will not call upon our government for one cent of it. Georgia is well able to do the like for her own seaport and her own territory, and there must be some movement of our chief men to secure so honorable an act. It will relieve our new government, and enable it to appropriate its funds in other directions for our honor and our defense.

We are favored again, in providence, by the belligerent acts and declarations of Mr. Lincoln, which have precipitated the border states upon a decision in our favor precisely at the moment most favorable to us. I never believed we should have war until after Lincoln's inaugural address—and not altogether then, thinking that there were some preventing considerations of interest and self-preservation, and some residuum of humanity and respect for the opinions of the civilized world in the Black Republican party. But in this I have been mistaken. Christianity with its enlightening and softening influences upon the human soul—at least so far as the great subject dividing our country is concerned—finds no lodgment in the soul of that party, destitute of justice and mercy, without the fear of God, supremely selfish and arrogant, unscrupulous in its acts and measures, intensely malignant and vituperative, and persecuting the innocent even unto blood and utter destruction. That party is essentially *infidel!* And these are our enemies, born and reared in our own political family, for whom we are to pray, and from whom we are to defend ourselves!

The conduct of the government of the old United States towards the Confederate States is an outrage upon Christianity and the civilization of the age, and upon the great and just principles of popular sovereignty which we have contended for and embraced for near an hundred years, and brands it with a deserved and indelible infamy. We have nothing left us but to work out our independence, relying, as our good President instructs us, upon "a just and superintending Providence." The ordering out of such large bodies of men is an easy matter; but to *officer*, to *equip*, to *maintain*, and (*more than all*) to *maneuver and bring these forces into safe action with the enemy*— these are the burdens and the arts and realities of war. And we wait Lincoln's success. He is not training and educating the people up to the point of war gradually and familiarizing them with it, but he plunges them up to their necks in it at once. But enough. What is it all for? Are the people of the free states going to attempt *the subjugation* of our Confederacy under the fanatical and brutal lead of Black Republicans? I agree with you fully in your view of the character and conduct of this party. It would be a sublime spectacle to see the conservative portion of the free states uniting with our Confederacy in overthrowing the present government in Washington and installing a better one in its place—not for us, but for themselves. But I fear that portion of the free states have not the decision and daring and patriotism for the effort. *Douglas* leads off for coercion! A miserable politican and patriot he.

No man can even conjecture where this strife is to end. Yet it is under the control of God. He can "still the tumult of the people," and we can but cast this care upon Him and humbly await His interposition. It may be long delayed; it may be immediate. We must maintain our equanimity, go to our daily duties and by His help faithfully discharge them as in times past, and stand ready for emergencies when they arise, and keep in good heart all around us. The Lord keep you, my dear son, and strengthen you to serve Him and to fear His great and holy name, and to discharge your various and responsible duties to your family and country with cheerfulness and self-possession, with purity and integrity, and with intelligence, decision, and kindness. Seek to do all things well, and everything in its proper time.

Am glad you have consented to deliver the address to your company the 1st of May. You may do good by it, and should like to come and hear you.

The package from Mr. —— was his finish of the copy of the first volume of my church history. Arrived safe. . . .

The news from Baltimore and Washington is out here in the form of rumor. The events of the morning are old by the evening. The scenes succeed almost as rapidly as those of a play. Marvelous if Lincoln, who gave us twenty days to disperse, is in less than ten dispersed himself! As our mails North are stopped, send us what news of interest you can spare. Special prayer should be offered for the *life* of our President; I hope he will not expose his person.

Your affectionate father,
C. C. Jones.

# John B. Jones: Diary, April 15–22, 1861

The editor of the *Southern Monitor*, a weekly journal published in Philadelphia, John B. Jones feared that he would be arrested as a Confederate sympathizer once war began. Anticipating that hostilities would soon break out, Jones left his home in Burlington, New Jersey, on April 9 and arrived in Richmond three days later, where the Virginia convention had been meeting since February. After weeks of debate, on April 4 the convention rejected a motion to secede, 90–45, but remained in session. On April 17, three days after the surrender of Fort Sumter, the convention reversed itself and voted 88–55 to leave the Union—a decision that would be overwhelmingly approved in a referendum held on May 23. Virginia would soon be followed by Arkansas (May 6), North Carolina (May 20), and Tennessee (June 8), resulting in the formation of an eleven-state Confederacy.

---

APRIL 15TH.—To-day the secession fires assumed a whiter heat. In the Convention the Union men no longer utter denunciations against the disunionists. They merely resort to pretexts and quibbles to stave off the inevitable ordinance. They had sent a deputation to Washington to make a final appeal to Seward and Lincoln to vouchsafe them such guarantees as would enable them to keep Virginia to her moorings. But in vain. They could not obtain even a promise of concession. And now the Union members as they walk the streets, and even Gov. Letcher himself, hear the indignant mutterings of the impassioned storm which threatens every hour to sweep them from existence. Business is generally suspended, and men run together in great crowds to listen to the news from the North, where it is said many outrages are committed on Southern men and those who sympathize with them. Many arrests are made, and the victims thrown into Fort Lafayette. These crowds are addressed by the most inflamed members of the

Convention, and never did I hear more hearty responses from the people.

APRIL 16TH.—This day the Spontaneous People's Convention met and organized in Metropolitan Hall. The door-keeper stood with a drawn sword in his hand. But the scene was orderly. The assembly was full, nearly every county being represented, and the members were the representatives of the most ancient and respectable families in the State. David Chalmers, of Halifax County, I believe, was the President, and Willoughby Newton, a life-long Whig, among the Vice-Presidents. P. H. Aylett, a grandson of Patrick Henry, was the first speaker. And his eloquence indicated that the spirit of his ancestor survived in him. But he was for moderation and delay, still hoping that the other Convention would yield to the pressure of public sentiment, and place the State in the attitude now manifestly desired by an overwhelming majority of the people. He was answered by the gallant Capt. Wise, who thrilled every breast with his intrepid bearing and electric bursts of oratory. He advocated action, without reference to the other Convention, as the best means of bringing the Unionists to their senses. And the so-called Demosthenean Seddon, and G. W. Randolph (grandson of Thomas Jefferson), Lieut.-Gov. Montague, James Lyons, Judge Robertson, etc., were there. Never, never did I hear more exalted and effective bursts of oratory. And it was apparent that messages were constantly received from the other Convention. What they were, I did not learn at the moment; but it was evident that the Unionists were shaking in their shoes, and they certainly begged one—just one—day's delay, which was accorded them. The People's Convention agreed to adjourn till 10 o'clock A.M. the next day. But before we separated a commotion was observed on the stage, and the next moment a Mr. P., from Gov. Wise's old district, rushed forward and announced that he had just arrived from Norfolk, where, under instructions, and *with the acquiescence of Gov. Letcher*, he had succeeded in blocking the channel of the river; and this would either secure to us, or render useless to the United States, certain ships of the navy, stores, armament, etc., of the value of millions of dollars. This announcement was received with the wildest shouts of joy. Young men threw up their hats, and old men buttoned their coats and clapped their hands most vigorously. It was next hinted by some one who seemed to know something of the matter, that before another day elapsed, Harper's Ferry would fall into the hands of the secessionists.

At night the enthusiasm increases in intensity, and no further opposition is to be apprehended from the influence of Tim Rives, Baldwin, Clemens, etc. etc. It was quite apparent, indeed, that if an ordinance of secession were passed by the new Convention, its validity would be recognized and acted upon by the majority of the people. But this would be a complication of the civil war, now the decree of fate.

Perhaps the occurrence which has attracted most attention is the raising of the Southern flag on the capitol. It was hailed with the most deafening shouts of applause. But at a quiet hour of the night, the governor had it taken down, for the Convention had not yet passed the ordinance of secession. Yet the stars and stripes did not float in its stead; it was replaced by the flag of Virginia.

APRIL 17TH.—This was a memorable day. When we assembled at Metropolitan Hall, it could be easily perceived that we were on the threshold of momentous events. All other subjects, except that of a new political organization of the State, seemed to be momentarily delayed, as if awaiting action elsewhere. And this plan of political organization filled me with alarm, for I apprehended it would result in a new conflict between the old parties—Whig and Democrat. The ingenious discussion of this subject was probably a device of the Unionists, two or three of them having obtained seats in the Revolutionary Convention. I knew the ineradicable instincts of Virginia politicians, and their inveterate habit of public speaking, and knew there were well-grounded fears that we should be launched and lost in an illimitable sea of argument, when the business was Revolution, and death to the coming invader. Besides, I saw no hope of unanimity if the old party distinctions and designations were not submerged forever.

These fears, however, were groundless. The Union had received its *blessure mortelle*, and no power this side of the Potomac could save it. During a pause in the proceedings, one of the leading members arose and announced that he had information that the vote was about being taken in the other

Convention on the ordinance of secession. "Very well!" cried another member, "we will give them another chance to save themselves. But it is the last!" This was concurred in by a vast majority. Not long after, Lieut.-Gov. Montague came in and announced the passage of the ordinance by the other Convention! This was succeeded by a moment too thrilling for utterance, but was followed by tears of gladness and rapturous applause. Soon after, President Tyler and Gov. Wise were conducted arm-in-arm, and bare-headed, down the center aisle amid a din of cheers, while every member rose to his feet. They were led to the platform, and called upon to address the Convention. The venerable ex-President of the United States first rose responsive to the call, but remarked that the exhaustion incident to his recent incessant labors, and the nature of his emotions at such a momentous crisis, superadded to the feebleness of age, rendered him physically unable to utter what he felt and thought on such an occasion. Nevertheless, he seemed to acquire supernatural strength as he proceeded, and he spoke most effectively for the space of fifteen minutes. He gave a brief history of all the struggles of our race for freedom, from *Magna Charta* to the present day; and he concluded with a solemn declaration that at no period of our history were we engaged in a more just and holy effort for the maintenance of liberty and independence than at the present moment. The career of the dominant party at the North was but a series of aggressions, which fully warranted the steps we were taking for resistance and eternal separation; and if we performed our whole duty as Christians and patriots, the same benign Providence which favored the cause of our forefathers in the Revolution of 1776, would again crown our efforts with similar success. He said he might not survive to witness the consummation of the work begun that day; but generations yet unborn would bless those who had the high privilege of being participators in it.

He was succeeded by Gov. Wise, who, for a quarter of an hour, electrified the assembly by a burst of eloquence, perhaps never surpassed by mortal orator. During his pauses a silence reigned, pending which the slightest breathing could be distinctly heard, while every eye was bathed in tears. At times the vast assembly rose involuntarily to their feet, and every emotion and expression of feature seemed responsive to his own. During his speech he alluded to the reports of the press that the oppressors of the North had probably seized one of his children sojourning in their midst. "But," said he, "if they suppose hostages of my own heart's blood will stay my hand in a contest for the maintenance of sacred rights, they are mistaken. Affection for kindred, property, and life itself sink into insignificance in comparison with the overwhelming importance of public duty in such a crisis as this." He lamented the blindness which had prevented Virginia from seizing Washington before the Republican hordes got possession of it—but, said he, we must do our best under the circumstances. It was now Independence or Death—although he had preferred fighting in the Union—and when the mind was made up to die rather than fail, success was certain. For himself, he was eager to meet the ordeal, and he doubted not every Southern heart pulsated in unison with his own.

Hon. J. M. Mason, and many other of Virginia's distinguished sons were called upon, and delivered patriotic speeches. And finally, *Gov. Letcher* appeared upon the stage. He was loudly cheered by the very men who, two days before, would gladly have witnessed his execution. The governor spoke very briefly, merely declaring his concurrence in the important step that had been taken, and his honest purpose, under the circumstances, to discharge his whole duty as Executive of the State, in conformity to the will of the people and the provisions of the Constitution.

Before the *sine die* adjournment, it was suggested that inasmuch as the ordinance had been passed in secret session, and it was desirable that the enemy should not know it before certain preparations could be made to avert sudden injury on the border, etc., that the fact should not be divulged at present.

APRIL 18TH.—In spite of every precaution, it is currently whispered in the streets to-day that Virginia has seceded from the Union; and that the act is to be submitted to the people for ratification a month hence. This is perhaps a blunder. If the Southern States are to adhere to the old distinct sovereignty doctrine, God help them one and all to achieve their independence of the United States. Many are inclined to think the safest plan would be to obliterate State lines, and merge them

all into an indivisible nation or empire, else there may be incessant conflicts between the different sovereignties themselves, and between them and the General Government. I
doubt our ability to maintain the old cumbrous, complicated,
and expensive form of government. A national executive and
Congress will be sufficiently burdensome to the people without the additional expense of governors, lieutenant-governors,
a dozen secretaries of State, as many legislatures, etc. etc. It is
true, State rights gave the States the right to secede. But what
is in a name? Secession by any other name would smell as
sweet. For my part, I like the name of Revolution, or even Rebellion, better, for they are sanctified by the example of Washington and his compeers. And separations of communities are
like the separations of bees when they cannot live in peace in
the same hive. The time had come apparently for us to set up
for ourselves, and we should have done it if there had been no
such thing as State sovereignty. It is true, the Constitution
adopted at Montgomery virtually acknowledges the right of
any State to secede from the Confederacy; but that was necessary in vindication of the action of its fathers. That Constitution, and the *permanent* one to succeed it, will, perhaps, never
do. They too much resemble the governmental organization
of the Yankees, to whom we have bid adieu forever in disgust.

APRIL 19TH.—Dispatches from Montgomery indicate that
President Davis is as firm a States right man as any other, perfectly content to bear the burdens of government six years,
and hence I apprehend he will not budge in the business of
guarding Virginia until after the ratification of the secession
ordinance. Thus a month's precious time will be lost; and the
scene of conflict, instead of being in Pennsylvania, near Philadelphia, will be in Virginia. From the ardor of the volunteers
already beginning to pour into the city, I believe 25,000 men
could be collected and armed in a week, and in another they
might sweep the whole Abolition concern beyond the Susquehanna, and afterward easily keep them there. But this will not
be attempted, nor permitted, by the Convention, so recently
composed mostly of Union men.

To-night we have rumors of a collision in Baltimore. A regiment of Northern troops has been assailed by the mob. No
good can come of mob assaults in a great revolution.

Wrote my wife to make preparations with all expedition to escape into Virginia. Women and children will not be molested for some weeks yet; but I see they have begun to ransack their baggage. Mrs. Semple, daughter of President Tyler, I am informed, had her plate taken from her in an attempt to get it away from New York.

APRIL 20TH.—The news has been confirmed. It was a brickbat "Plug Ugly" fight—the result of animal, and not intellectual or patriotic instincts. Baltimore has better men for the strife than bar-room champions. The absence of dignity in this assault will be productive of evil rather than good. Maryland is probably lost—for her fetters will be riveted before the secession of Virginia will be communicated by the senseless form of ratification a month hence. Woe, woe to the politicians of Virginia who have wrought this delay! It is now understood that the very day before the ordinance was passed, the members were gravely splitting hairs over proposed amendments to the Federal Constitution!

Guns are being fired on Capitol Hill in commemoration of secession, and the Confederate flag now floats unmolested from the summit of the capitol. I think they had better save the powder, etc.

At night. We have a gay illumination. This too is wrong. We had better save the candles.

APRIL 21ST.—Received several letters to-day which had been delayed in their transmission, and were doubtless opened on the way. One was from my wife, informing me of the illness of Custis, my eldest son, and of the equivocal conduct of some of the neighbors. The Rev. Mr. D., son of the late B——p, raised the flag of the Union on his church.

The telegraphic wires are still in operation.

APRIL 22D.—Early a few mornings since, I called on Gov. Wise, and informed him that Lincoln had called out 70,000 men. He opened his eyes very widely and said, emphatically, "I don't believe it." The greatest statesmen of the South have no conception of the real purposes of the men now in power in the United States. They cannot be made to believe that the Government at Washington are going to wage war immediately. But when I placed the President's proclamation in his hand, he read it with deep emotion, and uttered a fierce

"Hah!" Nevertheless, when I told him that these 70,000 were designed to be merely the videttes and outposts of an army of 700,000, he was quite incredulous. He had not witnessed the Wide-Awake gatherings the preceding fall, as I had done, and listened to the pledges they made to subjugate the South, free the negroes, and hang Gov. Wise. I next told him they would blockade our ports, and endeavor to cut off our supplies. To this he uttered a most positive negative. He said it would be contrary to the laws of nations, as had been decided often in the Courts of Admiralty, and would be moreover a violation of the Constitution. Of course I admitted all this; but maintained that such was the intention of the Washington Cabinet. Laws and Courts and Constitutions would not be impediments in the way of Yankees resolved upon our subjugation. Presuming upon their superior numbers, and under the pretext of saving the Union and annihilating slavery, they would invade us like the army-worm, which enters the green fields in countless numbers. The real object was to enjoy our soil and climate by means of confiscation. He poohed me into silence with an indignant frown. He had no idea that the Yankees would *dare* to enter upon such enterprises in the face of an enlightened world. But I know them better. And it will be found that they will learn how to fight, and will not be afraid to fight.

# John W. Hanson: from Historical Sketch of the Old Sixth Regiment of Massachusetts Volunteers

On April 19 the 6th Massachusetts Regiment was attacked by a secessionist mob as it passed through Baltimore on its way to Washington. Four soldiers and a dozen Baltimore citizens were killed in the fighting, the first fatal casualties of the war. In Massachusetts the skirmish would take on special meaning because it fell on the anniversary of the battles of Lexington and Concord. John W. Hanson became the chaplain of the 6th Massachusetts in 1862 and later wrote the regimental history, in which he drew on three first-hand accounts of the riot.

----

Col. Jones, in his official report to Maj. William H. Clemence, Maj. Gen. B. F. Butler's Adjutant, dated in Washington, 22d April, says:—

\*   \*   \*   After leaving Philadelphia, I received intimation that our passage through the city of Baltimore would be resisted. I caused ammunition to be distributed, and arms loaded; and went personally through the cars, and issued the following order, viz.:—

"The regiment will march through Baltimore in column of sections, arms at will. You will undoubtedly be insulted, abused, and perhaps assaulted, to which you must pay no attention whatever; but march with your faces square to the front, and pay no attention to the mob, even if they throw stones, bricks, or other missiles; but if you are fired upon, and any one of you is hit, your officers will order you to fire. Do not fire into any promiscuous crowds; but select any man whom you see aiming at you, and be sure you drop him."

Reaching Baltimore, horses were attached the instant that the locomotive was detached, and the cars were driven at a rapid pace across the city. After the cars containing seven companies had reached the Washington depot, the track behind them was barricaded, and the cars containing the band and the following companies, viz.: company C, of Lowell, Capt. Follansbee; company D, of Lowell, Capt. Hart;

company I, of Lawrence, Capt. Pickering; and company L, of Stoneham, Capt. Dike, were vacated; and they proceeded to march in accordance with orders, and had proceeded but a short distance before they were furiously attacked by a shower of missiles, which came faster as they advanced. They increased their step to double-quick, which seemed to infuriate the mob, as it evidently impressed them with the idea that the soldiers dared not fire, or had no ammunition; and pistol-shots were numerously fired into the ranks, and one soldier fell dead. The order, "Fire!" was given, and it was executed; in consequence, several of the mob fell, and the soldiers again advanced hastily. The Mayor of Baltimore placed himself at the head of the column, beside Capt. Follansbee, and proceeded with them a short distance, assuring him that he would protect them, and begging him not to let the men fire; but the mayor's patience was soon exhausted, and he seized a musket from the hands of one of the men, and killed a man therewith; and a policeman, who was in advance of the column, also shot a man with a revolver.

They, at last, reached the cars, and they started immediately for Washington. On going through the train, I found there were about one hundred and thirty missing, including the band and field music. Our baggage was seized, and we have not as yet been able to recover any of it. I have found it very difficult to get reliable information in regard to the killed and wounded.

As the men went into the cars, I caused the blinds to be closed, and took every precaution to prevent any shadow of offence to the people of Baltimore; but still the stones flew thick and fast into the train, and it was with the utmost difficulty that I could prevent the troops from leaving the cars, and revenging the death of their comrades.    *    *    *

EDWARD F. JONES,
Col. Sixth Regt., M. V. M., in service of U. S.


## WHY THE MOB WAS SO LENIENTLY TREATED.

Those who have since been made familiar with scenes of war, and with the true method of dealing with such men as those who intercepted the march of the Sixth, might, at first thought, be surprised at the gentle treatment the mob received. But the regiment was anxious to reach Washington, then supposed to be in imminent danger; and it was hoped that the demonstration in Baltimore would not be serious. Besides, the people of the North were trying conciliation. No blood had been shed, and it was universally desired to treat Maryland and other border states with all the forbearance possible. The regiment had been drilled in street-firing, and was amply able to strew the streets of Baltimore with traitor dead, and would have done so but for these considerations. Place the same men under the same circumstances to-day, and there would be grief in hundreds of homes where one mourned on the 19th of April, 1861.

## CAPT. FOLLANSBEE'S ACCOUNT.

Capt. Follansbee, under date of Washington, April 20, wrote a letter to H. H. Wilder, Esq., of Lowell, which embodies the observations of as cool a head and brave a heart as were among the two hundred heroes of that day. He says:—

We arrived in Baltimore about 10 o'clock, A.M. The cars are drawn through the city by horses. There were about thirty cars in our train; there being, in addition to Col. Jones' command, about 1200 troops from Philadelphia, without uniforms or arms, they intending to get them here. After we arrived, the cars were taken, two at a time, and drawn to the depot at the lower part of the city, a mob assaulting them all the way. The Lowell Mechanic Phalanx car was the ninth; and we waited till after the rest had left, for our turn, till two men came to me and informed me that I had better take my command, and march to the other depot, as the mob had taken up the track to prevent the passage of the cars. I immediately informed Capt. Pickering, of the Lawrence Light Infantry, and we filed out of the cars in regular order. Capt. Hart's company, of Lowell, and Capt. Dike's, of Stoneham, did the same, and formed on the sidewalk. The captains consulted together, and decided that the command should devolve upon me. I immediately took my position upon the right, wheeled into column of sections, and requested them to march in close order. Before we had started, the mob was upon us, with a secession flag, attached to a pole, and told us we could never march through that city. They would kill every "white nigger" of us, before we could reach the other depot. I paid no attention to them, but, after I had wheeled the battalion, gave the order to march.

As soon as the order was given, the brick-bats began to fly into our ranks from the mob. I called a policeman, and requested him to lead the way to the depot. He did so. After we had marched about a hundred yards, we came to a bridge. The rebels had torn up most of the planks. We had to play "Scotch hop," to get over it. As soon as we had crossed the bridge, they commenced to fire upon us from the street and houses. I ordered the men to protect themselves; and then we returned their fire, and laid a great many of them away. I saw four fall on the sidewalk at one time. They followed us up, and we fought our way to the other depot,—about one mile. They kept at us till the cars started. Quite a number of the rascals were shot, after we entered the cars. We went very slow, for we expected the rails were torn up on the road.

I do not know how much damage we did. Report says, about forty were killed, but I think that is exaggerated: still it may be so. There is any quantity of them wounded. Quite a number of horses were killed. The mayor of the city met us almost half way. He said that there would be no trouble, and that we could get through, and kept with me for about a hundred yards; but the stones and balls whistled too near his head, and he left, took a gun from one of my company, fired, and brought his man down. That was the last I saw of him. We fought our way to the cars, and joined Col. Jones, and the seven companies that left us at the other end of the city; and now we are here, every man of the old Phalanx safe and sound, with the exception of a few marks made by brick-bats, and all we want now is a chance to go to Baltimore, and clean out all the roughs there. If Col. Jones would march his command there, we would do it. There are five or six of the regiment missing, and all of the band. I am in hopes that most, if not all of them are alive. Where a man in Baltimore showed his pistol, axe, or palmetto flag, he was about sure to drop.

## ANOTHER TESTIMONY.

A. S. Young, a member of the band, after relating that one of the musicians had left the car to consult with Gen. Small, of the unarmed Pennsylvanians, says:—

As he was returning, he was set upon, and driven into the car, followed by a number of the roughs. We fought them off as long as we could; but coming thicker and faster, some crawling from under the cars, others jumping from the tops, they forced their way in, in spite of our utmost exertions. The door was then partly thrown open by the exertions of our men inside, and partly torn open by the mob outside; and we attempted, by leaping from the car, and running in all directions, to escape from the mob. We were obliged to leave everything behind. Music, instruments, coats, caps, knapsacks, and haversacks. On our way we saw squads of police, who took no notice of us, evidently regarding the whole thing as a good joke. The writer of this saw and spoke to two of them, and was told to "run—run like the devil;" and he did. They could do nothing: they would take care of our property, but could do nothing for us. After running in this way for a half mile, as near as we could judge, we were encountered by a party of women, partly Irish, partly German, and some American, who took us into their houses, removed the stripes from our pants, and we were furnished with old clothes of every description for disguise. We were treated here as well as we could have been in our own homes. Everything we wished was furnished, and nothing would be taken therefor; but we were told that it would be an insult to offer it.

Under the protection of four hundred policemen, these unarmed musicians were able to reach the station, and take the cars back to Philadelphia.

# Ulysses S. Grant to Frederick Dent, April 19, 1861, and to Jesse Root Grant, April 21, 1861

An 1843 graduate of West Point, Ulysses S. Grant had served in Mexico before resigning from the army as a captain in 1854. When the war began, he was working as a clerk in his family's leather-goods store in Galena, Illinois. Grant responded to the news of Fort Sumter in letters to his father-in-law and his father.

———————————

Galena, April 19th 1861

MR. F. DENT;
DEAR SIR:

I have but very little time to write but as in these exciting times we are very anxious to hear from you, and know of no other way but but by writing first to you, I must make time.— We get but little news, by telegraph, from St. Louis but from most all other points of the Country we are hearing all the time. The times are indeed startling but now is the time, particularly in the border Slave states, for men to prove their love of country. I know it is hard for men to apparently work with the Republican party but now all party distinctions should be lost sight of and evry true patriot be for maintaining the integrity of the glorious old *Stars & Stripes*, the Constitution and the Union. The North is responding to the Presidents call in such a manner that the rebels may truly quaik. I tell you there is no mistaking the feelings of the people. The Government can call into the field not only 75000 troops but ten or twenty times 75000 if it should be necessary and find the means of maintaining them too. It is all a mistake about the Northern pocket being so sensative. In times like the present no people are more ready to give their own time or of their abundant means. No impartial man can conceal from himself

the fact that in all these troubles the South have been the aggressors and the Administration has stood purely on the defensive, more on the defensive than she would dared to have done
but for her consiousness of strength and the certainty of right
prevailing in the end. The news to-day is that Virginia has
gone out of the Union. But for the influance she will have on
the other border slave states this is not much to be regreted.
Her position, or rather that of Eastern Virginia, has been more
reprehensible from the begining than that of South Carolina.
She should be made to bear a heavy portion of the burthen of
the War for her guilt.—In all this I can but see the doom of
Slavery. The North do not want, nor will they want, to interfere with the institution. But they will refuse for all time to
give it protection unless the South shall return soon to their allegiance, and then too this disturbance will give such an impe-
tus to the production of their staple, cotton, in other parts of
the world that they can never recover the controll of the market again for that comodity. This will reduce the value of
negroes so much that they will never be worth fighting over
again.—I have just rec'd a letter from Fred. He breathes forth
the most patriotic sentiments. He is for the old Flag as long as
there is a Union of two states fighting under its banner and
when they desolve he will go it alone. This is not his language
but it is the idea not so well expressed as he expresses it.

Julia and the children are all well and join me in love to you
all. I forgot to mention that Fred. has another heir, with some
novel name that I have forgotten.

Yours Truly<br>U. S. GRANT

Get John or Lewis Sheets to write to me.

---

Galena, April 21st 1861

DEAR FATHER;

We are now in the midst of trying times when evry one must
be for or against his country, and show his colors too, by his
every act. Having been educated for such an emergency, at the
expense of the Government, I feel that it has upon me superior
claims, such claims as no ordinary motives of self-interest can

surmount. I do not wish to act hastily or unadvisadly in the matter, and as there are more than enough to respond to the first call of the President, I have not yet offered myself. I have promised and am giving all the assistance I can in organizing the Company whose services have been accepted from this place. I have promised further to go with them to the state Capital and if I can be of service to the Governer in organizing his state troops to do so. What I ask now is your approval of the course I am taking, or advice in the matter. A letter written this week will reach me in Springfield. I have not time to write you but a hasty line for though Sunday as it is we are all busy here. In a few minuets I shall be engaged in directing tailors in the style and trim of uniforms for our men.

Whatever may have been my political opinions before I have but one sentiment now. That is we have a Government, and laws and a flag and they must all be sustained. There are but two parties now, Traitors & Patriots and I want hereafter to be ranked with the latter, and I trust, the stronger party.—I do not know but you may be placed in an awkward position, and a dangerous one pecuniarily, but costs can not now be counted. My advice would be to leave where you are if you are not safe with the veiws you entertain. I would never stultify my opinions for the sake of a little security.

I will say nothing about our business. Orvil & Lank will keep you posted as to that.

Write soon and direct as above.

Yours Truly
U. S. GRANT.

# Jefferson Davis: Message to the Confederate Congress

Davis called the Provisional Confederate Congress into special session on April 29 and sent a message regarding the outbreak of hostilities.

---

MONTGOMERY, April 29, 1861.

*Gentlemen of the Congress:* It is my pleasing duty to announce to you that the Constitution framed for the establishment of a permanent Government for the Confederate States has been ratified by conventions in each of those States to which it was referred. To inaugurate the Government in its full proportions and upon its own substantial basis of the popular will, it only remains that elections should be held for the designation of the officers to administer it. There is every reason to believe that at no distant day other States, identified in political principles and community of interests with those which you represent, will join this Confederacy, giving to its typical constellation increased splendor, to its Government of free, equal, and sovereign States a wider sphere of usefulness, and to the friends of constitutional liberty a greater security for its harmonious and perpetual existence. It was not, however, for the purpose of making this announcement that I have deemed it my duty to convoke you at an earlier day than that fixed by yourselves for your meeting. The declaration of war made against this Confederacy by Abraham Lincoln, the President of the United States, in his proclamation issued on the 15th day of the present month, rendered it necessary, in my judgment, that you should convene at the earliest practicable moment to devise the measures necessary for the defense of the country. The occasion is indeed an extraordinary one. It justifies me in a brief review of the relations heretofore existing between us and the States which now unite in warfare against us and in a succinct statement of the events which have resulted in this warfare, to the end that mankind may pass intelligent and impartial judgment on its motives and objects. During the war waged against Great Britain by her colonies on this continent a common danger impelled them to a close alliance and to the formation of a Confederation, by the terms of which the colonies, styling themselves States, entered "*severally* into a firm league of friendship with each other for their common defense, the security of their liberties, and their mutual and general welfare, binding themselves to assist each other against all force offered to or attacks made upon them, or any of them, on account of religion, sovereignty, trade, or any other pretense whatever." In order to guard against any misconstruction of their compact, the several States made explicit declaration in a distinct article—that "*each* State *retains its* sovereignty, freedom, and independence, and every power, jurisdiction, and right which is not by this Confederation *expressly delegated* to the United States in Congress assembled."

Under this contract of alliance, the war of the Revolution was successfully waged, and resulted in the treaty of peace with Great Britain in 1783, by the terms of which the several States were *each by name* recognized to be independent. The Articles of Confederation contained a clause whereby all alterations were prohibited unless confirmed by the Legislatures of *every State* after being agreed to by the Congress; and in obedience to this provision, under the resolution of Congress of the 21st of February, 1787, the several States appointed delegates who attended a convention "for the *sole and express purpose* of revising the Articles of Confederation and reporting to Congress and the several Legislatures such alterations and provisions therein as shall, when agreed to in Congress *and confirmed by the States*, render the Federal Constitution adequate to the exigencies of Government and the preservation of the Union." It was by the delegates chosen by the *several States* under the resolution just quoted that the Constitution of the United States was framed in 1787 and submitted to the *several States* for ratification, as shown by the seventh article, which is in these words: "The ratification of the *conventions of nine States* shall be sufficient for the establishment of this Constitution *between the States* so ratifying the same." I have italicized certain words in the quotations just made for the purpose of attracting attention to the singular and marked caution with which the States endeavored in every possible form to exclude the idea that the separate and independent sovereignty of each State was merged into one common government and nation, and the earnest desire they evinced to impress on the Constitution its true character—that of a *compact between* independent States. The Constitution of 1787, having, however, omitted the clause already recited from the Articles of Confederation, which provided in explicit terms that each State *retained* its sovereignty and independence, some alarm was felt in the States, when invited to ratify the Constitution, lest this omission should be construed into an abandonment of their cherished principle, and they refused to be satisfied until amendments were added to the Constitution placing beyond any pretense of doubt the reservation by the States of all their sovereign rights and powers not expressly delegated to the United States by the Constitution.

Strange, indeed, must it appear to the impartial observer, but it is none the less true that all these carefully worded clauses proved unavailing to prevent the rise and growth in the Northern States of a political school which has persistently claimed that the government thus formed was not a compact *between* States, but was in effect a national government, set up *above* and *over* the States. An organization created by the States to secure the blessings of liberty and independence against *foreign* aggression, has been gradually perverted into a machine for their control in their *domestic* affairs. The *creature* has been exalted above its *creators*; the *principals* have been made subordinate to the *agent* appointed by themselves. The people of the Southern States, whose almost exclusive occupation was agriculture, early perceived a tendency in the Northern States to render the common government subservient to their own purposes by imposing burdens on commerce as a protection to their manufacturing and shipping interests. Long and angry controversies grew out of these attempts, often successful, to benefit one section of the country at the expense of the other. And the danger of disruption arising from this cause was enhanced by the fact that the Northern population was increasing, by immigration and other causes, in a greater ratio than the population of the South. By degrees, as the Northern

States gained preponderance in the National Congress, self-interest taught their people to yield ready assent to any plausible advocacy of their right as a majority to govern the minority without control. They learned to listen with impatience to the suggestion of any constitutional impediment to the exercise of their will, and so utterly have the principles of the Constitution been corrupted in the Northern mind that, in the inaugural address delivered by President Lincoln in March last, he asserts as an axiom, which he plainly deems to be undeniable, that the theory of the Constitution requires that in all cases the majority shall govern; and in another memorable instance the same Chief Magistrate did not hesitate to liken the relations between a State and the United States to those which exist between a county and the State in which it is situated and by which it was created. This is the lamentable and fundamental error on which rests the policy that has culminated in his declaration of war against these Confederate States. In addition to the long-continued and deep-seated resentment felt by the Southern States at the persistent abuse of the powers they had delegated to the Congress, for the purpose of enriching the manufacturing and shipping classes of the North at the expense of the South, there has existed for nearly half a century another subject of discord, involving interests of such transcendent magnitude as at all times to create the apprehension in the minds of many devoted lovers of the Union that its permanence was impossible. When the several States delegated certain powers to the United States Congress, a large portion of the laboring population consisted of African slaves imported into the colonies by the mother country. In twelve out of the thirteen States negro slavery existed, and the right of property in slaves was protected by law. This property was recognized in the Constitution, and provision was made against its loss by the escape of the slave. The increase in the number of slaves by further importation from Africa was also secured by a clause forbidding Congress to prohibit the slave trade anterior to a certain date, and in no clause can there be found any delegation of power to the Congress authorizing it in any manner to legislate to the prejudice, detriment, or discouragement of the owners of that species of property, or excluding it from the protection of the Government.

The climate and soil of the Northern States soon proved unpropitious to the continuance of slave labor, whilst the converse was the case at the South. Under the unrestricted free intercourse between the two sections, the Northern States consulted their own interests by selling their slaves to the South and prohibiting slavery within their limits. The South were willing purchasers of a property suitable to their wants, and paid the price of the acquisition without harboring a suspicion that their quiet possession was to be disturbed by those who were inhibited not only by want of constitutional authority, but by good faith as vendors, from disquieting a title emanating from themselves. As soon, however, as the Northern States that prohibited African slavery within their limits had reached a number sufficient to give their representation a controlling voice in the Congress, a persistent and organized system of hostile measures against the rights of the owners of slaves in the Southern States was inaugurated and gradually extended. A continuous series of measures was devised and prosecuted for the purpose of rendering insecure the tenure of property in slaves. Fanatical organizations, supplied with money by voluntary subscriptions, were assiduously engaged in exciting amongst the slaves a spirit of discontent and revolt; means were furnished for their escape from their owners, and agents secretly employed to entice them to abscond; the constitutional provision for their rendition to their owners was first evaded, then openly denounced as a violation of conscientious obligation and religious duty; men were taught that it was a merit to elude, disobey, and violently oppose the execution of the laws enacted to secure the performance of the promise contained in the constitutional compact; owners of slaves were mobbed and even murdered in open day solely for applying to a magistrate for the arrest of a fugitive slave; the dogmas of these voluntary organizations soon obtained control of the Legislatures of many of the Northern States, and laws were passed providing for the punishment, by ruinous fines and long-continued imprisonment in jails and penitentiaries, of citizens of the Southern States who should dare to ask aid of the officers of the law for the recovery of their property. Emboldened by success, the theater of agitation and aggression against the clearly expressed constitutional rights of the Southern States was transferred to the Congress; Senators and Representatives were sent to the common councils of the nation, whose chief title to this distinction consisted in the display of a spirit of ultra fanaticism, and whose business was not "to promote the general welfare or insure domestic tranquillity," but to awaken the bitterest hatred against the citizens of sister States by violent denunciation of their institutions; the transaction of public affairs was impeded by repeated efforts to usurp powers not delegated by the Constitution, for the purpose of impairing the security of property in slaves, and reducing those States which held slaves to a condition of inferiority. Finally a great party was organized for the purpose of obtaining the administration of the Government, with the avowed object of using its power for the total exclusion of the slave States from all participation in the benefits of the public domain acquired by all the States in common, whether by conquest or purchase; of surrounding them entirely by States in which slavery should be prohibited; of thus rendering the property in slaves so insecure as to be comparatively worthless, and thereby annihilating in effect property worth thousands of millions of dollars. This party, thus organized, succeeded in the month of November last in the election of its candidate for the Presidency of the United States.

In the meantime, under the mild and genial climate of the Southern States and the increasing care and attention for the well-being and comfort of the laboring class, dictated alike by interest and humanity, the African slaves had augmented in number from about 600,000, at the date of the adoption of the constitutional compact, to upward of 4,000,000. In moral and social condition they had been elevated from brutal savages into docile, intelligent, and civilized agricultural laborers, and supplied not only with bodily comforts but with careful religious instruction. Under the supervision of a superior race their labor had been so directed as not only to allow a gradual and marked amelioration of their own condition, but to convert hundreds of thousands of square miles of the wilderness into cultivated lands covered with a prosperous people; towns and cities had sprung into existence, and had rapidly increased in wealth and population under the social system of the South; the white population of the Southern slaveholding States had augmented from about 1,250,000 at the date of the adoption of the Constitution to more than 8,500,000 in 1860; and the productions of the South in cotton, rice, sugar, and tobacco, for the full development and continuance of which the labor of African slaves was and is indispensable, had swollen to an amount which formed nearly three-fourths of the exports of the whole United States and had become absolutely necessary to the wants of civilized man. With interests of such overwhelming magnitude imperiled, the people of the Southern States were driven by the conduct of the North to the adoption of some course of action to avert the danger with which they were openly menaced. With this view the Legislatures of the several States invited the people to select delegates to conventions to be held for the purpose of determining for themselves what measures were best adapted to meet so alarming a crisis in their history. Here it may be proper to observe that from a period as early as 1798 there had existed in *all* of the States of the Union a party almost uninterruptedly in the majority based upon the creed that each State was, in the last resort, the sole judge as well of its wrongs as of the mode and measure of redress. Indeed, it is obvious that under the law of nations this principle is an axiom as applied to the relations of independent sovereign States, such as those which had united themselves under the constitutional compact. The Democratic party of the United States repeated, in its successful canvass in 1856, the declaration made in numerous previous political contests, that it would "faithfully abide by and uphold the principles laid down in the Kentucky and Virginia resolutions of 1798, and in the report of Mr. Madison to the Virginia Legislature in 1799; and that it adopts those principles as constituting one of the main foundations of its political creed." The principles thus emphatically announced embrace that to which I have already adverted—the right of each State to judge of and redress the wrongs of which it complains. These principles were maintained by overwhelming majorities of the people of all the States of the Union at different elections, especially in the elections of Mr. Jefferson in 1805, Mr. Madison in 1809, and Mr. Pierce in 1852. In the exercise of a right so ancient, so well-established, and so necessary for self-preservation, the people of the Confederate States, in their conventions, determined that the wrongs which they had suffered and the evils with which they were menaced required that they should revoke the delegation of powers to the Federal Government which they had ratified in their several conventions. They consequently passed ordinances resuming all their rights as sovereign and independent States and dissolved their connection with the other States of the Union.

Having done this, they proceeded to form a new compact amongst themselves by new articles of confederation, which have been also ratified by the conventions of the several States with an approach to unanimity far exceeding that of the conventions which adopted the Constitution of 1787. They have organized their new Government in all its departments; the functions of the executive, legislative, and judicial magistrates are performed in accordance with the will of the people, as displayed not merely in a cheerful acquiescence, but in the enthusiastic support of the Government thus established by themselves; and but for the interference of the Government of the United States in this legitimate exercise of the right of a people to self-government, peace, happiness, and prosperity would now smile on our land. That peace is ardently desired by this Government and people has been manifested in every possible form. Scarce had you assembled in February last when, prior even to the inauguration of the Chief Magistrate you had elected, you passed a resolution expressive of your desire for the appointment of commissioners to be sent to the Government of the United States "for the purpose of negotiating friendly relations between that Government and the Confederate States of America, and for the settlement of all questions of disagreement between the two Governments upon principles of right, justice, equity, and good faith." It was my pleasure as well as my duty to coöperate with you in this work of peace. Indeed, in my address to you on taking the oath of office, and before receiving from you the communication of this resolution, I had said "as a necessity, not a choice, we have resorted to the remedy of separation, and henceforth our energies must be directed to the conduct of our own affairs and the perpetuity of the Confederacy which we have formed. If a just perception of mutual interests shall permit us peaceably to pursue our separate political career, my most earnest desire will have been fulfilled." It was in furtherance of these accordant views of the Congress and the Executive that I made choice of three discreet, able, and distinguished citizens, who repaired to Washington. Aided by their cordial cooperation and that of the Secretary of State, every effort compatible with self-respect and the dignity of the Confederacy was exhausted before I allowed myself to yield to the conviction that the Government of the United States was determined to attempt the conquest of this people and that our cherished hopes of peace were unattainable.

On the arrival of our commissioners in Washington on the 5th of March they postponed, at the suggestion of a friendly intermediary, doing more than giving informal notice of their arrival. This was done with a view to afford time to the President, who had just been inaugurated, for the discharge of other pressing official duties in the organization of his Administration before engaging his attention in the object of their mission. It was not until the 12th of the month that they officially addressed the Secretary of State, informing him of the purpose of their arrival, and stating, in the language of their instructions, their wish "to make to the Government of the United States overtures for the opening of negotiations, assuring the Government of the United States that the President, Congress, and people of the Confederate States earnestly desire a peaceful solution of these great questions; that it is neither their interest nor their wish to make any demand which is not founded on strictest justice, nor do any act to injure their late confederates."

To this communication no formal reply was received until the 8th of April. During the interval the commissioners had consented to waive all questions of form. With the firm resolve to avoid war if possible, they went so far even as to hold during that long period unofficial intercourse through an intermediary, whose high position and character inspired the hope of success, and through whom constant assurances were received from the Government of the United States of peaceful intentions, of the determination to evacuate Fort Sumter; and further, that no measure changing the existing status prejudicially to the Confederate States, especially at Fort Pickens, was in contemplation, but that in the event of any change of intention on the subject, notice would be given to the commissioners. The crooked paths of diplomacy can scarcely furnish an example so wanting in courtesy, in candor, and directness as was the course of the United States Government toward our commissioners in Washington. For proof of this I refer to the annexed documents marked ———, taken in connection with further facts, which I now proceed to relate.

Early in April the attention of the whole country, as well as that of our commissioners, was attracted to extraordinary preparations for an extensive military and naval expedition in New York and other Northern ports. These preparations commenced in secrecy, for an expedition whose destination was concealed, only became known when nearly completed, and on the 5th, 6th, and 7th of April transports and vessels of war with troops, munitions, and military supplies sailed from Northern ports bound southward. Alarmed by so extraordinary a demonstration, the commissioners requested the delivery of an answer to their official communication of the 12th of March, and thereupon received on the 8th of April a reply, dated on the 15th of the previous month, from which it appears that during the whole interval, whilst the commissioners were receiving assurances calculated to inspire hope of the success of their mission, the Secretary of State and the President of the United States had already determined to hold no intercourse with them whatever; to refuse even to listen to any proposals they had to make, and had profited by the delay created by their own assurances in order to prepare secretly the means for effective hostile operations. That these assurances were given has been virtually confessed by the Government of the United States by its sending a messenger to Charleston to give notice of its purpose to use force if opposed in its intention of supplying Fort Sumter. No more striking proof of the absence of good faith in the conduct of the Government of the United States toward this Confederacy can be required than is contained in the circumstances which accompanied this notice. According to the usual course of navigation the vessels composing the expedition designed for the relief of Fort Sumter might be expected to reach Charleston Harbor on the 9th of April. Yet, with our commissioners actually in Washington, detained under assurances that notice should be given of any military movement, the notice was not addressed to *them*, but a messenger was sent to Charleston to give the notice to the Governor of South Carolina, and the notice was so given at a late hour on the 8th of April, the eve of the very day on which the fleet might be expected to arrive.

That this maneuver failed in its purpose was not the fault of those who contrived it. A heavy tempest delayed the arrival of the expedition and gave time to the commander of our forces at Charleston to ask and receive the instructions of this Government. Even then, under all the provocation incident to the contemptuous refusal to listen to our commissioners, and the tortuous course of the Government of the United States, I was sincerely anxious to avoid the effusion of blood, and directed a proposal to be made to the commander of Fort Sumter, who had avowed himself to be nearly out of provisions, that we would abstain from directing our fire on Fort Sumter if he would promise not to open fire on our forces unless first attacked. This proposal was refused and the conclusion was reached that the design of the United States was to place the besieging force at Charleston between the simultaneous fire of the fleet and the fort. There remained, therefore, no alternative but to direct that the fort should at once be reduced. This order was executed by General Beauregard with the skill and success which were naturally to be expected from the well-known character of that gallant officer; and although the bombardment lasted but thirty-three hours our flag did not wave over its battered walls until after the appearance of the hostile fleet off Charleston. Fortunately, not a life was lost on our side, and we were gratified in being spared the necessity of a useless effusion of blood, by the prudent caution of the officers who commanded the fleet in abstaining from the evidently futile effort to enter the harbor for the relief of Major Anderson.

I refer to the report of the Secretary of War, and the papers which accompany it, for further details of this brilliant affair. In this connection I cannot refrain from a well-deserved tribute to the noble State, the eminent soldierly qualities of whose people were so conspicuously displayed in the port of Charleston. For months they had been irritated by the spectacle of a fortress held within their principal harbor as a standing menace against their peace and independence. Built in part with their own money, its custody confided with their own consent to an agent who held no power over them other than such as they had themselves delegated for their own benefit, intended to be used by that agent for their own protection against foreign attack, they saw it held with persistent tenacity as a means of offense against them by the very Government which they had established for their protection. They had beleaguered it for months, felt entire confidence in their power to capture it, yet yielded to the requirements of discipline, curbed their impatience, submitted without complaint to the unaccustomed hardships, labors, and privations of a protracted siege; and when at length their patience was rewarded by the signal for attack, and success had crowned their steady and gallant conduct, even in the very moment of triumph they evinced a chivalrous regard for the feelings of the brave but unfortunate officer who had been compelled to lower his flag. All manifestations of exultation were checked in his presence. Their commanding general, with their cordial approval and the consent of his Government, refrained from imposing any terms that could wound the sensibilities of the commander of the fort. He was permitted to retire with the honors of war, to salute his flag, to depart freely with all his command, and was escorted to the vessel in which he embarked with the highest marks of respect from those against whom his guns had been so recently directed.

Not only does every event connected with the siege reflect the highest honor on South Carolina, but the forbearance of her people and of this Government from making any harsh use of a victory obtained under circumstances of such peculiar provocation attest to the fullest extent the absence of any purpose beyond securing their own tranquillity and the sincere desire to avoid the calamities of war. Scarcely had the President of the United States received intelligence of the failure of the scheme which he had devised for the reënforcement of Fort Sumter, when he issued the declaration of war against this Confederacy which has prompted me to convoke you. In this extraordinary production that high functionary affects total ignorance of the existence of an independent Government, which, possessing the entire and enthusiastic devotion of its people, is exercising its functions without question over seven sovereign States, over more than 5,000,000 of people, and over a territory whose area exceeds half a million of square miles. He terms sovereign States "combinations too powerful to be suppressed by the ordinary course of judicial proceedings or by the powers vested in the marshals by law." He calls for an army of 75,000 men to act as a *posse comitatus* in aid of the process of the courts of justice in States where no courts exist whose mandates and decrees are not cheerfully obeyed and respected by a willing people. He avows that "the *first* service to be assigned to the forces called out" will be not to execute the process of courts, but to capture forts and strongholds situated within the admitted limits of this Confederacy and garrisoned by its troops; and declares that "this effort" is intended "to maintain the perpetuity of popular government." He concludes by commanding "the persons composing the combinations aforesaid"—to wit, the 5,000,000 of inhabitants of these States—"to retire peaceably to their respective abodes within twenty days." Apparently contradictory as are the terms of this singular document, one point is unmistakably evident. The President of the United States called for an army of 75,000 men, whose *first* service was to be to capture our forts. It was a plain declaration of war which I was not at liberty to disregard because of my knowledge that under the Constitution of the United States the President was usurping a power granted exclusively to the Congress. He is the sole organ of communication between that country and foreign powers. The law of nations did not permit me to question the authority of the Executive of a foreign nation to declare war against this Confederacy. Although I might have refrained from taking active measures for our defense, if the States of the Union had all imitated the action of Virginia, North Carolina, Arkansas, Kentucky, Tennessee, and Missouri, by denouncing the call for troops as an unconstitutional usurpation of power to which they refused to respond, I was not at liberty to disregard the fact that many of the States seemed quite content to submit to the exercise of the power assumed by the President of the United States, and were actively engaged in levying troops to be used for the purpose indicated in the proclamation. Deprived of the aid of Congress at the moment, I was under the necessity of confining my action to a call on the States for volunteers for the common defense, in accordance with the authority you had confided to me before your adjournment. I deemed it proper, further, to issue proclamation inviting application from persons disposed to aid our defense in private armed vessels on the high seas, to the end that preparations might be made for the immediate issue of letters of marque and reprisal which you alone, under the Constitution, have power to grant. I entertain no doubt you will concur with me in the opinion that in the absence of a fleet of public vessels it will be eminently expedient to supply their place by private armed vessels, so happily styled by the publicists of the United States "the militia of the sea," and so often and justly relied on by them as an efficient and admirable instrument of defensive warfare. I earnestly recommend the immediate passage of a law authorizing me to accept the numerous proposals already received. I cannot close this review of the acts of the Government of the United States without referring to a proclamation issued by their President, under date of the 19th instant, in which, after declaring that an insurrection has broken out in this Confederacy against the Government of the United States, he announces a blockade of all the ports of these States, and threatens to punish as pirates all persons who shall molest any vessel of the United States under letters of marque issued by this Government. Notwithstanding the authenticity of this proclamation you will concur with me that it is hard to believe it could have emanated from a President of the United States. Its announcement of a mere paper blockade is so manifestly a violation of the law of nations that it would seem incredible that it could have been issued by authority; but conceding this to be the case so far as the Executive is concerned, it will be difficult to satisfy the people of these States that their late confederates will sanction its declarations—will determine to ignore the usages of civilized nations, and will inaugurate a war of extermination on both sides by treating as pirates open enemies acting under the authority of commissions issued by an organized government. If such proclamation was issued, it could only have been published under the sudden influence of passion, and we may rest assured mankind will be spared the horrors of the conflict it seems to invite.

For the details of the administration of the different Departments I refer to the reports of the Secretaries, which accompany this message.

The State Department has furnished the necessary instructions for three commissioners who have been sent to England, France, Russia, and Belgium since your adjournment to ask our recognition as a member of the family of nations, and to make with each of those powers treaties of amity and commerce. Further steps will be taken to enter into like negotiations with the other European powers, in pursuance of your resolutions passed at the last session. Sufficient time has not yet elapsed since the departure of these commissioners for the receipt of any intelligence from them. As I deem it desirable that commissioners or other diplomatic agents should also be sent at an early period to the independent American powers south of our Confederacy, with all of whom it is our interest and earnest wish to maintain the most cordial and friendly relations, I suggest the expediency of making the necessary appropriations for that purpose. Having been officially notified by the public authorities of the State of Virginia that she had withdrawn from the Union and desired to maintain the closet political relations with us which it was possible at this time to establish, I commissioned the Hon. Alexander H. Stephens, Vice President of the Confederate States, to represent this Government at Richmond. I am happy to inform you that he has concluded a convention with the State of Virginia by which that honored Commonwealth, so long and justly distinguished among her sister States, and so dear to the hearts of thousands of her children in the Confederate States, has united her power and her fortunes with ours and become one of us. This convention, together with the ordinance of Virginia adopting the Provisional Constitution of the Confederacy, will be laid before you for your constitutional action. I have satisfactory assurances from other of our late confederates that they are on the point of adopting similar measures, and I cannot doubt that ere you shall have been many weeks in session the whole of the slaveholding States of the late Union will respond to the call of honor and affection, and by uniting their fortunes with ours promote our common interests and secure our common safety.

In the Treasury Department regulations have been devised

and put into execution for carrying out the policy indicated in your legislation on the subject of the navigation of the Mississippi River, as well as for the collection of revenue on the frontier. Free transit has been secured for vessels and merchandise passing through the Confederate States; and delay and inconvenience have been avoided as far as possible, in organizing the revenue service for the various railways entering our territory. As fast as experience shall indicate the possibility of improvement in these regulations no effort will be spared to free commerce from all unnecessary embarrassments and obstructions. Under your act authorizing a loan, proposals were issued inviting subscriptions for $5,000,000, and the call was answered by the prompt subscription of more than $8,000,000 by our own citizens, and not a single bid was made under par. The rapid development of the purpose of the President of the United States to invade our soil, capture our forts, blockade our ports, and wage war against us induced me to direct that the entire subscription should be accepted. It will now become necessary to raise means to a much larger amount to defray the expenses of maintaining our independence and repelling invasion. I invite your special attention to this subject, and the financial condition of the Government, with the suggestion of ways and means for the supply of the Treasury, will be presented to you in a separate communication.

To the Department of Justice you have confided not only the organization and supervision of all matters connected with the courts of justice, but also those connected with patents and with the bureau of public printing. Since your adjournment all the courts, with the exception of those of Mississippi and Texas, have been organized by the appointment of marshals and district attorneys and are now prepared for the exercise of their functions. In the two States just named the gentlemen confirmed as judges declined to accept the appointment, and no nominations have yet been made to fill the vacancies. I refer you to the report of the Attorney-General and concur in his recommendation for immediate legislation, especially on the subject of patent rights. Early provision should be made to secure to the subjects of foreign nations the full enjoyment of their property in valuable inventions, and to extend to our own citizens protection, not only for their own inventions, but for such as may have been assigned to them or may hereafter be assigned by persons not alien enemies. The Patent Office business is much more extensive and important than had been anticipated. The applications for patents, although confined under the law exclusively to citizens of our Confederacy, already average seventy per month, showing the necessity for the prompt organization of a bureau of patents.

The Secretary of War in his report and accompanying documents conveys full information concerning the forces –regular, volunteer, and provisional– raised and called for under the several acts of Congress—their organization and distribution; also an account of the expenditures already made, and the further estimates for the fiscal year ending the 18th of February, 1862, rendered necessary by recent events. I refer to his report also for a full history of the occurrences in Charleston Harbor prior to and including the bombardment and reduction of Fort Sumter, and of the measures subsequently taken for the common defense on receiving the intelligence of the declaration of war against us, made by the President of the United States. There are now in the field at Charleston, Pensacola, Forts Morgan, Jackson, Saint Philip, and Pulaski 19,000 men, and 16,000 are now *en route* for Virginia. It is proposed to organize and hold in readiness for instant action, in view of the present exigencies of the country, an army of 100,000 men. If further force should be needed, the wisdom and patriotism of Congress will be confidently appealed to for authority to call into the field additional numbers of our noble-spirited volunteers who are constantly tendering service far in excess of our wants.

The operations of the Navy Department have been necessarily restricted by the fact that sufficient time has not yet elapsed for the purchase or construction of more than a limited number of vessels adapted to the public service. Two vessels purchased have been named the Sumter and McRae, and are now being prepared for sea at New Orleans with all possible dispatch. Contracts have also been made at that city with two different establishments for the casting of ordnance– cannon shot and shell—with the view to encourage the manufacture of these articles, so indispensable for our defense, at as many points within our territory as possible. I call your attention to the recommendation of the Secretary for the establishment of a magazine and laboratory for preparation of ordnance stores and the necessary appropriation for that purpose. Hitherto such stores have usually been prepared at the navy yards, and no appropriation was made at your last session for this object. The Secretary also calls attention to the fact that no provision has been made for the payment of invalid pensions to our own citizens. Many of these persons are advanced in life; they have no means of support, and by the secession of these States have been deprived of their claim against the Government of the United States. I recommend the appropriation of the sum necessary to pay these pensioners, as well as those of the Army, whose claims can scarcely exceed $70,000 per annum.

The Postmaster General has already succeeded in organizing his Department to such an extent as to be in readiness to assume the direction of our postal affairs on the occurrence of the contingency contemplated by the act of March 15, 1861, or even sooner if desired by Congress. The various books and circulars have been prepared and measures taken to secure supplies of blanks, postage stamps, stamped envelopes, mail bags, locks, keys, etc. He presents a detailed classification and arrangement of his clerical force, and asks for its increase. An auditor of the Treasury for this Department is necessary, and a plan is submitted for the organization of his bureau. The great number and magnitude of the accounts of this Department require an increase of the clerical force in the accounting branch in the Treasury. The revenues of this Department are collected and disbursed in modes peculiar to itself, and require a special bureau to secure a proper accountability in the administration of its finances. I call your attention to the additional legislation required for this Department; to the recommendation for changes in the law fixing the rates of postage on newspapers, periodicals, and sealed packages of certain kinds, and specially to the recommendation of the Secretary, in which I concur, that you provide at once for the assumption by him of the control of our entire postal service.

In the military organization of the States provision is made for brigadier and major generals, but in the Army of the Confederate States the highest grade is that of brigadier general. Hence it will no doubt sometimes occur that where troops of the Confederacy do duty with the militia, the general selected for the command and possessed of the views and purposes of this Government will be superseded by an officer of the militia not having the same advantages. To avoid this contingency in the least objectionable manner I recommend that additional rank be given to the general of the Confederate Army, and concurring in the policy of having but one grade of generals in the Army of the Confederacy, I recommend that the law of its organization be amended so that the grade be that of general. To secure a thorough military education it is deemed essential that officers should enter upon the study of their profession at an early period of life and have elementary instruction in a military school. Until such school shall be established it is recommended that cadets be appointed and attached to companies until they shall have attained the age and have acquired the knowledge to fit them for the duties of lieutenants. I also call your attention to an omission in the law organizing the Army, in relation to military chaplains, and recommend that provision be made for their appointment.

In conclusion, I congratulate you on the fact that in every portion of our country there has been exhibited the most patriotic devotion to our common cause. Transportation companies have freely tendered the use of their lines for troops and supplies. The presidents of the railroads of the Confederacy, in company with others who control lines of communication with States that we hope soon to greet as sisters, assembled in convention in this city, and not only reduced largely the rates heretofore demanded for mail service and conveyance of troops and munitions, but voluntarily proffered to receive their compensation, at these reduced rates, in the bonds of the Confederacy, for the purpose of leaving all the resources of the Government at its disposal for the common defense. Requisitions for troops have been met with such alacrity that the numbers tendering their services have in every instance greatly exceeded the demand. Men of the highest official and social position are serving as volunteers in the ranks. The gravity of age and the zeal of youth rival each other in the desire to be foremost for the public defense; and though at no other point than the one heretofore noticed have they been stimulated by the excitement incident to actual engagement and the hope of distinction for individual achievement, they have borne what for new troops is the most severe ordeal—patient toil and constant vigil, and all the exposure and discomfort of active service, with a resolution and fortitude such as to command approbation and justify the highest expectation of their conduct when active valor shall be required in place of steady endurance. A people thus united and resolved cannot shrink from any sacrifice which they may be called on to make, nor can there be a reasonable doubt of their final success, however long and severe may be the test of their determination to maintain their birthright of freedom and equality as a trust which it is their first duty to transmit undiminished to their posterity. A bounteous Providence cheers us with the promise of abundant crops. The fields of grain which will within a few weeks be ready for the sickle give assurance of the amplest supply of food for man; whilst the corn, cotton, and other staple productions of our soil afford abundant proof that up to this period the season has been propitious. We feel that our cause is just and holy; we protest solemnly in the face of mankind that we desire peace at any sacrifice save that of honor and independence; we seek no conquest, no aggrandizement, no concession of any kind from the States with which we were lately confederated; all we ask is to be let alone; that those who never held power over us shall not now attempt our subjugation by arms. This we will, this we must, resist to the direst extremity. The moment that this pretension is abandoned the sword will drop from our grasp, and we shall be ready to enter into treaties of amity and commerce that cannot but be mutually beneficial. So long as this pretension is maintained, with a firm reliance on that Divine Power which covers with its protection the just cause, we will continue to struggle for our inherent right to freedom, independence, and self-government.

JEFFERSON DAVIS.

# Frederick Douglass: How to End the War

## May 1861

Up until the outbreak of hostilities Douglass worried that the North would resolve the secession crisis by offering new concessions regarding slavery. Once the war began he used his *Monthly* to advocate that it be waged radically, by enlisting black soldiers and making the destruction of slavery an essential aim.

---

To our mind, there is but one easy, short and effectual way to suppress and put down the desolating war which the slaveholders and their rebel minions are now waging against the American Government and its loyal citizens. Fire must be met with water, darkness with light, and war for the destruction of liberty must be met with war for the destruction of slavery. *The simple way, then, to put an end to the savage and desolating war now waged by the slaveholders, is to strike down slavery itself,* the primal cause of that war.

Freedom to the slave should now be proclaimed from the Capitol, and should be seen above the smoke and fire of every battle field, waving from every loyal flag! The time for mild measures is past. They are pearls cast before swine, and only increase and aggravate the crime which they would conciliate and repress. The weak point must be found, and when found should be struck with the utmost vigor. Any war is a calamity; but a peace that can only breed war is a far greater calamity. A long and tame war, waged without aim or spirit, paralyzes business, arrests the wheels of civilization, benumbs the national feeling, corrodes the national heart, and diffuses its baleful influence universally. Sharp, quick, wise, strong and sudden, are the elements for the occasion. The sooner this rebellion is put out of its misery, the better for all concerned. A lenient war is a lengthy war, and therefore the worst kind of war. Let us stop it, and stop it effectually—stop it before its evils are diffused throughout the Northern States—stop it on the soil upon which it originated, and among the traitors and rebels who originated the war. This can be done at once, by *"carrying the war into Africa."* Let the slaves and free colored people be called into service, and formed into a liberating army, to march into the South and raise the banner of Emancipation among the slaves. The South having brought revolution and war upon the country, and having elected and consented to play at that fearful game, she has no right to complain if some good as well as calamity shall result from her own act and deed.

The slaveholders have not hesitated to employ the sable arms of the Negroes at the South in erecting the fortifications which silenced the guns of Fort Sumter, and brought the star-spangled banner to the dust. They often boast, and not without cause, that their Negroes will fight for them against the North. They have no scruples against employing the Negroes to exterminate freedom, and in overturning the Government. They work with spade and barrow with them, and they will stand with them on the field of battle, shoulder to shoulder, with guns in their hands, to shoot down the troops of the U. S. Government.—They have neither pride, prejudice nor *pity* to restrain them from employing Negroes *against white men, where slavery is to be protected and made secure.* Oh! that this Government would only now be as true to liberty as the rebels, who are attempting to batter it down, are true to slavery. We have no hesitation in saying that ten thousand black soldiers might be raised in the next thirty days to march upon the South. One black regiment alone would be, in such a war, the full equal of two white ones. The very fact of color in this case would be more terrible than powder and balls. The slaves would learn more as to the nature of the conflict from the presence of one such regiment, than from a thousand preachers. Every consideration of justice, humanity and sound policy confirms the wisdom of calling upon black men just now to take up arms in behalf of their country.

We are often asked by persons in the street as well as by letter, what our people will do in the present solemn crisis in the affairs of the country. Our answer is, would to God you would let us do something! We lack nothing but your consent.

We are ready and would go, counting ourselves happy in being permitted to serve and suffer for the cause of freedom and free institutions. But you won't let us go. Read the heart-rending account we publish elsewhere of the treatment received by the brave fellows, who broke away from their chains and went through marvelous suffering to defend Fort Pickens against the rebels.—They were instantly seized and put in irons and returned to their guilty masters to be whipped to death! Witness Gen. Butler's offer to put down the slave insurrection in the State of Maryland. The colored citizens of Boston have offered their services to the Government, and were refused. There is, even now, while the slaveholders are marshaling armed Negroes against the Government, covering the ocean with pirates, destroying innocent lives, to sweep down the commerce of the country, tearing up railways, burning bridges to prevent the march of Government troops to the defence of its capital, exciting mobs to stone the Yankee soldiers; there is still, we say, weak and contemptible tenderness towards the blood thirsty, slaveholding traitors, by the Government and people of the country. Until the nation shall repent of this weakness and folly, until they shall make the cause of their country the cause of freedom, until they shall strike down slavery, the source and center of this gigantic rebellion, they don't deserve the support of a single sable arm, nor will it succeed in crushing the cause of our present troubles.

# Walt Whitman: First O Songs for a Prelude

In the spring of 1861 Walt Whitman was working as a freelance journalist in New York. He watched as a series of newly-formed Union
regiments paraded through the city, part of what Whitman would
later describe as the "volcanic upheaval of the nation, after that firing
on the flag at Charleston, . . . the grandest and most encouraging
spectacle yet vouchsafed in any age, old or new, to democracy." This
poem was first published in *Drum-Taps* in 1865.

---

FIRST O songs for a prelude,
Lightly strike on the stretch'd tympanum pride and joy in my
    city,
How she led the rest to arms, how she gave the cue,
How at once with lithe limbs unwaiting a moment she
    sprang,
(O superb! O Manhattan, my own, my peerless!
O strongest you in the hour of danger, in crisis! O truer than
    steel!)
How you sprang—how you threw off the costumes of peace
    with indifferent hand,
How your soft opera-music changed, and the drum and fife
    were heard in their stead,
How you led to the war, (that shall serve for our prelude,
    songs of soldiers,)
How Manhattan drum-taps led.

Forty years had I in my city seen soldiers parading,
Forty years as a pageant, till unawares the lady of this teeming
    and turbulent city,
Sleepless amid her ships, her houses, her incalculable wealth,
With her million children around her, suddenly,
At dead of night, at news from the south,
Incens'd struck with clinch'd hand the pavement.

A shock electric, the night sustain'd it,
Till with ominous hum our hive at daybreak pour'd out its
    myriads.

From the houses then and the workshops, and through all the
    doorways,
Leapt they tumultuous, and lo! Manhattan arming.

To the drum-taps prompt,
The young men falling in and arming,
The mechanics arming, (the trowel, the jack-plane, the black-
    smith's hammer, tost aside with precipitation,)
The lawyer leaving his office and arming, the judge leaving
    the court,
The driver deserting his wagon in the street, jumping down,
    throwing the reins abruptly down on the horses' backs,
The salesman leaving the store, the boss, book-keeper, porter,
    all leaving;
Squads gather everywhere by common consent and arm,
The new recruits, even boys, the old men show them how to
    wear their accoutrements, they buckle the straps care-
    fully,
Outdoors arming, indoors arming, the flash of the musket-
    barrels,
The white tents cluster in camps, the arm'd sentries around,
    the sunrise cannon and again at sunset,
Arm'd regiments arrive every day, pass through the city, and
    embark from the wharves,
(How good they look as they tramp down to the river,
    sweaty, with their guns on their shoulders!
How I love them! how I could hug them, with their brown
    faces and their clothes and knapsacks cover'd with dust!)
The blood of the city up—arm'd! arm'd! the cry everywhere,
The flags flung out from the steeples of churches and from all
    the public buildings and stores,
The tearful parting, the mother kisses her son, the son kisses
    his mother,
(Loth is the mother to part, yet not a word does she speak to
    detain him,)

The tumultuous escort, the ranks of policemen preceding,
    clearing the way,
The unpent enthusiasm, the wild cheers of the crowd for
    their favorites,
The artillery, the silent cannons bright as gold, drawn along,
    rumble lightly over the stones,
(Silent cannons, soon to cease your silence,
Soon unlimber'd to begin the red business;)
All the mutter of preparation, all the determin'd arming,
The hospital service, the lint, bandages and medicines,
The women volunteering for nurses, the work begun for in
    earnest, no mere parade now;
War! an arm'd race is advancing! the welcome for battle, no
    turning away;
War! be it weeks, months, or years, an arm'd race is advancing
    to welcome it.

Mannahatta a-march—and it's O to sing it well!
It's O for a manly life in the camp.

And the sturdy artillery,
The guns bright as gold, the work for giants, to serve well the
    guns,
Unlimber them! (no more as the past forty years for salutes
    for courtesies merely,
Put in something now besides powder and wadding.)

And you lady of ships, you Mannahatta,
Old matron of this proud, friendly, turbulent city,
Often in peace and wealth you were pensive or covertly
    frown'd amid all your children,
But now you smile with joy exulting old Mannahatta.

# Winfield Scott to George B. McClellan

A hero of the War of 1812 and the U.S.-Mexican War, Winfield Scott had served as general-in-chief of the army since 1841. He outlined his grand strategy for defeating the Confederacy in a letter to George B. McClellan, who at the time commanded the Ohio militia. When Scott's proposal was made public, it became popularly known as the "Anaconda Plan" because it sought to constrict the Confederacy by blockade.

---

HEADQUARTERS OF THE ARMY,
*Washington, May 3, 1861.*

Maj. Gen. GEORGE B. McCLELLAN,
*Commanding Ohio Volunteers, Cincinnati, Ohio:*

SIR: I have read and carefully considered your plan for a campaign, and now send you confidentially my own views, supported by certain facts of which you should be advised.

First. It is the design of the Government to raise 25,000 additional regular troops, and 60,000 volunteers for three years. It will be inexpedient either to rely on the three-months' volunteers for extensive operations or to put in their hands the best class of arms we have in store. The term of service would expire by the commencement of a regular campaign, and the arms not lost be returned mostly in a damaged condition. Hence I must strongly urge upon you to confine yourself strictly to the quota of three-months' men called for by the War Department.

Second. We rely greatly on the sure operation of a complete blockade of the Atlantic and Gulf ports soon to commence. In connection with such blockade we propose a powerful movement down the Mississippi to the ocean, with a cordon of posts at proper points, and the capture of Forts Jackson and Saint Philip; the object being to clear out and keep open this great line of communication in connection with the strict blockade of the sea-board, so as to envelop the insurgent

States and bring them to terms with less bloodshed than by any other plan. I suppose there will be needed from twelve to twenty steam gun-boats, and a sufficient number of steam transports (say forty) to carry all the personnel (say 60,000 men) and material of the expedition; most of the gun-boats to be in advance to open the way, and the remainder to follow and protect the rear of the expedition, &c. This army, in which it is not improbable you may be invited to take an important part, should be composed of our best regulars for the advance and of three-years' volunteers, all well officered, and with four months and a half of instruction in camps prior to (say) November 10. In the progress down the river all the enemy's batteries on its banks we of course would turn and capture, leaving a sufficient number of posts with complete garrisons to keep the river open behind the expedition. Finally, it will be necessary that New Orleans should be strongly occupied and securely held until the present difficulties are composed.

Third. A word now as to the greatest obstacle in the way of this plan—the great danger now pressing upon us—the impatience of our patriotic and loyal Union friends. They will urge instant and vigorous action, regardless, I fear, of consequences—that is, unwilling to wait for the slow instruction of (say) twelve or fifteen camps, for the rise of rivers, and the return of frosts to kill the virus of malignant fevers below Memphis. I fear this; but impress right views, on every proper occasion, upon the brave men who are hastening to the support of their Government. Lose no time, while necessary preparations for the great expedition are in progress, in organizing, drilling, and disciplining your three-months' men, many of whom, it is hoped, will be ultimately found enrolled under the call for three-years' volunteers. Should an urgent and immediate occasion arise meantime for their services, they will be the more effective. I commend these views to your consideration, and shall be happy to hear the result.

With great respect, yours, truly,

WINFIELD SCOTT.

# Charles B. Haydon: Diary, May 3 -12, 1861

A law clerk from Kalamazoo, Charles B. Haydon enlisted in the local militia on April 22, 1861, and soon became a sergeant in Company I, 2nd Michigan Infantry. In his diary he recorded his experiences at an encampment outside Detroit.

———  ——

MAY 3    Sergt. Ford & self quartered with the men last night. We had a straw bed & each a blanket & a shawl so that we were warm enough & slept well, but Ford complains considerably. Nearly all the men have bad colds & 3 are sick. The duties of the day commenced at 5 by washing at the pump &c. The day like the latter part of yesterday is cold & disagreeable with fair prospect of another storm which would make the parade ground impassable. I acted as second Sergt. this P.M. & was sharply berated by the Col. for not knowing my business. I very soon learned it however & shall not be caught again on that point. We are becoming more accustomed to camp life &c. Still there is some grumbling amg the men. Those who are living better now than they ever lived before grumble most in many cases. Such are always first to complain when they are away from home.

MAY 4    We had to day the first fine day of camp life. The weather was really comfortable. We could lounge in the sun. I could laugh as heartily to day to hear the Col. blow up others as they did yesterday at my berating. I had the satisfaction of seeing Lieut. Dake on the full run several times (a rare sight). The Capt. did not fare much better.

MAY 5    Sunday. Corpl. Ball & self went up to Ft. Wayne after breakfast to see how the other Regt. was faring. We had a fine ride up & back on a steam boat & saw the fort & men &c. We returned to a late dinner. At 3 P.M. we mustered 18 men in our Co. to march to religious services. We march before breakfast for one hour & after church we drilled 2 hrs. They were busy drilling at the Ft.

We are now quite comfortable & used to camp life. I am surprised to see how quick I came into it. Capt. C. S. May says we shall never know anything again except facing, flanking, filing, marching &c &c. I think he is to some extent correct. I can easily see that if we remain here 6 or 8 weeks it will be dull beyond all description. If we are to remain here for three months I shall be very sorry that I enlisted. I came because I thought we were needed & if we are I shall be well content.

We got news yesterday that one man who enlisted in our Co. at Kalamazoo was dead. His name was Henry Carrier—a good stout boy—he was taken sick the day before we started & died soon after. This is the first death in our Co. & I believe the first in the Regt. There are several on the sick list.

MAY 6  Some rain last night, weather fair this morning. If the men pursue the enemy as vigorously as they do the whores they will make very efficient soldiers.

A smart rain P.M. We were to day examined & took the oath of alligiance to the State. The examination was not rigid, & none were rejected on acct of physical incapacity. Abt a doz. spare men had to be thrown out & will very reluctantly (most of them) go. Some will return home & others will enter other companies of this Regt. to supply the place of those who have been thrown out or have deserted. Many enlisted hastily & from some Co's., especially the Adrian Guards, desertions have been frequent. Till to day the stay of all was merely voluntary, henceforth it will be compulsory. An opportunity was given before taking the oath by our Co. for any who desired to withdraw. Only one went & he (Dennis Stockwell) among abundant groans & hisses from the Co. He returned before the oath & would have come in again if he had been permitted.

Camp life is not much different from what I expected. Card playing, profanity & the stealing of provisions are among the most noted characteristics outside of the duties. There are 4 Co's. of us quartered together, 2 from Kalamazoo, the East Saginaw Guards, & Constantine Union Guards. I noticed at one time this P.M. 15 4-hand games of euchre going on at the same time. No gambling is allowed in camp & strong measures are taken to prevent stealing.

I have not as yet regretted that I enlisted. I went from a sense of duty & I expect that to sustain me in the hardships which I may be called to endure. Only one thing troubles me seriously. That is to get up at 5 A.M. & drill at double quick time before breakfast.

MAY 7   Rain A.M. light. I have been on the go pretty briskly for two days, acting as second & sometimes as first Sergt. owing to the sickness or absence of the other. The battalion drill makes busy work for a new guide & for one who is the only file closer for a large part of the time. The rascals steal everything they can put hands on—stole Ford's shawl (an important part of our bed clothes) to day.

It is reported that we cannot go into service unless we enlist for three years or during the war. I should very much dislike 3 years & I also very much dislike to return without doing anything. If it was not for business I would not hesitate for a moment. After all we can do little while the war continues & we should do all we can to aid the vigorous measures which the Administration is taking.

MAY 8   I am to day Sergt. of the Guard & I find it dull business. It will probably be duller yet before 10 A.M. to morrow. We are out in all abt 26 hours  —2 hours on & 4 off. This is the first time I have been on. There is something exceeding solitary in the looks of a sentinel placing slowly up & down in stillness of the night. The weather is fine & we shall have a good night.

The morals of camp life are bad & manners likewise. It is doubtful whether the effect which war has upon the morals of a people is not more to be regretted than its more ostensible evils. I believe I have kept on abt as usual. This open air life will be good for me I think. It seems like old times to be out doors all day.

MAY 9   Morning watch 6 A.M. We passed the night, which was a fine one, in comparative quiet. The Corporals Guard was called for but twice during my watches. The first time my Corpl., a very worthy German, ran without the countersign & was himself arrested & sent to the guard house. I laughed heartily at the joke on the Corpl. I slept well abt 3 hours. My head aches a little & I feel dull & tired this morning. This standing guard is the most tiresome service I have. I believe I

would rather march all the time. We were finally relieved abt
11 A.M. after abt 27 hours duty. I have not felt quite as well as
usual to day. I have a sour stomach & a tendency toward
looseness of the bowels. I do nothing for it save to stop eating.

MAY 10    It rains hard this morning & I am not sorry I can
assure on any account save the condition of the grounds. I feel
better this m'g but am not yet entirely well. Nearly all the men
have diarhea & several are in the hospital quite sick. This is
caused by the indiscretion of the men & by the quality of the
food. Our victuals are cooked & served out by a contractor at
one of the Fair buildings. The quantity is ample & the quality
before cooking is good enough. There is a good deal of dirt
mixed with it when we get it & some of it comes in very bad
shape. The butter is bad & I eat very little of it. We have soup
for dinner, made I presume from the fragments of breakfast. I
think this soup is one of the principal causes of sickness. The
potatoes are of poor quality. The bread thank God is good. We
have in addition fresh & salt beef & pork. The provisions
would be ample if well served. We have also tea, coffee, sugar
& sometimes milk.

It is certain that this Regt. will not be recd for 3 months. We
must enlist for 3 yrs during the war unless sooner discharged. I
have not yet positively decided to do that. The Co. will stand
abt half & half. If I had poorer prospects at home or a better
place here I would not hesitate.

Our grounds will be all afloat by night. I wish the state
could find dry land enough for us to camp. I would rather
sleep in the open air than be quartered in the mud. I fear we
shall all be sick when warm weather comes. The boys behaved
rather bad in some cases yesterday. The guard house was pretty
well filled & one came near being flogged.

MAY 11    It rained nearly all day yesterday & we had no drill
except a private one for a few who saw fit to take part in it. I
went to town once & spent the balance of the day in studying
Hardee &c. This m'g is fine but the grounds are very bad. We
have drilled but little to day owing to the state of the ground.

There is a good deal of reluctance to enlist for the war or
three years. There are all manner of doubts & excuses raised. I
can not wonder very much at it. A step which involves the possibility of 3 yrs in the army is a pretty serious one for most men.

I have pretty much decided to go. It seems to me that I cannot honorably do otherwise. I should very much dislike to return to Kalamazoo in this juncture of affairs.

There is a general laxity of discipline in the camp partly because of 2 days idleness & partly because many of the men expect soon to be discharged & having no prospect of fighting before them care very little whether they do anything or not. There was some disturbance last night at the other building. Several were sent to the Guard House & pistols were freely drawn but none fired. A new made acquaintance of mine, 3d Sergt. of the Hudson Guards, is on trial by a Court Martial to day in consequence. We have no uniform as yet & shall soon be a very ragged Regt. if we do not get it.

MAY 12  Sunday. A fine day, no drilling. Dissatisfaction among some Co's. because the uniform has not been furnished. Meetings were held last night & strong indignation expressed & resolutions passed not to drill after Monday noon if they were not supplied. The consequence is that the men who were foremost in them have gone to the Guard House. Capt. C. S. May has trouble with his Co. He will not be well liked.

Our Capt. was found fault with yesterday for the first time. There is a general outcry agt officers. It is without just cause. Many of the men seem to think they should never be spoken to unless the remarks are prefaced by some words of deferential politeness. Will the gentlemen who comprise the first platoon have the kindness to march forward, or will they please to halt, &c is abt what some of them seem to expect. An officer would need 3 yrs under a French dancing master before he could satisfy them.

I wanted to go to town to day to bathe & be shaved but they refuse to let us out. It surprises me to see how quickly I have fallen into this mode of life. I feel little more uneasiness or inconvenience than if I had been bred to it from youth. I have hardly a thought abt law. I eat, drink, sleep, drill & study Hardee's Tactics as much of course as if I knew no other business. I think I must have been intended for a soldier. If I were but Lieut. instead of 3d Sergt. I should be better satisfied than at present. My pay is very small. I have however money enough for the present.

The boys will upset the table before many days I think. The contractor gets over $3.25 per week for our board & might give better. I bought a pie & some cakes of a peddler this m'g & filled up for once.

We succeeded in getting out about 25 men to church to day. Many of them absolutely refused to go. We must have more discipline or we shall have nothing.

# Ulysses S. Grant to Jesse Root Grant

On April 29 Grant became military aide to Illinois governor Richard
Yates. He wrote to his father a week later.

———————————

Camp Yates, near Springfield
May 6th 1861

DEAR FATHER;

Your second letter, dated the 1st of May has just come to
hand. I commenced writing you a letter three or four days ago
but was interrupted so often that I did not finish it. I wrote
one to Mary which no doubt was duly recieved but do not
rember whether it answers your questions or not.

At the time our first Galena company was raised I did not
feel at liberty to engage in hot haste, but took an active interest in drilling them and emparting all the instruction I could,
and at the request of the members of the company, and of Mr.
Washburn, I come here for the purpose of assisting for a short
time in camp, and, if necessary, my services for the War. The
next two days after my arrival it was rainy and muddy so that
the troops could not drill and I concluded to go home. Governer Yates heard it and requested me to remain. Since that I
have been acting in that capacity, and for the last few days have
been in command of this camp. The last of the six Regiments
called for from this state will probably leave by to-morrow,
or the day following, and then I shall be relieved from this
command.

The Legislature of this state provided for the raising of
Eleven additional Regiments and a Battalion of Artillery, and a
portion of these the Governer will appoint me to muster into
the service of the State, when I presume my services may end.
I might have got the Colonelcy of a Regiment possibly, but I
was perfectly sickened at the political wire pulling for all these
commissions and would not engage in it. I shall be no ways

backward in offering my services when and where they are required, but I feel that I have done more now than I could do
serving as a Capt. under a green Colonel, and if this thing continues they will want more men at a later day.—

There has been full 30,000 more volunteers offered their
services than can be accepted under the present call, without
including the call made by the state; but I can go back to
Galena and drill the three or four companies there and render
them efficient for any future call.—My own opinion is that this
War will be but of short duration. The Administration has
acted moste prudently and sagaciously so far in not bringing
on a conflict before it had its forces fully martialed. When they
do strike our thoroughly loyal states will be fully protected and
a few decisive victories in some of the southern ports will send
the secession army howling and the leaders in the rebelion will
flee the country. All the states will then be loyal for a generation to come, negroes will depreciate so rapidly in value that
no body will want to own them and their masters will be the
loudest in their declaimations against the institution in a political and economic view. The nigger will never disturb this
country again. The worst that is to be apprehended from him
is now; he may revolt and cause more destruction than any
Northern man, except it be the ultra abolitionest, wants to see.
A Northern army may be required in the next ninety days to
go south to suppress a negro insurrection. As much as the
South have vilified the North they would go on such a mission
and with the purest motives.

I have just recieved a letter from Julia. All are well. Julia
takes a very sensible vue of our present difficulties. She would
be sorry to have me go but thinks the circumstances may war-
rent it and will not through a single obsticle in the way.

(There is no doubt but the *valiant* Pillow has been planning
an attac on Cairo, but as he will learn that that point is well
Garrisoned and they have their ditch on the out side, filled
with watter, he will probably desist. As however he would find
it necessary to receive a wound, on the first discharge of fire
arms he would not be a formidable enemy. I do not say he
would shoot himself, ah no! I am not so uncharitable as many
who served under him in Mexico. I think however he might
report himself wounded on the receipt of a very slight scratch,

recieved hastily in any way and might eritate the sore until he convinced himself that he had been wounded by the enemy.)

Tell Simp. that I hope he will be able to visit us this Summer. I should like very much to have him stay with us and I want him to make my house his home.

Remember me to all.

ULYSSES

# John Hay: Diary, May 7–10, 1861

Following his election in November 1860, Lincoln hired John Hay, a Brown graduate and nephew of one of his legal colleagues, to assist his secretary John G. Nicolay. In February 1861 Nicolay and Hay accompanied the president-elect from Springfield to Washington, where they lived in the Executive Mansion while serving as Lincoln's principal secretaries.

————————

7 MAY 1861, TUESDAY

I went in to give the President some little items of Illinois news, saying among other things that Singleton was behaving very badly. He replied with emphasis that Singleton was a miracle of meanness, calmly looking out of the window at the smoke of the two Navy steamers puffing up the way, resting the end of the telescope on his toes sublime.

I spoke of the proposition of Browning to subjugate the South, establish a black republic in lieu of the exterminated whites, and extend a protectorate over them, while they raised our cotton. He said, Some of our northerners seem bewildered and dazzled by the excitement of the hour. Doolittle seems inclined to think that this war is to result in the entire abolition of Slavery. Old Col. Hamilton a venerable and most respectable gentleman, impresses upon me most earnestly the propriety of enlisting the slaves in our army."

I told him his daily correspondence was thickly interspersed by such suggestions.

"For my own part," he said, "I consider the central idea pervading this struggle is the necessity that is upon us, of proving that popular government is not an absurdity. We must settle this question now, whether in a free government the minority have the right to break up the government whenever they choose. If we fail it will go far to prove the incapability of the people to govern themselves. There may be one consideration used in stay of such final judgement, but that is not for us to use in advance. That is, that there exists in our case, an instance of a vast and far reaching disturbing element, which the history of no other free nation will probably ever present. That however is not for us to say at present. Taking the government as we found it we will see if the majority can preserve it."

He is engaged in constant thought upon his Message: It will be an exhaustive review of the questions of the hour & of the future.

In the Afternoon we went up to see Ellsworth's Zouave Firemen. They are the largest sturdiest and physically the most magnificent men I ever saw collected together. They played over the sward like kittens, lithe and agile in their strength.

Ellsworth has been intensely disgusted at the wild yarns afloat about them which are for the most part, utterly untrue. A few graceless rascals have been caught in various lapses. These are in irons. One horrible story which has been terrifying all the maiden antiques of the city for several days, has the element of horror pretty well eliminated today, by the injured fair, who proves a most yielding seducee, offering to settle the matter for 25 dollars. Other yarns are due to the restless brains of the press-gang.

The youthful Colonel formed his men in a hollow square, and made a great speech at them. There was more common-sense, dramatic power, tact, energy, & that eloquence that naturally flowers into deeds in le petit Colonels fifteen minute harangue, than in all the speeches that stripped the plumes from our unfortunate ensign in the spread eagle days of the Congress that has flitted. He spoke to them as men, made them proud in their good name, spoke bitterly & witheringly of the disgrace of the recreant, contrasted with cutting emphasis which his men delighted in, the enlistment of the dandy regiment for thirty days, with *theirs* for the war—spoke solemnly & impressively of the disgrace of expulsion—roused them to wild enthusiasm by announcing that he had heard of one officer who treated his men with less consideration than himself and that, if on inquiry the rumor proved true, he would strip him & send him home in irons. The men yelled with delight clapped their hands & shouted "Bully for you." He closed with wonderful tact and dramatic spirit, by saying

"Now laddies, if any one of you wants to go home, he had better sneak around the back alleys, crawl over fences, and get out of sight before we see him." which got them again. He must have run with this crowd some time in his varied career. He knows them and handles them so perfectly.

## 8 May 1861, Wednesday

Eames called this morning & brought to my notice a singular omission in Jeff. Davis' manifesto, His ignoring all mention of the right of revolution and confining his defense of his position to the reserved constitutional right of a state to secede. By this means he estops his claim upon the recognition of the world. For even those cabinets that acknowledge the necessity of recognizing all governments, which by virtue of revolution have a defacto existence, would most naturally say to a new government basing its claim to nationality on the constitution of the government vs. which it rebels, "We can entertain no such question of legal construction. The contest as stated by you between you and your government is a municipal one. We have no right to interfere or prejudge the issue of such a case of conflicting interpretation." Jeff. Davis seems to have been so anxious to satisfy the restless consciences of the Borderers, that he utterly overlooks the importance of conciliating the good opinion of the outside world. "There is a hole in your best coat Master Davis.

## 9 May 1861, Thursday

Saw at breakfast this morning a quiet, shrewd looking man with unobtrusive spectacles, doing his devoir to an egg. I was informed that it was Anderson. The North has been strangely generous with that man. The red tape of military duty was all that bound his heart from its traitorous impulses. His Kentucky brigade will be like himself fighting weakly for a Union they scorn.

There was a very fine matinee at the Navy Yard given by some musical members of the 12th New York. They sang well the Band played well and the President listened well. After the programme, the President begged for the Marseillaise. The

prime gentleman gave the first verse and then generously repeated it, interpolating nonchalantly "Liberty or Death" in
place of "Abreuve nos sillons," which he had forgotten.

Then we went down to the Pensacola and observed the
shooting of the great Dahlgren gun Plymouth. Two ricochette
shots were sent through the target and one plumper. The
splendid course of the 11 inch shell [      ] through 1300 yds of
air, the lighting, the quick rebound & flight through the target
with wild skips, throwing up a 30 ft column of spray at every
jump, the decreasing leaps and the steady roll into the waves
were scenes as novel and pleasant to me as to all the rest of the
party. The Prest. was delighted. Capt. Gillis was bored at
Dahlgren for laughing at the bad firing from the Pocahontas.

This morning Ellsworths Zouaves covered themselves with
glory as with a blanket in saving Willard's Hotel and quench-
ing a most ugly looking fire. They are utterly unapproachable
in anything they attempt. Their respectful demeanor to their
Chief and his anxious solicitude for their comfort & safety are
absolutely touching to behold.


10 MAY 1861, FRIDAY

Carl Schurz loafed into my room this morning & we spoke
of the slaves & their ominous discontent. He agreed with me
that the Commandants at Pickens & Monroe were unnecessar-
ily squeamish in imprisoning & returning to their masters the
fugitives who came to their gates begging to be employed.
Their owners are in a state of open rebellion against the government & nothing would bring them to their senses more
readily than a gentle reminder that they are dependent upon
the good will of the Government for the security of their lives
and property. The action would be entirely just and eminently
practicable. Schurz says that thousands of Democrats are declaring that now is the time to remove the cause of all our
woes. What we could not have done in many lifetimes the
madness and folly of the South has accomplished for us. Slavery offers itself more vulnerable to our attack than at any point
in any century and the wild malignity of the South is excusing
us, before God & the World.

So we talked in the morning.

But tonight I saw a letter from Mrs. Whitman stating that Thomas Earl, T. W. Higginson the essayist of Boston and young John Brown, were "going to free the slaves." What we were dreaming of came over my mind with horrible distinctness and I shrunk from the apparition. This is not the time nor are these the men to do it. They should wait till the government gives some kind of sanction to the work. Otherwise the horrors of the brutal massacre will move the pity of the magnanimous North, and in the suppression of the insurrection the warring sections may fuse and compromise.

# *Judith W. McGuire: Diary, May 10, 1861*

Judith W. McGuire lived in Alexandria, Virginia, where her husband, John P. McGuire, was rector of the Episcopal High School of Virginia. When Union troops occupied Alexandria on May 24, 1861, the McGuires would flee their home on the school campus and spend the next four years as refugees; the school was turned into a Union army hospital.

---

*May* 10.—Since writing last, I have been busy, very busy, arranging and rëarranging. We are now hoping that Alexandria will not be a landing-place for the enemy, but that the forts will be attacked. In that case, they would certainly be repulsed, and we could stay quietly at home. To view the progress of events from any point will be sad enough, but it would be more bearable at our own home, and surrounded by our family and friends. With the supposition that we may remain, and that the ladies of the family at least may return to us, I am having the grounds put in order, and they are now so beautiful! Lilacs, crocuses, the lily of the valley, and other spring flowers, are in luxuriant bloom, and the roses in full bud. The greenhouse plants have been removed and grouped on the lawn, verbenas in bright bloom have been transplanted from the *pit* to the borders, and the grass seems unusually green after the late rains; the trees are in full leaf; every thing is so fresh and lovely. "All, save the spirit of man, is divine."

War seems inevitable, and while I am trying to employ the passing hour, a cloud still hangs over us and all that surrounds us. For a long time before our society was so completely broken up, the ladies of Alexandria and all the surrounding country were busily employed sewing for our soldiers. Shirts, pants, jackets, and beds, of the heaviest material, have been made by the most delicate fingers. All ages, all conditions, meet now on one common platform. We must all work for our country.

Our soldiers must be equipped. Our parlor was the rendezvous for our neighborhood, and our sewing-machine was in requisition for weeks. Scissors and needles were plied by all. The daily scene was most animated. The fires of our enthusiasm and patriotism were burning all the while to a degree which might have been consuming, but that our tongues served as safety-valves. Oh, how we worked and talked, and excited each other! One common sentiment animated us all; no doubts, no fears were felt. We all have such entire reliance in the justice of our cause and the valor of our men, and, above all, on the blessing of Heaven! These meetings have necessarily ceased with us, as so few of any age or degree remain at home; but in Alexandria they are still kept up with great interest. We who are left here are trying to give the soldiers who are quartered in town comfort, by carrying them milk, butter, pies, cakes, etc. I went in yesterday to the barracks, with the carriage well filled with such things, and found many young friends quartered there. All are taking up arms; the first young men in the country are the most zealous. Alexandria is doing her duty nobly; so is Fairfax; and so, I hope, is the whole South. We are very weak in resources, but strong in stout hearts, zeal for the cause, and enthusiastic devotion to our beloved South; and while men are making a free-will offering of their life's blood on the altar of their country, women must not be idle. We must do what we can for the comfort of our brave men. We must sew for them, knit for them, nurse the sick, keep up the faint-hearted, give them a word of encouragement in season and out of season. There is much for us to do, and we must do it. The embattled hosts of the North will have the whole world from which to draw their supplies; but if, as it seems but too probable, our ports are blockaded, we shall indeed be dependent on our own exertions, and great must those exertions be.

The Confederate flag waves from several points in Alexandria: from the Marshall House, the Market-house, and the several barracks. The peaceful, quiet old town looks quite warlike. I feel sometimes, when walking on King's street, meeting men in uniform, passing companies of cavalry, hearing martial music, etc., that I must be in a dream. Oh that it were a dream, and that the last ten years of our country's history were blotted out! Some of our old men are a little nervous, look doubt-

ful, and talk of the impotency of the South. Oh, I feel utter
scorn for such remarks. We must not admit weakness. Our soldiers do not think of weakness; they know that their hearts are
strong, and their hands well skilled in the use of the rifle. Our
country boys have been brought up on horseback, and hunt-
ing has ever been their holiday sport. Then why shall they feel
weak? Their hearts feel strong when they think of the justice of
their cause. In that is *our* hope.

Walked down this evening to see Mrs. Johns. The road
looked lonely and deserted. Busy life has departed from our
midst. We found Mrs. Johns packing up valuables. I have been
doing the same; but after they are packed, where are they to be
sent? Silver may be buried, but what is to be done with books,
pictures, etc.? We have determined, if we are obliged to go
from home, to leave every thing in the care of the servants.
They have promised to be faithful, and I believe they will be;
but my hope becomes stronger and stronger that we may remain here, or may soon return if we go away. Every thing is so
sad around us! We went to the Chapel on Sunday as usual, but
it was grievous to see the change—the organ mute, the organ-
ist gone; the seats of the students of both institutions empty;
but one or two members of each family to represent the ab-
sentees; the prayer for the President omitted. When Dr.
Packard came to it, there was a slight pause, and then he went
on to the next prayer—all seemed so strange! Tucker Conrad,
one of the few students who is still here, raised the tunes; his
voice seemed unusually sweet, because so sad. He was feebly
supported by all who were not in tears. There was night service, but it rained, and I was not sorry that I could not go.

# *William T. Sherman to John Sherman*

The outbreak of the war increased tensions between secessionist and unionist factions in Missouri, and Claiborne Jackson, the pro-Confederate governor, began planning the seizure of the federal arsenal in St. Louis. Captain Nathaniel Lyon, the commander of the arsenal garrison, led a force of regular soldiers and German American volunteers against a state militia encampment on the edge of the city on May 10. William T. Sherman, who had become president of a St. Louis street railroad company after he left Louisiana, witnessed the incident.

---------

Office St. Louis R. R. Co.
St. Louis, May 11, 1861

Hon. John Sherman
Dear Brother,
Very imprudently I was a witness of the firing on the People by the U.S. Militia at Camp Jackson yesterday. You will hear all manner of accounts and as these will be brought to bear on the present Legislature to precipitate events, may be secession I will tell you what I saw. My office is up in Bremen the extreme north of the city. The arsenal is at the extreme south. The State camp was in a pretty grove directly west of the City, bounded by Olive Street & Laclede Avenue. I went to my house on Locust between 11 & 12 at 3 P.M. and saw the whole city in commotion and heard that the U.S. troops were marching from the arsenal to capture the State camp. At home I found Hugh & Charley Ewing & John Hunter so excited they would not wait for dinner, but went out to see the expected Battle. I had no such curiosity and staid to dinner, after which I walked out and soon met a man who told me Gen. Frost had surrendered. I went back home & told Ellen—then took Willy to see the soldiers march back I kept on walking and about 5 1/2 P.M. found myself in the grove, with Soldiers all round standing at rest—I went into the Camp till turned aside by sentinels, and

found myself with a promiscuous crowd, men, women & children, inside the Grove, near Olive Street. On that street the disarmed State troops some 800 were in ranks. Soon a heavy column of U.S. Regulars, followed by militia came down Olive, with music & halted abreast of me. I went up and spoke to Some of the officers and fell back to a Knoll where I met Hugh & Charley & John Hunter. Soon the music again started, and as the Regulars got abreast of the Crowd about 60 yards to my front and right I observed them in confusion, using their bayonets to keep the crowd back as I supposed. Still they soon moved on, and as the militia reached the same point a similar confusion began. I heard a couple of shots then half a dozen & observed the militia were firing on the crowd at that point, but the fire kept creeping to the rear along the flank of the column & hearing balls cutting the leaves of trees over my head I fell down on the grass, and crept up to where Charley Ewing had my boy Willy. I also covered his person—probably a hundred shots passed over the ground, but none near us. As soon as the fire slackened, I picked Willy up, and ran with him till behind the rising ground, and continued at my leisure out of harms way, & went home—I saw no one shot—but some dozen were Killed, among them a woman & little girl. There must have been some provocation at the point where the Regulars charged bayonets, and when the militia began their fire—the rest was irregular & unnecessary—for the crowd, was back in the woods, a fence between them and the street—There was some cheering of the U.S. troops, and some halloos for Jeff Davis.

I hear all of Frosts command who would not take the oath of allegiance to the U.S. are prisoners at the arsenal—I suppose they will be held for the orders of the President—They were mostly composed of young men, who doubtless were secessionist—Frost is a New Yorker, was a graduate of West Point—served some years in the army & married a Miss Graham here, a lady of great wealth & large connections. He was encouraged by order of the Governor, and this brings up the old question of State & U.S. authority we cannot have two Kings—one is enough and of the two the U.S. must prevail, but in all the South, and even here there are plenty who think the State is their King. I think of course that both extremes are determined that Missouri should secede, one from Southern feeling and the other for the satisfaction of beating her. When I got back last evening to my house I found Turner. He gave me a letter for you which I mailed addressed to Mansfield as the More certain method of reaching you. Tom Turner has declined his appointment for reasons the Major gives. I enclose you the copy of a letter I wrote some days since to the Secretary of War—If I must embark in this war I prefer Regulars who can be controlled. I have just received your letter of the 9 from Philadelphia—to which point I have already written to you—As ever yours affectionately

W. T. Sherman

# Benjamin F. Butler to Winfield Scott

A successful lawyer and Democratic politician from Massachusetts, Benjamin F. Butler was appointed a brigadier general in the state militia at the start of the war. Commissioned as a major general of U.S. volunteers on May 16, he was given command of the Union forces at Fort Monroe in Virginia. (Located at the end of the peninsula between the York and James rivers, and commanding the entrance to Hampton Roads, the post remained in Union hands throughout the war.) Shortly after his arrival at the fort, Butler faced the question of how the Union army should treat runaway slaves.

———

HEADQUARTERS DEPARTMENT OF VIRGINIA,
*Fort Monroe, May 24, 1861.*

Lieut. Gen. WINFIELD SCOTT:

\*　　　\*　　　\*　　　\*　　　\*　　　\*　　　\*

*Saturday, May 25.—* I had written thus far when I was called away to meet Major Cary, of the active Virginia volunteers, upon questions which have arisen of very considerable importance both in a military and political aspect and which I beg leave to submit herewith.

On Thursday night three negroes, field hands belonging to Col. Charles K. Mallory now in command of the secession forces in this district, delivered themselves up to my picket guard and as I learned from the report of the officer of the guard in the morning had been detained by him. I immediately gave personal attention to the matter and found satisfactory evidence that these men were about to be taken to Carolina for the purpose of aiding the secession forces there; that two of them left wives and children (one a free woman) here; that the other had left his master from fear that he would be called upon to take part in the rebel armies. Satisfied of these facts from cautious examination of each of the negroes apart from the others I determined for the present and until better advised as these men were very serviceable and I had great need of labor in my quartermaster's department to avail myself of their services, and that I would send a receipt to Colonel Mallory that I had so taken them as I would for any other property of a private citizen which the exigencies of the service seemed to require to be taken by me, and especially property that was designed, adapted and about to be used against the United States.

As this is but an individual instance in a course of policy which may be required to be pursued with regard to this species of property I have detailed to the lieutenant-general this case and ask his direction. I am credibly informed that the negroes in this neighborhood are now being employed in the erection of batteries and other works by the rebels which it would be nearly or quite impossible to construct without their labor. Shall they be allowed the use of this property against the United States and we not be allowed its use in aid of the United States?

*     *     *     *     *     *     *

Major Cary demanded to know with regard to the negroes what course I intended to pursue. I answered him substantially as I have written above when he desired to know if I did not feel myself bound by my constitutional obligations to deliver up fugitives under the fugitive-slave act. To this I replied that the fugitive-slave act did not affect a foreign country which Virginia claimed to be and that she must reckon it one of the infelicities of her position that in so far at least she was taken at her word; that in Maryland, a loyal State, fugitives from service had been returned, and that even now although so much pressed by my necessities for the use of these men of Colonel Mallory's yet if their master would come to the fort and take the oath of allegiance to the Constitution of the United States I would deliver the men up to him and endeavor to hire their services of him if he desired to part with them. To this Major Cary responded that Colonel Mallory was absent.

*     *     *     *     *     *     *

Trusting that these dispositions and movements will meet the approval of the lieutenant-general and begging pardon for the detailed length of this dispatch, I have the honor to be, most respectfully, your obedient servant,

BENJ. F. BUTLER,
*Major-General, Commanding.*

# The New York Times: General Butler and the Contraband of War

June 2, 1861

Butler's decision not to return slaves who had escaped from Confederate territory was endorsed by the administration, and "contraband" became a common term for slaves who came within the Union lines.

---

## GENERAL BUTLER AND THE
## CONTRABAND OF WAR.

The correspondent of the Boston *Journal*, writing from Fortress Monroe on May 26, gives these interesting particulars of recent events at that point:

The "everlasting nigger" hath heretofore lain *perdu* in the wood pile of this Bailiwick, and the appearance of General BUTLER at the post was the signal for his becoming uproarious. Yesterday morning three negroes came to the picket-guard and gave themselves up. Upon a separate examination of these men it satisfactorily appeared that they were field hands, owned by one Colonel MALLORY, a resident of this neighborhood, heretofore a lawyer, and now engaged in the defence of the soil of Virginia—that's what they call it—as the commandant of the active militia of this immediate district; that MALLORY proposed to take them to Carolina, to be employed in military operations there; that one of them had a wife—a free woman—and several children in the neighborhood; and that they all objected to having anything to do with fighting. Under these circumstances, General BUTLER concluded that the property was contraband of war, seized upon it, and turned it over to the Quartermaster's Department, where labor is much wanted. He proposed to receipt to Colonel

MALLORY for the men, if desired, as he would for the same number of beeves coming into this inclosure under like circumstances.

Yesterday afternoon Gen. BUTLER, accompanied by Major FAY and Capt. HAGGERTY of the Staff, went out on the Hampton road to meet one Major CARY, who represents himself to be an officer of the "active Virginia Volunteers," who requested an interview for the purpose of discussing sundry topics. This Maj. CARY, be it remembered, was a member of the Charleston-Baltimore Convention, and in his company Gen. BUTLER seceded from the Front street Theatre concern and went over to the Hard Shells at the Maryland Institute. So this meeting was but a renewal of an old acquaintanceship. CARY first asked if a passage through the blockading fleet would be allowed to the families of citizens desiring to go North or South to a place of safety. To this the General replied that the presence of the families of belligerents was always the best hostage for the good behavior of citizens; that one of the objects of the blockade was to prevent the admission of supplies of provisions into Virginia while she continued in an attitude hostile to the Government; and that the reduction of the number of consumers would manifestly tend to the postponement of the object in view; and that, moreover, the passage of vessels through the blockade would involve an amount of labor, in the way of a surveillance, to prevent abuse, which it would be impossible to perform. The request must therefore be refused. The Major then desired to know whether or not the passage of persons and families wishing to go North by land, from Virginia, would be permitted. To this the General replied that, with the exception of an interruption at Baltimore, which had now been disposed of, the travel of peaceable citizens through the North had not been hindered; that of the internal line of travel through Virginia his friends had, for the present, entire control; and that, finally, the authorities at Washington could judge better than himself upon this subject, and travelers might well pass that way in going North.

The Major then wanted to know what the General proposed to do about his friend MALLORY's "niggers," and in reply Gen. BUTLER stated the circumstances and his reasons for detaining them, as above recited. Maj. CARY asked if the General wasn't mindful of his constitutional obligations to return fugitives, in accordance with the terms of the Fugitive Slave Act? To this query, answer was made that the slave act was not of force, as to a foreign country, which Virginia claimed to be, and she must count it among the infelicities of her position, that so far, at least, she was taken at her word. But that notwithstanding his great need of just such labor as had thus providentially fallen into his hands, if Col. MALLORY would come into the fortress and take the oath of allegiance to the Government, his negroes should be returned, or hired of him, as he chose. The General further suggested, that in Maryland, a loyal State, fugitives from service had been returned. To all this Maj. CARY had no reply to make, other than that Col. MALLORY was absent. So closed the first meeting for the discussion of the Slavery question in this camp.

Under date of May 27, the same correspondent writes:

Yesterday, eight negroes, belonging to various planters in this neighborhood, came into this camp, one of whom had been employed in the erection of the enemy's sand batteries. They all told the story that they had left their masters because they believed they were to be sent South; one objected that he didn't care to be employed in fighting on the secession side, as he had been heretofore; and one stated very frankly that he supposed that the gentlemen in Fortress Monroe were the friends of the colored population. "We had heard it," said he, in the genuine field-hand dialect, "since last Fall, that if LINCOLN was elected, you would come down and set us free. And the white-folks used to say so, but they don't talk so now; the colored people have talked it all over; we heard that if we could get in here we should be free, or, at any rate, we should be among friends." This morning forty seven came in one squad, embracing all ages from three months to 85 years. Most are owned in this neighborhood, but a few came from beyond —one from well up toward Richmond, and one, a woman, came from the other side of Hampton Roads. There were in this lot half a dozen entire families. Another lot of a dozen good field-hands, many from points far in the interior, also came and expressed their willingness to enroll in the new corps of "Virginia Union Volunteers," and they were forthwith accepted.

There is now $60,000 worth of this sort of property in camp, and the stock is hourly increasing. The subject is becoming one of very great moment. As long as only property contraband of war—that is to say, negroes adapted for, and about to be employed in military movement—come into our possession, the question was comparatively simple; it was simply military. But when women and children come, as they have by the score, it became a humanitarian question. And some in Massachusetts, who have been afflicted by the "ANDREW and BUTLER correspondence," will find solace in the fact that the Massachusetts stores have—by order of the General in command—been taken to feed these panting fugitives. For the present, and until better advised by Gen. SCOTT or President LINCOLN, or somebody else, I understand that the General has decided to retain all the negroes who have come. An officer has been appointed to take a general charge of them, taking receipts from all parties who select servants from his gang, and opening an account with the reputed owner of each negro, charging the expense of caring for and supporting the non-laborers, and crediting the services of the men and women employed. So much for the negro question in its present aspect.

To-day, a Prof. RAYMOND, who is the head of a Seminary in Hampton, called upon the General, and they two had a long confabulation. The Professor, it appears, has a son 15 yrs of age. The youth has been, unfortunately, impressed into the service of the rebels at Norfolk. The anxious parent first desired to know whether there was any law by which he could regain the custody of his son; and for answer he was told that traitors who are in armed rebellion against the Government would not be likely to hearken to its laws in this case. In the United States the laws would protect him in his parental rights. Then he wanted to go over to Norfolk to attempt to reclaim his son, but this could not be permitted. He took occasion to make some general observations on politics, and expressed a belief that Republicanism is a failure, and that the only way to govern men is through a limited monarchy. "That is just where we differ," replied the Colonel, "and we have come down here to teach

you the Republic is a success!" Whether or not, in the enforced service of his son in the Rebel army, he found any reason for losing his faith in the Republic, the Professor was
unable to say. The people of Hampton have nearly all left; indeed the country around is panic-stricken. Virginia is but just
beginning to learn that the path of rebellion is not a pleasant
one.

The latest news from the outposts is that the rebels have
succeeded, after several attempts, in destroying the bridges
each side of Hampton, and that Col. DURYEE had retaliated
by seizing every boat in town. Who has the bridge now?

# Kate Stone: Journal, May 15–27, 1861

At the start of the war, twenty-year-old Kate Stone was living with her family at Brokenburn, a prosperous cotton plantation near the Mississippi River in what is now Madison Parish, Louisiana, about thirty miles northwest of Vicksburg.

———————

*May 15*:   My Brother started at daybreak this morning for New Orleans. He goes as far as Vicksburg on horseback. He is wild to be off to Virginia. He so fears that the fighting will be over before he can get there that he has decided to give up the plan of raising a company and going out as Captain. He has about fifty men on his rolls and they and Uncle Bo have empowered him to sign their names as members of any company he may select. Mamma regrets so that My Brother would not wait and complete his commission. He could get his complement of men in two weeks, and having been educated at a military school gives him a great advantage at this time. And we think there will be fighting for many days yet.

We gave him quite a list of articles to be bought in the City, for it may be some time before we shop in New Orleans again.

*May 23*:   Mamma was busy all the morning having the carpets taken up and matting put down and summer curtains hung. Of course the house was dusty and disagreeable. Mr. Newton and the children were shut up in the schoolroom and so escaped it, but Uncle Bo wandered aimlessly around, seeking rest and finding none. I retired to the fastness of my room with a new novel and a plate of candy and was oblivious to discomfort until Frank came to say dinner was ready and "the house shorely do look sweet and cool."

In the afternoon Mamma lay down to rest as she was tired out. Mr. Newton and Uncle Bo rode out to Omega for the mail and to hear the news. The boys, Little Sister, and I all went down the bayou for a walk with a running accompaniment of leaping, barking hounds, ranging the fields for a scent of deer or maybe a rabbit. The boys are so disgusted if the dogs race off after a rabbit. They think it ruins them for deer dogs. How pleasant to have the smooth, dry ground underfoot again after so many months of mud. It has been such a long, muddy winter and spring. No one knows what mud is until he lives on a buckshot place and travels buckshot roads.

Tonight a little fire was pleasant and we all gathered around it to hear Mr. Newton read the papers. Nothing but "War, War" from the first to the last column. Throughout the length and breadth of the land the trumpet of war is sounding, and from every hamlet and village, from city and country, men are hurrying by thousands, eager to be led to battle against Lincoln's hordes. Bravely, cheerily they go, willing to meet death in defense of the South, the land we love so well, the fairest land and the most gallant men the sun shines on. May God prosper us. Never again can we join hands with the North, the people who hate us so. We take quite a number of papers: *Harper's Weekly* and *Monthly*, the *New York Tribune*, *Journal of Commerce*, *Littell's Living Age*, the *Whig* and *Picayune* of New Orleans, and the Vicksburg and local sheets. What shall we do when Mr. Lincoln stops our mails?

The Northern papers do make us so mad! Even Little Sister, the child of the house, gets angry. Why will they tell such horrible stories about us? Greeley is the worst of the lot; his wishes for the South are infamous and he has the imagination of Poe. What shall we do when our mails are stopped and we are no longer in touch with the world?

We hear that Mr. Peck has raised a company of Irishmen from the levee camp and that the Richmond company has disbanded and re-enlisted for the war. They were twelve-month men.

Wednesday Uncle Bo went out to the river to drill the men and soon returned with the news that the levee at Airlie came very near giving away last night. The river is very high and a break there would put us entirely under. There are great fears of a tremendous overflow. Men are watching and the Negroes are working on the levees day and night.

The Monticello company, 4th La. Regt., has been ordered

up the river and the Lake Providence Cadets are off for New Orleans.

Late this afternoon Mamma and I went down to see the wife of the new overseer. She seems entirely too nice a woman, for her fashion is evidently from the planter class. I wonder why she married him. She does not look like a contented woman.

Uncle Bo, Ashburn, and I walked back and forth on the gallery in the cool moonlight, talking of soldier life and wondering what we who are left behind will do when both of our men folks are off and away.

From Uncle Bo's room floats the soft sound of violin, flute, and guitar. They are enjoying perhaps their last practice together. May God bless and keep them.

*May 24:* A lovely spring day, as fair as a poet's dream of May. Mamma is busy doing some machine work on Jimmy's shirts and I have been embroidering so enthusiastically that tonight I am tired out. In the afternoon Mamma, Mrs. Hardison, and I called on Mrs. Graves, and Mrs. Hardison and I adjourned to the orchard and feasted on the best plums, our first this spring. Mrs. Graves promised Mamma a bulb of lovely crimson gladiolus.

The boys went over to the schoolhouse to hear Mr. Ewing's scholars "speak a piece." Mr. Ewing is tutor for the Curry and Hardison children. At the supper table they were rather severe in their criticisms of the speeches; of course they think they could have done better. And they were especially emphatic in their remarks on Mrs. Curry and her two youngest hopefuls. Mrs. Curry insisted on bossing the whole thing. As they were mostly her children and her tutor, I could not see why the boys should object.

Dr. Devine came up from the quarters, where he had been to see one of the sick Negroes, in high feather and his new Sunday suit. He did not have as much news as usual but perhaps more truth. It is a lovely moonlight night and Brother Walter is out riding the levee, watching in Mr. Newton's place. Ashburn and I walked a long time on the gallery after supper, he playing the flute and I repeating to myself poems recently learned—the last, "The Jacobite Fiddler," from a recent number of the *Living Age*.

*May 25*:   My Brother returned this evening. He did not succeed in joining the Monticello Guards from Carroll Parish. They had gone up the river, but he joined the Jeff Davis Guards at Vicksburg and was elected 3rd lieutenant. It is an Irish company officered by Americans. It was raised by Dr. Buckner and Capt. Manlove, and if My Brother had seen either of them on his way to New Orleans, they would have given him the captaincy. Tom Manlove is a captain. Uncle Bo cannot join it as a private, as the association would not be pleasant; and he is so disappointed not to be with My Brother. He hopes to get into the Volunteer Southerns, which will leave Vicksburg in a few days.

The Jeff Davis Guards leave for Richmond on Monday, and so My Brother and Uncle Bo get off in the morning as early as possible. My Brother told us much of the soldiers he saw in New Orleans: the Zouaves, with their gay, Turkish trousers and jackets and odd drill; the Tiger Rifles, recruited from the very dregs of the City and commanded by a man who has served a term in the penitentiary; and the Perrit Guards, the gambler's company—to be admitted one must be able to cut, shuffle, and deal on the point of a bayonet.

My Brother is in extravagant spirits. He is so glad to get off, and then he saw Kate and I think they have made it up again. Uncle Bo is very sad for he so wanted for them both to be in the same company. Now they can only hope to be in the same regiment. I can see them go, for I feel I know they will return. The parting will be dreadful for Mamma. She so depends on My Brother, her oldest and best beloved. The boys are disgruntled because they cannot go too.

*May 26*:   Our two loved ones left us this morning, but we cannot think it a last farewell. My heart tells me they will come again. They go to bear all hardships, to brave all dangers, and to face death in every form, while we whom they go to protect are lapped safe in luxurious ease. But oh! the weary days of watching and waiting that stretch before us! We who stay behind may find it harder than they who go. They will have new scenes and constant excitement to buoy them up and the consciousness of duty done.

Mr. Catlin came over to tell them good-bye. My Brother explained everything to him and gave him a letter for the men Brother had been drilling. I hope they will not blame him.

Mamma fitted them out with everything she thought they could need. And their three horses were well loaded down. Wesley went to wait on them and was very proud of the honor of being selected to "go to battle with Marse Will." We hope he will do, though he has not been much about the house. Uncle Bo would not take a man for himself. He says a private has no business with a body servant, but if he changes his mind, a boy can be sent to him at any time.

Both will belong to infantry companies, and they will be fitted out with uniforms in Vicksburg. Brother Coley went with them as far as Vicksburg. They left so quickly that none of their friends knew in time to come over to say good-bye. Mr. Valentine will be sorry. He is such a friend of My Brother's.

They said good-bye in the fairest, brightest of May mornings. Will they come again in the summer's heat, the autumn's grey, or the winter's cold?

Mr. Newton and the boys rode out to the river with them. As they rode away, out of the yard and through the quarters, all the house servants and fieldhands watched them go. And many a heartfelt "Good-bye, Marse William and Marse Bo— God bless you" went with them.

I hope we put up everything they need. We lined their heavy blankets with brown linen and put pockets at the top for soap, combs, brushes, handkerchiefs, etc. The linen is tied to the blankets with strong tapes so that it can be easily taken off and washed. And we impressed it on Wesley that he must keep everything clean and take the best care of both our soldiers as long as they are together. He promised faithfully to do his best. Mamma has been very brave and stood the separation better than I hoped.

*May 27*:   Mamma has been busy all day sewing on Jimmy's shirts and going through the vegetable and flower garden, all in a flourishing state. So many flowers, though our garden is but a new one yet. We must save all sorts of seeds, as we will get no more from the North. Mamma is having quantities of peas, potatoes, and all things eatable planted, as our only chance for anything from this time until the close of the war will be to raise it ourselves. Strict economy is to be the order of the day.

It is probable that meat will be very high, and by advice of Mr. Fellowes Mamma will try to raise enough to do the place. She has put Jeffery to devoting his whole time to the hogs and cattle. We have not a great quantity of either just now, but they will soon grow.

Times are already dreadfully hard. It was difficult for My Brother to raise enough money to fit them out—could only do it by pledging cotton at the bank.

Webster, who went to bring the horses back, came this morning. Wonka is the horse Uncle Bo gave me some time ago. He is such a lovely blood bay, so spirited, with every gait, and fleet as the wind when we start on a race. But I shall give him to Uncle Bo when he gets home. He will deserve a good horse after walking so long.

All Uncle Bo's jewelry, he left with me. He has quite an assortment of pins and rings and watch chains. One makes a lovely bracelet and I have often worn it.

Roanoke, a powerful hunter, will belong to Brother Walter until My Brother gets back. I am glad Dr. Buckner did not keep Roanoke.

Ashburn and Johnny, the youngest of the boys, brought us some mulberries from their ride in the woods, but nobody but children cares to eat mulberries. They report the blackberries as nearly ripe, and we will have a lovely trip for them deep in the green woods in an old clearing. They are the finest, glossy, sweet berries ever seen and with the dew on them—delicious.

We had a warm discussion after tea, Mr. Newton contending that the states had no right to secede immediately on Lincoln's election and that they should have remained quiet for four years and seen what would be the policy of the government. We all bitterly oppose this view of the subject. Why, in four years we would have no rights worth fighting for! He thinks that if the states had been patient there would have been no war for years and that it would have been better to submit to Lincoln's rule no matter how unjust than to have provoked a war. But oh, no! We cannot see it that way. We should make a stand for our rights—and a nation fighting for its own homes and liberty cannot be overwhelmed. Our Cause is just and must prevail.

# George Templeton Strong:
## Diary, May 29–June 2, 1861

George Templeton Strong visited Washington and the Union lines in northern Virginia in the late spring of 1861. Shortly after his return to New York, Strong became the treasurer of the newly-formed United States Sanitary Commission, a civilian organization dedicated to improving conditions in army camps and caring for sick and wounded soldiers.

———————

*May 29*, WEDNESDAY.   Off by early train after very early breakfast. Fine day; Wickham Hoffman joined me at the Jersey City depot. No incidents of travel; Baltimore, that nest of traitors and assassins, was traversed in peace. There were crowds at the corners of the streets watching the trains. They were looking out for the troops that were in a train we passed on a turn-off at Havre de Grace. But the crowd was silent and innocuous, for Fort McHenry is now strongly reinforced and Federal Hill is white with the tents of government troops. At Washington in due season, and to Willard's Hotel; densely crowded. We had to put up with one room, a very good one, however, on the second floor. The corridors downstairs are packed with a mob of civilians, army officers, motley militia men, and loafers of every class. The little reception parlor on the side street is the headquarters of Colonel Somebody (D'Utassy, I believe) of the "Garibaldi Guard," a very promising corps, and that end of the first floor passageway is permanently occupied by a guard of swarthy Italians and Hungarians.

Called on sundry people with letters and cards and lodged our pasteboard successfully with all but Mr. Secretary Blair, who was on his own front "stoop" and could not be escaped. We bored him about twenty minutes, not more. He tends a little to prose, but is courteous and intelligent. His talk is en-

couraging. He thinks there is little fight, if any, in the bluster-
ing fire-eating elements of the South; its bar-room swash-
bucklers will collapse whenever they are resolutely met. And
this element constitutes, he thinks, two-thirds of the secession
force. We were presented to Mrs. Blair, a lady-like person from
New England.

Met Dick Smith, whilom of West Point, who marched me
into General Sandford's parlor, where I had some talk with
that chieftain and with Clarence Brown and Aleck Hamilton
(not James A.'s Aleck, but John C.'s), who are on his staff.
Heard all about the Alexandrian movement, for the execution
of which Sandford takes much credit to himself. I hear Scott
ranks him high for a "trainband" general, experienced only in
marches down Broadway. I called with Hoffman at Scott's
quarters. Saw Schuyler Hamilton, one of his aids, but did not
disturb the meditations of the wily old Lieutenant-General,
who lies there like a great spider in the center of his net,
throwing out cords that will entangle his buzzing blue-bottle
of an antagonist, if all go well.

Many New Yorkers at Willard's. Clarence Cram, Sam Neill,
Willy Cutting, and others are begging for commissions. The
honorable F. B. Cutting is diligently backing his son's petition;
he has already secured a lieutenancy for Hayward Cutting, his
youngest son. The Cuttings begging office from Lincoln, and
these offices of all others, are a goodly spectacle to those who
remember their extravagant, treasonable talk of sixty days ago
and ever since last November. Many Republicans are soured by
seeing a share of public patronage given to late-converted ul-
tra-Southern Democrats. But the Administration is right. All
party lines are wiped out now.

Dan Messenger, Judge Cowles, and others are after jobs in
the Civil Service. The Rev. Dr. Bellows is concerned with the
proposed Sanitary Commission. President Felton, Peirce, and
Emory Washburn of Harvard, and Leutze are lookers-on.

*May 30.* Afternoon, parade and review of newly arrived
regiments. Garibaldi Guard, Colonel Blenker's Germans (very
promising corps both), the New York Ninth in their effective
black and red uniform, and a fourth that I've forgotten (the
"Brooklyn Zouaves").

*May 31.* Drove with Hoffman, Dan Messenger, and his

friend Charley Smith of Boston to Long Bridge. Our pass was inspected, and we went on. We invaded and (I suppose) "polluted" the Sacred Soil of Virginia. But it is so lacerated and insulted already by entrenchments, that our intrusion was a trifle. A very formidable *tête-du-pont* is in progress at the Virginia end of the bridge, and swarming with working parties. It is not armed yet, nor near completion, and it will need 2,000 men and upwards to occupy it when completed. Thence drove southwards, passing camps of New Jersey, Massachusetts, and other regiments, challenged every half mile, at least, by sentries and required to show our passes. Michiganders just outside Alexandria (fine looking fellows), and Pennsylvanians in the town. They do not seem to me very promising material. We drove to the famous Marshall House where Colonel Ellsworth was assassinated. It's a second-class hotel. Admitted with difficulty and formality; passes countersigned by the "provost-marshal." Explored the house, which is being carried off by relic hunters in little bits. Flag-staff is nearly cut through; stair-banisters, all gone; pieces of floor and stairs gouged out. Ordered dinner at Mansion House and drove a mile and a half northwest to Shooter's (or Sutter's) Hill, where Ellsworth's regiment (the New York Firemen Zouaves) is encamped and working at entrenchments, covering the extreme right of our line. Unfavorably impressed by the Zouaves. The men "sassed" the officers and the officers seemed loose in their notions of military subordination. One of them, a captain, and a rather scrubby specimen of a fire-company foreman in regimentals, said, "I guess we'll have the Colonel we want" (Ellsworth's successor); "if we don't, we'll let them fellows know we're about. We're firemen, we are." Probably a few of the Zouaves will have to be court-martialled and shot before the regiment can be relied on. With or near them are some Massachusetts soldiers and one of Sherman's light batteries. . . .

Returned from Alexandria by a back road, visiting the camp of the New York Twelfth in a secluded, picturesque place, surrounded by woods and enlivened by a rattling stream. The regiment is quartered partly in bush huts, partly in an old tumbledown cotton factory, built forty years ago and never worked from that day to this. . . .

We then visited all the lines south of Long Bridge. Spirit and temper of the men clearly good. Equipment imperfect in many particulars, but I heard no grumbling. One fact is apparent and unmistakable, that discipline and actual service produce good manners. We were challenged and called on to produce our passes a score of times, and the sentinels (except perhaps certain of the Massachusetts boys) were common men enough, country laborers or city roughs. But we experienced no incivility, even of manner. They scrutinized our passes, asked questions sometimes, but were always respectful and courteous, and generally dismissed us with a sort of apology for our detention and some reference to their orders as leaving them no discretion.

We recrossed the Long Bridge and drove to Colonel Burnside's Rhode Island camp, far away on the outskirts of the City of Distances, somewhere northwest of the Capitol. It's a model of neatness and order, with every provision for health and comfort; by far the most sensibly arranged camp I've seen. The huts are well built and ventilated, with convenient bunks, and a covered porch for the mess table. Talked with Goddard and other Providence millionaires who are serving in the ranks, and saw their evening parade, which was creditable and closed with an evening service by chaplain. Chapter in the Bible and extempore prayer. It suggested a field-preaching in the days of Lauderdale and Claverhouse, and though Puritanism is unlovely, the Rhode Island boys will fight none the worse for this daily inculcation of the truth that they are fighting for the laws of God and not merely for those of Congress. Thence to Burnside's quarters. He seems one of the strongest men I've seen in command.

*June 1*, SATURDAY.    Spent the morning at War Office on business. Visited the Capitol, Smithsonian, and so on, with Hoffman. The Capitol has suffered no damage from its occupation by the Northern hordes. Its beautiful frescos are unscathed by the mudsills who were quartered there. Dined with Wise of the navy; Mrs. Wise is a daughter of Edward Everett. Wise is extravagantly funny. He is now in a prominent and responsible position in the Department. After dinner, walked with the lady and her nice children, and N. P. Willis, in the grounds back of the White House, listening to the Marine

Band. Loungers numerous and the crowd bright with uniforms. Firing heard in direction of Alexandria. Excitement, rumors of battle, and rapid dispersion of the audience. It was
probably a salute. Returned to Wise's, and escorted Mrs. Wise
to reception at Secretary Blair's. Pleasant enough; Seward,
General Mansfield, Hamilton, Trowbridge, and others.

Called on Bache this morning and on Trowbridge. Coast
Survey office full of business. Surveys of southern ports not yet
published are so far advanced that they can be made useful to
the blockading squadrons, and copies are being got up and issued with all possible despatch. At two, I happened to see the
prisoners brought in who were taken at the Fairfax Court
House skirmish Thursday night. They were in a covered waggon, escorted by dragoons, revolver in hand, on their way to
Mansfield's headquarters.

This was a dashing little affair, though General McDowell
tells me it was injudicious and might have turned out very
badly. Fifty United States dragoons . . . were making a re-
connaissance, when they were fired on by a rebel guard of two
men. They shot one and captured the other, who was interro-
gated and said there were about 100 men in the village. Relying on this, the dragoons rode in, and found themselves in
presence of from 1,000 to 1,500 men. Their treacherous in-
formant was shot down at once and very properly. This I heard
in confidence. They charged and dispersed the rebels, rode
through the streets more than once under fire from windows
and from behind fences, and came off at last with trifling loss
and several prisoners. The rebels fired quite wildly. The prisoners begged and cried and knelt and seemed to expect instant
military execution. One of them (a son of Colonel Washington
who was lost on the *San Francisco*) was seized by the hair of
his head and dragged across the pommel of a saddle and carried through the village with the charging dragoons. He took
oath of allegiance very promptly when it was tendered him,
declaring he was a Union man, coerced into the rebel service,
and was liberated by Mansfield and provided with some cloak
or overcoat to cover his rebel uniform. . . .

*June 2*, SUNDAY. Drove with Hoffman to Arlington
House, the hereditary mansion of that fine old fellow, Colonel
Lee, now unhappily a traitor. A splendid place amid beautiful

grounds, through which we strolled a while. The sentinels refused us admission to the house and we were walking back to our carriage when General McDowell came riding up the road with his tail of staff and orderlies. He hailed me, dismounted, took us through the house, and was very kind and obliging. It's a queer place, an odd mixture of magnificence and meanness, like the castle of some illustrious, shabby, semi-insolvent old Irish family; for example, a grand costly portico with half-rotten wooden steps. Hall decorated with pictures, battle-pieces, by some illustrious Custis or other (fearful to behold); also with abundant stags' skulls and antlers. Thence to the camp of the Sixty-ninth, Colonel Corcoran's regiment. Inspected their battalion drill; rather rough. Then visited the New York Twenty-eighth and Fifth Regiments a little in advance, supported by the United States Dragoons, who charged through the streets of Fairfax Court House. Trained soldiers are easily distinguished from even the best volunteers. There was a little bugler of fifteen perhaps, a Brooklyn boy, whose narrative of the fray was spirited and modest. . . . The officers of the Twenty-eighth would not let us drive to Georgetown by the Chain Bridge. It was too hazardous. Rebel pickets were within a mile or two of the road, so we returned by the rope ferry. Orders were issued tonight by telegraph for a general advance. This I had from Wise. But they were countermanded.

Monday morning Hoffman returned to New York. At two I railroaded to Baltimore with Dan Messenger, Smith, and one Lamson of Boston, who is applying for a commission; a very good fellow he seems to be. We had agreed to visit Old Point Comfort and pay our respects to General Butler and Colonel Duryea. From depot to wharf, where we embarked in the *Adelaide*, heavily laden with stores for Fort Monroe, but built for first-class summer passengers to the fashionable hotel at the Point—the "Hygeia Hotel," a Baltimorean Newport in former days. Only half a dozen passengers with us, one a Virginian who wanted to get to Norfolk to look after some property there, and professed himself, in talk with us Union men, to be a sort of Union-lover, of a cold-blooded, anti-coercion type. A very fat and funny old fellow he was, Jenison by name. He was just from Harper's Ferry, where he had friends to see him through. Reports the rebel force at Harper's Ferry undisciplined and insubordinate, the officers and men "all mixed up together." Says he saw a captain enter a bar-room in great excitement and address himself to his commandant. "Colonel, what in H—— shall I do with the boys? They say they won't drill this morning." Colonel replies, "O, well, get two or three of them to turn out, and then I guess the others will come in by degrees." . . .

# *John Brown's Body*

Union veteran George Kimball wrote in an 1890 magazine article that the words to the "John Brown Song" were collectively composed by members of a Massachusetts militia battalion stationed at Fort Warren in Boston Harbor in the spring of 1861. They were inspired by the presence of "a jovial Scotchman in the battalion, named John Brown. . . . As he happened to bear the identical name of the old hero of Harper's Ferry, he became at once the butt of his comrades." Sung to the music of the hymn "Say, brothers, will you meet us?", the "John Brown Song" was sold as a street ballad in Boston in late May 1861, and would be sung by soldiers of the 12th Massachusetts, which many of the militiamen from Fort Warren had joined, as they marched through Boston and New York in July 1861. "John Brown's Body" soon became one of the most popular songs of the Union army. The "jovial Scotchman" who inspired it drowned in the Shenandoah River in June 1862 while serving with the 12th Massachusetts.

---

John Brown's body lies a-mouldering in the grave;
John Brown's body lies a-mouldering in the grave;
John Brown's body lies a-mouldering in the grave;
His soul's marching on!

CHORUS.

Glory, halle—hallelujah! Glory, halle—hallelujah!
Glory, halle—hallelujah!
His soul's marching on!

He's gone to be a soldier in the army of the Lord!
He's gone to be a soldier in the army of the Lord!
He's gone to be a soldier in the army of the Lord!
His soul's marching on!

CHORUS.

Glory, halle—hallelujah! Glory, halle—hallelujah!
Glory, halle—hallelujah!
His soul's marching on!

John Brown's knapsack is strapped upon his back!
John Brown's knapsack is strapped upon his back!
John Brown's knapsack is strapped upon his back!
His soul's marching on!

CHORUS.

Glory, halle—hallelujah! Glory, halle—hallelujah!
Glory, halle—hallelujah!
His soul's marching on!

His pet lambs will meet him on the way;
His pet lambs will meet him on the way;
His pet lambs will meet him on the way;
They go marching on!

CHORUS.

Glory, halle—hallelujah! Glory, halle—hallelujah!
Glory, halle—hallelujah!
They go marching on!

They will hang Jeff. Davis to a tree!
They will hang Jeff. Davis to a tree!
They will hang Jeff. Davis to a tree!
As they march along!

CHORUS.

Glory, halle—hallelujah! Glory, halle—hallelujah!
Glory, halle—hallelujah!
As they march along!

Now, three rousing cheers for the Union!
Now, three rousing cheers for the Union!
Now, three rousing cheers for the Union!
As we are marching on!

## CHORUS.

Glory, halle—hallelujah! Glory, halle—hallelujah!
Glory, halle—hallelujah!
Hip, hip, hip, hip, Hurrah!

# Roger B. Taney: Opinion in Ex parte Merryman, June 1, 1861

On April 27, 1861, President Lincoln authorized the military to suspend the writ of habeas corpus along the Philadelphia–Washington railroad line. When John Merryman was arrested by the army in Baltimore County on May 25 and imprisoned at Fort McHenry, his lawyer obtained a writ of habeas corpus from Chief Justice Roger B. Taney, who was sitting as a federal circuit judge for Maryland. General George Cadwalader, the commander at Fort McHenry, refused to respond to the writ, and when Taney ordered him to be attached (arrested) for contempt, the marshal carrying Taney's writ was barred from the fort. On May 28 the Chief Justice told a crowded courtroom in Baltimore that he would excuse the marshal from further attempts to enforce the attachment because "the power refusing obedience was so notoriously superior to any the marshal could command." Taney issued this opinion on June 1 and ordered the proceedings in the case sent to the President. Lincoln did not respond directly to the Chief Justice, but did address his unprecedented suspension of habeas corpus in his message to Congress on July 4 (see pp. 433.27–434.36 in this volume). By the end of 1861 Lincoln had authorized the suspension of habeas corpus along the railroad line from Philadelphia to New York City (July 2), from New York City to Bangor, Maine (October 14), and within the state of Missouri (December 2). John Merryman was indicted for treason on July 10, 1861, and released on bail, but was never tried.

———————

THE APPLICATION in this case for a writ of habeas corpus is made to me under the 14th section of the judiciary act of 1789, which renders effectual for the citizen the constitutional privilege of the writ of habeas corpus. That act gives to the courts of the United States, as well as to each justice of the supreme court, and to every district judge, power to grant writs of habeas corpus for the purpose of an inquiry into the cause of commitment. The petition was presented to me, at Washington, under the impression that I would order the prisoner to be brought before me there, but as he was confined in Fort McHenry, in the city of Baltimore, which is in my circuit, I resolved to hear it in the latter city, as obedience to the writ, under such circumstances, would not withdraw General Cadwalader, who had him in charge, from the limits of his military command.

The petition presents the following case: The petitioner resides in Maryland, in Baltimore county; while peaceably in his own house, with his family, it was at two o'clock on the morning of the 25th of May 1861, entered by an armed force, professing to act under military orders; he was then compelled to rise from his bed, taken into custody, and conveyed to Fort McHenry, where he is imprisoned by the commanding officer, without warrant from any lawful authority.

The commander of the fort, General George Cadwalader, by whom he is detained in confinement, in his return to the writ, does not deny any of the facts alleged in the petition. He states that the prisoner was arrested by order of General Keim, of Pennsylvania, and conducted as aforesaid to Fort McHenry, by his order, and placed in his (General Cadwalader's) custody, to be there detained by him as a prisoner.

A copy of the warrant or order under which the prisoner was arrested was demanded by his counsel, and refused: and it is not alleged in the return, that any specific act, constituting any offence against the laws of the United States, has been charged against him upon oath, but he appears to have been arrested upon general charges of treason and rebellion, without proof, and without giving the names of the witnesses, or specifying the acts which, in the judgment of the military officer, constituted these crimes. Having the prisoner thus in custody upon these vague and unsupported accusations, he refuses to obey the writ of habeas corpus, upon the ground that he is duly authorized by the president to suspend it.

The case, then, is simply this: a military officer, residing in Pennsylvania, issues an order to arrest a citizen of Maryland, upon vague and indefinite charges, without any proof, so far as appears; under this order, his house is entered in the night, he is seized as a prisoner, and conveyed to Fort McHenry, and there kept in close confinement; and when a habeas corpus is served on the commanding officer, requiring him to produce the prisoner before a justice of the supreme court, in order that he may examine into the legality of the imprisonment, the answer of the officer, is that he is authorized by the president to suspend the writ of habeas corpus at his discretion, and in the exercise of that discretion, suspends it in this case, and on that ground refuses obedience to the writ.

As the case comes before me, therefore, I understand that the president not only claims the right to suspend the writ of habeas corpus himself, at his discretion, but to delegate that discretionary power to a military officer, and to leave it to him to determine whether he will or will not obey judicial process that may be served upon him. No official notice has been given to the courts of justice, or to the public, by proclamation or otherwise, that the president claimed this power, and had exercised it in the manner stated in the return. And I certainly listened to it with some surprise, for I had supposed it to be one of those points of constitutional law upon which there was no difference of opinion, and that it was admitted on all hands, that the privilege of the writ could not be suspended, except by act of congress.

When the conspiracy of which Aaron Burr was the head, became so formidable, and was so extensively ramified, as to justify, in Mr. Jefferson's opinion, the suspension of the writ, he claimed, on his part, no power to suspend it, but communicated his opinion to congress, with all the proofs in his possession, in order that congress might exercise its discretion upon the subject, and determine whether the public safety required it. And in the debate which took place upon the subject, no one suggested that Mr. Jefferson might exercise the power himself, if, in his opinion, the public safety demanded it.

Having, therefore, regarded the question as too plain and too well settled to be open to dispute, if the commanding officer had stated that, upon his own responsibility, and in the exercise of his own discretion, he refused obedience to the writ, I should have contented myself with referring to the clause in the constitution, and to the construction it received from every jurist and statesman of that day, when the case of Burr was before them. But being thus officially notified that the privilege of the writ has been suspended, under the orders, and by the authority of the president, and believing, as I do, that the president has exercised a power which he does not possess under the constitution, a proper respect for the high office he fills, requires me to state plainly and fully the grounds of my opinion, in order to show that I have not ventured to question the legality of his act, without a careful and deliberate examination of the whole subject.

The clause of the constitution, which authorizes the suspension of the privilege of the writ of habeas corpus, is in the 9th section of the first article. This article is devoted to the legislative department of the United States, and has not the slightest reference to the executive department. It begins by providing "that all legislative powers therein granted, shall be vested in a congress of the United States, which shall consist of a senate and house of representatives." And after prescribing the manner in which these two branches of the legislative department shall be chosen, it proceeds to enumerate specifically the legislative powers which it thereby grants and legislative powers which it expressly prohibits; and at the conclusion of this specification, a clause is inserted giving congress "the power to make all laws which shall be necessary and proper for carrying into execution the foregoing powers, and all other powers vested by this constitution in the government of the United States, or in any department or officer thereof."

The power of legislation granted by this latter clause is, by its words, carefully confined to the specific objects before enumerated. But as this limitation was unavoidably somewhat indefinite, it was deemed necessary to guard more effectually certain great cardinal principles, essential to the liberty of the citizen, and to the rights and equality of the states, by denying to congress, in express terms, any power of legislation over them. It was apprehended, it seems, that such legislation might be attempted, under the pretext that it was necessary and proper to carry into execution the powers granted; and it was determined, that there should be no room to doubt, where rights of such vital importance were concerned; and accordingly, this clause is immediately followed by an enumeration of certain subjects, to which the powers of legislation shall not extend. The great importance which the framers of the constitution attached to the privilege of the writ of habeas corpus, to protect the liberty of the citizen, is proved by the fact, that its suspension, except in cases of invasion or rebellion, is first in the list of prohibited powers; and even in these cases the power is denied, and its exercise prohibited, unless the public safety shall require it.

It is true, that in the cases mentioned, congress is, of necessity, the judge of whether the public safety does or does not require it; and their judgment is conclusive. But the introduction of these words is a standing admonition to the legislative body of the danger of suspending it, and of the extreme caution they should exercise, before they give the government of the United States such power over the liberty of a citizen.

It is the second article of the constitution that provides for the organization of the executive department, enumerates the powers conferred on it, and prescribes its duties. And if the high power over the liberty of the citizen now claimed, was intended to be conferred on the president, it would undoubtedly be found in plain words in this article; but there is not a word in it that can furnish the slightest ground to justify the exercise of the power.

The article begins by declaring that the executive power shall be vested in a president of the United States of America, to hold his office during the term of four years; and then proceeds to prescribe the mode of election, and to specify, in precise and plain words, the powers delegated to him, and the duties imposed upon him. The short term for which he is elected, and the narrow limits to which his power is confined, show the jealousy and apprehension of future danger which the framers of the constitution felt in relation to that department of the government, and how carefully they withheld from it many of the powers belonging to the executive branch of the English government which were considered as dangerous to the liberty of the subject; and conferred (and that in clear and specific terms) those powers only which were deemed essential to secure the successful operation of the government.

He is elected, as I have already said, for the brief term of four years, and is made personally responsible, by impeachment, for malfeasance in office; he is, from necessity, and the nature of his duties, the commander-in-chief of the army and navy, and of the militia, when called into actual service; but no appropriation for the support of the army can be made by congress for a longer term than two years, so that it is in the power of the succeeding house of representatives to withhold the appropriation for its support, and thus disband it, if, in their judgment, the president used, or designed to use it for improper purposes. And although the militia, when in actual service, is under his command, yet the appointment of the officers is reserved to the states, as a security against the use of the military power for purposes dangerous to the liberties of the people, or the rights of the states.

So too, his powers in relation to the civil duties and authority necessarily conferred on him are carefully restricted, as well as those belonging to his military character. He cannot appoint the ordinary officers of government, nor make a treaty with a foreign nation or Indian tribe, without the advice and consent of the senate, and cannot appoint even inferior officers, unless he is authorized by an act of congress to do so. He is not empowered to arrest any one charged with an offence against the United States, and whom he may, from the evidence before him, believe to be guilty; nor can he authorize any officer, civil or military, to exercise this power, for the fifth article of the amendments to the constitution expressly provides that no person "shall be deprived of life, liberty or property, without due process of law"—that is, judicial process.

Even if the privilege of the writ of habeas corpus were suspended by act of congress, and a party not subject to the rules and articles of war were afterwards arrested and imprisoned by regular judicial process, he could not be detained in prison, or brought to trial before a military tribunal, for the article in the amendments to the constitution immediately following the one above referred to (that is, the sixth article) provides, that "in all criminal prosecutions, the accused shall enjoy the right to a speedy and public trial by an impartial jury of the state and district wherein the crime shall have been committed, which district shall have been previously ascertained by law; and to be informed of the nature and cause of the accusation; to be confronted with the witnesses against him; to have compulsory process for obtaining witnesses in his favor; and to have the assistance of counsel for his defence."

The only power, therefore, which the president possesses,

where the "life, liberty or property" of a private citizen is concerned, is the power and duty prescribed in the third section of the second article, which requires "that he shall take care that the laws shall be faithfully executed." He is not authorized to execute them himself, or through agents or officers, civil or military, appointed by himself, but he is to take care that they be faithfully carried into execution, as they are expounded and adjudged by the co-ordinate branch of the government to which that duty is assigned by the constitution. It is thus made his duty to come in aid of the judicial authority, if it shall be resisted by a force too strong to be overcome without the assistance of the executive arm; but in exercising this power he acts in subordination to judicial authority, assisting it to execute its process and enforce its judgments.

With such provisions in the constitution, expressed in language too clear to be misunderstood by any one, I can see no ground whatever for supposing that the president, in any emergency, or in any state of things, can authorize the suspension of the privileges of the writ of habeas corpus, or the arrest of a citizen, except in aid of the judicial power. He certainly does not faithfully execute the laws, if he takes upon himself legislative power, by suspending the writ of habeas corpus, and the judicial power also, by arresting and imprisoning a person without due process of law.

Nor can any argument be drawn from the nature of sovereignty, or the necessity of government, for self-defence in times of tumult and danger. The government of the United States is one of delegated and limited powers; it derives its existence and authority altogether from the constitution, and neither of its branches, executive, legislative or judicial, can exercise any of the powers of government beyond those specified and granted; for the tenth article of the amendments to the constitution, in express terms, provides that "the powers not delegated to the United States by the constitution, nor prohibited by it to the states, are reserved to the states, respectively, or to the people."

Indeed, the security against imprisonment by executive authority, provided for in the fifth article of the amendments to the constitution, which I have before quoted, is nothing more than a copy of a like provision in the English constitution, which had been firmly established before the declaration of independence. Blackstone states it in the following words: "To make imprisonment lawful, it must be either by process of law from the courts of judicature, or by warrant from some legal officer having authority to commit to prison." 1 Bl. Comm. 137.

The people of the United Colonies, who had themselves lived under its protection, while they were British subjects, were well aware of the necessity of this safeguard for their personal liberty. And no one can believe that, in framing a government intended to guard still more efficiently the rights and liberties of the citizen, against executive encroachment and oppression, they would have conferred on the president a power which the history of England had proved to be dangerous and oppressive in the hands of the crown; and which the people of England had compelled it to surrender, after a long and obstinate struggle on the part of the English executive to usurp and retain it.

The right of the subject to the benefit of the writ of habeas corpus, it must be recollected, was one of the great points in controversy, during the long struggle in England between arbitrary government and free institutions, and must therefore have strongly attracted the attention of the statesmen engaged in framing a new and, as they supposed, a freer government than the one which they had thrown off by the revolution. From the earliest history of the common law, if a person were imprisoned, no matter by what authority, he had a right to the writ of habeas corpus, to bring his case before the king's bench; if no specific offence were charged against him in the warrant of commitment, he was entitled to be forthwith discharged; and if an offence were charged which was bailable in its character, the court was bound to set him at liberty on bail. The most exciting contests between the crown and the people of England, from the time of Magna Charta, were in relation to the privilege of this writ, and they continued until the passage of the statute of 31 Car. II., commonly known as the great habeas corpus act.

This statute put an end to the struggle, and finally and firmly secured the liberty of the subject against the usurpation and oppression of the executive branch of the government. It nevertheless conferred no new right upon the subject, but only secured a right already existing; for, although the right could not justly be denied, there was often no effectual remedy against its violation. Until the statute of 13 Wm. III., the judges held their offices at the pleasure of the king, and the influence which he exercised over timid, time-serving and partisan judges, often induced them, upon some pretext or other, to refuse to discharge the party, although entitled by law to his discharge, or delayed their decision, from time to time, so as to prolong the imprisonment of persons who were obnoxious to the king for their political opinions, or had incurred his resentment in any other way.

The great and inestimable value of the habeas corpus act of the 31 Car. II. is, that it contains provisions which compel courts and judges, and all parties concerned, to perform their duties promptly, in the manner specified in the statute.

A passage in Blackstone's Commentaries, showing the ancient state of the law on this subject, and the abuses which were practised through the power and influence of the crown, and a short extract from Hallam's Constitutional History, stating the circumstances which gave rise to the passage of this statute, explain briefly, but fully, all that is material to this subject.

Blackstone says: "To assert an absolute exemption from imprisonment in all cases is inconsistent with every idea of law and political society, and in the end would destroy all civil liberty by rendering its protection impossible. But the glory of the English law consists in clearly defining the times, the causes and the extent, when, wherefore and to what degree, the imprisonment of the subject may be lawful. This it is which induces the absolute necessity of expressing upon every commitment the reason for which it is made, that the court, upon a habeas corpus, may examine into its validity, and according to the circumstances of the case, may discharge, admit to bail or remand the prisoner. And yet early in the reign of Charles I. the court of kings bench, relying on some arbitrary precedents (and those perhaps misunderstood) determined that they would not, upon a habeas corpus, either bail or deliver a prisoner, though committed without any cause assigned, in case he was committed by the special command of the king or by the lords of the privy council. This drew on a parliamentary inquiry, and produced the 'Petition of Right' (3 Car. I.) which recites this illegal judgment, and enacts that no freeman hereafter shall be so imprisoned or detained. But when, in the following year, Mr. Selden and others were committed by the lords of the council, in pursuance of his majesty's special command, under a general charge of 'notable contempts, and stirring up sedition against the king and the government,' the judges delayed for two terms (including also the long vacation) to deliver an opinion how far such a charge was bailable; and when at length they agreed that it was, they however annexed a condition of finding sureties for their good behavior, which still protracted their imprisonment, the chief justice, Sir Nicholas Hyde, at the same time, declaring that 'if they were again remanded for that cause, perhaps the court would not afterwards grant a habeas corpus, being already made acquainted with the cause of the imprisonment.' But this was heard with indignation and astonishment by every lawyer present, according to Mr. Selden's own account of the matter, whose resentment was not cooled at the distance of four and twenty years." 3 Bl. Comm. 133, 134.

It is worthy of remark, that the offences charged against the prisoner in this case, and relied on as a justification for his arrest and imprisonment, in their nature and character, and in the loose and vague manner in which they are stated, bear a striking resemblance to those assigned in the warrant for the arrest of Mr. Selden. And yet, even at that day, the warrant was regarded as such a flagrant violation of the rights of the subject that the delay of the time-serving judges to set him at liberty, upon the habeas corpus issued in his behalf, excited the universal indignation of the bar.

The extract from Hallam's Constitutional History is equally impressive and equally in point: "It is a very common mistake, and that not only among foreigners, but many from whom some knowledge of our constitutional laws might be expected, to suppose that this statute of Car. II. enlarged in a great degree our liberties, and forms a sort of epoch in their history. But though a very beneficial enactment, and eminently remedial in many cases of illegal imprisonment, it introduced no new principle, nor conferred any right upon the subject. From the earliest records of the English law, no freeman could be detained in prison, except upon a criminal charge or conviction, or for a civil debt. In the former case it was always in his power to demand of the court of king's bench a writ of habeas corpus ad subjiciendum, directed to the person detaining him in custody, by which he was enjoined to bring up the body of the prisoner, with the warrant of commitment, that the court might judge of its sufficiency, and remand the party, admit him to bail, or discharge him, according to the nature of the charge. This writ issued of right, and could not be refused by the court. It was not to bestow an immunity from arbitrary imprisonment, which is abundantly provided for in Magna Charta (if indeed it is not more ancient), that the statute of Car. II. was enacted, but to cut off the abuses by which the government's lust of power, and the servile subtlety of the crown lawyers, had impaired so fundamental a privilege." 3 Hall. Const. Hist. 19.

While the value set upon this writ in England has been so great, that the removal of the abuses which embarrassed its employment has been looked upon as almost a new grant of liberty to the subject, it is not to be wondered at, that the continuance of the writ thus made effective should have been the object of the most jealous care. Accordingly, no power in England short of that of parliament can suspend or authorize the suspension of the writ of habeas corpus. I quote again from Blackstone (1 Bl. Comm. 136): "But the happiness of our constitution is, that it is not left to the executive power to determine when the danger of the state is so great as to render this measure expedient. It is the parliament only or legislative power that, whenever it sees proper, can authorize the crown by suspending the habeas corpus for a short and limited time, to imprison suspected persons without giving any reason for so doing." If the president of the United States may suspend the writ, then the constitution of the United States has conferred upon him more regal and absolute power over the liberty of the citizen, than the people of England have thought it safe to entrust to the crown; a power which the queen of England cannot exercise at this day, and which could not have been lawfully exercised by the sovereign even in the reign of Charles the First.

But I am not left to form my judgment upon this great

question, from analogies between the English government and our own, or the commentaries of English jurists, or the decisions of English courts, although upon this subject they are entitled to the highest respect, and are justly regarded and received as authoritative by our courts of justice. To guide me to a right conclusion, I have the Commentaries on the Constitution of the United States of the late Mr. Justice Story, not only one of the most eminent jurists of the age, but for a long time one of the brightest ornaments of the supreme court of the United States; and also the clear and authoritative decision of that court itself, given more than half a century since, and conclusively establishing the principles I have above stated.

Mr. Justice Story, speaking, in his Commentaries, of the habeas corpus clause in the constitution, says: "It is obvious that cases of a peculiar emergency may arise, which may justify, nay, even require, the temporary suspension of any right to the writ. But as it has frequently happened in foreign countries, and even in England, that the writ has, upon various pretexts and occasions, been suspended, whereby persons apprehended upon suspicion have suffered a long imprisonment, sometimes from design, and sometimes because they were forgotten, the right to suspend it is expressly confined to cases of rebellion or invasion, where the public safety may require it. A very just and wholesome restraint, which cuts down at a blow a fruitful means of oppression, capable of being abused, in bad times, to the worst of purposes. Hitherto, no suspension of the writ has ever been authorized by congress, since the establishment of the constitution. It would seem, as the power is given to congress to suspend the writ of habeas corpus, in cases of rebellion or invasion, that the right to judge whether the exigency had arisen must exclusively belong to that body." 3 Story, Comm. Const. § 1336.

And Chief Justice Marshall, in delivering the opinion of the supreme court in the case of Ex parte Bollman and Swartwout, uses this decisive language, in 4 Cranch [8 U. S.] 95: "It may be worthy of remark, that this act (speaking of the one under which I am proceeding) was passed by the first congress of the United States, sitting under a constitution which had declared 'that the privilege of the writ of habeas corpus should not be suspended, unless when, in cases of rebellion or invasion, the

public safety may require it.' Acting under the immediate influence of this injunction, they must have felt, with peculiar
force, the obligation of providing efficient means, by which
this great constitutional privilege should receive life and activity; for if the means be not in existence, the privilege itself
would be lost, although no law for its suspension should be
enacted. Under the impression of this obligation, they give to
all the courts the power of awarding writs of habeas corpus."
And again on page 101: "If at any time, the public safety should
require the suspension of the powers vested by this act in the
courts of the United States, it is for the legislature to say so.
That question depends on political considerations, on which
the legislature is to decide; until the legislative will be expressed, this court can only see its duty, and must obey the
laws." I can add nothing to these clear and emphatic words of
my great predecessor.

But the documents before me show, that the military authority in this case has gone far beyond the mere suspension of
the privilege of the writ of habeas corpus. It has, by force of
arms, thrust aside the judicial authorities and officers to whom
the constitution has confided the power and duty of interpret-
ing and administering the laws, and substituted a military government in its place, to be administered and executed by
military officers. For, at the time these proceedings were had
against John Merryman, the district judge of Maryland, the
commissioner appointed under the act of congress, the district
attorney and the marshal, all resided in the city of Baltimore, a
few miles only from the home of the prisoner. Up to that time,
there had never been the slightest resistance or obstruction to
the process of any court or judicial officer of the United States,
in Maryland, except by the military authority. And if a military
officer, or any other person, had reason to believe that the prisoner had committed any offence against the laws of the
United States, it was his duty to give information of the fact
and the evidence to support it, to the district attorney; it
would then have become the duty of that officer to bring the
matter before the district judge or commissioner, and if there
was sufficient legal evidence to justify his arrest, the judge or
commissioner would have issued his warrant to the marshal to

arrest him; and upon the hearing of the case, would have held him to bail, or committed him for trial, according to the character of the offence, as it appeared in the testimony, or would have discharged him immediately, if there was not sufficient evidence to support the accusation. There was no danger of any obstruction or resistance to the action of the civil authorities, and therefore no reason whatever for the interposition of the military.

Yet, under these circumstances, a military officer, stationed in Pennsylvania, without giving any information to the district attorney, and without any application to the judicial authorities, assumes to himself the judicial power in the district of Maryland; undertakes to decide what constitutes the crime of treason or rebellion; what evidence (if indeed he required any) is sufficient to support the accusation and justify the commitment; and commits the party, without a hearing, even before himself, to close custody, in a strongly garrisoned fort, to be there held, it would seem, during the pleasure of those who committed him.

The constitution provides, as I have before said, that "no person shall be deprived of life, liberty or property, without due process of law." It declares that "the right of the people to be secure in their persons, houses, papers and effects, against unreasonable searches and seizures, shall not be violated; and no warrant shall issue, but upon probable cause, supported by oath or affirmation, and particularly describing the place to be searched, and the persons or things to be seized." It provides that the party accused shall be entitled to a speedy trial in a court of justice.

These great and fundamental laws, which congress itself could not suspend, have been disregarded and suspended, like the writ of habeas corpus, by a military order, supported by force of arms. Such is the case now before me, and I can only say that if the authority which the constitution has confided to the judiciary department and judicial officers, may thus, upon any pretext or under any circumstances, be usurped by the military power, at its discretion, the people of the United States are no longer living under a government of laws, but every citizen holds life, liberty and property at the will and pleasure of the army officer in whose military district he may happen to be found.*

In such a case, my duty was too plain to be mistaken. I have exercised all the power which the constitution and laws confer upon me, but that power has been resisted by a force too strong for me to overcome. It is possible that the officer who has incurred this grave responsibility may have misunderstood his instructions, and exceeded the authority intended to be given him; I shall, therefore, order all the proceedings in this case, with my opinion, to be filed and recorded in the circuit court of the United States for the district of Maryland, and direct the clerk to transmit a copy, under seal, to the president of the United States. It will then remain for that high officer, in fulfilment of his constitutional obligation to "take care that the laws be faithfully executed," to determine what measures he will take to cause the civil process of the United States to be respected and enforced.

---

*The constitution of the United States is founded upon the principles of government set forth and maintained in the Declaration of Independence. In that memorable instrument the people of the several colonies declared, that one of the causes which "impelled" them to "dissolve the political bands" which connected them with the British nation, and justified them in withdrawing their allegiance from the British sovereign, was that "he (the king) had affected to render the military independent of, and superior to, the civil power."

# Henry A. Wise: Speech at Richmond

## June 1, 1861

In late May 1861 the Confederacy moved its capital from Montgomery to Richmond, Virginia, where President Davis addressed a crowd on June 1. He was followed by former Virginia governor Henry A. Wise, who had been one of the leading secessionists in the state convention earlier in the year.

---

MY FRIENDS:—You all know that I am a civil soldier only, and that in that capacity I was nearly worn down in the siege of the Virginia Convention. Thank God, however, that with a little rest, some help, and some damage from the doctors, I have been enabled to recruit my exhausted energies.

The time of deliberation has given place to the time of action, and I have taken up my bed as an individual, in common with others, to march to Richmond to meet the President of our now separate and independent republic. I am ready to obey his orders, not only with pride, pleasure, and devotion to the cause, and respect to the office he fills, but with repect to the man himself as one who has our fullest confidence.

You have to meet a foe with whom you could not live in peace. Your political powers and rights, which were enthroned in that Capitol when you were united with them under the old constitutional bond of the Confederacy, have been annihilated. They have undertaken to annul laws within your own limits that would render your property unsafe within those limits. They have abolitionized your border, as the disgraced North-west will show. They have invaded your moral strongholds and the rights of your religion, and have undertaken to teach you what should be the moral duties of men.

They have invaded the sanctity of your homes and firesides, and endeavored to play master, father, and husband for you in your households; in a word, they have set themselves up as a petty Providence by which you are in all things to be guided and controlled. But you have always declared that you would not be subject to this invasion of your rights.

Though war was demanded, it was not for you to declare war. But now that the armies of the invader are hovering around the tomb of Washington, where is the Virginian heart that does not beat with a quicker pulsation at this last and boldest desecration of his beloved State? Their hordes are already approaching our metropolis, and extending their folds around our State as does the anaconda around his victim. The call is for action.

I rejoice in this war. Who is there that now dares to put on sanctity to depreciate war, or the "horrid glories of war." None. Why? Because it is a war of purification. You want war, fire, blood, to purify you; and the Lord of Hosts has demanded that you should walk through fire and blood. You are called to the fiery baptism, and I call upon you to come up to the altar. Though your pathway be through fire, or through a river of blood, turn not aside. Be in no hurry—no hurry and flurry.

Collect yourselves, summon yourselves, elevate yourselves to the high and sacred duty of patriotism. The man who dares to pray, the man who dares to wait until some magic arm is put into his hand; the man who will not go unless he have a Minié, or percussion musket, who will not be content with flint and steel, or even a gun without a lock, is worse than a coward—he is a renegade. If he can do no better, go to a blacksmith, take a gun along as a sample, and get him to make you one like it. Get a spear—a lance. Take a lesson from John Brown. Manufacture your blades from old iron, even though it be the tires of your cart-wheels. Get a bit of carriage spring, and grind and burnish it in the shape of a bowie knife, and put it to any sort of a handle, so that it be strong—ash, hickory, oak. But, if possible, get a double-barrelled gun and a dozen rounds of buckshot, and go upon the battle-field with these.

If their guns reach further than yours, reduce the distance; meet them foot to foot, eye to eye, body to body, and when you strike a blow, strike home. Your true-blooded Yankee will never stand still in the face of cold steel. Let your aim, there-

fore, be to get into close quarters, and with a few decided, vigorous movements, always pushing forward, never back, my
word for it, the soil of Virginia will be swept of the Vandals
who are now polluting its atmosphere.

The band then struck up "Dixie," which was followed by
"We may be Happy yet."

# Charles C. Jones Jr. to
# Charles C. Jones Sr. and Mary Jones

Educated at the College of New Jersey (Princeton) and the Dane Law School at Harvard, Charles C. Jones Jr. was elected mayor of Savannah in October 1860. Jones wrote to his parents while anticipating that a major battle would soon be fought in Virginia.

———————

Savannah, *Monday*, June 10th, 1861

My dear Father and Mother,

Ruth has returned after her short visit to Amanda looking pretty well. She suffered one day from an acute attack, but was soon relieved.

I presume you have observed the appointment of Judge Jackson as a brigadier general in the Confederate service. It is a position he has long and most ardently desired, and I doubt not when the hour of combat comes he will do the states no little service.

That hour must soon arrive. Sincerely do I trust and believe that the God of Battles will in that day send the victory where it of right belongs. I cannot bring my mind to entertain even the impression that a God of justice and of truth will permit a blinded, fanatical people, who already have set at naught all rules of equality, of right, and of honor; who flagrantly violate the inalienable right of private liberty by an arrogant suspension of the privilege of habeas corpus, a writ of right than which none can be dearer to the citizen—and that in the face of judicial process issued by the Chief Justice Taney, renowned for his profound legal attainments, respected for his many virtues and high position, and venerable for his many useful labors and constitutional learning; who set at defiance the right of private property by seizing Negroes, the personal chattels of others, without offer of remuneration or consent of the owner;

who permit their mercenaries to trifle at will with private virtue; who trample under foot sacred compacts and solemn engagements; who substitute military despotism in the place of constitutional liberty; and who without the fear of either God or man in their eyes recklessly pursue a policy subversive of all that is just and pure and high-minded—to triumph in this unholy war. We have our sins and our shortcomings, and they are many; but without the arrogance of the self-righteous Pharisee we may honestly thank God that we are not as they are. Should they be defeated in this fearful contest, how fearful the retribution! Who can appreciate the terrors of this lifted wave of fanaticism when, broken and dismayed, it recoils in confusion and madness upon itself? Agrarianism in ancient Rome will appear as naught in the contrast.

You will observe that I have issued a proclamation requesting the citizens of Savannah to abstain from their ordinary engagements on Thursday next, the day set apart by the President as a day of fasting and prayer, and with one consent to unite in the due observation of the day. You may also notice an anonymous communication in our city papers signed "Citizen," in which I recommend that the suggestion in reference to the taking up of a collection in all places of public worship on that day for the benefit of our army and of our government should meet with a generous, practical, and patriotic adoption. If this plan be pursued generally on that day throughout these Confederate States, the amount received will be large, and the fund thus realized will prove most acceptable to the present finances of the government. The idea is a good one, and should be everywhere carried into effect. I intend myself conscientiously to observe the day. We should all do so.

We are kept very much in the dark with reference to the true movements of our army in Virginia, and it is proper that this should be so. President Davis' presence inspires great enthusiasm and confidence. He appears to be in every respect the man raised for the emergency. At once soldier and statesman, he everywhere acknowledges our dependence upon and our hope in the guiding influence and the protection of a superintending Providence. I regret to know that his health is feeble. In the event of his death, where would we look for a successor?

The Central Railroad Company have declared a semi-annual

dividend payable on and after the 15th inst. of five percent. Very acceptable to all stockholders at the present. I send by this post a copy of Judge Jackson's recent eulogy upon the life and character of the Hon. Charles J. McDonald. We are all well, and unite, my dearest parents, in warmest love to you both. As ever,

Your affectionate son,<br>
Charles C. Jones, Jr.

What was done at Hinesville last Tuesday?

# Henry Adams to Charles Francis Adams Jr.

When Lincoln appointed Charles Francis Adams as the new American minister to Great Britain, his son Henry accompanied him to London, where he would serve as his father's confidential secretary. They arrived on May 13, 1861, just as the British government issued a proclamation of neutrality recognizing the Confederates as belligerents under international law, a measure widely seen as a possible prelude to full diplomatic recognition. Adams wrote to his brother in Boston.

———————————

London 10 June 1861.

My dear Charles

Your letters, to the family in general arrived this morning and gave great satisfaction in so far as they were letters, though they made the M. E. & Amb. Plen. as glum as an English Viscount. At that date you had not received our first letters, and as I have not written since then, I feel as though I ought to answer yours at once. It is a relief to know that you are out of the fort and I hope to the Lord that no unhappy chance will carry you off to the wars, however much you may want to go yourself. Not that I want you or anyone to shirk their duties, but simply because I can't see my way straight to where we shall be a year hence, and I don't like to see a man do his best pace on the first quarter. Talking of duties shirked, it has occurred to me that I am probably not innocent in that way myself, for I do not suppose that my property has been taxed. I am not of that mind which approves of neglecting these duties when most called for, and I therefore desire you to make a just estimate of my manifold possessions and hand it in to the authorities, paying said taxes out of such monies as may be received in the way of dividends or may be in your hands. The expenses in this city are enormous and if the Ambassador's private income fails, we must cut our establishment down to a very low figure, as one can do little here with less than forty thousand, and nothing with less than twenty five thousand dollars. People must occasionally live on less, but if so, they must have assistance from the public charities. The scale of living and the prices are curious examples of the beauties of a high civilization.

As for myself, I have only the same old story to sing which I have chanted many times, especially in my letters to you. I have done nothing whatever in the way of entering society, nor do I mean to take the plunge until after my presentation on the 19th. (Court suit = upwards of $200.00). Getting into society is a beastly repulsive piece of work here. Supposing you are invited to a ball. You arrive at eleven o'clock. A footman in powder asks your name and announces you. The lady or ladies of the house receive you and shake hands. You pass on and there you are. You know not a soul. No one offers to introduce you. No one even looks at you with curiosity. London society is so vast that the oldest habitués know only their own sets, and never trouble themselves even to look at anyone else. No one knows that you're a stranger. You see numbers of men and women just as silent and just as strange as yourself. You may go from house to house and from rout to rout and never see a face twice. You may labor for weeks at making acquaintances and yet go again and again to balls where you can't discover a face you ever saw before. And supposing you are in society, what does it amount to! The state dinners are dull, heavy, lifeless, affairs. The balls are solemn stupid crushes without a scintilla of the gaiety of our balls. No one enjoys them so far as I can hear. They are matters of necessity, of position. People have to entertain. They were born to it and it is one of the duties of life. My own wish is quietly to slide into the literary set and leave the heavy society, which without dancing is a frightful and irredeemable bore to me, all on one side.

After the 19th I must set to work to get a club and make acquaintances of my own age; no easy work with English. But I do not expect or wish to do a great deal in this way this season. There is time enough for all that.

You want to be posted up politically. If the Times has published my letters without mutilation, you will see what I think about it. We arrived here just as the Queen's Proclamation was issued. Of course the question arose what course to take.

Papa's instructions and especially a later despatch, would have justified him in breaking off at once all diplomatic relations with this Government, and we felt no doubt that, as you say, the Americans would have upheld him. But I must confess such a policy appeared to me to be the extreme of shallowness and folly. In the first place it would have been a tremendous load for the country. In the second place it would have been a mere wanton, mad windmill-hitting, for the sympathies and the policy of England are undoubtedly with us as has been already shown. In the third place it would have been ruin in a merely private point of view. Two such wars would grind us all into rags in America. One is already enough to cut down incomes to a dreadful extent.

Papa took the course that seems to me to have been the correct one. He had an interview with Lord John and told him, without bravado or bragg, how the matter was regarded in America, or was likely to be regarded, and announced plainly what course he should be compelled to take if the Government really entertained any idea of encouraging the insurgents, and demanded a categorical answer as to the course the Government meant to pursue. Lord John promised to send this answer by Lord Lyons, protesting at the same time the unreasonableness of the American feeling, and the perfect good-faith of his Government. Since that time no opportunity has escaped the Government of proving their good-will towards us and unless you in America are run mad, and are determined to run your heads right against a stone wall there need be no more difficulty whatever.

Feeling as I did in the matter, of course I did my best in my letters to the Times to quiet rather than inflame. If you choose you can suggest to the Advertiser a leader developing the view which I take, and pointing out the good sense of our worthy Ambassador in maintaining the dignity of the country and yet avoiding a rupture, as contrasted with those noisy jackasses Clay and Burlingame who have done more harm here than their weak heads were worth a thousand times over. I believe it to be essential to our interests now, that Europe should be held on our side. Our troubles have gone too far to be closed by foreign jealousies. The cotton-states would rather annex themselves to England or Spain than come back to us.

I have tried to get some influence over the press here but as yet have only succeeded in one case which has however been of some use. That is the Morning Herald, whose American editor, a young man named Edge, came to call on the Amb. He is going to America to correspond for his paper; at least he says so. If he brings you a letter, let him be asked out to dine and give him what assistance in the way of introductions he wants. He is withal of passing self-conceit and his large acquaintance is fudge, for he is no more than an adventurer in the press; but his manners are good, and so long as he asks nothing in return, it's better to have him an ally than an enemy.

As to the Article on the last Winter which I left in the drawer of your table at the house, I left with it a note of directions. It was merely to the purport that I had not succeeded in making it fit for publication, and as it stood, it was not to be published, but if on reading it you thought you could make anything of it, you might have it for your pains.

Our life here is not of the gayest, at least to my mind. Not that I care much so far as the outside of the house goes, but the Ambassador is more snappish and sulky than I have known him to be for a long time, and mamma has fits of homesickness that don't make us cheerful while Margaret thinks she's going insane with weeping—damn her, I wish she would,—and Bridget is little better, for Margaret infects her. Mary is of as little count in a house as anyone I ever saw and really is a problem to me, for she seems wholly different from all the rest of us. I'm afraid she won't improve with age. Poor Brooks I took off to boarding school this morning. He's a good boy as ever lived and I've become very fond of him though I treat him like a dog. He was very brave about it and indeed was rather glad to go, for our house is not over-cheerful especially for a boy of his age. His school seems pleasant and clean, and he'll learn to play cricket and be a man.

Tuesday. 11th.   To return to politics, and this in absolute secrecy, for I let you know what I've no business to. A despatch arrived yesterday from Seward, so arrogant in tone and so extraordinary and unparalleled in its demands that it leaves no doubt in my mind that our Government wishes to force a war with all Europe. That is the inevitable result of any attempt to

any reason why the Cherokee Nation should take any other course, for it seems to me to be dictated by their treaties and sanctioned by wisdom and humanity. It ought not give ground for complaint to either side, and should cause our rights to be respected by both. Our country and institutions are our own. However small the one or humble the others, they are as sacred and valuable to us as are those of your own populous and wealthy State to yourself and your people. We have done nothing to bring about the conflict in which you are engaged with your own people, and I am unwilling that my people shall become its victims. I am determined to do no act that shall furnish any pretext to either of the contending parties to overrun our country and destroy our rights. If we are destined to be overwhelmed, it shall not be through any agency of mine. The United States are pledged not to disturb us in our rights, nor can we suppose for a moment that your Government will do it, as the avowed principle upon which it is struggling for an acknowledged existence is the rights of the States and freedom from outside interference.

The Cherokee people and Government have given every assurance in their power of their sympathy and friendship for the people of Arkansas and of other Confederate States, unless it be in not voluntarily assuming an attitude of hostility toward the Government of the United States, with whom their treaties exist and from whom they are not experiencing any new burdens or exactions. That I cannot advise them to do, and hope that their good faith in adhering to the requirements of their treaties and of their friendship for all the whites will be manifested by strict observance of the neutrality enjoined.

Your demand that those people of the nation who are in favor of joining the Confederacy be allowed to organize into military companies as home guards for the purpose of defending themselves in case of invasion from the North is most respectfully declined. I cannot give my consent to any such organization for very obvious reasons:

1st. It would be a palpable violation of my position as a neutral.

2d. It will place in our midst organized companies not authorized by our laws, but in violation of treaty, and who would soon become efficient instruments in stirring up domestic strife and creating internal difficulties among the Cherokee people.

As in this connection you have misapprehended a remark which I made in conversation at our interview some eight or ten days ago, I hope you will allow me to repeat what I did say. I informed you that I had taken a neutral position and would maintain it honestly, but that in case of a foreign invasion old as I am I would assist in repelling it. I have not signified any purpose as to an invasion of our soil and interference with our rights from the United or Confederate States, because I have apprehended none and cannot give my consent to any.

I have the honor to be, sir, your obedient servant,

JNO. ROSS,
*Principal Chief Cherokee Nation.*

# James Russell Lowell:
# The Pickens-and-Stealin's Rebellion

June 1861

A prominent poet and literary critic, James Russell Lowell was professor of Romance languages at Harvard and the founding editor of *The
Atlantic Monthly*, where this article appeared.

---

HAD ANY one ventured to prophesy on the Fourth of March
that the immediate prospect of Civil War would be hailed by
the people of the Free States with a unanimous shout of
enthusiasm, he would have been thought a madman. Yet the
prophecy would have been verified by what we now see and
hear in every city, town, and hamlet from Maine to Kansas.
With the advantage of three months' active connivance in the
cabinet of Mr. Buchanan, with an empty treasury at Washington, and that reluctance to assume responsibility and to inaugurate a decided policy, the common vice of our politicians,
who endeavor to divine and to follow popular sentiment rather
than to lead it, it seemed as if Disunion were inevitable, and
the only open question were the line of separation. So assured
seemed the event, that English journalists moralized gravely
on the inherent weakness of Democracy. While the leaders of
the Southern Rebellion did not dare to expose their treason to
the risk of a popular vote in any one of the seceding States, the
"Saturday Review," one of the ablest of British journals,
solemnly warned its countrymen to learn by our example the
dangers of an extended suffrage.

Meanwhile the conduct of the people of the Free States,
during all these trying and perilous months, had proved, if it
proved anything, the essential conservatism of a population in
which every grown man has a direct interest in the stability of
the national government. So abstinent are they by habit and

principle from any abnormal intervention with the machine of administration, so almost superstitious in adherence to constitutional forms, as to be for a moment staggered by the claim to a *right* of secession set up by all the Cotton States, admitted by the Border Slave-States, which had the effrontery to deliberate between their plain allegiance and their supposed interest, and but feebly denied by the Administration then in power. The usual panacea of palaver was tried; Congress did its best to add to the general confusion of thought; and, as if that were not enough, a Convention of Notables was called simultaneously to thresh the straw of debate anew, and to convince thoughtful persons that men do not grow wiser as they grow older. So in the two Congresses the notables talked,—in the one, those who ought to be shelved, in the other, those who were shelved already,—while those who were too thoroughly shelved for a seat in either addressed Great Union Meetings at home. Not a man of them but had a compromise in his pocket, adhesive as Spalding's glue, warranted to stick the shattered Confederacy together so firmly, that, if it ever broke again, it must be in a new place, which was a great consolation. If these gentlemen gave nothing very valuable to the people of the Free States, they were giving the Secessionists what was of inestimable value to them,—Time. The latter went on seizing forts, navy-yards, and deposits of Federal money, erecting batteries, and raising and arming men at their leisure; above all, they acquired a prestige, and accustomed men's minds to the thought of disunion, not only as possible, but actual. They began to grow insolent, and, while compelling absolute submission to their rebellious usurpation at home, decried any exercise of legitimate authority on the part of the General Government as *Coercion*,—a new term, by which it was sought to be established as a principle of constitutional law, that it is always the Northern bull that has gored the Southern ox.

During all this time, the Border Slave-States, and especially Virginia, were playing a part at once cowardly and selfish. They assumed the right to stand neutral between the Government and rebellion, to contract a kind of morganatic marriage with Treason, by which they could enjoy the pleasant sin without the tedious responsibility, and to be traitors in everything but the vulgar contingency of hemp. Doubtless the aim of the political managers in these States was to keep the North amused with schemes of arbitration, reconstruction, and whatever other fine words would serve the purpose of hiding the real issue, till the new government of Secessia should have so far consolidated itself as to be able to demand with some show of reason a recognition from foreign powers, and to render it politic for the United States to consent to peaceable secession. They counted on the self-interest of England and the supineness of the North. As to the former, they were not wholly without justification,—for nearly all the English discussions of the "American Crisis" which we have seen have shown far more of the shop-keeping spirit than of interest in the maintenance of free institutions; but in regard to the latter they made the fatal mistake of believing our Buchanans, Cushings, and Touceys to be representative men. They were not aware how utterly the Democratic Party had divorced itself from the moral sense of the Free States, nor had they any conception of the tremendous recoil of which the long-repressed convictions, traditions, and instincts of a people are capable.

Never was a nation so in want of a leader; never was it more plain, that, without a head, the people "bluster abroad as beasts," with plenty of the iron of purpose, but purpose without coherence, and with no cunning smith of circumstance to edge it with plan and helve it with direction. What the country was waiting for showed itself in the universal thrill of satisfaction when Major Anderson took the extraordinary responsibility of doing his duty. But such was the general uncertainty, so doubtful seemed the loyalty of the Democratic Party as represented by its spokesmen at the North, so irresolute was the tone of many Republican leaders and journals, that a powerful and wealthy community of twenty millions of people gave a sigh of relief when they had been permitted to install the Chief Magistrate of their choice in their own National Capital. Even after the inauguration of Mr. Lincoln, it was confidently announced that Jefferson Davis, the Burr of the Southern conspiracy, would be in Washington before the month was out; and so great was the Northern despondency, that the chances of such an event were seriously discussed. While the nation was falling to pieces, there were newspapers and "distinguished statesmen" of the party so lately and so long in power base enough to be willing to make political capital out of the common danger, and to lose their country, if they could only find their profit. There was even one man found in Massachusetts, who, measuring the moral standard of his party by his own, had the unhappy audacity to declare publicly that there were friends enough of the South in his native State to prevent the march of any troops thence to sustain that Constitution to which he had sworn fealty in Heaven knows how many offices, the rewards of almost as many turnings of his political coat. There was one journal in New York which had the insolence to speak of *President* Davis and *Mister* Lincoln in the same paragraph. No wonder the "dirt-eaters" of the Carolinas could be taught to despise a race among whom creatures might be found to do that by choice which they themselves were driven to do by misery.

Thus far the Secessionists had the game all their own way, for their dice were loaded with Northern lead. They framed their sham constitution, appointed themselves to their sham offices, issued their sham commissions, endeavored to bribe England with a sham offer of low duties and Virginia with a sham prohibition of the slave-trade, advertised their proposals for a sham loan which was to be taken up under intimidation, and levied real taxes on the people in the name of the people whom they had never allowed to vote directly on their enormous swindle. With money stolen from the Government, they raised troops whom they equipped with stolen arms, and beleaguered national fortresses with cannon stolen from national arsenals. They sent out secret agents to Europe, they had their secret allies in the Free States, their conventions transacted all important business in secret session;—there was but one exception to the shrinking delicacy becoming a maiden government, and that was the openness of the stealing. We had always thought a high sense of personal honor an essential element of chivalry; but among the *Romanic* races, by which, as the wonderful ethnologist of "De Bow's Review" tells us, the Southern States were settled, and from which they derive a close entail of chivalric characteristics, to the exclusion of the vulgar Saxons of the North, such is by no means the case. For the first time in history the deliberate treachery of a general is deemed worthy of a civic ovation, and Virginia has the honor of being the first State claiming to be civilized that has decreed the honors of a triumph to a cabinet officer who had contrived to gild a treason that did not endanger his life with a peculation that could not further damage his reputation. Rebellion, even in a bad cause, may have its romantic side; treason, which had not been such but for being on the losing side, may challenge admiration; but nothing can sweeten larceny or disinfect perjury. A rebellion inaugurated with theft, and which has effected its entry into national fortresses, not over broken walls, but by breaches of trust, should take Jonathan Wild for its patron saint, with the run of Mr. Buchanan's cabinet for a choice of sponsors,—godfathers we should not dare to call them.

Mr. Lincoln's Inaugural Speech was of the kind usually called "firm, but conciliatory,"—a policy doubtful in troublous times, since it commonly argues weakness, and more than doubtful in a crisis like ours, since it left the course which the Administration meant to take ambiguous, and, while it weakened the Government by exciting the distrust of all who wished for vigorous measures, really strengthened the enemy by encouraging the conspirators in the Border States. There might be a question as to whether this or that attitude were expedient for the Republican Party; there could be none as to the only safe and dignified one for the Government of the Nation. Treason was as much treason in the beginning of March as in the middle of April; and it seems certain now, as it seemed probable to many then, that the country would have sooner rallied to the support of the Government, if the Government had shown an earlier confidence in the loyalty of the people. Though the President talked of "repossessing" the stolen forts, arsenals, and customhouses, yet close upon this declaration followed the disheartening intelligence that the Cabinet were discussing the propriety of evacuating not only Fort Sumter, which was of no strategic importance, but Fort Pickens, which was the key to the Gulf of Mexico, and to abandon which was almost to acknowledge the independence of the Rebel States. Thus far the Free States had waited with commendable patience for some symptom of vitality in the new Administration, something that should distinguish it from the piteous helplessness of its predecessor. But now their pride was too deeply outraged for endurance, indignant remonstrances were heard from all quarters, and the Government seemed for the first time fairly to comprehend that it had twenty millions of freemen at its back, and that forts might be taken and held by honest men as well as by knaves and traitors. The nettle had been stroked long enough; it was time to try a firm grip. Still the Administration seemed inclined to temporize, so thoroughly was it possessed by the notion of conciliating the Border States. In point of fact, the side which those States might take in the struggle between Law and Anarchy was of vastly more import to them than to us. They could bring no considerable reinforcement of money, credit, or arms to the rebels; they could at best but add so many mouths to an army whose commissariat was already dangerously embarrassed. They could not even, except temporarily, keep the war away from the territory of the seceding States, every one of which had a sea-door open to the invasion of an enemy who controlled the entire navy and shipping of the country. The position assumed by Eastern Virginia and Maryland was of consequence only so far as it might facilitate a sudden raid on Washington, and the policy of both these States was to amuse the Government by imaginary negotiations till the plans of the conspirators were ripe. In both States men were actively recruited and enrolled to assist in attacking the capital. With them, as with the more openly rebellious States, the new theory of "Coercion" was ingeniously arranged like a valve, yielding at the slightest impulse to the passage of forces for the subversion of legitimate authority, closing imperviously so that no drop of power could ooze through in the opposite direction. Lord de Roos, long suspected of cheating at cards, would never have been convicted but for the resolution of an adversary, who, pinning his hand to the table with a fork, said to him blandly, "My Lord, if the ace of spades is not under your Lordship's hand, why, then, I beg your pardon!" It seems to us that a timely treatment of Governor Letcher in the same energetic way would have saved the disasters of Harper's Ferry and Norfolk,—for disasters they were, though six months of temporizing had so lowered the public sense of what was due to the national dignity, that people were glad to see the Government active at length, even if only in setting fire to its own house.

We are by no means inclined to criticize the Administration, even if this were the proper time for it; but we cannot help thinking that there was great wisdom in Napoleon's recipe for saving life in dealing with a mob,—"First fire grape-shot *into* them; after that, over their heads as much as you like." The position of Mr. Lincoln was already embarrassed when he entered upon office, by what we believe to have been a political blunder in the leaders of the Republican Party. Instead of keeping closely to the real point, and the only point, at issue, namely, the claim of a minority to a right of rebellion when displeased with the result of an election, the bare question of Secession, pure and simple, they allowed their party to become divided, and to waste themselves in discussing terms of compromise and guaranties of slavery which had nothing to do with the business in hand. Unless they were ready to admit that popular government was at an end, those were matters already settled by the Constitution and the last election. Compromise was out of the question with men who had gone through the motions, at least, of establishing a government and electing an anti-president. The way to insure the loyalty of the Border States, as the event has shown, was to convince them that disloyalty was dangerous. That revolutions never go backward is one of those compact generalizations which the world is so ready to accept because they save the trouble of thinking; but, however it may be with revolutions, it is certain that rebellions most commonly go backward with disastrous rapidity, and it was of the gravest moment, as respected its moral influence, that Secession should not have time allowed it to assume the proportions and the dignity of revolution, in other words, of a rebellion too powerful to be crushed. The secret friends of the Secession treason in the Free States have done their best to bewilder the public mind and to give factitious prestige to a conspiracy against free government and civilization by talking about the *right* of revolution, as if it were some acknowledged principle of the Law of Nations. There is a right, and sometimes a duty, of rebellion, as there is also a right and sometimes a duty of hanging men for it; but rebellion continues to be rebellion until it has accomplished its object and secured the acknowledgment of it from the other party to the quarrel, and from the world at large. The Republican Party in the November elections had really effected a peaceful revolution, had emancipated the country from the tyranny of an oligarchy which had abused the functions of the Government almost from the time of its establishment, to the advancement of their own selfish aims and interests; and it was this legitimate change of rulers and of national policy by constitutional means which the Secessionists intended to prevent. To put the matter in plain English, they resolved to treat the people of the United States, in the exercise of their undoubted and lawful authority, as rebels, and resorted to their usual policy of intimidation in order to subdue them. Either this magnificent empire should be their plantation, or it should perish. This was the view even of what were called the moderate slave-holders of the Border States; and all the so-called compromises and plans of reconstruction that were thrown into the caldron where the hell-broth of anarchy was brewing had this extent,—no more,—What terms of *submission* would the people make to their natural masters? Whatever other result may have come of the long debates in Congress and elsewhere, they have at least convinced the people of the Free States that there can be no such thing as a moderate slave-holder,—that moderation and slavery can no more coexist than Floyd and honesty, or Anderson and treason.

We believe, then, that conciliation was from the first impossible,—that to attempt it was unwise, because it put the party of law and loyalty in the wrong,—and that, if it was done as a mere matter of policy in order to gain time, it was a still greater mistake, because it was the rebels only who could profit by it in consolidating their organization, while the seeming gain of a few days or weeks was a loss to the Government, whose great advantage was in an administrative system thoroughly established, and, above all, in the vast power of the national idea, a power weakened by every day's delay. This is so true, that already men began to talk of the rival governments at Montgomery and Washington, and Canadian journals recommend a strict neutrality, as if the independence and legitimacy of the mushroom despotism of New Ashantee were an acknowledged fact, and the name of the United States of America had no more authority than that of Jefferson Davis and Company, dealers in all kinds of repudiation and anarchy. For more than a month after the inauguration of President

Lincoln there seemed to be a kind of interregnum, during which the confusion of ideas in the Border States as to their rights and duties as members of the "old" Union, as it began to be called, became positively chaotic. Virginia, still professing neutrality, prepared to seize the arsenal at Harper's Ferry and the navy-yard at Norfolk; she would prevent the passage of the United States' forces "with a serried phalanx of her gallant sons," two regiments of whom stood looking on while a file of marines took seven wounded men in an engine-house for them; she would do everything but her duty,—the gallant Ancient Pistol of a commonwealth. She "resumed her sovereignty," whatever that meant; her Convention passed an ordinance of secession, concluded a league offensive and defensive with the rebel Confederacy, appointed Jefferson Davis commander-in-chief of her land-forces and somebody else of the fleet she meant to steal at Norfolk, and then coolly referred the whole matter back to the people to vote three weeks afterwards whether they *would* secede three weeks before. Wherever the doctrine of Secession has penetrated, it seems to have obliterated every notion of law and precedent.

The country had come to the conclusion that Mr. Lincoln and his cabinet were mainly employed in packing their trunks to leave Washington, when the "venerable Edward Ruffin of Virginia" fired that first gun at Fort Sumter which brought all the Free States to their feet as one man. That shot is destined to be the most memorable one ever fired on this continent since the Concord fowling-pieces said, "That bridge is ours, and we mean to go across it," eighty-seven Aprils ago. As these began a conflict which gave us independence, so that began another which is to give us nationality. It was certainly a great piece of good-luck for the Government that they had a fort which it was so profitable to lose. The people were weary of a masterly inactivity which seemed to consist mainly in submitting to be kicked. We know very well the difficulties that surrounded the new Administration; we appreciate their reluctance to begin a war the responsibility of which was as great as its consequences seemed doubtful; but we cannot understand how it was hoped to evade war, except by concessions vastly more disastrous than war itself. War has no evil comparable in its effect on national character to that of a craven submission

to manifest wrong, the postponement of moral to material interests. There is no prosperity so great as courage. We do not
believe that any amount of forbearance would have conciliated
the South so long as they thought us pusillanimous. The only
way to retain the Border States was by showing that we had
the will and the power to do without them. The little Bopeep
policy of

> "Let them alone, and they'll all come home
>    Wagging their tails behind them"

was certainly tried long enough with conspirators who had
shown unmistakably that they desired nothing so much as the
continuance of peace, especially when it was all on one side,
and who would never have given the Government the great
advantage of being attacked in Fort Sumter, had they not supposed they were dealing with men who could not be cuffed
into resistance. The lesson we have to teach them now is, that
we are thoroughly and terribly in earnest. Mr. Stephens's the-
ories are to be put to a speedier and sterner test than he expected, and we are to prove which is stronger,—an oligarchy
built *on* men, or a commonwealth built *of* them. Our structure
is alive in every part with defensive and recuperative energies;
woe to theirs, if that vaunted corner-stone which they believe
patient and enduring as marble should begin to writhe with intelligent life!

   We have no doubt of the issue. We believe that the strongest
battalions are always on the side of God. The Southern army
will be fighting for Jefferson Davis, or at most for the liberty of
self-misgovernment, while we go forth for the defence of principles which alone make government august and civil society
possible. It is the very life of the nation that is at stake. There
is no question here of dynasties, races, religions,—but simply
whether we will consent to include in our Bill of Rights—not
merely as of equal validity with all other rights, whether natural or acquired, but by its very nature transcending and abro-
gating them all—the Right of Anarchy. We must convince men
that treason against the ballot-box is as dangerous as treason
against a throne, and that, if they play so desperate a game,
they must stake their lives on the hazard. The one lesson that
remained for us to teach the political theorists of the Old

World was, that we are as strong to suppress intestine disorder as foreign aggression, and we must teach it decisively and thoroughly. The economy of war is to be tested by the value of the object to be gained by it. A ten years' war would be cheap that gave us a country to be proud of and a flag that should command the respect of the world because it was the symbol of the enthusiastic unity of a great nation.

The Government, however slow it may have been to accept the war which Mr. Buchanan's supineness left them, is acting now with all energy and determination. What they have a right to claim is the confidence of the people, and that depends in good measure on the discretion of the press. Only let us have no more weakness under the plausible name of Conciliation. We need not discuss the probabilities of an acknowledgment of the Confederated States by England and France; we have only to say, "Acknowledge them at your peril." But there is no chance of the recognition of the Confederacy by any foreign governments, so long as it is without the confidence of the brokers. There is no question on which side the strength lies. The whole tone of the Southern journals, so far as we are able to judge, shows the inherent folly and weakness of the Secession movement. Men who feel strong in the justice of their cause, or confident in their powers, do not waste breath in childish boasts of their own superiority and querulous depreciation of their antagonists. They are weak, and they know it. And not only are they weak in comparison with the Free States, but we believe they are without the moral support of whatever deserves the name of public opinion at home. If not, why does their Congress, as they call it, hold council always with closed doors, like a knot of conspirators? The first tap of the Northern drum dispelled many illusions, and we need no better proof of which ship is sinking than that Mr. Caleb Cushing should have made such haste to come over to the old Constitution with the stars and stripes at her mast-head.

We cannot think that the war we are entering on can end without some radical change in the system of African slavery. Whether it be doomed to a sudden extinction, or to a gradual abolition through economical causes, this war will not leave it where it was before. As a power in the State, its reign is already over. The fiery tongues of the batteries in Charleston harbor accomplished in one day a conversion which the constancy of Garrison and the eloquence of Phillips had failed to bring about in thirty years. And whatever other result this war is destined to produce, it has already won for us a blessing worth everything to us as a nation in emancipating the public opinion of the North.

# Abraham Lincoln:
# Message to Congress in Special Session

In his proclamation of April 15, President Lincoln had called the new 37th Congress, which was scheduled to meet in December 1861, into session on July 4.

---

*Fellow-citizens of the Senate and House of Representatives:*

Having been convened on an extraordinary occasion, as authorized by the Constitution, your attention is not called to any ordinary subject of legislation.

At the beginning of the present Presidential term, four months ago, the functions of the Federal Government were found to be generally suspended within the several States of South Carolina, Georgia, Alabama, Mississippi, Louisiana, and Florida, excepting only those of the Post Office Department.

Within these States, all the Forts, Arsenals, Dock-yards, Custom-houses, and the like, including the movable and stationary property in, and about them, had been seized, and were held in open hostility to this Government, excepting only Forts Pickens, Taylor, and Jefferson, on, and near the Florida coast, and Fort Sumter, in Charleston harbor, South Carolina. The Forts thus seized had been put in improved condition; new ones had been built; and armed forces had been organized, and were organizing, all avowedly with the same hostile purpose.

The Forts remaining in the possession of the Federal government, in, and near, these States, were either besieged or menaced by warlike preparations; and especially Fort Sumter was nearly surrounded by well-protected hostile batteries, with guns equal in quality to the best of its own, and outnumbering the latter as perhaps ten to one. A disproportionate share, of the Federal muskets and rifles, had somehow found their way into these States, and had been seized, to be used against the government. Accumulations of the public revenue, lying within them, had been seized for the same object. The Navy was scattered in distant seas; leaving but a very small part of it within the immediate reach of the government. Officers of the Federal Army and Navy, had resigned in great numbers; and, of those resigning, a large proportion had taken up arms against the government. Simultaneously, and in connection, with all this, the purpose to sever the Federal Union, was openly avowed. In accordance with this purpose, an ordinance had been adopted in each of these States, declaring the States, respectively, to be separated from the National Union. A formula for instituting a combined government of these states had been promulgated; and this illegal organization, in the character of confederate States was already invoking recognition, aid, and intervention, from Foreign Powers.

Finding this condition of things, and believing it to be an imperative duty upon the incoming Executive, to prevent, if possible, the consummation of such attempt to destroy the Federal Union, a choice of means to that end became indispensable. This choice was made; and was declared in the Inaugural address. The policy chosen looked to the exhaustion of all peaceful measures, before a resort to any stronger ones. It sought only to hold the public places and property, not already wrested from the Government, and to collect the revenue; relying for the rest, on time, discussion, and the ballot-box. It promised a continuance of the mails, at government expense, to the very people who were resisting the government; and it gave repeated pledges against any disturbance to any of the people, or any of their rights. Of all that which a president might constitutionally, and justifiably, do in such a case, everything was foreborne, without which, it was believed possible to keep the government on foot.

On the 5th of March, (the present incumbent's first full day in office) a letter of Major Anderson, commanding at Fort Sumter, written on the 28th of February, and received at the War Department on the 4th of March, was, by that Department, placed in his hands. This letter expressed the professional opinion of the writer, that re-inforcements could not be thrown into that Fort within the time for his relief, rendered necessary by the limited supply of provisions, and with a view of holding possession of the same, with a force of less than twenty thousand good, and well-disciplined men. This opinion was concurred in by all the officers of his command; and their *memoranda* on the subject, were made enclosures of Major Anderson's letter. The whole was immediately laid before Lieutenant General Scott, who at once concurred with Major Anderson in opinion. On reflection, however, he took full time, consulting with other officers, both of the Army and the Navy; and, at the end of four days, came reluctantly, but decidedly, to the same conclusion as before. He also stated at the same time that no such sufficient force was then at the control of the Government, or could be raised, and brought to the ground, within the time when the provisions in the Fort would be exhausted. In a purely military point of view, this reduced the duty of the administration, in the case, to the mere matter of getting the garrison safely out of the Fort.

It was believed, however, that to so abandon that position, under the circumstances, would be utterly ruinous; that the *necessity* under which it was to be done, would not be fully understood—that, by many, it would be construed as a part of a *voluntary* policy—that, at home, it would discourage the friends of the Union, embolden its adversaries, and go far to insure to the latter, a recognition abroad—that, in fact, it would be our national destruction consummated. This could not be allowed. Starvation was not yet upon the garrison; and ere it would be reached, *Fort Pickens* might be reinforced. This last, would be a clear indication of *policy*, and would better enable the country to accept the evacuation of Fort Sumter, as a military *necessity*. An order was at once directed to be sent for the landing of the troops from the Steamship Brooklyn, into Fort Pickens. This order could not go by land, but must take the longer, and slower route by sea. The first return news from the order was received just one week before the fall of Fort Sumter. The news itself was, that the officer commanding the Sabine, to which vessel the troops had been transferred from the Brooklyn, acting upon some *quasi* armistice of the late administration, (and of the existence of which, the present administration, up to the time the order was despatched, had only too vague and uncertain rumors, to fix attention) had refused to land the troops. To now re-inforce Fort Pickens, before

a crisis would be reached at Fort Sumter was impossible—
rendered so by the near exhaustion of provisions in the latter-
named Fort. In precaution against such a conjuncture, the
government had, a few days before, commenced preparing
an expedition, as well adapted as might be, to relieve Fort
Sumter, which expedition was intended to be ultimately used,
or not, according to circumstances. The strongest anticipated
case, for using it, was now presented; and it was resolved to
send it forward. As had been intended, in this contingency, it
was also resolved to notify the Governor of South Carolina,
that he might expect an attempt would be made to provision
the Fort; and that, if the attempt should not be resisted, there
would be no effort to throw in men, arms, or ammunition,
without further notice, or in case of an attack upon the Fort.
This notice was accordingly given; whereupon the Fort was attacked, and bombarded to its fall, without even awaiting the
arrival of the provisioning expedition.

It is thus seen that the assault upon, and reduction of, Fort
Sumter, was, in no sense, a matter of self defence on the part
of the assailants. They well knew that the garrison in the Fort
could, by no possibility, commit aggression upon them. They
knew—they were expressly notified—that the giving of bread
to the few brave and hungry men of the garrison, was all which
would on that occasion be attempted, unless themselves, by
resisting so much, should provoke more. They knew that this
Government desired to keep the garrison in the Fort, not to
assail them, but merely to maintain visible possession, and thus
to preserve the Union from actual, and immediate dissolution
—trusting, as herein-before stated, to time, discussion, and
the ballot-box, for final adjustment; and they assailed, and reduced the Fort, for precisely the reverse object—to drive out
the visible authority of the Federal Union, and thus force it to
immediate dissolution.

That this was their object, the Executive well understood;
and having said to them in the inaugural address, "You can
have no conflict without being yourselves the aggressors," he
took pains, not only to keep this declaration good, but also to
keep the case so free from the power of ingenious sophistry,
as that the world should not be able to misunderstand it. By
the affair at Fort Sumter, with its surrounding circumstances,

that point was reached. Then, and thereby, the assailants of the Government, began the conflict of arms, without a gun in sight, or in expectancy, to return their fire, save only the few in the Fort, sent to that harbor, years before, for their own protection, and still ready to give that protection, in whatever was lawful. In this act, discarding all else, they have forced upon the country, the distinct issue: "Immediate dissolution, or blood."

And this issue embraces more than the fate of these United States. It presents to the whole family of man, the question, whether a constitutional republic, or a democracy—a government of the people, by the same people—can, or cannot, maintain its territorial integrity, against its own domestic foes. It presents the question, whether discontented individuals, too few in numbers to control administration, according to organic law, in any case, can always, upon the pretences made in this case, or on any other pretences, or arbitrarily, without any pretence, break up their Government, and thus practically put an end to free government upon the earth. It forces us to ask: "Is there, in all republics, this inherent, and fatal weakness?" "Must a government, of necessity, be too *strong* for the liberties of its own people, or too *weak* to maintain its own existence?"

So viewing the issue, no choice was left but to call out the war power of the Government; and so to resist force, employed for its destruction, by force, for its preservation.

The call was made; and the response of the country was most gratifying; surpassing, in unanimity and spirit, the most sanguine expectation. Yet none of the States commonly called Slave-states, except Delaware, gave a Regiment through regular State organization. A few regiments have been organized within some others of those states, by individual enterprise, and received into the government service. Of course the seceded States, so called, (and to which Texas had been joined about the time of the inauguration,) gave no troops to the cause of the Union. The border States, so called, were not uniform in their actions; some of them being almost *for* the Union, while in others—as Virginia, North Carolina, Tennessee, and Arkansas—the Union sentiment was nearly repressed, and silenced. The course taken in Virginia was the most remarkable—perhaps the most important. A convention, elected by the people of that State, to consider this very question of disrupting the Federal Union, was in session at the capital of Virginia when Fort Sumter fell. To this body the people had chosen a large majority of *professed* Union men. Almost immediately after the fall of Sumter, many members of that majority went over to the original disunion minority, and, with them, adopted an ordinance for withdrawing the State from the Union. Whether this change was wrought by their great approval of the assault upon Sumter, or their great resentment at the government's resistance to that assault, is not definitely known. Although they submitted the ordinance, for ratification, to a vote of the people, to be taken on a day then somewhat more than a month distant, the convention, and the Legislature, (which was also in session at the same time and place) with leading men of the State, not members of either, immediately commenced acting, as if the State were already out of the Union. They pushed military preparations vigorously forward all over the state. They seized the United States Armory at Harper's Ferry, and the Navy-yard at Gosport, near Norfolk. They received—perhaps invited—into their state, large bodies of troops, with their warlike appointments, from the so-called seceded States. They formally entered into a treaty of temporary alliance, and co-operation with the so-called "Confederate States," and sent members to their Congress at Montgomery. And, finally, they permitted the insurrectionary government to be transferred to their capital at Richmond.

The people of Virginia have thus allowed this giant insurrection to make its nest within her borders; and this government has no choice left but to deal with it, *where* it finds it. And it has the less regret, as the loyal citizens have, in due form, claimed its protection. Those loyal citizens, this government is bound to recognize, and protect, as being Virginia.

In the border States, so called—in fact, the middle states—there are those who favor a policy which they call "armed neutrality"—that is, an arming of those states to prevent the Union forces passing one way, or the disunion, the other, over their soil. This would be disunion completed. Figuratively speaking, it would be the building of an impassable wall along the line of separation. And yet, not quite an impassable one;

for, under the guise of neutrality, it would tie the hands of the Union men, and freely pass supplies from among them, to the insurrectionists, which it could not do as an open enemy. At a stroke, it would take all the trouble off the hands of secession, except only what proceeds from the external blockade. It would do for the disunionists that which, of all things, they most desire—feed them well, and give them disunion without a struggle of their own. It recognizes no fidelity to the Constitution, no obligation to maintain the Union; and while very many who have favored it are, doubtless, loyal citizens, it is, nevertheless, treason in effect.

Recurring to the action of the government, it may be stated that, at first, a call was made for seventy-five thousand militia; and rapidly following this, a proclamation was issued for closing the ports of the insurrectionary districts by proceedings in the nature of Blockade. So far all was believed to be strictly legal. At this point the insurrectionists announced their purpose to enter upon the practice of privateering.

Other calls were made for volunteers, to serve three years, unless sooner discharged; and also for large additions to the regular Army and Navy. These measures, whether strictly legal or not, were ventured upon, under what appeared to be a popular demand, and a public necessity; trusting, then as now, that Congress would readily ratify them. It is believed that nothing has been done beyond the constitutional competency of Congress.

Soon after the first call for militia, it was considered a duty to authorize the Commanding General, in proper cases, according to his discretion, to suspend the privilege of the writ of habeas corpus; or, in other words, to arrest, and detain, without resort to the ordinary processes and forms of law, such individuals as he might deem dangerous to the public safety. This authority has purposely been exercised but very sparingly. Nevertheless, the legality and propriety of what has been done under it, are questioned; and the attention of the country has been called to the proposition that one who is sworn to "take care that the laws be faithfully executed," should not himself violate them. Of course some consideration was given to the questions of power, and propriety, before this matter was acted upon. The whole of the laws which were required to be faithfully executed, were being resisted, and failing of execution, in nearly one-third of the States. Must they be allowed to finally fail of execution, even had it been perfectly clear, that by the use of the means necessary to their execution, some single law, made in such extreme tenderness of the citizen's liberty, that practically, it relieves more of the guilty, than of the innocent, should, to a very limited extent, be violated? To state the question more directly, are all the laws, *but one*, to go unexecuted, and the government itself go to pieces, lest that one be violated? Even in such a case, would not the official oath be broken, if the government should be overthrown, when it was believed that disregarding the single law, would tend to preserve it? But it was not believed that this question was presented. It was not believed that any law was violated. The provision of the Constitution that "The privilege of the writ of habeas corpus, shall not be suspended unless when, in cases of rebellion or invasion, the public safety may require it," is equivalent to a provision—is a provision—that such privilege may be suspended when, in cases of rebellion, or invasion, the public safety *does* require it. It was decided that we have a case of rebellion, and that the public safety does require the qualified suspension of the privilege of the writ which was authorized to be made. Now it is insisted that Congress, and not the Executive, is vested with this power. But the Constitution itself, is silent as to which, or who, is to exercise the power; and as the provision was plainly made for a dangerous emergency, it cannot be believed the framers of the instrument intended, that in every case, the danger should run its course, until Congress could be called together; the very assembling of which might be prevented, as was intended in this case, by the rebellion.

No more extended argument is now offered; as an opinion, at some length, will probably be presented by the Attorney General. Whether there shall be any legislation upon the subject, and if any, what, is submitted entirely to the better judgment of Congress.

The forbearance of this government had been so extraordinary, and so long continued, as to lead some foreign nations to shape their action as if they supposed the early destruction of our national Union was probable. While this, on discovery, gave the Executive some concern, he is now happy to say that the sovereignty, and rights of the United States, are now everywhere practically respected by foreign powers; and a general sympathy with the country is manifested throughout the world.

The reports of the Secretaries of the Treasury, War, and the Navy, will give the information in detail deemed necessary, and convenient for your deliberation, and action; while the Executive, and all the Departments, will stand ready to supply omissions, or to communicate new facts, considered important for you to know.

It is now recommended that you give the legal means for making this contest a short, and a decisive one; that you place at the control of the government, for the work, at least four hundred thousand men, and four hundred millions of dollars. That number of men is about one tenth of those of proper ages within the regions where, apparently, *all* are willing to engage; and the sum is less than a twentythird part of the money value owned by the men who seem ready to devote the whole. A debt of six hundred millions of dollars *now*, is a less sum per head, than was the debt of our revolution, when we came out of that struggle; and the money value in the country now, bears even a greater proportion to what it was *then*, than does the population. Surely each man has as strong a motive *now*, to *preserve* our liberties, as each had *then*, to *establish* them.

A right result, at this time, will be worth more to the world, than ten times the men, and ten times the money. The evidence reaching us from the country, leaves no doubt, that the material for the work is abundant; and that it needs only the hand of legislation to give it legal sanction, and the hand of the Executive to give it practical shape and efficiency. One of the greatest perplexities of the government, is to avoid receiving troops faster than it can provide for them. In a word, the people will save their government, if the government itself, will do its part, only indifferently well.

It might seem, at first thought, to be of little difference whether the present movement at the South be called "secession" or "rebellion." The movers, however, well understand the difference. At the beginning, they knew they could never raise their treason to any respectable magnitude, by any name

which implies *violation* of law. They knew their people possessed as much of moral sense, as much of devotion to law and
order, and as much pride in, and reverence for, the history,
and government, of their common country, as any other civilized, and patriotic people. They knew they could make no advancement directly in the teeth of these strong and noble
sentiments. Accordingly they commenced by an insidious de-
bauching of the public mind. They invented an ingenious
sophism, which, if conceded, was followed by perfectly logical
steps, through all the incidents, to the complete destruction of
the Union. The sophism itself is, that any state of the Union
may, *consistently* with the national Constitution, and therefore
*lawfully*, and *peacefully*, withdraw from the Union, without
the consent of the Union, or of any other state. The little disguise that the supposed right is to be exercised only for just
cause, themselves to be the sole judge of its justice, is too thin
to merit any notice.

With rebellion thus sugar-coated, they have been drugging
the public mind of their section for more than thirty years;
and, until at length, they have brought many good men to a
willingness to take up arms against the government the day
*after* some assemblage of men have enacted the farcical pretence of taking their State out of the Union, who could have
been brought to no such thing the day *before*.

This sophism derives much—perhaps the whole—of its
currency, from the assumption, that there is some omnipotent,
and sacred supremacy, pertaining to a *State*—to each State of
our Federal Union. Our States have neither more, nor less
power, than that reserved to them, in the Union, by the
Constitution—no one of them ever having been a State *out* of
the Union. The original ones passed into the Union even
*before* they cast off their British colonial dependence; and the
new ones each came into the Union directly from a condition
of dependence, excepting Texas. And even Texas, in its temporary independence, was never designated a State. The new
ones only took the designation of States, on coming into the
Union, while that name was first adopted for the old ones, in,
and by, the Declaration of Independence. Therein the "United
Colonies" were declared to be "Free and Independent States";
but, even then, the object plainly was not to declare their in-

dependence of *one another*, or of the *Union*; but directly the contrary, as their mutual pledge, and their mutual action, before, at the time, and afterwards, abundantly show. The express plighting of faith, by each and all of the original thirteen, in the Articles of Confederation, two years later, that the Union shall be perpetual, is most conclusive. Having never been States, either in substance, or in name, *outside* of the Union, whence this magical omnipotence of "State rights," asserting a claim of power to lawfully destroy the Union itself? Much is said about the "sovereignty" of the States; but the word, even, is not in the national Constitution; nor, as is believed, in any of the State constitutions. What is a "sovereignty," in the political sense of the term? Would it be far wrong to define it "A political community, without a political superior"? Tested by this, no one of our States, except Texas, ever was a sovereignty. And even Texas gave up the character on coming into the Union; by which act, she acknowledged the Constitution of the United States, and the laws and treaties of the United States made in pursuance of the Constitution, to be, for her, the supreme law of the land. The States have their *status* IN the Union, and they have no other *legal status*. If they break from this, they can only do so against law, and by revolution. The Union, and not themselves separately, procured their independence, and their liberty. By conquest, or purchase, the Union gave each of them, whatever of independence, and liberty, it has. The Union is older than any of the States; and, in fact, it created them as States. Originally, some dependent colonies made the Union; and, in turn, the Union threw off their old dependence, for them, and made them States, such as they are. Not one of them ever had a State constitution, independent of the Union. Of course, it is not forgotten that all the new States framed their constitutions, before they entered the Union; nevertheless, dependent upon, and preparatory to, coming into the Union.

Unquestionably the States have the powers, and rights, reserved to them in, and by the National Constitution; but among these, surely, are not included all conceivable powers, however mischievous, or destructive; but, at most, such only, as were known in the world, at the time, as governmental powers; and certainly, a power to destroy the government itself, had never been known as a governmental—as a merely administrative power. This relative matter of National power, and State rights, as a principle, is no other than the principle of *generality*, and *locality*. Whatever concerns the whole, should be confided to the whole—to the general government; while, whatever concerns *only* the State, should be left exclusively, to the State. This is all there is of original principle about it. Whether the National Constitution, in defining boundaries between the two, has applied the principle with exact accuracy, is not to be questioned. We are all bound by that defining, without question.

What is now combatted, is the position that secession is *consistent* with the Constitution—is *lawful*, and *peaceful*. It is not contended that there is any express law for it; and nothing should ever be implied as law, which leads to unjust, or absurd consequences. The nation purchased, with money, the countries out of which several of these States were formed. Is it just that they shall go off without leave, and without refunding? The nation paid very large sums, (in the aggregate, I believe, nearly a hundred millions) to relieve Florida of the aboriginal tribes. Is it just that she shall now be off without consent, or without making any return? The nation is now in debt for money applied to the benefit of these so-called seceding States, in common with the rest. Is it just, either that creditors shall go unpaid, or the remaining States pay the whole? A part of the present national debt was contracted to pay the old debts of Texas. Is it just that she shall leave, and pay no part of this herself?

Again, if one State may secede, so may another; and when all shall have seceded, none is left to pay the debts. Is this quite just to creditors? Did we notify them of this sage view of ours, when we borrowed their money? If we now recognize this doctrine, by allowing the seceders to go in peace, it is difficult to see what we can do, if others choose to go, or to extort terms upon which they will promise to remain.

The seceders insist that our Constitution admits of secession. They have assumed to make a National Constitution of their own, in which, of necessity, they have either *discarded*, or *retained*, the right of secession, as they insist, it exists in ours. If they have discarded it, they thereby admit that, on principle, it ought not to be in ours. If they have retained it, by their own construction of ours they show that to be consistent they must secede from one another, whenever they shall find it the easiest way of settling their debts, or effecting any other selfish, or unjust object. The principle itself is one of disintegration, and upon which no government can possibly endure.

If all the States, save one, should assert the power to *drive* that one out of the Union, it is presumed the whole class of seceder politicians would at once deny the power, and denounce the act as the greatest outrage upon State rights. But suppose that precisely the same act, instead of being called "driving the one out," should be called "the seceding of the others from that one," it would be exactly what the seceders claim to do; unless, indeed, they make the point, that the one, because it is a minority, may rightfully do, what the others, because they are a majority, may not rightfully do. These politicians are subtle, and profound, on the rights of minorities. They are not partial to that power which made the Constitution, and speaks from the preamble, calling itself "We, the People."

It may well be questioned whether there is, to-day, a majority of the legally qualified voters of any State, except perhaps South Carolina, in favor of disunion. There is much reason to believe that the Union men are the majority in many, if not in every other one, of the so-called seceded States. The contrary has not been demonstrated in any one of them. It is ventured to affirm this, even of Virginia and Tennessee; for the result of an election, held in military camps, where the bayonets are all on one side of the question voted upon, can scarcely be considered as demonstrating popular sentiment. At such an election, all that large class who are, at once, *for* the Union, and *against* coercion, would be coerced to vote against the Union.

It may be affirmed, without extravagance, that the free institutions we enjoy, have developed the powers, and improved the condition, of our whole people, beyond any example in the world. Of this we now have a striking, and an impressive illustration. So large an army as the government has now on foot, was never before known, without a soldier in it, but who had taken his place there, of his own free choice. But more than this: there are many single Regiments whose members, one and another, possess full practical knowledge of all the arts,

sciences, professions, and whatever else, whether useful or ele-
gant, is known in the world; and there is scarcely one, from
which there could not be selected, a President, a Cabinet, a
Congress, and perhaps a Court, abundantly competent to administer the government itself. Nor do I say this is not true,
also, in the army of our late friends, now adversaries, in this
contest; but if it is, so much better the reason why the government, which has conferred such benefits on both them and us,
should not be broken up. Whoever, in any section, proposes to
abandon such a government, would do well to consider, in
deference to what principle it is, that he does it—what better
he is likely to get in its stead—whether the substitute will give,
or be intended to give, so much of good to the people. There
are some foreshadowings on this subject. Our adversaries
have adopted some Declarations of Independence; in which,
unlike the good old one, penned by Jefferson, they omit the
words "all men are created equal." Why? They have adopted a
temporary national constitution, in the preamble of which,
unlike our good old one, signed by Washington, they omit "We,
the People," and substitute "We, the deputies of the sovereign
and independent States." Why? Why this deliberate pressing
out of view, the rights of men, and the authority of the people?

This is essentially a People's contest. On the side of the
Union, it is a struggle for maintaining in the world, that form,
and substance of government, whose leading object is, to elevate the condition of men—to lift artificial weights from all
shoulders—to clear the paths of laudable pursuit for all—to afford all, an unfettered start, and a fair chance, in the race of
life. Yielding to partial, and temporary departures, from necessity, this is the leading object of the government for whose
existence we contend.

I am most happy to believe that the plain people understand, and appreciate this. It is worthy of note, that while in
this, the government's hour of trial, large numbers of those in
the Army and Navy, who have been favored with the offices,
have resigned, and proved false to the hand which had pam-
pered them, not one common soldier, or common sailor is
known to have deserted his flag.

Great honor is due to those officers who remain true, despite the example of their treacherous associates; but the great-

est honor, and most important fact of all, is the unanimous firmness of the common soldiers, and common sailors. To the last man, so far as known, they have successfully resisted the traitorous efforts of those, whose commands, but an hour before, they obeyed as absolute law. This is the patriotic instinct of the plain people. They understand, without an argument, that destroying the government, which was made by Washington, means no good to them.

Our popular government has often been called an experiment. Two points in it, our people have already settled—the successful *establishing*, and the successful *administering* of it. One still remains—its successful *maintenance* against a formidable internal attempt to overthrow it. It is now for them to demonstrate to the world, that those who can fairly carry an election, can also suppress a rebellion—that ballots are the rightful, and peaceful, successors of bullets; and that when ballots have fairly, and constitutionally, decided, there can be no successful appeal, back to bullets; that there can be no successful appeal, except to ballots themselves, at succeeding elections. Such will be a great lesson of peace; teaching men that what they cannot take by an election, neither can they take it by a war— teaching all, the folly of being the beginners of a war.

Lest there be some uneasiness in the minds of candid men, as to what is to be the course of the government, towards the Southern States, *after* the rebellion shall have been suppressed, the Executive deems it proper to say, it will be his purpose then, as ever, to be guided by the Constitution, and the laws; and that he probably will have no different understanding of the powers, and duties of the Federal government, relatively to the rights of the States, and the people, under the Constitution, than that expressed in the inaugural address.

He desires to preserve the government, that it may be administered for all, as it was administered by the men who made it. Loyal citizens everywhere, have the right to claim this of their government; and the government has no right to withhold, or neglect it. It is not perceived that, in giving it, there is any coercion, any conquest, or any subjugation, in any just sense of those terms.

The Constitution provides, and all the States have accepted

the provision, that "The United States shall guarantee to every State in this Union a republican form of government." But, if a State may lawfully go out of the Union, having done so, it may also discard the republican form of government; so that to prevent its going out, is an indispensable *means*, to the *end*, of maintaining the guaranty mentioned; and when an end is lawful and obligatory, the indispensable means to it, are also lawful, and obligatory.

It was with the deepest regret that the Executive found the duty of employing the war-power, in defence of the government, forced upon him. He could but perform this duty, or surrender the existence of the government. No compromise, by public servants, could, in this case, be a cure; not that compromises are not often proper, but that no popular government can long survive a marked precedent, that those who carry an election, can only save the government from immediate destruction, by giving up the main point, upon which the people gave the election. The people themselves, and not their servants, can safely reverse their own deliberate decisions. As a private citizen, the Executive could not have consented that these institutions shall perish; much less could he, in betrayal of so vast, and so sacred a trust, as these free people had confided to him. He felt that he had no moral right to shrink; nor even to count the chances of his own life, in what might follow. In full view of his great responsibility, he has, so far, done what he has deemed his duty. You will now, according to your own judgment, perform yours. He sincerely hopes that your views, and your action, may so accord with his, as to assure all faithful citizens, who have been disturbed in their rights, of a certain, and speedy restoration to them, under the Constitution, and the laws.

And having thus chosen our course, without guile, and with pure purpose, let us renew our trust in God, and go forward without fear, and with manly hearts.

July 4, 1861.

# Kate Stone: Journal, July 4, 1861

On the day that Congress met in Washington, Kate Stone reflected on the changes caused by the war.

---

*July 4*:   Mamma is still in bed but is better. The boys have holiday in honor of the Fourth but more I think to keep up old customs than for any feeling of respect for the day. This is the first Fourth in our memory to pass without a public merrymaking of some kind, but we do not hear of the day's being celebrated in town or country. There are other and sterner duties before us. It would ill become us as a Nation to be celebrating a day of independence when we are fighting for our very existence.

This July sun has set on a Nation in arms against itself, host against host. Those who have clasped each other's hands in kindest spirits less than one short year ago, as friends, as countrymen, as children of one common Mother, now stand opposing each other in deadliest hate, eager to water Old Mother Earth with the blood of her children. Our Cause is right and God will give us the victory. Will the next July sun rise on a Nation peaceful, prosperous, and happy, or on a land desolate and disgraced? He alone knows.

Congress meets today. The lives of thousands hang on its decision. Will it be for peace or war? We should know by Saturday.

Brother Coley returned tonight. He had gone to Memphis with Aunt Sarah. Mr. Miller is stationed only seven hours from Memphis and can run in quite frequently. He is trying to get the Colonelcy of a regiment and is stirring around in his usual style. He says he spends $2,000 a month and lives delightfully. Hope he will make an equal division with Aunt Sarah. Brother Coley enjoyed the trip greatly.

# Ulysses S. Grant: from
# Personal Memoirs of U. S. Grant

Grant had been appointed commander of the 21st Illinois Volunteers in June 1861, and in July he was ordered to cross into Missouri with his regiment. He would later recall the experience in *Personal Memoirs of U. S. Grant* (1885).

---

MY SENSATIONS as we approached what I supposed might be "a field of battle" were anything but agreeable. I had been in all the engagements in Mexico that it was possible for one person to be in; but not in command. If some one else had been colonel and I had been lieutenant-colonel I do not think I would have felt any trepidation. Before we were prepared to cross the Mississippi River at Quincy my anxiety was relieved; for the men of the besieged regiment came straggling into town. I am inclined to think both sides got frightened and ran away.

I took my regiment to Palmyra and remained there for a few days, until relieved by the 19th Illinois infantry. From Palmyra I proceeded to Salt River, the railroad bridge over which had been destroyed by the enemy. Colonel John M. Palmer at that time commanded the 13th Illinois, which was acting as a guard to workmen who were engaged in rebuilding this bridge. Palmer was my senior and commanded the two regiments as long as we remained together. The bridge was finished in about two weeks, and I received orders to move against Colonel Thomas Harris, who was said to be encamped at the little town of Florida, some twenty-five miles south of where we then were.

At the time of which I now write we had no transportation and the country about Salt River was sparsely settled, so that it took some days to collect teams and drivers enough to move the camp and garrison equipage of a regiment nearly a thousand strong, together with a week's supply of provision and some ammunition. While preparations for the move were going on I felt quite comfortable; but when we got on the road and found every house deserted I was anything but easy. In the twenty-five miles we had to march we did not see a person, old or young, male or female, except two horsemen who were on a road that crossed ours. As soon as they saw us they decamped as fast as their horses could carry them. I kept my men in the ranks and forbade their entering any of the deserted houses or taking anything from them. We halted at night on the road and proceeded the next morning at an early hour. Harris had been encamped in a creek bottom for the sake of being near water. The hills on either side of the creek extend to a considerable height, possibly more than a hundred feet. As we approached the brow of the hill from which it was expected we could see Harris' camp, and possibly find his men ready formed to meet us, my heart kept getting higher and higher until it felt to me as though it was in my throat. I would have given anything then to have been back in Illinois, but I had not the moral courage to halt and consider what to do; I kept right on. When we reached a point from which the valley below was in full view I halted. The place where Harris had been encamped a few days before was still there and the marks of a recent encampment were plainly visible, but the troops were gone. My heart resumed its place. It occurred to me at once that Harris had been as much afraid of me as I had been of him. This was a view of the question I had never taken before; but it was one I never forgot afterwards. From that event to the close of the war, I never experienced trepidation upon confronting an enemy, though I always felt more or less anxiety. I never forgot that he had as much reason to fear my forces as I had his. The lesson was valuable.

Inquiries at the village of Florida divulged the fact that Colonel Harris, learning of my intended movement, while my transportation was being collected took time by the forelock and left Florida before I had started from Salt River. He had increased the distance between us by forty miles. The next day I started back to my old camp at Salt River bridge. The citizens living on the line of our march had returned to their houses after we passed, and finding everything in good order, nothing carried away, they were at their front doors ready to greet us now. They had evidently been led to believe that the National troops carried death and devastation with them wherever they went.

# *Sallie Brock: from*
# Richmond During the War

A Virginia native, Sallie Brock was working as a tutor in King and Queen County in 1860. As the war began she returned to Richmond, where her father owned a hotel. In a memoir published in 1867, Brock describes learning of the Confederate defeats in western Virginia at Rich Mountain, July 11, and Carrick's Ford, July 13.

------

### DISASTER IN WESTERN VIRGINIA.

THE SMOKE of battle had scarcely cleared away, and the shouts of victory died upon the ear, after the animating contest at Great Bethel, before the news of disaster to our forces in Western Virginia came to dampen the ardor arising from our recent successes. We were to be blessed no longer with bloodless victories. The trial of soul had begun.

The Confederate camp at Philippi had been surprised and dispersed. This disaster, as stated in the Richmond *Dispatch*, was caused by a sentinel sleeping on his post. Intimations of a contemplated attack upon the Confederate camp had been conveyed to them by two heroic women, who rode thirty miles on horseback in the night to warn them of the approach of the Federals, but too late to prevent the confusion that followed. By this misfortune to the Confederates these valorous women were cut off from their homes, and without a change of apparel were compelled to come on to Richmond, where they remained until they could conveniently return to their former places of abode.

The defeat at Rich Mountain occurred a few days after the dispersion at Philippi, and Colonel John Pegram and his entire command of sixteen hundred men were captured.

Nor with this was the measure of disaster in Western Virginia complete. General Garnett was in command of all the forces in the northwestern section of the State. With only about three thousand men he had intrenched himself at Laurel Hill; but from the well-intentioned blunders of inexperienced officers and men, and from the defeat of Colonel Pegram at Rich Mountain, he was compelled to retreat, which he managed to do in good order. Closely pressed by the enemy until he reached the second ford of Cheat River, being himself in the rear, his riderless horse announced to the vanguard that their brave commander had fallen. At Carrick's Ford, where he was killed, the enemy abandoned the pursuit, and the Confederates succeeded in forming a junction with the force under General Jackson.

Although the numbers in killed, wounded and missing were comparatively so small, this disaster was truly discouraging, as it caused the surrender of a very important portion of Northwestern Virginia, and was keenly felt as the very first check to Southern arms. Our troops had not, however, shown any failure in courage; and the fatigue endured by them in the undertaking, and the success of the retreat had not then a parallel in the history of the war. But the deepest regret was experienced at the untimely end of the gallant General Garnett. He was the first officer of high rank who had fallen in battle in the Confederate army, and his death cast the deepest gloom over the hearts of the many who loved and honored him for his bravery and nobility of spirit. He was a native of Essex County, Virginia, and belonged to an old and highly respectable family, numbering in its connection several men of distinguished talent and position. He had himself received a military education, and was thought to possess the genius which would insure him success in his profession.

There is no denying that these reverses were the cause of much anxiety to the Southern people, and for the first time a gloom spread over the souls of many whose sanguine temperaments precluded the idea of possibility of defeat to Southern arms.

But the Richmond people, although they might for a few days be bowed down by defeat, were generally reassured by the very accommodating press, which conveniently and wisely, doubtless, appropriated the proverb, "What cannot be cured must be endured;" and thus succeeded in allaying the usual discouragement and mistrust arising from petty defeats and disappointments.

We had, however, very little time to devote to the luxury of lamentation over our fallen brave, or to the sad misfortunes to our cause in Western Virginia. The sad strains of mournful music, the dull sounds of the muffled drum, as borne in the procession of the lamented Garnett, were only just lost in the busy hum of every-day life in Richmond, when our attention was called to the condition of things in a different portion of the State. Over the Potomac, and especially in the vicinity of Harper's Ferry, which had been evacuated by the Federals, the war-clouds hung heavily and ominously, and it seemed altogether evident to us that it could not be long ere the dark and sombre masses would burst upon us in the lurid lightnings and hoarse thunders of battle. We knew that somewhere in that section of Virginia would be enacted fierce scenes of sanguinary strife. July, 1861, opened upon us with a knowledge of the fact that two of the largest armies that the continent of America had ever seen were ranged in hostile defiance, and awaited with anxiety the signal to measure the relative strength of the North and South. All hearts were directed to that portion of the State over which the storm must soon break.

Our women for a time suspended the busy operations of the needle, and set aside the more expeditious and labor-saving sewing machine, to apply themselves more industriously to the preparation of lint, the rolling of bandages, and the many other nameless necessaries which the signs of the times made apparent would soon be in requisition for the unfortunates which the chances of battle would send among us mutilated and helpless. No longer the sempstress, every woman of Richmond began to prepare herself for the more difficult and responsible duties of the nurse. What pen can describe in fitting terms the history of the anxious hearts hidden behind the busy exterior, in those labors which patriotism dignified into duty, and which were lightened by cheerfulness and love? What pencil can paint the rainbow tints that glowed in the briny tear as it fell upon the snowy pile of lint which accumulated under the hands of her who had laid her heart's idol upon the altar of her country? What imagination can picture the midnight experiences of the restless, anxious ones from whose eyelids sleep had fled, as day after day and night after night brought nearer and nearer the dreaded day, which might close over in the darkness of death all we held most dear? Who can enumerate the prayers wafted on every breath, which in the humble and simple language of the publican went up continually in the cry, "Lord have mercy?"

# Sullivan Ballou to Sarah Ballou

A lawyer who had served in the Rhode Island legislature and campaigned for Lincoln in 1860, Sullivan Ballou was commissioned as a
major in the 2nd Rhode Island Volunteers on June 11, 1861. A week
before the battle of Bull Run, he wrote a farewell letter to his wife and
left it in his trunk at camp. During the battle a six-pound cannon shot
shattered his leg, and Ballou died of his wounds on July 28, 1861.

---

HEAD-QUARTERS, CAMP CLARK,
WASHINGTON, D. C., July 14, 1861.

MY VERY DEAR WIFE:

The indications are very strong that we shall move in a few
days, perhaps to-morrow. Lest I should not be able to write
you again, I feel impelled to write a few lines, that may fall
under your eye when I shall be no more.

Our movement may be one of a few days duration and full
of pleasure—and it may be one of severe conflict and death to
me. Not my will, but thine, O God, be done. If it is necessary
that I should fall on the battle-field for my country, I am ready.
I have no misgivings about, or lack of confidence in, the cause
in which I am engaged, and my courage does not halt or falter.
I know how strongly American civilization now leans upon the
triumph of the government, and how great a debt we owe to
those who went before us through the blood and suffering of
the Revolution, and I am willing, perfectly willing to lay down
all my joys in this life to help maintain this government, and to
pay that debt.

But, my dear wife, when I know, that, with my own joys, I
lay down nearly all of yours, and replace them in this life with
cares and sorrows,—when, after having eaten for long years the
bitter fruit of orphanage myself, I must offer it, as their only
sustenance, to my dear little children, is it weak or dishonorable, while the banner of my purpose floats calmly and proudly
in the breeze, that my unbounded love for you, my darling

wife and children, should struggle in fierce, though useless, contest with my love of country.

I cannot describe to you my feelings on this calm summer night, when two thousand men are sleeping around me, many of them enjoying the last, perhaps, before that of death,—and I, suspicious that Death is creeping behind me with his fatal dart, am communing with God, my country and thee.

I have sought most closely and diligently, and often in my breast, for a wrong motive in thus hazarding the happiness of those I loved, and I could not find one. A pure love of my country, and of the principles I have often advocated before the people, and "the name of honor, that I love more than I fear death," have called upon me, and I have obeyed.

Sarah, my love for you is deathless. It seems to bind me with mighty cables, that nothing but Omnipotence can break; and yet, my love of country comes over me like a strong wind, and bears me irresistibly on with all those chains, to the battle-field. The memories of all the blissful moments I have spent with you, come crowding over me, and I feel most deeply grateful to God and you, that I have enjoyed them so long. And how hard it is for me to give them up, and burn to ashes the hopes of future years, when, God willing, we might still have lived and loved together, and seen our boys grow up to honorable manhood around us.

I know I have but few claims upon Divine Providence, but something whispers to me, perhaps it is the wafted prayer of my little Edgar, that I shall return to my loved ones unharmed. If I do not, my dear Sarah, never forget how much I love you, nor that, when my last breath escapes me on the battle-field, it will whisper your name.

Forgive my many faults, and the many pains I have caused you. How thoughtless, how foolish I have oftentimes been! How gladly would I wash out with my tears, every little spot upon your happiness, and struggle with all the misfortune of this world, to shield you and my children from harm. But I cannot. I must watch you from the spirit land and hover near you, while you buffet the storms with your precious little freight, and wait with sad patience till we meet to part no more.

But, O Sarah, if the dead can come back to this earth, and flit unseen around those they loved, I shall always be near you—in the garish day, and the darkest night—amidst your happiest scenes and gloomiest hours—always, always; and, if the soft breeze fans your cheek, it shall be my breath; or the cool air cools your throbbing temples, it shall be my spirit passing by.

Sarah, do not mourn me dead; think I am gone, and wait for me, for we shall meet again.

As for my little boys, they will grow as I have done, and never know a father's love and care. Little Willie is too young to remember me long, and my blue-eyed Edgar will keep my frolics with him among the dimmest memories of his childhood. Sarah, I have unlimited confidence in your maternal care, and your development of their characters. Tell my two mothers, I call God's blessing upon them. O Sarah, I wait for you *there!* Come to me, and lead thither my children.

SULLIVAN.

## *Charles Minor Blackford: from*
# Letters from Lee's Army

After the Provisional Confederate Congress voted in late May to move the Confederate capital from Montgomery to Richmond, political pressure increased in the North for the army at Washington to take offensive action in Virginia. At a meeting held on June 29 General Irvin McDowell asked for more time to train his troops, but was ordered by Lincoln to move against the Confederate army of 20,000 men under General Pierre G. T. Beauregard defending the key railroad junction at Manassas. McDowell began his advance with 30,000 troops on July 16 and attacked across Bull Run on the morning of July 21. By this time General Joseph Johnston had brought most of his 11,000 men by rail to reinforce Beauregard from the Shenandoah Valley. A lawyer from Lynchburg, Charles Minor Blackford was a first lieutenant in Company B, 30th Virginia Volunteers (later the 2nd Virginia Cavalry) who had previously fought in a skirmish at Vienna, Virginia, in June. He was recovering from an attack of dysentery when the battle began.

———————————

*July 20th.*

    This day I spent lying down and taking remedies. By night I was so much better I determined to go back to duty. So, with some pain, I mounted my horse and rode back to my company reaching them about nine o'clock much worn down by my ride. The men welcomed me gladly. They had seen no yankees and very little expected the storm that was to break over our heads so soon. A bed of leaves was made for me and I laid down to rest. My own opinion was that a great battle was going to be fought the next day. The thoughts of a thinking man the day before a battle are necessarily solemn, he may be buoyant and hopeful, yet there is a dread uncertainty that comes over his thoughts both as to himself and those dependent on him which makes him grave and almost sad. I was tired and despite the thoughts of the next day's work I soon dropped off to sleep and never moved until roused by my servant, John Scott, early Sunday morning. He told me to get up, something was going on, he did not know what but I'd better get up and make ready. I soon discovered what was about to happen. All the troops around me were up and cooking their breakfast, though it was scarcely light, and every one seemed to think an attack was about to be made upon our lines, but no one knew where. We supposed it would be made down towards the center where it was made on the 18th.

The bivouac of our squadron was on the extreme left near the Henry house as it was called. Mrs. Henry, who lived in it, and was so very old and infirm she refused to move out of it. She was said to have been a Miss Carter, and to have been one of the family who once owned the Sudley farm nearby. Mrs. Henry's house during the day became a strategic point of great importance and was much torn up by shot and shell, by one of which she was killed. In her yard General Bee was killed and near it Colonel Bartow. Near it also it was that General Jackson formed his heroic brigade and received the baptism of fire during which he received the immortal name of "Stonewall." A few days after the battle I got a piece of cedar post from the ruins of the house, and cut some crosses and other things which I sent home as mementoes, and which I still have.

We were thrown into line about sunrise on the brow of a hill which overlooked Bull Run, with quite a wide valley (two hundred yards at least), below us. On the other side the bluff rose quite steeply, but on the top of it there was an open field. We were placed in that position to support a battery of artillery, whose I did not find out for it was moved very soon after the battle began to rage on our extreme left above the stone bridge.

I was still weak and John Scott brought me out to the line of battle another cup of coffee. He also brought some oats for my horse, which had not finished eating when I mounted him. He got an ammunition box to put the oats in and the horse was eating while I drank the coffee. We could distinctly hear the rumble of the yankee artillery on the pike beyond the run, and there was no doubt they were moving in force towards the stone bridge and the Sudley farm and proposed to turn our left wing and sweep down on our side the run and our line.

While we stood thus listening to the rumbling artillery and watching the dust as it arose from many hostile feet, we noticed a Federal battery of four guns suddenly dash out of the woods and throw itself into battery in the open space on the other side of the run above the bluff. We were much interested in the beauty of the movement, all of which we could see plainly, as it was not more than five hundred yards distant, but in a moment they opened upon our lines. The first shells went high above us, but the second were better aimed, and one of them struck the box out of which my horse was eating and shattered it to fragments, and then went on amongst the infantry behind us. John Scott did not move, or show any signs of fear. Having fired those two rounds they limbered up and left us as quickly as they came, and before our battery had done them any injury. When I noticed the first fire in some way I never dreamed the creatures were firing at us, so I went on drinking my coffee, but I was very rudely awakened from the dream by the second round when my indifference was changed to indignation, that they should actually have the impudence to fire at us on our own ground, and when we were doing them no harm.

After this there was a lull for a half hour while we remained in line of battle, but with no enemy in sight, then we heard the sound of cannon and musketry on our left, towards the stone bridge. We were moved up nearer the fighting, two other companies having joined us, and the whole thing being under the command of Lieut.-Col. Thomas T. Munford, of our regiment. The sounds indicated that the battle was growing fast and furious on our left, and that our lines were slowly being driven back, at which we were not surprised, as we knew we had but a small force on our left, and it was then obvious that the enemy was hurling upon it their whole force. We waited orders with great impatience and anxiety, for we saw our people were giving way and we could not see why we could not be of use. The battery we were supporting had been moved and there were no other troops very near us. I think Colonel Cocke forgot us, at all events we remained in the same position until near three o'clock in the evening.

About nine o'clock Generals Beauregard and Johnston, with their respective staffs, dashed by us, about fifty persons, handsomely dressed and mounted, and making a very grand show, and one which appealed to our enthusiasm very much, though all of us thought that one of the two generals should have been up with Colonel Cocke much earlier. Doubtless, however, they had good cause for the delay. Immediately behind them, at a sweeping gallop, came the "Washington Artillery," a battalion of sixteen guns. This was the most inspiring sight I ever saw, and fills me with emotion whenever I think of it now. One not familiar with artillery can little imagine how grand a sight it was. Each gun had four horses, with outriders and officers on horseback and several men mounted on the gun; then the caisson of each gun with its four horses and the like equipment of men, making thirty-two in all. Their ammunition wagons, forges and ambulances, all at full speed, making a procession, which under the circumstances, was very inspiring. Following the battalion next came "Hampton's Legion" of infantry under Col. Wade Hampton. Then a long and continuous line of infantry came pouring by as our troops were moved from the center and right wing to meet the attack on the left.

It is very easy, of course to criticise the conduct of the battle, and it is very unfair, as the critic does not know the inside causes, but while we stood there in nervous anxiety we all concluded our generals had been out-generaled, and the enemy had gained a great point upon them in transferring so many troops without their knowledge to the left, and forcing that wing back as they did. Our troops were put to a great disadvantage when run directly into a fight after moving at almost double-quick from six to ten miles on a hot July day, yet many of them were put to the test. We wondered also why, after it was discovered how the attack was made and that the enemy had stretched out his column from Centreville parallel to our front in the march towards Sudley, an attack was not made on his column, or upon the rear of the column, cutting him off from his base. Instead large forces, even after sending troops to the left, were idle all day at Mitchell's and Blackburn's Fords. No use was made of the cavalry until late in the day and then it was scattered about in small detachments, each acting under different orders, its attack was of little avail except to increase the panic of the enemy inducing a greater loss to them of the material of war. If when the enemy commenced to break, a column of cavalry had crossed Bull Run half way between Manassas and the stone bridge, and opened fire upon them as they moved back on the Warrenton Pike the victory would have been far more disastrous to the enemy and our gain in material so much the greater.

As these troops were passing towards the enemy another dismal line was moving back in the opposite direction. I shall never forget them. They were the wounded, some walking, some on stretchers, some in ambulances, all seeking the field hospital, which was near us in the woods, and all giving proof of their persons as well as their tongues of the terrible carnage on the left, and many giving discouraging tidings that our line was slowly giving way. Troops, certainly none but veterans, should never, if possible, be taken into action so as to see a field hospital or to meet the wounded or demoralized men. It has a bad effect and renders them unsteady.

The news given by the wounded men made us very impatient. We felt there was certainly something for us to do but no orders came. About eleven o'clock we were moved again further to the left, but though within range of artillery we had no actual fighting. The enemy continued to advance and at last, about mid-morning we saw signs of demoralization on the part of some of our troops; but about that time we saw a long column of troops in the same direction moving towards us, which, at first, we thought was the enemy, but to our infinite relief we found was General Jackson's brigade which had just been put off a train of cars on the Manassas road. They doubled quick into action and met the enemy's line and were soon heavily engaged. I was not near enough to mark the fighting, or rather my view was too much obstructed to get a view, but we could tell by the constant roar of cannon and musketry that the contest was severe. It was soon after this that Jackson won his "Stonewall," as I have stated before. I got permission to ride a little distance from our command to get a closer view, and while out in an open field viewing the contest the best I could a bright-eyed boy of some sixteen years of age came up to me with a wounded hand and arm and spoke to me by name. I did not remember ever having seen him before, but he said he remembered me when I was a student at the University of Virginia and that his name was Everett B. Early, of Charlottesville. He had run away from home and gone into the fight and been wounded. He had dressed his wound and was on his way back to take a hand again. He gave me a very intelligent account of the battle.

I was kept in a state of great excitement all day and found it hard to set on my horse from weakness induced by my recent sickness. We had nothing to eat. About four it became obvious that the advance of the enemy had been stopped. Then there was a sudden pause in the firing on their side, and then we could hear cheers and shouts on our lines. We were told by a wounded man that Sherman's and Ricketts' battery had been captured and that the enemy were slowly retiring. Still we were kept waiting though the sound of firing showed us the enemy was now in full retreat and the time for the cavalry had come. About five o'clock an officer came up and told Col. Munford the enemy were in full retreat across Bull Run, and ordered him to cross the stream and make for the pike to cut them off if possible and that Col. Radford with the rest of the regiment had already gone. Both parts of the regiment crossed about the same time, and we dashed up the hill, but the order had come too late for much good to be done. We were received by a scattering fire from the routed column, but they had generally thrown away their arms, and those who had not done so did so as soon as they saw us. It was a terrible rout and the face of the earth was covered with blankets, haversacks, overcoats, and every species of arms. We joined Col. Radford and the other six companies of the regiment as we reached the pike and followed the fleeing yankees, capturing many prisoners, until we came to a block in the road made by a great number of abandoned wagons, cannon and caissons, ambulances and other material at a bridge over a creek about two miles of Centreville. Further advance was checked, or at all events we went no further. From the other side of the creek and on top of the hill the enemy had been able to halt a battery long enough to fire one or two shots at our column, one of which killed Captain Winston Radford, of Bedford, a most excellent man and citizen and the brother of our Colonel. Beyond this our loss was very small and my company had only one or two wounded slightly.

Just as we crossed Bull Run I saw Edmund Fontaine, of

Hanover, resting on a log by the roadside. I asked him what was the matter, and he said he was wounded and dying. He said it very cheerfully and did not look as if anything was the matter. As we came back we found him dead and some of his comrades about to remove the body. It was a great shock to me, as I had known him from boyhood, and though he was younger than I was we had met during many visits to Hanover when I was younger. We went into bivouac a little after dark, for it had become cloudy and was very dark.

It was a day long to be remembered, and such a Sunday as men seldom spend. To all but a scattered few it was our first battle, and its sights and wonders were things of which we had read but scarcely believed or understood until seen and experienced. The rout of the enemy was complete but our generals showed much want of skill in not making the material advantages greater. The Federal army was equipped with every species of munition and property, while ours was wanting in everything. They were stricken with a panic; wherever the panic was increased by the sight of an armed rebel it discovered itself by the natural impulse to throw away arms and accoutrements and to abandon everything in the shape of cannon, caissons, wagons, ambulances and provisions that might impede their flight, yet they managed, despite their flight, to carry off much. They only lost some thirty-odd cannon for example, while with proper management on our part they would not have reached the Potomac with two whole batteries and so with other properties.

Had there been even a slight demonstration on Centreville that evening the panic would have been so increased that we would have made more captures in cannon, small arms and wagons.

During the evening as I was riding over part of the field where there were many dead yankees lying who had been killed, I thought by some of Stuart's regiment, I noticed an old doll-baby with only one leg lying by the side of a Federal soldier just as it dropped from his pocket when he fell writhing in the agony of death. It was obviously a memento of some little loved one at home which he had brought so far with him and had worn close to his heart on this day of danger and death. It was strange to see that emblem of childhood, that token of a father's love lying there amidst the dead and dying where the storm of war had so fiercely raged and where death had stalked in the might of its terrible majesty. I dismounted, picked it up and stuffed it back into the poor fellow's cold bosom that it might rest with him in the bloody grave which was to be forever unknown to those who loved and mourned him in his distant home.

The actual loss of the enemy I do not know but their dead extended for miles and their wounded filled every house and shed in the neighborhood. The wounded doubtless suffered much. Their own surgeons abandoned their field hospitals and joined the fleeing cohorts of the living, and our surgeons had all they could do to look after their own wounded, who of course were the first served. They received kind treatment however, and as soon as our surgeons were free they rendered all the aid in their power.

The enemy had permitted no doubt of the result to cross their minds, and had not kept it a secret in Washington that the final attack was to be made on Sunday. The day was therefore made a gala day by the people of all classes, and they came in great numbers in every possible conveyance to enjoy the rebel rout and possible share in the rebel spoils. Members of Congress and cabinet ministers, department clerks and idle citizens followed the advancing column in all the confidence of exhorting confidence, and there were not wanting many a hack-load of the *demi-monde* with their admirers to complete the motley crew. Along the road and amidst abandoned cannon and wagons we found many a forsaken carriage and hack with half-eaten lunches and half-used baskets of champagne, and we received most laughable accounts from the citizens on the roadside of the scenes they saw and the sharp contrast between the proud and confident advance and the wild panic of the flight. The men of our company got many a spoil not known to the ordnance department or used by those who filled the ranks.

We bivouacked in the field and without tent or any shelter but the oilcloths, a vast supply of which we had laid in from those upon which our foes had slept the night before. They were of the very best material and we gladly abandoned ours or kept them to throw over our saddles in the rain. A battle is not a sanitarium for the sick or the cold ground a good bed for a feverish and chilly man. I was so worn and weary that I had no doubt whatever that when I awoke in the morning I would be very ill. Before I laid down I fortunately found an opportunity to send a telegram to my wife and owing to a fortunate accident it got off the next morning and relieved the minds of my people at home and the friends of all my men.

Despite my gloomy anticipations as to the effect on my health I slept like a top and awoke the next morning after daylight feeling very much better. I was aroused by a hard rain falling on my face. I got up at once and crawled into my wagon, which fortunately had come up during the night, and then I had my breakfast owing to John Scott's thoughtfulness. I had heard nothing about my brothers, Capt. Eugene Blackford of the Fourth Alabamas and Lieut. W. W. Blackford, of Stuart's regiment of Cavalry. Both, I knew, had been engaged but I could not hear anything of them. Of course I was anxious.

About eight o'clock a staff officer from somewhere rode up and delivered an order calling for details to gather up arms and spoils from the field and to carry prisoners to the rear. I was sent with twenty men to report to Colonel Evans on the latter duty. When I reported I found also a small detail of infantry and the Colonel put me in charge of the whole detachment and turned over to me several hundred prisoners, who looked very uncomfortable in the rain, with orders to take them to Manassas, six miles to the rear. Before we started Colonel Evans took me into a house in the yard of which he had his headquarters and introduced me to Colonel O. B. Willcox and Captain Ricketts of the Federal army, both of whom were wounded and prisoners. Willcox and Evans seemed very good friends and called each other Orlando and Shanks respectively —"Shanks" being Evans' nickname at West Point. Willcox was very courteous but Ricketts was surly and bitter and complained of his accommodations, which were very much better than those of his captor in the yard or than those of the vast proportion of our wounded men and officers. He had a comfortable room and bed and two surgeons to attend his wounds. One would suppose he expected the rebels to have a first-class hotel on the battlefield ready to receive him and that they had violated all the rules of civilized warfare in failing to do so.

We carried the two officers, placed under my care, in an ambulance, and made them as comfortable as possible. We made rapid progress and I soon delivered my charge to some officer at General Beauregard's headquarters. I had some pleasant chats with Colonel Willcox.

The sights of this day were terrible and more heartrending than those of the day before. Our preparations for the battle, so far as the care of the wounded was concerned, were very imperfect and we were called on to provide for those of both sides. The result was that many of both sides suffered much, but no difference was shown them save in the matter of priority of service. The surgeons were busy all day but still many wounds remained undressed for full twenty-four hours. Luckily it was not very hot and the rain was a comfort.

# William Howard Russell: from
# My Diary North and South

The Union attack across Bull Run against the Confederate left flank was initially successful, but was halted by determined resistance on Henry House Hill. When the last Confederate reinforcements from the Shenandoah Valley reached the battlefield in the afternoon, Beauregard launched a successful counterattack. The Union forces began a retreat that soon turned into a rout. William Howard Russell left Washington in a hired carriage shortly after daybreak on July 21, hoping to catch up with the advance of McDowell's army. His subsequent report on the battle for *The Times* of London would be denounced in the Northern press for describing "the disgraceful conduct" of the Union troops as an instance of "miserable, causeless panic."

———————————

PUNCTUAL to time, our carriage appeared at the door, with a spare horse, followed by the black quadruped on which the negro boy sat with difficulty, in consequence of its high spirits and excessively hard mouth. I swallowed a cup of tea and a morsel of bread, put the remainder of the tea into a bottle, got a flask of light Bordeaux, a bottle of water, a paper of sandwiches, and having replenished my small flask with brandy, stowed them all away in the bottom of the gig; but my friend, who is not accustomed to rise very early in the morning, did not make his appearance, and I was obliged to send several times to the legation to quicken his movements. Each time I was assured he would be over presently; but it was not till two hours had elapsed, and when I had just resolved to leave him behind, that he appeared in person, quite unprovided with *viaticum*, so that my slender store had now to meet the demands of two instead of one. We are off at last. The amicus and self find contracted space behind the driver. The negro boy, grinning half with pain and "the balance" with pleasure, as the

Americans say, held on his rampant charger, which made continual efforts to leap into the gig, and thus through the deserted city we proceeded towards the Long Bridge, where a sentry examined our papers, and said with a grin, "You'll find plenty of Congressmen on before you." And then our driver whipped his horses through the embankment of Fort Runyon, and dashed off along a country road, much cut up with gun and cart wheels, towards the main turnpike.

The promise of a lovely day, given by the early dawn, was likely to be realised to the fullest, and the placid beauty of the scenery as we drove through the woods below Arlington, and beheld the white buildings shining in the early sunlight, and the Potomac, like a broad silver riband dividing the picture, breathed of peace. The silence close to the city was unbroken. From the time we passed the guard beyond the Long Bridge, for several miles we did not meet a human being, except a few soldiers in the neighbourhood of the deserted camps, and when we passed beyond the range of tents we drove for nearly two hours through a densely-wooded, undulating country; the houses, close to the road-side, shut up and deserted, window-high in the crops of Indian corn, fast ripening for the sickle; alternate field and forest, the latter generally still holding possession of the hollows, and, except when the road, deep and filled with loose stones, passed over the summit of the ridges, the eye caught on either side little but fir-trees and maize, and the deserted wooden houses, standing amidst the slave quarters.

The residences close to the lines gave signs and tokens that the Federals had recently visited them. But at the best of times the inhabitants could not be very well off. Some of the farms were small, the houses tumbling to decay, with unpainted roofs and side walls, and windows where the want of glass was supplemented by panes of wood. As we got further into the country the traces of the debateable land between the two armies vanished, and negroes looked out from their quarters, or sickly-looking women and children were summoned forth by the rattle of the wheels to see who was hurrying to the war. Now and then a white man looked out, with an ugly scowl on his face, but the country seemed drained of the adult male population, and such of the inhabitants as we saw were neither as comfortably dressed nor as healthy looking as the shambling

slaves who shuffled about the plantations. The road was so cut
up by gun-wheels, ammunition and commissariat waggons,
that our horses made but slow way against the continual draft
upon the collar; but at last the driver, who had known the
country in happier times, announced that we had entered the
high road for Fairfax Court-house. Unfortunately my watch
had gone down, but I guessed it was then a little before nine
o'clock. In a few minutes afterwards I thought I heard,
through the eternal clatter and jingle of the old gig, a sound
which made me call the driver to stop. He pulled up, and we
listened. In a minute or so, the well-known boom of a gun,
followed by two or three in rapid succession, but at a considerable distance, reached my ear. "Did you hear that?" The driver
heard nothing, nor did my companion, but the black boy on
the led horse, with eyes starting out of his head, cried, "I hear
them, massa; I hear them, sure enough, like de gun in de navy
yard;" and as he spoke the thudding noise, like taps with a
gentle hand upon a muffled drum, were repeated, which were
heard both by Mr. Warre and the driver. "They are at it! We
shall be late! Drive on as fast as you can!" We rattled on still
faster, and presently came up to a farm-house, where a man
and woman, with some negroes beside them, were standing
out by the hedge-row above us, looking up the road in the direction of a cloud of dust, which we could see rising above the
tops of the trees. We halted for a moment. "How long have the
guns been going, sir?" "Well, ever since early this morning,"
said he; "they've been having a fight. And I do really believe
some of our poor Union chaps have had enough of it already.
For here's some of them darned Secessionists marching down
to go into Alexandry." The driver did not seem altogether
content with this explanation of the dust in front of us, and
presently, when a turn of the road brought to view a body of
armed men, stretching to an interminable distance, with bayonets glittering in the sunlight through the clouds of dust,
seemed inclined to halt or turn back again. A nearer approach
satisfied me they were friends, and as soon as we came up with
the head of the column I saw that they could not be engaged
in the performance of any military duty. The men were marching without any resemblance of order, in twos and threes or
larger troops. Some without arms, carrying great bundles on

their backs; others with their coats hung from their firelocks; many foot sore. They were all talking, and in haste; many plodding along laughing, so I concluded that they could not belong to a defeated army, and imagined M'Dowell was effecting some flank movement. "Where are you going to, may I ask?"

"If this is the road to Alexandria, we are going there."

"There is an action going on in front, is there not?"

"Well, so we believe, but we have not been fighting."

Although they were in such good spirits, they were not communicative, and we resumed our journey, impeded by the straggling troops and by the country cars containing their baggage and chairs, and tables and domestic furniture, which had never belonged to a regiment in the field. Still they came pouring on. I ordered the driver to stop at a rivulet, where a number of men were seated in the shade, drinking the water and bathing their hands and feet. On getting out I asked an officer, "May I beg to know, sir, where your regiment is going to?" "Well, I reckon, sir, we are going home to Pennsylvania." "This is the 4th Pennsylvania Regiment, is it not, sir?" "It is so, sir; that's the fact." "I should think there is severe fighting going on behind you, judging from the firing" (for every moment the sound of the cannon had been growing more distinct and more heavy)?" "Well, I reckon, sir, there is." I paused for a moment, not knowing what to say, and yet anxious for an explanation; and the epauletted gentleman, after a few seconds' awkward hesitation, added, "We are going home because, as you see, the men's time's up, sir. We have had three months of this sort of work, and that's quite enough of it." The men who were listening to the conversation expressed their assent to the noble and patriotic utterances of the centurion, and, making him a low bow, we resumed our journey.

It was fully three and a half miles before the last of the regiment passed, and then the road presented a more animated scene, for white-covered commissariat waggons were visible, wending towards the front, and one or two hack carriages, laden with civilians, were hastening in the same direction. Before the doors of the wooden farm-houses the coloured people were assembled, listening with outstretched necks to the repeated reports of the guns. At one time, as we were descending the wooded road, a huge blue dome, agitated by some internal convulsion, appeared to bar our progress, and it was only after infinite persuasion of rein and whip that the horses approached the terrific object, which was an inflated balloon, attached to a waggon, and defying the efforts of the men in charge to jockey it safely through the trees.

It must have been about eleven o'clock when we came to the first traces of the Confederate camp, in front of Fairfax Court-house, where they had cut a few trenches and levelled the trees across the road, so as to form a rude abattis; but the works were of a most superficial character, and would scarcely have given cover either to the guns, for which embrasures were left at the flanks to sweep the road, or to the infantry intended to defend them.

The Confederate force stationed here must have consisted, to a considerable extent, of cavalry. The bowers of branches, which they had made to shelter their tents, camp tables, empty boxes, and packing-cases, in the *débris* one usually sees around an encampment, showed they had not been destitute of creature comforts.

Some time before noon the driver, urged continually by adjurations to get on, whipped his horses into Fairfax Court-house, a village which derives its name from a large brick building, in which the sessions of the county are held. Some thirty or forty houses, for the most part detached, with gardens or small strips of land about them, form the main street. The inhabitants who remained had by no means an agreeable expression of countenance, and did not seem on very good terms with the Federal soldiers, who were lounging up and down the streets, or standing in the shade of the trees and doorways. I asked the sergeant of a picket in the street how long the firing had been going on. He replied that it had commenced at half-past seven or eight, and had been increasing ever since. "Some of them will lose their eyes and back teeth," he added, "before it is over." The driver, pulling up at a roadside inn in the town, here made the startling announcement, that both he and his horses must have something to eat, and although we would have been happy to join him, seeing that we had no breakfast, we could not afford the time, and were not displeased when a thin-faced, shrewish woman, in black, came out into the verandah, and said she could not let us have anything unless we liked to wait till the regular dinner hour of the house, which was at one o'clock. The horses got a bucket of water, which they needed in that broiling sun; and the cannonade, which by this time had increased into a respectable tumult that gave evidence of a well-sustained action, added vigour to the driver's arm, and in a mile or two more we dashed in to a village of burnt houses, the charred brick chimney stacks standing amidst the blackened embers being all that remained of what once was German Town. The firing of this village was severely censured by General M'Dowell, who probably does not appreciate the value of such agencies employed "by our glorious Union army to develope loyal sentiments among the people of Virginia."

The driver, passing through the town, drove straight on, but after some time I fancied the sound of the guns seemed dying away towards our left. A big negro came shambling along the roadside—the driver stopped and asked him, "is this the road to Centreville?" "Yes, sir; right on, sir; good road to Centreville, massa," and so we proceeded, till I became satisfied from the appearance of the road that we had altogether left the track of the army. At the first cottage we halted, and inquired of a Virginian, who came out to look at us, whether the road led to Centreville. "You're going to Centreville, are you?" "Yes, by the shortest road we can." "Well, then—you're going wrong—right away! Some people say there's a bend of road leading through the wood a mile further on, but those who have tried it lately have come back to German Town and don't think it leads to Centreville at all." This was very provoking, as the horses were much fatigued and we had driven several miles out of our way. The driver, who was an Englishman, said, "I think it would be best for us to go on and try the road anyhow. There's not likely to be any Seceshers about there, are there, sir?"

"What did you say, sir," inquired the Virginian, with a vacant stare upon his face.

"I merely asked whether you think we are likely to meet with any Secessionists if we go along that road?"

"Secessionists!" repeated the Virginian, slowly pronouncing

each syllable as if pondering on the meaning of the word—
"Secessionists! Oh no, *sir*; I don't believe there's such a thing
as a Secessionist in the whole of this country."

The boldness of this assertion, in the very hearing of Beauregard's cannon, completely shook the faith of our Jehu in any
information from that source, and we retraced our steps to
German Town, and were directed into the proper road by some
negroes, who were engaged exchanging Confederate money at
very low rates for Federal copper with a few straggling soldiers.
The faithful Muley Moloch, who had been capering in our rear
so long, now complained that he was very much burned, but
on further inquiry it was ascertained he was merely suffering
from the abrading of his skin against an English saddle.

In an hour more we had gained the high road to Centreville, on which were many buggies, commissariat carts, and
waggons full of civilians, and a brisk canter brought us in sight
of a rising ground, over which the road led directly through a
few houses on each side, and dipped out of sight, the slopes
of the hill being covered with men, carts, and horses, and the
summit crested with spectators, with their backs turned
towards us, and gazing on the valley beyond. "There's Centreville," says the driver, and on our poor panting horses were
forced, passing directly through the Confederate bivouacs,
commissariat parks, folds of oxen, and two German regiments,
with a battery of artillery, halting on the rising-ground by the
road-side. The heat was intense. Our driver complained of
hunger and thirst, to which neither I nor my companion were
insensible; and so pulling up on the top of the hill, I sent the
boy down to the village which we had passed, to see if he
could find shelter for the horses, and a morsel for our break-
fastless selves.

It was a strange scene before us. From the hill a densely
wooded country, dotted at intervals with green fields and
cleared lands, spread five or six miles in front, bounded by a
line of blue and purple ridges, terminating abruptly in escarp-
ments towards the left front, and swelling gradually towards
the right into the lower spines of an offshoot from the Blue-
Ridge Mountains. On our left the view was circumscribed by a
forest which clothed the side of the ridge on which we stood,
and covered its shoulder far down into the plain. A gap in the

nearest chain of the hills in our front was pointed out by the bystanders as the Pass of Manassas, by which the railway from the West is carried into the plain, and still nearer at hand, before us, is the junction of that rail with the line from Alexandria, and with the railway leading southwards to Richmond. The intervening space was not a dead level; undulating lines of forest marked the course of the streams which intersected it, and gave, by their variety of colour and shading, an additional charm to the landscape which, enclosed in a framework of blue and purple hills, softened into violet in the extreme distance, presented one of the most agreeable displays of simple pastoral woodland scenery that could be conceived.

But the sounds which came upon the breeze, and the sights which met our eyes, were in terrible variance with the tranquil character of the landscape. The woods far and near echoed to the roar of cannon, and thin frayed lines of blue smoke marked the spots whence came the muttering sound of rolling musketry; the white puffs of smoke burst high above the treetops, and the gunners' rings from shell and howitzer marked the fire of the artillery.

Clouds of dust shifted and moved through the forest; and through the wavering mists of light blue smoke, and the thicker masses which rose commingling from the feet of men and the mouths of cannon, I could see the gleam of arms and the twinkling of bayonets.

On the hill beside me there was a crowd of civilians on horseback, and in all sorts of vehicles, with a few of the fairer, if not gentler sex. A few officers and some soldiers, who had straggled from the regiments in reserve, moved about among the spectators, and pretended to explain the movements of the troops below, of which they were profoundly ignorant.

The cannonade and musketry had been exaggerated by the distance and by the rolling echoes of the hills; and sweeping the position narrowly with my glass from point to point, I failed to discover any traces of close encounter or very severe fighting. The spectators were all excited, and a lady with an opera-glass who was near me was quite beside herself when an unusually heavy discharge roused the current of her blood— "That is splendid. Oh, my! Is not that first-rate? I guess we will be in Richmond this time to-morrow." These, mingled with coarser exclamations, burst from the politicians who had come out to see the triumph of the Union arms. I was particularly irritated by constant applications for the loan of my glass. One broken-down looking soldier observing my flask, asked me for a drink, and took a startling pull, which left but little between the bottom and utter vacuity.

"Stranger, that's good stuff and no mistake. I have not had such a drink since I come South. I feel now as if I'd like to whip ten Seceshers."

From the line of the smoke it appeared to me that the action was in an oblique line from our left, extending farther outwards towards the right, bisected by a road from Centreville, which descended the hill close at hand and ran right across the undulating plain, its course being marked by the white covers of the baggage and commissariat waggons as far as a turn of the road, where the trees closed in upon them. Beyond the right of the curling smoke clouds of dust appeared from time to time in the distance, as if bodies of cavalry were moving over a sandy plain.

Notwitstanding all the exultation and boastings of the people at Centreville, I was well convinced no advance of any importance or any great success had been achieved, because the ammunition and baggage waggons had never moved, nor had the reserves received any orders to follow in the line of the army.

The clouds of dust on the right were quite inexplicable. As we were looking, my philosophic companion asked me in perfect seriousness, "Are we really seeing a battle now? Are they supposed to be fighting where all that smoke is going on? This is rather interesting, you know."

Up came our black boy. "Not find a bit to eat, sir, in all the place." We had, however, my little paper of sandwiches, and descended the hill to a bye lane off the village, where, seated in the shade of the gig, Mr. Warre and myself, dividing our provision with the driver, wound up a very scanty, but much relished, repast with a bottle of tea and half the bottle of Bordeaux and water, the remainder being prudently reserved at my request for contingent remainders. Leaving orders for the saddle horse, which was eating his first meal, to be brought up the moment he was ready—I went with Mr. Warre to the hill once more and observed that the line had not sensibly altered whilst we were away.

An English gentleman, who came up flushed and heated from the plain, told us that the Federals had been advancing steadily in spite of a stubborn resistance and had behaved most gallantly.

Loud cheers suddenly burst from the spectators, as a man dressed in the uniform of an officer, whom I had seen riding violently across the plain in an open space below, galloped along the front, waving his cap and shouting at the top of his voice. He was brought up by the press of people round his horse close to where I stood. "We've whipped them on all points," he cried. "We have taken all their batteries. They are retreating as fast as they can, and we are after them." Such cheers as rent the welkin! The Congress men shook hands with each other, and cried out, "Bully for us. Bravo, didn't I tell you so." The Germans uttered their martial cheers and the Irish hurrahed wildly. At this moment my horse was brought up the hill, and I mounted and turned towards the road to the front, whilst Mr. Warre and his companion proceeded straight down the hill.

By the time I reached the lane, already mentioned, which was in a few minutes, the string of commissariat waggons was moving onwards pretty briskly, and I was detained until my friends appeared at the road-side. I told Mr. Warre I was going forward to the front as fast as I could, but that I would come back, under any circumstances, about an hour before dusk, and would go straight to the spot where we had put up the gig by the road-side, in order to return to Washington. Then getting into the fields, I pressed my horse, which was quite recovered from his twenty-seven mile's ride and full of spirit and mettle, as fast as I could, making detours here and there to get through the ox fences, and by the small steams which cut up the country. The firing did not increase but rather diminished in volume, though it now sounded close at hand.

I had ridden between three and a half and four miles, as well as I could judge, when I was obliged to turn for the third and fourth time into the road by a considerable stream, which was spanned by a bridge, towards which I was threading my way, when my attention was attracted by loud shouts in advance, and I perceived several waggons coming from the direction of the battle-field, the drivers of which were endeavouring to force their horses past the ammunition carts going in the contrary direction near the bridge; a thick cloud of dust rose behind them, and running by the side of the waggons, were a number of men in uniform whom I supposed to be the guard. My first impression was that the waggons were returning for fresh supplies of ammunition. But every moment the crowd increased, drivers and men cried out with the most vehement gestures, "Turn back! Turn back! We are whipped." They seized the heads of the horses and swore at the opposing drivers. Emerging from the crowd a breathless man in the uniform of an officer with an empty scabbard dangling by his side, was cut off by getting between my horse and a cart for a moment. "What is the matter, sir? What is all this about?" "Why it means we are pretty badly whipped, that's the truth," he gasped, and continued.

By this time the confusion had been communicating itself through the line of waggons towards the rear, and the drivers endeavoured to turn round their vehicles in the narrow road, which caused the usual amount of imprecations from the men and plunging and kicking from the horses.

The crowd from the front continually increased, the heat, the uproar, and the dust were beyond description, and these were augmented when some cavalry soldiers, flourishing their sabres and preceded by an officer, who cried out, "Make way there—make way there for the General," attempted to force a covered waggon in which was seated a man with a bloody handkerchief round his head, through the press.

I had succeeded in getting across the bridge with great difficulty before the waggon came up, and I saw the crowd on the road was still gathering thicker and thicker. Again I asked an officer, who was on foot, with his sword under his arm, "What is all this for?" "We are whipped, sir. We are all in retreat. You are all to go back." "Can you tell me where I can find General M'Dowell?" "No! nor can any one else."

A few shells could be heard bursting not very far off, but there was nothing to account for such an extraordinary scene. A third officer, however, confirmed the report that the whole army was in retreat, and that the Federals were beaten on all

points, but there was nothing in this disorder to indicate a
general rout. All these things took place in a few seconds. I got
up out of the road into a corn-field, through which men were
hastily walking or running, their faces streaming with perspi-
ration, and generally without arms, and worked my way for
about half a mile or so, as well as I could judge, against an increasing stream of fugitives, the ground being strewed with
coats, blankets, fire-locks, cooking tins, caps, belts, bayonets—
asking in vain where General M'Dowell was.

Again I was compelled by the condition of the fields to
come into the road; and having passed a piece of wood and a
regiment which seemed to be moving back in column of march
in tolerably good order, I turned once more into an opening
close to a white house, not far from the lane, beyond which
there was a belt of forest. Two field-pieces unlimbered near the
house, with panting horses in the rear, were pointed towards
the front, and along the road beside them there swept a tolerably steady column of men mingled with field ambulances and
light baggage carts, back to Centreville. I had just stretched
out my hand to get a cigar-light from a German gunner, when
the dropping shots which had been sounding through the
woods in front of us, suddenly swelled into an animated fire.
In a few seconds a crowd of men rushed out of the wood
down towards the guns, and the artillerymen near me seized
the trail of a piece, and were wheeling it round to fire, when an
officer or sergeant called out, "Stop! stop! They are our own
men;" and in two or three minutes the whole battalion came
sweeping past the guns at the double, and in the utmost disorder. Some of the artillerymen dragged the horses out of the
tumbrils; and for a moment the confusion was so great I could
not understand what had taken place; but a soldier whom I
stopped, said, "We are pursued by their cavalry; they have cut
us all to pieces."

Murat himself would not have dared to move a squadron on
such ground. However, it could not be doubted that something serious was taking place; and at that moment a shell burst
in front of the house, scattering the soldiers near it, which was
followed by another that bounded along the road; and in a few
minutes more out came another regiment from the wood,
almost as broken as the first. The scene on the road had now

assumed an aspect which has not a parallel in any description I have ever read. Infantry soldiers on mules and draught horses, with the harness clinging to their heels, as much frightened as their riders; negro servants on their masters' chargers; ambulances crowded with unwounded soldiers; waggons swarming with men who threw out the contents in the road to make room, grinding through a shouting, screaming mass of men on foot, who were literally yelling with rage at every halt, and shrieking out, "Here are the cavalry! Will you get on?" This portion of the force was evidently in discord.

There was nothing left for it but to go with the current one could not stem. I turned round my horse from the deserted guns, and endeavoured to find out what had occurred as I rode quietly back on the skirts of the crowd. I talked with those on all sides of me. Some uttered prodigious nonsense, describing batteries tier over tier, and ambuscades, and blood running knee deep. Others described how their boys had carried whole lines of entrenchments, but were beaten back for want of reinforcements. The names of many regiments were mentioned as being utterly destroyed. Cavalry and bayonet charges and masked batteries played prominent parts in all the narrations. Some of the officers seemed to feel the disgrace of defeat; but the strangest thing was the general indifference with which the event seemed to be regarded by those who collected their senses as soon as they got out of fire, and who said they were just going as far as Centreville, and would have a big fight to-morrow.

By this time I was unwillingly approaching Centreville in the midst of heat, dust, confusions, imprecations inconceivable. On arriving at the place where a small rivulet crossed the road, the throng increased still more. The ground over which I had passed going out was now covered with arms, clothing of all kinds, accoutrements thrown off and left to be trampled in the dust under the hoofs of men and horses. The runaways ran alongside the waggons, striving to force themselves in among the occupants, who resisted tooth and nail. The drivers spurred, and whipped, and urged the horses to the utmost of their bent. I felt an inclination to laugh, which was overcome by disgust, and by that vague sense of something extraordinary taking place which is experienced when a man sees a number of people acting as if driven by some unknown terror. As I rode in the crowd, with men clinging to the stirrup-leathers, or holding on by anything they could lay hands on, so that I had some apprehension of being pulled off, I spoke to the men, and asked them over and over again not to be in such a hurry. "There's no enemy to pursue you. All the cavalry in the world could not get at you." But I might as well have talked to the stones.

For my own part, I wanted to get out of the ruck as fast as I could, for the heat and dust were very distressing, particularly to a half-starved man. Many of the fugitives were in the last stages of exhaustion, and some actually sank down by the fences, at the risk of being trampled to death. Above the roar of the flight, which was like the rush of a great river, the guns burst forth from time to time.

The road at last became somewhat clearer; for I had got ahead of some of the ammunition train and waggons, and the others were dashing up the hill towards Centreville. The men's great-coats and blankets had been stowed in the trains; but the fugitives had apparently thrown them out on the road, to make room for themselves. Just beyond the stream I saw a heap of clothing tumble out of a large covered cart, and cried out after the driver, "Stop! stop! All the things are tumbling out of the cart." But my zeal was checked by a scoundrel putting his head out, and shouting with a curse, "If you try to stop the team, I'll blow your —— brains out." My brains advised me to adopt the principle of non-intervention.

It never occurred to me that this was a grand débâcle. All along I believed the mass of the army was not broken, and that all I saw around was the result of confusion created in a crude organisation by a forced retreat; and knowing the reserves were at Centreville and beyond, I said to myself, "Let us see how this will be when we get to the hill." I indulged in a quiet chuckle, too, at the idea of my philosophical friend and his stout companion finding themselves suddenly enveloped in the crowd of fugitives; but knew they could easily have regained their original position on the hill. Trotting along briskly through the fields, I arrived at the foot of the slope on which Centreville stands, and met a German regiment just deploying into line very well and steadily—the men in the rear companies laughing, smoking, singing, and jesting with the fugitives, who were filing past; but no thought of stopping the waggons, as the orders repeated from mouth to mouth were that they were to fall back beyond Centreville.

The air of the men was good. The officers were cheerful, and one big German with a great pipe in his bearded mouth, with spectacles on nose, amused himself by pricking the horses with his sabre point, as he passed, to the sore discomfiture of the riders. Behind the regiment came a battery of brass field-pieces, and another regiment in column of march was following the guns. They were going to form line at the end of the slope, and no fairer position could well be offered for a defensive attitude, although it might be turned. But it was getting too late for the enemy wherever they were to attempt such an extensive operation. Several times I had been asked by officers and men, "Where do you think we will halt? Where are the rest of the army?" I always replied "Centreville," and I had heard hundreds of the fugitives say they were going to Centreville.

I rode up the road, turned into the little street which carries the road on the right-hand side to Fairfax Courthouse and the hill, and went straight to the place where I had left the buggy in a lane on the left of the road beside a small house and shed, expecting to find Mr. Warre ready for a start, as I had faithfully promised Lord Lyons he should be back that night in Washington. The buggy was not there. I pulled open the door of the shed in which the horses had been sheltered out of the sun. They were gone. "Oh," said I, to myself, "of course! What a stupid fellow I am. Warre has had the horses put in and taken the gig to the top of the hill, in order to see the last of it before we go." And so I rode over to the ridge; but arriving there, could see no sign of our vehicle far or near. There were two carriages of some kind or other still remaining on the hill, and a few spectators, civilians and military, gazing on the scene below, which was softened in the golden rays of the declining sun. The smoke wreaths had ceased to curl over the green sheets of billowy forest as sea foam crisping in a gentle breeze breaks the lines of the ocean. But far and near yellow and dun-coloured piles of dust seamed the landscape, leaving behind them long trailing clouds of lighter vapours which were dotted now and then by white puff balls from the bursting of shell.

On the right these clouds were very heavy and seemed to approach rapidly, and it occurred to me they might be caused by an advance of the much spoken-of and little seen cavalry; and remembering the cross road from German Town, it seemed a very fine and very feasible operation for the Confederates to cut right in on the line of retreat and communication, in which case the fate of the army and of Washington could not be dubious. There were now few civilians on the hill, and these were thinning away. Some were gesticulating and explaining to one another the causes of the retreat, looking very hot and red. The confusion among the last portion of the carriages and fugitives on the road, which I had outstripped, had been renewed again, and the crowd there presented a remarkable and ludicrous aspect through the glass; but there were two strong battalions in good order near the foot of the hill, a battery on the slope, another on the top, and a portion of a regiment in and about the houses of the village.

A farewell look at the scene presented no new features. Still the clouds of dust moved onwards denser and higher; flashes of arms lighted them up at times; the fields were dotted by fugitives, among whom many mounted men were marked by their greater speed, and the little flocks of dust rising from the horses' feet.

I put up my glass, and turning from the hill, with difficulty forced my way through the crowd of vehicles which were making their way towards the main road in the direction of the lane, hoping that by some lucky accident I might find the gig in waiting for me. But I sought in vain; a sick soldier who was on a stretcher in front of the house near the corner of the lane, leaning on his elbow and looking at the stream of men and carriages, asked me if I could tell him what they were in such a hurry for, and I said they were merely getting back to their bivouacs. A man dressed in civilian's clothes grinned as I spoke. "I think they'll go farther than that," said he; and then added, "If you're looking for the waggon you came in, it's pretty well back to Washington by this time. I think I saw you down there with a nigger and two men." "Yes. They're all off, gone more than an hour and a-half ago, I think, and a stout man—I thought was you at first—along with them."

Nothing was left for it but to brace up the girths for a ride to the Capitol, for which, hungry and fagged as I was, I felt very little inclination. I was trotting quietly down the hill road beyond Centreville, when suddenly the guns on the other side, or from a battery very near, opened fire, and a fresh outburst of artillery sounded through the woods. In an instant the mass of vehicles and retreating soldiers, teamsters, and civilians, as if agonised by an electric shock, quivered throughout the tortuous line. With dreadful shouts and cursings, the drivers lashed their maddened horses, and leaping from the carts, left them to their fate, and ran on foot. Artillerymen and foot soldiers, and negroes mounted on gun horses, with the chain traces and loose trappings trailing in the dust, spurred and flogged their steeds down the road or by the side paths. The firing continued and seemed to approach the hill, and at every report the agitated body of horsemen and waggons was seized, as it were, with a fresh convulsion.

Once more the dreaded cry, "The cavalry! cavalry are coming!" rang through the crowd, and looking back to Centreville I perceived coming down the hill, between me and the sky, a number of mounted men, who might at a hasty glance be taken for horsemen in the act of sabreing the fugitives. In reality they were soldiers and civilians, with, I regret to say, some officers among them, who were whipping and striking their horses with sticks or whatever else they could lay hands on. I called out to the men who were frantic with terror beside me, "They are not cavalry at all; they're your own men"—but they did not heed me. A fellow who was shouting out, "Run! run!" as loud as he could beside me, seemed to take delight in creating alarm; and as he was perfectly collected as far as I could judge, I said, "What on earth are you running for? What are you afraid of?" He was in the roadside below me, and at once turning on me, and exclaiming, "I'm not afraid of you," presented his piece and pulled the trigger so instantaneously, that had it gone off I could not have swerved from the ball. As the scoundrel deliberately drew up to examine the nipple, I judged it best not to give him another chance, and spurred on through the crowd, where any man could have shot as many as he pleased without interruption. The only conclusion I came to was, that he was mad or drunken. When I was passing by the line of the bivouacs a battalion of men came tumbling

down the bank from the field into the road, with fixed bayonets, and as some fell in the road and others tumbled on top of
them, there must have been a few ingloriously wounded.

I galloped on for a short distance to head the ruck, for I
could not tell whether this body of infantry intended moving
back towards Centreville or were coming down the road; but
the mounted men galloping furiously past me, with a cry of
"Cavalry! cavalry!" on their lips, swept on faster than I did,
augmenting the alarm and excitement. I came up with two
officers who were riding more leisurely; and touching my hat,
said, "I venture to suggest that these men should be stopped,
sir. If not, they will alarm the whole of the post and pickets on
to Washington. They will fly next, and the consequences will
be most disastrous." One of the two, looking at me for a moment, nodded his head without saying a word, spurred his
horse to full speed, and dashed on in front along the road. Following more leisurely I observed the fugitives in front were
suddenly checked in their speed; and as I turned my horse into
the wood by the road-side to get on so as to prevent the
chance of another block-up, I passed several private vehicles, in
one of which Mr. Raymond, of the *New York Times*, was seated
with some friends, looking by no means happy. He says in his
report to his paper, "About a mile this side of Centreville a
stampedo took place amongst the teamsters and others, which
threw everything into the utmost confusion, and inflicted very
serious injuries. Mr. Eaton, of Michigan, in trying to arrest the
flight of some of these men, was shot by one of them, the ball
taking effect in his hand." He asked me, in some anxiety, what
I thought would happen. I replied, "No doubt M'Dowell will
stand fast at Centreville to-night. These are mere runaways,
and unless the enemy's cavalry succeed in getting through at
this road, there is nothing to apprehend."

And I continued through the wood till I got a clear space in
front on the road, along which a regiment of infantry was advancing towards me. They halted ere I came up, and with levelled firelocks arrested the men on horses and the carts and
waggons galloping towards them, and blocked up the road to
stop their progress. As I tried to edge by on the right of the
column by the left of the road, a soldier presented his firelock
at my head from the higher ground on which he stood, for

the road had a deep trench cut on the side by which I was endeavouring to pass, and sung out, "Halt! Stop—or I fire!" The officers in front were waving their swords and shouting out, "Don't let a soul pass! Keep back! keep back!" Bowing to the officer who was near me, I said, "I beg to assure you, sir, I am not running away. I am a civilian and a British subject. I have done my best as I came along to stop this disgraceful rout. I am in no hurry; I merely want to get back to Washington to-night. I have been telling them all along there are no cavalry near us." The officer to whom I was speaking, young and somewhat excited kept repeating, "Keep back, sir! keep back! you must keep back." Again I said to him, "I assure you I am not with this crowd; my pulse is as cool as your own." But as he paid no attention to what I said, I suddenly bethought me of General Scott's letter, and addressing another officer, said, "I am a civilian going to Washington; will you be kind enough to look at this pass, specially given to me by General Scott." The officer looked at it, and handed it to a mounted man, either adjutant or colonel, who, having examined it, returned it to me, saying, "Oh, yes! certainly. Pass that man!" And with a cry of "Pass that man!" along the line, I rode down the trench very leisurely, and got out on the road, which was now clear, though some fugitives had stolen through the woods on the flanks of the column and were in front of me.

A little further on there was a cart on the right hand side of the road, surrounded by a group of soldiers. I was trotting past when a respectable-looking man in a semi-military garb, coming out from the group, said, in a tone of much doubt and distress—"Can you tell me, sir, for God's sake, where the 69th New York are? These men tell me they are all cut to pieces." "And so they are," exclaimed one of the fellows, who had the number of the regiment on his cap.

"You hear what they say, sir?" exclaimed the man.

"I do, but I really cannot tell you where the 69th are."

"I'm in charge of these mails, and I'll deliver them if I die for it; but is it safe for me to go on? You are a gentleman, and I can depend on your word."

His assistant and himself were in the greatest perplexity of mind, but all I could say was, "I really can't tell you; I believe the army will halt at Centreville to-night, and I think you may go on there with the greatest safety, if you can get through the crowd." "Faith, then, he can't," exclaimed one of the soldiers. "Why not?" "Shure, arn't we cut to pieces. Didn't I hear the kurnel himsilf saying we was all of us to cut and run, every man on his own hook, as well as he could. Stop at Cinthreville, indeed!"

I bade the mail agent* good evening and rode on, but even in this short colloquy stragglers on foot and on horseback, who had turned the flanks of the regiment by side paths or through the woods, came pouring along the road once more.

Somewhere about this I was accosted by a stout, elderly man, with the air and appearance of a respectable mechanic, or small tavern-keeper, who introduced himself as having met me at Cairo. He poured out a flood of woes on me, how he had lost his friend and companion, nearly lost his seat several times, was unaccustomed to riding, was suffering much pain from the unusual position and exercise, did not know the road, feared he would never be able to get on, dreaded he might be captured and ill-treated if he was known, and such topics as a selfish man

---

*I have since met the person referred to, an Englishman living in Washington, and well known at the Legation and elsewhere. Mr. Dawson came to tell me that he had seen a letter in an American journal, which was copied extensively all over the Union, in which the writer stated he accompanied me on my return to Fairfax Court-house, and that the incident I related in my account of Bull Run did not occur, but that he was the individual referred to, and would swear with his assistant that every word I wrote was true. I did not need any such corroboration for the satisfaction of any who know me; and I was quite well aware that if one came from the dead to bear testimony in my favour before the American journals and public, the evidence would not countervail the slander of any characterless scribe who sought to gain a moment's notoriety by a flat contradiction of my narrative. I may add, that Dawson begged of me not to bring him before the public, "because I am now sutler to the ——th, over in Virginia, and they would dismiss me." "What! For certifying to the truth?" "You know, sir, it might do me harm." Whilst on this subject, let me remark that some time afterwards I was in Mr Brady's photographic studio in Pennsylvania Avenue, Washington, when the very intelligent and obliging manager introduced himself to me, and said that he wished to have an opportunity of repeating to me personally what he had frequently told persons in the place, that he could bear the fullest testimony to the complete accuracy of my account of the panic from Centreville down the road at the time I left, and that he and his assistants, who were on the spot trying to get away their photographic van and apparatus, could certify that my description fell far short of the disgraceful spectacle and of the excesses of the flight.

in a good deal of pain or fear is likely to indulge in. I calmed his apprehensions as well as I could, by saying, "I had no doubt M'Dowell would halt and show fight at Centreville, and be able to advance from it in a day or two to renew the fight again; that he couldn't miss the road; whiskey and tallow were good for abrasions;" and as I was riding very slowly, he jogged along, for he was a burr, and would stick, with many "Oh dears! Oh! dear me!" for most part of the way joining me at intervals till I reached Fairfax Court House. A body of infantry were under arms in a grove near the Court House, on the right hand side of the road. The door and windows of the houses presented crowds of faces black and white; and men and women stood out upon the porch, who asked me as I passed, "Have you been at the fight?" "What are they all running for?" "Are the rest of them coming on?" to which I gave the same replies as before.

Arrived at the little inn where I had halted in the morning, I perceived the sharp-faced woman in black, standing in the verandah with an elderly man, a taller and younger one dressed in black, a little girl, and a woman who stood in the passage of the door. I asked if I could get anything to eat. "Not a morsel; there's not a bit left in the house, but you can get something, perhaps, if you like to stay till supper time." "Would you oblige me by telling me where I can get some water for my horse?" "Oh, certainly," said the elder man, and calling to a negro he directed him to bring a bucket from the well or pump, into which the thirsty brute buried his head to the eyes. Whilst the horse was drinking the taller or younger man, leaning over the verandah, asked me quietly "What are all the people coming back for?—what's set them a running towards Alexandria?"

"Oh, it's only a fright the drivers of the commissariat waggons have had; they are afraid of the enemy's cavalry."

"Ah," said the man, and looking at me narrowly he inquired, after a pause, "are you an American?"

"No, I am not, thank God; I'm an Englishman."

"Well, then," said he, nodding his head and speaking slowly through his teeth, "There *will* be cavalry after them soon enough; there is 20,000 of the best horsemen in the world in old Virginny."

Having received full directions from the people at the inn
for the road to the Long Bridge, which I was most anxious to
reach instead of going to Alexandria or to Georgetown, I bade
the Virginian good evening; and seeing that my stout friend,
who had also watered his horse by my advice at the inn, was
still clinging alongside, I excused myself by saying I must press
on to Washington, and galloped on for a mile, until I got into
the cover of a wood, where I dismounted to examine the
horse's hoofs and shift the saddle for a moment, wipe the
sweat off his back, and make him and myself as comfortable as
could be for our ride into Washington, which was still seventeen or eighteen miles before me. I passed groups of men,
some on horseback, others on foot, going at a more leisurely
rate towards the capital; and as I was smoking my last cigar by
the side of the wood, I observed the number had rather increased, and that among the retreating stragglers were some
men who appeared to be wounded.

The sun had set, but the rising moon was adding every moment to the lightness of the road as I mounted once more and
set out at a long trot for the capital. Presently I was overtaken
by a waggon with a small escort of cavalry and an officer riding
in front. I had seen the same vehicle once or twice along the
road, and observed an officer seated in it with his head bound
up with a handkerchief, looking very pale and ghastly. The
mounted officer leading the escort asked me if I was going
into Washington and knew the road. I told him I had never
been on it before, but thought I could find my way, "at any
rate we'll find plenty to tell us." "That's Colonel Hunter inside the carriage, he's shot through the throat and jaw, and I
want to get him to the doctor's in Washington as soon as I
can. Have you been to the fight?"

"No, sir."

"A member of Congress, I suppose, sir?"

"No, sir; I'm an Englishman."

"Oh indeed, sir, then I'm glad you did not see it, so mean a
fight, sir, I never saw; we whipped the cusses and drove them
before us, and took their batteries and spiked their guns, and
got right up in among all their dirt works and great batteries
and forts, driving them before us like sheep, when up more of
them would get, as if out of the ground, then our boys would

drive them again till we were fairly worn out; they had nothing to eat since last night and nothing to drink. I myself have not tasted a morsel since two o'clock last night. Well, there we were waiting for reinforcements and expecting M'Dowell and the rest of the army, when whish! they threw open a whole lot of masked batteries on us, and then came down such swarms of horsemen on black horses, all black as you never saw, and slashed our boys over finely. The colonel was hit, and I thought it best to get him off as well as I could, before it was too late; And, my God! when they did take to running they did it first-rate, I can tell you," and so, the officer, who had evidently taken enough to affect his empty stomach and head, chattering about the fight, we trotted on in the moonlight: dipping down into the valleys on the road, which seemed like inky lakes in the shadows of the black trees, then mounting up again along the white road, which shone like a river in the moonlight—the country silent as death, though once as we crossed a small water-course and the noise of the carriage wheels ceased, I called the attention of my companions to a distant sound, as of a great multitude of people mingled with a faint report of cannon. "Do you hear that?" "No, I don't. But it's our chaps, no doubt. They're coming along fine, I can promise you." At last some miles further on we came to a picket, or main guard, on the roadside, who ran forward, crying out "What's the news—anything fresh—are we whipped? —is it a fact?" "Well, gentlemen," exclaimed the Major, reining up for a moment, "we are knocked into a cocked hat— licked to h——l." "Oh, pray don't say that," I exclaimed, "It's not quite so bad, it's only a drawn battle, and the troops will occupy Centreville to-night, and the posts they started from this morning."

A little further on we met a line of commissariat carts, and my excited and rather injudicious military friend appeared to take the greatest pleasure in replying to their anxious queries for news. "We are whipped! Whipped like h——."

At the cross-roads now and then we were perplexed, for no one knew the bearings of Washington, though the stars were bright enough; but good fortune favoured us and kept us straight, and at a deserted little village, with a solitary church on the road-side, I increased my pace, bade good-night and good speed to the officer, and having kept company with two men in a gig for some time, got at length on the guarded road leading towards the capital, and was stopped by the pickets, patrols, and grand rounds, making repeated demands for the last accounts from the field. The houses by the road-side were all closed up and in darkness, I knocked in vain at several for a drink of water, but was answered only by the angry barkings of the watch-dogs from the slave quarters. It was a peculiarity of the road that the people, and soldiers I met, at points several miles apart, always insisted that I was twelve miles from Washington. Up hills, down valleys, with the silent, grim woods for ever by my side, the white roads and the black shadows of men, still I was twelve miles from the Long Bridge, but suddenly I came upon a grand guard under arms, who had quite different ideas, and who said I was only about four miles from the river; they crowded round me. "Well, man, and how is the fight going?" I repeated my tale. "What does he say?" "Oh, begorra, he says we're not bet at all; it's all lies they have been telling us; we're only going back to the ould lines for the greater convaniency of fighting to-morrow again; that's illigant, hooro!"

All by the sides of the old camps the men were standing, lining the road, and I was obliged to evade many a grasp at my bridle by shouting out "Don't stop me; I've important news; it's all well!" and still the good horse, refreshed by the cool night air, went clattering on, till from the top of the road beyond Arlington I caught a sight of the lights of Washington and the white buildings of the Capitol, and of the Executive Mansion, glittering like snow in the moonlight. At the entrance to the Long Bridge the sentry challenged, and asked for the countersign. "I have not got it, but I've a pass from General Scott." An officer advanced from the guard, and on reading the pass permitted me to go on without difficulty. He said, "I have been obliged to let a good many go over to-night before you, Congress men and others. I suppose you did not expect to be coming back so soon. I fear it's a bad business." "Oh, not so bad after all; I expected to have been back to-night before nine o'clock, and crossed over this morning without the countersign." "Well, I guess," said he, "we don't do such quick fighting as that in this country."

As I crossed the Long Bridge there was scarce a sound to dispute the possession of its echoes with my horse's hoofs. The poor beast had carried me nobly and well, and I made up my mind to buy him, as I had no doubt he would answer perfectly to carry me back in a day or two to M'Dowell's army by the time he had organised it for a new attack upon the enemy's position. Little did I conceive the greatness of the defeat, the magnitude of the disasters which it had entailed upon the United States or the interval that would elapse before another army set out from the banks of the Potomac onward to Richmond. Had I sat down that night to write my letter, quite ignorant at the time of the great calamity which had befallen his army, in all probability I would have stated that M'Dowell had received a severe repulse, and had fallen back upon Centreville, that a disgraceful panic and confusion had attended the retreat of a portion of his army, but that the appearance of the reserves would probably prevent the enemy taking any advantage of the disorder; and as I would have merely been able to describe such incidents as fell under my own observation, and would have left the American journals to narrate the actual details, and the despatches of the American Generals the strategical events of the day, I should have led the world at home to believe, as, in fact, I believed myself, that M'Dowell's retrograde movement would be arrested at some point between Centreville and Fairfax Court House.

The letter that I was to write occupied my mind whilst I was crossing the Long Bridge, gazing at the lights reflected in the Potomac from the city. The night had become overcast, and heavy clouds rising up rapidly obscured the moon, forming a most phantastic mass of shapes in the sky.

At the Washington end of the bridge I was challenged again by the men of a whole regiment, who, with piled arms, were halted on the chaussée, smoking, laughing, and singing. "Stranger, have you been to the fight?" "I have been only a little beyond Centreville." But that was quite enough. Soldiers, civilians, and women, who seemed to be out unusually late, crowded round the horse, and again I told my stereotyped story of the unsuccessful attempt to carry the Confederate position, and the retreat to Centreville to await better luck next time. The soldiers alongside me cheered, and those next them took it up till it ran through the whole line, and must have awoke the night owls.

As I passed Willard's hotel a little further on, a clock—I think the only public clock which strikes the hours in Washington—tolled out the hour; and I supposed, from what the sentry told me, though I did not count the strokes, that it was eleven o'clock. All the rooms in the hotel were a blaze of light. The pavement before the door was crowded, and some mounted men and the clattering of sabres on the pavement led me to infer that the escort of the wounded officer had arrived before me. I passed on to the livery-stables, where every one was alive and stirring.

"I'm sure," said the man, "I thought I'd never see you nor the horse back again. The gig and the other gentleman has been back a long time. How did he carry you?"

"Oh, pretty well; what's his price?"

"Well, now that I look at him, and to you, it will be 100 dollars less than I said. I'm in good heart to-night."

"Why so? A number of your horses and carriages have not come back yet, you tell me."

"Oh, well, I'll get paid for them some time or another. Oh, such news! such news!" said he, rubbing his hands. "Twenty thousand of them killed and wounded! May-be they're not having fits in the White House to-night!"

I walked to my lodgings, and just as I turned the key in the door a flash of light made me pause for a moment, in expectation of the report of a gun; for I could not help thinking it quite possible that, somehow or another, the Confederate cavalry would try to beat up the lines, but no sound followed. It must have been lightning. I walked up-stairs, and saw a most welcome supper ready on the table—an enormous piece of cheese, a sausage of unknown components, a knuckle-bone of ham, and a bottle of a very light wine of France; but I would not have exchanged that repast and have waited half an hour for any banquet that Soyer or Careme could have prepared at their best. Then, having pulled off my boots, bathed my head, trimmed candles, and lighted a pipe, I sat down to write. I made some feeble sentences, but the pen went flying about the paper as if the spirits were playing tricks with it. When I screwed up my utmost resolution, the "y's" would still run into long streaks, and the letters combine most curiously, and my eyes closed, and my pen slipped, and just as I was aroused from a nap, and settled into a stern determination to hold my pen straight, I was interrupted by a messenger from Lord Lyons, to inquire whether I had returned and if so, to ask me to go up to the Legation, and get something to eat. I explained, with my thanks, that I was quite safe, and had eaten supper, and learned from the servant that Mr. Warre and his companion had arrived about two hours previously. I resumed my seat once more, haunted by the memory of the Boston mail, which would be closed in a few hours, and I had much to tell, although I had not seen the battle. Again and again I woke up, but at last the greatest conqueror but death overcame me, and with my head on the blotted paper, I fell fast asleep.

## Samuel J. English to his Mother

In a letter home Corporal Samuel English of the 2nd Rhode Island
Volunteers—the regiment Sullivan Ballou served in—described his
part in the battle that would be known in the North as Bull Run and
in the South as Manassas. The Union army lost about 2,900 men
killed, wounded, or missing, the Confederates about 1,900.

——————————

                                    Camp Clark, July 24th/61
Dear Mother                         Washington, D.C.
    I rec'd your letter of the 21st shortly after our return to
camp and take the earliest opportunity of writing. Yes, we have
been & gone and done it. Last Thursday the 16th our brigade
consisting of the two Rhode Island regiments, the New York
71st and the New Hampshire 2nd took up our line of march for
Fairfax Court House. We crossed Long Bridge about 3 o'clock
and continued on for six miles where we bivouacked for the
night. Nothing occurred of importance to disturb our slum-
bers except the passing of troops bound on the same expedition. We commenced our march early in the morning, the 2nd
R.I. regiment taking the lead and acting as skirmishers, Co. A
taking the advance on the right; Co. D acting as flankers; Co.
F acting as rear advance on the right of the column, Co. K acting as advance on the left. Co. C as flankers and Co. G as rear
guard. I cannot state exactly the strength of our forces at the
time, but should judge there were seven or eight thousand, including 1500 cavalry and two Batteries of artillery with two
howitzers belonging to the New York 71st Regt. When within
half a mile of the village of Fairfax, word was sent that the
rebels' battery was directly in our line of march. Our artillery
was immediately ordered to the front and fired three shots into
it, making the sand fly, and showing pretty conclusively that
the birds had flown. All the time this was taking place your

humble servant was skirting around in the woods as a skir-
misher and arrived in the village ahead of the main column. As
our company arrived the streets presented the scene of the
wildest confusion: old negroes running around, some laughing, some crying and some swearing at a fearful rate. The
streets were strewn with the knapsacks, haversacks, canteens,
blankets, shirts and most every article pertaining to camp life.
The houses were deserted and in some places the tables were
set for dinner and coffee warm on the stove. After strolling
around a short time we quartered ourselves in the park of Gen.
Lee and made ourselves as comfortable as circumstances
would permit. The cavalry in the meantime pursuing the retreating rebels and capturing 30 of their men. What particularly pleased me was that the company that lost the mess was
the Palmetto Guards and Brooks Guards of South Carolina,
having lost all of their camp equipage and barely escaped with
their lives. But to continue, the next day our colors started for
Manassas but halted and camped three miles this side of Centreville, waiting for our troops and reinforcements to come up;
the second regiment being somewhat in advance of the main
army; we stay here for three days and Sunday the 21st about 2
o'clock the drums beat the assembly and in ten minutes we
were on our march for Bull Run having heard the enemy were
waiting to receive us, our troops then numbering 25 or 30
thousand which were divided into three columns ours under
Col Hunter taking the right through a thick woods. About
eleven o'clock as our pickets were advancing through the
woods a volley was poured in upon them from behind a fence
thickly covered with brush; the pickets after returning the
shots returned to our regiment and we advanced double quick
time yelling like so many devils. On our arrival into the open
field I saw I should judge three or four thousand rebels retreating for a dense woods, firing as they retreated, while from
another part of the woods a perfect hail storm of bullets,
round shot and shell was poured upon us, tearing through our
ranks and scattering death and confusion everywhere; but with
a yell and a roar we charged upon them driving them again
into the woods with fearful loss. In the mean time our battery
came up to our support and commenced hurling destruction
among the rebels. Next orders were given for us to fall back

and protect our battery as the enemy were charging upon it from another quarter, and then we saw with dismay that the second R.I. regiment were the only troops in the fight; the others having lagged so far behind that we had to stand the fight alone for 30 minutes; 1100 against 7 or 8 thousand. It was afterwards ascertained from a prisoner that the rebels thought we numbered 20 or 30 thousand from the noise made by us while making the charge. While preparing to make our final effort to keep our battery out of their hands, the 1st R.I. regiment then came filing over the fence and poured a volley out to them that drove them under cover again; they were followed by the New York 71st and the New Hampshire 2nd regiments; with 2,000 regulars bringing up the rear who pitched into the "Sechers" most beautifully. Our regiments were then ordered off the field and formed a line for a support to rally on in case the rebels over powered our troops. When the line had formed again I started off for the scene of action to see how the fight was progressing. As I emerged from the woods I saw a bomb shell strike a man in the breast and literally tear him to pieces. I passed the farm house which had been appropriated for a hospital and the groans of the wounded and dying were horrible. I then descended the hill to the woods which had been occupied by the rebels at the place where the Elsworth zouaves made their charge; the bodies of the dead and dying were actually three and four deep, while in the woods where the desperate struggle had taken place between the U.S. Marines and the Louisiana zouaves, the trees were spattered with blood and the ground strewn with dead bodies. The shots flying pretty lively round me I thought best to join my regiment; as I gained the top of the hill I heard the shot and shell of our batteries had given out, not having but 130 shots for each gun during the whole engagement. As we had nothing but infantry to fight against their batteries, the command was given to retreat; our cavalry not being of much use, because the rebels would not come out of the woods. The R.I. regiments, the New York 71st and the New Hampshire 2nd were drawn into a line to cover the retreat, but an officer galloped wildly into the column crying the enemy is upon us, and off they started like a flock of sheep every man for himself and the devil take the hindermost; while the rebels' shot and shell fell like rain among our exhausted troops. As we gained the cover of the woods the stampede became even more frightful, for the baggage wagons and ambulances became entangled with the artillery and rendered the scene even more dreadful than the battle, while the plunging of the horses broke the lines of our infantry and prevented any successful formation out of the question. The rebels being so badly cut up supposed we had gone beyond the woods to form on for a fresh attack and shelled the woods for full two hours, supposing we were there, thus saving the greater part of our forces, for if they had begun an immediate attack, nothing in heaven's name could have saved us. As we neared the bridge the rebels opened a very destructive fire upon us, mowing down our men like grass, and caused even greater confusion than before. Our artillery and baggage wagons became fouled with each other, completely blocking the bridge, while the bomb shells bursting on the bridge made it "rather unhealthy" to be around. As I crossed on my hands and knees, Capt. Smith who was crossing by my side at the same time was struck by a round shot at the same time and completely cut in two. After I crossed I started up the hill as fast as my legs could carry and passed through Centreville and continued on to Fairfax where we arrived about 10 o'clock halting about 15 minutes, then kept on to Washington where we arrived about 2 o'clock Monday noon more dead than alive, having been on our feet 36 hours without a mouthful to eat, and traveled a distance of 60 miles without twenty minutes halt. The last five miles of that march was perfect misery, none of us having scarcely strength to put one foot before the other, but I tell you the cheers we rec'd going through the streets of Washington seemed to put new life into the men for they rallied and marched to our camps and every man dropped on the ground and in one moment the greater part of them were asleep. Our loss is estimated at 1,000, but I think it greater, the rebels loss from three to five thousand.

# Emma Holmes: Diary, July 22–23, 1861

Emma Holmes, the young daughter of a plantation owner, recorded the reaction in Charleston to news of the Confederate victory in Virginia.

---

*July 22*

The telegraph this morning announces a great and glorious victory gained yesterday at Bull's Run after ten hours hard fighting. The enemy were completely routed, with tremendous slaughter; the loss on either side is of course not yet known, but ours is light compared to theirs. They have besides lost the whole of the celebrated Sherman Battery, two or three others, and a quantity of ammunition, baggage, etc. Their whole force amounted to about 80,000 while ours was only 35,000; only our left wing, however, commanded by Genl. Johnson, 15,000 in number against 35,000 of the enemy, were mostly engaged. The centre commanded by the President, who arrived on the field about noon, & the right wing, led by Beauregard, were only partially engaged. The Georgia Regiment commanded by Col. Francis S. Bartow seems to have suffered very severely, the Ogelthorpe Light I. from Savannah especially. Col. Bartow was killed as was also Gen. Barnard Bee and Col. B. F. Johnson of the Hampton Legion. The latter arrived only three hours before the battle and seem to have taken a conspicuous part in it. In Gen. Bee the Confederate Army has lost an officer whose place cannot readily be supplied. He stood so high in his profession that, immediately after his arrival quite late from the distant western frontiers, a captain, he was raised to the rank of Brigadier General; he was one of Carolina's noblest sons, and, though we glory in the victory won by the prowess of our gallant men, tears for the honored dead mingle with our rejoicings. Col. Bartow was

one of the most talented and prominent men in Savannah and
very much beloved; he left Congress to go to Va. with the
O. L. I. as their captain, but was made Col. & was acting
Brigadier Gen. during the battle. Col. Johnson's loss will also
be much felt; he leaves a wife & eight children. A great many
Charlestonians are wounded but only three of Kershaw's R.
which must have been in the right wing. . . . Rumors are, of
course, flying in every direction, none of which are to be relied
on, but Willie Heyward went on tonight to see after some of
his friends, whom he hears are wounded.


*July 23*

The telegraph today only confirms what we heard yesterday
without additional information, as the wires from Manassas to
Richmond were down for some hours. Several gentlemen
went on last night with servants & nurses to attend our
wounded, and societies for their relief are being organized in
the city. The *northern* account of the battle & the dreadful
panic which seized their troops, followed by complete demoralization, is most graphic. They admit that the carnage was
fearful. The "brag" regiment of N.Y., the 69th, was cut to
pieces; the *infamous* Fire Zouaves went into battle 1100 strong
and came out 206. The New Orleans Zouaves were let loose
on them & most amply were the murder of Jackson & the outrages on women avenged on these fiends; 60 pieces of artillery
were taken including Sherman's which was celebrated as Ring-
gold's during the Mexican War. Carlisle's, Griffin's, the West
Point Batteries, & the 8 siege 32-pounder rifle cannon, with
which Scott was marching upon Richmond. The Federal Army
left Washington commanded by Scott in all the pomp & pag-
eantry of the panoply of war—all so grand and impressive in
their own eyes that they did not dream that we would strike a
blow but would lay down our arms in terror. They carried 550
pair of handcuffs & invited immense numbers of ladies to follow and see Beauregard and Lee put into irons, expecting to
march directly on to Richmond. The contrast of the picture
may be imagined—gloom and terror reign in Washington, and
they are multiplying fortifications and reinforcing the city.
    Today, by Col. Anderson's order, a salute was fired of twenty-
one guns, from Forts Moultrie & Sumter, at 12 o'clock, in

honor of the victory, & tomorrow their flags will be placed at half-mast and guns fired hourly from 6:00 A.M. till sunset in honor of the illustrious dead. Preparations are being made to receive the bodies in state; the City Hall is draped in mourning as when Calhoun lay in state, & now his statue gleams intensely white through the funeral hangings surrounding the three biers. I have not yet visited the hall but those who have say the impression is awfully solemn. It seems really the "Chamber of the Dead." The bodies were expected today, but a delay occurred & they may not come till Friday. This afternoon the Ladies Charleston Volunteer Aid Society held a meeting at the S.C. Hall, 192 ladies were there and nearly $1000 collected from subscriptions and donations. Miss Hesse Drayton was appointed Superintendent, & Hesse, Assistant, Emily Rutledge, Secy. & Treasurer, & 12 Managers to cut out the work and distribute it. We are to have monthly as well as quarterly meetings. The ladies all seemed to enjoy seeing their friends as well as the purpose for which they came. Mrs. Geo. Robertson & Mrs. Amy Snowden have got up another called Soldiers' Relief Assn. not only for sending clothes, but comforts & necessaries for the sick and wounded, while the ladies interested in the Y.M.C.A. have got up another & already sent on supplies for the hospitals. All are most liberally supported. . . .

## Elizabeth Blair Lee to Samuel Phillips Lee

Elizabeth Blair Lee related the aftermath of the Union defeat to her husband, who had returned to the United States and was now on blockade duty off Charleston.

———————————

Philadelphia   July 23, 1861

Dear Phil   The most comfortable sensation I have about this move from my home is that it will be a relief to you & that after this you will never have an anxious thought about us— feeling we have the most cautious care taken of us—

News from Washington indicates a revival of energy in Washn   They are sad & the secessionist too are equally busy over their dead & wounded   Mr. Pryor a brother of the M.C. says their loss was awful even before he was taken prisoner early in the day— It must have been or they would have followed up their Victory more vigorously which they had not done at 2 olk today Patterson's men are ready to mob him so one of them told me today They say he is as more of an ally to the South than even Genl Jo Johnston The rumors about our loss is all uncertain for the rolls were not called at midday to day & I saw many of the soldiers straggling in late last night & early the morning— One of them sat in the rain on the stone foundation of brother's front fence— I asked if he was hungry? No! Thirsty? no, sick? no,— wounded no no only mad— we are beat & badly because we have no generals— no competent officers He was almost heart broken from his tone & manner— a very respectable looking man— The Citizens treated them well— fed & sheltered them from the storm— Maryland seems *steady*— All was quiet in Balt— as we came thro it— & I saw 50 flags where I saw ten in June—

I shall still stay here a few days & then go to Bethlehem for Mary Blairs party without Dr Hodge advises me to go to the

Sea shore for these headaches which I think comes from the same cause that makes specs comfortable— & if he advises me to go to the sea— Ill go with Mira & Mr. Dick to the Atlantic City— across New Jersey & just 2 hours from here & until this is settled I'll home here under Aunt Becky's care— Blair & Becky are my best protection in my wanderings— & our dear child is certainly a great comfort— He was joyous today in the Cars with hope of going to see Papa    I do hope you will soon come into port— tho this Rhode Island provision looks like keeping you all out but the rest have had their turn & you ought to have yours-Ever yr devoted Lizzie

Betty & Apo go to New York tomorrow— Betty to Martins & Apo to Connecticut

## Walt Whitman: from Specimen Days

Walt Whitman was at his home in Brooklyn when he learned of Bull
Run from the New York newspapers. In 1863 Whitman moved to
Washington, and it is likely that he spoke there with witnesses to the
aftermath of the battle. He described the return of the defeated army
to the capital in *Specimen Days* (1882), drawing on accounts he had
previously published in "'Tis But Ten Years Since," a series of six articles that appeared in the *New York Weekly Graphic* in 1874, and in
*Memoranda During the War* (1875).

---

### CONTEMPTUOUS FEELING

Even after the bombardment of Sumter, however, the gravity of the revolt, and the power and will of the slave States for
a strong and continued military resistance to national authority, were not at all realized at the North, except by a few. Nine-
tenths of the people of the free States look'd upon the
rebellion, as started in South Carolina, from a feeling one-half
of contempt, and the other half composed of anger and in-
credulity. It was not thought it would be join'd in by Virginia,
North Carolina, or Georgia. A great and cautious national official predicted that it would blow over "in sixty days," and
folks generally believ'd the prediction. I remember talking
about it on a Fulton ferry-boat with the Brooklyn mayor, who
said he only "hoped the Southern fire-eaters would commit
some overt act of resistance, as they would then be at once so
effectually squelch'd, we would never hear of secession again
—but he was afraid they never would have the pluck to really
do anything." I remember, too, that a couple of companies of
the Thirteenth Brooklyn, who rendezvou'd at the city armory,
and started thence as thirty days' men, were all provided with
pieces of rope, conspicuously tied to their musket-barrels, with
which to bring back each man a prisoner from the audacious

South, to be led in a noose, on our men's early and triumphant
return!

### BATTLE OF BULL RUN, JULY, 1861

All this sort of feeling was destin'd to be arrested and re-
vers'd by a terrible shock—the battle of first Bull Run—certainly, as we now know it, one of the most singular fights on
record. (All battles, and their results, are far more matters of
accident than is generally thought; but this was throughout a
casualty, a chance. Each side supposed it had won, till the last
moment. One had, in point of fact, just the same right to be
routed as the other. By a fiction, or series of fictions, the national forces at the last moment exploded in a panic and fled
from the field.) The defeated troops commenced pouring into
Washington over the Long Bridge at daylight on Monday,
22d—day drizzling all through with rain. The Saturday and
Sunday of the battle (20th, 21st,) had been parch'd and hot to
an extreme—the dust, the grime and smoke, in layers, sweated
in, follow'd by other layers again sweated in, absorb'd by those
excited souls—their clothes all saturated with the clay-powder
filling the air—stirr'd up everywhere on the dry roads and
trodden fields by the regiments, swarming wagons, artillery,
&c.—all the men with this coating of murk and sweat and rain,
now recoiling back, pouring over the Long Bridge—a horrible
march of twenty miles, returning to Washington baffled, humiliated, panic-struck. Where are the vaunts, and the proud
boasts with which you went forth? Where are your banners,
and your bands of music, and your ropes to bring back your
prisoners? Well, there isn't a band playing—and there isn't a
flag but clings ashamed and lank to its staff.

The sun rises, but shines not. The men appear, at first sparsely
and shame-faced enough, then thicker, in the streets of Washington—appear in Pennsylvania avenue, and on the steps and
basement entrances. They come along in disorderly mobs, some
in squads, stragglers, companies. Occasionally, a rare regiment,
in perfect order, with its officers (some gaps, dead, the true
braves,) marching in silence, with lowering faces, stern, weary
to sinking, all black and dirty, but every man with his musket,
and stepping alive; but these are the exceptions. Sidewalks of

Pennsylvania avenue, Fourteenth street, &c., crowded, jamm'd with citizens, darkies, clerks, everybody, lookers-on; women in the windows, curious expressions from faces, as those swarms of dirt-cover'd return'd soldiers there (will they never end?) move by; but nothing said, no comments; (half our lookers-on secesh of the most venomous kind—they say nothing; but the devil snickers in their faces.) During the forenoon Washington gets all over motley with these defeated soldiers—queer-looking objects, strange eyes and faces, drench'd (the steady rain drizzles on all day) and fearfully worn, hungry, haggard, blister'd in the feet. Good people (but not over-many of them either,) hurry up something for their grub. They put wash-kettles on the fire, for soup, for coffee. They set tables on the side-walks—wagon-loads of bread are purchas'd, swiftly cut in stout chunks. Here are two aged ladies, beautiful, the first in the city for culture and charm, they stand with store of eating and drink at an improvis'd table of rough plank, and give food, and have the store replenish'd from their house every half-hour all that day; and there in the rain they stand, active, silent, white-hair'd, and give food, though the tears stream down their cheeks, almost without intermission, the whole time. Amid the deep excitement, crowds and motion, and desperate eagerness, it seems strange to see many, very many, of the soldiers sleeping—in the midst of all, sleeping sound. They drop down anywhere, on the steps of houses, up close by the basements or fences, on the sidewalk, aside on some vacant lot, and deeply sleep. A poor seventeen or eighteen year old boy lies there, on the stoop of a grand house; he sleeps so calmly, so profoundly. Some clutch their muskets firmly even in sleep. Some in squads; comrades, brothers, close together—and on them, as they lay, sulkily drips the rain.

As afternoon pass'd, and evening came, the streets, the bar-rooms, knots everywhere, listeners, questioners, terrible yarns, bugaboo, mask'd batteries, our regiment all cut up, &c.—stories and story-tellers, windy, bragging, vain centres of street-crowds. Resolution, manliness, seem to have abandon'd Washington. The principal hotel, Willard's, is full of shoulder-straps—thick, crush'd, creeping with shoulder-straps. (I see them, and must have a word with them. There you are, shoul-der-straps!—but where are your companies? where are your men? Incompetents! never tell me of chances of battle, of getting stray'd, and the like. I think this is your work, this retreat, after all. Sneak, blow, put on airs there in Willard's sumptuous parlors and bar-rooms, or anywhere—no explanation shall save you. Bull Run is your work; had you been half or one-tenth worthy your men, this would never have happen'd.)

Meantime, in Washington, among the great persons and their entourage, a mixture of awful consternation, uncertainty, rage, shame, helplessness, and stupefying disappointment. The worst is not only imminent, but already here. In a few hours— perhaps before the next meal—the secesh generals, with their victorious hordes, will be upon us. The dream of humanity, the vaunted Union we thought so strong, so impregnable—lo! it seems already smash'd like a china plate. One bitter, bitter hour—perhaps proud America will never again know such an hour. She must pack and fly—no time to spare. Those white palaces—the dome-crown'd capitol there on the hill, so stately over the trees—shall they be left—or destroy'd first? For it is certain that the talk among certain of the magnates and officers and clerks and officials everywhere, for twenty-four hours in and around Washington after Bull Run, was loud and undisguised for yielding out and out, and substituting the southern rule, and Lincoln promptly abdicating and departing. If the secesh officers and forces had immediately follow'd, and by a bold Napoleonic movement had enter'd Washington the first day, (or even the second,) they could have had things their own way, and a powerful faction north to back them. One of our returning colonels express'd in public that night, amid a swarm of officers and gentlemen in a crowded room, the opinion that it was useless to fight, that the southerners had made their title clear, and that the best course for the national government to pursue was to desist from any further attempt at stopping them, and admit them again to the lead, on the best terms they were willing to grant. Not a voice was rais'd against this judgment, amid that large crowd of officers and gentlemen. (The fact is, the hour was one of the three or four of those crises we had then and afterward, during the fluctuations of four years, when human eyes appear'd at least just as likely to see the last breath of the Union as to see it continue.)

# Abraham Lincoln:
# Memoranda on Military Policy

On the afternoon of July 21 President Lincoln followed the fighting from the War Department, where he read telegrams sent every fifteen minutes from Fairfax Station, about four miles east of the Bull Run battlefield. Between 4 P.M. and 6 P.M. a series of messages reported that the Confederate lines had been driven back. After the President went out for his evening ride, Secretary of State Seward arrived at the Executive Mansion and told John Nicolay and John Hay: "The battle is lost. The telegraph says that McDowell is in full retreat, and calls on General Scott to save the Capitol." When Lincoln learned of the defeat he went to confer with General Scott, and then spent the night hearing the accounts of senators and congressmen who had gone out to watch the battle. In the week following Bull Run he would write two memoranda on future military actions.

———————————

July 23. 1861.

1   Let the plan for making the Blockade effective be pushed forward with all possible despatch.

2   Let the volunteer forces at Fort-Monroe & vicinity—under Genl. Butler—be constantly drilled, disciplined, and instructed without more for the present.

3.   Let Baltimore be held, as now, with a gentle, but firm, and certain hand.

4   Let the force now under Patterson, or Banks, be strengthened, and made secure in it's possition.

5.   Let the forces in Western Virginia act, till further orders, according to instructions, or orders from Gen. McClellan.

6.   Gen. Fremont push forward his organization, and opperations in the West as rapidly as possible, giving rather special attention to Missouri.

7   Let the forces late before Manassas, except the three months men, be reorganized as rapidly as possible, in their camps here and about Arlington

8.  Let the three months forces, who decline to enter the longer service, be discharged as rapidly as circumstances will permit.

9  Let the new volunteer forces be brought forward as fast as possible; and especially into the camps on the two sides of the river here.

### July 27, 1861

When the foregoing shall have been substantially attended to—

1.  Let Manassas junction, (or some point on one or other of the railroads near it;); and Strasburg, be seized, and permanently held, with an open line from Washington to Manassas; and an open line from Harper's Ferry to Strasburg—the military men to find the way of doing these.

2.  This done, a joint movement from Cairo on Memphis; and from Cincinnati on East Tennessee.

# Mary Chesnut: Diary, July 24, 1861

Mary Chesnut was in Richmond during the battle of Manassas, and witnessed the reaction in the Confederate capital to the victory.

*July 24, 1861.* Here Mr. Chesnut opened my door—and walked in. Of the fullness of the heart the mouth speaketh. I had to ask no questions. He gave me an account of the battle as he saw it (walking up and down my room, occasionally seating himself on a window sill, but too restless to remain still many moments). Told what regiments he was sent to bring up. He took orders to Colonel Jackson—whose regiment stood so stock-still under fire they were called a stone wall. Also, they call Beauregard "Eugene" and Johnston "Marlboro" (s'en va—en guerre). Mr. C rode with Lay's cavalry after the retreating enemy, in the pursuit, they following them until midnight. There then came such a rain—rain such as is only known in semitropical lands.

In the drawing room Colonel Chesnut was the "belle of the ball"—they crowded him so for news. He was the first arrival that they could get at, from the field of battle—handle, so to speak. But the women had to give way to the dignitaries of the land, who were as filled with curiosity as themselves—Mr. Barnwell, Mr. Hunter, the Cobbs, Captain Ingraham, &c&c.

Wilmot DeSaussure says Wilson of Massachusetts, senator U.S.A., came to Manassas en route to Richmond, with his dancing shoes ready for the festive scene which was to celebrate a triumph.

The *Tribune* said: "In a few days" they would have Richmond, Memphis, New Orleans. "They must be taken and at once." For "a few days" maybe now they will modestly substitute "in a few years."

They brought me a Yankee soldier's portfolio from the battle-field. The letters were franked by Senator Harlan. One might shed a few tears over some of his letters. Women—wives and mothers—are the same everywhere.

What a comfort the spelling was. We were willing to admit their universal free school education put their rank and file ahead of us *literarily*. Now, these letters do not attest that fact. The spelling is comically bad.

Not so bad as Wigfall's man, however, who spelt "fi-ar" à la mode de "li-ar."

Mrs. Davis's drawing room last night was brilliant, and she was in great force. Outside a mob collected and called for the president. He did speak. He is an old war-horse—and scents the battlefields from afar. His enthusiasm was contagious. The president took all the credit to himself for the victory—said the wounded roused and shouted for Jeff Davis and the men rallied at the sight of him and rushed on and routed the enemy. The truth is, Jeff Davis was not two miles from the battlefield, but he is greedy for military fame. They called for Colonel Chesnut, and he gave them a capital speech, too. As the public speakers say sometimes, "It was the proudest moment of my life." My life—the woman who writes here, now. I did not hear a great deal of it, for always when anything happens of any moment, my heart beats up in my ears. But the distinguished Carolinians that crowded round me told me how good a speech he made. I was dazed. He gave the glory of the victory to Beauregard and said if the president had not said so much for himself, he would have praised him.

Mrs. McLean was very angry with Joe Davis: he forgot her presence and wished all Yankees were dead.

Somebody said he did remember ladies' presence, for the habit of our men was to call them "Damn Yankees." Mrs. Davis was at her wits' end what to do with Joe Davis, for she is devoted to Mrs. McLean. And when she consults anyone, they only grin, the sentiment being one which meets with almost universal sympathy just now.

There goes the Dead March for some poor soul.

———————

Mrs. Wigfall said when her children were small, she broke them of ever using bad words by washing their mouths with soap and water to cleanse them. Joe Davis is not small, alas! And then somebody told a story—a little girl came running to tell on her brother: "Oh, mama, Charlie is using bad language —curse words."

"What is it?"

"He says 'Damn Yankees' are here prisoners."

"Well, mama, is not that their name? I never hear them called anything else."

---

Today the president told us at dinner that Mr. Chesnut's eulogy of Bartow in the Congress was highly praised. Men liked it. Two eminently satisfactory speeches in twenty-four hours is doing pretty well. And now I would be happy, but this cabinet of ours are in such bitter quarrels among themselves. Everybody abusing everybody.

---

Last night, while those splendid descriptions of the battles were being given to the crowd below, from our windows I said, "Then why do we not go on to Washington?"

"You mean, why did they not. The time has passed—the opportunity is lost." Mr. Barnwell said to me: "Silence. We want to listen to the speaker." And Mr. Hunter smiled compassionately: "Don't ask awkward questions."

---

Mr. C said: "They were lapping round Hampton, and I saw they would flank us. Then that fine fellow Elzey came in view —when I saw it was our flag! At first we thought it was the enemy! And we had our hands full before. They were pushing us hard. Almost at the moment that joyful sight of our flag had relieved my mind. I saw confusion in the enemy's wagon train. Then their panic began."

---

Kirby Smith came down on the turnpike at the very nick of time. Still, the heroes who fought all day and held the Yankees in check deserve credit beyond words. *Or* it would all have been over before the Joe Johnston contingent came. It is another case of the *eleventh-hour* scrape. The eleventh-hour men claim all the credit, and they who bore the heat and brunt and burden of the day do not like that.

---

Mrs. Wigfall busy as a bee, making a flag for her Texians. Louis is colonel of the regiment.

Everybody said at first: "Pshaw! There will be no war." Those who foresaw evil were called "Ravens"—ill foreboders. Now the same sanguine people all cry "the war is over"—the very same who were packing to leave Richmond a few days ago. Many were ready to move on at a moment's warning, when the good news came.

There are such owls everywhere. But to revert to the other kind—the sage and circumspect, those who say very little, but that little shows they think the war barely begun. Mr. Rives and Mr. Seddon have just called. Arnoldus VanderHorst came to see me at the same time. He said there was no great show of victory on our side until two o'clock, but when we began to win, we did it in double-quick time. I mean, of course, the battle last Saturday.

———————

I was talking with Hon. Mr. Clingman and the friendly Brewster—when a U.S. surgeon on parole came to see Mrs. McLean. A terrible Confederate female of ardent patriotism and a very large damp mouth said, "How I would like to scalp that creature."

"A descendant of Pocahontas, evidently," said Brewster, with a faint snigger. "She must mean Mrs. McLean, who has a beautiful head of hair. The man is shorn to the quick—no hair to get a purchase, to tear his scalp off."

Mr. Clingman could not look more disgusted than he always does.

———————

Arnold Harris told Mr. Wigfall the news from Washington last Saturday. For hours the telegrams reported at rapid intervals: "great victory," "defeating them at all points."

About three o'clock the telegrams began to come in on horseback—at least, after two or three o'clock there was a sudden cessation of all news. About nine, bulletins came on foot or on horseback, wounded, weary, draggled, footsore, panic-stricken, spreading in their path on every hand terror and dismay.

That was our opportunity. Wigfall can see nothing to stop

us. And when they explain why we did not go, I understand it all less than ever.

---

Yes, here we will dillydally and Congress orate and generals parade, until they get up an army three times as large as Mc-Dowell's that we have just defeated.

---

Trescot says this victory will be our ruin. It lulls us into a fool's paradise of conceit at our superior valor.

And the shameful farce of their flight will wake every inch of their manhood. It was the very fillip they needed.

There are a quieter sort here who know their Yankees well. They say if the thing begins to pay—government contracts and all that—we will never hear the end of it. At least, until they get their pay out of us. They will not lose money by us. Of that we may be sure. Trust Yankee shrewdness and vim for that.

---

There seems to be a battle raging at Bethel, but no mortal here can be got to think of anything but Manassas.

---

Mrs. McLean says she does not see that it was such a great victory, and if it be so great, how can one defeat hurt a nation like the North. What a villain that woman is.

John Waties fought the whole battle over for me. Now I understand it. Before this, nobody could take time to tell the thing consecutively, rationally, and in order.

Again the crowd came, to get Mr. Davis to speak to them. They wanted to hear all about it again.

Afterward they called for Chesnut of South Carolina—who could not be found. He had retired into Mrs. Preston's room.

---

Mr. Venable said he did not see a braver thing done than the cool performance of a Columbia negro. He brought his master a bucket of ham and rice which he had cooked for him, and he cried, "You must be so tired and hungry, Marster—make haste and eat." This was in the thickest of the fight, under the heaviest of the enemies' guns.

The Federal congressmen were making a picnic of it. Their luggage was all ticketed to Richmond.

"It is a far cry to Lochow"—as the clansmen say.

Cameron has issued a proclamation. They are making ready to come after us on a magnificent scale. They acknowledge us at last—foemen worthy of their steel.

The Lord help us, since England and France won't—or don't. If we could only get a friend outside and open a port.

Mr. Mason came and would march me in state on his arm into Mrs. Davis's drawing room (Maxcy Gregg and Mr. Miles were with me when Mr. Mason and Mr. Seddon called. Mr. Miles and Co. meekly followed). I looked back and wished I was with the unobserved rear guard.

Mr. Mason is a high and mighty Virginian. He brooks no opposition to his will.

They say it is Douglas Ramsay who was killed, and not our friend Wadsworth.

One of these men told me he had seen a Yankee prisoner who asked him what sort of a diggins Richmond was for trade. He was tired of the old concern and would like to take the oath and settle here.

They brought us handcuffs found in the debacle of the Yankee army.

For whom were they? Jeff Davis, no doubt. And the ringleaders.

Tell that to the Marines. We have outgrown the handcuff business on this side of the water.

---

Russell, the Englishman, was in Alexandria. Why did we not follow them there? That's the question.

---

After the little unpleasantness &c&c between Mrs. Davis and Mrs. Wigfall, there was a complete reconciliation, and Mrs. Wigfall in all amity presented Mrs. Davis with the most hideous Chinese monster I ever saw. A Mandarin, I meant to say.

---

All day I was in bed. The night before, sat up too late hearing Mrs. Davis abuse and disabuse Mrs. McLean. Mrs. Joe Johnston and Mrs. McLean have gone to Orange Court House. I am truly glad they did not get to Manassas. Mrs. Davis, Wigfall, &c&c sat with me and told me unutterable stories of the war, but I forget after so much opium. Mr. Chesnut

would not go to bed but sat up and gave me such a scolding.
. . . Jeff Davis offers Mr. Chesnut anything he wants—and is
going to give Mr. Preston a commission. . . .

---

Dr. Gibbes says he was at a country house near Manassas
when a Federal soldier who had lost his way came in, exhausted. He asked for brandy, which the lady of the house
gave him. Upon second thought he declined it. She brought it
to him so promptly, he said he thought it might be poisoned.
His mind was.

She was enraged.

"Sir, I am a Virginia woman. Do you think I could be as
base as that? Here—Bill, Tom, disarm this man. He is our prisoner." The negroes came running, and the man surrendered
without more ado. Another Federal was drinking at the well. A
negro girl said, "You go in and see Missis." The man went in,
and she followed crying triumphantly, "Look here—Missis, I
got a prisoner too!"

They were not ripe for John Brown, you see.

This lady sent in her two prisoners, and Beauregard complimented her on her pluck and patriotism and presence of mind.

---

These negroes were rewarded by their owners. Now if slavery is as disagreeable as we think it, why don't they all march
over the border, where they would be received with open arms?
It amazes me. I am always studying these creatures. They are
to me inscrutable in their ways and past finding out.

Dr. Gibbes says the faces of the dead grow as black as charcoal on the battlefield, and they shine in the sun.

---

Now this horrible vision of the dead on the battlefield
haunts me.

---

Old Ruffin has promised me a John Brown pike—and Dr.
Gibbes a handcuff—for my very own, trophies for future generations—more especially, as they see I do not believe any stories of pikes or handcuffs or a cage for Jeff Davis.

---

Hon. Mr. Hammond is here. Our world collects here—gravitates to Richmond, as it did to Charleston and Montgomery.

---

These young men say the war is doing them good. Hugh Rose, who has a room in this hotel, offered to share it with his father. It was that or the street for the old gentleman—so great is the crowd. They seem to think it an act of superhuman virtue "to have your father in your room." At least they know it was on Hugh Rose's part.

---

Camden DeLeon is sure to lose his place as surgeon general. Dr. Gibbes wants it. Dr. Nott is looked upon by many as a fit person for it. DeLeon is always drunk.

---

Somebody sent me a caricature of Jeff Davis trying to throw sand in John Bull's eyes and stuff wool in his ears.

---

There are so many wonderful tales here about everybody. That strange-looking man Clingman—I thought the first story funny enough. Dancing is a serious business with him. Some young lady spoke to him while he was dancing with her. "Pray withhold all remarks. It puts me out. I cannot do two things at once. If you will talk, I shall have to stop dancing."

Then, when he was presented to Miss Lane, he bowed low and immediately held his nose. Holding it firmly, he said: "Pardon me. I will retire now. I may come back and make a few remarks." He had bowed so low his nose began to bleed, and he had to hold it with all his might.

Fancy Miss Lane's face. The very queen of the proprieties. I cannot imagine her laughing in the wrong place or at the wrong time.

And yet she must have laughed then. Stories of Clingman abound. He cut his throat because he was not as clever as Mr. Calhoun. Made a failure then, too, for it was sewed up—and he lives still.

---

One of Mr. Chesnut's anecdotes of Manassas:
He had in his pocket a small paper of morphine. He put it

there to alleviate pain. Ever since Tom Withers's frightful frac-
tured leg, when the doctors would not give him anodyne
enough to put him to sleep and quiet his agony for a time, at
least, Mr. C always carried morphine powders in his pocket.
These he gave Tom in the night, in spite of the faculty, and the
soothing of that poor boy's anguish he considered one of the
good deeds of his life.

Now a man was howling with pain on the outskirts of the
battlefield—by the way, the only one that made any outcry, at
least, that he heard that day, be their wounds as grievous as
they might. This man proved to be only a case of pain in the
stomach. Him he relieved with the opiate and passed on rapidly
where he was sent. Later in the day he saw a man lying under a
tree who begged for water. He wore the Federal uniform.

As Mr. C carried him the water, he asked him where he was
from. The man refused to answer.

"Poor fellow—you have no cause to care about all that
now—you can't hurt me. And God knows I would not harm
you. What else do you want?"

"Straighten my legs—they are doubled up under me." The
legs were smashed. He gave him some morphine to let him at
least know a few moments of peace. He says: "This is my first
battle. I hope my heart will not grow harder."

———————

Clingman said he credited the statement that they wanted
water, for he remembered the avidity with which he drank
water himself from dirty pools.

Captain Ingraham told Captain Smith Lee: "Don't be so
conceited about your looks. Mrs. Chesnut thinks your brother
Robert a handsomer man than you."

I did not contradict the statement, as Clingman would say,
and yet it was false.

———————

This is how I saw Robert E. Lee for the first time. I had
heard of him, strange to say, in this wise. Though his family,
who then lived at Arlington, called to see me in Washington (I
thought because of Mrs. Chesnut's intimacy with Nelly Custis
in the old Philadelphia days—and Mrs. Lee was Nelly Custis's
niece), I had not known the head of the Lee family. He was
somewhere with the army then.

Last summer at the White Sulphur, Roony Lee and his wife, that sweet little Charlotte Wickham, was there, and I spoke of Roony with great praise.

Mrs. Izard said: "Don't waste your admiration on him. Wait till you see his father. He is the nearest to a perfect man I ever saw." "How?" "Every way—handsome, clever, agreeable, high-bred, &c&c."

Mrs. Stanard came for Mrs. Preston and me, to drive to the camp. She was in an open carriage. A man riding a beautiful horse joined us. He wore a hat with somehow a military look to it. He sat his horse gracefully, and he was so distinguished at all points that I very much regretted not catching the name as Mrs. Stanard gave it to us. He, however, heard ours and bowed as gracefully as he rode, and the few remarks he made to each of us showed he knew all about us.

But Mrs. Stanard was in ecstasies of pleasurable excitement. I felt she had bagged a big fish. Just then they abounded in Richmond. Mrs. Stanard accused him of being ambitious &c. He remonstrated—said his tastes were of the simplest. He "only wanted a Virginia farm—no end of cream and fresh butter—and fried chicken. Not one fried chicken or two—but unlimited fried chicken."

To all this light chat did we seriously incline because the man and horse and everything about him was so fine looking. Perfection—no fault to be found if you hunted for one. As he left us, I said, "Who is it?" eagerly.

"You did not know! Why, it is Robert E. Lee, son of Light Horse Harry Lee, the first man in Virginia"—raising her voice as she enumerated his glories.

All the same, I like Smith Lee better, and I like his looks, too. I know Smith Lee well. Can anybody say they know his brother? I doubt it. He looks so cold and quiet and grand.

---

And so Dr. Moore was made surgeon general. Dr. Gibbes has the sulks.

---

Reading the *Herald*—filled with excuses for their disaster. Excuses don't count. We must accept facts.

It is wonderful. Kirby Smith, our Blücher, who came on the field in the nick of time—as at Waterloo. And now we are as

the British, who do not remember Blücher. It is all Wellington.
So every individual man I see fought and won the battle. From
Kershaw up and down—all the eleventh-hour men won the
battle, turned the tide—the Marylanders. Elzey & Co. one
never hears of—as little as one hears of Blücher in the English
Waterloo stories.

---

Had a painful adventure, in a small way. The poor soul who
was debarred the pleasure of rushing to Mrs. Bartow with
the news of her husband's death—they call her "bad accident
maker to the evening news"—today she came into my room.
Adèle Auzé said, "That woman Cousin Mary calls 'bad
accident' "—and there was a look of consternation—for she was
among us. Mrs. Davis applauded my adroitness: "Is it true your
son has met with a bad accident? We are so sorry to hear it."

"Oh, yes—it is a dreadful wound. He was punched in the
side by the butt end of a musket."

The deep and absorbing interest I evinced in that wound
and the frowns that I gave Adèle when I could turn my head
and Adèle's reckless making of comic faces over her blunder—
it was overheating, at this state of the thermometer.

Letter from Columbia, S.C.

Home

*July 28, 1861*

Many thanks to you, my dear Mrs. C, for your kind letter,
which I have vainly hoped would have been followed by many
more.

Letters from Virginia are like water to the thirsty, fainting
body. We look for tidings with that aching of the heart that
seems almost beyond endurance. Such tidings as we have had!
Exultingly singing and praising God with one voice and the
next moment finding us low at His footstool in weeping and
prayer and deep humility. His mercies abound and we will not
sully the bright glories of the 21st by more than *natural* tears,
in grieving over our brave soldiers. I think every man on that
battlefield *on our side* was a hero. And we must admit that a
*portion* of the "bad cause" fought as bravely as *ours*, but the
heart and principle were wanting, and so God gave us the victory. Our brave and noble men! May the merciful God of

battles shield them every moment. I feel that they may be again in conflict—this very hour! When Beauregard puts the seal of secrecy upon his doings and prohibits all intercourse, I look for some great achievement to follow.

That was a *dear-bought*, but such a grand, victory. It seems incredible.

I think Havelock's great movement in the East the only recorded event that outstrips it. God help and keep our brave soldiers! This opens the way to a request from John Means to you. He begs you will oblige him by discovering the where-abouts of a young soldier, John Means Thompson (a nephew of Gen. Waddy Thompson), who was wounded slightly. He belongs to the Washington Light Infantry, Captain Conner, from Charleston. His friends apprehend increased dangers in his case from a delicate constitution with pulmonary tendencies. If not in Richmond, would you get a line to Mrs. Singleton at her post, or Mrs. Carrington in Charlottesville? The arrangements for our soldiers we do not exactly take in—are they scattered in the different hospitals or principally in Richmond and Charlottesville? Stark Means, belonging to the Sixth Regiment S.C.V. Colonel Winder is in Virginia. His mother is here and says I must beg you and Mrs. Singleton or any and all of our friends to remember *her*, if anything happens to her son. She is here now with her daughter Emma—very, very ill, and we fear her case will end in consumption, if not already that. John is down today just to see his child and will return tomorrow. Their hearts are torn between these only darling ones—God help them. How little all these things make me feel.

Old Scott! I only wish every disaster on that battlefield could be photographed on his heart and brain—stereotyped on his *vision*—that mortification, remorse, and shame might balance in some degree the horrors he has brought on our country.

Please say to Mrs. Preston, too, to bear in mind our boys. Oh! If you could realize all we dread and yet long to hear, I am sure you ladies would write. There is no detail that is not pre-cious to us—nothing from the seat of war that has not its value to our anxious hearts, worn with suspense, and taking "*all*" our brave ones into the circle of love and care.

Tell Mrs. Preston her dear old mother turned out today for

the national thanksgiving. But our ministers were all absent, and she had to go back home without joining in the *public* praise, but God has heard her hosannas and prayers.

Tell Mrs. Preston I am glad to hear "she is such a charming old lady." Mrs. Taylor says the next thing, you will be calling her an old lady! She joins me, as well as my sisters, in much love to you—to Mrs. P—and *any* and *all* of our dear Columbia friends. You do not know how grieved and mortified I feel that South Carolina and Virginia should feel their "identities" at such a time as this. I cannot realize *individual feeling, personal* sensitiveness. Each man is a modicum of his *country*, and must aim to be the best portion without reference to his neighbors. It is a grand and glorious cause and should not be sullied by petty envyings and jealousies and strife.

All friends here are quite well, or as well as we can be. John Means begs to be most 'specially remembered to you.

If Theo was here he would send you a message of thanks for your successful effort in John West's behalf. Tell me of our ladies, their whereabouts and doings. Let us know what we can do for the hospitals.

I was delighted at the appropriation from Congress, consecrated as it was by prayer, fasting, and tears. God bless you all.

Most truly yours,

Mary Stark

Copy of a letter I wrote to Harriet—

July 25

Dear H,

Mrs. Carrington from Charlottesville writes that there is a great deal needed there for the South Carolina wounded. Today Mrs. George Randolph, who is president of the Ladies' Association here, tells me she wants arrowroot and tamarinds, and there are none to be found. Tomorrow I am going the rounds of the hospitals with her.

Whatever you have to send, direct to Mrs. G. Randolph, Franklin St., Richmond. Always send by express. She is the head and distributes to Winchester, Culpeper, &c&c, and every other place where things are needed.

Ask Kate Williams to get us arrowroot from Florida.

I feel somewhat easy in mind, now Mr. C is once more with

the Congress here. But they will try again. It is not all over. We will have a death struggle.

Everyone who comes from Manassas brings a fresh budget of news. We are still finding batteries—at any rate, rifles and muskets. We had eighteen cannons on our side and we captured 63 (pretty good for beginners), mostly rifled cannon.

The negroes come in loaded like mules.

One man brought four overcoats and, when they cheered him, said, "You never mind—I done give the best one to Marster."

There is no end to the stories and talk. Write to Mary Witherspoon to send her things to Mrs. Randolph's care.

Yours, etc.

M. B. C.

---

Kept a copy, in case anything goes wrong. Camden is cranky.

---

A note from Mrs. Randolph:

My dear Mrs. C,

I am much obliged to you for the money sent by the Camden ladies and will hand it to the treasure on Monday. We have received two boxes from South Carolina and sent them to Charlottesville, with other articles purchased here. I am in doubt what it is best to do at this time but will call upon the ladies, if they can be of service at any time. I am as yet sending nothing to Culpeper, expecting orders from the ladies and surgeons there, having told them to call on us when they have need.

I think many comforts were captured. I know 52 barrels of white sugar were taken.

I will see you in a few days and tell you what we are about.

Yours truly,

M. G. Randolph

Franklin St.
July 27

---

Mr. Venable was praising Hugh Garden and Kershaw's regiment generally. This was delightful. They are my friends and neighbors from home. Showed him Miss Mary Stark's letter—

and we agreed with her. At the bottom of our hearts we believe every Confederate soldier to be a hero. Sans peur, sans reproche.

———————

Hope for the best today. Things must be on a pleasanter footing all over the world. Why? Met the president in the corridor. He took me by both hands. "Have you breakfasted? Come in and breakfast with me?"

Alas, I had had my breakfast. And he said, laughing at his own French, "J'en suis fâché—de tout mon coeur."

———————

When he jokes it is a good sign. "Moi! malheureux! Or is it 'que je suis malheureux?' " he said.

———————

At the public dining room, where I had taken my breakfast with Mr. Chesnut, Mrs. Davis came to him while we were at table. She said she had been to our rooms. She wanted Wigfall hunted up. Mr. Davis thought Chesnut would be apt to know his whereabouts. I ran to Mrs. Wigfall's room, who tells me she was sure he could be found with his regiment in camp. But Mr. C had not to go to the camp, for Wigfall came to his wife's room while I was there. Mr. Davis and Wigfall would be friends, if—if—

———————

We have sent the captured white sugar to Charlottesville hospital.

The Northern papers say we hung and quartered a Zouave —cut him in 4 pieces—and that we tie prisoners to a tree and bayonet them. In other words, we are savages. It ought to teach us not to credit what our papers say of them. It is so absurd an imagination of evil.

We are absolutely treating their prisoners as well as our own men. It is complained of here. I am going to the hospitals here for the enemy's sick and wounded to see for myself.

Mr. C is devoted to Mrs. Long and Mrs. McLean. They do not seem to take his compliments to Sumner l'oncle, or cousin—I do not know which he is—in bad part.

Trescot says Keitt, Boyce, Hammond, and many others hate Jeff Davis. He says disintegration has already begun. Sat up until twelve—he abusing Davis and Mrs. Davis. . . .

Like Martin Luther, he had a right to protest and free himself from the thralldom of Roman Catholic church, but when everybody began to protest against Luther—as it seemed good to them—freely exercising their right of private interpretation—!

Seceding can go on indefinitely with the dissatisfied seceders.

Why did we not follow the flying foe across the Potomac? That is the question of the hour in the drawing room—those of us who are not contending as to "who took Ricketts's Battery?" Allen Green—for one—took it. Allen told us that finding a portmanteau with nice clean shirts, he was so hot and dusty he stepped behind a tree and put on a clean Yankee shirt. And was more comfortable.

---

I was made to do an awfully rude thing. Trescot wanted to see Mr. C on particular business. I left him on the stairs, telling him to wait for me there, I would be back in an instant.

Mr. C listened until I had finished my story—then locked the door and put the key in his pocket. Said I should not be running up and down stairs on Trescot's errands. Today saw Trescot. He waited on the stairs an hour, he said. He was very angry, you may be sure.

---

The *Tribune* soothes the Yankee self-conceit, which has received a shock—the national vanity, you know—by saying we had 100,000 men on the field at Manassas. We had about 15,000 effective men in all.

And then the *Tribune* tries to inflame and envenom them against us by telling lies as to our treatment of prisoners.

They say when they come against us next, it will be in overwhelming force.

---

Lord Lyons, who is not our friend, says to them gravely, "Now, perhaps we may be allowed to call them belligerents."

I long to see Russell's letter to the *Times* about Bulls Run and Manassas. It will be rich and rare.

In Washington it is crimination and recrimination. Well—let them abuse one another to their hearts' content.

Mr. Chesnut met his old flame Miss Lizzie Dallas, now Mrs. Tucker. Found her, he *said*, *old* but very agreeable. Did not mention it to me for several days.

# Crittenden-Johnson Resolutions, July 22–25, 1861

These resolutions were introduced in the House of Representatives by John J. Crittenden of Kentucky, who had been elected to Congress in June after completing his Senate term in March 1861, and in the Senate by Andrew Johnson of Tennessee, a unionist who had kept his seat after his state seceded. They were adopted by the House on July 22 and by the Senate on July 25.

---

*Resolved by the House of Representatives of the Congress of the United States*, That the present deplorable civil war has been forced upon the country by the disunionists of the southern States, now in arms against the constitutional Government, and in arms around the capital; that in this national emergency, Congress, banishing all feelings of mere passion or resentment, will recollect only its duty to the whole country; that this war is not waged on their part in any spirit of oppression, or for any purpose of conquest or subjugation, or purpose of overthrowing or interfering with the rights or established institutions of those States, but to defend and maintain the *supremacy* of the Constitution, and to preserve the Union with all the dignity, equality, and rights of the several States unimpaired; and that as soon as these objects are accomplished the war ought to cease.

---

*Resolved*, That the present deplorable civil war has been forced upon the country by the disunionists of the southern States now in revolt against the constitutional Government and in arms around the capital; that in this national emergency Congress, banishing all feeling of mere passion or resentment, will recollect only its duty to the whole country; that this war is not prosecuted upon our part in any spirit of oppression, nor for any purpose of conquest or subjugation, nor for the purpose of overthrowing or interfering with the rights or established institutions of those States, but to defend and maintain the supremacy of the Constitution and all laws made in pursuance thereof, and to preserve the Union, with all the dignity, equality, and rights of the several States unimpaired; that as soon as these objects are accomplished the war ought to cease.

# George B. McClellan to
# Mary Ellen McClellan

An 1846 graduate of West Point who served in Mexico before resigning from the army as a captain in 1857, George B. McClellan was the president of the eastern division of the Ohio and Mississippi Railroad when the war began. Commissioned as a major general in May 1861, McClellan commanded the successful Union offensive in western Virginia in early July, and he was summoned to Washington the day after Bull Run to take command of the defeated army. The texts of the letters McClellan wrote to his wife printed in this volume are taken from partial copies he made in the 1870s while assembling material for his memoirs; the original letters are not known to have survived.

─────────────

July 27/61 Washington D.C. Saturday

I have been assigned to the command of a Division—composed of Depts of N.E. Va (that under McDowell) & that of Washington (now under Mansfield)—neither of them like it much—especially Mansfield, but I think they must ere long become accustomed to it, as there is no help for it. . . .

I find myself in a new & strange position here—Presdt, Cabinet, Genl Scott & all deferring to me—by some strange operation of magic I seem to have become *the* power of the land. I almost think that were I to win some small success now I could become Dictator or anything else that might please me—but nothing of that kind would please me—*therefore* I *won't* be Dictator. Admirable self denial! I see already the main causes of our recent failure—I am *sure* that I can remedy these & am confident that I can lead these armies of men to victory once more. I start tomorrow very early on a tour through the lines on the other side of the river—it will occupy me all day long & a rather fatiguing ride it will be—but I will be able to make up my mind as to the state of things. Refused invitations to dine today from Genl Scott & four Secy's—had too many things to attend to. . . .

I will endeavor to enclose with this the "thanks of Congress" which please preserve. I feel very proud of it. Genl Scott objected to it on the ground that it ought to be accompanied by a gold medal. I cheerfully acquiesce in the Thanks by themselves, hoping to win the medal by some other action, & the sword by some other fait d'éclat.

# William T. Sherman to
# Ellen Ewing Sherman

Sherman had been commissioned as the colonel of the new 13th U.S. Infantry on May 14 and was given command of the Third Brigade, First Division in June 30. He led his brigade at Bull Run and later wrote to his wife Ellen from Arlington, Virginia, about his first experience of combat.

———————

Fort Corcoran July 28,
Saturday—

Dearest Ellen,

I have already written to you since my return from the Unfortunate defeat at Bulls Run—I had previously conveyed to you the doubts that oppressed my mind on the Score of discipline. Four large columns of poorly disciplined militia left this place—the Long bridge and Alexandria—all concentrating at a place called Centreville 27 miles from Washington. We were the first column to reach Centreville the Enemy abandoning all defenses en route. The first day of our arrival our Commander Genl. Tyler advanced on Bulls Run, about 2 1/2 miles distant, and against orders engaged their Batteries. He sent back to Centreville and I advanced with our Brigade, where we lay for half an hour, amidst descending shots killing a few of our men—The Batteries were full a mile distant and I confess I, nor any person in my Brigade saw an enemy.

Towards evening we returned to Centreville.

That occurred on Thursday. We lay in camp till Saturday night by which the whole army was assembled in and about Centreville. We got orders for march at 2 1/2 Sunday morning. Our column of 3 Brigades—Schenck, Sherman & Keyes—to move straight along a Road to Bulls Run—another of about 10,000 men to make a circuit by the Right (Hunters) and come upon the enemy in front of us—Heintzelmans column of about similar strength also to make a wide circuit to sustain Hunter—We took the road first and about 6 A.M. came in sight of Bull Run—we saw in the grey light of morning men moving about—but no signs of batteries: I rode well down to the Stone Bridge which crosses the Stream, saw plenty of trees cut down—some brush huts such as soldiers use on picket Guard, but none of the Evidences of Strong fortification we had been led to believe. Our business was simply to threaten, and give time for Hunter & Heintzelman to make their circuit. We arranged our troops to this end. Schenck to the left of the Road, & I to the right—Keyes behind in reserve. We had with us two six gun batteries, and a 30 pd. Gun—This was fired several times, but no answer—we shifted positions several times, firing wherever we had reason to suppose there were any troops. About 10 or 11 o.c. we saw the clouds of dust in the direction of Hunters approach. Saw one or more Regiments of the Enemy leave their cover, and move in that direction—soon the firing of musketry, and guns showing the engagement had commenced—early in the morning I saw a flag flying behind some trees. Some of the Soldiers seeing it Called out Colonel, there's a flag—a flag of truce—a man in the Field with his dog & gun—called out—No it is no flag of truce, but a flag of defiance—I was at the time studying the Ground and paid no attention to him—about 9 oclock I was well down to the River—with some skirmishes and observed two men on horseback ride along a hill, descend, cross the stream and ride out towards us—he had a gun in his hand which he waved over his head, and called out to us, You D——d black abolitionists, come on &c.—I permitted some of the men to fire on him—but no damage was done he remained some time thus waiting the action which had begun on the other side of Bulls Run—we could See nothing, but heard the firing and could judge that Hunters column steadily advanced: about 2 P.M. they came to a stand, the firing was severe and stationary—Gen. Tyler rode up to me and remarked that he might have to Send the N.Y. 69th to the relief of Hunter—a short while after he came up and ordered me with my whole Brigade, some 3400 men to cross over to Hunter. I ordered the movement, led off—found a place where the men could cross, but the Battery could not follow. We crossed the stream, and ascended the Bluff Bank, moving slowly to permit the Ranks to close up—When about half a mile back from the Stream I saw the parties in the fight, and the first danger was that we might be mistaken for Secessionists & fired on—One of my Regiments had on the grey uniform of the Virginia troops—We first fired on some retreating Secessionists, our Lt. Col. Haggerty was killed, and my bugler by my side had his horse shot dead—I moved on and Joined Hunters column. They had had a pretty severe fight—Hunter was wounded, and the unexpected arrival of my brigade seemed a great relief to all. I joined them on a high field with a house—and as we effected the junction the secessionists took to the woods and were *seemingly* retreating and Gen. McDowell who had accompanied Hunter's column ordered me to join in the pursuit—I will not attempt to describe you the scene—their Batteries were on all the high hills overlooking the ground which we had to cross, and they fired with great vigor—our horse batteries pursued from point to point returning the fire, whilst we moved on, with shot shells, and cannister over and all round us. I kept to my horse and head of the Brigade, and moving slowly, came upon their heavy masses of men, behind all kinds of obstacles. They knew the ground perfectly, and at every turn we found new ground, over which they poured their fire. At last we came to a stand, and with my Regiments in succession we crossed a Ridge and were exposed to a very heavy fire, first one Regiment & then another and another were forced back—not by the bayonet but by a musketry & rifle fire, which it seemed impossible to push our men through. After an hour of close contest our men began to fall into confusion. 111 had been killed some 250 wounded and the Soldiers began to fall back in disorder—My horse was shot through the foreleg—my knee was cut round by a ball, and another had hit my Coat collar and did not penetrate an aid Lt. Bagley was missing, and spite of all exertions the confusion increased, and the men would not reform—Similar confusion had already occurred among other Regiments & I saw we were gone. Had they kept their Ranks we were the gainers up to that point—only our field Batteries exposed had been severely cut up, by theirs partially covered. Then for the first time I saw the Carnage of battle—men lying in every conceivable shape, and mangled in a horrible way—but this did not make a particle of impression on me—but horses running about riderless with blood streaming from their nostrils—lying on the ground hitched to guns, gnawing their sides in death— I sat on my horse on the ground where Ricketts Battery had been shattered to fragments, and saw the havoc done. I kept my Regiments under cover as much as possible, till the last moment, when it became necessary to cross boldly a Ridge and attack the enemy by that time gathered in great strength behind all sorts of cover—The Volunteers up to that time had done well, but they were repulsed regiment by Regiment, and I do think it was impossible to stand long in that fire. I did not find fault with them but they fell into disorder—an incessant clamor of tongues, one saying that they were not properly supported, another that they could not tell friend from foe—but I observed the gradual retreat going on and did all I could to stop it. At last it became manifest we were falling back, and as soon as I perceived it, I gave it direction by the way we came, and thus we fell back to Centreville some four miles—we had with our Brigade no wagons, they had not crossed the River. At Centreville came pouring in the confused masses of men, without order or system. Here I supposed we should assemble in some order the confused masses and try to Stem the tide— Indeed I saw but little evidence of being pursued, though once or twice their cavalry interposed themselves between us and our Rear. I had read of retreats before—have seen the noise and confusion of crowds of men at fires and Shipwrecks but nothing like this. It was as disgraceful as words can portray, but I doubt if volunteers from any quarter could do better. Each private thinks for himself—If he wants to go for water, he asks leave of no one. If he thinks right he takes the oats & corn, and even burns the house of his enemy. As we could not prevent these disorders on the way out—I always feared the result—for everywhere we found the People against us—no curse could be greater than invasion by a Volunteer Army. No goths or vandals ever had less respect for the lives & property of friends and foes, and henceforth we ought never to hope for any friends in Virginia—McDowell & all the Generals tried their best to stop these disorders, but for us to say we commanded that army is no such thing—they did as they pleased. Democracy has worked out one result, and the next step is to be seen—Beauregard & Johnston were enabled to effect a Junction, by the failure of Patterson to press the latter, and they had such accurate accounts of our numbers & movements that they had all the men they wanted—We had never more than 18,000 engaged, though Some 10 or 12,000 were within a few miles. After our Retreat here, I did my best to stop the flying masses, and partially succeeded, so that we once more present a front: but Beauregard has committed a sad mistake in not pursuing us promptly. Had he done so, he could have stampeded us again, and gone into Washington. As it is I suppose their plan is to produce Riot in Baltimore, cross over above Leesburg, and come upon Washington through Maryland. Our Rulers think more of who shall get office, than who can save the Country. No body—no one man can save the country. The difficulty is with the masses—our men are not good Soldiers—They brag, but dont perform—complain sadly if they dont get everything they want—and a march of a few miles uses them up. It will take a long time to overcome these things, and what is in store for us in the future I know not. I propose trying to defend this place if Beauregard approaches Washington by this Route, but he has now deferred it Some days and I rather think he will give it up.

The newspapers will tell ten thousand things none of which are true. I have had no time to read them, but I know no one now has the moral courage to tell the truth. Public opinion is a more terrible tyrant than Napoleon—My own hope is now in the Regulars, and if I can escape this Volunteer command I will do so, and stick by my Regular Regiment. Gen. McClellan arrived today with Van Vliet—Stoneman, Benham—Biddle—and many others of my acquaintance. Affecy. &c.

W. T. Sherman

July 28, 1861

# Horace Greeley to Abraham Lincoln

Beginning on June 26, Horace Greeley ran a daily "On to Richmond!" editorial in the New York *Tribune*, calling for the capture of the city before the opening on July 20 of the next session of the Confederate Congress. In the aftermath of Bull Run, Greeley sent this letter to President Lincoln. There is no record that Lincoln ever replied to it, but in April 1864 he would retrieve the letter and show it to his secretaries John Hay and John G. Nicolay. Hay, who called the letter "the most insane specimen of pusillanimity that I have ever read," wrote in his diary that when Nicolay suggested Greeley's rival James Bennett of the New York *Herald* would willingly pay $10,000 for a copy, Lincoln replied: "I need $10,000 very much but he could not have it for many times that."

---

New York, Monday, July 29, 1861.
Midnight.

Dear Sir:

This is my seventh sleepless night—yours too, doubtless—yet I think I shall not die, because I have no right to die. I must struggle to live, however, bitterly. But to business.

You are not considered a great man, and I am a hopelessly broken one. You are now undergoing a terrible ordeal, and God has thrown the gravest responsibility upon you. Do not fear to meet them.

Can the Rebels be beaten after all that has occurred, and in view of the actual state of feeling caused by our late awful disaster? If they can—and it is your business to ascertain and decide—write me that such is your judgment, so that I may know and do my duty.

And if they *cannot* be beaten—if our recent disaster is fatal—do not fear to sacrifice yourself to your country. If the Rebels are not to be beaten—if that is your judgment in view of all the light you can get—then every drop of blood henceforth shed in this quarrel will be wantonly, wickedly shed, and the guilt will rest heavily on the soul of every promoter of the crime. I pray you to decide quickly, and let me know my duty.

If the Union is irrevocably gone, an Armistice for thirty, sixty, ninety, 120 days—better still, for a year—ought at once to be proposed with a view to a peaceful adjustment. Then Congress should call a National convention to meet at the earliest possible day. And there should be an immediate and mutual exchange or release of prisoners and a disbandment of forces.

I do not consider myself at present a judge of any thing but the public sentiment. That seems to me every where gathering and deepening against a prosecution of the war. The gloom in this city is funereal for our dead at Bull Run were many, and they lie unburied yet. On every brow sits sullen, scowling, black despair.

It would be easy to have Mr. Crittenden move any proposition that ought to be adopted, or to have it come from any proper quarter. The first point is to ascertain what is best that can be done—which is the measure of our duty—and do that very thing at the earliest moment.

This letter is written in the strictest confidence, and is for your eye alone. But you are at liberty to say to members of your Cabinet that you *know* I will second any move you may see fit to make. But do nothing timidly nor by halves.

Send me word what to do. I will live till I can hear it at all events. If it is best for the country and for mankind that we make peace with the Rebels at once and on their own terms, do not shrink even from that. But bear in mind the greatest truth—"Whoso would lose his life for my sake shall save it," do the thing that is the highest right, and tell me how I am to second you.

> Yours, in the depths of bitterness,
> Horace Greeley

# George B. McClellan:
# Memorandum for the President

In response to a presidential request, McClellan offered his strategy for prosecuting the war, including recommendations for operations far outside the area of his command.

---

Memorandum for the Consideration
of His Excellency the President,
submitted at his request.

The object of the present war differs from those in which nations are usually engaged, mainly in this; that the purpose of ordinary war is to conquer a peace and make a treaty on advantageous terms; in this contest it has become necessary to crush a population sufficiently numerous, intelligent and warlike to constitute a nation; we have not only to defeat their armed and organized forces in the field but to display such an overwhelming strength, as will convince all our antagonists, especially those of the governing aristocratic class, of the utter impossibility of resistance. Our late reverses make this course imperative; had we been successful in the recent battle it is possible that we might have been spared the labor and expense of a great effort; now we have no alternative; their success will enable the political leaders of the rebels to convince the mass of their people that we are inferior to them in force and courage, and to command all their resources. The contest began with a class; now it is with a people. Our military success can alone restore the former issue. By thoroughly defeating their armies, taking their strong places, and pursuing a rigidly protective policy as to private property and unarmed persons, and a lenient course as to common soldiers, we may well hope for the permanent restoration of peaceful Union; but in the first instance the authority of the Government must be supported by overwhelming physical force. Our foreign relations and financial credit also imperatively demand that the military action of the Government should be prompt and irresistible.

The rebels have chosen Virginia as their battle-field—and it seems proper for us to make the first great struggle there; but while thus directing our main efforts, it is necessary to diminish the resistance there offered us, by movements on other points, both by land and water. Without entering at present into details, I would advise that a strong movement be made on the Mississippi, and that the rebels be driven out of Missouri. As soon as it becomes perfectly clear that Kentucky is cordially united with us, I would advise a movement through that state into Eastern Tennessee, for the purpose of assisting the Union men of that region, and of seizing the Railroads leading from Memphis to the East. The possession of those roads by us, in connection with the movement on the Mississippi, would go far towards determining the evacuation of Virginia by the rebels. In the mean time all the passes into Western Virginia from the East should be securely guarded; but I would make no movement from that quarter towards Richmond unless the political condition of Kentucky renders it impossible or inexpedient for us to make the movement upon Eastern Tennessee through that state; every effort should however be made to organize, equip, and arm as many troops as possible in Western Virginia, in order to render the Ohio and Indiana regiments available for other operations.

At as early a day as practicable it would be well to protect and reopen the Baltimore & Ohio Railroad. Baltimore & Fort Monroe should be occupied by *garrisons* sufficient to retain them in our possession.

The importance of Harper's Ferry and the line of the Potomac in the direction of Leesburg will be very materially diminished as soon as our force in this vicinity becomes organized, strong and efficient; because no capable general will cross the river north of this city, when we have a strong army here ready to cut off his retreat.

To revert to the West. It is probable that no very large additions to the troops now in Missouri will be necessary to secure that state. I presume that the force required for the movement down the Mississippi will be determined by its commander and the President.

If Kentucky assumes the right position, not more than 20,000 troops will be needed, together with those that can be raised in that state and Eastern Tennessee, to secure the latter region and its railroads; as well as ultimately to occupy Nashville. The Western Virginia troops with not more than from 5 to 10,000 from Ohio and Indiana should under proper management, suffice for its protection. When we have reorganized our main army here, 10,000 men ought to be enough to protect the Balt. & Ohio R.R. and the Potomac—5000 will *garrison* Baltimore—3000 Fort Monroe; and not more than 20,000 will be necessary, at the utmost, for the defence of Washington.

For the main Army of Operations I urge the following composition.

| | | |
|---|---|---|
| 250 | Regt's Infantry—say | 225,000 men |
| 100 | Field Batteries—600 guns | 15,000 " |
| 28 | Regts. Cavalry | 25,500 " |
| 5 | " Engineer troops | 7,500 " |
| | Total | 273,000 " |

This force must be supplied with the necessary engineer and ponton trains, and with transportation for everything save tents. Its general line of operations should be directed that water transportation can be availed of from point to point, by means of the ocean and the rivers emptying into it.

An essential feature of the plan of operations will be the employment of a strong naval force, to protect the movement of a fleet of transports, intended to convoy a considerable body of troops from point to point of the enemy's seacoast; thus either creating diversions and rendering it necessary for them to detach largely from their main body in order to protect such of their cities as may be threatened; or else landing and forming establishments on their coast at any favorable places that opportunity might offer. This naval force should also cooperate with the main army in its efforts to seize the important seaboard towns of the rebels.

It cannot be ignored that the construction of railroads has introduced a new and very important element into war, by the great facilities thus given for concentrating at particular positions large masses of troops from remote sections, and by creating new strategic points and lines of operations. It is intended to overcome this difficulty by the partial operations suggested, and such others as the particular case may require; we must endeavor to seize places on the railways in the rear of the enemy's points of concentration; and we must threaten their seaboard cities in order that each state may be forced by the necessity of its own defence to diminish its contingent to the Confederate Army.

The proposed movement down the Mississippi will produce important results in this connection. That advance and the progress of the main army at the East will materially assist each other by diminishing the resistance to be encountered by each. The tendency of the Mississippi movement upon all questions connected with cotton are too well understood by the President and Cabinet to need any illustration from me.

There is another independent movement which has often been suggested and which has always recommended itself to my judgment. I refer to a movement from Kansas and Nebraska through the Indian Territory upon Red river and Western Texas, for the purpose of protecting and developing the latent Union and free state sentiment well known to predominate in Western Texas, and which like a similar sentiment in Western Virginia, will, if protected, ultimately organize that section into a free state. How far it will be possible to support this movement by an advance through New Mexico from California is a matter which I have not sufficiently examined to be able to express a decided opinion; if at all practicable, it is eminently desirable as bringing into play the resources and warlike qualities of the Pacific States, as well as identifying them with our cause and cementing the bond of Union between them and the General Government. If it is not departing too far from my province I will venture to suggest the policy of an intimate alliance and cordial understanding with Mexico; their sympathies and interests are with us; their antipathies exclusively against our enemies and their institutions. I think it would not be difficult to obtain from the Mexican Government the right to use, at least during the present contest, the road from Guaymas to New Mexico; this concession would very materially reduce the obstacles of the column moving from the Pacific; a similar permission to use their territory for the passage of troops between the Panuco and the Rio Grande would enable us to throw a column by a good road from Tampico or some of the small harbors north of it upon and across the Rio Grande into the country of our friends, and without risk, and scarcely firing a shot. To what extent if any it would be desirable to take into service, and employ Mexican soldiers is a question entirely political, on which I do not venture to offer any opinion.

The force I have recommended is large—the expense is great. It is possible that a smaller force might accomplish the object in view, but I understand it to be the purpose of this great Nation to reestablish the power of the Government, and to restore peace to its citizens, in the shortest possible time. The question to be decided is simply this; shall we crush the rebellion at one blow, terminate the war in one campaign, or shall we leave it as a legacy for our descendants? When the extent of the possible line of operations is considered, the force asked for, for the main army under my command, cannot be regarded as unduly large. Every mile we advance carries us further from our base of operations and renders detachments necessary to cover our communications; while the enemy will be constantly concentrating as he falls back. I propose with the force which I have requested, not only to drive the enemy out of Virginia and occupy Richmond, but to occupy Charleston, Savannah, Montgomery, Pensacola, Mobile, and New Orleans; in other words to move into the heart of the enemy's country, and crush out this rebellion in its very heart. By seizing and repairing the railroads as we advance, the difficulties of transportation will be materially diminished.

It is perhaps unnecessary to state that in addition to the forces named in this memorandum strong reserves should be formed, ready to supply any losses that may occur. In conclusion, I would submit that the exigencies of the treasury may be lessened by making only partial payments to our troops when in the enemy's country and by giving the obligations of the United States for such supplies as may there be obtainable.

Geo B McClellan<br>Maj Genl USA

Washington D.C. Aug 2 1861

# Confiscation Act, August 6, 1861

Two weeks after declaring in the Crittenden-Johnson resolutions that it had no intention of "overthrowing or interfering" with slavery in the Southern states, Congress passed the Confiscation Act, authorizing the seizure of slaves being used to militarily aid the rebellion. The act gave legislative endorsement to the "contraband" policy originated at Fort Monroe in May by General Benjamin Butler.

---

### Chap. LX—An Act to confiscate Property used for Insurrectionary Purposes.

*Be it enacted by the Senate and House of Representatives of the United States of America in Congress assembled*, That if, during the present or any future insurrection against the Government of the United States, after the President of the United States shall have declared, by proclamation, that the laws of the United States are opposed, and the execution thereof obstructed, by combinations too powerful to be suppressed by the ordinary course of judical proceedings, or by the power vested in the marshals by law, any person or persons, his, her, or their agent, attorney, or employé, shall purchase or acquire, sell or give, any property of whatsoever kind or description, with intent to use or employ the same, or suffer the same to be used or employed, in aiding, abetting, or promoting such insurrection or resistance to the laws, or any person or persons engaged therein; or if any person or persons, being the owner or owners of any such property, shall knowingly use or employ, or consent to the use or employment of the same as aforesaid, all such property is hereby declared to be lawful subject of prize and capture wherever found; and it shall be the duty of the President of the United States to cause the same to be seized, confiscated, and condemned.

Sec. 2. *And be it further enacted*, That such prizes and capture shall be condemned in the district or circuit court of the

United States having jurisdiction of the amount, or in admiralty in any district in which the same may be seized, or into which they may be taken and proceedings first instituted.

SEC. 3. *And be it further enacted*, That the Attorney General, or any district attorney of the United States in which said property may at the time be, may institute the proceedings of condemnation, and in such case they shall be wholly for the benefit of the United States; or any person may file an information with such attorney, in which case the proceedings shall be for the use of such informer and the United States in equal parts.

SEC. 4. *And be it further enacted*, That whenever hereafter, during the present insurrection against the Government of the United States, any person claimed to be held to labor or service under the law of any State, shall be required or permitted by the person to whom such labor or service is claimed to be due, or by the lawful agent of such person, to take up arms against the United States, or shall be required or permitted by the person to whom such labor or service is claimed to be due, or his lawful agent, to work or to be employed in or upon any fort, navy-yard, dock, armory, ship, intrenchment, or in any military or naval service whatsoever, against the Government and lawful authority of the United States, then, and in every such case, the person to whom such labor or service is claimed to be due shall forfeit his claim to such labor, any law of the State or of the United States to the contrary notwithstanding. And whenever thereafter the person claiming such labor or service shall seek to enforce his claim, it shall be a full and sufficient answer to such claim that the person whose service or labor is claimed had been employed in hostile service against the Government of the United States, contrary to the provisions of this act.

APPROVED, August 6, 1861.

# George B. McClellan to
# Mary Ellen McClellan

General McClellan expressed his increasing frustration with General Scott and President Lincoln in a series of letters to his wife. The "'pronunciamento'" McClellan refers to in the first letter was a memorandum he sent to Lincoln and Scott on August 8, warning that Washington was in "*imminent danger*" of being attacked by "at least 100,000 men"; at the time the Confederates had about 40,000 men in northern Virginia.

———————

Aug 8

. . . Rose early today (having retired at 3 am) & was pestered to death with Senators etc & a row with Genl Scott until about 4 o'clock, then crossed the river & rode beyond & along the line of pickets for some distance—came back & had a long interview with Seward about my "pronunciamento" against Genl Scott's policy. . . .

How does he think that I can save this country when stopped by Genl Scott—I do not know whether he is a *dotard* or a *traitor!* I can't tell which. He *cannot* or *will* not comprehend the condition in which we are placed & is entirely unequal to the emergency. If he cannot be taken out of my path I will not retain my position, but will resign & let the admn take care of itself. I have hardly slept one moment for the last three nights, knowing well that the enemy intend some movement & fully recognizing our own weakness. If Beauregard does not attack tonight I shall look upon it as a dispensation of Providence—he *ought* to do it. Every day strengthens me—I am leaving nothing undone to increase our force—but that confounded old Genl always comes in the way—he is a perfect imbecile. He understands nothing, appreciates nothing & is ever in my way.

Washington Aug 9 1861 1 am.

I have had a busy day—started from here at 7 in the morning & was in the saddle until about 9 this evening—rode over the advanced positions on the other side of the river, was soundly drenched in a hard rain & have been busy ever since my return. Things are improving daily—I received 3 new rgts today—fitted out one new battery yesterday, another today—two tomorrow—about five day after. Within four days I hope to have at least 21 batteries—say 124 field guns—18 co's. of cavalry & some 70 rgts of infantry. Genl Scott is the great obstacle—he will not comprehend the danger & is either a traitor or an incompetent. I have to fight my way against him & have thrown a bombshell that has created a perfect stampede in the Cabinet—tomorrow the question will probably be decided by giving me absolute control independently of him. I suppose it will result in a mortal enmity on his part against me, but I have no choice—the people call upon me to save the country—I *must* save it & cannot respect anything that is in the way.

I receive letter after letter—have conversation after conversation calling on me to save the nation—alluding to the Presidency, Dictatorship &c. As I hope one day to be united with you forever in heaven, I have no such aspirations—I will never accept the Presidency—I will cheerfully take the Dictatorship & agree to lay down my life when the country is saved. I am *not* spoiled by my unexpected & new position—I feel sure that God will give me the strength & wisdom to preserve this great nation—but I tell *you*, who share all my thoughts, that I have no selfish feeling in the matter. I feel that God has placed a great work in my hands—I have not sought it—I know how weak I am—but I know that I mean to do right & I believe that God will help me & give me the wisdom I do not possess. Pray for me, darling, that I may be able to accomplish my task —the greatest, perhaps, that any poor weak mortal ever had to do. . . .

God grant that I may bring this war to an end & be permitted to spend the rest of my days quietly with you. . . .

I met the Prince at Alexandria today & came up with him. He says that Beauregard's head is turned & that he acts like a fool. That Joe Johnston is quiet & sad, & that he spoke to him in very kind terms of me.

———————————

16th
. . . I am here in a terrible place—the enemy have from 3 to 4 times my force—the Presdt is an idiot, the old General in his dotage—they cannot or will not see the true state of affairs. Most of my troops are demoralized by the defeat at Bull Run, some rgts even mutinous—I have probably stopped that—but you see my position is not pleasant. . . .

I have, I believe, made the best possible disposition of the few men under my command—will quietly await events & if the enemy attacks will try to make my movements as rapid & desperate as may be—if my men will only fight I think I can thrash him notwithstanding the disparity of numbers. As it is I trust to God to give success to our arms—tho' he is not wont to aid those who refuse to aid themselves. . . .

I am weary of all this. I have no ambition in the present affairs—only wish to save my country—& find the incapables around me will not permit it! They sit on the verge of the precipice & cannot realize what they see—their reply to everything is "Impossible! Impossible!" They think nothing possible which is against their wishes.

6 p.m.— . . . Gen. Scott is at last opening his eyes to the fact that I am right & that we are in imminent danger. Providence is aiding me by heavy rains, which are swelling the Potomac, which may be impassable for a week—if so we are saved. If Beauregard comes down upon us soon I have everything ready to make a manoeuvre which will be decisive. Give me two weeks & I will defy Beauregard—in a week the chances will be at least even.

August 16, 1861

# *E. F. Ware: from*
# The Lyon Campaign in Missouri

Nathaniel Lyon was commissioned as a brigadier general after his successful defense of the St. Louis arsenal and given command of the Union forces in Missouri. By the beginning of August he had gained control of most of the state, but now faced a force of 11,000 Confederates advancing from the southwest on his headquarters in Springfield. Despite his numerical inferiority, Lyon decided to attack the enemy encampment along Wilson's Creek. Dividing his force of 5,400 men, Lyon led the main body attacking from the north, while 1,200 men under Colonel Franz Sigel advanced from the south on the early morning of August 10. E. F. Ware, at the time a young harness-maker from Burlington serving as a private in Company E, 1st Iowa Infantry, described the battle in a memoir published in 1907.

ON AUGUST 9th shortly before sundown the bugle was blown and we were commanded to "fall in." There were no tents to mark our regimental line. We were sleeping in the open air; the position of the companies was marked by the ashes where the company camp-kettles and mess-pans were standing. Each company of our regiment fell in, making an irregular line which was quite long, owing to the distances between the companies. After standing in line for some minutes General Lyon was seen approaching on his large dapple-gray horse; this was the horse he generally used. Lyon, as he rode by the companies, made a brief speech to each. We could not hear what he said to the companies on each side of us, owing to the distance apart of the companies and the low tones of his voice. When he came to our company his words were:

"Men, we are going to have a fight. We will march out in a short time. Don't shoot until you get orders. Fire low—don't aim higher than their knees; wait until they get close; don't get scared; it's no part of a soldier's duty to get scared."

This is all he said, and is, I believe, a verbatim report, for we often talked it over, and compared notes, practically committing it to memory. He said the same to the other companies, stopping about a minute at each. It was a tactless and chilling speech; there was nothing in it of dash, vim, or encouragement. It was spoken in a low tone and with a solemn look, and apparently with a feeling of exhaustion. He was dressed in uniform, buttoned up to the chin, as if he were cold, although the weather was dry and roasting. We boys considered the speech as a very poor effort and entirely wanting in enthusiasm. He had better not have made it. The absurdity of the last expression struck every one of us,—that it was "no part of a soldier's duty to get scared." It had no sense to it. As Bill Huestis said, "How is a man to help being skeered when he is skeered?" But the speech represented Lyon. His idea was duty; every soldier was to him a mere machine; it was not the "duty" of a soldier to think, and hence he was not to get scared until his superior officer told him so. Lyon might have spoken a few sentences that would have raised his men up to the top notch and endeared himself in their memory for all time; but that was not Lyon; he did not care to endear himself to anybody. This speech of his seemed to me just the kind of speech he would make. On the other hand, dear old Irish General Sweeney, who did not get killed, made a speech to his cavalry, of which I have no notes except that he said (so his boys told) among other things, "Stay together, boys, and we'll saber hell out of them." This had enthusiasm to it.

Among the men Lyon had bitter enemies for his occasional severity and want of consideration. The boys thought, as they had agreed to stay with him voluntarily, that he ought to act better. He seemed to go upon the theory that he did not want his men to think kindly of him; that what he wanted of them was to have them understand that he was not to be fooled with, and that as they were in the employ of the Government it was his duty to see that the Government got everything out of them that could be got for the time being. On the other hand, the boys felt that strange confidence which soldiers always feel in an officer who they believe understands his business. So that speech which General Lyon made produced no particular effect one way or another, and had he not been killed would have been entirely forgotten. In fact, the boys did not like Lyon. They wanted a fight so that they could go home creditably, to themselves and their sweethearts; they knew just exactly how to fire a musket, and they did not intend to be scared, whether it was part of their duty or not, if they could help it.

———————

About sundown we were all marched into the city of Springfield; only about 70 of our company were in line; the balance of our company had broken down and were things of the past. We soon found that we were going southwest. The city was in frightful disorder. Every available means of transportation was being used by the merchants on the city square to load up and haul off their goods. We had brought nothing along with us but fighting material, and had left behind, where we had camped, our blankets and cooking utensils. Storekeepers brought us out, during our very brief stop of a few minutes, tobacco, sugar, and things of that kind. Starting west, it was twilight. When we got out of town we marched along past cornfields. The day had been hot, and as the night began to grow cool, life became more endurable, and the marching was anything but a funeral procession. The boys gave each other elaborate instructions as to the material out of which they wanted their coffins made, and how they wanted them decorated. Bill Huestis said he wanted his coffin made out of sycamore boards, with his last words put on with brass tacks, which were: "I am a-going to be a great big he-angel." (Bill still lives.*) After going several miles in the night, the path we were following became a dim timber road leading tortuously around among the rocks and trees and brush among the hills, and we were ordered to keep still and to make no noise. About that time a cavalryman passed us from the front, and we noticed that he was going slowly, and that his horse's feet had cloths tied around them, banded at the fetlock. During the

*At Ferndale, Calif.

stoppage there was a passing to and fro along the line, and some one said that blankets had been tied around the artillery wheels. We moved short distances from twenty to a hundred yards at a time, and kept halting and closing up, and making very slow progress. Finally we were practically involved in the timber and among the side-hills of a watercourse. There were some little light clouds, but it was light enough to see a short distance around us, by starlight; it was in the dark of the moon. Finally word was passed along the line that we were inside the enemy's pickets, but were two or three miles from their camps. Rumor magnified the number of the enemy to twenty-five thousand. We could see the sheen in the sky of vast camp-fires beyond the hills, but could not see the lights. We also heard at times choruses of braying mules.

About this time, while we were moving along we passed around the brow of a low, rocky hill, and the line stopped at a place where our company stood on a broad ledge of rock. It must have been about 11 o'clock. I never did know the hour; I had traded my watch for ammunition. We all laid down on this rock to get rested. The cool, dewy night air made me feel chilly in the "linings" which I was wearing; but the radiating heat which the rock during the day had absorbed, was peculiarly comfortable. I went to sleep in from five to ten seconds and slept deliciously. I had made up my mind that if we were going to have a battle I certainly would not get killed, but might need all my strength and ability in getting away from the enemy's cavalry. The anxiety which novelists describe, and the wakefulness on the eve of battle, are creatures I presume of the imagination of the novelists respectively, who were never there. I do not know what took place, until, early in the morning, just as there was a slight flush of dawn in the east, somebody came along and woke us all up, and told us to keep still and fall into line. We marched a short distance and struck an open piece of ground where we could see all who were marching, those in our front and those in our rear. The cavalry, artillery and infantry were marching in companies, abreast, and in close order. In a short time as it began to grow a little light we heard a gun fire. In a short time two or three more. Then some regular troops were detailed as skirmishers, and circled around to our left. In a short time we found that the enemy were alive and active. Our regiment was ordered to go in a direction to the left, and to take a position on a low ridge; the enemy in straggling numbers were shooting at us from the ridge. The skirmishers fell back. As we marched up the hill, it came in my way to step over one of the skirmishers who was shot right in front of us. He was a blue-eyed, blonde, fine-looking young man, with a light mustache, who writhed around upon the ground in agony. While I was walking past, I asked him where he was shot, but he seemed unable to comprehend or answer, and perhaps in the noise heard nothing. As we started up the ridge a yell broke from our lines that was kept up with more or less accent and with slight intermissions for six hours. We took a position on the ridge, and the country seemed alive on both our right and left. Wilson's creek was in our front, with an easy descending hillside and a broad meadow before us, in which about five acres of Confederate wagons were parked, axle to axle. The hills bore some scattering oaks, and an occasional bush, but we could see clearly, because the fires had kept the undergrowth eaten out, and the soil was flinty and poor. Since that time a large portion of the country has been covered with a very dense thicket of small oaks. But in those days the few trees were rather large, scrawling, and straggling, and everything could be distinctly seen under them all around. Across the creek, which was not very far, perhaps about a third of a mile, a battery of artillery made a specialty of our ranks, opening out thunderously. We all lay down on the ground, and for some time the shells, round shot and canister were playing closely over our heads. Some few of the canister fell into our ranks. They were coarse cast-iron balls, about an inch to an inch and a half in diameter. Where they struck in the ground the boys hunted for them with their hands. The shells were shrapnels, being filled with leaden balls run together with sulphur. Our company did not have much to do for a while in the way of shooting; we simply laid down on the ridge and watched the battery in front of us, or sat up or kneeled down. When we saw the puff of the artillery we dodged and went down flat, and in the course of fifteen minutes gained so much confidence that we felt no hesitation in walking around and seeing what we could see, knowing that we could dodge the artillery ammunition. This battery was making a specialty of us, but we could evade their missiles; we could see the shells in the air when they were coming toward us, and could calculate their routes.

In a little while two pieces of artillery were run up on the ridge between our company and the company on the right. These were Totten's, and were afterwards increased. They started in to silence the enemy's artillery, and a concentration of fire began in our neighborhood near the cannon. The duel was very interesting, and our boys stayed close to the earth. Considerable damage was done to our artillery, but they were not silenced. One of the large roan artillery horses was standing back of the gun and over the crest of the hill. A shell from the battery in front of us struck this horse somehow and tore off its left shoulder. Then began the most horrible screams and neighing I ever heard. I have since that time seen wounded horses, and heard their frantic shrieks, and so have all other soldiers, but the voice of this roan horse was the limit; it was so absolutely blood-curdling that it had to be put to an end immediately. One of the soldiers shot the horse through the heart.

In a little while, in front of us, appeared, advancing in the meadow, a body of men that we estimated at about one thousand. They seemed to be going to attack somebody on our left. Our artillery stopped firing over their heads at the enemy's battery, and turned upon the meadow; in a short time the enemy were in confusion.

On the edge of the meadow toward us, and between us, was a low rail fence; the enemy rallied under the shelter of it, and, as if by some inspiration or some immediate change of orders, they broke it down in places and started for our artillery. As they got nearer to us, their own artillery ceased to fire, because it endangered them. When they got close the firing began on both sides. How long it lasted I do not know. It might have been an hour; it seemed like a week; it was probably twenty minutes. Every man was shooting as fast, on our side, as he could load, and yelling as loud as his breath would permit. Most were on the ground, some on one knee. The enemy stopped advancing. We had paper cartridges, and in loading we had to bite off the end, and every man had a big quid of paper in his mouth, from which down his chin ran the dissolved gunpowder. The other side were yelling, and if any orders were given nobody heard them. Every man assumed the responsibility of doing as much shooting as he could.

Finally, the field was so covered with smoke that not much could be known as to what was going on. The day was clear and hot. As the smoke grew denser, we stood up and kept inching forward, as we fired, and probably went forward in this way twenty-five yards. We noticed less noise in front of us, and only heard the occasional boom of a gun. The wind, a very light breeze, was in our favor, blowing very gently over us upon the enemy.

Our firing lulled, and as the smoke cleared away, sitting on the fence in front of us, on the edge of the meadow, was a standard-bearer, waving a hostile flag. I do not know its description, but it was not a Union flag. The firing having ceased, we were ordered back and told to lie down, but the boys would not do it until the Rebel artillery opened on us again. Several wanted to shoot at the man on the fence, but the officers went along the line threatening to kill the first man that raised a musket, which was all right, that being the way the game is played. In the mean time, however, a little Irish sergeant, who appeared to stand about five feet high, and sported a large fiery mustache, turned a twelve-pounder on the man who was waving the flag on the fence in such a foolhardy way. The gun went off, the Rebel flag pitched up in the air, and the man fell to pieces gradually over the fence; and at least a thousand men on our side, who saw it, cheered in such loud unison that it could have been heard as far as the report of the twelve-pounder.

I am not able to give, in any moderate limits, the history of the charges and counter-charges on the slope of that hill, but they kept coming. In one of them the Rebel infantry, in its charge, worn down to a point, with its apex touched the twelve-pounder, and one man with his bayonet tried to get the Irish sergeant, who, fencing with his non-commissioned officer's sword, parried the thrusts of the bayonet. I fired at this "apex" at a distance of not over 30 feet. Other secesh were around the guns, but none of them got away. The main body were started back down the slope; the twelve-pounder was then loaded, and assisted their flight.

At one time we were charged by a large detachment of Louisiana troops. They made the most stubborn fight of the day. They had nice new rifled muskets from the armory at Baton Rouge, which armory had by the secession leaders been judiciously filled, before the war, from Northern arsenals. We were borne back by the charge of the Louisiana regiment, slowly in the course of the firing, as much as fifty feet. Squads of Rebel cavalry had been seen in our right rear, and while the enemy were safe in running, we were not. No man deserted the ranks. During that fight Corporal Bill* received a minie ball on the crest of the forehead. The ball went over his head, tearing the scalp, sinking the skull at the point of impact about one-eighth of an inch. He bled with a sickening profusion all over his face, neck, and clothing; and as if half-unconscious and half-crazed, he wandered down the line, asking for me; he was my blanket-mate. He said, "Link, have you got any water in your canteen?" I handed him my canteen and sat him down by the side of a tree that stood near our line, but he got up and wandered around with that canteen, perfectly oblivious; going now in one direction and then in another. From that depression in the skull, wasted to a skeleton, he, an athlete, died shortly after his muster-out, with consumption. How could it be?

We succeeded in repulsing the Louisiana troops, although we were not numerically superior. Our former victory had given us great confidence, and no man broke ranks or ran. As the Louisiana troops yielded back we followed them some little distance down the slope, and when they were gone we put in about fifteen or twenty minutes gathering up fine shot-guns and fine rifled muskets, and looking over the poor fellows that were killed and wounded on the hill in front of us.

I was afraid I would run out of ammunition, and I helped myself to the cartridges in the box of a dead soldier who was labeled as a "Pelican Ranger." He had the same kind of gun that I had, and used the same kind of ammunition. I now have two bullets left that I took from that cartridge-box, my only mementoes of the battle. The Louisiana boys showed lots of grit.

After a few minutes another attack was made, but it was

---

*William J. Fuller.

weak and feeble; it must have been a sort of "Butternut Militia" gang. One of them behind a tree, perhaps 50 yards in front of us, after his associates had retired, rose up and deliberately, fired a double-barrel shotgun, both barrels, at us. He injured no one that we knew of, but some one dropped him suddenly, and Seeger of our company ran forward and got his shotgun, kept it, and took it back home to Iowa, a splendid stub-and-twist gun. I saw it all done—in fact I fired at the man behind the tree while he was reloading his shotgun, but don't think I hit him.

About this time we heard yelling in the rear, and we saw a crowd of cavalry coming on a grand gallop, very disorderly, with their apex pointing steadily at our pieces of artillery. We were ordered to face about and step forward to meet them. We advanced down the hill toward them about forty yards to where our view was better, and rallied in round squads of fifteen or twenty men as we had been drilled to do, to repel a cavalry charge. We kept firing, and awaited their approach with fixed bayonets. Our firing was very deadly, and the killing of horses and riders in the front rank piled the horses and men together as they tumbled over one another, from the advancing rear. The charge, so far as its force was concerned, was checked before it got within fifty yards of us. There were 800 of them. This cavalry charge was led by a man named Laswell, formerly from our State,—Ottumwa, Iowa,—who had gone to Texas; we got him.

In the mean time, over our heads our artillery took up the fight; then the cavalry scattered through the woods, leaving the wounded horses and men strewn around. We captured several dismounted men by ordering them in under cover of a gun. A flag was seen lying on the ground about 150 yards in front of us, but no one was ordered or cared to undertake to go and bring it in. In a few minutes a solitary horseman was seen coming towards us, as if to surrender, and the cry therefore rose from us, "Don't shoot!" When within about twenty yards of that flag the horseman spurred his horse, and, leaning from his saddle, picked the flag from the grass, and off he went with it a-flying. The flag bore the "Lone Star" of Texas, and we didn't shoot at the horseman because we liked his display of nerve.

In a few minutes a riderless horse came dashing over the ground, and as he passed a bush, a man with a white shirt, covered with blood, rose from the ground, stopped the horse, slowly and painfully mounted, and rode off. The cry passed, "Don't shoot!" and the man escaped. In the mean time artillery fire concentrated on us, and the Irish sergeant yelled, "They are shooting Sigel's ammunition at us!" Sigel had been whipped. We resumed our place on the ridge.

Some few spasmodic efforts were made to dislodge us, all of which we repulsed. Finally the hostile artillery in front ceased firing, and there came a lull; finally the last charge of the day was made, which we easily repulsed, and the field was ours.

This last charge was not very much of a charge. It was a mixed, heterogeneous charge. I remember one very funny thing that happened in it. We were down on one knee, firing and loading as fast as possible, expecting to rise soon and repel them, for the enemy had slacked up and almost stopped advancing; along came a man in a Union lieutenant's uniform, inquiring for his regiment,—he was lost; we of course did not know where his regiment was; I was near the end of our company line; he pulled out a long plug of chewing-tobacco, thin and black; I grabbed it and bit off a chew; the man next to me wanted a chew; I handed it to him; then it went to the next, and so on down the line; the lieutenant followed it for a while and then gave up and passed on, leaving the remnant of the plug with the company. Every man that took a chew first blew out a big wad of cartridge-paper blackened with gunpowder, which he had bitten off in loading.

Word had been passed along the line that Lyon was killed. A big regular army cavalry soldier on a magnificent horse rode down alongside of the rear of our company, and along the line; he appeared to have been sent for the purpose of bracing us up. He shouted and swore in a manner that was attractive even on the battle-field, and wound up with a great big oath and the expression, "Life ain't long enough for them to lick us in." After this last repulse the field was ours, and we sat down on the ground and began to tell the funny incidents that had happened. We looked after boys who were hurt, sent details off to fill the canteens, and we ate our dinners, saving what we did not want of our big crusts and hanging them over our shoulders again on our gun-slings. We regretted very much the death of General Lyon, but we felt sanguine over our success, and thought the war was about ended.

Our drill had given us more than one advantage: in the *first* place, not much of us could be seen by an advancing regiment while we lay on the ground; we were sort of an unknown quantity, and could only be guessed at. *Second*, we could take a rest and deadly aim and pour in a terrific volley while lying on the ground; this would shock the advancing line if it indeed did not bring them to a dead halt. It embarrassed their alignment and reduced their momentum. *Third*, when they began to fire we rose on one knee; the air was soon full of smoke, and while they always shot over our heads we could see them under the cloud of smoke. The smoke was inclined to rise, but if they were advancing they were on foot and could not see under the smoke. If they advanced they were soon enveloped in their own smoke, their officers could not see their own men, and the men became bewildered at their situation and by their losses in killed and wounded. On the other hand, the air was clear behind us and our officers could manage their men, and we were not staggered by losses. *Fourth*, our men could not break to the rear and run, because they could be seen; while the ranks of the enemy could dissolve and the skulkers get to the rear in the smoke practically unseen. Hence by reason of our drill and situation we could not be dislodged by anything but a very strong force. And we were comparatively safe in comparison with an attacking column. Above all other factors of safety was our drill.

# W. E. Woodruff: from
# With the Light Guns in '61–'65

Following Lyon's death, the Union forces retreated to Springfield and then to Rolla, 100 miles to the north. The battle cost the Union about 1,300 men killed, wounded, or missing, the Confederates about 1,200. Woodruff, a lawyer from Little Rock, Arkansas, serving as an artillery officer, recorded his experiences during the battle in a memoir published in 1903.

———————

IN AN old package of papers, yellow with age, is found a substantial copy of the report of the Pulaski battery's participation in the battle of the 10th of August. It has never been published within the knowledge of this writer, and it appears now, as having been made when matters were fresh in mind:

"Camp on Wilson's Creek, Mo., Aug. 11, 1861.
"Col. Joseph Hebert, Commanding Advance:—
"Sir:—My battery having been asigned to your command, it becomes my duty to report its participation in the action of yesterday on the ground it occupies. If I am in error, please forward to proper headquarters.

"On the morning of the 9th inst., I was ordered to be in readiness to move promptly against the enemy, at 9 p. m. Later, in consequence of the rain, I was ordered to be 'ready to move at a moment's notice.' My officers and men were ordered to remain at and near their posts, with teams harnessed and hitched, parked at full distance, and remained so all night.

"About 6 a. m. on the 10th, just as my men had finished breakfast, a great commotion was observed on the Springfield road, in a direction northwesterly (as I take it) from my camp. Men, horses and other animals, with and without wagons, carriages, etc., were seen rushing hurriedly and confusedly in great numbers down the roads and to the fords on the west and south. It seemed to be a repetition of the affair at Crane Creek a few days ago, and we were not greatly disturbed. Nevertheless, I ordered officers and men to posts and mounted drivers while awaiting orders. A minute or two later, on the hill five or six hundred yards northwest a rush of teams was observed, which rapidly developed into a light battery, that quickly unlimbered and commenced firing, seemingly in the direction of General McCulloch's headquarters, or of the crowd flying down the main road towards Sharp's house. Almost simultaneously a second battery or section rushed forward to the right and in front of the first, about 200 yards, unlimbered and commenced firing, apparently in the direction of McRae's battalion, or Third Louisiana regiment.* My men had been held a minute or two in expectation of orders, but satisfied the situation was grave, I passed my caissons to the rear and ordered "in battery," at the appearance of the first mentioned force. The second battery or section of the enemy observed my movement, and opened fire on us. We were able to answer the enemy's third or fourth †shot. Generals Pearce and McCulloch were soon on the ground and approved the action taken. Within a few minutes after the enemy opened, the report of a few shots of artillery to the southwest was heard, or at both extremities of our camp. Feeling the importance of staying the assault until our infantry lines were established, the cannonade with the hostile battery was continued half an hour or more, with the double purpose of checking it and for effect on his infantry lines behind.‡

"Early in the action, the Missouri cavalry regiment of Colonel Graves reported, in support of the battery. The colonel was requested to take position on our flanks and rear, if he approved. A considerable force of the enemy was observed in the cornfield near one-half mile immediately north of our position. Foreseeing that it was intended to attack our

---

*Curiously, the tactics outlined in Exodus 4-4 flashed in mind at this time.

†Gen. Price "was greatly aided from the beginning by Woodruff, who had, with true soldierly instinct, thrown his pieces into battery, on the bluff east of the ford, at the sound of Totten's guns, and opened on Lyon a fire which checked his advance and gave the Missourians time to reach Cawthon's position and form a line of battle there."—Snead's Fight for Missouri, p. 274.

‡See p. 277; Snead Ib.

position and dislodge us, the appearance and position of this force, regulars, infantry, cavalry and a battery, was quickly reported to General McCulloch,* who speedily opposed it with McRae's battalion, part of the Third Louisiana, and, I think, Flanagin's regiment, all under Colonel McIntosh. They had to pass under the fire of our guns, stationed at a higher level, to reach the enemy. With the rest of the Third Louisiana regiment, General McCulloch, in a little while, moved rapidly to the west or southwest. Our infantry line being formed, and the threatened attack from the hill north checked, our fire was thereafter directed where it could be advantageously used without injury to our own troops, sometimes at the opposing battery, at others against the assaults of the enemy on the hill to the northwest, in support of Colonel McIntosh, and after in support of our infantry line on the enemy, when the latter was uncovered. About 9 a. m., Colonel Gratiot's Third Arkansas reported in support, and was requested to take the position vacated by Graves' Missouri cavalry. An hour later the Third Arkansas, Colonel Gratiot, passed down the hill to the left of our position, directed by General Pearce, and crossed the creek, and in a little while went into action. Observing a Federal regiment, uniformed in gray, advancing in fine order to meet Gratiot, and having an excellent opportunity to enfilade it while Gratiot was uncovered, we opened on it with the effect of breaking its beautiful line and scattering it its full length, to the depth of a company front or more, when Gratiot met and dispersed it gallantly. The enemy commenced falling back about noon, to the northwest, in good order, their rear covered by artillery and cavalry. We opened on the retreating force, which gave our artillery antagonists opportunity to send a few spiteful shots at us in return.

## "CASUALTIES.

"I have to report a loss of four officers and men, killed, wounded and missing. First Lieutenant Omer R. Weaver and Private Hugh Byler were killed by cannon shot; Private Richard C. Byrd, Jr., was wounded in the leg by a minnie ball, sufficiently to disable him from service for some time; two

*See last paragraph of Note 1 to appendix.

horses were also killed. The death of Weaver is an irreparable loss to the battery and the cause. Byler was a brave and useful and exemplary soldier. Their loss is all the more deplorable, because if a surgeon had been attached, their valuable lives might possibly have been saved. The missing man had gone to the corral without permission at dawn, and was cut off from return by position of the enemy and his line of fire.

"During a lull in the action, by General Pearce's order, the battery was limbered up and moved to more elevated ground some one hundred yards to the right and rear of the first position.

"Very respectfully, etc.,

"W. E. WOODRUFF, Jr.,

"Captain Pulaski (Arkansas) Light Battery."

The average excellence of behavior of the company was very high. There was only one absentee, and he, a boy, caught away from camp when the battle opened, had no exemplar to point the way to duty. His name is not mentioned. The army roll is challenged for superiors or peers of Tom Cavanaugh, Pat Connolly, Higgins, Cook, Lowe and Quinn, as cannoneers. They were all artists in the service of the piece. The names of a few others are given alphabetically, special mention of whom will excite no jealousy: Blocher, Brodie, Button, Campbell, Curry, Davis, W. R. Douglass George, Halliburton, Hugh Hardy, Jennings, Kimbell, Lewis, Marshall, Mears, Merrick, Mills, Osborne, the two Parks brothers, Pollock, Visart, Watkins, Williams and Woodard, as deserving of commendation. Judgment forbids extending the list, lest the heart run away with the pen and cause it to copy the roll. Ten or more were boys between 15 and 17, and their youth alone prevented some from being placed as sergeants and corporals. All seemed to vie as if each member felt desirous of averting from the State of Arkansas, the odium of an overwhelming disgrace, responsibility for which might be settled upon each.

Many of the incidents of the fight are recalled. It had been arranged between the company officers long before, that in our first engagement each should take the post of gunner at designated pieces. Weaver to take No. 1, I to take No. 2 (to be near the center) Reyburn No. 3, and Brown No. 4, assisted and rested by the proper gunner of the respective pieces. From the shape of the gun, the tendency is to "over-shoot" the mark, the outer surface of the gun being much thicker at the breech than at the muzzle. The difference is more than an inch according to calibre, and in a distance of several hundred yards the overshot is considerable. Only experience can qualify a gunner to determine what elevation to give his piece, to strike with certainty a particular object. It was a fortunate incident that our overshots were effective on the Federal lines and reserve behind. I fired the first shot and the others followed. Weaver was struck within the first hour. He had just been relieved by his gunner, Sergeant Blocher, I believe, and, was struck a moment after with a solid shot, which broke his right arm and crushed his breast. Some one told me Weaver was wounded and wanted to see me. I went to him immediately, and he said, lying on the ground, his wounded arm across his breast: "I am done for; can't you have me moved?" I said, "Yes, immediately, and I will try to get a surgeon." He said, "All right; you had better go back to your gun or post." I called Sergeant Button and told him to detail men to move Weaver, and to get a surgeon if he could. The fight was going on all the time. A little later Byler was struck by a solid shot above the knee. He was removed also. Within an hour Byrd was shot in the leg with a minnie ball and was also removed. Button managed to find Dr. Dunlap, of Fort Smith, who ministered to all while there was life. A wheel horse of the limber of Weaver's gun, one of the "overland" white team, was also killed. All the casualties happened at the same gun and its caisson—a piece of shell splintered the latter and fell inside the chest—except another horse which was killed near us to the left—a sergeant's horse hitched to a small tree.

During the "cornfield fight," a battery, I think Bledsoe's Missouri Battery, opened at a point considerably to the left, west and south of us, and fired apparently at the Federal regulars in the cornfield four or five shots. At the time I thought it was Reed. It may be, however, that it was Guibor's Missouri Battery,* which was camped over a mile to the left and rear of

---

*It was Guibor, as learned from Snead's book long after Woodruff's official report was made. See note to appendix. Guibor had to "move more than a

us as we fired. Neither Reed, Bledsoe or Guibor was in sight. This was the only participation in the fight by the Missouri batteries that I am aware of. It occurred to me at the time, that the missiles of this battery were as dangerous to McIntosh as to the enemy. I had partially discontinued firing in that direction for that reason. The guns sounded beautifully and inspiringly, however. Reed fired a few shots at Sigel's battery, which we heard only, as he was out of sight. All the reports of the Pulaski battery "whipping Totten" are foundationless. He manifested himself a courageous and capable officer. He was in the fight from "end to end" and in the very forefront. He fired, I think, his last shot at us on the retreat, as stated in my report— though there was another regular battery, Du Bois',* in the close vicinity of the Federal force that made the cornfield fight. Totten's guns were abandoned at one stage. Colonel De Rosey Carroll's regiment (he told me) went over his, Totten's ground, and found them abandoned. They were recovered, however and drawn away. I freely say that while our post was dangerous enough, I am glad the conditions were not reversed. He was afterwards dismissed from the army on account of dissipation, a weakness which President Grant might well have overlooked, as Totten suggested to him, when notified of that President's approval of his dismissal. The unkindest thing I ever heard of Captain Totten was a remark of Captain C. C. Danley, in '60 or '61, who remarked: "T. was always a bosom friend of the man he drank with last." Certainly a testimonial to his generous nature, and I can testify to his soldierly qualities.

Generals McCulloch, Price, Pearce and Colonel McIntosh visited our position several times during the day; also President David Walker of the State convention. The demeanor of all was fearless. It is recalled that Price wore throughout the fight a black "plug" hat, which ranged over the field like an orri flamme, to the Missourians.

The bearing of General Lyon was in plain view, and was very gallant. There was another Federal officer, a one-armed Irishman, named Sweeny, as afterwards learned, whose actions were

---

mile" to reach his post in Price's line, which he could not have done at the time Totten opened fire with his battery, and for a half hour after that time.

*It was DuBois. See note to appendix, next to last paragraph.

most gallant in bringing up and encouraging his infantry as his battallions were put into the fight successively. He was always in the thick of it. We did not know the names of either until later. One factor aided the Federals greatly; all their infantry had long range guns; our men had very few; the Federals could pick their distance out of range of our old muskets, squirrel rifles and shot guns, when the two lines clashed. This was signally manifested when Gratiot's minnie rifles were pitted against the last regiment put in the fight, which was arrested long before a return fire was expected. The difference in arms explains the heavy loss of the Confederates.

Next day after the battle the captain went to take a look at the "dutch" prisoners. As we passed a group of Price's Missourians, one of them spoke out so that he could be heard: "There goes the little captain of the battery that saved us yesterday." Then it was assured our boys had done well.

# John C. Frémont: Proclamation

A former army officer who had gained fame for his western explorations and his service in California during the U.S.-Mexican War, John C. Frémont became the first Republican presidential nominee in 1856. Commissioned as a major general in May 1861, Frémont arrived in St. Louis on July 25 and assumed command of the Union forces in Missouri. As Confederate guerrilla activity increased following the Union defeat at Wilson's Creek, the new commander issued a proclamation.

---

HEADQUARTERS WESTERN DEPARTMENT,

Saint Louis, August 30, 1861.

Circumstances, in my judgment, of sufficient urgency render it necessary that the commanding general of this department should assume the administrative powers of the State. Its disorganized condition, the helplessness of the civil authority, the total insecurity of life, and the devastation of property by bands of murderers and marauders, who infest nearly every county of the State, and avail themselves of the public misfortunes and the vicinity of a hostile force to gratify private and neighborhood vengeance, and who find an enemy wherever they find plunder, finally demand the severest measures to repress the daily increasing crimes and outrages which are driving off the inhabitants and ruining the State.

In this condition the public safety and the success of our arms require unity of purpose, without let or hinderance to the prompt administration of affairs. In order, therefore, to suppress disorder, to maintain as far as now practicable the public peace, and to give security and protection to the persons and property of loyal citizens, I do hereby extend and declare established martial law throughout the State of Missouri.

The lines of the army of occupation in this State are for the present declared to extend from Leavenworth, by way of the posts of Jefferson City, Rolla, and Ironton, to Cape Girardeau, on the Mississippi River.

All persons who shall be taken with arms in their hands within these lines shall be tried by court-martial, and if found guilty will be shot.

The property, real and personal, of all persons in the State of Missouri who shall take up arms against the United States, or who shall be directly proven to have taken an active part with their enemies in the field, is declared to be confiscated to the public use, and their slaves, if any they have, are hereby declared freemen.

All persons who shall be proven to have destroyed, after the publication of this order, railroad tracks, bridges, or telegraphs shall suffer the extreme penalty of the law.

All persons engaged in treasonable correspondence, in giving or procuring aid to the enemies of the United States, in fomenting tumults, in disturbing the public tranquillity by creating and circulating false reports or incendiary documents, are in their own interests warned that they are exposing themselves to sudden and severe punishment.

All persons who have been led away from their allegiance are required to return to their homes forthwith. Any such absence, without sufficient cause, will be held to be presumptive evidence against them.

The object of this declaration is to place in the hands of the military authorities the power to give instantaneous effect to existing laws, and to supply such deficiencies as the conditions of war demand. But this is not intended to suspend the ordinary tribunals of the country, where the law will be administered by the civil officers in the usual manner, and with their customary authority, while the same can be peaceably exercised.

The commanding general will labor vigilantly for the public welfare, and in his efforts for their safety hopes to obtain not only the acquiescence but the active support of the loyal people of the country.

J. C. FRÉMONT,
Major-General, Commanding.

# Abraham Lincoln to John C. Frémont

John G. Nicolay recorded that when Frémont's proclamation reached Washington, it "at once troubled the Prest and Gen. Scott exceedingly," causing both men to worry that the provision for emancipating slaves would have "an exceedingly discouraging effect" on unionists in Kentucky. Although Lincoln hoped to keep his modification of the proclamation private, Frémont would respond to his letter of September 2 by refusing to modify the proclamation unless he was publicly ordered to do so, a request the President "very cheerfully" granted in a subsequent communication.

---

*Private and confidential.*

Major General Fremont:     Washington D.C. Sept. 2, 1861.

My dear Sir: Two points in your proclamation of August 30th give me some anxiety. First, should you shoot a man, according to the proclamation, the Confederates would very certainly shoot our best man in their hands in retaliation; and so, man for man, indefinitely. It is therefore my order that you allow no man to be shot, under the proclamation, without first having my approbation or consent.

Secondly, I think there is great danger that the closing paragraph, in relation to the confiscation of property, and the liberating slaves of traiterous owners, will alarm our Southern Union friends, and turn them against us—perhaps ruin our rather fair prospect for Kentucky. Allow me therefore to ask, that you will as of your own motion, modify that paragraph so as to conform to the *first* and *fourth* sections of the act of Congress, entitled, "An act to confiscate property used for insurrectionary purposes," approved August, 6th, 1861, and a copy of which act I herewith send you. This letter is written in a spirit of caution and not of censure.

I send it by a special messenger, in order that it may certainly and speedily reach you. Yours very truly     A. LINCOLN

Copy of letter sent to Gen. Fremont, by special messenger leaving Washington Sep. 3. 1861.

## Frederick Douglass: Fighting Rebels with Only One Hand

September 1861

The disillusionment and frustration Douglass expressed at the administration's policy in his *Monthly* increased after Lincoln revoked Frémont's proclamation.

———————

WHAT UPON EARTH is the matter with the American Government and people? Do they really covet the world's ridicule as well as their own social and political ruin? What are they thinking about, or don't they condescend to think at all? So, indeed, it would seem from their blindness in dealing with the tremendous issue now upon them. Was there ever any thing like it before? They are sorely pressed on every hand by a vast army of slaveholding rebels, flushed with success, and infuriated by the darkest inspirations of a deadly hate, bound to rule or ruin. Washington, the seat of Government, after ten thousand assurances to the contrary, is now positively in danger of falling before the rebel army. Maryland, a little while ago considered safe for the Union, is now admitted to be studded with the materials for insurrection, and which may flame forth at any moment.—Every resource of the nation, whether of men or money, whether of wisdom or strength, could be well employed to avert the impending ruin. Yet most evidently the demands of the hour are not comprehended by the Cabinet or the crowd. Our Presidents, Governors, Generals and Secretaries are calling, with almost frantic vehemence, for men.— "Men! men! send us men!" they scream, or the cause of the Union is gone, the life of a great nation is ruthlessly sacrificed, and the hopes of a great nation go out in darkness; and yet these very officers, representing the people and Government, steadily and persistently refuse to receive the very class of men which have a deeper interest in the defeat and humiliation of the rebels, than all others.—Men are wanted in Missouri—wanted in Western Virginia, to hold and defend what has been already gained; they are wanted in Texas, and all along the sea coast, and though the Government has at its command a class in the country deeply interested in suppressing the insurrection, it sternly refuses to summon from among the vast multitude a single man, and degrades and insults the whole class by refusing to allow any of their number to defend with their strong arms and brave hearts the national cause. What a spectacle of blind, unreasoning prejudice and pusillanimity is this! The national edifice is on fire. Every man who can carry a bucket of water, or remove a brick, is wanted; but those who have the care of the building, having a profound respect for the feeling of the national burglars who set the building on fire, are determined that the flames shall only be extinguished by Indo-Caucasian hands, and to have the building burnt rather than save it by means of any other. Such is the pride, the stupid prejudice and folly that rules the hour.

Why does the Government reject the Negro? Is he not a man? Can he not wield a sword, fire a gun, march and countermarch, and obey orders like any other? Is there the least reason to believe that a regiment of well-drilled Negroes would deport themselves less soldier-like on the battle field than the raw troops gathered up generally from the towns and cities of the State of New York? We do believe that such soldiers, if allowed now to take up arms in defence of the Government, and made to feel that they are hereafter to be recognized as persons having rights, would set the highest example of order and general good behavior to their fellow soldiers, and in every way add to the national power.

If persons so humble as we can be allowed to speak to the President of the United States, we should ask him if this dark and terrible hour of the nation's extremity is a time for consulting a mere vulgar and unnatural prejudice? We should ask him if national preservation and necessity were not better guides in this emergency than either the tastes of the rebels, or the pride and prejudices of the vulgar? We would tell him that General Jackson in a slave State fought side by side with

Negroes at New Orleans, and like a true man, despising mean-ness, he bore testimony to their bravery at the close of the war. We would tell him that colored men in Rhode Island and Con-necticut performed their full share in the war of the Revolu-tion, and that men of the same color, such as the noble Shields Green, Nathaniel Turner and Denmark Vesey stand ready to peril every thing at the command of the Government. We would tell him that this is no time to fight with one hand, when both are needed; that this is no time to fight only with your white hand, and allow your black hand to remain tied.

Whatever may be the folly and absurdity of the North, the South at least is true and wise. The Southern papers no longer indulge in the vulgar expression, "free n—rs." That class of bipeds are now called "colored residents." The Charleston papers say:

"The colored residents of this city can challenge comparison with their class, in any city or town, in loyalty or devotion to the cause of the South. Many of them individually, and without ostentation, have been contributing liberally, and on Wednesday evening, the 7th inst., a very large meeting was held by them, and a Committee appointed to provide for more efficient aid. The proceedings of the meeting will appear in results hereinafter to be reported."

It is now pretty well established, that there are at the present moment many colored men in the Confederate army doing duty not only as cooks, servants and laborers, but as real sol-diers, having muskets on their shoulders, and bullets in their pockets, ready to shoot down loyal troops, and do all that sol-diers may to destroy the Federal Government and build up that of the traitors and rebels. There were such soldiers at Manassas, and they are probably there still. There is a Negro in the army as well as in the fence, and our Government is likely to find it out before the war comes to an end. That the Negroes are numerous in the rebel army, and do for that army its heaviest work, is beyond question. They have been the chief laborers upon those temporary defences in which the rebels have been able to mow down our men. Negroes helped to build the batteries at Charleston. They relieve their gentle-manly and military masters from the stiffening drudgery of the camp, and devote them to the nimble and dexterous use of arms. Rising above vulgar prejudice, the slaveholding rebel accepts the aid of the black man as readily as that of any other. If a bad cause can do this, why should a good cause be less wisely conducted? We insist upon it, that one black regiment in such a war as this is, without being any more brave and orderly, would be worth to the Government more than two of any other; and that, while the Government continues to refuse the aid of colored men, thus alienating them from the national cause, and giving the rebels the advantage of them, it will not deserve better fortunes than it has thus far experienced.—Men in earnest don't fight with one hand, when they might fight with two, and a man drowning would not refuse to be saved even by a colored hand.

# Abraham Lincoln to Orville H. Browning

Lincoln explained his decision to revoke Frémont's proclamation to his friend Orville H. Browning, who had recently been appointed to fill the Senate seat left vacant by the death of Stephen A. Douglas.

---

*Private & confidential.*

Hon. O. H. Browning                    Executive Mansion
My dear Sir                    Washington Sept 22d 1861.

Yours of the 17th is just received; and coming from you, I confess it astonishes me. That you should object to my adhering to a law, which you had assisted in making, and presenting to me, less than a month before, is odd enough. But this is a very small part. Genl. Fremont's proclamation, as to confiscation of property, and the liberation of slaves, is *purely political*, and not within the range of *military* law, or necessity. If a commanding General finds a necessity to seize the farm of a private owner, for a pasture, an encampment, or a fortification, he has the right to do so, and to so hold it, as long as the necessity lasts; and this is within military law, because within military necessity. But to say the farm shall no longer belong to the owner, or his heirs forever; and this as well when the farm is not needed for military purposes as when it is, is purely political, without the savor of military law about it. And the same is true of slaves. If the General needs them, he can seize them, and use them; but when the need is past, it is not for him to fix their permanent future condition. That must be settled according to laws made by law-makers, and not by military proclamations. The proclamation in the point in question, is simply "dictatorship." It assumes that the general may do *anything* he pleases—confiscate the lands and free the slaves of *loyal* people, as well as of disloyal ones. And going the whole figure I have no doubt would be more popular with some thoughtless people, than that which has been done! But I cannot assume this reckless position; nor allow others to assume it on my responsibility. You speak of it as being the only means of *saving* the government. On the contrary it is itself the surrender of the government. Can it be pretended that it is any longer the government of the U.S.—any government of Constitution and laws,—wherein a General, or a President, may make permanent rules of property by proclamation?

I do not say Congress might not with propriety pass a law, on the point, just such as General Fremont proclaimed. I do not say I might not, as a member of Congress, vote for it. What I object to, is, that I as President, shall expressly or impliedly seize and exercise the permanent legislative functions of the government.

So much as to principle. Now as to policy. No doubt the thing was popular in some quarters, and would have been more so if it had been a general declaration of emancipation. The Kentucky Legislature would not budge till that proclamation was modified; and Gen. Anderson telegraphed me that on the news of Gen. Fremont having actually issued deeds of manumission, a whole company of our Volunteers threw down their arms and disbanded. I was so assured, as to think it probable, that the very arms we had furnished Kentucky would be turned against us. I think to lose Kentucky is nearly the same as to lose the whole game. Kentucky gone, we can not hold Missouri, nor, as I think, Maryland. These all against us, and the job on our hands is too large for us. We would as well consent to separation at once, including the surrender of this capitol. On the contrary, if you will give up your restlessness for new positions, and back me manfully on the grounds upon which you and other kind friends gave me the election, and have approved in my public documents, we shall go through triumphantly.

You must not understand I took my course on the proclamation *because* of Kentucky. I took the same ground in a private letter to General Fremont before I heard from Kentucky.

You think I am inconsistent because I did not also forbid Gen. Fremont to shoot men under the proclamation. I understand that part to be within military law; but I also think, and so privately wrote Gen. Fremont, that it is impolitic in this, that our adversaries have the power, and will certainly exercise it, to shoot as many of our men as we shoot of theirs. I did not say this in the public letter, because it is a subject I prefer not to discuss in the hearing of our enemies.

There has been no thought of removing Gen. Fremont on any ground connected with his proclamation; and if there has been any wish for his removal on any ground, our mutual friend Sam. Glover can probably tell you what it was. I hope no real necessity for it exists on any ground.

Suppose you write to Hurlbut and get him to resign. Your friend as ever                                          A. LINCOLN

# John Ross: Message to the National Council

During the summer of 1861 John Ross became concerned that the Confederacy would seek an alliance with his rival Stand Watie, the leader of a powerful tribal faction. Seeking to avoid a split in the Cherokee Nation, Ross announced on August 21 his intention to negotiate a treaty with the Confederacy. The alliance was concluded on October 7, and two days later Ross successfully argued for its ratification.

---

*Message of the Principal Chief of the Cherokee Nation.*

*To the National Committee and Council in National Council convened:*

FRIENDS AND FELLOW-CITIZENS: Since the last meeting of the National Council events have occurred that will occupy a prominent place in the history of the world. The United States have been dissolved and two governments now exist. Twelve of the States composing the late Union have erected themselves into a government under the style of the Confederate States of America, and, as you know, are now engaged in a war for their independence. The contest thus far has been attended with success almost uninterrupted on their side and marked by brilliant victories. Of its final result there seems to be no ground for a reasonable doubt. The unanimity and devotion of the people of the Confederate States must sooner or later secure their success over all opposition and result in the establishment of their independence and a recognition of it by the other nations of the earth.

At the beginning of the conflict I felt that the interests of the Cherokee people would be best maintained by remaining quiet and not involving themselves in it prematurely. Our relations had long existed with the United States Government and bound us to observe amity and peace alike with all the States. Neutrality was proper and wise so long as there remained a reasonable probability that the difficulty between the two sections of the Union would be settled, as a different course would have placed all our rights in jeopardy and might have led to the sacrifice of the people. But when there was no longer any reason to believe that the Union of the States would be continued there was no cause to hesitate as to the course the Cherokee Nation should pursue. Our geographical position and domestic institutions allied us to the South, while the developments daily made in our vicinity and as to the purposes of the war waged against the Confederate States clearly pointed out the path of interest.

These considerations produced a unanimity of sentiment among the people as to the policy to be adopted by the Cherokee Nation, which was clearly expressed in their general meeting held at Tahlequah on the 21st of August last. A copy of the proceedings of that meeting is submitted for your information.

In accordance with the declarations embodied in the resolutions then adopted the Executive Council deemed it proper to exercise the authority conferred upon them by the people there assembled. Messengers were dispatched to General Albert Pike, the distinguished Indian Commissioner of the Confederate States, who, having negotiated treaties with the neighboring Indian nations, was then establishing relations between his Government and the Comanches and other Indians in the Southwest, who bore a copy of the proceedings of the meeting referred to, and a letter from the executive authorities, proposing on behalf of the nation to enter into a treaty of alliance, defensive and offensive, with the Confederate States.

In the exercise of the same general authority, and to be ready as far as practicable to meet any emergency that might spring up on our northern border, it was thought proper to raise a regiment of mounted men and tender its services to General McCulloch. The people responded with alacrity to the call, and it is believed the regiment will be found as efficient as any other like number of men. It is now in the service of the Confederate States for the purpose of aiding in defending their homes and the common rights of the Indian nations about us. This regiment is composed of ten full companies, with two reserve companies, and, in addition to the force previously authorized to be raised to operate outside of the nation by General McCulloch, will show that the Cherokee people are ready to do all in their power in defense of the Confederate cause, which has now become their own. And it is to be hoped that our people will spare no means to sustain them, but contribute liberally to supply any want of comfortable clothing for the approaching season.

In years long since past our ancestors met undaunted those who would invade their mountain homes beyond the Mississippi. Let not their descendants of the present day be found unworthy of them, or unable to stand by the chivalrous men of the South by whose side they may be called to fight in self-defense. The Cherokee people do not desire to be involved in war, but self-preservation fully justifies them in the course they have adopted, and they will be recreant to themselves if they should not sustain it to the utmost of their humble abilities.

A treaty with the Confederate States has been entered into and is now submitted for your ratification. In view of the circumstances by which we are surrounded and the provisions of the treaty it will be found to be the most important ever negotiated on behalf of the Cherokee Nation, and will mark a new era in its history. Without attempting a recapitulation of all its provisions, some of its distinguishing features may be briefly enumerated.

The relations of the Cherokee Nation are changed from the United to the Confederate States, with guarantees of protection and a recognition in future negotiations only of its constitutional authorities. The metes and boundaries, as defined by patent from the United States, are continued, and a guarantee given for the neutral land or a fair consideration in case it should be lost by war or negotiation, and an advance thereon to pay the national debt and to meet other contingencies. The payment of all our annuities and the security of all our investments are provided for. The jurisdiction of the Cherokee courts over all members of the nation, whether by birth, marriage, or adoption, is recognized.

Our title to our lands is placed beyond dispute. Our relations with the Confederate States is that of a ward; theirs to us that of a protectorate, with powers restricted. The district court, with a limited civil and criminal jurisdiction, is admitted into the country instead of being located in Van Buren, as was the United States court. This is perhaps one of the most important provisions of the treaty, and secures to our own citizens the great constitutional right of trial by a jury of their vicinage, and releases them from the petty abuses and vexations of the old system, before a foreign jury and in a foreign country. It gives us a Delegate in Congress on the same footing with Delegates from the Territories, by which our interests can be represented; a right which has long been withheld from the nation and which has imposed upon it a large expense and great injustice. It also contains reasonable stipulation in regard to the appointing powers of the agent and in regard to licensed traders. The Cherokee Nation may be called upon to furnish troops for the defense of the Indian country, but is never to be taxed for the support of any war in which the States may be engaged.

The Cherokee people stand upon new ground. Let us hope that the clouds which overspread the land will be dispersed and that we shall prosper as we have never before done. New avenues to usefulness and distinction will be opened to the ingenuous youth of the country. Our rights of self-government will be more fully recognized, and our citizens be no longer dragged off upon flimsy pretexts, to be imprisoned and tried before distant tribunals. No just cause exists for domestic difficulties. Let them be buried with the past and only mutual friendship and harmony be cherished.

Our relations with the neighboring tribes are of the most friendly character. Let us see that the white path which leads from our country to theirs be obstructed by no act of ours, and that it be open to all those with whom we may be brought into intercourse.

Amid the excitement of the times it is to be hoped that the interests of education will not be allowed to suffer and that no interruption be brought into the usual operations of the government. Let all its officers continue to discharge their appropriate duties.

As the services of some of your members may be required

elsewhere and all unnecessary expense should be avoided, I respectfully recommend that the business of the session be promptly discharged.

JNO. ROSS.,

EXECUTIVE DEPARTMENT,
*Tahlequah, C. N., October* 9, 1861.

# Henry Livermore Abbott to
# Josiah Gardner Abbott

Several Union regiments crossed the Potomac upriver from Washington on October 21 in an attempt to dislodge Confederate troops from Leesburg, Virginia. Henry Livermore Abbott was a nineteen-year-old Harvard graduate serving as a second lieutenant in Company I, 20th Massachusetts Volunteers. He wrote to his father from an army camp near Poolesville, Maryland, and described his regiment's baptism of fire in the Battle of Ball's Bluff.

———————

Camp Benton
Oct 22nd

Dear Papa,

I suppose you have by this got my telegraphic dispatch & know that we are all safe. I will give you a brief description of the affair, only brief because I am rather played out by 2 days hard work.

It seems that upon Sunday the quartermaster of the 15th Mass. had got across & discovered that there were no pickets on the other side; accordingly to them was given the honor of crossing to attack a rebel camp about 2 miles off from the shore. One company of a hundred men from the 20th was ordered to follow the 15th & take possession of the opposite height as a reserve. Co. I & 57 of Caspar's men with Caspar & George were the reserve.

Sunday night the passage was made by the 15th. We followed, getting over about 5 o'clock & taking the heights. Now look at the absurdity of the thing. To cross the river we had two little row boats that together carried over 30 men at a time. We landed on the hill almost perpendicular & very thickly wooded. When we get on the top, we are drawn up on the only open space there is, about wide enough for a front of two

regiments, & about a short rifle shot in length, surrounded on
every side by large, unexplored woods. It was in fact one of the
most complete slaughter pens ever devised. Here we were
kept, while the 15th marched off to surprise the rebel camp.

In the meantime we sent off scouts which resulted in our
first sergeant, Riddle, being shot in the arm. The Fifteenth, of
course, lose their way, are attacked & send word they are surrounded & we must cover their retreat. It was rather an un
comfortable thing. A hundred men in an unknown country,
surrounded by the hidden enemy & cut off virtually, by the
badness of transport, from reinforcement. The col. told us
there was no doubt it was all up with us.

The 15th, however, held their ground nobly till now, when
they fell back on us & shortly after we were reinforced by the
rest of our regiment on hand (making only 300) & by Baker's
brigade & a couple of howitzers, who came in by boatloads of
30. After a while, however, they got a boat which carried 60, so
that the reinforcements came in faster.

Now to begin with the order of battle. I have no right to
criticize it in terms. It will be enough to describe it. The uncovered space I have spoken of was the battle ground. Part of
Baker's brigade was drawn up on the right flank, on the edge
of the wood, with the 15th. The rest was drawn across the opening, back towards the river, 30 feet from the top of the bank.
15 feet behind them the 318 men of our regiment were drawn
up in a second, parallel line, under command of Col. Lee. The
whole was the command of Gen. Baker. The two howitzers in
front entirely unprotected. The enemy in the woods. Here is a
rough sketch:

[    ]

You can see from the sketch that 2 of the regts. on our side
were left in open view, when they might just as well have been
in the woods, while the rebels were conveniently posted in the
woods, just at good rifle shot, from which they didn't venture
out till the conclusion of the fight.

In the first half hour, the gunners & horses of the howitzers
were all killed; the line in front of our regiment was broken &
fled so that we were the only force in the open field & from 2
to 6, we kept that field under a heavy fire of rifles & musketry.
It seemed as if every square inch of air within six feet of the

ground was traversed by bullets as they whistled by us. Tremblet's company got the worst of it. The col. tried to save ours as a reserve. But we foolishly hung all our company's great coats on the trees just behind us. Their red lining was so conspicuous as to draw the enemy's fire at a great rate. Though we were lying down, our men were shot on every side of us. And yet Capt. Bartlett, though standing up nearly all the time, wasn't so much as scratched.

The fight was made up of charges. You would see our capts. rush out in front & cry forward & their companies would follow them at full speed under a tremendous fire till they were obliged to fall back. And this was repeated over & over during the 4 hours fight.

Our company made the last charge. The general was killed, shot by 5 balls; nobody knew who was the senior in command & Col. Lee ordered a retreat. But we were determined to have one more shot. So Frank ordered a charge & we rushed along, followed by all our men without an exception, & by Lieut. Hallowell with 20 men, making about 60 in all. So we charged across the field about half way, when we saw the enemy in full sight. They had just come out of the wood & had halted at our advance. There they were in their dirty gray clothes, their banner waving, cavalry on the flank. For a moment there was a pause. And then, simultaneously, we fired & there came a murderous discharge from the full rebel force. Of course we retreated, but not a man went faster than a walk.

When we got back to the wood, we found the whole regiment cut to pieces & broken up, all the other forces gone & Col. Lee sitting under a tree, swearing he wouldn't go another step, but had rather be taken prisoner. However, we got him to go & we all started down the bank, every body knowing, however, that there was no chance of an escape. The col. ordered a surrender & had a white flag raised but the rebels fired on us & we were obliged to retreat to the river's edge, the rebels pouring down a murderous fire.

When we got down we had lost the col., but heard that the adjutant & major had got him into a boat & carried him across. After that, of course, we had only to look to our own safety. We rallied our men & then proposed to swim across in case they could all do it. We found there were four that couldn't swim, so we were obliged to stay with them, and we sent the rest over. It was hard work to make them leave us, but we insisted upon it, & most of them reached the opposite shore in safety, notwithstanding a heavy fire opened on the swimmers immediately.

With the rest of our men & with Capt. Tremblet & his men, we marched along the shore, picking up about 50 men of Baker's, meaning to surrender ourselves, if we could only get a chance. After we got a mile & a half we found an old nigger who got us a boat & in this we sent across by fives the 70 men with us & then went over ourselves. And so we escaped.

The col., major & adjutant are prisoners, it seems by later intelligence. Capt. Dreher is nearly dead, shot through the head. Capt. Putnam's arm is amputated close to the shoulder. Capt. Babo is killed. Capt. Schmidt has 3 bullets in the legs. Capt. Crowninshield a slight flesh wound. Lieut. Putnam will probably die, shot through the stomach. Lieut. Holmes shot through the breast, will recover, as will Lieut. Lowell, shot in the thigh. Lieut. Wessleheft is dead.

We are now at camp trying to rally enough men to form a company, so as to join it to the two companies that were not engaged & make a battalion of 3 under the command of Col. Palfrey, who was not in the fight, but has since crossed the river with the two unengaged companies.

Gen. Lander has just got back from Washington & is in a horrible rage, swearing that the thing is nothing less than murder. Gen. Banks' column crosses here tomorrow & there will probably be a retreat of the rebels. The little midnight adventure of ours has started the whole thing; now we shall have our revenge.

The good of the action is this. It shows the pluck of our men. They followed their commanders admirably, except in the last charge that we made. Cas wanted to go with us but his men, who had been pretty well cut up, refused to follow. He swore & raved awfully, but it was no go.

The men of our company couldn't possibly have behaved better. They never fired once without an order. They never advanced without an order, as all the rest did. They never retreated without an order, as some of the others did. In short, they never once lost their presence of mind, & behaved as well as if on the parade ground.

Give my love to mamma & the rest.

Your aff. son,
H. L. Abbott
October 22, 1861

# George B. McClellan to
# Mary Ellen McClellan

The battle of Ball's Bluff cost the Union more than 900 men killed, wounded, or missing, six times the Confederate losses. Its political impact was magnified by the death of Colonel Edward D. Baker, a Republican senator from Oregon, former congressman from Illinois, and friend of President Lincoln. McClellan escaped blame for the defeat, and when Winfield Scott retired on November 1, McClellan replaced him as general-in-chief while retaining command of the Army of the Potomac.

---

Oct 25

. . . How weary I am of all this business—case after case—blunder after blunder—trick upon trick—I am well nigh tired of the world, & were it not for you would be fully so.

That affair of Leesburg on Monday last was a terrible butchery —the men fought nobly, but were penned up by a vastly superior force in a place where they had no retreat. The whole thing took place some 40 miles from here without my orders or knowledge—it was entirely unauthorized by me & I am in no manner responsible for it.

The man *directly* to blame for the affair was Col Baker who was killed—he was in command, disregarded entirely the instructions he had received from Stone, & violated all military rules & precautions. Instead of meeting the enemy with double their force & a good ferry behind him, he was outnumbered three to one, & had no means of retreat. Cogswell is a prisoner—he behaved very handsomely. Raymond Lee is also taken. We lost 79 killed, 141 wounded & probably 400 wounded & prisoners—stragglers are constantly coming in however, so that the number of missing is gradually being decreased & may not go beyond 300. I found things in great confusion when I arrived there—Genl Banks having assumed command &

having done *nothing*. In a very short time order & confidence
were restored. During the night I withdrew everything &
everybody to this side of the river—which in truth they should
never have left.

———————

Oct 26

For the last 3 hours I have been at Montgomery Blair's talking with Senators Wade, Trumbull & Chandler about war
matters—they will make a desperate effort tomorrow to have
Genl Scott retired at once. Until that is accomplished I can
effect but little good—he is ever in my way & I am sure does
not desire effective action—I want to get thro' with the war as
rapidly as possible. . . .

I go out soon after bkft to review Porter's Divn, about 5
miles from here.

———————

. . . You remember my wounded friend Col Kelley, whom
we met at Wheeling? He has just done a very pretty thing at
Romney—thrashed the enemy severely, taken all their guns
etc. I am very glad to hear it. You may have heard from the
papers etc of the small row that is going on just now between
Genl Scott & myself—in which the vox populi is coming out
strongly on my side. The affair had got among the soldiers, &
I hear that offs & men all declare that they will fight under no
one but "our George," as the scamps have taken it into their
heads to call me. I ought to take good care of these men, for I
believe they love me from the bottom of their hearts. I can see
it in their faces when I pass among them. I presume the Scott
war will culminate this week—& as it is now very clear that the
people will not permit me to be passed over it seems easy to
predict the result.

Whatever it may be I will try to do my duty to the army &
to the country—with God's help & a single eye to the right I
hope that I may succeed. I appreciate all the difficulties in my
path—the impatience of the people, the venality & bad faith
of the politicians, the gross neglect that has occurred in ob-

taining arms clothing etc—& also I feel in my innermost soul how small is my ability in comparison with the gigantic dimensions of the task, & that, even if I had the greatest intellect that was ever given to man, the result remains in the hands of God. I do not feel that I am an instrument worthy of the great task, but I *do* feel that I did not seek it—it was thrust upon me. I was called to it, my previous life seems to have been unwittingly directed to this great end, & I know that God can accomplish the greatest results with the weakest instruments—therein lies my hope. I feel too that, much as we in the North have erred, the rebels have been far worse than we—they seem to have deserted from the great cardinal virtues.

*October 30, 1861*

---

. . . I have been at work all day nearly on a letter to the Secy of War in regard to future military operations.

I have not been home for some 3 hrs, but am "concealed" at Stanton's to dodge all enemies in shape of "browsing" Presdt etc. . . .

I have been very busy today writing & am pretty thoroughly tired out. The paper is a very important one—as it is intended to place on record the fact that I have left nothing undone to make this army what it ought to be & that the necessity for delay has not been my fault. I have a set of scamps to deal with—unscrupulous & false—if possible they will throw whatever blame there is on my shoulders, & I do not intend to be sacrificed by such people. It is perfectly sickening to have to work with such people & to see the fate of the nation in such hands. I still trust that the all wise Creator does not intend our destruction, & that in his own good time he will free the nation from the imbeciles who curse it & will restore us to his favor. I know that as a nation we have grieviously sinned, but I trust that there is a limit to his wrath & that ere long we will begin to experience his mercy. But it is terrible to stand by & see the cowardice of the Presdt, the vileness of Seward, & the rascality of Cameron—Welles is an old woman—Bates an old fool. The only man of courage & sense in the Cabinet is Blair, & I do not altogether fancy him!

I cannot guess at my movements for they are not within my

own control. I cannot move without more means & I do not possess the power to control those means. The people think me all powerful. Never was there a greater mistake—I am thwarted & deceived by these incapables at every turn. I am doing all I can to get ready to move before winter sets in—but it now begins to look as if we are condemned to a winter of inactivity. If it is so the fault will not be mine—there will be that consolation for my conscience, even if the world at large never knows it. . . .

I have one great comfort in all this—that is that I did not seek this position, as you well know, & I still trust that God will support me & bear me out—he could not have placed me here for nothing. . . .

I am. I have just returned from a ride over the river where I went pretty late, to seek refuge in Fitz Porter's camp. You would have laughed if you could have seen me dodge off. I quietly told the little duke (Chartres) to get our horses saddled, & then we slipped off without escort or orderlies & trotted away for Fitz John's camp where we had a quiet talk over the camp fire.

I saw yesterday Genl Scott's letter asking to be placed on the Retired List & saying nothing about Halleck. The offer was to be accepted last night & they propose to make me at once Commander in Chief of the Army. I cannot get up any especial feeling about it—I feel the vast responsibility it imposes upon me. I feel a sense of relief at the prospect of having my own way untrammelled, but I cannot discover in my own heart one symptom of gratified vanity or ambition.

*October 31, 1861*

# Charles Francis Adams Jr. to Henry Adams

Charles Francis Adams Jr. expressed his unhappiness with the Lincoln administration in a letter written from Boston to his brother in London.

---

*Boston*, November 5, 1861

By the last mail I got a letter from you intended for the press. I have not however used it as intended. . . . The great facts of the case stand out. Six months of this war have gone and in them we have done much; and by we I mean our rulers. But if we have done much with our means, the rebels have performed miracles with theirs. At the end of six months have we a policy? Are traitors weeded out of our departments? Is our blockade effective? Is the war prosecuted honestly and vigorously? To all these questions there is but one answer. The President is not equal to the crisis; that we cannot now help. The Secretary of War is corrupt and the Secretary of the Navy is incompetent; that we can help and ought to. With the rebels showing us what we can do, we ought to be ashamed not to do more. But for me I despair of doing more without a purification of the Cabinet. With Seward I am satisfied, and so is the country at bottom, for our foreign affairs are creditable. Chase will do and to Blair I make no objection. But all the rest I wish the people would drive from power. Your historical examples are not good. When was England greatest? Was it not when an angry people drove the drivellers from office and forced on an unwilling King the elder Pitt, who reversed at once the whole current of a war? I want to see Holt in the War Department and a New York shipowner in that of the Navy, or else Mr. Dana. I am tired of incompetents and I want to see Lincoln forced to adopt a manly line of policy which all men may comprehend. The people here call for energy, not change, and if

Lincoln were only a wise man he could unite them in spite of party cries, and with an eye solely to the public good.

Herewith you will receive three Independents, in each of which you will find an article by me for your delectation. They answer at some length your suggestion that I am an "abolitionist." I am also assured that they met with favor in the eyes of Wendell Phillips, which indeed I do not understand. I imagine they will not meet your and my father's views, but on the whole I am not dissatisfied with the two last in general and the last in particular. . . .

Please notice the leader in the Independent of the 24th. I did more than I expected in influencing the editorials of the Independent.

# George B. McClellan to Samuel L. M. Barlow

McClellan discussed his plans in a letter to his friend Samuel Barlow, a New York lawyer and railroad executive active in Democratic politics.

---

My dear Samuel L. F. X. Q. Q.     Washington Nov 8 1861

Better late than never is a pretty good adage—& never better applied in this instance. I am pretty well fagged out, for it is 1 am, & as I have still more work to do, it suggested itself to me that I would refresh myself by an interlude in the way of a few words to an old friend whom I have treated shamefully. First let me thank you for that "carpet bag" which has been the companion of my woes in Western Va & here—I never shave without thinking of you, & religiously determining to write to you before the close of the day—you can therefore judge how little my promises are to be relied upon! Next let me say that that fine blanket you sent me by Van Vliet (our revered & venerable friend) shall comfort me when we advance. Speaking of an advance let me beg of you not to be impatient (I do not know that you are)—do you & all your friends trust implicitly in me—I am more anxious to advance than any other person in this country—there is no one whose interests would be so much subserved by prompt success as myself.

I feel however that the issue of this struggle is to be decided by the next great battle, & that I owe it to my country & myself not to advance until I have reasonable chances in my favor. The strength of the Army of the Potomac has been vastly overrated in the public opinion. It is now strong enough & well disciplined enough to hold Washington against *any* attack—I care not in what numbers. But, leaving the necessary garrisons here, at Baltimore etc—I cannot yet move in force equal to that which the enemy probably has in my front. We are rapidly increasing in numbers & efficiency. My intention is simply this —I will pay no attention to popular clamor—quietly, & quickly as possible, make this Army strong enough & effective enough to give me a reasonable certainty that, if I am able to handle the form, I will win the first battle. I expect to fight a terrible battle—I know full well the capacity of the Generals opposed to me, for by a singular chance they were once my most intimate friends—tho' we can never meet except as mortal foes hereafter—I appreciate too the courage & discipline of the rebel troops—I believe I know the obstacles in our path. I will first be sure that I have an Army strong enough & well enough instructed to fight with reasonable chances of success —I do not ask for perfect certainty. When I am ready I will move without regard to season or weather—I can overcome *these* difficulties. I think that the interests of the country demand the "festina lente" policy. But of one thing you can rest assured—when the blow *is* struck it will be heavy, rapid, & decisive. Help me to dodge the nigger—we want nothing to do with him. *I* am fighting to preserve the integrity of the Union & the power of the Govt—on no other issue. To gain that end we cannot afford to raise up the negro question—it must be incidental & subsidiary. The Presdt is perfectly honest & is really sound on the nigger question—I will answer for it now that things go right with him. As far as you can, keep the papers & the politicians from running over me—that speech that some rascal made the other day that I did *not dare* to advance, & had said so, was a lie—I have always said, when it was necessary to say anything, that I was not yet strong enough— but, did the public service require it, I would *dare* to advance with 10,000 men & throw my life in the balance.

I have said enough for tonight—& must go back to my work. I hope some time next week to have a review of from 30,000 to 50,000 good troops—can you not bring Madame on to it? If you come alone I can certainly accommodate you in my new house (that once occupied by Bayard Smith, corner of H & 15th)—I *think* I will have my ménage so arranged within two days that I shall be glad to have *her* come too. Telegraph me whether she can accompany you, & I will frankly reply whether my *cook* is ready—I *think* I can have everything ready for it. Do write to me often, & don't get mad if I delay replies—for I am rather busy.

Ever your sincere friend
Geo B McClellan

*All this is confidential.*

I think that it is now best to resign the Presidency of the O & M—Qu'en pensez vous? Do come on here & see me.

# Ulysses S. Grant to Jesse Root Grant

Ulysses S. Grant assumed command in early September of the Union forces at Cairo, Illinois, at the junction of the Ohio and Mississippi rivers. On November 7 he led 3,000 men in a raid on the Confederate camp at Belmont, Missouri.

––––––––––––––

Cairo, November 8th 1861

Dear Father,

It is late at night and I want to get a letter into the Mail for you before it closes. As I have just finished a very hasty letter to Julia that contains about what I would write, and having something els to do myself, I will have my clerk copy it on to this.

Day before yesterday, I left here with about 3000 men in five steamers, convoyed by two Gun Boats, and proceeded down the river, to within about twelve miles of Columbus. The next morning the Boats were dropped down just out of range of the enemies Batteries, and the troops debarked—

During this operation our Gun-Boats exercised the rebels by throwing shells into their Camps and Batteries—

When all ready we proceeded about one mile towards Belmont opposite Columbus: where I formed the troops into lines, and ordered two Companies from each Regiment to deploy as skirmishers, and push on through the woods and discover the position of the enemy. They had gone but a little way when they were fired upon and the *Ball* may be said to have fairly opened.

The whole command with the exception of a small reserve, were then deployed in like manner with the first, and ordered forward. The order was obeyed with great alacrity, the men all showing great courage. I can say with gratification that every Colonel without a single exception, set an example to their commands that inspired a confidence that will always insure victory when there is the slightest possibility of gaining one. I feel truly proud to command such men. From here we fought our way from tree to tree through the woods to Belmont, about 2 1/2 miles, the enemy contesting every foot of ground. Here the enemy had strengthened their position by felling the trees for two or three hundred yards, and sharpening the limbs making a sort of Abattis. Our men charged through making the victory complete, giving us possession of their Camp and Garrison Equipage Artillery and every thing else.

We got a great many prisoners, the majority however succeeded in getting aboard their Steamers, and pushing across the river  We burned every thing possible and started back having accomplished all that we went for, and even more. Belmont is entirely covered by the Batteries from Columbus and is worth nothing as a Military Position. Cannot be held without Columbus

The object of the expedition was to prevent the enemy from sending a force into Missouri to cut off troops I had sent there for a special purpose, and to prevent reinforcing Price

Besides being well fortified at Columbus their numbers far exceed ours, and it would have been folly to have attacked them. We found the Confederates well armed and brave. On our return stragglers that had been left in our rear, *now front*, fired into us and more recrossed the river and gave us Battle for full a mile and afterwards at the Boats when we were embarking. There was no hasty retreating or running away. Taking into account the object of the expedition the victory was most complete. It has given me a confidence in the Officers and men of this command, that will enable me to lead them in any future engagement without fear of the result. Genl. McClernand, (who by the way acted with great coolness and courage throughout, and proved that he is a soldier as well as statesman) and my self each had our Horses shot under us. Most of the Field Officers met with the same loss, besides nearly one third of them being Killed or wounded themselves. As near as I can ascertain our loss was about 250 Killed wounded and missing  I write in great haste to get this in the Office tonight

U. S. GRANT

# Lunsford P. Yandell Jr. to Lunsford Yandell Sr.

The fighting at Belmont cost each side more than 600 men killed, wounded, or missing. A surgeon from Kentucky serving with the Confederate army, Lunsford Yandell Jr. wrote about the battle to his father, a prominent Louisville physician.

———————

COLUMBUS, November 10.

MY DEAR FATHER: I know you have been impatient to hear from me since news reached you of the battle, but I have not had time till this morning. Thursday morning two gunboats, with five steamboats, landed six or eight miles above us on the Missouri shore, and were seen to disembark infantry, artillery, and cavalry in large numbers. Troops were thrown across from our side of the river about eight or nine o'clock, and about eleven o'clock the battle commenced and raged till three or four o'clock P.M. The gunboats came down within range of our camp and commenced throwing shot and shell about eight o'clock. One or two shots fell inside our line—one piece near my tent. Hamilton's artillery replied to the boats, and they soon moved out of range, when Captain Stewart, with his Parrott guns, went two miles up the bluff and opened on the boats. Most of his guns threw over the boats, and the enemy's balls did not reach us. Adjutant Hammond and I were with Captain Stewart, and helped the men to place the guns in position a number of times. They were just going to fire one of the guns, when Hammond and I retired some ten or twelve yards. The gun was fired—the explosion was terrific—and some one yelled out "Two men killed!" I rushed up immediately and saw at once that they were killed. The gun had exploded into a thousand atoms. One of the men had his right arm torn to pieces, and the ribs on that side pulpified, though the skin was not broken. He breathed half an hour. The other poor fellow received a piece of iron under the chin, which passed up into the brain—the blood gushing from his nose and ears. He never breathed afterward. A third man received a slight wound of the arm. The fragments of the gun flew in every direction, and I can only wonder that more of us were not killed. A horse hitched near mine received a glancing wound from a piece of the gun.

Our brigade was ordered under arms about noon—or rather, it was kept under arms all the morning, but I was ordered across the river about noon. Our men were previously anxious to be led over soon in the morning; but Gen. Polk would not allow it, as he expected an attack from this side of the river—which was certainly the plan of the enemy, but it was not carried out.

We did not get on the ground till the enemy were in full retreat, and we never got near them; in fact, only one regiment of our brigade pursued them at all, and they only for a mile or two. I went with Col. Scott's regiment, belonging to Col. Neeley's brigade. When about two miles out we were ordered back, as the enemy had reached his boats. I had fifty or eighty men detailed from Scott's regiment to scour the woods with me to pick up the wounded. We found none but Federals, but they were in such numbers we could only take back a few and return for the others. In one cornfield they were lying, dead and wounded, as thick as stumps in a new field. I saw sixty or seventy, and others report as many as two hundred in this field. They were mostly of the Sixth Iowa regiment, and some of the Twenty-seventh Illinois. The Lieutenant-Colonel and three captains I know to have been killed, or wounded and taken prisoners. The Seventh Iowa was almost annihilated. The scene upon the battle-field was awful.

The wounded men groaned and moaned, yelled and shrieked with pain. I had opium, brandy, and water, with which I alleviated their torture, and, poor creatures, they were exceedingly grateful. I was out until two o'clock that night with Col. Neeley and a battalion of the Fourth regiment picking up the wounded. In the woods and in the field the dead were so thick that it required careful riding to keep from tramping their bodies. The only means I had of knowing the road that night was by the corpses I had noticed in the afternoon. In one place

there were eleven bodies lying side by side; further on were
five; in another place were fifteen near together. These were
the only groups that I noticed, but I sometimes found six or
eight within a space of twenty yards. Some of the poor creatures had crawled to the foot of trees, and laid their heads
upon the roots and crossed their arms; others lay upon their
backs with arms and legs outstretched; some were doubled up,
and, in fact, they were in every imaginable position. As to the
variety of expression depicted upon the faces of the corpses, of
which I heard so much, I saw nothing of it. They all looked
pretty much alike—as much alike as dead men from any other
cause. Some had their eyes open, some closed; some had their
mouths open, and others had them closed. There is a terrible
sameness in the appearance of all the dead men I have ever
seen. The only faces which were disfigured were those that
were burned, or shot, or blackened with powder.

There were not many wounds from cannon balls or shells,
but I saw almost every variety of wounds from musket and
rifle balls. I saw almost all the battle from our camp, which is
on top of the high bluff. The Missouri side is low and flat, and
much of the battle-ground is open. The battle swayed back
and forth many times. Once our men were driven clear under
the river bank, having got out of cartridges. For several hours
General Pillow held the enemy in check with two thousand
men, the enemy having seven thousand infantry, four hundred
and fifty cavalry, and I don't recollect their artillery. Pillow
acted with great bravery. So did Polk and Cheatham, but they
were not in the fight for several hours after Pillow. Pillow's escape is miraculous. Every one of his staff officers had his horse
shot under him. One of them, Gus. Henry, had two shot under
him. One of his aids was shot through the hip, and his horse
was riddled with balls. Pillow wore a splendid uniform, very
conspicuous, and rode the handsomest gray mare in the army.
As we watched the fighting from the bluff, and saw our men
advance and retreat, waver and fall back, and then saw the
Arkansas troops' tents on fire, and the Stars and Stripes advancing toward the river, and some of our men crowding
down to the very water's edge, I tell you my feelings were indescribable. The scene was grand, but it was terrible, and
when I closed my eyes about four o'clock next morning, I

could see regiments charging and retreating—men falling and yelling—horses and men torn and mangled—and myriads of horrid spectacles. It was a bloody enjoyment, but we do not know the loss on either side yet.

It is roughly estimated that we lost two hundred and fifty in killed, wounded, and missing, and the enemy five hundred in killed and wounded. An immense number of horses were killed. I rode over the battle-field yesterday. For several miles the trees are torn and barked by balls, and many horses lie upon the ground, some torn open by shells and others riddled by balls. You can see innumerable stains of blood upon the ground. Where poor, gallant Armstrong was killed, there were eleven dead bodies. At the time of his death, he had a cap upon his sword waving it, rallying his men. My friend Captain Billy Jackson was shot in the hip while leading a portion of Russell's brigade. I think he will recover. I am afraid Jimmy Walker (James' son) will not recover. I think he is shot through the rectum.

The day before the battle, Jackson, Major Butler, of the Eleventh Louisiana regiment, Wilson, of Watson's battery, Lieut. Ball, of same regiment, and Major Gus. Henry, and myself dined at Gen. Pillow's. Butler was shot through and died yesterday. Lieut. Ball was dangerously injured, and Henry had two horses shot under him. Jackson I have spoken of. I have given you but a poor account of what I saw, but I have not time to go more into details now, and I am out of kelter besides. You will see a full account in the papers of the fight. I wish the war would close. Such scenes as that of Thursday are sickening; and this destruction of life is so useless. I believe we shall have some terrible fighting very soon on the coast, in Virginia and in Kentucky. Much love to mother and sister when you see them. Mr. Law gave me the letter.

I am your devoted son,

LUNSFORD P. YANDELL.

November 10, 1861

## Samuel Francis Du Pont to Sophie Du Pont

A career naval officer who had served in the U.S.-Mexican War, Captain Samuel Francis Du Pont commanded the fleet that captured the forts guarding Port Royal Sound on November 7. His victory gave the Union possession of an excellent natural harbor that served as a base for the squadron blockading the coast from South Carolina to Florida. In a letter to his wife Du Pont described the abandoned plantations of the region, now occupied by troops under the command of General Thomas W. Sherman (no relation to William T. Sherman).

――――――――

*Wabash*, Port Royal, 13 Nov. 1861

My precious Sophie,

I sent a letter by that hard-named steamer, the *Coatzacoalcos* —in a very bad condition, by the way.

Yesterday I made an excursion in the *Seneca* to Beaufort, seventeen miles from this anchorage up the Beaufort River. The scenery, owing to the cabbage palm, is tropical; the mansions of the planters and the Negro quarters, more or less prominent or embowered in the trees, gave a good deal of picturesqueness to the scene. The day was lovely, though warm. General Sherman was with me; my staff, Captains Comstock and Eldridge of the *Baltic* and *Atlantic* I also invited. Ammen, the commander of the *Seneca*, is a kindly and hospitable person as well as a good officer—and had found oysters, boasting he was the only officer who had had the prévoyance to bring oyster tongs for taking them.

You approach Beaufort on its full seaward façade; the houses are two and three stories, with verandas, large, and have a beautiful effect; the streets are wide, the gardens and shrubbery in the yards show the refinements of educated people but without the order of Northern towns of this description.

And now comes, my dear, the saddest picture that you can well conceive of, an *inside* view of this nefarious secession. We

596

landed, three gunboats covering, but in addition the armed
launches of this ship we towed up, and the crews went on
shore with their howitzers, and we placed pickets, to provide
against a treacherous foe, or a cavalry rush, [      ] astern, not
that we believed in such a thing, for the terror still continues.

Before our gunboats got up, the Negroes had commenced
plundering—the stores were all rifled and looked like a sacked
town; by this time our officers stopped the robbery of the private houses, though much had been carried off, in hopes the
whites would return. On my asking an old blacky of Mr. Nat
Heyward's, as he is called, a millionaire gentleman, why the remainder of the furniture in his handsome mansion was not carried off, he replied, "Massa, because Yankee tell 'em they
shoot 'em."

A sadder picture of desolation from the *desertion* of the population cannot be imagined; and the inhabitants fled not from
fear of *us* but from the dread of their own Negroes; a few
household servants followed their masters, but the field hands
they dare not attempt to control, and the overseers had run
with the masters. There are fifteen slaves to one white in this
part; the latter threatened to shoot if they did not follow them
into the interior, but I believe dare not attempt to execute this
threat. The Negroes, anxious to show everything, said to Captain Collins, *Unadilla*, "Massa, they more afraid us, than you"
—this was often repeated. Yet these are people whose very
slaves were to drive us into the sea, fleeing from the institution
with terror in their hearts, not taking a thing with them—the
center tables with lamps upon them, books and writing cards,
safes *unopened* which had defied the strength and ingenuity of
the Negroes. The latter, for want of means of carrying things,
cut open all the bedding to get the ticking with which to tie up
things. Such a mess. Outside the beautiful oleanders and chry-
santhemums smiled on this scene of robbery and confusion.

We took all the *public* property, a fine Fresnel lens, and
buoys for the channels; and General Sherman having declined
holding it as a military point, and as it only absorbs my force
from what is more necessary, and exposing it, when the rebels
recover from their panic, to devices of fire vessels and masked
batteries too far from my support, I have withdrawn the force.
I regret to leave the place to the Negroes, but why should I

expose my people to save the property of those who are planning their destruction and who disregard the ordinary rules of
war?

Mr. *Rhett*'s house was visited, and General Drayton's headquarters—all the same aspect. On our way down we stopped
at the ruins of an old Huguenot fort, built by Mons. de Rib-
audiere, said to have sustained successfully an assault from a
Spanish force from St. Augustine, under Philip the 2d. The
outline is left—but we were rejoiced more than anything at
seeing such a live-oak grove as I never saw in Florida. We
walked through it, touched by the hanging moss—and came
up to a large open space covered with sea-island cotton, un-
gathered and dropping from the pods. The Negroes were all
there, their quarters were curious; two were grinding corn
between two stones, the earliest form of such a process known.
Some fifty bales of cotton, unginned, lay in a building. The
Negroes were filthy but friendly, with scarcely any modification of the pure African feature. I had been carrying in my
pocket ever since I had left New York some quarters and
dimes, and I got a basket of eggs from them—the Negroes
running about and gathering them in all directions; others got
turkeys. All was paid for, and during the visit of the gunboats
and their five days at Beaufort not an article was taken by our
men, though things were laying about in all directions. *One*
thing we did take, we rescued Mr. Pope's large quarto family
Bible from some rubbish and furniture going into a boat. Mr.
Dorrance took it to return to its owner at some future day.
General Drayton's wife was a Miss Pope.

On our return we found *two* arrivals, water vessels, bringing
dates to the 7th. John Goldsborough put back and seems to
have *injured himself* much by so doing—he was halfway and
could have come here as well as return.

I see the gale was stronger in New York than with us, and
causing anxiety for us at home. I saw an absurd general order
from Sherman in the *Herald* of the 6th regulating the order of
sailing of his transports, etc.—after he knew we had arranged
the thing, established the signals, and instructed the transport
captains. Then his orders about *landing*; not one item of either
could they execute.

Captains Comstock and Eldridge spoke in the warmest

terms of the battle; the gallantry and lead of this ship they dwelt on with earnestness, saying more to others than they did to me, but neither did *other* matters escape them; one of them said to Davis, "The *Susquehanna* stuck to you like wax and was a true supporter, why was the line broken off after her?" Of course this inquiry was turned off. There was no want of courage anywhere, but *entre nous*, a want of head. I think Godon was hurt at something I said, not in reference to the above but to his preventing me from using my port broadside by being in the way during a certain part of the engagement. My remark involved a compliment, by saying he wanted a fight on his *own hook*—but he connected this with the other affair, but I hope he will get over it soon.

Have you heard today of our doings? Davis and Rodgers and myself are always speculating about this, and how much of our doings reached you by the Southern papers. I forgot to tell you to get the *Herald* for the accounts. It will be more full and more friendly.

We are busy tinkering up the engines—some of them are very worthless. Firing off the harbor this morning; I have sent out *Seneca* to see what it means. Probably *Augusta* chasing a vessel off Savannah.

Our Marine battalion was established on Bay Point—they behaved well during the gale on the *Governor*, for which they deserve credit, for it showed *moral* courage, so rare with that class of people; the people of the *Governor* behaved very badly.

8 o'clock. My dearest Sophie, the *Florida* is in and I have your dear letter by her—it was a great treat; though another whole week you will have to have passed before you were relieved by the news from us, except what will have oozed out from the Southern account. Your account of the intensity of interest in the expedition also struck me much and I read some paragraphs of it to Davis and Rodgers. A letter of great interest from Turner conveys the same thing from Philadelphia. But my! What would this have produced if we had not been successful? Drayton thinks the blow was the severest that could have been struck in the whole South—and, in my judgment, far beyond the capture of Charleston or Savannah, for in neither could we have got ships of all sizes. Strange that more vessels are here now than ever entered before in all time!—to

say nothing of the size. One of the finest harbors in the world, it possesses, besides, what we call the roadstead.

I send in the morning the gunboats up to Beaufort, General Sherman writing to a clergyman who has asked protection and wants to send an officer to Port Royal Ferry, three or four miles from Beaufort, and I do not think it prudent to send one boat alone.

I got newspapers in abundance up to the 9th but have not time scarcely to read them. I was sorry for Goldsborough but he bore his disappointment like a man—he was boarded from the *San Jacinto* and told of Mason and Slidell being on board!

*15 Nov. 1861*　　Friday. My dearest Sophie, we are overwhelmed here by events. Yesterday the *Rhode Island*, Trenchard, from the Gulf and now today the *Connecticut*, Woodhull, from New York and Hampton Roads—passed the *Bienville* going into latter place on Tuesday morning a few hours earlier than I thought. I have three letters from you and two notes, Nos. 11, 12, and 13, and though they came this morning I have only read one of them—so great is the pressure upon me of the official correspondence. I only got up on deck once today, for ten minutes after tea, to breathe the fresh air, and yet nothing I like so well as to go there and look at the ships in the harbor and dwell on the wonderful change a few days have wrought in one of the finest harbors in the known world.

The *Atlantic* goes at daylight and McKinley is copying the last of my *detailed* account of our battle—it has given me great labor, but it is accomplished and I feel relieved from its incubus. Davis, who has been on shore on Hilton Head side for the first time, thinks our achievement much greater than he did before seeing the fort and does not wonder that Generals Drayton and Ripley felt sure of destroying us.

I have received all you sent me—the pants, tablecloths, books, and before that the map by Goldsborough's ship. How kind you are—all these things are very acceptable to me and they make me to think of your devotion. I received the *North American* with the notice of the expedition and of myself, and I am free to confess that it is the first time in my life that a newspaper panegyric gratified me. I don't mean of course that I felt that I deserved it all, but its taste and sentiment were so much above those notices generally, and so free from vulgar puffing that it touched me sensibly. The portrait in *Harper's Weekly* is the most miserable of all likenesses I ever saw. But, my dear Sophie, I agree with you—we are not chastened yet by this war as we should be; it is fearful to think how God might chastise us and yet fall short of what we deserve.

This vaingloriousness is bad, and when I see what a reverse would have been to us, however unavoidable, under such absurd expectations, it makes me shrink from men and turn to God with a thankful heart.

In your last you express very properly one of the dangers I am liable to, viz., yielding my own judgment to pressure from without, or to meet exaggerated expectations—but I have had the moral courage to resist this already. Had I engaged Wednesday afternoon when the wind subsided, we should have been discomfited for that day certainly. But I said to myself, as I wrote you I think, if no troops were present, I never should put the thing in question; it would be so wrong—and I determined to do what was right. I knew a success would wipe away all the misgivings of the class who doubt everybody, and these were loudest afterwards in my praise.

Thank Eleu for her pincushion. Write to Peter Kemble I have the shirts and thank him much. I have not time to write to him by this mail. Please also ask Peter to do me the favor to purchase an opera nautical spyglass, the best he can find in New York, to go as high as $25 or $30—perhaps Pike's would be a good place—and to send it to me by Captain Eldridge on the return of the steamer *Atlantic*; and apologize for my troubling him, though from his kind letter I am sure it will give him pleasure. Mr. George W. Blunt also knows about such glasses.

I was glad to see Henry had been to Washington. I will begin soon another letter and note things in yours. I have to write a report about Beaufort. Sherman's flag of truce ended in nothing but being received with hauteur. I think he ought not to have issued a proclamation without showing it to me. I like him, but I think he has one or two intrigants with him who are jealous of us. I hope Sherman will come up to a commander in chief's requirements.

If we were to withdraw the moral effect and physical force of this squadron, I think he and his army would be prisoners of war in one month from this time.

Love to all; I long to hear how our work is received. I see the New York *Times* of 10 November, in his Washington correspondent, says the public will be disappointed in the place.

Every day convinces me it was the point of all others to strike, not *at all* excepting Savannah or Charleston.

Please get me some nice paper of the best quality when you go to Philadelphia, and note and letter, and stubbedy pen— envelopes of all sizes except the long official ones.

Good night and love to all, dearest. Ever your own devoted,

F.

Missroon came in today, not his ship, and I posted him up about Savannah; he looks very well and happy.

# Sam Mitchell: Narrative of the capture of the Sea Islands

Sam Mitchell, an eleven year-old boy tending cows on a plantation on Lady's Island, was one of the thousands of slaves liberated by the Union victory at Port Royal. In a 1937 interview with the Federal Writers' Project of the Works Progress Administration, Mitchell, now eighty-seven, recalled the arrival of the Du Pont's ships and the sudden flight of his owner, John Chaplin.

———————

Maussa had nine chillen, six boy been in Rebel army. Dat Wednesday in November w'en gun fust shoot to Bay Pint (Point) I t'ought it been t'under rolling, but dey ain't no cloud. My mother say, 'son, dat ain't no t'under, dat Yankee come to gib you Freedom.' I been so glad, I jump up and down and run. My father been splitting rail and Maussa come from Beaufort in de carriage and tear by him yelling for de driver. He told de driver to git his eight-oar boat name Tarrify and carry him to Charleston. My father he run to his house and tell my mother w'at Maussa say. My mother say, 'You ain't gonna row no boat to Charleston, you go out dat back door and keep a-going. So my father he did so and w'en dey git 'nuf nigger to row boat and Maussa and his family go right away to Charleston.

After Freedom come everybody do as he please. De Yankee open school for nigger and teacher lib in Maussa house to Brickyaa'd. My father git job as carpenter wid Yankee and buy ten acre ob land on Ladies Island.

———————

Did I ebber hear ob Abraham Lincoln? I got his history right here in my house. He was de president of de United

States that freed four million slave. He come to Beaufort befo'
de war and et dinner to Col. Paul Hamilton house at de Oaks.
He left his gold-headed walking cane dere and ain't nobody
know de president of de United States been to Beaufort 'till he
write back and tell um to look behind de door and send um his
gold-headed walking cane.

# Henry Tucker: God in the War

November 15, 1861

Tucker, a Baptist minister, delivered this sermon before the Georgia legislature in the state capitol at Milledgeville.

---

## SERMON.

*"Come behold the works of the Lord, what desolations He hath made in the earth.*

*He maketh wars to cease unto the end of the earth; He breaketh the bow, and cutteth the spear in sunder; He burneth the chariot in the fire."*

*PSALMS XLVI, 8:9.*

Desolation! Desolation! Thousands of our young men have been murdered. Thousands of fathers and mothers among us have been bereaved of their sons. Thousands of widows are left disconsolate and heart-broken, to struggle through life alone. The wail of thousands of orphans is heard through the land, the Ægis of a father's protection being removed from over their defenceless heads. Thousands of brave men are at this moment lying on beds of languishing, some prostrated by the diseases incident to the army and camp, and some by cruel wounds. Every house within reach of the seat of war is a hospital, and every hospital is crowded. Huge warehouses emptied of their merchandize, and churches, and great barns, are filled with long rows of pallets beside each other, containing each a sufferer, pale, emaciated and ghastly. Some writhe with pain; some rage with delirium; some waste with fever; some speak of *home*, and drop bitter tears at the recollection of wives soon to be widows, and babes soon to be fatherless. The nurse hurries with noiseless step, ministering from bedside to bedside. The pious chaplain whispers of Jesus to the dying. The surgeon is in frightful practice, bloody though beneficent; and as his knife glides through the quivering flesh and his saw grates through the bone and tears through the marrow, the suppressed groan bears witness to the anguish. A father stands by perhaps, to see his son mutilated. Mother and wife and sisters at home witness the scene by a dreadful clairvoyance, and with them the operation lasts not for moments but for weeks. Every groan in the hospital or tent, or on the bloody field, wakes echoes at home. There is not a city, nor village, nor hamlet, nor neighborhood that has not its representatives in the army, and scarcely a heart in our whole Confederacy that is not either bruised by strokes already fallen, or pained by a solicitude scarcely less dreadful than the reality. Desolation! Desolation! Hearts desolate, homes desolate, the whole land desolate! Our young men, our brave young men, our future statesmen, and scholars and divines, to whom we should bequeath this great though youthful empire with all its destinies; the flower of our society,—contributions from that genuine and proper aristocracy which consists of intelligence and virtue,—thousands, thousands of them laid upon the altar! And alas! the end is not yet. Another six months may more than double the desolation. Relentless winter may aid the enemy in his work of death. The youth accustomed at home to shelter, and bed, and fire, and all the comforts of high civilization, standing guard on wintry night, exposed to freezing rain and pealing blasts, and having completed his doleful task, retiring to his tent, to lie upon the bare ground, in clothes encrusted with ice, may not falter in *spirit* in view of his hardships; the fires of patriotism may still keep up the warmth at his heart; when he remembers that he is fighting for the honor of his father, and for the purity of his mother and sisters, and for all that is worth having in the world, he may cheerfully brave the terrors of a winter campaign; but though his soul be undaunted, his body will fail. Next spring when the daisies begin to blow, thousands of little hillocks dotted all over the country on mountain side and in valley, marked at each end with a rough memorial stone, and a brief and rude inscription made perhaps with the point of a bayonet, will silently but ah! how impressively, confirm the sad prophecy of this hour. Thus the work of desolation may go on winter after winter, until the malice of our foes is satiated, and until our young men are all gone. But let us not anticipate. The present alone presents subjects of contemplation, enough to fill the imagination and to break the heart.

These are the desolations of war. Do you ask why I present this sad, this melancholy picture? Why I make this heart-rending recital of woes enough to make heaven weep? In so doing I am but following the example of the Psalmist when he says, "Come behold the works of the Lord, what *desolations* He hath made in the earth!" If in the midst of victory when the God of Israel had given success to the arms of his people, their leader and king called upon them to forget their successes and meditate on the desolations of war, it must be right for the man of God now, to call upon his countrymen in the midst of a series of victories such as perhaps were never won in a war before, to forget their triumphs, and contemplate for a little the expense of life and of sorrow which those triumphs have cost.

Come then my countrymen, and behold the desolation. What emotion does it excite? What passion does it stimulate? To what action does it prompt? Indignation at the fanaticism, folly and sin of those who brought it all about. Rage at the authors of our ruin. Retaliation! To arms! To arms! Let us kill! Let us destroy! Let us exterminate the miscreants from the earth! Up with the black flag! They deserve no quarter! They alone are to blame for this horror of horrors. We had no hand in bringing it on. We asked for nothing but our rights. Our desire was for peace. They tormented us without cause while we were with them. What we cherish as a heaven-ordained institution they denounce as the "sum of all villainies." They regarded us as worse than heathen and pirates; they degraded us from all equality; they spurned us from all fellowship; they taught their children to hate us; their ministers of religion chased us like bloodhounds, actually putting weapons of death in the hands of their agents with instructions to murder us. They made a hero and a martyr of him, who at Harper's Ferry openly avowed his design, to enact over in all our land the horrid scenes of St. Domingo,—thus by the popular voice dooming us to death and our wives and daughters to worse than death; and when after these outrages, we sought no retaliation but besought them to let us go in peace, they still clutched us with frantic grasp, in order to filch away our substance, and reduce us to a bondage more degrading than that which they affect to pity in the negro.

I will not continue to give expression to thoughts which alas! have already taken too deep hold on us all. But in the midst of all the rage, resentment, and fury, which a contemplation of these facts of history is calculated to engender, let me repeat to you the words of the text, with an emphasis which perhaps will lift your minds above the consideration of second causes. "Come behold the works of the *Lord*, what desolations *He* hath made in the earth!" If it be important to regard the desolations of war, it is still more so, to be mindful of the source whence they come. This perhaps was the chief object of the Psalmist. If he pointed to the rod, it was that all hearts should be turned towards Him who held it. And this my countrymen it is all important for *us* to remember,—that GOD is in the war. *He* brought it upon us. The wickedness and folly of our enemies may have been the *occasion* of it, but these could not in any proper sense be the *cause*. That is but a shallow philosophy which sees a cause in anything outside of God. The idea of cause involves by necessity the idea of power, and what power is there independent of God? Aside from the will of God, what nexus can there be, between an effect and the antecedent which by a sad misnomer we denominate the cause? Satisfied with a slovenly nomenclature, we apply the term cause to that in which there resides no power. That profounder wisdom which we learn from the inspired oracles demands a better vocabulary; it calls for a word to designate the cause of so-called causes. In want of this, it disallows to earthly antecedents even if invariable, a name which describes that which is to be found only in the Almighty. The guilt of our enemies is what we term a *second* cause, that is to say, it is no cause at all, but only the occasion of a chastisement inflicted by an Almighty arm. God is in the war. God is in everything; in the doings of earth, for "He knoweth our downsitting and our uprising;" in the raptures of paradise, in the flames of perdition. Yea saith the Psalmist, "If I ascend up into heaven Thou art there. If I make my bed in hell, behold Thou art there!" *Psalms* cxxxix, 8.

In the economy of God the wicked are often used as instruments for the accomplishment of divine ends. Satan, when he introduced sin into the world, was the instrument of preparing the way for a brighter display of God's goodness than ever yet had amazed the universe, and was as really the herald of Jesus of Nazareth as was John the Baptist. Those who cried out "Crucify him! crucify him! his blood be upon us and upon our children!" all guilty as they were;—in piercing the veins of a Savior opened the fountain of eternal life to the millions of them who shall be redeemed unto God by his blood, out of every kindred and tongue and people and nation.*

Thus does God cause the wrath of man to praise him. If there be any possible wrath, such as could not by divine almightiness, be so perverted from its wicked end as to promote the glory and exhibit the goodness of God, that remainder of wrath is restrained. In other words, sin is allowed only in so far as God brings good out of it. Thus every evil is the precursor of blessing. The greatest calamities that ever befel the Universe were but the harbingers of glory.

A christian poet has said

> We should suspect some danger nigh
> When we possess delight.

Thank God it is also true, that whenever evil comes, we may know there is good at hand. In national or in individual experience, when the godless soul sees only a dark cloud, fraught with terror and with wrath, to the christian the cloud resolves itself into a blazing star that guides to the best of blessings. When God says to his children "All things work together for good to them that love God," the heart of the believer makes no exceptions, and thus "rejoices in tribulations, also."

It is also a part of the divine economy to use the wicked as instruments for the chastisement of each other.—Two individuals indulge in mutual animosity. Each is wrong; and each by a series of unkindnesses, or acts that deserve a harsher name, inflicts upon the other a well deserved penalty. Neighborhoods give way to ill-will.—Nothing short of a miracle could prevent

*Many parallel cases might be referred to; for an interesting one see Gen. 45. 6.

them from distressing each other; and Providence works no
such miracle. Nations burn with hate against nations, and as an
appropriate punishment for their crimes God turns them loose
upon each other, and their perpetual wars result in mutual
ruin. History, profane as well as sacred, is full of examples
where "Nation was destroyed of nation, and city of city; for
God did vex them with all adversity." 2 Chron. xv. 5.

Even in the control of his own children God makes use of
the wicked as his instruments of discipline. When Israel did evil
in the sight of the Lord, the inspired record declares that "The
Lord delivered them into the hand of Midian; and the hand of
Midian prevailed against Israel; and Israel was impoverished
because of the Midianites." Judges vi. 6. Individual experience
too, may often make appropriate the prayer of David when he
says "Deliver my soul from the wicked, *which is thy sword*; from
men *which are thy hand*." Ps. xvii. 13.

The sin of the wicked is not diminished by the fact that it is
over-ruled for good by a superior power. There can be no interference with the personal responsibility of moral creatures.
Thus the guilt of those who wage this diabolical war on the
unoffending people of these Confederate States, finds no apology in the providence of God. "It must needs be that offences
come but woe unto him by whom they come." Luke xvii. 1.
Our aggressors must answer for their awful account before the
bar of God.—There let us leave them. Our text which was
written when the death-smell was fresh on the field of battle,
makes no reference to the outrages of the enemy, but points
only to God, as the author of the desolation. The Psalmist
does not confound the cause of trouble with the occasion of it.
He is engrossed, not with the doings of earth, but with those
of heaven. He has no eyes to see the wickedness of his foes. He
forgets he ever had a foe, and sees only God in the war. Let his
example be for our imitation. Surely it is as contrary to religion
as it is to a sound philosophy to banish God from the most
striking act of his Providence that has occurred within the
memory of living man. If it be true then that the hand of God
is in this thing (and who can doubt it?) and if we lose sight of
that fact, surely a worse evil will come upon us. Among other
evils, we may expect to receive in our own souls the consequences of our sin. Resentment, rage, and hate, will be so de-

veloped as to take entire possession of us. We shall become blood-thirsty as tigers, cruel as death, and malicious as fiends. All that we expect to accomplish by the war, if bought at such expense to our own character, would cost more than it is worth. If we cannot be free without transforming ourselves into devils, it were better not to be free; for any thraldom is to be preferred before slavery to sin. But if we exclude God from our thoughts, and regard the desolations around us as coming only from the enemy, how is it possible to keep from violating the injunction "avenge not yourselves!" Whose blood would not be set on fire, whose soul would not be carried away with fiercest passions, by contemplation of the frightful evils we sustain, if they be traced to no cause outside the wicked hearts of our enemies! Alas, all of us are too prone to confine our attention to second causes. Methinks I see the apparition of the spirit of David rising from the sleep of centuries, as that of Samuel did under the incantations of the witch of Endor. His form is venerable, his beard is flowing, and on his brow rests the crown of Israel. He touches the harp of solemn sound, and peals forth the notes of the sublime ode whence our text is taken. He waves his hand to the scenes of sorrow wrought by the war now upon us, and making no allusion to our foes, says "Come behold the works of the Lord, what desolations He hath made in the earth!"

When we regard the evils we suffer as the chastisement of the Almighty, there arises within us no spirit of resentment. The fiercer elements of our nature all subside.—We humbly submit to the judgments of the Almighty. Our eyes instead of flashing fire, are melted to tears; our tongues instead of curses and defiance, utter words of penitence and contrition. Whatever comes from God we can bear. We acknowledge his authority. We know that at *his* hands we deserve nothing but indignation and wrath, tribulation and anguish. We know that he is a gracious Father as well as a righteous judge; and we recognise his benevolence even in his chastisements; for "whom the Lord loveth he chasteneth." We only say "It is the Lord, let him do as seemeth him good." Surely this is a better spirit than results from a view of second causes. Surely this is more likely to secure the divine approbation and the divine aid; and if God be for us who can be against us? This is the

very spirit which his chastisements are intended to excite; and
when the end is accomplished the means will be laid aside.
Thus shall war afflict us no more, and God will not allow "the
wicked which is his sword" to harm us further. But that other
spirit which instead of forgetting the enemy and looking to
God, reverses the order and forgetting God looks to the enemy, and which stimulates to frenzy the worst passions known
to human nature, tends only to make us more wicked than we
were before, and therefore to perpetuate the very causes which
made these chastisements necessary. If instead of profiting by
the afflictions which God sends upon us, we make them the
occasions of additional guilt, what can we expect but that billow after billow of his wrath will overtake us until we shall be
utterly destroyed.

The sweet singer of Israel having depicted the desolations
which God sends by war, devotes the next strain of his inspired
verse to the announcement of the truth that "He maketh wars
to *cease* unto the end of the earth." It is He who brings these
evils upon us and it is He who takes them away. Nor is it need-
less for the Psalmist to remind us of what we might have
known, that the blessings of peace are from the hand of the
Almighty. Here too as in the former case, we are prone to be
satisfied with second causes. We are anxious for wise legislation
and for skillful generalship. We congratulate ourselves on
having such able statesmen as Davis and Stephens, such able
generals as Johnston and Beauregard. We glory in the belief
that our troops are as brave as the bravest in the world, and that
our enemies though outnumbering us four to one as they did
at Leesburg, cannot stand before Southern valor in the open
field for one moment. We exult (alas! our exultation is not
unmixed with sin) when we see the terror-stricken fugitives
leaping by hundreds over the steep embankment, and like
devil-possessed swine plunging headlong into the Potomac.
We are making abundant arrangements to supply ourselves
with all the munitions of war. We are casting cannon, manufacturing arms, and fortifying our coasts. Hundreds of thousand of us are already under arms, and hundreds of thousands
more are ready and anxious to step into the ranks. We feel safe
when we remember that we are so many and so strong, and so
brave, and so well prepared to re-enact the scenes of Sumter,

and Bethel, and Manassas, and Springfield, and Lexington, and Leesburg, and Columbus. We feel sure that if the enemy will only give us battle once more on the Potomac, our brave boys will again send them shrieking and screaming back to their Northern homes. We doubt not that we shall whip them whenever we come in conflict with them. We shall whip them, and whip them, and whip them again. We shall whip them again and again. We shall whip them until they are satisfied to their hearts' content, that the only safety for themselves is in letting us alone.

My countrymen! it is right for us to resort to all the means of defence which Providence has placed within our reach. It is proper to call into action our best civil and military talent, to strain every energy to the utmost in supplying the material of war. As for that sublime faith which we have in the unconquerable valor of our troops, I admire it, I partake in it. But we are here on dangerous ground. We must not step over the line where God says "Thus far shalt thou go, and no farther." Let us not lean on an arm of flesh. Saith the prophet, "Cease ye from man whose breath is in his nostrils, for wherein is he to be accounted of." Isa. ii. 22. Is our confidence in our success based on the wisdom of our statesmen and generals? That Providence which sustains the flight of the sparrow and numbers the hairs of our head might direct the death-bringing bullet to the vitals of our greatest chieftain. Instead of the horse, the rider might have been slain. "It is better to trust in the Lord than to put confidence in man. It is better to trust in the Lord than to put confidence in Princes." Ps. cxviii. 8–9. Is our trust in the valor of our troops? The same God who struck terror into the hearts of the Midianites when they heard the cry "The sword of the Lord and of Gideon!" the same God who sent confusion and dismay into the ranks of our enemies when the sword of the Lord and of the South prevailed at Manassas, might send a panic among *us* which would scatter us like chaff before the wind. He might send his angels in armies to descend upon us, and filling the air with their unseen presence, every heart might quiver with undefinable dread from unknown cause, and they might smite us with invisible weapons, the very touch of which would curdle our blood. Oh! there is no bravery that can stand before the hosts of the living God. The outward appliances of war, the chieftains and captains, the arms and munitions, the shot and shell, the rifles, infantry, artillery, cavalry, all these are useful in their proper places. But let us not put our confidence in them. They are not to be trusted.—They all may fail. They never yet have made a war to cease. This is the very sentiment of the scripture which says "There is no King saved by the multitude of an host; a mighty man is not delivered by much strength. An horse is a vain thing for safety, neither shall he deliver any by his great strength. Behold the eye of the Lord is upon them that *fear* him!" Ps. xxxiii. 16. "Battle is the Lord's." 2 Chron. xx. 15. "He shall cut off the spirit of princes; he is terrible to the kings of the earth. At thy rebuke O God of Jacob both the chariot and the horse are cast into a dead sleep." Ps. lxxvi. 6–12. "He maketh wars to cease unto the end of the earth!" So earnest is the Psalmists in declaring that the ending of the war as well as the beginning of it is from God, that he reiterates the sentiment four times in the text. First in literal terms, "he maketh wars to cease;" then in figure of speech "he breaketh the bow;" again in similar figure, "he cutteth the spear in sunder;" and for the fourth time he enunciates the same idea in another figure when he says, "he burneth the chariot in the fire." The destruction of the bow, the spear, and the chariot, ancient instruments of war, was a symbolical way of describing peace. The figurative expressions then, mean the same as that which is literal; and if this portion of the ode were stripped of its poetic dress and expressed in plainest terms, it would be simply a fourfold declaration of a single truth. "He maketh wars to cease! *He maketh wars to cease*! HE MAKETH WARS TO CEASE! HE MAKETH WARS TO CEASE unto the end of the earth!" Let this tremendous energy of quadruple emphasis, be for the rebuke, and discomfiture and silencing of those who look to earthly sources for the power to stop this awful war. Ye worshippers of human Deities, who by supposing that the efforts of mortals can terminate the bloody strife, exalt the creature to a level with omnipotence, listen to the voice of the Almighty! "Be still and know that *I* am God! I will be exalted among the heathen, I will be exalted in the earth!"

While it is true that we need constant admonition to wean us from trust in human resources and lift our thoughts to a higher Power, yet it is also a fact, and one most gratifying to the christian, that thus far in the war, there has been a wonderful turning of the hearts of the people to God.—When Col. Hill wrote to the Governor of North Carolina that the Lord of Hosts had given us the victory at Bethel, he spoke the sentiment of the whole army. Our soldiers, from the highest officer to the humblest private in the ranks, habitually ascribe our victories to God. Even the irreligious seem to pause for a moment when they speak of Bethel or Manassas, and reverently acknowledge God in the battle. So universally does this feeling pervade our troops that it excites the wonder of all who have had an opportunity of observing it. When Mr. Memminger introduced into the Confederate Congress the ever-memorable and sublime resolutions ascribing the victory of the 21st of July to the King of kings and Lord of lords, a thrill of acquiescence and hearty appreciation flashed over the whole Confederacy, and the hearts of all the people were melted together. When the news reached this Legislative Hall only day before yesterday, that the Providence of God had brought across the ocean to our shores a ship laden with weapons of defence, and shoes for our feet, and other articles of necessity and comfort, the Representatives of the people here assembled, almost unanimously and simultaneously fell to their knees, and while tears of gratitude streamed from many a cheek, and amid a wide spread murmur of scarcely suppressed sobs, their presiding officer as the spokesman of the Assembly, offered up to God a tribute of prayer and thanksgiving!—Oh! that was a thrilling spectacle, and on which doubtless angels looked with beaming eyes and a new delight. Surely such a scene never occurred before. The record has been entered on the Journal and is now a chronicle of the times. Posterity will read it centuries hence with moistening eyes. Heartstrings will quiver and bosoms will heave with emotion all over the world on perusing this sublimest page in history. It is cheering to believe that the record is copied in heaven, and that this outburst of gratitude which thrilled the breasts of men and angels with such sweet and strange emotion, was not unacceptable to Him, to whom the tribute was paid and whose goodness was the cause of it. And now that His Excellency the President of the Confederate States has set apart this 15th day of November as a day of fasting, humiliation and prayer, calling on all the people to flock to a throne of grace, as a father calls on his children to surround the family altar, the whole people respond; all business has ceased, and the nation is prostrate before God.

The scoffer and the infidel may question the sincerity of the christian, or if not, they will perhaps be surprised to learn that to *his* mind the most cheering evidence of our success in this war is this acknowledgment of God so wide spread in the hearts of the people. This pious and reverent feeling is not the natural offspring of the human heart. If it comes to us from external sources it comes from none that are bad. Satan never turns the heart to God. None but God himself could have inspired this confidence in himself: and he never inspires confidence merely to betray it.—This then is the chief reliance of the christian patriot in this emergency. It is gratifying to see that this devout and proper spirit so generally prevails, and it should be the great aim of all who love God to cultivate and cherish it. The very best of us though we acknowledge God with one breath, are prone to forget him at the next; and while we ascribe the victories of the past to him, we are apt to trust for future victories to our own strong arms and stout hearts, and abundant preparations. No greater calamity could possibly overtake us than to yield to this disposition to forget God. If I were to say that it would be the certain precursor of overwhelming defeat, I should be only repeating what the prophet Isaiah said three thousand years ago, but which like all other truth is not impaired by time:—"Woe to them that stay on horses and trust in chariots because they are many, and in horsemen because they are very strong, but they look not unto the Holy One of Israel, neither seek the Lord."—Is. xxi.i. Woe to you then ye people of Georgia! Woe to you all ye people of these Confederate States! if you are engrossed with outward preparations for battle, and seek not the Lord nor put your trust in the Holy One of Israel, and in the King of glory! Who is this King of glory? "The Lord strong and mighty, the Lord mighty in *battle!*"—Ps. xxiv.8.

Many of the ways of God are past finding out, for "his thoughts are very deep," but in regard to the matter before us, it is not surprising that high and unfaltering faith in God should be the precursor of success. On the contrary it can be shown to be in keeping with all the dealings of his providence with us.

Of course when faith is spoken of, reference is had to real faith, not to counterfeits. Real faith either in God or in anything else is never an inert and unproductive principle. There is in its nature an element which prompts to action. Faith in God prompts to obedience, and if to obedience then to repentance, to reformation and to every virtue. The apostle not without reason places faith first, and hope and charity afterwards. For though charity be the greatest of the three, yet faith is the seed-virtue from which the others spring, certainly without which the others could not exist.

Now let us remember the point already made, that God is in the war. Let us further remember that he has not brought these calamities upon us without a purpose. Without presuming to know any of the secrets of Infinite wisdom, the Almighty has revealed himself to us sufficiently to warrant us in saying, that these afflictions must have been brought upon us either as a punishment for sins that are past, or as a means of making us better in future, or for both these ends. Suppose the object be the first of these. Then such faith in him as prompts to repentance and reformation while it might not logically remove the chastisement, would at least prevent further occasion for it from accruing; and there is reason to hope, that the divine benevolence would not be bound by so strict a logic as not to remove the penalty when the sin that occasioned it is repented of and abandoned. Suppose the object be to make us a better people. When the object is accomplished, there will be no further use for the instrumentality which brought it about. Suppose the object be both retrospective and prospective. The same reasoning that applied to the cases separately will apply to both together; except that the former case being coupled with the latter would receive strength by the connexion, and we should have still better reason to hope that if we cease to sin our Heavenly Parent would cease to chastise.

It is not irreverent to suppose that the divine procedure would be governed by the same principles which control us in the discipline of our children. What father ever continues to

use the rod when he is convinced that his child is so heartily
sorry for his fault that he will never commit it again? What
master would chastise his servant if he knew the servant's grief
for his fault to be sincere and profound enough to prevent him
from repeating the offence? We are God's children. He is chas-
tising us. Let us acknowledge him; and say "though he slay me
yet will I trust in him." Let us confess the sins that brought
these evils upon us. Let us repent of them, and so repent as to
abandon. Let us do all this, and this war will come to an end.
"He maketh wars to cease." He will make *this* war to cease.
When we become what we ought to be there can be no motive
in the divine mind to continue the chastisement, and the war
will cease. The skeptic may ridicule this conclusion. Let him
ridicule. "A brutish man knoweth not neither doth a fool understand this."—Ps. xcii.6. He who is enlightened from above,
without stopping to ask the opinions of politicians, soldiers or
philosophers, and preferring higher authority, goes straight to
the oracles of God for a solution of the problem, and is satisfied when he reads: "He maketh wars to cease unto the end
of the earth; he breaketh the bow and cutteth the spear in
sunder; he burneth the chariot in the fire." The caviller may
object, and talk about military and political necessities, and
physical and moral impossibilities, and philosophic difficulties.
But while he is prating, the providences of God will go right
on, and will say to him in due time, "Be still and know that I
am God." How strange that we should ask men to predict
what the end will be, without asking God who knows all
things from the beginning. How strange that we should rely
on our puny efforts to bring this dreadful strife to a close,
when we know that God only can stop it. For is it not *He* who
makes wars to cease? We have been trusting in horses and in
chariots. Let us rather remember the name of the Lord our
God. Let us pay our vows unto him, and we shall have no further use for these dread instruments of war.—Here then is
great good news for the people of these Confederate States!
These desolations may be stopped! The red tide of life that
flows from the veins of your sons may be staunched! Prosperity may again be established!—"What," exclaims one, "can we
entice the enemy from their entrenchments into open field?
Then indeed we shall soon destroy them and the remainder

will sue for peace!" No my friend, there is no certainty that that would close the war. "What then? shall we cross the Potomac, deliver Maryland, push on to Philadelphia and still farther North until we conquer a peace?" No, no. There can be no assurance of success in such an enterprise. "Shall we then court the friendship of foreign powers, and thus reinforce our army, and re-supply our wasting resources?" Yes! Let us court the friendship, not indeed of a foreign power, for the God of our fathers is not foreign to us, but let us court the favor of heaven, and verily an alliance with the Almighty will make *us* omnipotent!

My countrymen, before God! in my heart and from my soul, I do believe that if the people of this Confederacy were to turn with one heart and one mind to the Lord and walk in his ways, he would drive the invader from our territories and restore to us the blessings of peace. I wish I could express myself with more plainness and with more force. Let me say again, I believe that the quickest and easiest way to terminate this war, and that favorably to ourselves, is for us all to *be good*. We imagine that the only way to get out of our difficulties is to fight out. There is a more excellent way. Let us by faith, obedience and love, so engage the Lord of Hosts on our side that he will fight for us; and when he undertakes our case we are safe, for "he maketh wars to cease," and he will break the bow of the enemy, and cut his spear in sunder, and burn his chariot in the fire, and say unto him, "Be still and know that I am God!" Call it superstition if you please ye men of the world. Say that we are deluded by a religious enthusiasm. But know ye that faith in Israel's God is not superstition, and that confidence in an over ruling providence is no delusion. Enthusiasm there may be, there is, there ought to be, we avow it, we glory in it. The heathen may rage and the people imagine a vain thing, but we rejoice when we can say,—"God is our refuge and strength, a very present help in trouble. Therefore will not we fear though the earth be removed, and though the mountains be carried into the midst of the sea, though the mountains shake with the swelling thereof, Selah! The Lord of Hosts is with us, the God of Jacob is our refuge, Selah!"

Lay what plans you will, and set what schemes you please in operation, and at the summing up of all things at the end of the world, it will be found that God ruled and overruled all things according to the working of his power; and that the great statesmen and great captains who figure so largely in history, were but the unwitting instruments of accomplishing his purposes. We look back over the past and see God in history. We look forward and see him bringing generation after generation upon the earth to work out his designs and not theirs, for before they existed they could have had no designs. Why should the present be an exception? Let us then do justly, and love mercy and walk humbly before God, and by thus falling in with his plans, we shall be on his side and he will be on ours, and those who make war upon us will either see their folly and cease, or if they continue will do nothing more than work out their own ruin. They have no power to harm us. We have no power to make ourselves safe. "Once hath God spoken, yea twice have I heard this, that *power* belongeth unto *God*."—Ps. lxii.ii. Let us fly to that Power and engage it in our behalf, and he who smote great nations and slew mighty kings, Sihon king of Amorites, and Og king of Bashan for his people's sake, will smite the hypocritical nation that wars against us, and will give to us and to our children the heritage of our fathers forever.

I have said that the way to enlist this almightiness on our side is to make the law of God the law of every man's life. Perhaps these terms are too general to convey the idea with power. What then more particularly is to be done. What specific duties must we discharge? What special evils must we forsake? All, all! The whole head is sick, the whole heart is faint, the whole body is corrupt. How small a proportion of our population are disciples of Jesus!—Counting out avowed unbelievers and false professors, how few are left! Here is the place to begin. A pure Gospel is our only hope—I repeat it, a pure Gospel is our only hope. If the Kingdom of Christ be not set up in the hearts of the people no government can exist except by force. All you then who have no personal experience of the grace of the Gospel are so far, in the way of your country's prosperity. The first step for you to take is to believe in the Lord Jesus Christ, confessing your sins and giving him your heart. But aside from this, let us look at our public morals. Passing by profanity, for we are a nation of swearers; passing by drunkenness, for we are a nation of drunkards; passing by Sabbath-breaking, for our cars thunder along the track on the Sabbath as on any other day, and our convivial gatherings are too often on the day of the Lord; passing by covetousness and lying, for too many of our citizens alas! will for the sake of defrauding the public out of a few dollars make false oath in giving in their tax returns; passing by neglect of our children, for too few of them receive that religious instruction and training which is their due; passing by injustice to servants, for while their physical wants are in some cases unsupplied their moral wants are too generally neglected; passing by all these things, and each of the sins of private life which ought to be exchanged for its opposite virtue; let me call especial attention to three things of more public nature, and which are fairer samples of the average of public morals.

In the first place, how is it that in the State of Georgia it is almost impossible to convict a culprit of crime? The most atrocious murders and other outrages are committed with impunity, in the very face of our so-called Courts of Justice. Is the Bench prostituted? Is the Bar prostituted? Or is it the Jury box? In either case it is clear that public virtue is at fault; otherwise these evils would not be tolerated. So notoriously defective is the administration of justice, that in many cases fresh within the memory of us all, citizens have felt it necessary in self-defence to execute criminals without the forms of law. Is not this a step towards barbarism? The example of disregarding the law being set by reputable citizens, will be followed by others not so reputable. When this system is inaugurated where will it stop? Whose life will be safe? This reign of the mob, this lawless execution of men which is little short of murder, will become the rule and not the exception, unless a more healthy public opinion shall correct the evils in our Courts of Justice.

The second evil is kindred to the first. How is it that in all the history of this Legislative body pardon has been granted to every criminal, almost without exception who has ever applied for it? Can it be that all who have been pardoned were innocent? If so there must have been horrid injustice in the Courts which convicted them. The bloodthirsty Jeffreys would scarcely have sent so many innocent men to the gallows. No; under the loose administration of justice already referred to, none but the most glaring cases (with possibly a rare exception) could ever be convicted.—How comes it then that our Legislators turn loose these culprits upon society? It is because they are more anxious to secure a re-election than to promote the good of the State. How comes it that a vote adverse to pardon would endanger their re-election? It is because public opinion is rotten. The fault lies in the low standard of public morals.

But for the third item. Without meaning to indulge in wholesale denunciation of any class of my fellow citizens, it may yet be pertinent to inquire, how is it that so few of our public men are *good* men? Is it to be supposed that all the talent, and all the learning, and all the wisdom, have been vouchsafed to the bad rather than to the good? Does Satan claim a monopoly of all the intellectual power and administrative ability in the world? Perhaps it is not surprising that he should; for he once offered to give to their rightful owner "all the Kingdoms of this world and the glory of them" on condition of receiving his homage in return. But it is preposterous to suppose that there are no good men to be found capable of discharging the highest public trusts.—Why then are they not oftener found in eminent position? It is because the public in estimating a man's fitness for office, throw his morals out of the account; and because popularity can be obtained by means which bad men freely resort to, but which good men eschew. How sad a comment on public virtue! Every voter who allows personal interests, or preferences, or prejudices, or party zeal or anything to influence his suffrage in favor of a bad man in preference to a good one, if the latter be capable, is doing what he can to banish virtue from our councils and God from our support. It might be a fair subject of inquiry, whether he or the outbreaking felon whose place is in the Penitentiary inflicts the greatest injury upon society.

It is time that the preachers of the Gospel, who ought to be if they are not, the great conservators of public morals, had made way upon these monster evils; and I rejoice that I have the opportunity on this public day, before this Legislative body, and before the people of the whole State, to bear my testimony against them.

The three evils just specified are only outward manifestations of an internal distemper, the mere efflorescence of evil deep seated in the public heart. The disappearance of these would indicate a radical change. Suppose public justice to be rightly administered, suppose the influence of virtue in our councils to be predominant; and this is to suppose that thousands upon thousands of individual men have grown wiser and better, that myriads of private faults have been exchanged for corresponding virtues, that the whole complexion of society is changed, and its whole nature improved. Suppose that the Gospel of Christ *which alone can work these changes*, should continue thus to elevate, refine, ennoble and sanctify, until every heart were brought under its sacred influence. How much like heaven our earth would be! Can any one suppose that in such a state of society as this, the heavenly tranquility would ever be disturbed by the clangor of war! Let our whole people at once renounce their evil works and ways with grief, and follow hard after God, and I confidently declare that he would with a mighty hand and an outstretched arm deliver us from our enemies and restore peace and prosperity.—Think you that I ought to modify this positive declaration into a mere expression of opinion? I reiterate the same sentiment in words which no man will dare to question:—"When a man's ways please the Lord he maketh even his enemies to be at peace with him."—Prov. xvi.7. And again. "Let the wicked forsake his way and the unrighteous man his thoughts, and let him turn unto the Lord, and he will have mercy upon him, and unto our God for he will abundantly pardon."—Is. lv.7. Is it said that these words refer to individuals and are not applicable to States? The same conditions of mercy that would suffice for one man would suffice for two, and if for two then for any number, for nations and for all.

From these teachings of Holy Writ, it appears my countrymen, that in carrying on this war which the providence of God has brought upon us, we ought to use a new set of instrumentalities; instrumentalities the object of which shall be not to injure our enemies but to benefit ourselves; to benefit us not in things visible and tangible but in the inner man. Thus shall those faults in our character which made these chastisements necessary be removed, and as matter of moral certainty the sad consequences which we suffer would cease.

Here then is joyful news to thousands of Christian patriots

who burn with desire to aid their country's cause, but who know not what to do. All you have to do is to be good, and in *being* good you are *doing* good; and in doing good you are securing the favor of God and contributing your share towards enlisting Him on the side of our armies. Joy to our venerable fathers, who bowing beneath the weight of years, are unable to gratify their intense desire to fly to arms! Fathers, learn from the word of God; the sins peculiar to old age. Struggle against them. Fixed as your habits may be, try to improve your hearts and lives; and be sure that every success you meet with in the improvement of your graces will tell upon our enemies with more power than the missile from the musket. Joy to our mothers and wives and sisters and daughters! While with busy fingers you ply the needle and the loom for the benefit of our brave defenders, remember that you can render aid far more efficient. Cultivate the graces and practice the virtues enjoined in the Gospel; and though no famous report will be made to the world, God will observe it; though no influence be seen going out from it, yet its influence will be felt in heaven and will descend to earth again. God yearns towards them who seek Him; and when His affections are drawn out towards us, He will be more ready to defend and deliver us. Joy to the invalid, to the blind, and deaf and dumb, and maimed, and poor, and all who by afflictive dispensations are seemingly helpless and apparently a burden to their country in these times of peril. You too can help us in the war. Bear your sorrows with patience, receive the attentions of your friends with gratitude, copy the spirit of Jesus, and as little as the world may think of it, you too will help to drive the invaders from our soil. Scoff sceptic if you please, but we rejoice in the assurance that whatever brings God nigh to us will drive our enemies far away; and what brings God so nigh as the exercise of the spirit and the practice of the duties which His word enjoins? Joy, Joy to you ye preachers of the Gospel! Know ye that whatever makes the people better makes them stronger; that in spreading truth and virtue you are supplying the true sinews of war. Your mission is one of love and peace, and yet in more senses than one you are warriors. Your profession may be thought valueless in these times of bloody strife, but in truth yours is the most efficient branch of the service. The influence of the Gospel is a wall of defence against enemies carnal no less than spiritual. Every pulpit is a battlement whence great moral Columbiads hurl huge thunders against all who would harm us. Joy, joy! ye ministers of the Gospel of peace, for you can fight for your country and yet keep your hands unstained with blood.

See what an accession there is here to our forces in the field. We thought we had an army of some two hundred thousand. Here we have added the whole army of the saints, male and female, of every age, and color, and condition;—a motley band whose uneven ranks excite the sneers of men and devils. But on their banner is inscribed, "Not by might nor by power but by my Spirit saith the Lord." Zech. iv. 6. By that sign they will conquer. Each in his sphere moves quietly along, and men of the world think they are doing nothing, but they are the best soldiers in the war. Their spiritual weapons make no loud report; no blood is seen to follow their stroke; the stroke itself is not seen. The still closet is remote from the scene of battle. But when our enemies rush on a praying people, they rush on their own destruction. Every closet is a masked battery, from whose mysterious depths there goes forth an influence unseen and unheard, but carrying swift disaster to the ranks of our foes. Terror seizes upon them; they feel the dread influence but know not whence it comes, and bewildered and confounded by these assaults on their spiritual nature while yet their bodies are unhurt, they fly, they fly, supposing that they fly not from men but from devils. They know not that they are flying from before the saints of God, from before the armies of the Most High.

My countrymen, we are certain of success in this war if we but use the right means. But those means which are the last that men think of, and the last that they adopt, are the first in order and the first in importance in the Divine estimation. The first and last and only thing that men are apt to do, is to gather together the implements of war and prepare for battle. God forbids not the use of these things; nay, to lay them aside would be but to tempt His Providence. But paramount to this is the purifying of the heart. Let us "seek first the kingdom of God and his righteousness," and trust that all other things will be added. Mat. vi. 33. Let our people forsake their sins and practice goodness, so that it can be said of our land, "thy people shall all be righteous," and the sweet prophecy will be fulfilled in us, which declares, "Violence shall no more be heard in thy land, wasting nor destruction within thy borders; but thou shall call thy walls Salvation and thy gates Praise. A little one shall become a thousand and a small one a strong nation. I the Lord will hasten it in his time." Is. xvi. 18. Yes! when this happy day comes it will be of God, for "He maketh wars to cease unto the end of the earth; He breaketh the bow, and cutteth the spear in sunder; He burneth the chariot in the fire." Suppose every nation were thus to turn to the Lord. Then every nation would secure his blessing. Nation would rise up against nation no more, nor would men longer learn the arts of war. The spears would be beaten into pruning hooks and the swords into ploughshares; the days of Millenial glory would come, and the whole world would be subject to the gentle reign of the Prince of Peace!

# Jefferson Davis:
# Message to the Confederate Congress

The Confederacy held elections for congress, president, and vice-president on November 6. Running unopposed, Jefferson Davis and Alexander Stephens were elected to six-year terms that would begin in February 1862. Twelve days after the election Davis sent a message to the Provisional Confederate Congress as it began its fifth session.

---

RICHMOND, November 18, 1861.

THE CONGRESS of the Confederate States.

The few weeks which have elapsed since your adjournment have brought us so near the close of the year that we are now able to sum up its general results. The retrospect is such as should fill the hearts of our people with gratitude to Providence for his kind interposition in their behalf. Abundant yields have rewarded the labor of the agriculturist, whilst the manufacturing industry of the Confederate States was never so prosperous as now. The necessities of the times have called into existence new branches of manufactures and given a fresh impulse to the activity of those heretofore in operation. The means of the Confederate States for manufacturing the necessaries and comforts of life within themselves increase as the conflict continues, and we are gradually becoming independent of the rest of the world for the supply of such military stores and munitions as are indispensable for war.

The operations of the Army, soon to be partially interrupted by the approaching winter, have afforded a protection to the country and shed a luster upon its arms through the trying vicissitudes of more than one arduous campaign which entitle our brave volunteers to our praise and our gratitude. From its commencement to the present period the war has been enlarging its proportions and expanding its boundaries so as to include new fields. The conflict now extends from the shores of the Chesapeake to the confines of Missouri and Arizona; yet sudden calls from the remotest points for military aid have been met with promptness enough not only to avert disaster in the face of superior numbers, but also to roll back the tide of invasion from the border.

When the war commenced the enemy were possessed of certain strategic points and strong places within the Confederate States. They greatly exceeded us in numbers, in available resources, and in the supplies necessary for war. Military establishments had been long organized and were complete; the Navy, and for the most part the Army, once common to both, were in their possession. To meet all this we had to create not only an Army in the face of war itself, but also the military establishments necessary to equip and place it in the field. It ought indeed to be a subject of gratulation that the spirit of the volunteers and the patriotism of the people have enabled us, under Providence, to grapple successfully with these difficulties. A succession of glorious victories at Bethel, Bull Run, Manassas, Springfield, Lexington, Leesburg, and Belmont has checked the wicked invasion which greed of gain and the unhallowed lust of power brought upon our soil, and has proved that numbers cease to avail when directed against a people fighting for the sacred right of self-government and the privileges of freemen. After more than seven months of war the enemy have not only failed to extend their occupancy of our soil, but new States and Territories have been added to our Confederacy, while, instead of their threatened march of unchecked conquest, they have been driven, at more than one point, to assume the defensive, and, upon a fair comparison between the two belligerents as to men, military means, and financial condition, the Confederate States are relatively much stronger now than when the struggle commenced.

Since your adjournment the people of Missouri have conducted the war in the face of almost unparalleled difficulties with a spirit and success alike worthy of themselves and of the great cause in which they are struggling. Since that time Kentucky, too, has become the theater of active hostilities. The Federal forces have not only refused to acknowledge her right to be neutral, and have insisted upon making her a party to the war, but have invaded her for the purpose of attacking the

Confederate States. Outrages of the most despotic character have been perpetrated upon her people; some of her most eminent citizens have been seized and borne away to languish in foreign prisons, without knowing who were their accusers or the specific charges made against them, while others have been forced to abandon their homes, families, and property, and seek a refuge in distant lands.

Finding that the Confederate States were about to be invaded through Kentucky, and that her people, after being deceived into a mistaken security, were unarmed and in danger of being subjugated by the Federal forces, our armies were marched into that State to repel the enemy and prevent their occupation of certain strategic points which would have given them great advantages in the contest—a step which was justified not only by the necessities of self-defense on the part of the Confederate States, but also by a desire to aid the people of Kentucky. It was never intended by the Confederate Government to conquer or coerce the people of that State; but, on the contrary, it was declared by our generals that they would withdraw their troops if the Federal Government would do likewise. Proclamation was also made of the desire to respect the neutrality of Kentucky and the intention to abide by the wishes of her people as soon as they were free to express their opinions. These declarations were approved by me, and I should regard it as one of the best effects of the march of our troops into Kentucky if it should end in giving to her people liberty of choice and a free opportunity to decide their own destiny according to their own will.

The Army has been chiefly instrumental in prosecuting the great contest in which we are engaged, but the Navy has also been effective in full proportion to its means. The naval officers, deprived to a great extent of an opportunity to make their professional skill available at sea, have served with commendable zeal and gallantry on shore and upon inland waters, further detail of which will be found in the reports of the Secretaries of the Navy and War. In the transportation of the mails many difficulties have arisen, which will be found fully developed in the report of the Postmaster General. The absorption of the ordinary means of transportation for the movements of troops and military supplies; the insufficiency of the rolling stock of railroads for the accumulation of business resulting both from military operations and the obstruction of water communication by the presence of the enemy's fleet; the failure, and even refusal, of contractors to comply with the terms of their agreements; the difficulties inherent in inaugurating so vast and complicated a system as that which requires postal facilities for every town and village in a territory so extended as ours, have all combined to impede the best-directed efforts of the Postmaster General, whose zeal, industry, and ability have been taxed to the utmost extent. Some of these difficulties can only be overcome by time and an improved condition of the country upon the restoration of peace, but others may be remedied by legislation, and your attention is invited to the recommendations contained in the report of the head of that Department.

The condition of the Treasury will doubtless be a subject of anxious inquiry on your part. I am happy to say that the financial system already adopted has worked well so far, and promises good results for the future. To the extent that Treasury notes may be issued the Government is enabled to borrow money without interest, and thus facilitate the conduct of the war. This extent is measured by the portion of the field of circulation which these notes can be made to occupy. The proportion of the field thus occupied depends again upon the amount of the debts for which they are receivable; and when dues, not only to the Confederate and State governments, but also to corporations and individuals, are payable in this medium, a large amount of it may be circulated at par. There is every reason to believe that the Confederate Treasury note is fast becoming such a medium. The provision that these notes shall be convertible into Confederate stock bearing 8 per cent interest, at the pleasure of the holder, insures them against a depreciation below the value of that stock, and no considerable fall in that value need be feared so long as the interest shall be punctually paid. The punctual payment of this interest has been secured by the act passed by you at the last session, imposing such a rate of taxation as must provide sufficient means for that purpose.

For the successful prosecution of this war it is indispensable that the means of transporting troops and military supplies be furnished, as far as possible, in such manner as not to interrupt the commercial intercourse between our people nor place a check on their productive energies. To this end the means of transportation from one section of our country to the other must be carefully guarded and improved. And this should be the object of anxious care on the part of State and Confederate governments, so far as they may have power over the subject.

We have already two main systems of through transportation from the north to the south—one from Richmond along the seaboard; the other through Western Virginia to New Orleans. A third might be secured by completing a link of about forty miles between Danville, in Virginia, and Greensboro, in North Carolina. The construction of this comparatively short line would give us a through route from north to south in the interior of the Confederate States and give us access to a population and to military resources from which we are now in great measure debarred. We should increase greatly the safety and capacity of our means for transporting men and military supplies. If the construction of this road should, in the judgment of Congress as it is in mine, be indispensable for the most successful prosecution of the war, the action of the Government will not be restrained by the constitutional objection which would attach to a work for commercial purposes, and attention is invited to the practicability of securing its early completion by giving the needful aid to the company organized for its construction and administration.

If we husband our means and make a judicious use of our resources, it would be difficult to fix a limit to the period during which we could conduct a war against the adversary whom we now encounter. The very efforts which he makes to isolate and invade us must exhaust his means, whilst they serve to complete the circle and diversify the productions of our industrial system. The reconstruction which he seeks to effect by arms becomes daily more and more palpably impossible. Not only do the causes which induced us to separate still exist in full force, but they have been strengthened, and whatever doubt may have lingered in the minds of any must have been completely dispelled by subsequent events. If instead of being a dissolution of a league it were indeed a rebellion in which we are engaged, we might find ample vindication for the course we have adopted in the scenes which are now being enacted in the United States. Our people now look with contemptuous astonishment on those with whom they had been so recently associated. They shrink with aversion from the bare idea of renewing such a connection. When they see a President making war without the assent of Congress; when they behold judges threatened because they maintain the writ of *habeas corpus* so sacred to freemen; when they see justice and law trampled under the armed heel of military authority, and upright men and innocent women dragged to distant dungeons upon the mere edict of a despot; when they find all this tolerated and applauded by a people who had been in the full enjoyment of freedom but a few months ago—they believe that there must be some radical incompatibility between such a people and themselves. With such a people we may be content to live at peace, but the separation is final, and for the independence we have asserted we will accept no alternative.

The nature of the hostilities which they have waged against us must be characterized as barbarous wherever it is understood. They have bombarded undefended villages without giving notice to women and children to enable them to escape, and in one instance selected the night as the period when they might surprise them most effectually whilst asleep and unsuspicious of danger. Arson and rapine, the destruction of private houses and property, and injuries of the most wanton character, even upon noncombatants, have marked their forays along our borders and upon our territory. Although we ought to have been admonished by these things that they were disposed to make war upon us in the most cruel and relentless spirit, yet we were not prepared to see them fit out a large naval expedition, with the confessed purpose not only to pillage, but to incite a servile insurrection in our midst. If they convert their soldiers into incendiaries and robbers, and involve us in a species of war which claims noncombatants, women, and children as its victims, they must expect to be treated as outlaws and enemies of mankind. There are certain rights of humanity which are entitled to respect even in war, and he who refuses to regard them forfeits his claims, if captured, to be considered as a prisoner of war, but must expect to be dealt with as an offender against all law, human and divine.

But not content with violating our rights under the law of nations at home, they have extended these injuries to us within other jurisdictions. The distinguished gentlemen whom, with your approval at the last session, I commissioned to represent the Confederacy at certain foreign courts, have been recently seized by the captain of a U. S. ship of war on board a British steamer on their voyage from the neutral Spanish port of Havana to England. The United States have thus claimed a general jurisdiction over the high seas, and entering a British ship, sailing under its country's flag, violated the rights of embassy, for the most part held sacred even amongst barbarians, by seizing our ministers whilst under the protection and within the dominions of a neutral nation. These gentlemen were as much under the jurisdiction of the British Government upon that ship and beneath its flag as if they had been on its soil, and a claim on the part of the United States to seize them in the streets of London would have been as well founded as that to apprehend them where they were taken. Had they been malefactors and citizens even of the United States they could not have been arrested on a British ship or on British soil, unless under the express provisions of a treaty and according to the forms therein provided for the extradition of criminals.

But rights the most sacred seem to have lost all respect in their eyes. When Mr. Faulkner, a former minister of the United States to France, commissioned before the secession of Virginia, his native State, returned in good faith to Washington to settle his accounts and fulfill all the obligations into which he had entered, he was perfidiously arrested and imprisoned in New York, where he now is. The unsuspecting confidence with which he reported to his Government was abused, and his desire to fulfill his trust to them was used to his injury. In conducting this war we have sought no aid and proposed no alliances offensive and defensive abroad. We have asked for a recognized place in the great family of nations, but in doing so we have demanded nothing for which we did not offer a fair equivalent. The advantages of intercourse are mutual amongst nations, and in seeking to establish diplomatic relations we were only endeavoring to place that intercourse under the regulation of public law. Perhaps we had the right, if we had chosen to exercise it, to ask to know whether the principle that "blockades to be binding must be effectual," so solemnly announced by the great powers of Europe at Paris, is to be generally enforced or applied only to particular parties. When the Confederate States, at your last session, became a party to the declaration reaffirming this principle of international law, which has been recognized so long by publicists and governments, we certainly supposed that it was to be universally enforced. The customary law of nations is made up of their practice rather than their declarations; and if such declarations are only to be enforced in particular instances at the pleasure of those who make them, then the commerce of the world, so far from being placed under the regulation of a general law, will become subject to the caprice of those who execute or suspend it at will. If such is to be the course of nations in regard to this law, it is plain that it will thus become a rule for the weak and not for the strong.

Feeling that such views must be taken by the neutral nations of the earth, I have caused the evidence to be collected which proves completely the utter inefficiency of the proclaimed blockade of our coast, and shall direct it to be laid before such governments as shall afford us the means of being heard. But, although we should be benefited by the enforcement of this law so solemnly declared by the great powers of Europe, we are not dependent on that enforcement for the successful prosecution of the war. As long as hostilities continue the Confederate States will exhibit a steadily increasing capacity to furnish their troops with food, clothing, and arms. If they should be forced to forego many of the luxuries and some of the comforts of life, they will at least have the consolation of knowing that they are thus daily becoming more and more independent of the rest of the world. If in this process labor in the Confederate States should be gradually diverted from those great Southern staples which have given life to so much of the commerce of mankind into other channels, so as to make them rival producers instead of profitable customers, they will not be the only or even the chief losers by this change in the direction of their industry. Although it is true that the cotton supply from the Southern States could only be totally cut off by the subversion of our social system, yet it is plain that a long continuance of this blockade might, by a diversion of labor and an investment of capital in other employments, so diminish the supply as to bring ruin upon all those interests of foreign countries which are dependent on that staple. For every laborer who is diverted from the culture of cotton in the South, perhaps four times as many elsewhere, who have found subsistence in the various employments growing out of its use, will be forced also to change their occupation.

While the war which is waged to take from us the right of self government can never attain that end, it remains to be seen how far it may work a revolution in the industrial system of the world, which may carry suffering to other lands as well as to our own. In the meantime we shall continue this struggle in humble dependence upon Providence, from whose searching scrutiny we cannot conceal the secrets of our hearts, and to whose rule we confidently submit our destinies. For the rest we shall depend upon ourselves. Liberty is always won where there exists the unconquerable will to be free, and we have reason to know the strength that is given by a conscious sense not only of the magnitude but of the righteousness of our cause.

JEFF'N DAVIS.

# Harper's Weekly: The Great Review

December 7, 1861

On November 20 General McClellan staged a grand review of the Army of the Potomac at Bailey's Crossroads in Fairfax County, Virginia. The military spectacle demonstrated the progress made during the fall in organizing, equipping, and drilling the main Union fighting force in the eastern theater.

---

IN THE upper and lower divisions, General M'Call's and General Heintzelman's, from which a march of some eight or ten miles had to be made, the troops were astir at from two to three o'clock in the morning, and were on the march long before daylight. All of the seven divisions on the Virginia side of the Potomac were represented in the review, but enough were left in each to supply double the usual picket force to guard the camps, and a reserve in addition strong enough to repel any attack in force the enemy could make.

As early as nine o'clock the head of the column of General Blenker's division, the head-quarters of which are nearest to Bailey's, began to arrive at the grounds from the Washington road. Soon after General M'Dowell's advance-guard appeared on the road, entering the grounds from the same direction, but further to the west. Next came the head of General Franklin's column, approaching from the Alexandria road; and soon after the division of General Smith began to enter the grounds from the direction of Fall's Church. General Fitz John Porter was next on the ground, bringing his forces by still another road. The troops now poured in from all directions, those under General Heintzelman following General Franklin's division, and the column of General McCall succeeding that of General Smith, and continued without cessation until half past eleven o'clock.

For the last hour the scene was enlivening and brilliant beyond description. The whole immense area of the review grounds was covered with moving masses of men. More than twenty generals, commanding divisions and brigades, with five times the number of staff officers, mounted upon high mottled and richly caparisoned horses, were dashing through the grounds in every direction, superintending the placing in position of the various divisions, brigades, and regiments. Brigades are marching toward every possible point of the compass—some slowly, some in double-quick time, some wheeling into line, others standing in position. Here comes a regiment of cavalry, moving toward its designated station, wheeling to the right at this point and to the left at that, to avoid coming in contact with the moving masses of infantry. There goes a column of artillery, a mile in length, pursuing its way to its destination through bodies of infantry and cavalry.

And so the movements go on, seemingly in confusion, and yet, under the admirable management of General McDowell, who directs every thing, in most perfect order, until there have arrived and taken the various positions assigned not less than seventy thousand men, including seven regiments of cavalry, numbering some eight thousand men, and twenty batteries of artillery, numbering a hundred and twenty pieces.

After the arrival of the President and Cabinet and Commander-in-Chief, preparation was made for marching the troops in review. The honor of leading the column was assigned to the First Rifle Regiment of Pennsylvania Reserve, familiarly known as the "Bucktail Regiment." This regiment was with General M'Clellan in Western Virginia, and was particularly admired for the steadiness and regularity of its movements, and the soldierlike bearing of the men. Some three hours were occupied by the troops in passing. The divisions passed in the following order:

First. General M'Call's division, composed of the brigades of Generals Meade, Reynolds, and Ord.

Second. General Heintzelman's division, composed of the brigades of Generals Sedgwick, Jamison, and Richardson.

Third. General Smith's division, composed of the brigades of Generals Hancock, Brooks, and Benham.

Fourth. General Franklin's division, composed of the brigades of Generals Slocum, Newton, and Kearney.

Fifth. The division of General Blenker, composed of the brigade of General Stahl, and of two brigades commanded by senior Colonels.

Sixth. The division of General Fitz John Porter, composed of the brigades of Generals Morell, Martindale, and Butterfield.

Seventh. The division of General M'Dowell, composed of the brigades of Generals King and Wadsworth, and a brigade now commanded by Colonel Frisbie.

The passage of this large army of volunteers elicited the strongest praise from the very formidable body of old army officers who sat in review. General Sumner, who now for the first time since his return from the Pacific witnessed an exhibition of the progress in drill of the volunteers, expressed much surprise that men coming from civil life should, in so short a period, have been able to compete in soldierly appearance with the veterans of the regular army.

# Ulysses S. Grant to Jesse Root Grant

Grant would write in his memoirs that from the battle of Belmont to early February 1862 "the troops under my command did little except prepare for the long struggle which proved to be before them." During this period he wrote to his father about the expectations created by the Northern press.

———————

Cairo, Illinois,
November 27th, 1861.

DEAR FATHER:

Your letter enclosed with a shawl to Julia is just received.

In regard to your stricture about my not writing I think that you have no cause of complaint. My time is all taken up with public duties.

Your statement of prices at which you proposed furnishing harness was forwarded to Maj. Allen as soon as received and I directed Lagow, who received the letter enclosing it, to inform you of the fact. He did so at once.

I cannot take an active part in securing contracts. If I were not in the army I should do so, but situated as I am it is necessary both to my efficiency for the public good and my own reputation that I should keep clear of Government contracts.

I do not write you about plans, or the necessity of what has been done or what is doing because I am opposed to publicity in these matters. Then too you are very much disposed to criticise unfavorably from information received through the public press, a portion of which I am sorry to see can look at nothing favorably that does not look to a war upon slavery. My inclination is to whip the rebellion into submission, preserving all constitutional rights. If it cannot be whipped in any other way than through a war against slavery, let it come to that legitimately. If it is necessary that slavery should fall that the Republic may continue its existence, let slavery go. But that portion of the press that advocates the beginning of such a war now, are as great enemies to their country as if they were open and avowed secessionists.

There is a desire upon the part of people who stay securely at home to read in the morning papers, at their breakfast, startling reports of battles fought. They cannot understand why troops are kept inactive for weeks or even months. They do not understand that men have to be disciplined, arms made, transportation and provisions provided. I am very tired of the course pursued by a portion of the Union press.

Julia left last Saturday for St. Louis where she will probably spend a couple of weeks and return here should I still remain. It costs nothing for her to go there, and it may be the last opportunity she will have of visiting her father. From here she will go to Covington, and spend a week or two before going back to Galena.

It was my bay horse (cost me $140) that was shot. I also lost the little pony, my fine saddle and bridle, and the common one. What I lost cost about $250. My saddle cloth which was about half the cost of the whole, I left at home.

I try to write home about once in two weeks and think I keep it up pretty well. I wrote to you directly after the battle of Belmont, and Lagow and Julia have each written since.

Give my love to all at home. I am very glad to get letters from home and will write as often as I can. I am somewhat troubled lest I lose my command here, though I believe my administration has given general satisfaction not only to those over me but to all concerned. This is the most important command within the department however, and will probably be given to the senior officer next to General Halleck himself.

There are not so many brigadier generals in the army as there are brigades, and as to divisions they are nearly all commanded by brigadiers.

Yours,
ULYSSES.

## Sallie Brock: from
# Richmond During the War

In her memoir Sallie Brock described conditions in Richmond in the
first autumn of the war.

---

### RICHMOND A CITY OF REFUGE-EXTORTIONS.

RICHMOND had already become a "city of refuge." Flying
before the face of the invader, thousands sought within its
hospitable walls that security they could not hope to receive in
exposed and isolated places. Tales of suffering were even then
the theme of thousands of tongues, as the homeless and destitute crowded into our city for safety and support. The usual
hotel and boarding-house accommodations were found altogether insufficient to supply comfortable places of sojourn for
the great numbers demanding sympathy and shelter. From the
first day that war was declared against the South, Richmond
was taxed to the utmost extent of her capacity to take care of
the surplus population that accumulated within her limits.

Many of the citizens received and entertained these wander-
ers; but many, by the suspension of the ordinary business pursuits of the city, were so reduced in income that it became an
impossibility for them to extend to such numbers the assistance which a native kindness and generosity prompted.

From the extraordinary influx of population, and the existence of the blockade, which prevented the importation of
supplies in proportion to the demand, we were compelled to
submit to the vilest extortions by which any people were ever
oppressed. It was first observed in the increased prices placed
upon goods of domestic manufacture. Cotton and woolen
fabrics soon brought double prices, even before there was a
general circulation of the money issued by the Confederate

641

Treasury. The wisest laid in supplies sufficient to stock a small shop, and had enough to last during the entire war; but an overwhelming majority, unsupplied with means to use providently, waited for each day to provide for the peculiar wants of the day, and at length suffered for the simplest necessaries of life.

A lady in conversation with a friend, as early as May, 1861, said, "If you need calico, you had better purchase at once, for our ninepence goods have gone up to sixteen cents, and very soon we shall have to pay twenty-five cents. Our ten cent cotton domestics are now retailing at sixteen cents, and before the end of June it is said to be doubtful whether there will be any left in Richmond, and if any, we shall have to pay three prices." Could she have foreseen the time when for a yard of the goods in question she would have to pay as many dollars, and later still twice the amount in dollars, she would indeed have urged her friend, who was incredulous to the truth, to purchase supplies sufficient for a number of years.

The same fact was observable in regard to imported articles of food. The extraordinary increase in price was first noticeable in that demanded for coffee. An old lady, one of the most famous of the many distinguished housewives of Virginia, in great astonishment, said in August, 1861: "Only think! coffee is now thirty cents per pound, and my grocer tells me I must buy at once, or very soon we shall have to pay double that price. Shameful! Why, even in the war of 1812 we had not to pay higher than sixty cents. And now, so soon! We must do without it, except when needed for the sick. If we can't make some of the various proposed substitutes appetizing, why, we can use water. Thank God, no blockade can restrict the supply of that. That, at least, is abundant, and given without money and without price."

Could this conscientious economist then have foreseen the cost of the berry for her favorite beverage at fifty dollars per pound, she would not grudgingly have paid the grocer his exorbitant demand of fifty cents.

During the existence of the war, coffee was a luxury in which only the most wealthy could constantly indulge; and when used at all, it was commonly adulterated with other things which passed for the genuine article, but was often so nauseous that it was next to impossible to force it upon the stomach. Rye, wheat, corn, sweet potatoes, beans, ground-nuts, chestnuts, chiccory, ochre, sorghum-seed, and other grains and seeds, roasted and ground, were all brought into use as substitutes for the bean of Araby; but after every experiment to make coffee of what was not coffee, we were driven to decide that there was nothing coffee but coffee, and if disposed to indulge in extravagance at all, the people showed it only by occasional and costly indulgence in the luxurious beverage.

Tea, sugar, wines, and all imported liquors, increased rapidly in expense as the supply grew scarce, but not in the same ratio as coffee, which had been in universal use at the South—the low price at which it had been purchased, and its stimulating and pleasant effects making it agreeable, necessary and possible for even the poorest to indulge in its use.

The leaves of the currant, blackberry, willow, sage, and other vegetables, were dried and used as substitutes for tea by those who could not or did not feel justified in encouraging the exorbitant demands of successful blockade runners and dealers in the article. When sugar grew scarce, and so expensive that many were compelled to abandon its use altogether, there were substituted honey, and the syrup from sorghum, or the Chinese sugar cane, for all ordinary culinary purposes. The cultivation of the latter has become a very important consideration with the agriculturists of the more northern of the Southern States, being peculiarly adapted to the soil and climate, and furnishing a cheap and excellent substitute for the syrup of the sugar cane of the Gulf States and the West Indies.

With an admirable adaptation to the disagreeable and inconvenient circumstances entailed upon us by the blockade, the necessary self denial practiced by the people was in a spirit of cheerful acquiescence, and with a philosophical satisfaction and contentment that forgot the present in a hopeful looking for better and brighter days in the future.

Cheerfully submitting to inconveniences, and deprived from the first of the usual luxuries and many of the necessaries of life, the people were buoyed up with the hope and belief that their sufferings would be of short duration, and that an honorable independence and exemption from the evils which surrounded them, would soon compensate amply for the self denial they were called upon to practice. The remembrance then would be rather glorious than disagreeable in the reflection that they, too, had shared the travail which wrought the freedom of their country.

If there were any who sighed after the flesh-pots of Egypt, the sighs were breathed in the silence of retirement, and not where the ardor of the more hopeful could be chilled by such signs of discontent.

There was, however, a class in Richmond who very ill endured the severe simplicity and the rigid self-denial to which they were compelled to conform in the Confederate Capital. Gradually and insidiously innovations were permitted, until at last the license tolerated in fashionable society elsewhere grew to be tolerated somewhat in Richmond, and in the course of time prosy Richmond was acknowledged "fast" enough for the fastest.

# Benjamin Moran: Journal,
# November 27–December 3, 1861

Acting on his own initiative, Captain Charles Wilkes of the U.S.S. *San Jacinto* stopped the British steamer *Trent* off Cuba on November 8 and seized James Mason and John Slidell, Confederate diplomats on missions to Great Britain and France. His action was widely hailed in the North, but soon provoked an international crisis. Benjamin Moran, a secretary at the American legation in London, recorded the reaction in England to the *Trent* incident.

---

*Wed. 27 Nov. '61.* We have received a long note from Earl Russell, dated yesterday, in reply to Mr. Adams' letter of last Friday, announcing the revocation of Mr. Bunch's Exequatur. It is to me a hostile document. His Lordship defends Bunch, and boastfully states that his negotiations with the rebels on the last three articles of the Paris Declaration were authorized, and that Her Majesty's Gov't will continue to make such like communications to both the State Gov'ts & Central Govt. of the South whenever it sees fit to do so, & it will not regard such proceedings with the rebels as inconsistent with its obligations as a friendly power to the Federal Govt. This is an affront these people would not have dared commit, were we not in a crippled state. It seems to me that Lord Palmerston has deliberately determined to force us into a war with England, and I believe this has been his purpose from the beginning. All his movements point to that end. With a malicious wickedness his worst enemy could hardly think of charging him with, he has been playing into the hands of the rebels from the first: and with the aid of the *Times* he has been disseminating falsehoods about our enmity to England, until he has succeeded in making the people of these realms believe that enormous lie that we are doing all we can to involve them in a war. He is a foe to freedom: and if he succeeds in his satanic object of hostilities between the Federal Gov't & Great Britain he will deserve the execrations of mankind. His hatred of us is a boyish passion, strengthened by accumulated years. As he was Secretary at War in 1812 he feels that his life and name will not be free from tarnish unless he can expunge us from the earth, and to do so he must be quick. Age will soon lead him to the grave, and he must glut his ire before he goes. In case he succeeds in this mad scheme, he will have the whole English people with him, and they will religiously believe his monstrous imposition that we picked the quarrel. He is one of their idols, and being a Lord, all he has to do is to put adroitly forth a shameful misrepresentation, bearing the semblance of truth, and with the backing of The Times, it will take such firm hold of the public mind that ages will not eradicate it in case of war.

That such a result will follow I much fear, for it seems as if the demons of darkness were against us. At about 1/2 past 12 this morning we received a telegram from Capt. Britton at Southampton announcing that the West India steamer at that port brought news in there this morning that Capt. Wilkes, of the U.S. Ship of War San Jacinto, had stopped the British mail steamer Trent in the Bahama Channel, not far from St. Thomas, on the 9th Inst, & had forcibly taken Mason, Slidell, Eustis, & Macfarlane out of her: and at 1 o'clk a telegram from Reuter confirmed the statement. That the capture of these arch-rebels gave us great satisfaction at the first blush, was natural: & we gave free vent to our exultation. But on reflection I am satisfied that the act will do more for the Southerners than ten victories, for it touches John Bull's honor, and the honor of his flag. At present the people have hardly recovered from the paralysing effect of the news; but they are beginning to see that their flag has been insulted, and if that devil *The Times*, feeds their ire to-morrow, as it assuredly will, nothing but a miracle can prevent their sympathies running to the South, and Palmerston getting up a war. We have no particulars, but from what we hear, it would seem that Capt. Wilkes acted on his own responsibility, and not on that of the Govt.

I telegraphed the news at once to Mr. Adams, and fear it has not added to his enjoyment of rural retirement. It is odd that he never goes out of town that some thing serious don't arise to call him home.

*Thursday, 28 Nov. '61.*   This morning I went to a Mass at the French Chapel in King St., Portman Square, for the repose of the soul of Dom Pedro the 5th, late King of Portugal. I went directly from the house, & wore my Levee Dress, with crape on the arm, sword hilt, &c. I was the first there of the Diplomatic Corps, not belonging to the Portuguese Mission. Others soon came in, & shortly after 11 o'clock there were about 50 Ambassadors, Secretaries & Attachés, their rich uniforms presenting a gay appearance, as contrasted with the sable hangings on the catafalque and altar. Mass was performed by Cardinal Wiseman, a burly butcher looking man, assisted by some 20 other priests of various grades, & notwithstanding the stupidities of some of the ceremonies, the whole affair was impressive, and had the edifice been even ordinarily respectable, would have been solemn and overpowering. There were several splendid male voices among the singers, and the music was grand. The audience was large, & among them were Queen Amelie, widow of Louis Phillippe, an aristocratic and pensive old lady.

I was addressed by a number of the Diplomatic Corps & asked if we were going to have war with England about Mason & Slidell; but I thought it prudent to be quiet. On leaving, I drove to the Legation in my uniform, where I found Mr. Bright, M.P. deploring Capt. Wilkes act. There was a note from Earl Russell, asking an interview of Mr. Adams at 2 o'ck to-day, and as no answer had been made to it, I drove at once to the F. Office, and told Mr. Layard of Mr. A.'s absence. He told me that he sent the request up at 12 last night.

The newspapers are violent in the extreme, and yet seem in a mist. In all this there is still an ugly look of war. We have had a great deal to do to-day, and many American visitors in a great state of excitement. Wilson and Henry Adams seem to me very indiscreet in some of their remarks about the business to strangers.

*Friday, 29 Nov. 61.*   Mr. Adams returned to town last night. It appears he got my telegram promptly. He regards the Trent affair as serious, and is very grave about it. To-day he has been writing home concerning it, and I have had a vast deal of hard work. Earl Russell fixed quarter to two for an interview, but beyond asking a few questions about the orders of the Capt. of the James Adger, his Lordship said nothing. It is quite evident that Ministers consider the question as serious, and many of them feel very sore and hostile about it. As I was detained late, I remained to dinner. Mr. Adams expressed apprehensions that we would not be here a month and from this I suspect he has reason to believe that the people at the head of the Gov't are not altogether capable of dealing wisely with so delicate a question. We shall certainly be in an unpleasant state of mind concerning this affair for a month, or until we hear from Washington. We ought to hear something next Monday, but of this there is no certainty. Things now are by no means agreeable, and Mrs. Adams assured me that she was miserable at Moncton Milnes after the receipt of my telegram. She felt that they were provoked at what had occurred, friendly as they were, and she couldn't enjoy herself knowing how uncomfortable her presence must necessarily make them after such news. In future she will not go on such visits, for it seems something painful is sure to occur while Mr. Adams is away on such pleasure.

There has been a great crowd of anxious visitors to-day, mostly Americans, to know if war will result, but we can't tell.

*Sat. 30 Nov. '61.*   I got down early, and have been at hard work through the whole of this duly day. Joseph L. Spofford, a youth from New York, whose father is half owner of the Nashville, was the only person I noticed particularly. He is a well-behaved, sensible young man.

*Monday, 2 Dec. '61.*   There is no time for rest now. I was here nearly all day yesterday recording, and putting our accumulated documents to rights. During the morning Mr. Adams called our attention to a curious statement in the *Observer* about American *espionage* in England, in which there are some facts strangely mingled up with a great deal of speculation. From this it is quite clear to me that some person either in the

Foreign Office, or Lord Palmerston's confidence, communicates facts to this *Observer*, and does the work very clumsily.

After having finished my work I dined at Horatio Ward's, and then returned to the Legation for news. There was an ambiguous telegram from Reuter, showing that Capt. Wilkes had acted on his own responsibility, & in that there was some consolation. But I confess I went home sick at heart at the news of the safe arrival of the Fingal at Savannah with her cargo of war material. Her escape from capture is a disgrace to our Navy, & I fear treason in the Squadron is the cause.

This state of feeling was not improved on finding this morning that no despatches had arrived. All the evil spirits are at work against us, and the Despatch bag is shuffling about somewhere between this and Cork.

I went over to see Van de Weyer, the Belgian Minister, & enquire about a Baron de Reiffenberg, who has offered his services to our Govt. The result was damaging to the Baron, who instead of being a military man, is a *litterateur*, and never smelt powder, so far as Van de Weyer knows. I found His Ex.y suffering from illness, and very grumpy.

Col. Jos. L. Chester was here to-day, & presented me with a copy of his "John Rogers, the Martyr." The volume looks well & is finely gotten up. As Chester owes me over £80, I hope the book will not be the only return I shall get therefore.

We have had some forty people here to-day—all anxious, and all gloomy. Among them were A. S. Goodall & Lammot Dupont.

Mr. Adams continues to entertain very gloomy apprehensions of the future, but I don't know what he founds his fears upon. He probably has private advices of which I know nothing.

*Tuesday 3 Dec. '61.* I stayed here at work until 7.30 last evening, and had to go away without hearing of the arrival of the bag. On my return this morning, I was sick at heart to hear there was nothing from Washington on this trouble. Our despatches, which only arrived this morning, are silent. This is what may be called the extreme of cruel folly. And on all such momentous questions, the Department at Washington, no matter what may be its political cast, has, in all my time here, been equally indifferent about supplying the Minister at an early moment with its views. He, of all men, ought to be advised at once of intentions at Head Quarters, whereas he is generally the last to receive information as to their nature.

At present the excitement in England is truly terrific. The Europa was detained at Cork or Queenstown, until last night, or this morning, to carry out an Ultimatum, and the purport of that is indicated by the London papers of yesterday and to-day. It is alleged that the Law Officers of the Crown have decided that Wilkes did not insult England enough, and the result is a demand for an apology, and the restoration of the men. By harping on this, and asserting that Capt. Wilkes' act was an authorized and deliberate insult of our Gov't, the journals have lashed the nation into a most indecent rage, and the consequence is that mob rule reigns supreme, and the natural English hatred of the American people, which is ordinarily concealed, has been allowed to gush up in its full bitterness from all hearts, high and low. This polite and calm nation is in the throes of a vulgar and coarse excitement such as one might naturally look for among a crowd of the London Fancy, but the like of which no one, not even their worst enemy, would ever expect to seize upon the inoffensive and harmless upper classes of the realm. That pink of modesty and refinement, *The Times*, is filled with such slatternly abuse of us and ours, that it is fair to conclude that all the Fishwifes of Billingsgate have been transferred to Printing House Square to fill the ears of the writers there with their choicest phraseology. There is something positively infernal in the way these assassins are goading the nation on to a war. They daily feed the public mind with the most palpable lies, & stick at nothing. If a war should follow this wicked conduct, reflecting Englishmen will blush in after years at the bigotry and blindness which hurried them into the struggle.

# Henry Adams to Charles Francis Adams Jr.

Henry Adams expressed his apprehension that an Anglo-American war would break out over the *Trent* affair to his brother in Boston. On December 19 Lord Lyons, the British minister in Washington, formally demanded the release of the Confederate envoys. The crisis was resolved on December 25, when Lincoln and his cabinet decided to release Mason and Slidell. In his reply to Lyons, Secretary of State Seward asserted that Wilkes had rightfully considered the envoys to be "contraband of war," but had erred by not bringing the *Trent* into an American port so that the matter could be tried in a prize court.

---

London 30 Nov. 1861.

My dear Boy

If I thought the state of things bad last week you may imagine what I think of them now. In fact I consider that we are dished, and that our position is hopeless. If the Administration ordered the capture of those men, I am satisfied that our present authorities are very unsuitable persons to conduct a war like this or to remain in the direction of our affairs. It is our ruin. Do not deceive yourself about the position of England. We might have preserved our dignity in many ways without going to war with her, and our party in the Cabinet was always strong enough to maintain peace here and keep down the anti-blockaders. But now all the fat's in the fire, and I feel like going off and taking up my old German life again as a permanency. It is devilish disagreeable to act the part of Sisyphus especially when it is our own friends who are trying to crush us under the rock.

What part it is reserved to us to play in this very tragical comedy I am utterly unable to tell. The Government has left us in the most awkward and unfair position. They have given no warning that such an act was thought of, and seem almost to have purposely encouraged us to waste our strength in trying to maintain the relations which it was itself intending to destroy. I am half-mad with vexation and despair. If papa is ordered home I shall do as Fairfax did, and go into the war with 'peace' on my mind and lips.

Our position here is of course very unpleasant just now. We were to have gone to Lord Hatherton's on Monday, but now our visit is put off, and I am not without expectations that a very few weeks may see us either on our way home or on the continent. I think that the New Year will see the end.

This nation means to make war. Do not doubt it. What Seward means is more than I can guess. But if he means war also, or to run as close as he can without touching, then I say that Mr Seward is the greatest criminal we've had yet.

We have friends here still, but very few. Bright dined with us last night, and is with us, but is evidently hopeless of seeing anything good. Besides, his assistance at such a time as this is evidently a disadvantage to us, for he is now wholly out of power and influence. Our friends are all very much cast down and my friends of the Spectator sent up to me in a dreadful state and asked me to come down to see them, which I did, and they complained bitterly of the position we were now in. I had of course the pleasure of returning the complaint to any extent, but after all this is poor consolation.

Our good father is cool but evidently of the same mind as I am. He has seen Lord Russell but could give him no information, and my Lord did not volunteer any on his side. You will know very soon what you are to expect.

The house is not cheerful, and our good mother is in a state that does not tend to raise our spirits. Still we manage to worry along and I reserve my complaints for paper. Our minds have been so kept on the stretch for the last week that I feel a sort of permanent lowness and wretchedness which does not prevent laughing and gossiping though it does not give them much zest. Theodore writes me from Paris. No news of importance has yet reached my ears, but you will see my views as usual in the Times. We are preparing for a departure, though as yet we have taken no positive steps towards making future arrangements.

Beaufort was good. It gave me one glorious day worth a large share of all the anxiety and trouble that preceded and have followed it. Our cry now must be emancipation and arming the slaves.

Ever Yrs     HB.A.

# Abraham Lincoln:
# Annual Message to Congress

In his first annual message to Congress Lincoln reviewed the progress of the conflict and recommended a series of war-related measures, including a program for the emancipation and colonization of slaves confiscated from Confederate owners.

---

## Annual Message to Congress

FELLOW CITIZENS of the Senate and House of Representatives:

In the midst of unprecedented political troubles, we have cause of great gratitude to God for unusual good health, and most abundant harvests.

You will not be surprised to learn that, in the peculiar exigencies of the times, our intercourse with foreign nations has been attended with profound solicitude, chiefly turning upon our own domestic affairs.

A disloyal portion of the American people have, during the whole year, been engaged in an attempt to divide and destroy the Union. A nation which endures factious domestic division, is exposed to disrespect abroad; and one party, if not both, is sure, sooner or later, to invoke foreign intervention.

Nations, thus tempted to interfere, are not always able to resist the counsels of seeming expediency, and ungenerous ambition, although measures adopted under such influences seldom fail to be unfortunate and injurious to those adopting them.

The disloyal citizens of the United States who have offered the ruin of our country, in return for the aid and comfort which they have invoked abroad, have received less patronage and encouragement than they probably expected. If it were just to suppose, as the insurgents have seemed to assume, that foreign nations, in this case, discarding all moral, social, and treaty obligations, would act solely, and selfishly, for the most speedy restoration of commerce, including, especially, the acquisition of cotton, those nations appear, as yet, not to have seen their way to their object more directly, or clearly, through the destruction, than through the preservation, of the Union. If we could dare to believe that foreign nations are actuated by no higher principle than this, I am quite sure a sound argument could be made to show them that they can reach their aim more readily, and easily, by aiding to crush this rebellion, than by giving encouragement to it.

The principal lever relied on by the insurgents for exciting foreign nations to hostility against us, as already intimated, is the embarrassment of commerce. Those nations, however, not improbably, saw from the first, that it was the Union which made as well our foreign, as our domestic, commerce. They can scarcely have failed to perceive that the effort for disunion produces the existing difficulty; and that one strong nation promises more durable peace, and a more extensive, valuable and reliable commerce, than can the same nation broken into hostile fragments.

It is not my purpose to review our discussions with foreign states, because whatever might be their wishes, or dispositions, the integrity of our country, and the stability of our government, mainly depend, not upon them, but on the loyalty, virtue, patriotism, and intelligence of the American people. The correspondence itself, with the usual reservations, is herewith submitted.

I venture to hope it will appear that we have practiced prudence, and liberality towards foreign powers, averting causes of irritation; and, with firmness, maintaining our own rights and honor.

Since, however, it is apparent that here, as in every other state, foreign dangers necessarily attend domestic difficulties, I recommend that adequate and ample measures be adopted for maintaining the public defences on every side. While, under this general recommendation, provision for defending our sea-coast line readily occurs to the mind, I also, in the same connexion, ask the attention of Congress to our great lakes and rivers. It is believed that some fortifications and depots of arms and munitions, with harbor and navigation improvements, all at well selected points upon these, would be of great importance to the national defence and preservation. I ask attention to the views of the Secretary of War, expressed in his report, upon the same general subject.

I deem it of importance that the loyal regions of East Tennessee and western North Carolina should be connected with Kentucky, and other faithful parts of the Union, by railroad. I therefore recommend, as a military measure, that Congress provide for the construction of such road, as speedily as possible. Kentucky, no doubt, will co-operate, and, through her legislature, make the most judicious selection of a line. The northern terminus must connect with some existing railroad; and whether the route shall be from Lexington, or Nicholasville, to the Cumberland Gap; or from Lebanon to the Tennessee line, in the direction of Knoxville; or on some still different line, can easily be determined. Kentucky and the general government co-operating, the work can be completed in a very short time; and when done, it will be not only of vast present usefulness, but also a valuable permanent improvement, worth its cost in all the future.

Some treaties, designed chiefly for the interests of commerce, and having no grave political importance, have been negotiated, and will be submitted to the Senate for their consideration.

Although we have failed to induce some of the commercial powers to adopt a desirable melioration of the rigor of maritime war, we have removed all obstructions from the way of this humane reform, except such as are merely of temporary and accidental occurrence.

I invite your attention to the correspondence between her Britannic Majesty's minister accredited to this government, and the Secretary of State, relative to the detention of the British ship Perthshire in June last, by the United States steamer Massachusetts, for a supposed breach of the blockade. As this detention was occasioned by an obvious misapprehension of the facts, and as justice requires that we should commit no belligerent act not founded in strict right, as sanctioned by public law, I recommend that an appropriation be made to satisfy the reasonable demand of the owners of the vessel for her detention.

I repeat the recommendation of my predecessor, in his annual message to Congress in December last, in regard to the disposition of the surplus which will probably remain after satisfying the claims of American citizens against China, pursuant to the awards of the commissioners under the act of the 3rd of March, 1859. If, however, it should not be deemed advisable to carry that recommendation into effect, I would suggest that authority be given for investing the principal, over the proceeds of the surplus referred to, in good securities, with a view to the satisfaction of such other just claims of our citizens against China as are not unlikely to arise hereafter in the course of our extensive trade with that Empire.

By the act of the 5th of August last, Congress authorized the President to instruct the commanders of suitable vessels to defend themselves against, and to capture pirates. This authority has been exercised in a single instance only. For the more effectual protection of our extensive and valuable commerce, in the eastern seas especially, it seems to me that it would also be advisable to authorize the commanders of sailing vessels to re-capture any prizes which pirates might make of United States vessels and their cargoes, and the consular courts, now established by law in eastern countries, to adjudicate the cases, in the event that this should not be objected to by the local authorities.

If any good reason exists why we should persevere longer in withholding our recognition of the independence and sovereignty of Hayti and Liberia, I am unable to discern it. Unwilling, however, to inaugurate a novel policy in regard to them without the approbation of Congress, I submit for your consideration the expediency of an appropriation for maintaining a chargé d'affaires near each of those new states. It does not admit of doubt that important commercial advantages might be secured by favorable commercial treaties with them.

The operations of the treasury during the period which has elapsed since your adjournment have been conducted with signal success. The patriotism of the people has placed at the disposal of the government the large means demanded by the public exigencies. Much of the national loan has been taken by citizens of the industrial classes, whose confidence in their country's faith, and zeal for their country's deliverance from present peril, have induced them to contribute to the support of the government the whole of their limited acquisitions. This fact imposes peculiar obligations to economy in disbursement and energy in action.

The revenue from all sources, including loans, for the financial year ending on the 30th June, 1861, was eighty six million, eight hundred and thirty five thousand, nine hundred dollars, and twenty seven cents, ($86,835,900.27,) and the expenditures for the same period, including payments on account of the public debt, were eighty four million, five hundred and seventy eight thousand, eight hundred and thirty four dollars and forty seven cents, ($84,578,834.47;) leaving a balance in the treasury, on the 1st July, of two million, two hundred and fifty seven thousand, sixty five dollars and eighty cents, ($2,257,065.80.) For the first quarter of the financial year, ending on the 30th September, 1861, the receipts from all sources, including the balance of first of July, were $102,532,509.27, and the expenses $98,239,733.09; leaving a balance on the 1st of October, 1861, of $4,292,776.18.

Estimates for the remaining three quarters of the year, and for the financial year 1863, together with his views of ways and means for meeting the demands contemplated by them, will be submitted to Congress by the Secretary of the Treasury. It is gratifying to know that the expenditures made necessary by the rebellion are not beyond the resources of the loyal people, and to believe that the same patriotism which has thus far sustained the government will continue to sustain it till Peace and Union shall again bless the land.

I respectfully refer to the report of the Secretary of War for information respecting the numerical strength of the army, and for recommendations having in view an increase of its efficiency and the well being of the various branches of the service intrusted to his care. It is gratifying to know that the patriotism of the people has proved equal to the occasion, and that the number of troops tendered greatly exceeds the force which Congress authorized me to call into the field.

I refer with pleasure to those portions of his report which make allusion to the creditable degree of discipline already attained by our troops, and to the excellent sanitary condition of the entire army.

The recommendation of the Secretary for an organization of the militia upon a uniform basis, is a subject of vital importance to the future safety of the country, and is commended to the serious attention of Congress.

The large addition to the regular army, in connexion with the defection that has so considerably diminished the number of its officers, gives peculiar importance to his recommendation for increasing the corps of cadets to the greatest capacity of the Military Academy.

By mere omission, I presume, Congress has failed to provide chaplains for hospitals occupied by volunteers. This subject was brought to my notice, and I was induced to draw up the form of a letter, one copy of which, properly addressed, has been delivered to each of the persons, and at the dates respectively named and stated, in a schedule, containing also the form of the letter, marked A, and herewith transmitted.

These gentlemen, I understand, entered upon the duties designated, at the times respectively stated in the schedule, and have labored faithfully therein ever since. I therefore recommend that they be compensated at the same rate as chaplains in the army. I further suggest that general provision be made for chaplains to serve at hospitals, as well as with regiments.

The report of the Secretary of the Navy presents in detail the operations of that branch of the service, the activity and energy which have characterized its administration, and the results of measures to increase its efficiency and power. Such have been the additions, by construction and purchase, that it may almost be said a navy has been created and brought into service since our difficulties commenced.

Besides blockading our extensive coast, squadrons larger than ever before assembled under our flag have been put afloat and performed deeds which have increased our naval renown.

I would invite special attention to the recommendation of the Secretary for a more perfect organization of the navy by introducing additional grades in the service.

The present organization is defective and unsatisfactory, and the suggestions submitted by the department will, it is believed, if adopted, obviate the difficulties alluded to, promote harmony, and increase the efficiency of the navy.

There are three vacancies on the bench of the Supreme Court—two by the decease of Justices Daniel and McLean, and one by the resignation of Justice Campbell. I have so far forborne making nominations to fill these vacancies for reasons which I will now state. Two of the outgoing judges resided within the States now overrun by revolt; so that if successors were appointed in the same localities, they could not now serve upon their circuits; and many of the most competent men there, probably would not take the personal hazard of accepting to serve, even here, upon the supreme bench. I have been unwilling to throw all the appointments northward, thus disabling myself from doing justice to the south on the return of peace; although I may remark that to transfer to the north one which has heretofore been in the south, would not, with reference to territory and population, be unjust.

During the long and brilliant judicial career of Judge McLean his circuit grew into an empire—altogether too large for any one judge to give the courts therein more than a nominal attendance—rising in population from one million four hundred and seventy-thousand and eighteen, in 1830, to six million one hundred and fifty-one thousand four hundred and five, in 1860.

Besides this, the country generally has outgrown our present judicial system. If uniformity was at all intended, the system requires that all the States shall be accommodated with circuit courts, attended by supreme judges, while, in fact, Wisconsin, Minnesota, Iowa, Kansas, Florida, Texas, California, and Oregon, have never had any such courts. Nor can this well be remedied without a change of the system; because the adding of judges to the Supreme Court, enough for the accommodation of all parts of the country, with circuit courts, would create a court altogether too numerous for a judicial body of any sort. And the evil, if it be one, will increase as new States come into the Union. Circuit courts are useful, or they are not useful. If useful, no State should be denied them; if not useful, no State should have them. Let them be provided for all, or abolished as to all.

Three modifications occur to me, either of which, I think, would be an improvement upon our present system. Let the Supreme Court be of convenient number in every event. Then, first, let the whole country be divided into circuits of convenient size, the supreme judges to serve in a number of them corresponding to their own number, and independent circuit judges be provided for all the rest. Or, secondly, let the supreme judges be relieved from circuit duties, and circuit judges provided for all the circuits. Or, thirdly, dispense with circuit courts altogether, leaving the judicial functions wholly to the district courts and an independent Supreme Court.

I respectfully recommend to the consideration of Congress the present condition of the statute laws, with the hope that Congress will be able to find an easy remedy for many of the inconveniences and evils which constantly embarrass those engaged in the practical administration of them. Since the organization of the government, Congress has enacted some five thousand acts and joint resolutions, which fill more than six thousand closely printed pages, and are scattered through many volumes. Many of these acts have been drawn in haste and without sufficient caution, so that their provisions are often obscure in themselves, or in conflict with each other, or at least so doubtful as to render it very difficult for even the best informed persons to ascertain precisely what the statute law really is.

It seems to me very important that the statute laws should be made as plain and intelligible as possible, and be reduced to as small a compass as may consist with the fullness and precision of the will of the legislature and the perspicuity of its language. This, well done, would, I think, greatly facilitate the labors of those whose duty it is to assist in the administration of the laws, and would be a lasting benefit to the people, by placing before them, in a more accessible and intelligible form, the laws which so deeply concern their interests and their duties.

I am informed by some whose opinions I respect, that all the acts of Congress now in force, and of a permanent and general nature, might be revised and re-written, so as to be embraced in one volume (or at most, two volumes) of ordinary and convenient size. And I respectfully recommend to Congress to consider of the subject, and, if my suggestion be approved, to devise such plan as to their wisdom shall seem most proper for the attainment of the end proposed.

One of the unavoidable consequences of the present insurrection is the entire suppression, in many places, of all the ordinary means of administering civil justice by the officers and in the forms of existing law. This is the case, in whole or in part, in all the insurgent States; and as our armies advance upon and take possession of parts of those States, the practical evil becomes more apparent. There are no courts nor officers to whom the citizens of other States may apply for the enforcement of their lawful claims against citizens of the insurgent States; and there is a vast amount of debt constituting such claims. Some have estimated it as high as two hundred million dollars, due, in large part, from insurgents, in open rebellion, to loyal citizens who are, even now, making great sacrifices in the discharge of their patriotic duty to support the government.

Under these circumstances, I have been urgently solicited to establish, by military power, courts to administer summary justice in such cases. I have thus far declined to do it, not because I had any doubt that the end proposed—the collection of the debts—was just and right in itself, but because I have been unwilling to go beyond the pressure of necessity in the unusual exercise of power. But the powers of Congress I suppose are equal to the anomalous occasion, and therefore I refer the whole matter to Congress, with the hope that a plan may be devised for the administration of justice in all such parts of the insurgent States and Territories as may be under the control of this government, whether by a voluntary return to allegiance and order or by the power of our arms. This, however, not to be a permanent institution, but a temporary substitute, and to cease as soon as the ordinary courts can be re-established in peace.

It is important that some more convenient means should be provided, if possible, for the adjustment of claims against the government, especially in view of their increased number by reason of the war. It is as much the duty of government to render prompt justice against itself, in favor of citizens, as it is to administer the same, between private individuals. The investigation and adjudication of claims, in their nature belong to the judicial department; besides it is apparent that the attention of Congress, will be more than usually engaged, for some time to come, with great national questions. It was intended, by the organization of the court of claims, mainly to remove this branch of business from the halls of Congress; but while the court has proved to be an effective, and valuable means of investigation, it in great degree fails to effect the object of its creation, for want of power to make its judgments final.

Fully aware of the delicacy, not to say the danger, of the subject, I commend to your careful consideration whether this power of making judgments final, may not properly be given to the court, reserving the right of appeal on questions of law to the Supreme Court, with such other provisions as experience may have shown to be necessary.

I ask attention to the report of the Postmaster General, the following being a summary statement of the condition of the department:

The revenue from all sources during the fiscal year ending June 30. 1861, including the annual permanent appropriation of seven hundred thousand dollars ($700,000) for the transportation of "free mail matter," was nine million, forty nine thousand, two hundred and ninety six dollars and forty cents ($9,049,296.40) being about two per cent. less than the revenue for 1860.

The expenditures were thirteen million, six hundred and six thousand, seven hundred and fifty nine dollars and eleven cents. ($13,606,759.11) showing a decrease of more than eight per cent. as compared with those of the previous year, and leaving an excess of expenditure over the revenue for the last fiscal year of four million, five hundred and fifty seven thousand, four hundred and sixty two dollars and seventy one cents ($4,557,462.71.)

The gross revenue for the year ending June 30, 1863, is estimated at an increase of four per cent. on that of 1861, making eight million, six hundred and eighty three thousand dollars ($8,683,000) to which should be added the earnings of the department in carrying free matter, viz: seven hundred thousand dollars ($700,000.) making nine million, three hundred and eighty three thousand dollars, ($9,383,000.)

The total expenditures for 1863 are estimated at $12,528,000, leaving an estimated deficiency of $3,145,000, to be supplied from the treasury, in addition to the permanent appropriation.

The present insurrection shows, I think, that the extension of this District across the Potomac river, at the time of establishing the capital here, was eminently wise, and consequently that the relinquishment of that portion of it which lies within the State of Virginia was unwise and dangerous. I submit for your consideration the expediency of regaining that part of the District, and the restoration of the original boundaries thereof, through negotiations with the State of Virginia.

The report of the Secretary of the Interior, with the accompanying documents, exhibits the condition of the several branches of the public business pertaining to that department. The depressing influences of the insurrection have been especially felt in the operations of the Patent and General Land Offices. The cash receipts from the sales of public lands during the past year have exceeded the expenses of our land system only about $200,000. The sales have been entirely suspended in the southern States, while the interruptions to the business of the country, and the diversion of large numbers of men from labor to military service, have obstructed settlements in the new States and Territories of the northwest.

The receipts of the Patent Office have declined in nine months about $100,000, rendering a large reduction of the force employed necessary to make it self sustaining.

The demands upon the Pension Office will be largely increased by the insurrection. Numerous applications for pensions, based upon the casualties of the existing war, have already been made. There is reason to believe that many who are now upon the pension rolls and in receipt of the bounty of the government, are in the ranks of the insurgent army, or giving them aid and comfort. The Secretary of the Interior has directed a suspension of the payment of the pensions of such persons upon proof of their disloyalty. I recommend that Congress authorize that officer to cause the names of such persons to be stricken from the pension rolls.

The relations of the government with the Indian tribes have been greatly disturbed by the insurrection, especially in the southern superintendency and in that of New Mexico. The Indian country south of Kansas is in the possession of insurgents from Texas and Arkansas. The agents of the United States appointed since the 4th. of March for this superintendency have been unable to reach their posts, while the most of those who were in office before that time have espoused the insurrectionary cause, and assume to exercise the powers of agents by virtue of commissions from the insurrectionists. It has been stated in the public press that a portion of those Indians have been organized as a military force, and are attached to the army of the insurgents. Although the government has no official information upon this subject, letters have been written to the Commissioner of Indian Affairs by several prominent chiefs, giving assurance of their loyalty to the United States, and expressing a wish for the presence of federal troops to protect them. It is believed that upon the repossession of the country by the federal forces the Indians will readily cease all hostile demonstrations, and resume their former relations to the government.

Agriculture, confessedly the largest interest of the nation, has, not a department, nor a bureau, but a clerkship only, assigned to it in the government. While it is fortunate that this great interest is so independent in its nature as to not have demanded and extorted more from the government, I respectfully ask Congress to consider whether something more cannot be given voluntarily with general advantage.

Annual reports exhibiting the condition of our agriculture, commerce, and manufactures would present a fund of information of great practical value to the country. While I make no suggestion as to details, I venture the opinion that an agricultural and statistical bureau might profitably be organized.

The execution of the laws for the suppression of the African slave trade, has been confided to the Department of the Interior. It is a subject of gratulation that the efforts which have been made for the suppression of this inhuman traffic, have been recently attended with unusual success. Five vessels being fitted out for the slave trade have been seized and condemned. Two mates of vessels engaged in the trade, and one person in equipping a vessel as a slaver, have been convicted and subjected to the penalty of fine and imprisonment, and one captain, taken with a cargo of Africans on board his vessel, has been convicted of the highest grade of offence under our laws, the punishment of which is death.

The Territories of Colorado, Dakotah and Nevada, created by the last Congress, have been organized, and civil administration has been inaugurated therein under auspices especially gratifying, when it is considered that the leaven of treason was found existing in some of these new countries when the federal officers arrived there.

The abundant natural resources of these Territories, with the security and protection afforded by organized government, will doubtless invite to them a large immigration when peace shall restore the business of the country to its accustomed channels. I submit the resolutions of the legislature of Colorado, which evidence the patriotic spirit of the people of the Territory. So far the authority of the United States has been upheld in all the Territories, as it is hoped it will be in the future. I commend their interests and defence to the enlightened and generous care of Congress.

I recommend to the favorable consideration of Congress the interests of the District of Columbia. The insurrection has been the cause of much suffering and sacrifice to its inhabitants, and as they have no representative in Congress, that body should not overlook their just claims upon the government.

At your late session a joint resolution was adopted authorizing the President to take measures for facilitating a proper representation of the industrial interests of the United States at the exhibition of the industry of all nations to be holden at London in the year 1862. I regret to say I have been unable to give personal attention to this subject,—a subject at once so interesting in itself, and so extensively and intimately connected with the material prosperity of the world. Through the Secretaries of State and of the Interior a plan, or system, has been devised, and partly matured, and which will be laid before you.

Under and by virtue of the act of Congress entitled "An act to confiscate property used for insurrectionary purposes," approved August, 6, 1861, the legal claims of certain persons to the labor and service of certain other persons have become forfeited; and numbers of the latter, thus liberated, are already dependent on the United States, and must be provided for in some way. Besides this, it is not impossible that some of the States will pass similar enactments for their own benefit respectively, and by operation of which persons of the same class will be thrown upon them for disposal. In such case I recommend that Congress provide for accepting such persons from such States, according to some mode of valuation, in lieu, *pro tanto*, of direct taxes, or upon some other plan to be agreed on with such States respectively; that such persons, on such acceptance by the general government, be at once deemed free; and that, in any event, steps be taken for colonizing both classes, (or the one first mentioned, if the other shall not be brought into existence,) at some place, or places, in a climate congenial to them. It might be well to consider, too,—whether the free colored people already in the United States could not, so far as individuals may desire, be included in such colonization.

To carry out the plan of colonization may involve the acquiring of territory, and also the appropriation of money beyond that to be expended in the territorial acquisition. Having practiced the acquisition of territory for nearly sixty years, the question of constitutional power to do so is no longer an open one with us. The power was questioned at first by Mr. Jefferson, who, however, in the purchase of Louisiana, yielded his scruples on the plea of great expediency. If it be said that the only legitimate object of acquiring territory is to furnish homes for white men, this measure effects that object; for the emigration of colored men leaves additional room for white men remaining or coming here. Mr. Jefferson, however, placed the importance of procuring Louisiana more on political and commercial grounds than on providing room for population.

On this whole proposition,—including the appropriation of money with the acquisition of territory, does not the expediency amount to absolute necessity—that, without which the government itself cannot be perpetuated? The war continues. In considering the policy to be adopted for suppressing the insurrection, I have been anxious and careful that the inevitable conflict for this purpose shall not degenerate into a violent and remorseless revolutionary struggle. I have, therefore, in every case, thought it proper to keep the integrity of the Union prominent as the primary object of the contest on our part, leaving all questions which are not of vital military importance to the more deliberate action of the legislature.

In the exercise of my best discretion I have adhered to the blockade of the ports held by the insurgents, instead of putting in force, by proclamation, the law of Congress enacted at the late session, for closing those ports.

So, also, obeying the dictates of prudence, as well as the obligations of law, instead of transcending, I have adhered to the act of Congress to confiscate property used for insurrectionary purposes. If a new law upon the same subject shall be proposed, its propriety will be duly considered.

The Union must be preserved, and hence, all indispensable means must be employed. We should not be in haste to determine that radical and extreme measures, which may reach the loyal as well as the disloyal, are indispensable.

The inaugural address at the beginning of the Administration, and the message to Congress at the late special session, were both mainly devoted to the domestic controversy out of which the insurrection and consequent war have sprung. Nothing now occurs to add or subtract, to or from, the principles or general purposes stated and expressed in those documents.

The last ray of hope for preserving the Union peaceably, expired at the assault upon Fort Sumter; and a general review of what has occurred since may not be unprofitable. What was painfully uncertain then, is much better defined and more distinct now; and the progress of events is plainly in the right direction. The insurgents confidently claimed a strong support from north of Mason and Dixon's line; and the friends of the Union were not free from apprehension on the point. This, however, was soon settled definitely and on the right side. South of the line, noble little Delaware led off right from the first. Maryland was made to *seem* against the Union. Our soldiers were assaulted, bridges were burned, and railroads torn up, within her limits; and we were many days, at one time, without the ability to bring a single regiment over her soil to the capital. Now, her bridges and railroads are repaired and open to the government; she already gives seven regiments to the cause of the Union and none to the enemy; and her people, at a regular election, have sustained the Union, by a larger majority, and a larger aggregate vote than they ever before gave to any candidate, or any question. Kentucky, too, for some time in doubt, is now decidedly, and, I think, unchangeably, ranged on the side of the Union. Missouri is comparatively quiet; and I believe cannot again be overrun by the insurrectionists. These three States of Maryland, Kentucky, and Missouri, neither of which would promise a single soldier at first, have now an aggregate of not less than forty thousand in the field, for the Union; while, of their citizens, certainly not more than a third of that number, and they of doubtful whereabouts, and doubtful existence, are in arms against it. After a somewhat bloody struggle of months, winter closes on the Union people of western Virginia, leaving them masters of their own country.

An insurgent force of about fifteen hundred, for months dominating the narrow peninsular region, constituting the counties of Accomac and Northampton, and known as eastern shore of Virginia, together with some contiguous parts of Maryland, have laid down their arms; and the people there have renewed their allegiance to, and accepted the protection of, the old flag. This leaves no armed insurrectionist north of the Potomac, or east of the Chesapeake.

Also we have obtained a footing at each of the isolated points, on the southern coast, of Hatteras, Port Royal, Tybee Island, near Savannah, and Ship Island; and we likewise have some general accounts of popular movements, in behalf of the Union, in North Carolina and Tennessee.

These things demonstrate that the cause of the Union is advancing steadily and certainly southward.

Since your last adjournment, Lieutenant General Scott has retired from the head of the army. During his long life, the nation has not been unmindful of his merit; yet, on calling to mind how faithfully, ably and brilliantly he has served the country, from a time far back in our history, when few of the now living had been born, and thenceforward continually, I cannot but think we are still his debtors. I submit, therefore, for your consideration, what further mark of recognition is due to him, and to ourselves, as a grateful people.

With the retirement of General Scott came the executive duty of appointing, in his stead, a general-in-chief of the army. It is a fortunate circumstance that neither in council nor country was there, so far as I know, any difference of opinion as to the proper person to be selected. The retiring chief repeatedly expressed his judgment in favor of General McClellan for the position; and in this the nation seemed to give a unanimous concurrence. The designation of General McClellan is therefore in considerable degree, the selection of the Country as well as of the Executive; and hence there is better reason to hope there will be given him, the confidence, and cordial support thus, by fair implication, promised, and without which, he cannot, with so full efficiency, serve the country.

It has been said that one bad general is better than two good ones; and the saying is true, if taken to mean no more than that an army is better directed by a single mind, though inferior, than by two superior ones, at variance, and cross-purposes with each other.

And the same is true, in all joint operations wherein those engaged, *can* have none but a common end in view, and *can* differ only as to the choice of means. In a storm at sea, no one on board *can* wish the ship to sink; and yet, not unfrequently, all go down together, because too many will direct, and no single mind can be allowed to control.

It continues to develop that the insurrection is largely, if not exclusively, a war upon the first principle of popular government —the rights of the people. Conclusive evidence of this is found in the most grave and maturely considered public documents, as well as in the general tone of the insurgents. In those documents we find the abridgement of the existing right of suffrage and the denial to the people of all right to participate in the selection of public officers, except the legislative boldly advocated, with labored arguments to prove that large control of the people in government, is the source of all political evil. Monarchy itself is sometimes hinted at as a possible refuge from the power of the people.

In my present position, I could scarcely be justified were I to omit raising a warning voice against this approach of returning despotism.

It is not needed, nor fitting here, that a general argument should be made in favor of popular institutions; but there is one point, with its connexions, not so hackneyed as most others, to which I ask a brief attention. It is the effort to place *capital* on an equal footing with, if not above *labor*, in the structure of government. It is assumed that labor is available only in connexion with capital; that nobody labors unless somebody else, owning capital, somehow by the use of it, induces him to labor. This assumed, it is next considered whether it is best that capital shall *hire* laborers, and thus induce them to work by their own consent, or *buy* them, and drive them to it without their consent. Having proceeded so far, it is naturally concluded that all laborers are either *hired* laborers, or what we call slaves. And further it is assumed that whoever is once a hired laborer, is fixed in that condition for life.

Now, there is no such relation between capital and labor as assumed; nor is there any such thing as a free man being fixed for life in the condition of a hired laborer. Both these assumptions are false, and all inferences from them are groundless.

Labor is prior to, and independent of, capital. Capital is only the fruit of labor, and could never have existed if labor had not first existed. Labor is the superior of capital, and deserves much the higher consideration. Capital has its rights, which are as worthy of protection as any other rights. Nor is it denied that there is, and probably always will be, a relation between labor and capital, producing mutual benefits. The error is in assuming that the whole labor of community exists within that relation. A few men own capital, and that few avoid labor themselves, and, with their capital, hire or buy another few to labor for them. A large majority belong to neither class—neither work for others, nor have others working for them. In most of the southern States, a majority of the whole people of all colors are neither slaves nor masters; while in the northern a large majority are neither hirers nor hired. Men with their families—wives, sons, and daughters—work for themselves, on their farms, in their houses, and in their shops, taking the whole product to themselves, and asking no favors of capital on the one hand, nor of hired laborers or slaves on the other. It is not forgotten that a considerable number of persons mingle their own labor with capital—that is, they labor with their own hands, and also buy or hire others to labor for them; but this is only a mixed, and not a distinct class. No principle stated is disturbed by the existence of this mixed class.

Again: as has already been said, there is not, of necessity, any such thing as the free hired laborer being fixed to that condition for life. Many independent men everywhere in these States, a few years back in their lives, were hired laborers. The prudent, penniless beginner in the world, labors for wages awhile, saves a surplus with which to buy tools or land for himself; then labors on his own account another while, and at length hires another new beginner to help him. This is the just, and generous, and prosperous system, which opens the way to all—gives hope to all, and consequent energy, and progress, and improvement of condition to all. No men living are more worthy to be trusted than those who toil up from poverty—none less inclined to take, or touch, aught which they have not honestly earned. Let them beware of surrendering a political power which they already possess, and which, if surrendered, will surely be used to close the door of advancement against such as they, and to fix new disabilities and burdens upon them, till all of liberty shall be lost.

From the first taking of our national census to the last are seventy years; and we find our population at the end of the period eight times as great as it was at the beginning. The increase of those other things which men deem desirable has been even greater. We thus have at one view, what the popular principle applied to government, through the machinery of the States and the Union, has produced in a given time; and also what, if firmly maintained, it promises for the future. There are already among us those, who, if the Union be preserved, will live to see it contain two hundred and fifty millions. The struggle of today, is not altogether for today—it is for a vast future also. With a reliance on Providence, all the more firm and earnest, let us proceed in the great task which events have devolved upon us.

December 3, 1861

# Charles Francis Adams Jr. to Henry Adams

Shortly after writing to his brother, Charles Francis Adams Jr. was commissioned as a first lieutenant in the 1st Massachusetts Cavalry. He would sail with his regiment for Port Royal, South Carolina, at the end of the year.

---

*Boston*, December 10, 1861

YOURS of the 23d of last month reached me yesterday. . . . If we are going to have such a storm as you intimate, I should have to go, so anyhow, and if indeed "all that remains is to drop gracefully," it will not do me or any one else any good for me to anxiously hang on here a few days longer. Yet it does make me feel terribly. We have blundered all summer long and now we have capstoned our blunders by blundering into a war with England. So be it. While there's life there's hope; but I go into the army with a bitter feeling against those under whose lead we have come to this pass, and amid all the shattered idols of my whole life I don't feel as if I cared much when my turn came. I suppose now I shall go into the field against a foreign enemy and I ought to rejoice at that. Still, I don't. Against the rebels I could fight with a will and in earnest. They are traitors, they war for a lie, they are the enemies of morals, of government, and of man. In them we fight against a great wrong— but against England, we shall have forced her into war when she only asked for peace; we shall have made that a cause of quarrel which a few soft words might have turned away. It will be a wicked and causeless war wantonly brought about by us and one in which I most unwillingly would go to my death.

As for Seward I cannot comprehend his policy and so I cannot judge of it, and most slowly and reluctantly will I surrender my faith in him. His policy has been to keep a firm front, and in this it was wise; but I think he might have made himself less offensive to foreign powers in doing it, and I somewhat doubt the expediency of bragging yourself out of the game, as you tell me he has done. Still we have made our bed and now we must lie on it.

I shall probably have joined my regiment this week or early next. You will be surprised to hear that I shall probably regularly enlist and make my début as a simple sergeant in Caspar Crowninshield's company. The truth is they have so backed and filled, and hesitated and delayed, that, having determined to go, I have lost my patience, and have signified to them that I am ready to wait in the ranks until they are ready to give me a commission. Caspar got his company as a promotion for his behavior at Balls Bluff, and I shall get mine, I suppose, at some indefinite future period, when Sargent ceases to be a gas-bag and Williams feels the regiment under his thumb. Meanwhile I shall rough and fight it out with the rest, sleep fifteen in a tent with stable-boys, groom horses, feed like a hog and never wash, and such is my future! Well, it is better than my present, for I shall at least, by going into the army, get rid of the war.

Your last letter, and your statement that there was nothing left but a suspension of relations with England, came peculiarly unpleasantly just now. I had again begun to hope. Our blockade has become so effective and we are developing such enormous strength, that in spite of blunders, the confederates seemed likely to be crushed by brute force and starved to death, while we are really more prosperous than we have been for a year, and our poor more comfortable than they have been for four years. The confederates already, before winter begins, are regulating by law the profit on "articles of prime necessity," and what would it have been before spring? I had begun to hope yet to see this rebellion collapse. Of course a war with England exactly reverses positions. It will be short and desperate, and end in the establishment of a confederate government, I suppose. However, a glorious indifference is coming over me. I can live on my pay, the world will not come to an end this time, and if I do, I shall doubtless be very comfortable in my grave. But I do hate to be blundered out of existence and, before a foreign war just as we were getting the whip-hand. Even Balls Bluff will hide a diminished head; it will stand forth in all history as the Koh-i-noor of blunders. . . .

# Let My People Go

The Reverend Lewis Lockwood was sent by the American Missionary Association to Fort Monroe, Virginia, in September 1861 to assist the former slaves living within the Union lines. While he was at the fort Lockwood recorded the words to the song from the dictation of Carl Hollosay and other "contrabands," who told him that it had been sung in Virginia and Maryland for at least fifteen or twenty years. Lockwood sent his transcription to Harwood Vernon of the YMCA, who published it in the *New-York Daily Tribune* on December 2, 1861. The transcription also appeared in the *National Anti-Slavery Standard* on December 21.

---

## Let My People Go

### A Song of the "Contrabands"

When Israel was in Egypt's land,
    O let my people go!
Oppressed so hard they could not stand,
    O let my people go!

> *O go down, Moses*
> *Away down to Egypt's land,*
> *And tell King Pharaoh,*
> *To let my people go!*

Thus saith the Lord, bold Moses said,
    O let my people go!
If not, I'll smite your first born dead,
    O let my people go!

No more shall they in bondage toil,
    O let my people go!
Let them come out with Egypt's spoil,

O let my people go!

Then Israel out of Egypt came,
   O let my people go!
And left the proud oppressive land,
   O let my people go!

O 'twas a dark and dismal night,
   O let my people go!
When Moses led the Israelites,
   O let my people go!

'Twas good old Moses, and Aaron, too,
   O let my people go!
'Twas they that led the armies through,
   O let my people go!

The Lord told Moses what to do,
   O let my people go!
To lead the children of Israel through,
   O let my people go!

O come along Moses, you'll not get lost,
   O let my people go!
Stretch out your rod and come across,
   O let my people go!

As Israel stood by the water side,
   O let my people go!
At the command of God it did divide,
   O let my people go!

When they had reached the other shore,
   O let my people go!
They sang a song of triumph o'er,
   O let my people go!

Pharaoh said he would go across,
O let my people go!
But Pharaoh and his host were lost,
O let my people go!

O Moses, the cloud shall cleave the way,
O let my people go!
A fire by night, a shade by day,
O let my people go!

You'll not get lost in the wilderness,
O let my people go!
With a lighted candle in your breast,
O let my people go!

Jordan shall stand up like a wall,
O let my people go!
And the walls of Jericho shall fall,
O let my people go!

Your foe shall not before you stand,
O let my people go!
And you'll possess fair Canaan's land,
O let my people go!

'Twas just about in harvest time,
O let my people go!
When Joshua led his host Divine,
O let my people go!

O let us all from bondage flee,
O let my people go!
And let us all in Christ be free,
O let my people go!

We need not always weep and mourn,
O let my people go!
And wear these Slavery chains forlorn,
O let my people go!

This world's a wilderness of woe,
   O let my people go!
O let us on to Canaan go,
   O let my people go!

What a beautiful morning that will be!
   O let my people go!
When time breaks up in eternity,
   O let my people go!

# Robert E. Lee to
## George Washington Custis Lee

Robert E. Lee spent the first three months of the war organizing troops and building fortifications in Virginia. Lee was then sent to western Virginia, where he unsuccessfully tried to regain territory lost to the Union during the summer. On November 5 he was given command of the coastal defenses of South Carolina, Georgia, and east Florida, a position Lee would hold until March 1862, when he was recalled to Richmond to serve as military adviser to Jefferson Davis. He wrote to his son while inspecting coastal defenses in South Carolina.

———————————

Coosawhatchie, South Carolina
December 29, 1861

I have received my dear son your letter of the 21 & am happy that you have arranged with Mr. Stewart about his house. I feel badly about not having paid rent for it all this time as I fear now I ought to have done. But was misled by what was told me at the time. I am willing to do it now if it can be arranged with propriety & if you can do so let me know. Not having had to pay for my quarters in Richmond I never charged for any or fuel either, & thought that the State would gain by Mr. Stewart's liberality if I did not. I find it would have been better for me & him too now, to have done so. If you can get pleasant people to join in taking the house, it would certainly be more agreable for you to live there than at a hotel, but I know how expensive a bachelor's mess is &c., unless there is someone who will attend to it & conduct it economically. If you can make the arrangement, however, do so, & I will pay my share. I feel extremely obliged to Mr. Stewart for his considerate kindness & for his more than kind sentiments & I hope when you see him you will make my acknowledgements. I heard recently from your mother & hope that you were able to get to spend Xmas with them all at the W H. Mary, she thought, would be there, & if she gets to Richmond it will be a good opportunity for her to pay a visit to her Uncle Carter. I hope C will get into a good regiment & get promoted too. His friend Long is with me as Chief of Ordnance & Arthur Shaaff reported to me a few days since. I sent him to Savannah to organize & instruct some regiments coming into the service there. I wish indeed I could have you with me if it was best for you, but that no man can say & I am content to leave it to him who orders all for the best. I have two officers of the old service as my aids now, but may have to part with them as soon as I can do better for them. I suppose it is in vain for me to expect to keep an instructed officer, there is such demand for their services with troops. I have wished to get one of our young relatives with me if I could find one to whom it would be agreable & useful to me at the same time, for I have so much to attend to, that I must have those with me who can be of service. I have thought of Johnny Lee or Henry, Bev. Turner &c., &c., for there are a host of our relatives in the army. Who can you recommend to me? I have had numerous applications for the post of aid from citizens, but do not want a retinue around me who seek nominal duty or an excuse to get off of real service elsewhere. I have a great deal of work to do & want men able & willing to do it. I received not long since, a letter from Lewis Conrad applying for the appointment of aid to me. I was unable to grant it, for as I have said I have two now. I should like you to tell me, however, what sort of a youth he is & also your opinion of other youths of our house. All that I have said I of course wish you keep profoundly secret. If I had one of them in service with me I could soon see whether they would suit me, or I them. I should dislike to invite them & then for us to be obliged to part. The news from Europe is indeed good, but I think the United States government, notwithstanding their moral & political commitment to Wilkes' act, if it finds that England is in earnest & that it will have to fight or retract, will retract. We must make up our minds to fight our battles ourselves. Expect to receive aid from no one. Make every necessary sacrifice of comfort, money & labour to bring the war to a successful issue & then we will succeed. The cry is too much for help. I am mortified to hear it. We want no aid. We want to be true to ourselves, to be prudent, just, fair, & bold. I am dreadfully disappointed at the spirit here. They have all of a sudden realized the asperities of war, in what they must encounter, & do not seem to be prepared for it. If I only had some veteran troops to take the brunt, they would soon rally & be inspired with the great principle for which we are contending. The enemy is quiet & safe in his big boats. He is threatening every avenue. Pillaging, burning & robbing where he can venture with impunity & alarming women & children. Every day I have reports of landing in force, marching &c. which turns out to be some marauding party. The last was the North Edisto. I yesterday went over the whole line in that region from the Ashepro to the Wadalaw & found everything quiet & could only see their big black ships lying down the Edisto where the water is too broad for anything we have to reach them. They will not venture as yet in the narrow waters. I went yesterday 115 miles but only 35 on horseback. I did not get back till 11 p.m. I took Greenbrier the whole distance. Take good care of Richmond. Draw his forage on my account. Send him to me if opportunity offers, if you do not want him. I have two horses now with me.

Good bye my dear son
R. E. LEE

# Edward Bates: Diary, December 31, 1861

Attorney General Edward Bates records the uncertainty caused at the
end of 1861 by General McClellan's illness and by what Bates saw as
President Lincoln's unwillingness to assert himself.

———————————

*Dec 31.* Since last date the weather has been and is remarkably
fine. Mr. Eads has been here, bringing his wife, Miss
Genevieve and little Mattie—He has returned, by way of N. Y.
to St Louis (leaving Genevieve with us, untill his return again
in a few weeks). He was sadly disappointed about gitting
money, and went away in no good humor with Q. M. G
Meigs. I hope it will be all right soon.

I think he has made a very favorable impression upon the
Navy Dept, especially with Mr. Fox, asst. Sect: He will probably contract for the building of 4 of the 20 *iron ships* ordered
for the Navy, at $500.000 a piece—perhaps a little more.

Mr. Gibson shewed me to day a letter from Gov Gamble in
very low spirits—Genl Halleck rules out the malitia. The
goods sent from here—those clothes and blanketts—expressly
for Gambles malitia are taken and transfered to other troops,
this is too bad.

<*Note.* Jany 3    Mr. Gibson read me another letter from Gov
Gamble in much better spirits. He thinks, in the main that
Halleck is doing very well.>

Genl McClellan and his chief of staff, Genl Marcey, are both
very sick—Said to be typhoid fever—and this is making much
difficulty.

The Genl: it seems, is very reticent. Nobody knows his plans.
The Sec of war and the President himself are kept in ignorance
of the actual condition of the army and the intended movements of the General—if indeed they intend to move at all—In
fact the whole administration is lamentably deficient in the lack

of unity and co-action. There is no quarrell among us, but an absalute want of community of intelligence, purpose and action.

In truth, it is not *an* administration but the separate and disjointed action of seven independent officers, each one ignorant of what his colleagues are doing.

To day in council, Mr. Chase stated the condition of things in sorrowful plainness; and then, as usual, we had a "bald, disjointed chat" about it, coming to no conclusion.

It seemed as if all military operations were to stop, just because Genl McClellan is sick! Some proposed that there should be a council of war composed of Maj: Genls, in order that somebody besides the Genl in chief, may know something about the army; and be able to take command in case Genl McC should die or continue sick.

I differed, and told the President that *he* was commander in chief, and that it was not his *privilege* but his *duty* to command; and *that* implied the necessity to *know* the true condition of things.

That if I was in his place, I *would know*; and if things were not done to my liking, I would order them otherwise. That I believed he could get along easier and much better by the free use of his power, than by this injurious deference to his subordinates.

I said, the Sec of War is but the Adjutant Genl. and the Sec of the Navy the Admiral of the commander in chief, and through them, he ought to know all that is necessary to be known about the army and Navy. And I urged upon him (as often heretofore) the propriety of detailing at least two active and skillful officers to act as his aids, to write and carry his orders, collect his information, keep his military books and papers, and do his bidding generally in military affairs.

But I fear that I spoke in vain. The Prest. is an excellent man, and, in the main wise; but he lacks *will* and *purpose*, and, I greatly fear he, has not *the power to command*.

# Irwin McDowell:
# Memorandum, January 10–13, 1862

This selection is taken from a memorandum written by General Irvin McDowell and first printed in *The Life and Public Services of Abraham Lincoln* (1865), a biography published by Henry J. Raymond of the *New York Times* after Lincoln's assassination. Raymond wrote that he submitted a copy of McDowell's memorandum to the President in 1864, and that Lincoln returned it to him in October with an endorsement: "I well remember the meetings herein narrated. See nothing for me to object to in the narrative as being made by General McDowell, except the phrase attributed to me '*of the Jacobinism of Congress*,' which phrase I do not remember using literally or in substance, and which I wish not to be published in any event."

---

*January 10, 1862.*—At dinner at Arlington, Virginia. Received a note from the Assistant Secretary of War, saying the President wished to see me that evening at eight o'clock, if I could safely leave my post. Soon after, I received a note from Quartermaster-General Meigs, marked "Private and confidential," saying the President wished to see me. Note herewith.

Repaired to the President's house at eight o'clock P. M. Found the President alone. Was taken into the small room in the northeast corner. Soon after, we were joined by Brigadier-General Franklin, the Secretary of State, Governor Seward, the Secretary of the Treasury, and the Assistant Secretary of War. The President was greatly disturbed at the state of affairs. Spoke of the exhausted condition of the Treasury; of the loss of public credit; of the Jacobinism in Congress; of the delicate condition of our foreign relations; of the bad news he had received from the West, particularly as contained in a letter from General Halleck on the state of affairs in Missouri; of the want of co-operation between General Halleck and General Buell; but, more than all, the sickness of General McClellan.

The President said he was in great distress, and, as he had been to General McClellan's house, and the General did not ask to see him, and as he must talk to somebody, he had sent for General Franklin and myself, to obtain our opinion as to the possibility of soon commencing active operations with the Army of the Potomac.

To use his own expression, if something was not soon done, the bottom would be out of the whole affair; and, if General McClellan did not want to use the army, he would like to "*borrow it*," provided he could see how it could be made to do something.

The Secretary of State stated the substance of some information he considered reliable, as to the strength of the forces on the other side, which he had obtained from an Englishman from Fortress Monroe, Richmond, Manassas, and Centreville, which was to the effect that the enemy had twenty thousand men under Huger at Norfolk, thirty thousand at Centreville, and, in all, in our front an effective force, capable of being brought up at short notice, of about one hundred and three thousand men—men not suffering, but well shod, clothed, and fed. In answer to the question from the President, what could soon be done with the army, I replied that the question as to the *when* must be preceded by the one as to the *how* and the *where*. That, substantially, I would organize the army into four army corps, placing the five divisions on the Washington side on the right bank. Place three of these corps to the front, the right at Vienna or its vicinity, the left beyond Fairfax Station, the centre beyond Fairfax Court-House, and connect the latter place with the Orange and Alexandria Railroad by a railroad now partially thrown up. This would enable us to supply these corps without the use of horses, except to distribute what was brought up by rail, and to act upon the enemy without reference to the bad state of country roads.

The railroads all lead to the enemy's position. By acting upon them in force, besieging his strongholds, if necessary, or getting between them, if possible, or making the attempt to do so, and pressing his left, I thought we should, in the first place, cause him to bring up all his forces, and mass them on the flank mostly pressed—the left—and, possibly, I thought probably, we should again get them out of their works, and bring on a general engagement on favorable terms to us, at all events keeping him fully occupied and harassed. The fourth corps, in connection with a force of heavy guns afloat, would operate on his right flank, beyond the Occoquan, get behind the batteries on the Potomac, take Aquia, which, being supported by the Third Corps over the Occoquan, it could safely attempt, and then move on the railroad from Manassas to the Rappahannock. Having a large cavalry force to destroy bridges, I thought by the use of one hundred and thirty thousand men thus employed, and the great facilities which the railroads gave us, and the compact position we should occupy, we must succeed by repeated blows in crushing out the force in our front, even if it were equal in numbers and strength. The road by the Fairfax Court-House to Centreville would give us the means to bring up siege mortars and siege materials, and even if we could not accomplish the object immediately, by making the campaign one of positions instead of one of manœuvres, to do so eventually, and without risk. That this saving of wagon transportation should be effected at once, by connecting the Baltimore and Ohio Railroad with the Alexandria roads by running a road over the Long Bridge. That when all this could be commenced, I could better tell when I knew something more definite as to the general condition of the army.

General Franklin being asked, said he was in ignorance of many things necessary to an opinion on the subject, knowing only as to his own division, which was ready for the field. As to the plan of operations, on being asked by the President if he had ever thought what he would do with this army if he had it, he replied that he had, and that it was his judgment that it should be taken—what could be spared from the duty of protecting the capital—*to York River to operate on Richmond*. The question then came up as to the means at hand of transporting a large part of the army by water. The Assistant Secretary of War said the means had been fully taxed to provide transportation for twelve thousand men. After some further conversation, and in reference to our ignorance of the actual condition of the army, the President wished we should come together the next night at eight o'clock, and that General Franklin and I should meet in the mean time, obtain such further information as we might need, and to do so from the staff of the head-quarters of the Army of the Potomac. Immediate orders were to be given to make the railroad over Long Bridge.

*January 11.*—Held a meeting with General Franklin in the morning at the Treasury building, and discussed the question of the operations which in our judgment were best under existing circumstances of season, present position of the forces, present condition of the country, to be undertaken before going into the matter as to when those operations could be set on foot. I urged that we should now find fortifications in York River, which would require a movement in that direction to be preceded by a naval force of heavy guns to clear them out, as well as the works at West Point. That Richmond was now fortified, that we could not hope to carry it by a simple march after a successful engagement, that we should be obliged to take a siege train with us. That all this would take time, which would be improved by the enemy to mass his forces in our front, and we should find that we had not escaped any of the difficulties we have now before this position, but simply lost time and money to find those difficulties where we should not have so strong a base to operate from, nor so many facilities, nor so large a force as we have here, nor, in proportion, so small a one to overcome. That the war now had got to be one of positions till we should penetrate the line of the enemy. That to overcome him in front, or cut his communication with the South, would, by its moral as well as physical effect, prostrate the enemy, and enable us to undertake any future operations with ease and certainty of success; but that, in order of time as of importance, the first thing to be done was to overcome this army in our front, which is beleaguering our capital, blockading the river, and covering us day by day with the reproach of impotence, and lowering us in the eyes of foreign nations and of our people, both North and South, and that nothing but what is not necessary for this purpose should go elsewhere.

General Franklin suggested whether Governor Chase, in view of what we were charged to do, might not be at liberty to tell us where General Burnside's expedition had gone. I went and asked him. He told me that under the circumstances he felt he ought to do so, and said he was destined for Newbern, North Carolina, by way of Hatteras Inlet and Pamlico Sound, to operate on Raleigh and Beaufort, or either of them. That General McClellan had, by direction of the President, acquainted him with his plan, which was to go with a large part of this Army of the Potomac to Urbana or Toppahannock, on the Rappahannock, and then with his bridge train move directly on Richmond. On further consultation with General Franklin, it was agreed that our inquiries were to be directed to both cases, of going from our present position, and of removing the large part of the force to another base further South.

A question was raised by General Franklin, whether, in deference to General McClellan, we should not inform him of the duty we were ordered to perform. I said the order I received was marked "private and confidential," and as they came from the President, our Commander-in-Chief, I conceived, as a common superior to General McClellan and both of us, it was for the President to say, and not us, and that I would consult the Secretary of the Treasury, who was at hand, and could tell us what was the rule in the Cabinet in such matters. The Secretary was of opinion that the matter lay entirely with the President. We went to Colonel Kingsbury, Chief of Ordnance of the Army of the Potomac, Brigadier-General Van Vliet, Chief Quartermaster, and Major Shivers, Commissary of Subsistence, and obtained all the information desired.

Met at the President's in the evening at eight o'clock. Present the same as on the first day, with the addition of the Postmaster-General, Judge Blair, who came in after the meeting had begun the discussion. I read the annexed paper, marked (A), as containing both General Franklin's and my own views, General Franklin agreeing with me, in view of time, &c., required to take this army to another base, that the operation could best *now* be undertaken from the present base, substantially as proposed. The Postmaster-General opposed the plan, and was for having the army, or as much of it as could be spared, go to York River or Fortress Monroe, either to operate against Richmond, or to Suffolk and cut off Norfolk, that being in his judgment the point (Fortress Monroe or York) from which to make a decisive blow; that the plan of going to the front from this position was Bull Run over again, that it was strategically defective as was the effort last July, as then we would have the operations upon exterior lines, and that it involved too much risk; that there was not as much difficulty as had been supposed in removing the army down the Chesapeake; that only from the Lower Chesapeake could any thing decisive result against the army at Manassas; that to drive them from their present position by operating from our present base would only force them to another behind the one they now occupy, and we should have all our work to do over again. Mr. Seward thought if we only had a victory over them, it would answer, whether obtained at Manassas, or further South. Governor Chase replied, in general terms, to Judge Blair, to the effect that the moral power of a victory over the enemy in his present position would be as great as one elsewhere, all else equal; and the danger lay in the probability that we should find, after losing time and millions, that we should have as many difficulties to overcome below as we now have above.

The President wished to have General Meigs in consultation on the subject of providing water transportation, and desired General Franklin and myself to see him in the morning, and meet again at three o'clock P. M. the next day.

*January 12.*—Met General Franklin at General Meigs's. Conversed with him on the subject of our mission at his own house. I expressed my views to General Meigs, who agreed with me in the main as to concentrating our efforts against the enemy in front by moving against him from our present position. As to the time in which he could assemble water transportation for thirty thousand men, he thought in about from four to six weeks.

Met at the President's. General Meigs mentioned the time in which he could assemble transports as a month to six weeks. The general subject of operations from the present base was again discussed, General Meigs agreeing that it was best to do so, and to concentrate our forces for the purpose. The President and Mr. Seward said that General McClellan had been out to see the President, and was looking quite well; and that now, as he was able to assume the charge of the army, the President would drop any further proceedings with us. The general drift of the conversation was as to the propriety of moving the army further South, and as to the destination of Burnside's expedition. The Postmaster-General said that if it was the intention to fight out here (Manassas), then we ought to *concentrate*. It was suggested and urged somewhat on the President to countermand, or to have General McClellan countermand, General Burnside's expedition, and bring it up to Acquia. The President was, however, exceedingly averse from interfering, saying he disliked exceedingly to stop a thing long since planned, just as it was ready to strike. Nothing was done but to appoint another meeting the next day at 11 o'clock, when we were to meet General McClellan, and again discuss the question of the movement to be made, &c., &c.

*January 13, Monday.*—Went to the President's with the Secretary of the Treasury. Present, the President, Governor Chase, Governor Seward, Postmaster-General, General McClellan, General Meigs, General Franklin, and myself, and I think the Assistant Secretary of War. The President, pointing to a map, asked me to go over the plan I had before spoken to him of. He, at the same time, made a brief explanation of how he came to bring General Franklin and General McDowell before him. I mentioned, in as brief terms as possible, what General Franklin and I had done under the President's order, what our investigations had been directed upon, and what were our conclusions, giving as nearly as I could the substance of the paper hereto annexed, marked (B), referring to going to the front from our present base in the way I have hereinbefore stated, referring also to a transfer of a part of the army to another base further south; that we had been informed that the latter movement could not be commenced under a month to six weeks, and that a movement to the front could be undertaken in all of the present week. General Franklin dissented only as to the time I mentioned for beginning operations in the front, not thinking we could get the roads in order by that time. I added, *commence* operations in all of the week, to which he assented.

I concluded my remarks by saying something apologetic in explanation of the position in which we were, to which General McClellan replied somewhat coldly, if not curtly: "You are entitled to have any opinion you please!" No discussion was entered into by him whatever, the above being the only remark he made.

General Franklin said, that, in giving his opinion as to going to York River, he did it knowing it was in the direction of General McClellan's plans.

I said that I had acted entirely in the dark.

General Meigs spoke of his agency in having us called in by the President.

The President then asked what and when any thing could be done, again going over somewhat the same ground he had done with General Franklin and myself.

General McClellan said the case was so clear a blind man could see it, and then spoke of the difficulty of ascertaining what force he could count upon; that he did not know whether he could let General Butler go to Ship Island, or whether he could re-enforce General Burnside. Much conversation ensued, of rather a general character, as to the discrepancy between the number of men paid for and the number effective.

The Secretary of the Treasury then put a direct question to General McClellan, to the effect as to what he intended doing with his army, and when he intended doing it. After a long silence, General McClellan answered that the movement in Kentucky was to precede any one from this place, and that that movement might now be *forced*. That he had directed General Buell, if he could not hire wagons for his transportation, that he must take them. After another pause, he said he must say he was very unwilling to develop his plans, always believing that in military matters the fewer persons who were knowing to them the better; that he would tell them if he was *ordered* to do so. The President then asked him if he had counted upon any particular time; he did not ask what that time was, but had he in his own mind any particular time fixed, when a movement could be commenced. He replied he had. "Then," rejoined the President, "I will adjourn this meeting."

# Montgomery C. Meigs:
## Memoir of Meetings with President Lincoln

Montgomery C. Meigs served as quartermaster general of the Union army from May 1861 to the end of the war. His account of events in January 1862 is taken from a manuscript Meigs submitted to *The Century Magazine* in 1888, "The Relations of President Lincoln and Secretary Stanton to the Military Commanders in the Civil War," that was first published in 1921.

---

ON FRIDAY, January 10th, 1862, the President, in great distress, entered my office. He took a chair in front of the open fire and said, "General, what shall I do? The people are impatient; Chase has no money and he tells me he can raise no more; the General of the Army has typhoid fever. The bottom is out of the tub. What shall I do?"

I said, "If General McClellan has typhoid fever, that is an affair of six weeks at least; he will not be able sooner to command. In the meantime, if the enemy in our front is as strong as he believes, they may attack on any day, and I think you should see some of those upon whom in such case, or in case any forward movement becomes necessary, the control must fall. Send for them to meet you soon and consult with them; perhaps you may select the responsible commander for such an event."

The council was called. On Sunday, January 12th, McDowell and Franklin called on me with a summons to the White House for one P.M. These officers, and Messrs. Seward, Chase and Blair of the Cabinet attended. The President announced that he had called this meeting in consequence of the sickness of General McClellan, but he had that morning heard from him that he was better, and would be able to be present the next day; and that, on this promise, he adjourned the discussion for twenty four hours.

The next day, Jany. 13th, the same persons and General McClellan appeared at the rendezvous. The President opened the proceedings by making a statement of the cause of his calling the Council. Mr. Chase, and Mr. Blair, if memory is accurate, both spoke. All looked to McClellan, who sat still with his head hanging down, and mute. The situation grew awkward. The President spoke again a few words. One of the Generals said something; McClellan said something which evidently did not please the speaker, and again was mute.

I moved my chair to the side of McClellan's and urged him, saying, "The President evidently expects you to speak; can you not promise some movement towards Manassas? You are strong." He replied, "I cannot move on them with as great a force as they have." "Why, you have near 200,000 men, how many have they?" "Not less than 175,000 according to my advices." I said, "Do you think so?" and "the President expects something from you." He replied, "If I tell him my plans they will be in the New York Herald tomorrow morning. He can't keep a secret, he will tell them to Tadd." I said: "That is a pity, but he is the President,—the Commander-in-Chief; he has a right to know; it is not respectful to sit mute when he so clearly requires you to speak. He is superior to all."

After some further urging, McClellan moved, and seemed to prepare to speak. He declined to give his plans in detail, but thought it best to press the movement of Buell's troops in the central line of operation. After a few words that brought out nothing more, Mr. Lincoln said, "Well, on this assurance of the General that he will press the advance in Kentucky, I will be satisfied, and will adjourn this Council."

# Edwin M. Stanton to Charles A. Dana

Former attorney general Edwin M. Stanton replaced Simon Cameron in the cabinet on January 15, 1862, amid charges of widespread incompetence and corruption in the War Department. The new Secretary of War stated his intentions in a letter to Charles A. Dana of the *New-York Daily Tribune*.

---

WASHINGTON, *January 24, 1862.*

MY DEAR SIR: Yours of the 22d only reached me this evening. The facts you mention were new to me, but there is too much reason to fear they are true. But that matter will, I think, be corrected *very speedily.*

You can not tell how much obligation I feel myself under for your kindness. Every man who wishes the country to pass through this trying hour should stand on watch, and aid me. Bad passions and little passions and mean passions gather around and hem in the great movements that should deliver this nation.

Two days ago I wrote you a long letter—a three pager—expressing my thanks for your admirable article of the 21st, stating my position and purposes; and in that letter I mentioned some of the circumstances of my unexpected appointment. But, interrupted before it was completed, I will not inflict, or afflict, you with it.

I know the task that is before us—I say *us*, because the Tribune has its mission as plainly as I have mine, and they tend to the same end. But I am not in the smallest degree dismayed or disheartened. By God's blessing we shall prevail. I feel a deep, *earnest* feeling growing up around me. We have no jokes or trivialities, but all with whom I act show that they are now in dead earnest.

I know you will rejoice to know this.

As soon as I can get the machinery of the office working, the rats cleared out, and the rat holes stopped we shall *move*. This army has got to fight or run away; and while men are striving nobly in the West, the champagne and oysters on the Potomac must be stopped. But patience for a short while only is all I ask, if you and others like you will rally around me.

                              Yours truly,
                              EDWIN M. STANTON.

# Chronology
## April 1860–January 1862

Democratic Party national convention meets in Charleston, South Carolina, on April 23. Convention rejects platform plank calling for congressional legislation protecting slavery in the federal territories, endorsing instead the right of each territorial legislature to permit or prohibit slavery. Vote causes some fifty delegates, including most of six delegations from the Deep South, to bolt the convention on April 30. Senator Stephen A. Douglas of Illinois, the leading Democratic presidential candidate, is unable to secure the two-thirds majority needed for the nomination through fifty-seven ballots, and the deadlocked convention adjourns for six weeks on May 3.

Constitutional Union Party, made up of former members of the Whig and American (Know-Nothing) parties, meets in Baltimore on May 9. The convention nominates John Bell of Tennessee for president and Edward Everett of Massachusetts for vice president, but does not adopt a platform beyond a pledge to support the Constitution, the Union, and the enforcement of the laws. Republican Party national convention meets in Chicago on May 16 with Senator William H. Seward of New York as the leading candidate for the nomination. Seward is unable to gain a majority of the delegates during the first two ballots, and on May 18 Abraham Lincoln of Illinois is nominated on the third ballot. Convention chooses Senator Hannibal Hamlin of Maine as his running mate and adopts a platform opposing the extension of slavery.

Democratic Party reconvenes in Baltimore on June 18. Dispute over seating of rival delegations from the Deep South results in walkout by delegates from the Upper South and border states. Douglas is nominated for president on the second ballot, and former governor of Georgia Herschel V. Johnson becomes the vice-presidential candidate after Senator Benjamin Fitzpatrick of Alabama declines nomination. Southern Democrats meet in Baltimore on June 28 and nominate Vice President John C. Breckinridge

of Kentucky for president and Senator Joseph Lane of
Oregon for vice president. While Lincoln, Breckinridge,
and Bell follow precedent and do not actively campaign,
Douglas makes series of speaking tours through the
North and South, warning against disunion. Election of
Republican governors in key states of Indiana and Penn-
sylvania on October 9 indicate likelihood of Republican
victory in the presidential contest.

Lincoln wins election on November 6, gaining
1,866,452 popular and 180 electoral votes and carrying
every free state except New Jersey, whose electoral votes
are divided between Lincoln and Douglas. Douglas receives 1,376,957 popular votes, mostly in the free states
and the Upper South, but secures only twelve electoral
votes in New Jersey and Missouri. Breckinridge wins
849,781 popular and seventy-two electoral votes, carrying
eleven slave states, while Bell receives 588,879 popular and
thirty-nine electoral votes, winning Kentucky, Tennessee,
and Virginia. While Lincoln wins some votes in the border
states and Virginia, he does not appear on the ballot in
nine Southern states. (There is no popular vote for president in South Carolina, where electors are chosen by the
state legislature.)

Election of Lincoln begins movement for immediate
secession in South Carolina. President James Buchanan
meets with his cabinet to discuss secession and the situation of the federal garrison at Charleston, November 9–
10. Cabinet divides along sectional lines, and Buchanan
decides to address the crisis in his annual message to Congress on December 3. South Carolina legislature calls for
a convention to meet at Columbia on December 17 to
consider secession. By the end of November, conventions
have been called for January 1861 in Alabama, Mississippi,
Florida, and Georgia.

Second session of the 36th Congress meets on December 3. In his message, Buchanan declares secession to be
unconstitutional while asserting that the federal government has no right to "coerce" a state attempting to secede. House of Representatives forms a select Committee
of Thirty-Three on December 4 to consider responses to
the crisis. Presidential electors cast their ballots on December 5. South Carolina convention meets in Columbia
on December 17, then adjourns to Charleston due to
smallpox epidemic. Senator John J. Crittenden of Kentucky

proposes series of constitutional amendments on December 18 that would restore the Missouri Compromise line while offering new protections for slavery; his measures are referred to a select Committee of Thirteen. (The "Crittenden Compromise" is opposed by Lincoln, who writes a series of letters to Republican leaders from Springfield, Illinois, urging them not to permit any further extension of slavery.) South Carolina convention adopts ordinance of secession, 169–0, on December 20. Major Robert Anderson transfers federal garrison at Charleston from Fort Moultrie to Fort Sumter on December 26.

1861   Georgia state troops occupy Fort Pulaski on January 3; by the end of January, state forces seize federal forts and arsenals without bloodshed in Alabama, Florida, Mississippi, Louisiana, and North Carolina. South Carolina batteries open fire on the chartered civilian steamer *Star of the West*, which is carrying supplies and reinforcements for the Fort Sumter garrison, January 9. The ship withdraws without casualties, and Major Anderson does not return fire from Fort Sumter. Mississippi convention votes in favor of secession, 85–15, January 9. Florida convention votes to secede, 62–7, January 10. Alabama convention approves secession, 61–39, January 11. Kentucky legislature meets in special session on January 17 and rejects recommendation by Governor Beriah Magoffin that it call a secession convention. Georgia convention votes to secede from the Union, 208–39, on January 19. Virginia legislature proposes holding a peace convention attended by representatives of all the states, January 19. Louisiana convention approves secession, 113–17, on January 26. Congress admits Kansas as the thirty-fourth state under a constitution prohibiting slavery, January 29.

Convention in Texas votes to secede, 166–8, on February 1. Representatives from South Carolina, Mississippi, Florida, Alabama, Georgia, and Louisiana meet in Montgomery, Alabama, on February 4 to form the Confederate States of America. Peace convention meets in Washington, February 4, with only twenty-one of thirty-four states represented. Montgomery convention adopts a provisional constitution, February 8, and unanimously elects Jefferson Davis of Mississippi as the provisional president and Alexander H. Stephens of Georgia as the provisional vice president of the Confederacy, February 9. Tennessee voters reject holding a secession convention, 69,387–57,798, on February 9. Abraham Lincoln leaves Springfield, Illinois, by train on February 11; during his trip to Washington, D.C., he will make short speeches and appearances in Indiana, Ohio, Pennsylvania, New York, and New Jersey. Jefferson Davis leaves his plantation in Warren County, Mississippi, on February 11 for his inauguration at Montgomery, Alabama. Electoral votes are counted in Congress, February 13, and Lincoln is formally declared president-elect. Davis is inaugurated as provisional president of the Confederacy at Montgomery on February 18. His cabinet includes Robert Toombs (secretary of state), Christopher Memminger (secretary of the treasury), Leroy Walker (secretary of war), Stephen Mallory (secretary of the navy), Judah Benjamin (attorney general), and John Reagan (postmaster general).

In San Antonio, General David E. Twiggs surrenders U.S. army installations in Texas to the state authorities, February 18. Warned in Philadelphia that he might be assassinated in Baltimore, Lincoln travels secretly to Washington on night of February 22–23. Texas voters approve secession, 46,153–14,747, on February 23. Washington peace conference presents plan to Congress similar to the Crittenden Compromise. North Carolina voters reject holding a secession convention, 47,323–46,672, on February 28. Republican opposition prevents adoption of compromise measures permitting the extension of slavery, but on March 3 Congress proposes a Thirteenth Amendment to the Constitution that would prohibit the federal government from abolishing or interfering with slavery in the states (amendment will be ratified by only two states).

Abraham Lincoln is inaugurated as the sixteenth president of the United States on March 4. His cabinet includes the other major contenders for the 1860 Republican nomination: William H. Seward (secretary of state), Salmon P. Chase (secretary of the treasury), Simon Cameron (secretary of war), and Edward Bates (attorney general), as well as Gideon Welles (secretary of the navy), Montgomery Blair (postmaster general), and Caleb B. Smith (secretary of the interior). Lincoln learns on March 5 that the garrison at Fort Sumter will run out of supplies by mid-April, forcing its evacuation. Confederate Provisional Congress adopts permanent constitution on March 11 and submits it to the states for ratification. In a meeting on March 15, Lincoln requests the formal advice of his cabinet on whether to resupply Fort Sumter; five of the seven secretaries recommend evacuating the fort. Arkansas convention votes against secession, 39–35, March 18, and Missouri convention rejects secession, 98–1, March 21. Lincoln decides on March 29 to attempt to reprovision Fort Sumter and to hold Fort Pickens, in Pensacola Bay, Florida; his decision is supported by a majority of the cabinet.

On April 1 Secretary of State Seward sends Lincoln a memorandum recommending that Fort Sumter be evacuated; that the administration should confront a European power as a way of reestablishing national unity; and that the president consider giving the authority to execute both domestic and foreign policy to a member of the cabinet. Lincoln responds by reminding Seward that it is the president who decides which policies to pursue. Virginia convention votes against secession, 90–45, on April 4, but remains in session. Lincoln sends message on April 6 to Francis Pickens, the governor of South Carolina, informing him of the attempt to resupply Fort Sumter. On April 8 the Davis administration authorizes Braxton Bragg, the Confederate commander at Pensacola, to engage any force resupplying or reinforcing Fort Pickens. Union resupply expedition sails for Charleston on April 9. Davis and his cabinet meet on April 9 and order General Pierre G. T. Beauregard to demand the surrender of Fort Sumter. Major Anderson refuses to surrender, April 11. Confederates begin bombardment of the fort at 4:30 A.M. on April 12; the garrison begins to return fire at 7 A.M. Reinforcements land at Fort Pickens, April 12 (the fort will remain in Union hands throughout the war). Anderson surrenders, April 13, and the Confederates occupy Fort Sumter on April 14. (Although there are no fatalities during the bombardment, two members of the garrison are killed by an accidental explosion during the surrender ceremony.)

President Lincoln issues proclamation on April 15 calling forth 75,000 militia and summoning Congress to meet in special session on July 4. Virginia convention votes to secede, 88–55, on April 17. Missouri Governor Claiborne Jackson denounces Lincoln's call for troops and begins planning seizure of the federal arsenal at St. Louis. Federal garrison evacuates U.S. arsenal at Harpers

Ferry, Virginia, April 18. Pro-secessionist mob attacks the 6th Massachusetts Volunteers as it changes trains in Baltimore on April 19. Lincoln declares a blockade of the original seven Confederate states, April 19 (blockade is later extended to Virginia and North Carolina). Federal forces evacuate navy yard at Norfolk, Virginia, April 20. In response to the destruction of railroad bridges and telegraph lines in Maryland, Lincoln suspends the writ of habeas corpus along the rail corridor from Washington to Philadelphia on April 27. Maryland assembly rejects secession, 53–13, on April 29.

Lincoln issues a call for 42,034 volunteers to serve for three years and expands the authorized size of the regular army, May 3. Arkansas convention reassembles and votes to secede, 65–5, May 6; on the same day, the Tennessee legislature declares independence from the United States and schedules referendum on secession. Secessionists riot in St. Louis after Captain Nathaniel Lyon, commander of the garrison guarding the arsenal, captures pro-secessionist militia encampment near the city on May 10. Union troops occupy Baltimore on May 13, securing the movement of supplies and men into Washington. Great Britain declares neutrality in the conflict, May 13, while recognizing both the Union and the Confederacy as belligerent powers under international law. North Carolina convention votes unanimously for secession on May 20, creating an eleven-state Confederacy. Governor Beriah Magoffin proclaims Kentucky's neutrality, May 20. Provisional Congress votes on May 20 to relocate the Confederate capital to Richmond, Virginia. Secession referendum is approved in Virginia, 128,884–32,134, on May 23, although it is opposed by most voters in the western part of the state. Union troops cross the Potomac River and occupy Alexandria, Virginia, on May 24. The same day, at Fort Monroe, Virginia, General Benjamin F. Butler refuses to return escaped slaves who had worked on Confederate fortifications, declaring them contraband of war. While sitting as a U.S. circuit court judge in Baltimore, Chief Justice Roger B. Taney rules on May 28 in *Ex parte Merryman* that President Lincoln lacks the constitutional authority to suspend the writ of habeas corpus. (The administration ignores Taney's opinion, and Lincoln extends the suspension of the writ along the northeastern rail line to New York City, July 2, and to Bangor, Maine,

October 14.) Nathaniel Lyon replaces General William Harney as the Union commander in Missouri on May 31, ending a truce arranged between Harney and Sterling Price, the commander of the pro-secession state militia.

Union troops rout Confederates at Philippi, Virginia, on June 3, marking the start of the Union offensive into northwestern Virginia. Stephen A. Douglas dies in Chicago, June 3. Secession referendum is passed in Tennessee, 104,471–47,183, on June 8, although it is opposed by voters in eastern Tennessee. Attack by 4,400 Union troops against outpost at Big Bethel, Virginia, on June 10 is repulsed by 1,100 defenders, encouraging Confederate belief in the superiority of its soldiers. Unionist delegates meet in Wheeling on June 11 and organize a new Virginia state government that is recognized by Congress and the Lincoln administration. Union force under command of Nathaniel Lyon occupies Jefferson City, Missouri, on June 15 and defeats secessionist forces at Boonville on June 17, securing control of the Missouri River for the Union.

Congress meets in special session in Washington on July 4. Confederates halt Union advance into southwestern Missouri at Carthage on July 5. Union forces under the overall command of General George B. McClellan defeat Confederates at Rich Mountain, Virginia, on July 11, and overrun Confederate rear guard at Carrick's Ford on July 13, ending campaign that gives the Union control of northwestern Virginia. On July 16 Union army of 30,000 men under General Irvin McDowell advances into northeastern Virginia with the aim of defeating the 20,000 Confederate troops under Pierre G. T. Beauregard that are defending Manassas Junction. As Union advance elements skirmish with Confederates at Blackburn's Ford on July 18, General Joseph E. Johnston shifts his command of 11,000 men by rail out of the Shenandoah Valley to reinforce Beauregard at Manassas. Confederate Congress meets for the first time at Richmond, July 20. Union army attacks across Bull Run on morning of July 21, beginning the first major battle of the war. Confederate counterattack in the afternoon sends Union army into retreat; the Union loses about 2,900 men killed, wounded, or missing, the Confederates about 1,900.

Convention of Missouri Unionists meets in Jefferson City on July 22 and chooses new governor to replace Claiborne Jackson. Congress adopts Johnson-Crittenden resolutions on July 25, declaring that the purpose of the war is to preserve the Union and not to overthrow or interfere with "established institutions" (slavery) in the Southern states. Robert M. T. Hunter replaces Robert Toombs as Confederate secretary of state. General George B. McClellan assumes command of the forces around Washington on July 27 (command will later become the Army of the Potomac).

Congress passes revenue act, August 5, establishing the first national income tax, and confiscation act, August 6, authorizing the seizure of slaves being used to militarily aid the rebellion. Nathaniel Lyon is killed on August 10 at Wilson's Creek while leading 5,400 men in an unsuccessful attack against 11,000 Confederates under the command of Benjamin McCulloch and Sterling Price. Victory gives Confederates control of southwestern Missouri. Union naval expedition captures Fort Hatteras, North Carolina, August 29. General John C. Frémont, the Union commander in Missouri, issues proclamation on August 30 declaring martial law throughout the state and emancipating the slaves of secessionists.

Lincoln asks Frémont to withdraw his proclamation, September 2. Concerned by increasing political strength of Kentucky Unionists, Confederates send troops under General Gideon Pillow into the state on September 3 with orders to seize Columbus on the east bank of the Mississippi. Union forces under General Ulysses S. Grant occupy Paducah, Kentucky, at the junction of the Ohio and Tennessee rivers, on September 6. (By the end of the year Confederates will have established a defensive line across southern Kentucky.) When Frémont fails to comply with the president's request, Lincoln orders him to rescind the provisions of his proclamation concerning emancipation, September 11. General Robert E. Lee launches unsuccessful offensive against Union forces at Cheat Mountain in western Virginia, September 11–15. Confederates begin siege of Lexington, Missouri, September 12. Leroy Walker resigns as Confederate secretary of war and is succeeded by Judah Benjamin, who continues to serve as attorney general until November. Lincoln orders the arrest of thirty-one members of the Maryland legislature suspected of disloyalty. Union garrison of 3,600 men surrenders at Lexington, Missouri, on September 20, strengthening the Confederate position in the state.

Union attack across the Potomac at Ball's Bluff, near Leesburg, Virginia, on October 21 is repulsed with the loss of 900 men killed, wounded, or missing; among the dead is Colonel Edward D. Baker, a Republican senator from Oregon and friend of President Lincoln. Secessionist members of the Missouri legislature meet in Neosho on October 31 and vote to join the Confederacy.

George B. McClellan replaces the retiring Winfield Scott as general-in-chief of the Union army on November 1. John C. Frémont is removed from command in Missouri, November 2. Running unopposed, Jefferson Davis is elected to a six-year term as president of the Confederacy on November 6. Union naval expedition led by Commodore Samuel Du Pont captures Port Royal Sound, South Carolina, on November 7, securing a base between Savannah and Charleston for use by the blockade. Ulysses S. Grant leads raid against Confederate camp at Belmont, Missouri, across the Mississippi from Columbus, Kentucky, on November 7. Captain Charles Wilkes, commanding the U.S.S. *San Jacinto*, boards the British mail packet *Trent* off Cuba on November 8 and seizes James M. Mason, the Confederate commissioner to Great Britain, and John Slidell, the Confederate commissioner to France. Unionists in eastern Tennessee launch an unsuccessful uprising against the Confederate authorities on November 8. Port Royal expedition captures Beaufort, South Carolina, on November 9 (victory at Port Royal brings 10,000 former slaves in the Sea Islands under Union control). On November 9 General Henry W. Halleck is placed in command of the new Union Department of the Missouri, with responsibility for operations in Missouri and Kentucky west of the Cumberland River, while General Don C. Buell is given command of the Department of the Ohio, with responsibility for Kentucky east of the Cumberland. Thomas Bragg succeeds Judah Benjamin as Confederate attorney general. Unionist convention at Wheeling adopts constitution on November 26 for proposed new state of West Virginia.

President Lincoln sends his first annual message to Congress on December 3, calling for the gradual abolition of slavery with compensation for slaveowners and the voluntary colonization of former slaves outside the United States. Congress forms the Joint Committee on the Conduct of the War, December 9. Lincoln administration decides on December 26 to release Mason and Slidell to British authorities in order to avoid a possible war between the United States and Great Britain.

1862    Amid charges of widespread corruption and incompetence in the War Department, Lincoln replaces Simon Cameron with Edwin M. Stanton, a Democrat who had served as attorney general in the final months of the Buchanan administration. Stanton takes office as the new secretary of war on January 20.

# Biographical Notes

**Henry Livermore Abbott** (January 21, 1842–May 6, 1864) Born in Lowell, Massachusetts, the son of a lawyer active in Democratic politics. Graduated from Harvard College in 1860 and began studying law in his father's office. Commissioned second lieutenant, 20th Massachusetts Volunteer Infantry Regiment, July 10, 1861. Formed close friendship with his fellow officer Oliver Wendell Holmes Jr. Fought at Ball's Bluff. Promoted to first lieutenant, November 1861. Fought at Fair Oaks and in the Seven Days' Battles, where he was wounded in the arm at Glendale. Older brother Edward killed at Cedar Mountain. Fought at Fredericksburg (December 1862 and May 1863) and Gettysburg; promoted to captain, December 1862, and major, October 1863. Became acting commander of the 20th Massachusetts after all of the regimental officers senior to him were killed or wounded at Gettysburg. Led the regiment at Briscoe Station and at the Battle of the Wilderness, where he was fatally wounded on May 6, 1864.

**Charles Francis Adams Jr.** (May 27, 1835–March 20, 1915) Born in Boston, Massachusetts, brother of Henry Adams, son of lawyer Charles Francis Adams and Abigail Brooks Adams, grandson of John Quincy Adams, great-grandson of John Adams. Graduated Harvard College, 1856. Read law in Boston and passed bar, 1858. Commissioned first lieutenant, 1st Massachusetts Cavalry, December 1861. Served at Hilton Head, South Carolina, 1862, and with the Army of the Potomac, 1862–63, including Antietam and Gettysburg campaigns; promoted captain, October 1862. Commanded detached company on guard service at Army of the Potomac headquarters, spring 1864. Commissioned as lieutenant colonel of the 5th Massachusetts Cavalry, a black regiment, in July 1864, and as its colonel, February 1865; the regiment guarded Confederate prisoners at Point Lookout, Maryland, until March 1865, when it was sent to Virginia. Left army and married Mary Ogden in November 1865. Served on Massachusetts Railroad Commission, 1869–79. President of Union Pacific Railroad, 1884–90. Published series of historical works, including *Three Episodes of Massachusetts History* (1892) and biographies of Richard Henry Dana (1890) and Charles Francis Adams (1900). Died in Washington, D.C.

**Henry Adams** (February 16, 1838–March 27, 1918) Born in Boston, Massachusetts. Brother of Charles Francis Adams Jr., son of lawyer Charles Francis Adams and Abigail Brooks Adams, grandson of John Quincy Adams, great-grandson of John Adams. Graduated Harvard 1858; studied law in Berlin and Dresden until 1860. Served as secretary to father while Charles Francis Adams served in Congress, 1860–61, and as U.S. minister to Great Britain, 1861–68. Reported British reaction to the American Civil War as anonymous London correspondent of *The New York Times*, 1861–62. Returned to Washington, D.C., in 1868 to work as journalist. Appointed assistant professor of history at Harvard (1870–77); assumed editorship of *North American Review* (1870–76). Married Marion Hooper in 1872. Published *The Life of Albert Gallatin* (1879), biography; *Democracy* (1880), a novel that appeared anonymously; *John Randolph* (1882), a biography; *Esther* (1884) a novel that appeared pseudonymously; *History of the United States during the Administrations of Thomas Jefferson and James Madison* (1889–91); *Mont-Saint-Michel and Chartres: A Study of Thirteenth-Century Unity* (1904); *The Education of Henry Adams* (1907). Died in Washington.

**Sullivan Ballou** (March 28, 1827–July 28, 1861) Born in Smithfield, Rhode Island, the son of a merchant tailor. Educated at Brown University and the National Law School in Ballston Spa, New York. Admitted to Rhode Island bar in 1853 and began practice in Woonsocket. Served as clerk of the Rhode Island house of representatives, 1854–56. Married Sarah Hart Shumway in 1855. Served in the Rhode Island house of representatives, 1857–59. Unsuccessful Republican candidate for state attorney general, April 1861. Commissioned as major of 2nd Rhode Island Infantry, June 11, 1861. Hit by cannon shot at First Battle of Bull Run, July 21, 1861, and had leg amputated. Died of wounds at Sudley, Virginia a week after the battle.

**Edward Bates** (September 4, 1793–March 25, 1869) Born Belmont, Virginia, the son of a planter and merchant. Attended Charlotte Hall Academy in Maryland for three years. Served in militia company in 1813 but did not see action. Moved to St. Louis, Missouri, in 1814. Admitted to the bar, 1816. Delegate to the state constitutional convention in 1820. Attorney general of Missouri, 1820–21. Married Julia Coalter in 1823. Served in state house of representatives, 1822–24 and 1834–36, and state senate, 1830–34. U.S. attorney for Missouri, 1824–26. Served in Congress, 1827–29, but was defeated for reelection. Became leader of Whig Party in Missouri. Candidate for 1860 Republican presidential nomination. Served as attorney general in the Lincoln administration, March 1861–November 1864, before resigning. Opposed Radical Reconstruction in Missouri. Died in St. Louis.

**Charles Minor Blackford** (October 17, 1833–March 10, 1903) Born in Fredericksburg, Virginia, the son of a newspaper editor. Graduated from University of Virginia law school in 1855 and began practice in Lynchburg. Married Susan Leigh Colston in 1856. Commissioned lieutenant in 2nd Virginia Cavalry in May 1861 and saw action at First Manassas. Elected captain of his company in May 1862. Appointed judge advocate of the Confederate First Corps, commanded by General James Longstreet, in December 1862 and held this position for the remainder of the war. Served with the corps in the Gettysburg campaign, in northern Georgia and eastern Tennessee (September 1863–April 1864), and in Virginia, 1864–65. Returned to law practice in Lynchburg after the war. Worked with his wife on editing their wartime letters and had them privately printed, along with writings by his father and brother William, as *Memoirs of Life In and Out of the Army in Virginia during the War between the States* (1894). Published *Campaign and Battle of Lynchburg, Virginia* (1901). Died in Lynchburg.

**Sallie Brock** (March 18, 1831–March 22, 1911) Born Sarah Ann Brock in Madison County, Virginia, the daughter of a hotel owner. Moved with her family to Richmond in 1858. Began working as a tutor in King and Queen County, Virginia, in 1860, but returned to Richmond in 1861 and remained there for the duration of the war. Moved to New York City in 1865. Published *Richmond During the War: Four Years of Personal Observations* (1867). Edited *The Southern Amaranth* (1869), collection of poetry about the Confederacy and the war, and published a novel, *Kenneth, My King* (1873). Married Richard F. Putnam in 1882. Died in Brooklyn.

**Joseph E. Brown** (April 15, 1821–November 30, 1894) Born in Pickens District, South Carolina, son of a farmer. Family moved to Union County, Georgia. Attended Calhoun Academy in Anderson District, South Carolina. Taught school and studied law in Canton, Georgia. Admitted to the Georgia bar, 1845. Attended Yale Law School, 1845–46. Married Elizabeth Grisham in 1847. Served in state senate, 1850, and as circuit judge, 1855–57. Won Democratic nomination for governor and defeated American (Know-Nothing) candidate Benjamin Hill in 1857. Governor of Georgia, 1857–65. Supported secession; came into conflict with Jefferson Davis over assertion of state sovereignty and opposition to conscription. Chief justice of the Georgia Supreme Court, 1868–70. President of the Western and Atlanta Railroad, 1870–90. Served as a Democrat in the U.S. Senate, 1880–91. Died in Atlanta.

**William G. Brownlow** (August 29, 1805–April 29, 1877) Born in Wythe County, Virginia, the son of a farmer. Moved with family to eastern Tennessee. Learned carpentry before entering the Methodist ministry in 1826. Spent ten years as an itinerant minister. Married Eliza O'Brien in 1837. Founded the *Tennessee Whig* in Elizabethton, 1839. Moved the newspaper to Jonesboro, 1840, and to Knoxville, 1849. Opposed secession in the *Whig* until it was suppressed in October 1861. Arrested by Confederate authorities in December 1861 and expelled into Union territory in March 1862. Went on Northern lecture tour and published *Sketches of the Rise, Progress, and Decline of Secession* (1862). Returned to Knoxville after its capture by the Union army in November 1863. Governor of Tennessee, 1865–69. Republican senator from Tennessee, 1869–75. Died in Knoxville.

**James Buchanan** (April 23, 1791–June 1, 1868) Born near Mercersburg in Franklin County, Pennsylvania, son of a storekeeper and landowner. Graduated from Dickinson College, 1809, and admitted to the bar, 1812. Served in the Pennsylvania house of representatives, 1814–15, and in Congress, 1821–31. U.S. minister to Russia, 1832–34. Served in the U.S. Senate as a Democrat, 1834–45. Secretary of State in the Polk administration, 1845–49. U.S. minister to Great Britain, 1853–56. Won Democratic nomination in 1856 and defeated Republican John C. Frémont and American (Know-Nothing) Millard Fillmore in the presidential election. President of the United States, 1857–61. Died at his home near Lancaster, Pennsylvania.

**Benjamin F. Butler** (November 5, 1818–January 11, 1893) Born in Deerfield, New Hampshire, the son of a merchant. Graduated from Waterville (now Colby) College in 1838. Admitted to the bar in 1840 and began practicing law in Lowell, Massachusetts. Married Sarah Hildreth in 1844. Served as a Democrat in the Massachusetts house of representatives, 1853, and in the Massachusetts senate, 1859. Commissioned as brigadier general of Massachusetts militia in April 1861 and as a major general of U.S. volunteers in May 1861. Led occupation of Baltimore in May 1861 before becoming commander at Fort Monroe, Virginia. Commanded troops that captured Fort Hatteras, North Carolina, in August 1861. Military governor of New Orleans, May–December 1862. Commanded the Army of the James in Virginia, 1864. Relieved of command by Ulysses S. Grant after his failed assault on Fort Fisher, North Carolina, in December 1864. Served in Congress as a Republican, 1867–75 and 1877–79, and was one of the House managers at the impeachment trial of Andrew Johnson in 1868. Elected governor of Massachusetts as a Democrat and served one-year term in 1883. Presidential candidate of the Greenback and Anti-Monopolist parties in 1884. Died in Washington, D.C.

**Mary Chesnut** (March 31, 1823–November 22, 1886) Born Mary Boykin Miller in Statesburg, Sumter County, South Carolina, the daughter of Stephen Miller, a former congressman who later served as governor of South Carolina and in the U.S. Senate, and Mary Boykin Miller. Educated at a French boarding school in Charleston. Married James Chesnut Jr. in 1840 and lived on Mulberry, the Chesnut family plantation near Camden, South Carolina. Lived in Washington, D.C., while husband served in the Senate, 1859–60. Spent much of the Civil War in Richmond, Virginia, where her husband served as an advisor to Jefferson Davis, and formed close friendship with Varina Davis. Wrote three unfinished novels after the war, and extensively revised and expanded her wartime journal between 1881 and 1884. Died in Camden.

**John J. Crittenden** (September 10, 1786–July 26, 1863) Born near Versailles, Woodford County, Kentucky, the son of a farmer. Graduated from the College of William and Mary in 1807 and was admitted to the Kentucky bar. Twice widowed, he married Sarah Lee, 1811, Maria Todd, 1826, and Elizabeth Ashley, 1853. Served in the Kentucky house of representatives, 1811–17, and as an aide-de-camp on the frontier, 1812–13. U.S. senator from Kentucky, 1817–19, 1835–41, 1842–48, and 1855–61. Served as attorney general of the United States, 1841 and 1850–53. Governor of Kentucky, 1848–50. Elected to Congress after leaving the Senate in 1861 and served until his death at Frankfort, Kentucky.

**Jefferson Davis** (June 3, 1808–December 6, 1889) Born in Christian (now Todd) County, Kentucky, the son of a farmer. Moved with his family to Mississippi. Graduated from West Point in 1828 and served in the Black Hawk War. Resigned his commission in 1835 and married Sarah Knox Taylor, who died later in the year. Became a cotton planter in Warren County, Mississippi. Married Varina Howell in 1845. Elected to Congress as a Democrat and served 1845–46, then resigned to command a Mississippi volunteer regiment in Mexico, 1846–47, where he fought at Monterrey and was wounded at Buena Vista. Elected to the Senate and served from 1847 to 1851, when he resigned to run unsuccessfully for governor. Secretary of war in the cabinet of Franklin Pierce, 1853–57. Elected to the Senate and served from 1857 to January 21, 1861, when he withdrew following the secession of Mississippi. Inaugurated as provisional president of the Confederate States of America on February 18, 1861. Elected without opposition to six-year term in November 1861 and inaugurated on February 22, 1862. Captured by Union cavalry near Irwinville, Georgia, on May 10, 1865. Imprisoned at Fort Monroe, Virginia, and indicted for treason. Released on bail on May 13, 1867; the indictment was dropped in 1869 without trial. Published *The Rise and Fall of the Confederate Government* in 1881. Died in New Orleans.

**J.D.B. DeBow** (July 10, 1820–February 27, 1867) Born James Dunwoody Bronson DeBow in Charleston, South Carolina, the son of a merchant. Graduated from the College of Charleston, 1843. Admitted to the bar. Became associate editor of the *Southern Quarterly Review* in 1844. Moved to New Orleans, where he founded the political and economic journal *Commercial Review of the South and West*, popularly known as *DeBow's Review*, 1846–62. Appointed professor of political economy and statistics at the University of Louisiana, 1849. Served as superintendent of the U.S. Census, 1853–55, and published *Statistical View of the United States* (1854). Married Caroline Poe in 1854, and after her death, Martha Johns in 1860. Served as cotton purchasing agent for the Confederacy. Revived the *Review* in 1866. Died in Elizabeth, New Jersey.

**Abner Doubleday** (June 26, 1819–January 26, 1893) Born in Ballston Spa, New York, the son of a newspaper editor. Attended school at Cooperstown (his supposed role in inventing baseball is now discounted). Graduated from West Point in 1842 and served as an artillery officer in the U.S.-Mexican War and the Third Seminole War. Married Mary Hewitt in 1852. Fired the first shot in defense of Fort Sumter in April 1861. Appointed brigadier general of volunteers, February 1862, and major general of volunteers, November 1862. Commanded a brigade at Second Bull Run and a division at South Mountain, Antietam, Fredericksburg, Chancellorsville, and Gettysburg; served as acting corps commander on the first day of the Battle of Gettysburg after the death of Major General John Reynolds. Held no further field commands after Gettysburg. Retired from the army in 1873. Published *Reminiscences of Forts Sumter and Moultrie in 1860–'61* (1876) and *Chancellorsville and Gettysburg* (1882). Died in Mendham, New Jersey.

**Frederick Douglass** (February 1818–February 20, 1895) Born Frederick Bailey in Talbot County, Maryland, the son of a slave mother and an unknown white man. Worked on farms and in Baltimore shipyards. Escaped to Philadelphia in 1838. Married Anna Murray, a free woman from Maryland, and settled in New Bedford, Massachusetts, where he took the name Douglass. Became a lecturer for the American Anti-Slavery Society, led by William Lloyd Garrison, in 1841. Published *Narrative of the Life of Frederick Douglass, An American Slave* (1845). Began publishing *North Star*, first in a series of antislavery newspapers, in Rochester, New York, in 1847. Broke with Garrison and became an ally of Gerrit Smith, who advocated an antislavery interpretation of the Constitution and participation in electoral politics. Published *My Bondage and My Freedom* (1855). Advocated emancipation and the enlistment of black soldiers at the outbreak of the Civil War. Met with Abraham Lincoln in Washington in August 1863 and August 1864, and wrote public letter supporting his reelection in September 1864. Continued his advocacy of racial equality and woman's rights after the Civil War. Served as U.S. marshal for the District of Columbia, 1877–81, and as its recorder of deeds, 1877–86. Published *Life and Times of Frederick Douglass* (1881). After the death of his wife Anna, married Helen Pitts in 1884. Served as minister to Haiti, 1889–91. Died in Washington, D.C.

**Samuel Francis Du Pont** (September 27, 1803–June 23, 1865) Born in Bergen Point, New Jersey, the son of a former French diplomat. Moved with family to Delaware, where his uncle had founded the Du Pont gunpowder works. Appointed a midshipman in the U.S. Navy in 1815. Promoted to lieutenant, 1826. Married first cousin Sophie Madeleine du Pont in 1833. Promoted commander, 1842. Commanded sloop *Cyane* along the Pacific coast during the Mexican War. Promoted to captain, 1855, and flag officer, September 1861. Led South Atlantic blockading squadron in capture of Port Royal, South Carolina, in November 1861. Appointed rear admiral, 1862. Failed to capture Charleston in April 1863 while leading fleet of seven ironclad monitors. Relieved of command in July 1863 at his request. Died in Philadelphia.

**Catherine Edmondston** (October 10, 1823–January 3, 1875) Born Catherine Ann Devereux in Halifax County, North Carolina, the daughter of a plantation owner. Married Patrick Edmondston in 1846. Lived on Looking Glass, plantation in Halifax County. Published pamphlet *The Morte d'Arthur: Its Influence on the Spirit and Manners of the Nineteenth Century* (1872), in which she accused the Union army of barbarism. Died in Raleigh.

**Samuel J. English** Enlisted for three years in the 2nd Rhode Island Infantry at Providence in June 1861. Fought at First Bull Run in July 1861. Promoted to second lieutenant, November 1861, first lieutenant, July 1862, and captain, February 1863. Served as company commander before mustering out in June 1864.

**John C. Frémont** (January 21, 1813–July 13, 1890) Born in Savannah, Georgia, the son of a school teacher. Educated at College of Charleston. Mathematics instructor in the U.S. Navy, 1833–35. Appointed second lieutenant in the U.S. Army corps of topographical engineers, 1838. Conducted series of western explorations and surveys, 1838–46. Married Jessie Benton, daughter of Senator Thomas

Hart Benton, 1841. Appointed lieutenant colonel, 1846, and helped seize California for the United States, 1846–47. Served as U.S. senator from California, 1850–51. Nominated for president by the Republican Party in 1856 and finished second in three-way race with Democrat James Buchanan and American (Know-Nothing) Millard Fillmore. Commissioned major general in the U.S. Army, May 1861, and given command of Missouri, July 1861. Relieved of command, November 1861. Commanded troops in the Shenandoah Valley, March–June 1862. Again relieved of command, and spent remainder of war awaiting further orders. Nominated for president by faction of Radical Republicans in May 1864, but withdrew from race in September in exchange for the resignation of Montgomery Blair from the Lincoln administration. Governor of Arizona Territory, 1878–81. Died in New York City.

**Ulysses S. Grant** (April 22, 1822–July 23, 1885) Born in Point Pleasant, Ohio, the son of a tanner. Graduated from West Point in 1843. Served in the U.S.-Mexican War, 1846–48, and promoted to first lieutenant in 1847. Married Julia Dent in 1848. Promoted to captain, 1854, and resigns commission. Worked as a farmer, real estate agent, and general store clerk, 1854–61. Commissioned colonel, 21st Illinois Volunteers, June 1861, and brigadier general of volunteers, August 1861. Promoted major general of volunteers, February 1862, after victories at Forts Henry and Donelson. Defeated Confederates at Shiloh, April 1862, and captured Vicksburg, Mississippi, July 1863. Promoted to major general in the regular army, July 1863, and assigned to command of Military Division of the Mississippi, covering territory between the Alleghenies and the Mississippi, October 1863. Won Battle of Chattanooga, November 1863. Promoted lieutenant general, March 1864, and named general-in-chief of the Union armies. Accepted surrender of Robert E. Lee at Appomattox Court House, April 9, 1865. Promoted to general, July 1866. Served as secretary of war ad interim, August 1867–January 1868. Nominated for president by the Republican Party in 1868. Defeated Democrat Horatio Seymour, and won reelection in 1872 by defeating Liberal Republican Horace Greeley. President of the United States, 1869–77. Made world tour, 1877–79. Failed to win Republican presidential nomination, 1880. Worked on Wall Street, 1881–84, and was financially ruined when private banking firm of Grant & Ward collapsed. Wrote *Personal Memoirs of U.S. Grant*, 1884–85, while suffering from throat cancer, and completed them days before his death at Mount McGregor, New York.

**Horace Greeley** (February 3, 1811–November 29, 1872) Born in Amherst, New Hampshire, the son of a farmer. Learned printing trade in Vermont, upstate New York, and Pennsylvania. Moved to

New York City in 1831. Founded and edited weekly *New Yorker*, 1834–41. Married Mary Cheney in 1836. Edited Whig campaign newspapers *Jeffersonian*, 1838, and *Log Cabin*, 1840. Founded *New York Tribune*, 1841, and used it to advocate for social reforms and anti-slavery positions. Served in Congress, 1848–49. Active in Whig and Republican politics. Nominated for president by the Liberal Republicans and the Democrats in 1872, but was defeated by Ulysses S. Grant. Died in New York City.

**Stephen F. Hale** (January 31, 1816–July 18, 1862) Born in Crittenden County, Kentucky, the son of a Baptist minister. Educated at Cumberland University and the law school of Transylvania University. Moved to Greene County, Alabama, where he practiced law. Married Mary Kirksey in 1844. Served as a lieutenant in the Mexican War, 1846–48. Elected to the Alabama legislature as a Whig, 1843, 1857, and 1859. Traveled to Kentucky in December 1860 as an Alabama commissioner advocating secession. Served in the Provisional Confederate Congress, 1861. Became lieutenant colonel of the 11th Alabama Infantry. Wounded in the Battle of Gaines' Mill, June 27, 1862, and died in Richmond.

**John W. Hanson** (May 12, 1823–December 14, 1901) Born in Boston, Massachusetts. Ordained as Universalist minister at Wentworth, New Hampshire, in 1845. Married Eliza Holbrook in 1846. Served as pastor in Danvers, Massachusetts, Gardiner, Maine, and Haverhill, Massachusetts. Edited the *Gospel Banner*, 1854–60. Served as chaplain of the 6th Massachusetts Volunteers, 1862–64, and published history of the regiment in 1865. Helped found the Soldiers' Mission, a Universalist organization for aiding Union troops. Edited the *New Covenant*, 1869–84, and wrote more than thirty works on theology. Died in Flagstaff, Arizona.

**John Hay** (October 8, 1838–July 1, 1905) Born Salem, Indiana, the son of a doctor. Family moved to Warsaw, Illinois. Graduated from Brown University in 1858. Studied law in office of his uncle in Springfield, Illinois. Traveled to Washington in 1861 as assistant private secretary to Abraham Lincoln, serving until early in 1865. First secretary to American legation in Paris, 1865–67, chargé d'affaires in Vienna, 1867–68, and legation secretary in Madrid, 1868–70. Published *Castilian Days* (1871) and *Pike County Ballads and Other Pieces* (1871). Married Clara Louise Stone in 1874. Served as assistant secretary of state 1879–81. Political novel *The Bread-Winners*, an attack on labor unions, published anonymously in 1884. In collaboration with John G. Nicolay, wrote *Abraham Lincoln: A History* (10 volumes, 1890) and edited *Complete Works of Abraham Lincoln* (2 volumes,

1894). Ambassador to Great Britain, 1897–98. Served as Secretary of State in the administrations of William McKinley and Theodore Roosevelt, 1898–1905. Among first seven members elected to American Academy of Arts and Letters in 1904. Died in Newbury, New Hampshire.

**Charles B. Haydon** (1834–March 14, 1864) Born in Vermont. Raised in Decatur, Michigan. Graduated from the University of Michigan in 1857, then read law in Kalamazoo. Joined the Kalamazoo Home Guard on April 22, 1861, then enlisted on May 25 for three years service in the 2nd Michigan Infantry. Fought at Blackburn's Ford during the First Bull Run campaign. Commissioned second lieutenant in September 1861 and promoted to first lieutenant in February 1862. Fought at Williamsburg, Fair Oaks, the Seven Days' Battles, Second Bull Run, and Fredericksburg; promoted captain in September 1862. Regiment was sent to Kentucky in April and to Vicksburg in June as part of the Ninth Corps. Wounded in the shoulder while leading his company at Jackson, Mississippi, on July 11, 1863. Returned to active duty in December 1863 and was made lieutenant colonel of the 2nd Michigan. Died of pneumonia in Cincinnati while returning to Michigan on a thirty-day furlough after reenlisting.

**Benjamin Hill** (September 14, 1823–August 16, 1882) Born in Jasper County, Georgia, the son of a farmer. Moved with family to Troup County. Graduated from the University of Georgia in 1844. Studied law and began practice in La Grange. Married Caroline Holt in 1845. Served as a Whig in the state house of representatives, 1851. Unsuccessful American (Know-Nothing) candidate for governor in 1857. Served in the state senate, 1859–60. Opposed immediate secession at the 1861 state convention. Served in the Provisional Confederate Congress, 1861, and in the Confederate Senate, 1862–65. Resumed law practice after the war. Served as a Democrat in Congress, 1875–77, and in the U.S. Senate from 1877 until his death in Atlanta.

**Emma Holmes** (December 17, 1838–January 1910) Born in Charleston, South Carolina, the daughter of a physician and plantation owner. Family moved to Camden, South Carolina, in June 1862, where she began teaching. Returned after the war to Charleston, where she continued to teach and tutor. Died in Charleston.

**Sam Houston** (March 2, 1793–July 26, 1863) Born near Lexington, Rockbridge County, Virginia, the son of an army officer. Family moved to Blount County, Tennessee, around 1808. Enlisted in army in 1813 and fought under Andrew Jackson against the Creeks. Resigned commission in 1818 and began to practice law in Lebanon, Tennessee. Served in Congress, 1823–27, and as governor of Tennessee, 1827–29. Moved in 1829 to Indian Territory, where he became a successful trader and a member of the Cherokee Nation. Settled in Texas, 1835, and commanded the army that defeated and captured General Santa Anna at San Jacinto, 1836. President of the Republic of Texas, 1836–38 and 1841–44; served in the Texas congress, 1838–40. Married Margaret Lea in 1840. Served in the U.S. Senate as a Democrat, 1846–59. Governor of Texas, 1859–61. Opposed secession, and was removed from office when he refused to swear allegiance to the Confederacy. Died in Huntsville.

**Andrew Johnson** (December 29, 1808–July 31, 1875) Born in Raleigh, North Carolina, the son of a bank porter. Learned tailoring and moved to Greenville, Tennessee, in 1826. Married Eliza McArdle, 1827. Elected alderman, 1829–33, and mayor of Greenville, 1834–35 and 1837–38. Served in the Tennessee house of representatives, 1835–37 and 1839–41, in the state senate, 1841–43, and in Congress as a Democrat, 1843–53. Governor of Tennessee, 1853–57. Served in the U.S. Senate, 1857–62. Candidate for Democratic presidential nomination in 1860. Served as military governor of Tennessee, 1862–64, with rank of brigadier general. Nominated for vice president by the National Union (Republican) convention in 1864. Became president following the assassination of Abraham Lincoln in April 1865. Conflict with Republicans in Congress over Reconstruction led to his impeachment in 1868. Acquitted at trial in the U.S. Senate. Failed to win presidential nomination of the Democratic Party in 1868. Returned to the U.S. Senate in March 1875 and served until his death near Elizabethton, Tennessee.

**Charles C. Jones Sr.** (December 20, 1804–March 16, 1863) Born in Liberty County, Georgia, the son of a plantation owner. Educated at Phillips Andover Academy, Andover Theological Seminary, and Princeton Theological Seminary. Married first cousin Mary Jones in 1830. Pastor of the First Presbyterian Church, Savannah, 1831–32. Returned to Liberty County, where he owned three plantations. Taught at Columbia Theological Seminary, South Carolina, 1837–38 and 1848–50. Published *Catechism of Scripture Doctrine and Practice* (1837) and *The Religious Instruction of the Negroes of the United States* (1842). Lived in Philadelphia, 1850–53, while serving as the corresponding secretary of the board of domestic missions of the Presbyterian Church. Died in Liberty County.

**Charles C. Jones Jr.** (October 28, 1831–July 19, 1893) Born in Savannah, Georgia, the son of minister Charles C. Jones and Mary Jones. Educated at South Carolina College and the College of New Jersey (Princeton). Graduated from Dane Law School at Harvard,

1855. Practiced law in Savannah, where he served as alderman, 1859–60, and mayor, 1860–61. Married Ruth Berrien Whitehead, 1858, and after her death, Eva Berrien Eve, 1863. Commissioned lieutenant in Chatham Artillery, August 1861. Promoted to lieutenant colonel and made chief of artillery for Georgia, October 1862. Practiced law in New York City, 1866–77, then returned to Georgia. Published several historical and archaeological studies, including *Indian Remains in Southern Georgia* (1859), *The Monumental Remains of Georgia* (1861), *Antiquities of the Southern Indians* (1873), and *The History of Georgia* (1883). Died in Augusta.

**John B. Jones** (March 6, 1810–February 4, 1866) Born in Baltimore, Maryland. Lived in Kentucky and Missouri as a boy. Married Frances Custis in 1840. Became editor of the *Saturday Visiter* in Baltimore, 1841. Published several novels, including *Wild Western Scenes* (1841), *The War Path* (1858), and *Wild Southern Scenes* (1859). Established weekly newspaper *Southern Monitor* in Philadelphia, 1857. Fearing arrest as a Confederate sympathizer, Jones moved in 1861 to Richmond, Virginia, where he worked as a clerk in the Confederate war department. Died in Burlington, New Jersey, shortly before the publication of *A Rebel War Clerk's Diary*.

**Mary Jones** (September 24, 1808–April 23, 1869) Born in Liberty County, Georgia, the daughter of a plantation owner. Educated at Carter Academy in Savannah, 1823–27. Married first cousin Charles C. Jones in 1830. Moved to New Orleans in 1868 to live with her daughter. Died in New Orleans.

**Elizabeth Blair Lee** (June 20, 1818–September 13, 1906) Born Frankfort, Kentucky, daughter of journalist Francis Preston Blair and Elizabeth Gist Blair, sister of Montgomery Blair (postmaster general, 1861–64) and Frank Blair (a Union major general, 1862–65). Moved with family in 1830 to Washington, D.C., where her father edited the *Globe* and advised Andrew Jackson. Educated at boarding school in Philadelphia. Married naval officer Samuel Phillips Lee, a cousin of Robert E. Lee, in 1843. Became board member and active patron of the Washington City Orphan Asylum in 1849. Lived in Washington and at the Blair estate in Silver Spring, Maryland. Died in Washington.

**Robert E. Lee** (January 19, 1807–October 12, 1870) Born in Westmoreland County, Virginia, the son of Revolutionary War hero Henry "Light-Horse Harry" Lee and Ann Carter Lee. Graduated from West Point in 1829. Married Mary Custis, great-granddaughter of Martha Washington, in 1831. Served in the U.S.-Mexican War, and as superintendant of West Point, 1852–55. Promoted to colonel in March 1861. Resigned commission on April 20, 1861, after declining offer of field command of the Federal army. Served as commander of Virginia military forces, April–July, 1861; commander in western Virginia, August–October 1861; commander of the southern Atlantic coast, November 1861–March 1862; and military advisor to Jefferson Davis, March–May 1862. Assumed command of the Army of Northern Virginia on June 1, 1862, and led it until April 9, 1865, when he surrendered to Ulysses S. Grant at Appomattox. Named general-in-chief of all Confederate forces, January 1865. Became president of Washington College (now Washington and Lee), September 1865. Died in Lexington, Virginia.

**Abraham Lincoln** (February 12, 1809–April 15, 1865) Born near Hodgenville, Kentucky, the son of a farmer and carpenter. Family moved to Indiana in 1816 and to Illinois in 1830. Settled in New Salem, Illinois, and worked as a storekeeper, surveyor, and postmaster. Served as a Whig in the state legislature, 1834–41. Began law practice in 1836 and moved to Springfield in 1837. Married Mary Todd in 1842. Elected to Congress as a Whig and served from 1847 to 1849. Became a public opponent of the extension of slavery after the passage of the Kansas-Nebraska Act in 1854. Helped found the Republican Party of Illinois in 1856. Campaigned in 1858 for Senate seat held by Stephen A. Douglas and debated him seven times on the slavery issue; although the Illinois legislature reelected Douglas, the campaign brought Lincoln national prominence. Received Republican presidential nomination in 1860 and won election in a four-way contest; his victory led to the secession of seven Southern states. Responded to the Confederate bombardment of Fort Sumter by calling up militia, proclaiming the blockade of Southern ports, and suspending habeas corpus. Issued preliminary and final emancipation proclamations on September 22, 1862, and January 1, 1863. Appointed Ulysses S. Grant commander of all Union forces in March 1864. Won reelection in 1864 by defeating Democrat George B. McClellan. Died in Washington, D.C., after being shot by John Wilkes Booth.

**James Russell Lowell** (February 22, 1819–August 12, 1891) Born in Cambridge, Massachusetts, the son of a Unitarian minister. Graduated Harvard College, 1838, and Harvard Law School, 1840. Published first collection of poetry, *A Year's Life* (1841), followed by *Poems* (1844). Married Maria White in 1844; after her death, married Frances Dunlap in 1857. Became contributing editor to *National Anti-Slavery Standard*. Published *Poems: Second Series, A Fable for Critics, The Biglow Papers*, and *The Vision of Sir Launfal*, all in 1848. Professor of French and Spanish languages and literatures at Harvard, 1855–86. Became founding editor of *The Atlantic Monthly*, 1857–61.

Co-edited *The North American Review*, 1864–72. Three of his nephews died serving in the Union army. Delivered widely acclaimed "Ode" at Harvard Commemoration of July 21, 1865, in honor of Harvard men killed in the Civil War. Continued to publish poetry and essays. Served as U.S. minister to Spain, 1877–80, and Great Britain, 1880–85. Died in Cambridge, Massachusetts.

**George B. McClellan** (December 3, 1826–October 29, 1885) Born in Philadelphia, the son of a surgeon. Graduated from West Point in 1846. Served in the U.S.-Mexican War. Resigned from the army in 1857 to become chief engineer of the Illinois Central Railroad. Became president of the Ohio & Mississippi Railroad in 1860. Married Ellen Marcy, 1860. Appointed major general in the regular army, May 1861. Commanded offensive that drove Confederate troops from western Virginia, July 1861. Assumed command of the Military Division of the Potomac on July 25, 1861, following the Union defeat at First Bull Run. Served as general-in-chief of the Union armies, November 1861–March 1862. Commanded the Army of the Potomac on the Peninsula, in the Second Bull Run campaign, and at Antietam. Relieved of command by President Lincoln on November 7, 1862. Nominated for president by the Democratic Party in 1864, but was defeated by Lincoln. Governor of New Jersey, 1878–81. Died in Orange, New Jersey.

**Irvin McDowell** (October 15, 1818–May 4, 1885) Born in Columbus, Ohio. Graduated from West Point in 1839. Served in U.S.-Mexican War. Married Helen Burden in 1849. Promoted to major in 1856. Named brigadier general and commander of Union forces at Washington through patronage of Secretary of the Treasury Salmon P. Chase, May 1861. Defeated at First Bull Run, July 1861. Commanded division, October 1861–March 1862, and corps, March–September 1862. Criticized for his performance during the Second Bull Run campaign and relieved of command; held no further field assignments during the war. Retired from the army in 1882. Died in San Francisco.

**Judith W. McGuire** (March 19, 1813–March 21, 1897) Born Judith White Brockenbrough near Richmond, Virginia, the daughter of a judge. Married John P. McGuire, an Episcopalian rector, in 1846. Moved to Alexandria in 1852 when husband became principal of the Episcopal High School of Virginia. Fled Alexandria in May 1861 and settled in Richmond in February 1862. Worked as a clerk in the Confederate commissary department, November 1863–April 1864. Published *Diary of a Southern Refugee, during the war* (1867). Kept a school with her husband in Essex County in the 1870s. Published *General Robert E. Lee, The Christian Soldier* (1873). Died in Richmond.

**Montgomery C. Meigs** (May 3, 1816–January 2, 1892) Born Augusta, Georgia, the son of a physician. Moved with family to Philadelphia. Graduated from West Point in 1836 and began service in engineering corps. Married Louisa Rodgers in 1841. Supervised construction of the Washington Aqueduct, 1852–60, and of the wings and dome of the Capitol, 1853–59. Promoted to brigadier general, May 1861, and made army quartermaster general, a post he held throughout the war. Designed the Pension Building in Washington, D.C., after retiring from the army in 1882. Died in Washington.

**Herman Melville** (August 1, 1819–September 28, 1891) Born in New York City, the son of a merchant. Educated at schools in New York City and in upstate New York. Worked as bank clerk, bookkeeper, and schoolteacher. Sailed for Pacific on whaling ship in 1841 and returned in 1844 on frigate *United States*. Published *Typee* (1846) and *Omoo* (1847), fictionalized accounts of his experiences in the South Seas. Married Elizabeth Shaw in 1847. Published *Mardi* (1849), *Redburn* (1849), *White-Jacket* (1850), *Moby-Dick* (1851), *Pierre; or, The Ambiguities* (1852), *Israel Potter* (1855), *The Piazza Tales* (1856), and *The Confidence-Man* (1857). Visited Union lines in Virginia in spring 1864. Published poetry collection *Battle-Pieces and Aspects of the War* (1866). Worked as customs inspector in New York City, 1866–85. Published long poem *Clarel* (1876) and two small books of poetry, *John Marr and Other Sailors* (1888) and *Timoleon* (1891). Died in New York City, leaving *Billy Budd, Sailor* in manuscript.

**Sam Mitchell** (c. 1848–after 1937) Born on plantation of John Chaplin on Ladies Island, Beaufort, South Carolina, the son of slave parents. Remained with his family in Beaufort after Union occupation in November 1861. Educated in a school established in the plantation house during the war. Lived in Beaufort after the war and was married twice.

**Benjamin Moran** (August 1, 1820–June 20, 1886) Born West Marlboro, Pennsylvania, the son of a cotton mill owner. Worked for bookseller and printer John Grigg in Philadelphia. Traveled to England in 1851. Published *The Footpath and Highway: or, Wanderings of an American in Great Britain, in 1851 and '52* (1853). Married Catherine Goulder, an English mill worker. Became private secretary to James Buchanan, then U.S. minister to Great Britain, in 1854. Assistant secretary of the American legation in London, 1857–64, and secretary, 1864–74. Served as minister resident in Portugal, 1874–76, and as chargé d'affaires at Lisbon, 1876–82. Returned to England in 1882 and died at Braintree, Essex.

**John G. Nicolay** (February 26, 1832–September 26, 1901) Born in Essingen, Rhineland-Palatinate, Bavaria. Family emigrated to the United States in 1838 and eventually settled in Pike County, Illinois. Worked for the *Pike County Free Press* in Pittsfield and as a clerk in the office of the Illinois secretary of state. Became private secretary to Abraham Lincoln in 1860. With his friend John Hay, accompanied Lincoln to Washington, D.C., where Nicolay and Hay served as the president's principal secretaries. Married Therena Bates in 1865. Served as consul in Paris, 1865–69, and as marshal of the U.S. Supreme Court, 1872–87. Collaborated with Hay in writing *Abraham Lincoln: A History* (10 volumes, 1890) and editing *Complete Works of Abraham Lincoln* (2 volumes, 1894). Died in Washington.

**John Ross** (October 3, 1790–August 1, 1866) Born in Turkeytown, Alabama, the son of a trader; by ancestry, seven-eighths Scottish and one-eighth Cherokee. Family moved to Cherokee lands in southern Tennessee, where father owned a store. Educated at academy in Kingston, Tennessee. Married Elizabeth Henley in 1813; after her death, married Mary Stapler in 1844. Joined Cherokee volunteers who served under Andrew Jackson in the Creek War, 1813–14, and fought at Battle of Horsehoe Bend in Alabama. Helped negotiate treaties between Cherokee Nation and the United States in 1816 and 1819. President of the Cherokee National Committee, 1818–26. Became slaveholding landowner in western Georgia, 1827. Elected principal chief of the eastern Cherokee, 1828. Resisted attempts to relocate Cherokee to Indian Territory, but was unable to prevent rival faction from signing treaty in 1835 ceding Cherokee lands and agreeing to removal. Helped organize movement of Cherokees to Indian Territory along "Trail of Tears," 1838–39. Elected principal chief of the united Cherokee in 1839. Advocated neutrality at the outbreak of the Civil War, but signed treaty of alliance with the Confederacy in October 1861 in unsuccessful effort to avoid factional split within the Cherokee Nation. Fled Indian Territory in August 1862 and spent remainder of the war in Washington, D.C., where he sought to restore Cherokee relations with the United States. Died in Washington during post-war treaty negotiations.

**William Howard Russell** (March 28, 1820–February 10, 1907) Born in Tallaght, Ireland, the son of a businessman. Educated at Trinity College, Dublin. Became journalist for *The Times* of London in 1843. Married Mary Burrowes in 1846; after her death, married the Countess Antoinette Malvezzi in 1884. Reported on the Crimean War,

1854–56, and the Indian Rebellion, 1858–59. Sent to the United States by *The Times* to cover the secession crisis and arrived in March 1861. Traveled through the South until June, when he returned to Washington, D.C. Reported on the Union retreat from Bull Run in July 1861. Remained in the United States until April 1862, when he returned to England after failing to secure a pass to travel with the Union army in Virginia. Published *My Diary North and South* (1863). Reported on the Austro-Prussian War, 1866, and the Franco-Prussian war, 1870–71, for *The Times* and the Anglo-Zulu war, 1879, for *The Daily Telegraph*. Knighted in 1895. Died in London.

**Winfield Scott** (June 13, 1786–May 29, 1866) Born in Dinwiddie County, Virginia, the son of a farmer. Studied at the College of William and Mary. Practiced law and served in the Virginia militia, 1807, before being commissioned as captain in the U.S. Army in 1808. Served with distinction in the War of 1812, and was promoted to brigadier general in 1814. Married Mary Mayo in 1817. Commanded troops in South Carolina during the nullification crisis, 1832–33. Organized removal of Cherokees from the southeastern United States, 1838. Helped settle Anglo-American dispute over Maine border with Canada, 1838–39. Commissioned major general, 1841, and named general-in-chief of the U.S. Army. Commanded expedition that landed at Vera Cruz and captured Mexico City, 1847. Nominated for president by the Whig Party in 1852, but was defeated by Democrat Franklin Pierce. Helped settle Anglo-American border dispute over Puget Sound, 1859. Retired from army on November 1, 1861. Died at West Point, New York.

**William H. Seward** (May 16, 1801–October 10, 1872) Born in Florida, New York, the son of a doctor. Graduated from Union College in 1820 and was admitted to the bar in 1822. Married Frances Miller in 1824. Elected to the New York senate as an Anti-Masonic candidate and served until 1834. Unsuccessful Whig candidate for governor in 1834. Elected governor in 1838 and served until 1842. Elected to the U.S. Senate as a Whig and reelected as a Republican, serving from 1849 to 1861. Unsuccessful candidate for the Republican presidential nomination in 1860. Secretary of state in the cabinet of Abraham Lincoln, 1861–65. Wounded by a co-conspirator of John Wilkes Booth on April 14, 1865, but recovered and served as secretary of state under Andrew Johnson, 1865–69. Negotiated the purchase of Alaska in 1867. Died in Auburn, New York.

**William T. Sherman** (February 8, 1820–February 14, 1891) Born in Lancaster, Ohio, the son of an attorney. Graduated from West Point in 1840. Served in Florida and California, but did not see action in the U.S.-Mexican War. Married Ellen Ewing in 1850. Promoted to captain; resigned his commission in 1853. Managed bank branch in San Francisco, 1853–57. Moved in 1858 to Leavenworth, Kansas, where he worked in real estate and was admitted to the bar. Named first superintendent of the Louisiana State Seminary of Learning and Military Academy at Alexandria (now Louisiana State University) in 1859. Resigned position when Louisiana seceded in January 1861. Commissioned colonel, 13th U.S. Infantry, May 1861. Commanded brigade at First Bull Run, July 1861. Appointed brigadier general of volunteers, August 1861, and ordered to Kentucky. Assumed command of the Department of the Cumberland, October 1861, but was relieved in November at his own request. Returned to field in March 1862 and commanded division under Ulysses S. Grant at Shiloh. Promoted major general of volunteers, May 1862. Commanded corps under Grant during Vicksburg campaign, and succeeded him as commander of the Army of the Tennessee, October 1863, and as commander of the Military Division of the Mississippi, March 1864. Captured Atlanta, September 1864, and led march through Georgia, November–December 1864. Marched army through the Carolinas and accepted the surrender of Confederate General Joseph E. Johnston at Durham Station, North Carolina, April 26, 1865. Promoted to lieutenant general, 1866, and general, 1869, when he became commander of the army. Published controversial memoirs (1875, revised 1886). Retired from army in 1884 and moved to New York City. Rejected possible Republican presidential nomination, 1884. Died in New York City.

**Edwin M. Stanton** (December 19, 1814–December 24, 1869) Born in Steubenville, Ohio, the son of a physician. Attended Kenyon College. Admitted to bar in 1836. Married Mary Lamson in 1844; after her death, married Ellen Hutchinson in 1856. Practiced law in Cadiz, Ohio, and Steubenville before moving to Pittsburgh, Pennsylvania, in 1847 and Washington, D.C., in 1856. Served as attorney general of the United States, December 1860–March 1861; advised President Buchanan not to evacuate Fort Sumter. Appointed secretary of war in January 1862 by President Lincoln. Continued in office under President Andrew Johnson until August 1867, when Johnson attempted to remove him because of Stanton's support for congressional Reconstruction measures. Restored to office by the Senate in January 1868 under the Tenure of Office Act, but resigned in May 1868 after Johnson was acquitted at his impeachment trial. Appointed to the Supreme Court by Ulysses S. Grant and confirmed by the Senate, but died in Washington before he could be sworn in.

**Alexander H. Stephens** (February 11, 1812–March 4, 1883) Born in Taliaferro County, Georgia, the son of a farmer. Graduated from the

University of Georgia in 1832. Admitted to the bar in 1834. Served in the Georgia house of representatives, 1836–41, and the Georgia senate, 1842. Elected to Congress as a Whig and then as a Democrat and served from 1843 to 1859. Opposed immediate secession at the Georgia convention in January 1861. Elected provisional vice president of the Confederate States of America in February 1861 and vice president in November 1861. Opposed conscription, the suspension of habeas corpus, and other measures of the Davis administration, and spent much of the war in Georgia. Held unsuccessful peace conference with Abraham Lincoln and William H. Seward at Hampton Roads, Virginia, on February 3, 1865. Arrested by Union troops on May 11, 1865, and imprisoned for five months in Boston. Published *A Constitutional View of the Late War Between the States* (1868–70). Elected to Congress as a Democrat and served from 1873 to 1882. Governor of Georgia from 1882 until his death in Atlanta.

**Kate Stone** (May 8, 1841–December 28, 1907) Born Sarah Katherine Stone in Hinds County, Mississippi, the daughter of a plantation owner. Family moved to plantation in Madison Parish, Louisiana, thirty miles northwest of Vicksburg. Educated at boarding school in Nashville. Two of her five brothers died while serving in the Confederate army in 1863. Family fled plantation in April 1863 during the Vicksburg campaign and went to eastern Texas. Returned to plantation in November 1865. Married Henry Bry Holmes in 1869. Founded local chapter of the United Daughters of the Confederacy. Died in Tallulah, Louisiana.

**George Templeton Strong** (January 26, 1820–July 21, 1875) Born in New York City, the son of an attorney. Graduated from Columbia College in 1838. Read law in his father's office and was admitted to the bar in 1841. Joined father's firm. Married Ellen Ruggles in 1848. Served on Columbia board of trustees and as vestryman of Trinity Episcopal Church. Helped found the U.S. Sanitary Commission, June 1861, and served as its treasurer through the end of the war; also helped found the Union League Club of New York in 1863. Died in New York City.

**Roger B. Taney** (March 17, 1777–October 12, 1864) Born in Calvert County, Maryland, son of a plantation owner. Graduated from Dickinson College in 1795. Read law in Annapolis and began practicing in 1799. Served as Federalist in the Maryland house of delegates, 1799–1800, and in the Maryland senate, 1816–21. Married Anne Key in 1806. Began manumitting his slaves in 1818. Attorney general of Maryland, 1827–31. Served in the Jackson administration as attorney general, 1831–33, and as secretary of the treasury, 1833–34. Appointed chief justice of the U.S. Supreme Court by Jackson; served 1836–64. Wrote opinion of the court in the *Dred Scott* case, 1857. While sitting as a circuit judge in Maryland, ruled in *Ex parte Merryman* (1861) that President Lincoln lacked the authority to suspend the writ of habeas corpus. Dissented in the *Prize Cases* (1863), in which the Court upheld the legality of the blockade proclamation issued by Lincoln in April 1861. Died in Washington, D.C.

**Henry Tucker** (May 10, 1819–September 9, 1889) Born in Warren County, Georgia. Educated at the University of Pennsylvania and Columbian College (George Washington University). Admitted to the Georgia bar in 1846. Married Mary Catherine West in 1848; after her death, married Sarah O. Stevens in 1853. Ordained as a Baptist minister in 1851 and became pastor of a Baptist church in Alexandria, Virginia, 1854. Professor of literature and metaphysics at Mercer University in Penfield, Georgia, 1856–62. Opposed secession initially, but supported the Confederacy during the war; organized the Georgia Relief and Hospital Association to care for sick and wounded soldiers. Served as president of Mercer University, 1866–71, and as chancellor of the University of Georgia, 1874–78. Editor of the *Christian Index*, 1878–89. Died in Atlanta.

**Benjamin F. Wade** (October 27, 1800–March 2, 1878) Born in Feeding Hills, Massachusetts, the son of a farmer. Moved with family to Andover, Ohio, in 1821. Worked as a laborer on the Erie Canal, taught school, and studied medicine in Albany, New York, before being admitted to the Ohio bar in 1828. Served in Ohio senate as a Whig, 1837–38 and 1841–42. Married Caroline Rosekrans, 1841. Judge of circuit court of common pleas, 1847–51. Served in the U.S. Senate as a Whig and then as a Republican, 1851–69. Chairman of the Joint Committee on the Conduct of the War, 1861–65. Co-sponsored the Wade-Davis Bill on Reconstruction, 1864, which was pocket vetoed by President Lincoln. Elected president pro tempore of the Senate in 1867, he would have succeeded Andrew Johnson as president if had Johnson been convicted during his impeachment trial. Unsuccessful candidate for Republican vice-presidential nomination in 1868. Died in Jefferson, Ohio.

**E. F. Ware** (May 29, 1841–July 1, 1911) Born Eugene Fitch Ware in Hartford, Connecticut, the son of a leather worker. Moved with family to Burlington, Iowa, in 1844. Apprenticed in father's harness-making shop. Served in 1st Iowa Infantry, April–August 1861, and fought in the Battle of Wilson's Creek. Enlisted in 4th Iowa Cavalry, November 1861, and saw action in Missouri and Arkansas before mustering out in October 1862. Joined Iowa 7th Cavalry in February

1863 and served with the regiment on the Nebraska frontier. Mustered out as captain in 1866. Settled in Kansas in 1867. Worked on farm and as harness maker before becoming editor of the *Fort Scott Monitor*. Admitted to the bar in 1871. Married Jeanette Huntington in 1874. Served as a Republican in the Kansas senate, 1879–83. U.S. Pension Commissioner, 1902–5. Published a popular collection of poetry, *The Rhymes of Ironquill* (1885); a legal handbook, *From Court to Court* (1901); a collection of essays on psychology, *The Autobiography of Ithuriel* (1909); and two memoirs, *The Lyon Campaign in Missouri* (1907) and *The Indian War of 1864* (1911). Died in Cascade, Colorado.

**Gideon Welles** (July 1, 1802–February 11, 1878) Born in Glastonbury, Connecticut, the son of a merchant. Educated in Vermont at the American Literary, Scientific, and Military Academy (now Norwich University). Editor of the *Hartford Times*, 1826–36. Served as a Democrat in the Connecticut house of representatives, 1827–35. Married Mary Hale in 1835. Postmaster of Hartford, 1836–41. Served as chief of the bureau of provisions and clothing in the navy department, 1846–49. Helped organize Republican Party in Connecticut. Wrote for the *Hartford Evening Press*, the *New York Evening Post*, and other Republican newspapers. Secretary of the navy in the Lincoln and Andrew Johnson administrations, 1861–69. Died in Hartford.

**Walt Whitman** (May 31, 1819–March 26, 1892) Born in Huntington Township, New York, the son of a farmer and carpenter. Moved with family to Brooklyn in 1823. Learned printing trade at Brooklyn newspapers. Taught school on Long Island, 1836–38. Became freelance journalist and printer in New York and Brooklyn. Published first edition of *Leaves of Grass* in 1855 (revised editions appear in 1856, 1860, 1867, 1870, 1881, and 1891). Traveled to northern Virginia in December 1862 after learning that his brother George had been wounded at Fredericksburg. Became volunteer nurse in Washington, D.C., army hospitals. Published *Drum Taps* and *Sequel to Drum-Taps* in 1865. Worked as clerk at the interior department, 1865, and the office of the attorney general, 1865–73. Published prose recollections of his war experiences in *Memorandum During the War* (1875) and *Specimen Days and Collect* (1882). Died in Camden, New Jersey.

**Henry A. Wise** (December 3, 1806–September 12, 1876) Born in Drummondtown, Accomack County, Virginia, the son of a lawyer. Graduated from Washington College in Pennsylvania, 1825. Married Ann Jennings in 1828; after her death, he married Sarah Sergeant in 1840. Began legal practice in Accomack County, 1830. Served in Congress, 1833–44, and as U.S. minister to Brazil, 1844–47. Governor of

Virginia, 1856–60. Supported secession in the Virginia convention, 1861. Appointed brigadier general in the Confederate army, 1861, and served until the end of the war in Virginia and the Carolinas. Resumed legal career. Died in Richmond.

**W. E. Woodruff** (June 8, 1831–July 8, 1907) Born William Edward Woodruff Jr. in Little Rock, Arkansas, the son of the founder of the *Arkansas Gazette*. Graduated from the Western Military Institute in Georgetown, Kentucky, in 1852. Worked for father's land agency before beginning legal practice in Little Rock, 1859. Served as Confederate artillery officer in Missouri, Arkansas, and Indian Territory, and as commissary officer in Texas. Wounded at Battle of Prairie Grove in Arkansas, December 1862, and suffered major hearing loss from artillery service. Ended war as major. Publisher and editor of the *Arkansas Gazette*, 1866–76. Married Ruth Blocher in 1868. Served as state treasurer of Arkansas, 1881–91. Convicted of stealing state funds, but verdict was overturned on appeal. Published *With the Light Guns '61–'65* (1903). Died in Little Rock.

**Lunsford P. Yandell** (June 6, 1837–March 12, 1884) Born in Rutherford County, Tennessee, the son of a physician. Graduated from the University of Louisville medical school in 1857. Began practicing medicine in Memphis, 1858, and taught at the Memphis Medical College. Served as a surgeon with the Confederate army in the western theater, 1861–65. Married Louise Elliston in 1867. Taught medicine at the University of Louisville from 1869 until his death. Died in Louisville from an overdose of chloral hydrate.

# Note on the Texts

This volume collects nineteenth- and early twentieth-century writing about secession and the Civil War, bringing together public and private letters, newspaper and magazine articles, memoranda, speeches, narratives, journal and diary entries, proclamations and declarations, messages, judicial opinions, legislative enactments, poems, songs, sermons, and excerpts from memoirs written by participants and observers and dealing with events in the period between November 1860 and January 1862. Most of these documents were not written for publication, and most of them existed only in manuscript form during the lifetimes of the persons who wrote them. The texts presented in this volume are taken from the best printed sources available. In cases where there is only one printed source for a document, the text offered here comes from that source. Where there is more than one printed source for a document, the text printed in this volume is taken from the source that contains the fewest editorial alterations in the spelling, capitalization, paragraphing, and punctuation of the document.

The present volume prints texts as they appear in the sources listed below, but with a few alterations in editorial procedure. The bracketed conjectural readings of editors, in cases where original manuscripts or printed texts were damaged or difficult to read, are accepted without brackets in this volume when those readings seem to be the only possible ones; but when they do not, or when the editor made no conjecture, the missing word or words are indicated by a bracketed two-em space, i.e., [    ]. In cases where a typographical error or obvious misspelling in a manuscript was marked by earlier editors with "[*sic*]," the present volume omits the "[*sic*]" and corrects the typographical error or slip of the pen. In some cases, obvious errors were not marked by earlier editors with "[*sic*]" but were printed and then followed by a bracketed correction; in these instances, this volume removes the brackets and accepts the editorial emendation. Bracketed editorial insertions used in the source texts to identify persons or places, expand contractions and abbreviations, or to clarify meaning, have been deleted in this volume. In instances where canceled, but still legible, words were printed in the source texts with lines through the deleted material, this volume omits the canceled words. The texts of the memorandum sent by William H. Seward to President Lincoln and of the letter from Sullivan Ballou to Sarah Ballou were presented as quoted material in the sources used in this volume, with quotation marks placed at the beginning of each paragraph and at the end of the text; this volume omits the quotation marks.

*Mary Chesnut's Civil War* (1981), edited by C. Vann Woodward, prints the text of the narrative Chesnut prepared between 1881 and 1884, using her journal from the 1860s as a source, but also inserted significant passages from the 1860s journal that Chesnut omitted from her 1880s manuscript, and in some cases restored sensitive material that Chesnut had canceled in her journal. In the selections from *Mary Chesnut's Civil War* included in this volume, the inserted and restored material from the 1860s journal is printed without the single and double angle brackets used to indicate it in the Woodward edition. The inserted material appears at 253.3–4, "News so warlike . . . joining the artillery"; at 253.5–6, "Mr. Manning read . . . very complimentary."; at 259.33, "Everybody laughs at John Manning's brag."; at 260.27–28, "Manning, Wigfall, . . . us at night."; at 507.14–19, "The president took all . . . greedy for military fame."; at 507.26–28, "He gave the glory . . . have praised him."; at 510.19, "What a villain that woman is."; at 511.32–512.3, "All day I was . . . Mr. Preston a commission."; at 513.12, "DeLeon is always drunk."; at 520.35–36, "Sat up until . . . and Mrs. Davis."; at 521.35–37, "Mr. Chesnut met his . . . for several days." At 253.4–5, "last night I find he is my all, and I would go mad without him" was canceled by Chesnut in the manuscript.

*Inside Lincoln's White House: The Complete Civil War Diary of John Hay* (1997), edited Michael Burlingame and John R. Turner Ettlinger, prints a paragraph criticizing Major Robert Anderson in the May 9, 1861, entry (page 352.26–32 in this volume) as canceled material because it was crossed out in the manuscript. This volume prints the paragraph without cancellation marks because it is likely that it was crossed out by someone other than Hay, possibly after his death.

*Diary of a Southern Refugee* was first published in New York in 1867, with its author identified as "A Lady of the South" and with dashes substituted for the names of a number of persons referred to in the text. The book was reprinted in 1889 in Richmond by J. W. Randolph & English, with Judith McGuire identified as its author, and with an appended list of "Corrections" supplying the omitted names. In the selection from *Diary of a Southern Refugee* presented in this volume, the names supplied in the "Corrections" section of the 1889 printing have been incorporated into the text. The text of the judicial opinion *Ex parte Merryman* presented in this volume is taken from *The Federal Cases, Comprising Cases Argued and Determined in the Circuit and District Courts of the United States* (1895), which used as its source the reports of Chief Justice Roger B. Taney's circuit cases prepared by James Mason Campbell, but which also inserted in brackets a passage taken from the *American Law Register* that is omitted from the Campbell report. This volume prints the inserted passage without brackets.

The text of the letter sent by Henry Livermore Abbott to Josiah Gardner Abbott on October 22, 1861, is taken from *Fallen Leaves: The Civil War Letters of Major Henry Livermore Abbott* (1991), edited by Robert Garth Scott, but with several errors of transcription corrected by referring to the original manuscript in the Houghton Library, Harvard University, MS Am 800.26 (37). At 576.19, "on" becomes "upon"; at 576.30, "two row boats" becomes "two little row boats"; at 576.31, "perpendicular & thickly" becomes "perpendicular & very thickly"; at 577.6, "15th" becomes "Fifteenth"; at 577.15, "regiment . . . (making" becomes "regiment on hand (making"; at 577.20, "criticize it. . . . It will" becomes "criticize it in terms. It will"; at 577.26–27, "under command of Gen. Baker" becomes "under command of Col. Lee. The whole was the command of Gen. Baker"; at 577.27–29, "in front. . . . The rebels had 2 inf[antry] & one cavalry regt.; how full is not known" becomes "in front entirely unprotected. The enemy in the woods. Here is a rough sketch"; at 577.30, ". . . 2 of the regts." becomes "You can see from the sketch that 2 of the regts."; at 577.37–38, "2 [P.M.] to 6" becomes "2 till 6"; at 578.19, "with about 20 men" becomes "with 20 men"; at 578.39–579.1, "across [if] they could" becomes "across in case they could"; at 579.13–14, "it seems . . . Capt. Dreher" becomes "it seems by later intelligence. Capt. Dreher"; at 579.21, "are now in camp" becomes "We are now at camp."

The following is a list of the documents included in this volume, in the order of their appearance, giving the source of each text.

*Charleston Mercury*: What Shall the South Carolina Legislature Do? *Charleston Mercury*, November 3, 1860.

John G. Nicolay: Memoranda Regarding Abraham Lincoln, November 5–6, 1860. *With Lincoln in the White House: Letters, Memoranda, and other Writings of John G. Nicolay, 1860–1865*, ed. Michael Burlingame (Carbondale and Edwardsville: Southern Illinois University Press, 2000), 7–8. Copyright © 2000 by the Board of Trustees, Southern Illinois University.

*New-York Daily Tribune*: Going to Go. *New-York Daily Tribune*, November 9, 1860.

Jefferson Davis to Robert Barnwell Rhett Jr., November 10, 1860. *The Papers of Jefferson Davis*, Volume 6, ed. Lynda Laswell Crist and Mary Seaton Dix (Baton Rouge: Louisiana State University Press, 1989), 368–69. Copyright © 1989 by the Louisiana State University Press.

Benjamin Hill: Speech at Milledgeville, November 15, 1860. Benjamin H. Hill, Jr., *Senator Benjamin H. Hill of Georgia: His Life, Speeches and Writings* (Atlanta: T.H.P. Bloodworth, 1893), 238–50.

*New York Daily News*: The Right of States to Secede. *New York Daily News*, November 16, 1860.

Sam Houston to H. M. Watkins and Others, November 20, 1860. *The Writings of Sam Houston*, Volume VIII, ed. Amelia W. Williams and Eugene C. Barker (Austin: The University of Texas Press, 1943), 192–97.

George Templeton Strong: Diary, November 20, November 26–December 1, 1860. George Templeton Strong, *Diary of the Civil War, 1860–1865*, ed. Allan Nevins (New York: The Macmillan Company, 1962), 64, 65–68. Reprinted with permission of Scribner, a Division of Simon & Schuster, Inc., from *The Diary of George Templeton Strong* by Allan Nevins and Milton Halsey Thomas. Copyright © 1952 by Macmillan Publishing Company; copyright renewed © 1980 by Milton Halsey Thomas. All rights reserved.

Edward Bates: Diary, November 22, 1860. *The Diary of Edward Bates*, ed. Howard K. Beale (Washington: United States Government Printing Office, 1933), 157–58.

William G. Brownlow to R. H. Appleton, November 29, 1860. W. G. Brownlow, *Sketches of the Rise, Progress, and Decline of Secession; with a Narrative of Personal Adventures among the Rebels* (Philadelphia: George W. Childs, 1862), 38–48.

Frederick Douglass: The Late Election, December 1860. Philip S. Foner, *The Life and Writings of Frederick Douglass*, volume 2 (New York: International Publishers Co. Inc., 1950), 526–30. Reprinted from *The Life and Writings of Frederick Douglass*, published by International Publishers, copyright © 1950.

William T. Sherman to Thomas Ewing Sr. and to John Sherman, December 1, 1860. *Sherman's Civil War: Selected Correspondence of William T. Sherman, 1860–1865*, ed. Brooks D. Simpson and Jean V. Berlin (Chapel Hill: The University of North Carolina Press, 1999), 13–15. Copyright © 1999 The University of North Carolina Press.

James Buchanan: from the Annual Message to Congress, December 3, 1860. *A Compilation of the Messages and Papers of the Presidents*, vol. VII, ed. James Richardson (New York: Bureau of National Literature, Inc., 1897), 3157–70.

J.D.B. DeBow: The Non-Slaveholders of the South, December 5, 1860. *The Interest in Slavery of the Southern Non-Slaveholder; The*

*Right of Peaceful Secession; Slavery in the Bible* (Charleston, S.C.: Evans & Cogswell, 1860), 3–12.

Joseph E. Brown to Alfred H. Colquitt and Others, December 7, 1860. *Secession Debated: Georgia's Showdown in 1860*, ed. William W. Freehling and Craig M. Simpson (New York: Oxford University Press, 1992), 145–59. Copyright © 1992 by William W. Freehling, Craig M. Simpson. By permission of Oxford University Press, Inc.

Abraham Lincoln to John A. Gilmer, December 15, 1860. *The Collected Works of Abraham Lincoln*, Volume IV, ed. Roy P. Basler (New Brunswick, N.J.: Rutgers University Press, 1953), 151–53. Copyright © 1953 by the Abraham Lincoln Association.

*New-York Daily Tribune*: The Right of Secession, December 17, 1860. *Northern Editorials on Secession*, volume I, ed. Howard Cecil Perkins (New York: D. Appleton-Century, 1942), 199–201. Copyright 1942 by the American Historical Association.

Benjamin F. Wade: Remarks in the U.S. Senate, December 17, 1860. *Congressional Globe*, 36th Congress, 2nd session, 102–04.

John J. Crittenden: Remarks in the U.S. Senate, December 18, 1860. *Congressional Globe*, 36th Congress, 2nd session, 112–14.

Henry Adams to Charles Francis Adams Jr., December 18–20, 1860. *The Letters of Henry Adams*, volume I, ed. J. C. Levenson, Ernest Samuels, Charles Vandersee, Viola Hopkins Winner (Cambridge: The Belknap Press of Harvard University Press, 1982), 208–10. Copyright © 1982 by the Massachusetts Historical Society. Reprinted courtesy of the Adams Family Papers, Massachusetts Historical Society.

John G. Nicolay: Memorandum Regarding Abraham Lincoln, December 22, 1860. *With Lincoln in the White House: Letters, Memoranda, and other Writings of John G. Nicolay, 1860–1865*, ed. Michael Burlingame (Carbondale and Edwardsville: Southern Illinois University Press, 2000), 21. Copyright © 2000 by the Board of Trustees, Southern Illinois University.

South Carolina Declaration of the Causes of Secession, December 24, 1860. *Journal of the Convention of the People of South Carolina, Held in 1860, 1861, and 1862, together with the Ordinances, Reports, Resolutions, etc.* (Columbia, S.C.: R. W. Gibbes, 1862), 461–66.

Abner Doubleday: from *Reminiscences of Forts Sumter and Moultrie in 1860–'61*. Abner Doubleday, *Reminiscences of Forts Sumter and Moultrie in 1860–'61* (New York: Harper & Brothers, 1876), 34–35, 41–43, 58–67.

Catherine Edmondston: Diary, December 26–27, 1861. *"Journal of a Secesh Lady": The Diary of Catherine Ann Devereux Edmondston,*

*1860–1866*, ed. Beth G. Crabtree and James W. Patton (Raleigh: North Carolina Division of Archives and History, 1979), 29–30. Copyright © 1979 by the North Carolina Division of Archives and History.

Stephen F. Hale to Beriah Magoffin, December 27, 1860. *The War of the Rebellion: a Compilation of the Official Records of the Union and Confederate Armies*, series 4, volume I (Washington, D.C.: Government Printing Office, 1900), 4–11.

Herman Melville: Misgivings. Herman Melville, *Battle-Pieces and Aspects of the War* (New York: Harper & Brothers, 1866), 13.

Mary Jones to Charles C. Jones Jr., January 3, 1861. *The Children of Pride: A True Story of Georgia and the Civil War*, Abridged Edition, ed. Robert Manson Myers (New Haven: Yale University Press, 1984), 38–39. Copyright © 1972 by Robert Manson Myers.

Henry Adams to Charles Francis Adams Jr., January 8, 1861. *The Letters of Henry Adams*, volume I, ed. J. C. Levenson, Ernest Samuels, Charles Vandersee, Viola Hopkins Winner (Cambridge: The Belknap Press of Harvard University Press, 1982), 218–20. Copyright © 1982 by the Massachusetts Historical Society. Reprinted courtesy of the Adams Family Papers, Massachusetts Historical Society.

Mississippi Declaration of the Causes of Secession, January 9, 1861. *Journal of the State Convention and Ordinances and Resolutions Adopted in January, 1861* (Jackson, Miss.: E. Barksdale, 1861), 86–88.

Elizabeth Blair Lee to Samuel Phillips Lee, December 25, January 9–10, 1861. *Wartime Washington: The Civil War Letters of Elizabeth Blair Lee*, ed. Virginia Jeans Laas (Urbana: University of Illinois Press, 1991), 19–21. Copyright © 1991 by the Board of Trustees of the University of Illinois.

Catherine Edmondston: Diary, January 9–13, 1861. *"Journal of a Secesh Lady": The Diary of Catherine Ann Devereux Edmondston, 1860–1866*, ed. Beth G. Crabtree and James W. Patton (Raleigh: North Carolina Division of Archives and History, 1979), 32–34. Copyright © 1979 by the North Carolina Division of Archives and History.

Jefferson Davis: Farewell Address in the U.S. Senate, January 21, 1861. *The Papers of Jefferson Davis*, Volume 7, ed. Lynda Laswell Crist and Mary Seaton Dix (Baton Rouge: Louisiana State University Press, 1992), 18–23. Copyright © 1992 by Louisiana State University Press.

Robert E. Lee to George Washington Custis Lee, January 23, 1861. J. William Jones, *Life and Letters of Robert Edward Lee, Soldier and Man* (New York: Neale Publishing Company, 1906), 120–21.

Jefferson Davis: Inaugural Address, February 18, 1861. *A Compilation* of the *Messages and Papers of the Confederacy, including the diplomatic correspondence, 1861–1865*, Volume I, ed. James D. Richardson (Nashville: United States Publishing Company, 1905), 32–36.

Frederick Douglass: The New President, March 1861. Philip S. Foner, *The Life and Writings of Frederick Douglass*, volume 3 (New York: International Publishers Co. Inc., 1952), 66–67. Reprinted from *The Life and Writings of Frederick Douglass*, published by International Publishers, copyright © 1950.

Abraham Lincoln: First Inaugural Address, March 4, 1861. *The Collected Works of Abraham Lincoln*, Volume IV, ed. Roy P. Basler (New Brunswick, N.J.: Rutgers University Press, 1953), 262–71. Copyright © 1953 by the Abraham Lincoln Association.

Catherine Edmondston: Diary, March 4, 1861. *"Journal of a Secesh Lady": The Diary of Catherine Ann Devereux Edmondston, 1860–1866*, ed. Beth G. Crabtree and James W. Patton (Raleigh: North Carolina Division of Archives and History, 1979), 39–40. Copyright © 1979 by the North Carolina Division of Archives and History.

Alexander H. Stephens: "Corner-Stone" Speech, March 21, 1861. Henry Cleveland, *Alexander H. Stephens in Public and Private* (Philadelphia: National Publishing Company, 1866), 717–29.

Edward Bates: Diary, March 9–April 8, 1861. *The Diary of Edward Bates*, ed. Howard K. Beale (Washington: United States Government Printing Office, 1933), 177–81.

Gideon Welles: Memoir of Events, March 1861. *Diary of Gideon Welles*, volume I (Boston: Houghton Mifflin Company, 1911), 9–14.

William H. Seward: Memorandum for the President, April 1, 1861. *The Collected Works of Abraham Lincoln*, Volume IV, ed. Roy P. Basler (New Brunswick, N.J.: Rutgers University Press, 1953), 317–18. Copyright © 1953 by the Abraham Lincoln Association.

Abraham Lincoln to William H. Seward, April 1, 1861. *The Collected Works of Abraham Lincoln*, Volume IV, ed. Roy P. Basler (New Brunswick, N.J.: Rutgers University Press, 1953), 316–17. Copyright © 1953 by the Abraham Lincoln Association.

Mary Chesnut: Diary, April 7–15, 1861. *Mary Chesnut's Civil War*, ed. C. Vann Woodward (New Haven: Yale University Press, 1981), 42–50. Copyright © 1981 by C. Vann Woodward, Sally Bland Meets, Barbara C. Carpenter, Sally Bland Johnson, and Katherine W. Herbert.

Abner Doubleday: from *Reminiscences of Forts Sumter and Moultrie in 1860–'61*. Abner Doubleday, *Reminiscences of Forts Sumter and Moultrie in 1860–'61* (New York: Harper & Brothers, 1876), 143–46, 154–59, 162–65, 170–73.

George Templeton Strong: Diary, April 13–16, 1861. George Templeton Strong, *Diary of the Civil War, 1860–1865*, ed. Allan Nevins

(New York: The Macmillan Company, 1962), 118–21. Reprinted with permission of Scribner, a Division of Simon & Schuster, Inc., from *The Diary of George Templeton Strong* by Allan Nevins and Milton Halsey Thomas. Copyright © 1952 by Macmillan Publishing Company; copyright renewed © 1980 by Milton Halsey Thomas. All rights reserved.

*The New York Times*: The People and the Issue. *The New York Times*, April 15, 1861.

*Pittsburgh Post*: The War Begun—The Duty of American Citizens. *Pittsburgh Post*, April 15, 1861.

William Howard Russell: from *My Diary North and South. My Diary North and South*, vol. I (London: Bradbury and Evans, 1863), 143–61.

Charles C. Jones Sr. to Charles C. Jones Jr., April 20, 1861. *The Children of Pride: A True Story of Georgia and the Civil War*, Abridged Edition, ed. Robert Manson Myers (New Haven: Yale University Press, 1984), 52–54. Copyright © 1972 by Robert Manson Myers.

John B. Jones: Diary, April 15–22, 1861. J. B. Jones, *A Rebel War Clerk's Diary at the Confederate States Capital*, volume I (Philadelphia: J. B. Lippincott & Co., 1866), 19–26.

John W. Hanson: from *Historical Sketch of the Old Sixth Regiment of Massachusetts Volunteers*. John W. Hanson, *Historical Sketch of the Old Sixth Regiment of Massachusetts Volunteers* (Boston: Lee and Shepard, 1866), 37–42.

Ulysses S. Grant to Frederick Dent, April 19, 1861, and to Jesse Root Grant, April 21, 1861. *The Papers of Ulysses S. Grant*, Volume 2, ed. John Y. Simon (Carbondale and Edwardsville: Southern Illinois University Press, 1969), 3–4, 6–7. Published with the permission of the Ulysses S. Grant Association from *The Papers of Ulysses S. Grant*.

Jefferson Davis: Message to the Confederate Congress, April 29, 1861. *A Compilation of the Messages and Papers of the Confederacy, including the diplomatic correspondence, 1861–1865*, Volume I, ed. James D. Richardson (Nashville: United States Publishing Company, 1905), 63–82.

Frederick Douglass: How to End the War, May 1861. Philip S. Foner, *The Life and Writings of Frederick Douglass*, volume 3 (New York: International Publishers Co. Inc., 1952), 94–96. Reprinted from *The Life and Writings of Frederick Douglass*, published by International Publishers, copyright © 1950.

Walt Whitman: First O Songs for a Prelude. Walt Whitman, *Complete Poetry and Collected Prose*, ed. Justin Kaplan (New York: The Library of America, 1982), 416–18.

Winfield Scott to George B. McClellan, May 3, 1861. *The War of the Rebellion: a Compilation of the Official Records of the Union and*

*Confederate Armies*, series 1, volume LI, part 1 (Washington, D.C.: Government Printing Office, 1897), 369–70.

Charles B. Haydon: Diary, May 3–12, 1861. *For Country, Cause & Leader: The Civil War Journal of Charles B. Haydon*, ed. Stephen W. Sears (New York: Ticknor & Fields, 1993), 3–7. Copyright © 1993 by Stephen W. Sears. Reprinted by permission of Stephen W. Sears.

Ulysses S. Grant to Jesse Root Grant, May 6, 1861. *The Papers of Ulysses S. Grant*, Volume 2, ed. John Y. Simon (Carbondale and Edwardsville: Southern Illinois University Press, 1969), 20–22. Copyright © 1969 by the Ulysses S. Grant Association. Published with the permission of the Ulysses S. Grant Association from *The Papers of Ulysses S. Grant*.

John Hay: Diary, May 7–10, 1861. *Inside Lincoln's White House: The Complete Civil War Diary of John Hay*, ed. Michael Burlingame and John R. Turner Ettlinger (Carbondale and Edwardsville: Southern Illinois University Press, 1997), 19–23. Copyright © 1997 by the Board of Trustees, Southern Illinois University.

Judith W. McGuire: Diary, May 10, 1861. Judith W. McGuire, *Diary of a Southern Refugee, during the war*, 3rd edition (Richmond, Va.: J.W. Randolph & English, Publishers, 1889), 11–15.

William T. Sherman to John Sherman, May 11, 1861. *Sherman's Civil War: Selected Correspondence of William T. Sherman, 1860–1865*, ed. Brooks D. Simpson and Jean V. Berlin (Chapel Hill: The University of North Carolina Press, 1999), 81–82. Copyright © 1999 The University of North Carolina Press.

Benjamin F. Butler to Winfield Scott, May 24, 1861. *The War of the Rebellion: a Compilation of the Official Records of the Union and Confederate Armies*, series 2, volume I (Washington, D.C.: Government Printing Office, 1894), 752.

*The New York Times*: General Butler and the Contraband of War. *The New York Times*, June 2, 1861.

Kate Stone: Journal, May 15–27, 1861. *Brokenburn: The Journal of Kate Stone, 1861–1868*, ed. John Q. Anderson (Baton Rouge: Louisiana State University Press, 1955), 13–19. Copyright © 1989 by the Louisiana State University Press.

George Templeton Strong: Diary, May 29–June 2, 1861. George Templeton Strong, *Diary of the Civil War, 1860–1865*, ed. Allan Nevins (New York: The Macmillan Company, 1962), 150–55. Reprinted with permission of Scribner, a Division of Simon & Schuster, Inc., from *The Diary of George Templeton Strong* by Allan Nevins and Milton Halsey Thomas. Copyright © 1952 by Macmillan Publishing Company; copyright renewed © 1980 by Milton Halsey Thomas. All rights reserved.

John Brown's Body, May 1861. *The Rebellion Record: A Diary of American Events, with documents, narratives, illustrative incidents, poetry etc.*, volume II, ed. Frank Moore (New York: G. P. Putnam, 1862), poetry section, 105–06.

Roger B. Taney: Opinion in *Ex parte Merryman*, June 1, 1861. *The Federal Cases, Comprising Cases Argued and Determined in the Circuit and District Courts of the United States*, Book 17 (St. Paul: West Publishing Company, 1895), 147–53.

Henry A. Wise, Speech at Richmond, June 1, 1861. *The Rebellion Record: A Diary of American Events, with documents, narratives, illustrative incidents, poetry, etc.*, volume I, ed. Frank Moore (New York: G.P. Putnam, 1861), documents section, 323–24.

Charles C. Jones Jr. to Charles C. Jones Sr. and Mary Jones, June 10, 1861. *The Children of Pride: A True Story of Georgia and the Civil War*, ed. Robert Manson Myers (New Haven: Yale University Press, 1972), 694–96. Copyright © 1972 by Robert Manson Myers.

Henry Adams to Charles Francis Adams Jr., June 10–11, 1861. *The Letters of Henry Adams*, volume I, ed. J. C. Levenson, Ernest Samuels, Charles Vandersee, Viola Hopkins Winner (Cambridge: The Belknap Press of Harvard University Press, 1982), 237–40. Copyright © 1982 by the Massachusetts Historical Society. Reprinted courtesy of the Adams Family Papers, Massachusetts Historical Society.

John Ross to Benjamin McCulloch, June 17, 1861. *The War of the Rebellion: a Compilation of the Official Records of the Union and Confederate Armies*, series 1, volume XIII (Washington, D.C.: Government Printing Office, 1885), 495–97.

James Russell Lowell: The Pickens–and–Stealin's Rebellion. *The Atlantic Monthly*, June 1861.

Abraham Lincoln: Message to Congress in Special Session, July 4, 1861. *The Collected Works of Abraham Lincoln*, Volume IV, ed. Roy P. Basler (New Brunswick, N.J.: Rutgers University Press, 1953), 421–41. Copyright © 1953 by the Abraham Lincoln Association.

Kate Stone: Journal, July 4, 1861. *Brokenburn: The Journal of Kate Stone, 1861–1868*, ed. John Q. Anderson (Baton Rouge: Louisiana State University Press, 1955), 13–19. Copyright © 1989 by the Louisiana State University Press.

Ulysses S. Grant: from *Personal Memoirs of U. S. Grant*. Ulysses S. Grant, *Memoirs and Selected Letters*, ed. Mary Drake McFeely and William S. McFeely (New York: The Library of America, 1990), 163–65.

Sallie Brock: from *Richmond During the War*. Sallie Putnam, *Richmond During the War; Four Years of Personal Observation* (New York: G. W. Carleton & Co., 1867), 56–59.

Sullivan Ballou to Sarah Ballou, July 14, 1861. *Brown University in the Civil War. A Memorial*, ed. Henry Sweetser Burrage (Providence, R.I.: Providence Press Company, 1868), 105–08.

Charles Minor Blackford: from *Letters from Lee's Army. Letters from Lee's Army, or Memoirs of Life In and Out of the Army in Virginia During the War Between the States*, compiled by Susan Leigh Blackford, annotated by Charles Minor Blackford, edited and abridged for publication by Charles Minor Blackford III (New York: Charles Scribner's Sons, 1947), 26–36. Reprinted with permission of Scribner, a Division of Simon & Schuster, Inc., from *Letters from Lee's Army*, compiled by Susan L. Blackford. Copyright 1947 by Charles Scribner's Sons. All rights reserved.

William Howard Russell: from *My Diary North and South. My Diary North and South*, vol. II (London: Bradbury and Evans, 1863), 214–49.

Samuel J. English to his Mother, July 24, 1861. *All for the Union: A History of the 2nd Rhode Island Volunteer Infantry in the War of the Great Rebellion*, ed. Robert Hunt Rhodes (Lincoln, R.I.: Andrew Mowbray Inc., 1985), 24–31. Copyright © 1985 by Robert Hunt Rhodes.

Emma Holmes: Diary, July 22–23, 1861. *The Diary of Miss Emma Holmes*, ed. John F. Marszalek (Baton Rouge: Louisiana State University Press, 1979), 65–68. © 1979 by Louisana State University Press.

Elizabeth Blair Lee to Samuel Phillips Lee, July 23, 1861. *Wartime Washington: The Civil War Letters of Elizabeth Blair Lee*, ed. Virginia Jeans Laas (Urbana: University of Illinois Press, 1991), 68–69. Copyright © 1991 by the Board of Trustees of the University of Illinois.

Walt Whitman: from *Specimen Days. Walt Whitman: Complete Poetry and Collected Prose*, ed. Justin Kaplan (New York: The Library of America, 1982), 707–11.

Abraham Lincoln: Memoranda on Military Policy, July 23, 1861. *The Collected Works of Abraham Lincoln*, Volume IV, ed. Roy P. Basler (New Brunswick, N.J.: Rutgers University Press, 1953), 457–58. Copyright © 1953 by the Abraham Lincoln Association.

Mary Chesnut: Diary, July 24, 1861. *Mary Chesnut's Civil War*, ed. C. Vann Woodward (New Haven: Yale University Press, 1981), 108–22. Copyright © 1981 by C. Vann Woodward, Sally Bland Meets, Barbara C. Carpenter, Sally Bland Johnson, and Katherine W. Herbert.

Crittenden-Johnson Resolutions, July 22–25, 1861. *Congressional Globe*, 37th Congress, 1st session, 222, 257.

George B. McClellan to Mary Ellen McClellan, July 27, 1861. *The*

*Civil War Papers of George B. McClellan: Selected Correspondence, 1860–1865*, ed. Stephen W. Sears (New York: Ticknor & Fields, 1989), 70. Copyright © 1989 by Stephen W. Sears. Reprinted by permission of Stephen W. Sears.

William T. Sherman to Ellen Ewing Sherman, July 28, 1861. *Sherman's Civil War: Selected Correspondence of William T. Sherman, 1860–1865*, ed. Brooks D. Simpson and Jean V. Berlin (Chapel Hill: The University of North Carolina Press, 1999), 122–25. Copyright © 1999 The University of North Carolina Press.

Horace Greeley to Abraham Lincoln, July 29, 1861. Abraham Lincoln Papers at the Library of Congress. Transcribed and annotated by the Lincoln Studies Center, Knox College, Galesburg, Illinois.

George B. McClellan: Memorandum for the President, August 2, 1861. *The Civil War Papers of George B. McClellan: Selected Correspondence, 1860–1865*, ed. Stephen W. Sears (New York: Ticknor & Fields, 1989), 71–75. Copyright © 1989 by Stephen W. Sears. Reprinted by permission of Stephen W. Sears.

Confiscation Act, August 6, 1861. *Congressional Globe* Appendix, 37th Congress, 1st session, 42.

George B. McClellan to Mary Ellen McClellan, August 8, 10, and 16, 1861. *The Civil War Papers of George B. McClellan: Selected Correspondence, 1860–1865*, ed. Stephen W. Sears (New York: Ticknor & Fields, 1989), 81–82, 85. Copyright © 1989 by Stephen W. Sears. Reprinted by permission of Stephen W. Sears.

E. F. Ware: from *The Lyon Campaign in Missouri*. E. F. Ware, *The Lyon Campaign in Missouri* (Topeka, Kansas: Crane & Company, 1907), 310–12, 313–26.

W. E. Woodruff: from *With the Light Guns in '61–'65*. W. E. Woodruff, *With the Light Guns in '61–'65* (Little Rock, Ark.: Central Printing Company, 1903), 39–48.

John C. Frémont: Proclamation, August 30, 1861. *The War of the Rebellion: a Compilation of the Official Records of the Union and Confederate Armies*, series 1, volume III (Washington, D.C.: Government Printing Office, 1881), 466–67.

Abraham Lincoln to John C. Frémont, September 2, 1861. *The Collected Works of Abraham Lincoln*, Volume IV, ed. Roy P. Basler (New Brunswick, N.J.: Rutgers University Press, 1953), 506. Copyright © 1953 by the Abraham Lincoln Association.

Frederick Douglass: Fighting Rebels with Only One Hand, September 1861. Philip S. Foner, *The Life and Writings of Frederick Douglass*, volume 3 (New York: International Publishers Co. Inc., 1952), 151–54. Reprinted from *The Life and Writings of Frederick Douglass*, published by International Publishers, copyright © 1950.

Abraham Lincoln to Orville H. Browning, September 22, 1861. *The*

*Collected Works of Abraham Lincoln*, Volume IV, ed. Roy P. Basler (New Brunswick, N.J.: Rutgers University Press, 1953), 531–33. Copyright © 1953 by the Abraham Lincoln Association.

John Ross: Message to the National Council, October 9, 1861. *The War of the Rebellion: a Compilation of the Official Records of the Union and Confederate Armies*, series 1, volume XIII (Washington, D.C.: Government Printing Office, 1881), 500–02.

Henry Livermore Abbott to Josiah Gardner Abbott, October 22, 1861. *Fallen Leaves: The Civil War Letters of Major Henry Livermore Abbott*, ed. Robert Garth Scott (Kent, Ohio: The Kent State University Press, 1991), 60–66.

George B. McClellan to Mary Ellen McClellan, October 25, 26, 30, and 31, 1861. *The Civil War Papers of George B. McClellan: Selected Correspondence, 1860–1865*, ed. Stephen W. Sears (New York: Ticknor & Fields, 1989), 111–14. Copyright © 1989 by Stephen W. Sears. Reprinted by permission of Stephen W. Sears.

Charles Francis Adams Jr. to Henry Adams, November 5, 1861. *A Cycle of Adams Letters, 1861–1865*, ed. Worthington Chauncey Ford (Boston: Houghton Mifflin Company, 1920), 63–64.

George B. McClellan to Samuel L. M. Barlow, November 8, 1861. *The Civil War Papers of George B. McClellan: Selected Correspondence, 1860–1865*, ed. Stephen W. Sears (New York: Ticknor & Fields, 1989), 127–28. Copyright © 1989 by Stephen W. Sears. Reprinted by permission of Stephen W. Sears.

Ulysses S. Grant to Jesse Root Grant, November 8, 1861. *The Papers of Ulysses S. Grant*, Volume 3, ed. John Y. Simon (Carbondale and Edwardsville: Southern Illinois University Press, 1970), 136–38. Copyright © 1970 by the Ulysses S. Grant Association. Published with the permission of the Ulysses S. Grant Association from *The Papers of Ulysses S. Grant*.

Lunsford P. Yandell Jr. to Lunsford Yandell Sr., November 10, 1861. *The Rebellion Record: A Diary of American Events, with documents, narratives, illustrative incidents, poetry, etc.*, volume III, ed. Frank Moore (New York: G. P. Putnam, 1862), document pages 298–99.

Samuel Francis Du Pont to Sophie Du Pont, November 13–15, 1861 Samuel Francis DuPont, *A Selection From His Civil War Letters*, volume 1, ed. John D. Hayes (Ithaca, New York: Cornell University Press, 1969), 235–42. Copyright © 1969 by Eleutherian Mills-Hagley Foundation. Reprinted courtesy of Hagley Museum and Library.

Sam Mitchell: Narrative of the capture of the Sea Islands, November 1861. *The American Slave: A Composite Autobiography*, volume III, ed. George P. Rawick (Westport, Conn.: Greenwood Press, 1972), 202–03.

Henry Tucker: God in the War, November 15, 1861. Electronic text provided by The University of North Carolina at Chapel Hill: http://docsouth.unc.edu/imls/tuckerh/tuckerh.html.

Jefferson Davis: Message to the Confederate Congress, November 18, 1861. *A Compilation of the Messages and Papers of the Confederacy, including the diplomatic correspondence, 1861–1865*, Volume I, ed. James D. Richardson (Nashville: United States Publishing Company, 1905), 136–44.

*Harper's Weekly*: The Great Review. *Harper's Weekly*, December 7, 1861.

Ulysses S. Grant to Jesse Root Grant, November 27, 1861. *The Papers of Ulysses S. Grant*, Volume 3, ed. John Y. Simon (Carbondale and Edwardsville: Southern Illinois University Press, 1970), 226–28. Copyright © 1970 by the Ulysses S. Grant Association. Published with the permission of the Ulysses S. Grant Association from *The Papers of Ulysses S. Grant*.

Sallie Brock: from *Richmond During the War*. Sallie Putnam, *Richmond During the War; Four Years of Personal Observation* (New York: G. W. Carleton & Co., 1867), 78–81.

Benjamin Moran, Journal, November 27–December 3, 1861. *The Journal of Benjamin Moran, 1857–1865*, volume II, ed. Sarah Agnes Wallace and Frances Elma Gillespie (Chicago: The University of Chicago Press, 1949), 912–17. Copyright © 1949 by The University of Chicago.

Henry Adams to Charles Francis Adams Jr., November 30, 1861. *The Letters of Henry Adams*, volume I, ed. J. C. Levenson, Ernest Samuels, Charles Vandersee, Viola Hopkins Winner (Cambridge: The Belknap Press of Harvard University Press, 1982), 263–64. Copyright © 1982 by the Massachusetts Historical Society. Reprinted courtesy of the Adams Family Papers, Massachusetts Historical Society.

Abraham Lincoln, Annual Message to Congress, December 3, 1861. *The Collected Works of Abraham Lincoln*, Volume V, ed. Roy P. Basler (New Brunswick, N.J.: Rutgers University Press, 1953), 35–53. Copyright © 1953 by the Abraham Lincoln Association.

Charles Francis Adams Jr. to Henry Adams, December 10, 1861. *A Cycle of Adams Letters, 1861–1865*, ed. Worthington Chauncey Ford (Boston: Houghton Mifflin Company, 1920), 79–81.

Let My People Go. *American Poetry: The Nineteenth Century*, volume II, ed. John Hollander (New York: The Library of America, 1993), 786–88.

Robert E. Lee to George Washington Custis Lee, December 29, 1861. *The Wartime Papers of Robert E. Lee*, ed. Clifford Dowdey and Louis H. Manarin (Boston: Little, Brown, 1961), 97-99. Reprinted by permission of the National Archives.

Edward Bates: Diary, December 31, 1861. *The Diary of Edward Bates*, ed. Howard K. Beale (Washington: United States Government Printing Office, 1933), 219–20.

Irwin McDowell: Memorandum, January 10–13, 1862. Henry J. Raymond, *The Life and Public Services of Abraham Lincoln, Sixteenth President of the United States* (New York: Derby and Miller, 1865), 772–77.

Montgomery C. Meigs, Memoir of Meetings with President Lincoln, January 10–13, 1862. "General M. C. Meigs on the Conduct of the Civil War," *The American Historical Review*, vol. 26, no. 2 (January 1921), 292–93.

Edwin M. Stanton to Charles A. Dana, January 24, 1862. Charles A. Dana, *Recollections of the Civil War* (New York: D. Appleton and Company, 1899), 4–5.

This volume presents the texts of the printings chosen as sources here but does not attempt to reproduce features of their typographic design. The texts are printed without alteration except for the changes previously discussed and for the correction of typographical errors. All ellipses in the texts appeared in the printings chosen as sources. Spelling, punctuation, and capitalization are often expressive features, and they are not altered, even when inconsistent or irregular. The following is a list of typographical errors corrected, cited by page and line number: 2.3, unitedin; 24.32, 1703,; 39.3, "irrespresible; 48.30, of of; 49.24, 1880.; 61.8, odious.; 75.3, them directly; 86.26, truthfulnes,; 90.39–91.1, Massachussetts,; 93.37–38, non-slave. holder,; 99.14, imininent; 100.20, ballance; 107.25, retalitory; 107.30, staute; 108.3, nullifing; 166.27, subtantially; 232.11, become; 275.13, New York, City; 276.11, soveign; 279.19, citizens.; 280.19, direlect; 293.32, Rhelt.; 364.15, Balliwick; 372.21, penitenitary;; 387.16, General, George; 470.15, commssiariat; 474.21, from he; 476.31, inrceased; 477.10, could.; 479.37, theere; 484.5, and and; 531.29, you; 558.6, considerable..; 559.10, couragous; 605.10–11, to bow,; 606.30, when be; 607.30, villanies."; 608.39, ray bed; 608.39, there!; 611.2, Alt that; 616.27, —Woe; 617.37, proceedure; 618.20, he;; 619.33, —God; 621.3, two; 625.15, lond; 625.40, call be; 633.3, gentleman; 641.15, comfortaple; 642.13, have have.

# Notes

In the notes below, the reference numbers denote page and line of this volume (the line count includes headings, but not rule lines). No note is made for material included in the eleventh edition of *Merriam-Webster's Collegiate Dictionary*. Biblical references are keyed to the King James Version. Quotations from Shakespeare are keyed to *The Riverside Shakespeare*, ed. G. Blakemore Evans (Boston: Houghton, Mifflin, 1974). Footnotes and bracketed editorial notes within the text were in the originals. For further historical and biographical background, references to other studies, and more detailed maps, see James McPherson, *Battle Cry of Freedom: The Civil War Era* (New York: Oxford University Press, 1988); *Encyclopedia of the American Civil War: A Political, Social, and Military History*, edited by David S. Heidler and Jeanne T. Heidler (New York: W. W. Norton, 2002); and Aaron Sheehan-Dean, *Concise Historical Atlas of the U.S. Civil War* (New York: Oxford University Press, 2008).

2.33      Abolitionist colored man]    In a speech given at Charleston on July 9, 1860, Robert Barnwell Rhett, the secessionist publisher of the *Mercury*, alleged that Maine Senator Hannibal Hamlin (1809–1891), the Republican candidate for vice president, was a mulatto. His claim was repeated by Southern newspapers and orators during the campaign, although there was no evidence to support it.

4.16–17      Force Bill]    A South Carolina state convention passed a nullification ordinance on November 24, 1832, prohibiting the collection of the federal tariffs authorized in 1828 and 1832 and threatening secession if the federal government responded with force. At the urging of President Andrew Jackson, Congress passed a Force Bill, signed by Jackson on March 2, 1833, authorizing the president to use the military to enforce federal revenue laws; at the same time, Congress also passed a compromise tariff law lowering rates. The South Carolina convention met on March 11 and rescinded the nullification ordinance, ending the crisis.

5.14      SANFORD]    Henry Sanford (1823–1891) was a secretary in the American legation in Paris, 1849–54, then began representing American business interests in Central and South America. He served as the U.S. minister to Belgium, 1861–69, and later founded the town of Sanford in Florida.

5.33      irrepressible conflict]    In a speech delivered at Rochester, New York, on October 25, 1858, Senator William H. Seward described the "collision" between slavery and free labor as "an irrepressible conflict" that would result in the United States becoming "either entirely a slaveholding nation, or entirely a free-labor nation."

6.7     statement about Seward last year."] The New York Democratic Vigilant Association, a group of wealthy businessmen also known as the Fifth Avenue Hotel Committee, issued an address on October 27, 1859, denouncing John Brown's recent raid on the federal arsenal at Harpers Ferry, Virginia. Signed by thirty-one members of the Association's executive committee, the address quoted extensively from Seward's "irrepressible conflict" speech, asserting that "John Brown has only practiced what William H. Seward preaches," and accusing "republican Senators" of concealing knowledge of Brown's plans from the authorities.

8.27–29     Dogberry . . . must ride behind."] Cf. *Much Ado About Nothing*, III.v.36–37.

9.21–22     John Quincy Adams . . . dissolution of the Union.] As part of his campaign to overturn the rule forbidding the House of Representatives from considering antislavery petitions, congressman and former president John Quincy Adams (1767–1848) presented a petition on January 25, 1842, signed by forty-six residents of Haverhill, Massachusetts, seeking the peaceful dissolution of the Union because of a sectional imbalance in political power. Thomas Marshall (1801–1864), a Kentucky Whig, introduced a resolution censuring Adams for propositioning the House to commit perjury and high treason. After prolonged debate, the motion was defeated 106–93 on February 7, 1842.

16.21     acts nullifying the fugitive slave law] In response to the Fugitive Slave Act of 1850, Ohio, Michigan, Wisconsin, and the New England states passed personal liberty laws guaranteeing various due process protections to persons accused of being escaped slaves.

16.29–30     Northern courts, . . . unconstitutional] In 1854 the Supreme Court of Wisconsin ruled the Fugitive Slave Act of 1850 unconstitutional. Its decision was overturned by the U.S. Supreme Court in *Ableman v. Booth* (1859).

17.3–9     a Northern man . . . Governor of the State] William Dennison (1815–1882), the Republican governor of Ohio from 1860 to 1862, refused to extradite a man named Kennedy who had been indicted for taking slaves from Tennessee and selling them in Virginia.

17.18–19     to shield several . . . John Brown raid.] Seven of the twenty-one men who accompanied John Brown in his raid on Harpers Ferry, October 16–18, 1859, were able to flee the scene. Two of them were captured in Pennsylvania and extradited to Virginia, where they were tried and hanged, while the remaining five were able to escape arrest. When Virginia governor John Letcher sought the extradition of Barclay Coppoc from Iowa in January 1860, Governor Samuel Kirkwood, a Republican, rejected the request as improperly made out. Kirkwood accepted a second set of extradition papers in February, by which time Coppoc had gone into hiding. Letcher also sought the extradition of Owen Brown and Francis Merriam from Ohio, but Governor William Dennison rejected the request on the grounds that there was no proof that Brown and Merriam had fled from Virginia. In April 1860 federal authorities arrested Franklin B. Sanborn, one of the radical abolitionists who had financially supported Brown, for refusing to appear before the Senate committee investigating the Harpers Ferry raid. Sanborn was released on a state writ of habeas corpus, and the warrant for his arrest was rejected by the Massachusetts supreme judicial court as technically invalid.

17.29    most learned disciples of this party] Congregational minister Henry Ward Beecher (1813–1887), in a speech given at North Church, New Haven, Connecticut, on March 16, 1856. Beecher spoke at a meeting held to raise funds for the purchase of Sharps rifles for free-state settlers in Kansas.

17.37–39    honored senators . . . that party] John P. Hale (1806–1873) served in Congress as a Democrat from New Hampshire, 1843–45, and in the Senate as a Free-Soiler, 1847–53, and as a Republican, 1855–65. He spoke on June 17, 1856, at the Republican national convention that nominated John C. Frémont for president.

20.24    General Braddock] Major General Edward Braddock (1695–1755), the commander of British forces in North America, was fatally wounded on July 9, 1755, when his force was ambushed by the French and Indians near the Monongahela River in western Pennsylvania.

20.29    Newcastle] Thomas Pelham-Holles (1693–1768), Duke of Newcastle, was prime minister of Great Britain, 1754–56 and 1757–62.

23.17    abolished slavery in the West Indies] The Abolition Act, passed by Parliament in 1833, resulted in the emancipation of all slaves in the British West Indies in 1838.

24.26–27    In 1848 the Abolitionist . . . the Presidency] In 1848 former president Martin Van Buren (1782–1862) ran on the Free Soil Party ticket.

24.28–29    in 1852, . . . that party] New Hampshire senator John P. Hale headed the Free Soil ticket in 1852.

24.31–33    act of Massachusetts, . . . until 1855] The Massachusetts legislature passed a personal liberty law in 1843 prohibiting the participation of state officials and the use of state courtrooms and jails in the rendition of fugitive slaves. (Similar laws were adopted during the 1840s in Vermont, Connecticut, New Hampshire, Rhode Island, and Pennsylvania.) The personal liberty law passed in Massachusetts in 1855 authorized state judges to issue writs of habeas corpus in fugitive slave cases, releasing prisoners from federal custody and allowing their cases to be heard in state court, where they would be guaranteed the right to counsel and to trial by jury.

26.31–32 a fugitive is standing protected by a Northern mob] Possibly a reference to Eliza Grayson, a fugitive slave from Nebraska Territory who was arrested by a deputy U.S. marshal in Chicago on November 12, 1860. When a group of African Americans confronted the marshal, he turned Grayson over to the city police, who detained her in the city armory as the crowd outside vowed to prevent her removal from the city. The next morning Calvin DeWolf, an antislavery justice of the peace, issued a warrant charging her with breach of the peace. Grayson was then freed by the crowd and taken to safety while she was being brought to DeWolf's office by a deputy sheriff.

27.36 "Wide Awakes"] The Wide-Awake marching clubs, first organized by the Republicans during the 1856 campaign and revived in 1860, staged mass torchlight parades and other events in support of Lincoln's election.

34.30 first Congress passed the Bill of Rights] The Declaration and Resolves adopted by the First Continental Congress on October 14, 1774.

34.31–32 Bill of Rights . . . Charles the First] The Petition of Right adopted by Parliament in 1628.

38.8–9 candidates . . . Texas was declared] The Southern Democratic ticket of John C. Breckinridge for president and Joseph Lane for vice president.

40.29 the higher law principle] In a speech in the Senate on March 11, 1850, William H. Seward argued that the Constitution permitted the prohibition of slavery in the federal territories and that slavery was unjust under "a higher law than the Constitution."

41.24–25 In reply to Mr. Seward, . . . these words] Houston quotes from a speech he gave on April 20, 1858, advocating establishing an American protectorate over Mexico. In a speech in the Senate on March 3, 1858, opposing the admission of Kansas as a slave state, Seward had described the annexation of Texas as "a bold measure, of doubtful constitutionality, distinctly adopted as an act of intervention in favor of slave labor," and went on to say that the nation "has advanced another stage; it has reached the point where intervention by the Government for slavery and slave labor will no longer be tolerated. Free labor has at last apprehended its rights, its interests, its power, and its destiny; and is organizing itself to assume the government of the Republic."

43.11–12 First Board . . . the Second.] The First Board was the morning trading session, held between 10:30 A.M. and noon, and the Second Board was the afternoon session, held between 2:30 and 3:00 P.M.

43.31 mere nullities] Under the fugitive slave act of 1850, rendition cases were heard and decided by federal commissioners, not in state courts.

44.30–31 John C. Green] John C. Green (1800–1875), a New York merchant, railroad financier, and philanthropist.

45.8    Mr. Ruggles's friend, Senator Dixon]    Samuel B. Ruggles (1800–1881), a lawyer and real estate developer, created Gramercy Park in 1831 and later served as a Whig member of the New York assembly, 1838–39, and as a state canal commissioner. Strong had married his daughter Ellen in 1848. James Dixon (1814–1873) was a Whig congressman from Connecticut, 1845–49, and a Republican senator, 1857–69.

45.13    Tom Corwin]    Thomas Corwin (1794–1865) of Ohio was a Whig congressman, 1831–40, governor of Ohio, 1840–42, a U.S. senator, 1845–50, and secretary of the treasury, 1850–53. He served in Congress as a Republican, 1859–61, and was U.S. minister to Mexico, 1861–64. In December 1860 he became chairman of the House Committee of Thirty-Three that considered proposals for sectional compromise.

46.4    Willy Cutting]    William Cutting (1832–1897) was a New York lawyer who later became a major in the Union army and served as an aide-de-camp to Major General Ambrose Burnside.

46.21    the right of petition, and the Giddings business]    In response to an increasing number of petitions calling for the abolition of slavery in Washington, D.C., the House of Representatives adopted a rule on May 26, 1836, requiring that all petitions regarding slavery be tabled without being read or printed. After a prolonged struggle over the right to petition, the rule was revoked on December 3, 1844. Joshua R. Giddings (1795–1864) of Ohio was an antislavery Whig, and later Republican, who served in congress from 1838 to 1859. On March 21, 1842, he introduced nine resolutions in the House regarding the *Creole*, an American brig carrying slaves from Virginia to New Orleans that was seized by slave mutineers in November 1841 and taken to Nassau in the Bahamas, where British authorities freed the slaves who had not participated in the revolt (the mutineers were released in April 1842). Drafted by the abolitionist Theodore Weld, the resolutions declared that the slaves onboard the *Creole* had "violated no law of the United States, incurred no legal penalty, and are justly liable to no punishment" for "resuming their natural rights of personal liberty," and that attempts to reenslave them would be "unauthorized by the Constitution" and "incompatible with our national honor." The next day the House voted 125–69 to censure Giddings. He immediately resigned his seat and was returned to the House after winning a special election, 7,469–393.

46.22–23    the admission of California]    In a special message to Congress in January 1850 President Zachary Taylor recommended the immediate admission of California as a free state. His proposal aroused intense Southern opposition both in and out of Congress, including threats of disunion. In September 1850 Congress passed several separate acts that later became known as "the compromise of 1850." The legislation admitted California into the Union as a free state, organized territorial governments for New Mexico and Utah without a congressional prohibition of slavery in those territories, settled the Texas–New Mexico boundary dispute, assumed $10 million of the debt of the Texas republic, abolished the slave trade in the District of Columbia, and replaced the 1793 fugitive slave act with a stronger law.

46.31–32    S. A. Douglas . . . the Missouri Compromise.] In 1819 northern opposition prevented the admission of Missouri as a slave state. The following year Congress passed legislation admitting Missouri as a slave state and Maine as a free state while excluding slavery from the remainder of the Louisiana Purchase territory north of 36° 30′ latitude. In 1854 Democratic senator Stephen A. Douglas of Illinois secured passage of the Kansas-Nebraska Act, which repealed the Missouri Compromise line and allowed the question of whether slavery would be permitted in the newly-organized territories to be decided by their legislatures.

46.33    effort to force slavery on Kansas] In November 1857 a convention held at Lecompton in Kansas Territory approved a proslavery constitution, and in December it was approved in a referendum boycotted by free-state settlers, in which voters were denied the choice of rejecting the document outright. President James Buchanan asked Congress in February 1858 to approve the constitution and admit Kansas as a slave state. Despite the opposition of Senator Stephen A. Douglas, who denounced the Lecompton constitution as a violation of the principle of popular sovereignty, the admission of Kansas was approved by the Senate, 33–25, but was rejected by the House, 120–112. Both the House and the Senate then approved a bill resubmitting the Lecompton constitution under the guise of a land-grant referendum, and on August 2, 1858, it was rejected by the voters of Kansas, 11,300–1,788.

46.35–36    brutal beating . . . Sumner] In his antislavery speech, "The Crime Against Kansas," delivered in the Senate May 19–20, 1856, Charles Sumner (1811–1874) of Massachusetts described Senator Andrew Butler of South Carolina as having chosen "the harlot, Slavery" as his "mistress." On May 22 South Carolina congressman Preston Brooks (1819–1857), a cousin of Senator Butler, approached Sumner as he sat at his desk in the Senate chamber, accused him of libeling South Carolina and Butler, and beat him unconscious with a cane. After a measure to expel him from the House failed to win the necessary two-thirds majority, Brooks resigned his seat and was reelected by his district. Sumner did not return regularly to the Senate until December 1859.

46.37    the project to revive the slave trade] During the 1850s several prominent Southern proslavery advocates, including William Yancey, J.D.B. DeBow, and Leonidas Spratt, began calling for the reopening of the African slave trade, in part as a way of making slaveholding more affordable for Southern farmers. Their proposal failed to win the support of most Southerners, who opposed reopening the trade on moral, political, and economic grounds. (Many slaveholders in the Upper South profited from selling slaves to the cotton states and did not wish to see the price of slaves decline.)

50.1–2    General JACKSON's Message of 1833] President Andrew Jackson submitted a message to Congress on January 16, 1833, requesting the passage of a Force Bill in response to the South Carolina nullification ordinance of November 24, 1832; see note 4.16–17.

50.18–19    Cuba, . . . *two hundred millions*]    In 1854 the Pierce administration authorized the U.S. minister to Spain to offer as much as $130 million for the purchase of Cuba. Although Spain rejected the bid, proslavery expansionists continued to advocate the acquisition of the island.

53.7–8    "Except ye abide in the ship, ye cannot be saved."]    Acts 27:31.

53.32–33    Dr. PIERCE]    Lovick Pierce (1785–1879), a Methodist minister from Georgia.

55.31    message to Congress, January 7, 1833]    The message was sent on January 16, 1833.

58.10    Lord Mansfield]    William Murray, Lord Mansfield (1705–1793), was Lord Chief Justice of the King's Bench, 1756–88. In December 1771 he issued a writ of habeas corpus for James Somerset, a slave brought to England from North America in 1769 who had run away, been recaptured, and was about to be sent by his owner to Jamaica for sale. After hearing several pleadings, Lord Mansfield ruled on June 22, 1772, that slavery could exist only when supported by positive law, and that because no positive law in England authorized the forcible removal of slaves, Somerset should be set free.

58.12    Brougham denounced as the "wild and guilty fantasy"]    A leading British abolitionist, Henry Brougham (1778–1868) spoke in a debate in the House of Commons on July 13, 1830, of "the law written by the finger of God on the heart of man; and by that law, unchangeable and eternal, while men despise fraud, and loathe rapine, and abhor blood, they shall reject with indignation the wild and guilty fantasy that man can hold property in man." Brougham later served as Lord Chancellor, 1830–34, and was a member of the government, headed by Earl Grey, that passed an act in 1833 abolishing slavery in the West Indies.

59.35–36    The South . . . a Sardinia.]    At the beginning of 1860 Sicily and Naples were ruled by an absolutist branch of the Bourbon dynasty, while Sardinia and Piedmont were ruled by the more liberal House of Savoy. In May 1860 Giuseppe Garibaldi (1807–1882) landed in Sicily and led a campaign that succeeded in overthrowing Bourbon rule, and in October a plebiscite approved the union of Sicily with Sardinia-Piedmont.

60.4–5    consummation . . . to be wished."]    Cf. *Hamlet*, III.i.62–63.

60.30–31    reviving fires . . . slave trade]    In November 1858 the schooner *Wanderer* illegally landed about 400 slaves on the Georgia coast. After the ship was seized by federal authorities, press reports and rumors circulated of other attempts to smuggle slaves into the South.

61.38–39    Benj. Lundy and Wm. Lloyd Garrison]    Benjamin Lundy

(1789–1839) was a Quaker abolitionist who published and edited the *Genius of Universal Emancipation*, 1821–35, and the *National Enquirer and Constitutional Advocate of Universal Liberty*, 1836–38. An advocate of gradual emancipation, Lundy supported efforts to colonize free blacks outside the United States. William Lloyd Garrison (1805–1879) met Lundy in 1828 and was the co-editor of *The Genius of Universal Emancipation*, 1829–30. An advocate of immediate abolition who opposed colonization, Garrison edited *The Liberator*, 1831–65. He helped found the American Anti-Slavery Society in 1833 and served as its president, 1843–65.

62.6　Fusion party] In the 1860 presidential election supporters of Stephen A. Douglas (Northern Democratic), John C. Breckinridge (Southern Democratic), and John Bell (Constitutional Union) combined to run anti-Lincoln fusion tickets in New York, New Jersey, and Rhode Island; there was also a Douglas-Breckinridge ticket in Pennsylvania and a Douglas-Bell ticket in Texas.

63.2–3　*Thomas Ewing Sr. . . . John Sherman*] Thomas Ewing (1789–1871) served as a senator from Ohio, 1831–37 and 1850–51, as secretary of the treasury, 1841, and as secretary of the interior, 1849–50. William T. Sherman had married Ellen Ewing, his eldest daughter, in 1850. John Sherman (1823–1900) served as a Republican congressman from Ohio, 1855–61, as a senator, 1861–77 and 1881–97, as secretary of the treasury, 1877–81, and as secretary of state, 1897–98.

65.3　Clay] Sherman's horse, who was ill with glanders. He did not recover, and in early January 1861 Sherman had him shot.

68.39–40　In 1835 . . . inflammatory appeals] In 1835 the American Anti-Slavery Society began mailing thousands of abolitionist pamphlets to prominent Southerners. At the direction of Postmaster General Amos Kendall, Southern postmasters stopped delivering antislavery materials.

69.3–4　"to stimulate them . . . servile war."] From President Jackson's annual message to Congress, December 7, 1835, in which Jackson asked Congress to pass a law prohibiting the circulation through the mail of "incendiary" antislavery publications. The post office bill eventually passed by Congress in 1836 did not include a ban on antislavery mailings.

69.37–38　"a deliberate, . . . exercise"] From the Virginia resolutions, drafted by James Madison and adopted by the Virginia assembly on December 24, 1798. The resolutions condemned the Alien and Sedition Acts as unconstitutional and called upon the states to resist them.

70.28　"sufficient unto the day is the evil thereof."] Matthew 6:34.

70.36–37　the Supreme Court, . . . decided] In *Dred Scott v. Sandford* (1857).

72.10　a State court in Wisconsin] See note 16.29–30.

74.34–75.5    It was formed . . . committed to it.]  From a public letter written by James Madison to Edward Everett on August 28, 1830, and published in the October 1830 *North American Review*.

78.33    *posse comitatus*]  Literally, "power of the county"; a group of citizens summoned by a sheriff or federal marshal to keep the peace and enforce the law.

83.5    Mr. Madison's . . . in 1799]  In December 1799 James Madison began writing an extensive report on the response by other states to the Virginia resolutions of 1798. The report was adopted by the Virginia house of delegates on January 7, 1800.

85.27    Sydneys, Hampdens]  Algernon Sydney (1622–1683) was an English republican and opponent of Charles II who was executed for allegedly plotting his assassination. John Hampden (1594–1643) was a leader of the parliamentary opposition to Charles I. He was killed in battle during the English Civil War.

86.1    Senator Cass]  Lewis Cass (1782–1866) was a Democratic senator from Michigan, 1845–48 and 1849–57, and the Democratic presidential nominee in 1848. He served as secretary of state, 1857–60.

90.28–29    Senator Johnson, of Tennessee]  See Biographical Notes.

92.9    Owenites, Fourierites]  Followers of the British social reformer Robert Owen (1771–1858) and the French social theorist Charles Fourier (1772–1837). Several Owenite and Fourierist communal settlements were established in the northern United States in the early nineteenth century.

92.10    Millerites]  Followers of the American preacher William Miller (1782–1849) who had predicted that Christ would return to earth between March 1843 and March 1844.

94.8    the McDuffies, Langdon Cheves]  George McDuffie (1790–1851) served as a congressman from South Carolina, 1821–34, as governor, 1834–36, and as a senator, 1842–46. Langdon Cheves (1776–1857) was a congressman from South Carolina, 1810–15, and served as Speaker of the House, 1814–15.

94.9–11    Rusks, . . . Maunsel Whites]  Thomas J. Rusk (1803–1857) was a Democratic senator from Texas, 1846–57; James Henry Hammond (1807–1864) was governor of South Carolina, 1842–44, and a Democratic senator, 1857–60; William Lowndes Yancey (1814–1863) was a Democratic congressman from Alabama, 1844–46, and a prominent advocate of secession during the 1850s; James L. Orr (1822–1873) was a Democratic congressman from South Carolina, 1849–59, who served as Speaker of the House, 1857–59; Christopher G. Memminger (1803–1888) was a state legislator from South Carolina who later served as the Confederate secretary of the treasury, 1861–64; Judah P. Benjamin (1811–1884) was a Whig, and later Democratic, senator from Louisiana, 1853–61, and later served as the Confederate secretary of state,

1862–65; for Alexander H. Stephens, see Biographical Notes; Pierre Soulé (1801–1870) was a Democratic senator from Louisiana, 1849–53, and U.S. minister to Spain, 1853–55; Albert G. Brown (1813–1880) served as a Democratic congressman from Mississippi, 1839–41 and 1847–53, as governor, 1844–48, and as a senator, 1854–61; William E. Simms (1822–1898) was a Democratic congressman from Kentucky, 1859–61, who later served in the Confederate Senate, 1862–65; William D. Porter (1810–1883) was a South Carolina state senator, 1848–64, served as president of the state senate, 1858–64, and was also the president of the secessionist 1860 Association; Andrew G. Magrath (1813–1893) was U.S. district judge for South Carolina, 1856–60, and later served as governor, 1864–65; William Aiken (1806–1887) was governor of South Carolina, 1844–46, and a Democratic congressman, 1851–57; Maunsel White (1783–1863) was a Louisiana merchant and plantation owner who served in the state senate.

96.34    Mr. Kettell, of New York] Thomas Prentice Kettell (b. 1811), an editor of the *Democratic Review, United States Economist,* and *Hunt's Merchants' Magazine,* published *Southern Wealth and Northern Profits* in 1860.

101.10–11    4,500,000 slaves in the Southern States.] The 1860 census recorded 3,949,557 slaves living in the fifteen slave states.

107.24    my late message . . . Assembly] Brown sent a special message to the legislature on November 7, 1860.

109.3    *John A. Gilmer*] Gilmer (1805–1868) was an American (Know-Nothing) congressman from North Carolina, 1857–61. An opponent of secession in 1860–61, he later served in the Confederate Congress, 1864–65.

111.29–30    "madly shooting from its sphere,"] Cf. *A Midsummer Night's Dream,* II.i.106.

115.25    the Senator from Texas] Louis T. Wigfall (1816–1874) was a South Carolina native who moved to Texas in 1846. He served in the Texas house of representatives, 1850–57, in the Texas senate, 1857–59, in the U.S. Senate, 1859–61, and in the Confederate Senate, 1862–1865.

115.26    the Senator from Georgia] Alfred Iverson Sr. (1798–1873) was a Democratic congressman from Georgia, 1847–49, and a senator, 1855–61.

117.16–17    a Senator . . . a resolution] Lazarus W. Powell (1812–1867) was the Democratic governor of Kentucky, 1851–55, and a senator, 1859–65.

120.23    Senator from Mississippi] Albert G. Brown; see note 94.9–11.

121.28–29    Mr. Webster . . . Mr. Hayne] Robert Hayne (1791–1839) was a senator from South Carolina, 1823–32. In a speech delivered in the Senate on January 19, 1830, Hayne attacked federal land and tariff policies as an attempt by the eastern states to dominate the South and West and called for federal lands to be distributed to the states. Massachusetts Senator Daniel

Webster replied on January 20, defending federal land policies and praising the prohibition of slavery contained in the Northwest Ordinance of 1787. Hayne then responded with a lengthy speech, delivered on January 21 and 25, in which he defended slavery. On January 26–27 Webster gave his second reply to Hayne, which concluded with the phrase "Liberty *and* Union, now and for ever, one and inseparable!" More than 40,000 pamphlet copies of the "Second Reply" were printed within three months of its issue.

121.37     resolutions of 1798–99]   The Virginia resolutions of 1798, drafted by James Madison (see note 69.37–38), and the resolutions protesting the Alien and Sedition Acts, drafted by Thomas Jefferson, that were adopted by the Kentucky legislature on November 10, 1798, and November 14, 1799.

122.12     letter to Governor Hamilton]   Dated August 28, 1832, Calhoun's public letter was addressed to James Hamilton Jr. (1786–1857), governor of South Carolina, 1830–32.

124.13–14     Faneuil Hall.]   A public meeting place in Boston, Massachusetts.

126.10–11     Mr. DOUGLASS . . . Mr. PUGH]   Stephen A. Douglas (1813–1861) was a Democratic congressman from Illinois, 1843–47, and a senator, 1847–61. George Pugh (1822–1876) was a Democratic senator from Ohio, 1855–61.

129.10–11     the Missouri compromise]   See note 46.31–32.

130.35     *posse comitatus*]   See note 78.33

139.21     Mr. FITZPATRICK]   Benjamin Fitzpatrick (1802–1869) was the Democratic governor of Alabama, 1841–45, and a senator, 1848–49, 1853–55, and 1855–61.

139.25     Mr. GREEN]   James Green (1817–1870) was a Democratic congressman from Missouri, 1847–51, and a senator, 1857–61.

144.16     Reuben Davis of Miss.]   Reuben Davis (1813–1890) was a Democratic congressman from Mississippi, 1857–61. He withdrew from Congress in January 1861 and later served as a brigadier general in the Confederate army.

144.29     when Webster was pulled down]   In a Senate speech delivered on March 7, 1850, Daniel Webster endorsed a series of compromise measures regarding slavery introduced by Henry Clay, including the passage of a new fugitive slave law. His position was denounced by many antislavery Whigs in Massachusetts, who accused him of betraying his earlier antislavery principles. After Webster resigned from the Senate on July 22, 1850, to become secretary of state under Millard Fillmore, a Free Soil-Democratic coalition succeeded in electing Charles Sumner, an antislavery Whig, to his seat in April 1851.

144.33–34     Rice . . . Thayer]   Alexander H. Rice (1818–1895) was mayor of Boston, 1856–57, and a Republican congressman from Massachusetts,

1859–67. Eli Thayer (1819–1899) was a Republican congressman from Massachusetts, 1857–61.

144.36–37    John Adams . . . Dickinson.]  In 1775–76 John Adams was a leading advocate of American independence in the Second Continental Congress, while John Dickinson (1732–1808) of Pennsylvania opposed declaring independence and sought reconciliation with Great Britain.

145.4    Mr. Appleton and Mr. Amory]  William Appleton (1786–1862) was a Whig congressman from Massachusetts, 1851–55, who won election to the House of Representatives in 1860 as a Constitutional Unionist. William Amory (1804–1888) was a cotton manufacturer from Boston.

145.8    Mason]  James Mason (1798–1871) was a Democratic congressman from Virginia, 1837–39, and a senator, 1847–61. He later served as Confederate envoy to Great Britain and France, 1861–1865

145.15    Boston Courier and Caleb Cushing]  The Boston *Courier* was a conservative newspaper hostile to Sumner. Caleb Cushing (1800–1879) was a Whig congressman from Massachusetts, 1835–43, who became a Democrat and served as attorney general under Franklin Pierce, 1853–57. Cushing supported John C. Breckinridge in the 1860 election, but became a Republican during the Civil War.

145.21–22    Mr Etheridge . . . Anthony]  Emerson Etheridge (1819–1902) was a Whig, and then an American (Know-Nothing) congressman from Tennessee, 1853–57 and 1859–61. He remained loyal to the Union and served as the clerk of the House of Representatives, 1861–63. Henry B. Anthony (1815–1884) was the Whig governor of Rhode Island, 1849–51, and a Republican senator, 1859–84.

145.27    examples of Wellington and Peale]  Arthur Wellesley, Duke of Wellington (1769–1852) was the prime minister of a Tory government, 1828–30, in which Sir Robert Peel (1788–1850) served as home secretary and leader of the House of Commons. In 1829 Wellington and Peel secured the passage of an act allowing Catholics to sit in Parliament and hold public office, believing it was necessary to avoid civil strife in Ireland. The measure was opposed by many in their own party.

145.31–32    Pugh's speech]  Ohio Democrat George E. Pugh (1822–1876) had addressed the Senate on December 20, 1860, urging the adoption of the Crittenden compromise proposals and criticizing Republicans for their opposition to slavery.

145.37    Winter Davis]  Henry Winter Davis (1817–1865) was an American (Know Nothing) congressman from Maryland, 1855–61. He later won election as an Unconditional Unionist and served from 1863 to 1865.

146.5    Hale]  Charles Hale (1831–1882) was the editor and owner of the Boston *Daily Advertiser*. Henry Adams wrote seventeen unsigned letters from Washington, dated December 7, 1860–February 11, 1861, which were published in the *Daily Advertiser*.

146.23    Johnson's speech yesterday] In his speech in the Senate on December 19, 1860, Andrew Johnson of Tennessee called for the preservation of the Union, denounced secession as unconstitutional, and said that the federal government had the power to enforce the laws within states attempting to secede.

146.27    Alley] John B. Alley (1817–1896) was a Republican congressman from Massachusetts, 1859–67.

147.29    Washburne] Elihu Washburne (1816–1887) was a Whig, and then Republican, congressman from Illinois, 1853–69. He served as U.S. minister to France, 1869–77.

147.30    Gen. Scott] Winfield Scott (1786–1866) was general-in-chief of the U.S. Army from 1841 until his retirement on November 1, 1861.

148.5    Wm H Herndon] Herndon (1818–1891) had been Lincoln's law partner in Springfield since 1844.

151.25–26    two of the States . . . into operation] A quorum was achieved by both houses of the First Federal Congress on April 6, 1789, and George Washington was inaugurated on April 30. The Constitution was ratified by North Carolina on November 21, 1789, and by Rhode Island on May 29, 1790.

153.18–20    States of Ohio . . . State of Virginia.] See note 17.18–19.

154.21–22    "Government . . . half slave, half free,"] A paraphrase of a passage from the "House Divided" speech given by Abraham Lincoln at Springfield, Illinois, on June 16, 1858.

154.27–28    citizenship, persons, . . . becoming citizens] The Supreme Court had ruled in *Dred Scott v. Sandford* (1857) that free blacks were not citizens of the United States.

157.10    Anderson] Major Robert Anderson (1805–1871), a native of Kentucky, graduated from West Point in 1825 and was commissioned as an artillery officer. He was appointed brigadier general in May 1861 and commanded Union troops in Kentucky until early October 1861, when he resigned because of failing health. Anderson retired from the army in 1863.

157.13–14    Seminole Indians . . . Molino del Rey] Anderson served in Florida, 1837–38, during the Second Seminole War (1835–42). The Battle of Molino del Rey, fought outside of Mexico City on September 8, 1847, ended in an American victory.

158.25    Yancey] See note 94.9–11.

160.36    columbiads] Large cannons used for coastal defense.

165.2    *Beriah Magoffin*]    Magoffin (1815–1885) was the Democratic governor of Kentucky, 1859–62.

169.34    abolition incendiary . . . Texas]    On July 8, 1860, fires in north Texas destroyed much of the downtown areas of Dallas and Denton as well as a store in Pilot Point. Although the fires were initially attributed to the spontaneous combustion of volatile phosphorus matches during a period of exceptionally hot weather, on July 12 Charles A. Pryor, the editor of the *Dallas Herald*, wrote the first in a series of letters claiming that they were part of an abolitionist plot to stage a slave insurrection in Texas. Alarmed by reports of further fires and the alleged discovery of stockpiles of poison, vigilance committees were formed throughout northern and eastern Texas, and by September 1860 at least ten whites and twenty blacks were hanged without trial because of their suspected involvement in the purported conspiracy.

169.38–39    "Alarm to their sleep, . . . their food."]    In his message to the Virginia general assembly on December 5, 1859, Governor Henry A. Wise asserted that this was the "motto" of "secret societies for mischief" formed by the abolitionists responsible for the underground railroad.

172.14–15    San Domingo servile insurrection]    A slave revolt began in Saint-Domingue (Haiti) on August 22, 1791, that eventually resulted in the establishment of an independent republic in 1804.

173.30–32    West India emancipation . . . folly)]    Sugarcane production in the West Indies declined sharply after emancipation was completed in 1838 as many former slaves stopped working on plantations.

175.19–20    Jefferson . . . Chippewa]    In October 1859 settlers in present-day Colorado created the extralegal Territory of Jefferson, which included parts of the territories of Nebraska, Kansas, New Mexico, Utah, and Washington. The territory was never recognized by the federal government, and its administration disbanded after Congress organized Colorado Territory in February 1861. "Chippewa" probably refers to the unattached territory east of the Missouri River and west of Minnesota that became part of the new Dakota Territory in 1861.

180.20    Ben Crowninshield]    Benjamin William Crowninshield (1837–1892), a Harvard classmate of Henry Adams who later served with Charles Francis Adams Jr. as an officer in the 1st Massachusetts Cavalry.

180.23–25    Seward . . . his speech.]    Seward gave a conciliatory speech in the Senate on January 12, 1861, in which he stated his willingness to vote for a constitutional amendment protecting slavery in the states from interference by Congress.

181.11–12    Is thy servant . . . this thing.]    Cf. 2 Kings 8:13: "is thy servant a dog, that he should do this great thing?"

181.38    the Bayards . . . Florey]    James A. Bayard (1799–1880),

Democratic senator from Delaware, 1851–64 and 1867–69; his wife, Ann Willing Francis Bayard; and their daughter Florence Bayard (1842–1898).

182.4    Loo]    Louisa Catherine Adams Kuhn (1831–1870), older sister of Henry Adams.

184.15    Ordinance of 1787]    The Northwest Ordinance, adopted by the Confederation Congress on July 13, 1787, prohibited slavery in the territory north of the Ohio and east of the Mississippi.

184.20    dismembered Texas]    In 1850 Texas ceded to the United States land in present-day Kansas, Oklahoma, New Mexico, Colorado, and Wyoming in return for $10 million.

186.22    exhuberance of Blair]    Francis Preston Blair Lee, born in 1857, was the only child of Elizabeth Blair Lee and Samuel Phillips Lee.

186.31    Bates]    Edward Bates, who became attorney general. See Biographical Notes.

186.34    Our Maryland nominee]    Montgomery Blair (1813–1883) served as postmaster general from March 1861 until his resignation in September 1864.

187.1    Frank]    Francis Preston Blair Jr. (1821–1875) was a Republican congressman from Missouri, 1857–59, 1861–62, and 1863–64, and served as a general in the Union army, 1862–63 and 1864–65. An opponent of Radical Reconstruction, he was the Democratic candidate for vice president in 1868.

187.11    Mr. Bailey . . . Floyd]    Godard Bailey, a clerk in the Department of the Interior who was married to a cousin of Secretary of War John B. Floyd, had given $870,000 in Indian trust fund bonds to William Russell, a heavily indebted army contractor, in return for promissory notes endorsed by Floyd. Bailey confessed his role in the scheme to President Buchanan on December 22, 1860. Floyd (1806–1863) served as governor of Virginia, 1848–52, before becoming secretary of war in 1857. At a cabinet meeting held on December 27, 1860, he unsuccessfully sought to persuade Buchanan that the garrison at Fort Sumter should be ordered to return to Fort Moultrie. Floyd resigned on December 29 and was succeeded by Postmaster General Joseph Holt, a Kentucky unionist. He later became a brigadier general in the Confederate army, but was relieved of duty after the surrender of Fort Donelson in February 1862.

187.27    Mr. Slidell]    John Slidell (1793–1871) was a Democratic congressman from Louisiana, 1843–45, and a senator, 1853–61. He later served as a Confederate envoy to France, 1861–65.

188.2    Hartstene]    Henry J. Hartstene (d. 1868) was commissioned in the U.S. Navy in 1828 and served in expeditions to the Pacific, Antarctic, and Arctic. He joined the Confederate navy in 1861.

188.10    Cameron]    Simon Cameron (1799–1889) of Pennsylvania served in the Senate as a Democrat, 1845–49, and as a Republican, 1857–61 and 1867–77. An unsuccessful candidate for the Republican presidential nomination in 1860, Cameron became secretary of war in the Lincoln administration and served until January 1862, when he was forced to resign amid charges of widespread corruption and incompetence in the war department.

188.26 Thompson] Jacob Thompson (1810–1885) was a Democratic congressman from Mississippi, 1839–51, before becoming secretary of the interior in 1857. Thompson resigned from the cabinet on January 8, 1861, and later served as a Confederate commissioner in Canada, 1864–65.

191.23–24 "Gentlemen of the . . . fire first!"] In *Historie de Guerre de 1741* (1755), Voltaire wrote that when opposing lines of British and French Guards faced each other at the Battle of Fontenoy in 1745, Lord Charles Hay, a captain of the First Foot Guards, called out, "Gentlemen of the French Guards, fire." The Count d'Antroche, a lieutenant of Grenadiers, replied: "Gentlemen, we never fire first; fire yourselves."

196.3–6 Massachusetts was arraigned . . . fugitive slave in Boston.] Frederick "Shadrach" Minkins was rescued from the Boston federal courthouse by a group of African Americans on February 15, 1851, and later escaped to Canada. Davis spoke in the Senate on February 18, 1851, during a debate over a resolution asking President Millard Fillmore for information about the incident.

196.29–30 language of Mr. Jefferson] Jefferson wrote to Roger C. Weightman on June 24, 1826: "The general spread of the light of science has already laid open the palpable truth, that the mass of mankind has not been born with saddles on their backs, nor a favored few booted and spurred, ready to ride them legitimately, by the grace of God."

199.12 Everett's "Life of Washington"] Edward Everett, *The Life of George Washington* (1860).

210.25–26 one of those speeches] Lincoln's reply to Stephen A. Douglas at Ottawa, Illinois, on August 21, 1858, during the first of their seven debates.

213.9 Articles of Association in 1774.] The articles were adopted by the First Continental Congress.

213.39–214.1 The power confided . . . the government] In the first draft, written in Springfield in January 1861, this passage read: "All the power at my disposal will be used to reclaim the public property and places which have fallen; to hold, occupy and possess these, and all other property and places belonging to the government . . ." Lincoln followed the advice of his friend Orville H. Browning in revising this passage for the final version.

217.36 proposed amendment to the Constitution] A proposed Thirteenth Amendment to the Constitution forbidding Congress from abolishing or interfering with slavery in the states was approved by the House of

Representatives, 133–65, on February 28, and by the Senate, 24–12, on March 3. It was ratified by only two states.

219.10–16    I am loth . . . our nature.]  This paragraph was proposed and drafted by William H. Seward as follows: "I close. We are not we must not be aliens or enemies but ~~countrm~~ fellow countrymen and brethren. Although passion has strained our bonds of affection too hardly they must not ~~be broken they will not,~~ I am sure they will not be broken. The mystic chords which proceeding from ~~every ba~~ so many battle fields and ~~patriot~~ so many patriot graves ~~bind~~ pass through all the hearts and ~~hearths~~ all the hearths in this broad continent of ours will yet ~~harmon~~ again harmonize in their ancient music when ~~touched as they surely~~ breathed upon ~~again~~ by the ~~better angel~~ guardian angel of the nation."

220.24–25    Saul . . . multitude]  See 1 Samuel 9:2.

223.25–26    Palmetto State, . . . in 1833.]  A South Carolina state convention passed a nullification ordinance on November 24, 1832, prohibiting the collection of the federal tariffs authorized in 1828 and 1832 and threatening secession if the federal government responded with force. President Andrew Jackson responded by issuing a proclamation on December 10 asserting federal supremacy and denouncing nullification as illegal. On March 2, 1833, he signed a Force Bill authorizing the military to enforce the revenue laws, as well as a compromise tariff law lowering rates. The South Carolina convention met on March 11 and rescinded the nullification ordinance, ending the crisis.

228.18    curse against Canaan]  See Genesis 9:20–27. The passage was sometimes used to justify African slavery.

228.28–29    "one star . . . in glory"]  Cf. 1 Corinthians 15:41.

228.34–35    This stone . . . corner."]  Cf. Psalm 118:22

229.8–9    "in . . . bread,"]  Genesis 3:19.

237.12    General Scott, Genl. Totten]  Winfield Scott (1786–1866), general-in-chief of the U.S. Army from 1841 until his retirement on November 1, 1861; Joseph Totten (1788–1864), chief engineer of the U.S. Army from 1838 until his death.

237.18–19    Comodore Stringham, and Mr. Fox]  Silas Stringham (1798–1876) was a veteran of the War of 1812, the Algerine War, and the U.S.-Mexican War. He would command the North Atlantic blockading squadron, which patrolled the coasts of Virginia and North Carolina, until his retirement from active duty in December 1861. Gustavus Fox (1821–1883) served in the navy, 1838–56, before becoming a woolen manufacturer in Massachusetts. Fox served as an informal advisor on naval matters to Winfield Scott before becoming chief clerk of the navy department in May 1861. He was appointed assistant secretary of the navy in August 1861 and served until the end of the war.

241.18     Govr. Pickens]     Francis Pickens (1805–1869), governor of South Carolina, 1860–1862.

242.30     sent Mr. Lamon . . . Charleston]     Ward Hill Lamon (1828–1893) was Abraham Lincoln's law partner in Danville, Illinois, from 1852 to 1857. He spoke with Major Anderson and Governor Pickens during his visit to Charleston, March 24–25, 1861. Appointed the U.S. marshal for the District of Columbia in 1861, Lamon served as an unofficial presidential bodyguard during the war (he was not present when Lincoln was assassinated).

243.31–32     Commander Ward]     James Harmon Ward (1806–1861) served in the U.S.-Mexican War and wrote books on naval tactics, ordnance, and steam engineering. He was killed during fighting at Mathias Point on the Potomac River on June 27, 1861, the first Union naval officer to die in the Civil War.

244.31–32     Mr. Stanton . . . Mr. Buchanan's Cabinet]     Edwin M. Stanton became attorney general of the United States on December 22, 1860.

246.13     The elder Blair]     Francis Preston Blair (1791–1876), the father of Postmaster General Montgomery Blair, had edited the *Washington Globe*, 1830–45, and advised Andrew Jackson and Martin Van Buren. An opponent of the extension of slavery, Blair helped organize the 1856 Republican convention, and would serve as an adviser to President Lincoln.

246.31–32     orders . . . Captain Vogdes]     An army artillery officer, Captain Israel Vogdes (1816–1889) sailed with reinforcements for Fort Pickens onboard the sloop *Brooklyn* on January 24, 1861, but then received orders from the Buchanan administration not to land his troops unless the fort came under attack. On March 12 General Winfield Scott ordered him to land his men, but when Vogdes received his new instructions on March 31, Captain Henry A. Adams, the naval commander at Pensacola, refused to comply, believing himself still guided by the orders he had received from Buchanan's navy secretary, Isaac Toucey. On April 12 Adams received new orders from Secretary of the Navy Gideon Welles, and Vogdes began landing his troops at Fort Pickens.

249.18–20     explanations from *Spain* . . . Russia]     Spain was reannexing Santo Domingo, and it was rumored that France was planning to recolonize Haiti. Great Britain and France were threatening to send troops to Mexico to force the payment of debts owed to their citizens, and there were reports that Russia was considering recognizing the Confederacy.

252.23     Mrs. Wigfall]     Charlotte Maria Cross Wigfall (born 1818) had married Louis T. Wigfall in 1841.

252.30–31     "And she thinks . . . MacGregor."]     Cf. Sir Walter Scott, *Rob Roy* (1817): "my foot is on my native heath, and my name is MacGregor."

253.1      Margaret Fuller Ossoli]   Chesnut's journal from the 1860s indicates that she was reading an essay by Samuel Smiles in *Brief Biographies* (1860) about the American essayist and journalist Margaret Fuller Ossoli (1810–1850).

253.9      Charles Cotesworth Pinckney]   An officer in the Continental Army during the Revolutionary War, Pinckney (1746–1825) was a delegate to the Constitutional Convention and later served as a special envoy to France, 1797–98. He was the Federalist candidate for vice president, 1800, and for president, 1804 and 1808.

253.17     Governor Manning]   A wealthy plantation owner, John Lawrence Manning (1816–1889) served in the South Carolina house of representatives, 1842–46 and 1865–67, in the state senate, 1846–52 and 1861–65, and as governor, 1852–54. He was a member of the South Carolina secession convention in 1860.

253.23     Talbot and Chew]   Captain Theodore Talbot, an army officer, and Robert Chew, a clerk in the State Department, left Washington, D.C., on April 6 and arrived in Charleston on April 8. Chew delivered a message from President Lincoln to Governor Pickens, informing him that an attempt would be made to provision Fort Sumter, while Talbot was prevented from going to Fort Sumter and telling Major Anderson that a relief expedition was being sent to Charleston.

253.27     Wigfall]   See note 115.25.

253.27–28   "There was a . . . by night,]   Lord Byron, *Childe Harold's Pilgrimage*, Canto III (1816), stanza 21, describing a ball held in Brussels on the eve of the Battle of Waterloo.

254.3      Governor Means]   John Hugh Means (1812–1862) was governor of South Carolina, 1850–52. In 1862 he became the colonel of the 17th South Carolina Infantry, and was fatally wounded at the Second Battle of Manassas on August 30, 1862.

254.10–11   "Dame Placid"]   A character in *Everyone Has His Faults* (1793), play by Elizabeth Inchbald (1753–1821).

256.33     The *Harriet Lane* . . . smashed]   A Coast Guard revenue cutter requisitioned by the navy for the Fort Sumter expedition, the *Harriet Lane* was not damaged during the bombardment.

257.14     Sound and fury, signifying nothing.]   *Macbeth*, V.v.27–28.

257.30     Pryor of Virginia]   A leading secessionist, Roger A. Pryor (1828–1919) served in the House of Representatives, 1859–61.

259.34     *St. Valentine's . . . Perth*]   Novel (1828) by Sir Walter Scott, in which Conachar, a Highland chieftain who was suckled as an infant by a white doe, fulfills a prophecy by showing cowardice in combat.

261.10     Edmund Ruffin]   A Virginia planter, journalist, and influential writer on agriculture and soil replenishment, Ruffin (1794–1865) became a prominent defender of slavery and advocate of secession in the 1850s. Frustrated by Virginia's failure to secede in early 1861, he went to South Carolina and enlisted as a private in the Palmetto Guards. On June 17, 1865, Ruffin shot himself in Virginia after writing in his diary of his "unmitigated hatred" for the "perfidious, malignant, & vile Yankee race."

262.1     columbiads]   See note 160.36.

262.39     line of negroes . . . torpedoes at Mobile.]   The 1st Division, U.S. Colored Troops, participated in the successful Union assault on Fort Blakeley at Mobile, Alabama, on April 9, 1865, attacking through defensive obstacles that included torpedoes (land mines).

263.34     Ripley's incendiary shells]   Roswell Sabine Ripley (1823–1887), a former U.S. Army artillery officer serving in the South Carolina militia. Ripley later became a Confederate brigadier general.

264.33     case-shot]   Shrapnel shells.

266.31–32     Wigfall . . . the pistol.]   In 1840 Wigfall became involved in a political feud in South Carolina with Whitfield Brooks, Brooks's son Preston, and their ally, James Carroll. After posting Whitfield Brooks as a scoundrel and coward, Wigfall fatally shot Thomas Bird, Whitfield's nephew, in a gunfight outside the Edgefield District courthouse. He then fought a bloodless duel with Carroll, and a duel with Preston Brooks in which both men were seriously wounded. (While serving in Congress, Preston Brooks would assault Charles Sumner on the Senate floor in 1856.)

267.4     the Provisional Army]   Established on February 28, 1861, the Provisional Army of the Confederate States was made up of volunteers who enlisted for twelve months' service (later extended to three years, or for the duration of the war). A much smaller force, the Army of the Confederate States of America, was established on March 6, 1861, and was intended to serve as the regular standing army of the Confederacy.

268.17     shouting my name]   In an earlier passage in *Reminiscences of Forts Sumter and Moultrie in 1860–'61*, Doubleday wrote: "While the battle was going on, a correspondent of the *New York Tribune*, who was in Charleston, wrote that the populace was calling for my head. Fortunately I was not there to gratify them. My relations with the gentlemen of Charleston had always been friendly. The enmity of the mob was simply political, and was founded on the belief that I was the only 'Black Republican,' as they termed it, in the fort."

268.25     Moses . . . governor]   Franklin J. Moses (1838–1906) was Republican governor of South Carolina, 1872–74.

269.10–11     EXSURGAT DEUS . . . *facie ejus*]   Psalm 67:2 in the Latin Vulgate, translated in the Douay-Rheims Bible as: "Let God arise, and let his

enemies be scattered: and let them that hate him flee from before his face."
(In the King James Version, this is Psalm 68:1.)

270.25–26    "four . . . Balaklava]   During the Crimean War Battle of
Balaklava, October 25, 1854, confusing orders sent by Lord Raglan, the British
commander-in-chief, led the Light Brigade of British cavalry to attack down
a valley to their front instead of moving onto the ridge to their right. Of the
673 men in the brigade, 109 were killed and 159 were wounded in the battle.
An eyewitness account by correspondent William Howard Russell inspired
Alfred Tennyson to write his poem "The Charge of the Light Brigade,"
which was published on December 9, 1854.

270.31    Ossawattomie John Brown]   Brown settled near the town of
Osawatomie, Kansas, in 1855, and unsuccessfully defended it against an attack
by a large force of proslavery Missouri "Border Ruffians" on August 30, 1856.

271.1    Mr. Ruggles]   See note 45.8.

271.8    Punch and the Charivari]   Punch, or The London Charivari, a
British illustrated weekly magazine founded in 1841 and known for its satiric
articles and cartoons.

272.5    Mayor Wood]   Fernando Wood (1812–1881), a Democrat, served in
Congress, 1841–43, 1863–65, and 1867–81, and as mayor of New York, 1855–57
and 1860–61. In January 1861 he suggested to the aldermen that New York
protect its trade with the South by seceding and becoming a free city.

273.1    J. G. Bennett]   James Gordon Bennett (1795–1872), a Scottish immigrant, was the founder, publisher, and editor of the highly popular and influential New York Herald.

273.40    Major Burnside]   Ambrose Burnside (1824–1881) was appointed
a major general of volunteers in March 1862. He succeeded George B.
McClellan as commander of the Army of the Potomac in November 1862, but
was relieved in January 1863 in the aftermath of the Union defeat at Fredericksburg, Virginia. Burnside subsequently commanded the Department of
the Ohio in 1863 and a corps in Virginia in 1864. After the war he served as
governor of Rhode Island, 1866–68, and in the U.S. Senate, 1875–81.

278.12–13    "Unto . . . determined."]   Daniel 9:26.

281.22    Solferino.]   On June 24, 1859, a French and Piedmontese-Sardinian
army of approximately 130,000 defeated about 120,000 Austrians at Solferino
in northern Italy during the Second War of Italian Independence. Almost
40,000 men were killed, wounded, or captured in the battle.

283.16    Major Whiting]   William H. C. Whiting (1824–1865), a West Point
graduate, served in the U.S. Army engineers until his resignation in February
1861. He was appointed as a brigadier general in the Confederate army,
August 1861, and as a major general, February 1863. Whiting was fatally

wounded at Fort Fisher, North Carolina, on January 15, 1865, and died a prisoner on Governor's Island in New York harbor on March 10, 1865.

287.15    Bobadil]   A braggart soldier in *Every Man in his Humour* (1598, revised 1616) by Ben Jonson.

287.25    Edonian]   An ancient Thracian people known in Greek mythology for their love of wine.

287.35    St. Calhoun.]   John C. Calhoun (1782–1850) represented South Carolina in Congress, 1811–17, and in the Senate, 1832–43 and 1845–50, and served as secretary of war, 1817–25, as secretary of state, 1844–45, and as vice president of the United States, 1825–32. He became famous for his defense of states' rights and slavery.

288.10    *pain coupé*]   Literally, cut bread.

289.33    *sans bornes*]   Without limits

290.15    In my letter]   Russell's dispatch, dated April 21, was printed in *The Times* of London on May 14, 1861.

291.11    Ironsides.]   Name given to the cavalry commanded by Oliver Cromwell in the English Civil War.

291.40    assault on Senator Sumner]   See note 46.35–36.

292.9    Lord Lyons]   Richard Bickerton Pemell Lyons, Lord Lyons (1817–1887) was the British minister to the United States, 1858–65.

293.1–4    "Integer . . . pharetrâ."]   Horace, *Odes* 22.1: "The man of upright life and pure from wickedness, O Fuscus, has no need of the Moorish javelins or bow, or quiver loaded with poisoned darts."

293.10    Mr. Ransome Calhoun]   A nephew of John C. Calhoun, Ransom Calhoun (1827–1865) was a West Point graduate who became colonel of the 1st South Carolina Artillery. In August 1862 Calhoun challenged his subordinate Major Alfred Rhett (1829–1889), the son of Robert Barnwell Rhett, after learning that Rhett had called him a "damned puppy." In the resulting duel, fought on September 5, 1862, Rhett killed Calhoun.

293.12–13    letter copying-machine]   A letterpress machine.

296.5–6    "still the tumult . . . people,"]   Cf. Psalm 65:7.

296.26–27    Lincoln, . . . twenty days to disperse]   In his proclamation of April 15, 1861, calling forth 75,000 militia, President Lincoln commanded the "combinations" opposing federal authority in the South to disperse within twenty days.

297.26    Gov. Letcher]   John Letcher (1813–1884) served in Congress, 1851–59, and as governor of Virginia, 1860–64.

298.17        the gallant Capt. Wise]   Jennings Wise (1831–1862), son of former
governor Henry Wise and co-editor of the *Richmond Enquirer*. Wise was fatally wounded at the Battle of Roanoke Island in North Carolina, February
8, 1862.

298.21        Seddon]   James Seddon (1815–1880) was a congressman from
Virginia, 1845–47 and 1849–51, and served as the Confederate secretary of war,
November 1862–February 1865.

299.37        *blessure mortelle*]   Mortal wound.

300.8         President Tyler . . . Gov. Wise]   John Tyler (1790–1862) served
as a congressman from Virginia, 1816–21, as governor, 1825–27, as a U.S. senator, 1827–36, as vice president of the United States, 1841, and as president of
the United States, 1841–45. For Henry Wise, see Biographical Notes.

300.14        recent incessant labors]   Tyler had presided over the unsuccessful
peace conference held in Washington, D.C., February 4–27, 1861. Attended
by delegates from twenty-one states, the conference recommended a series of
compromise measures that failed to win approval from Congress.

301.18        Hon. J. M. Mason]   James M. Mason (1798–1871) was a congressman from Virginia, 1837–39, and a U.S. senator, 1847–61. He served as Confederate envoy to Great Britain and France, 1861–65.

303.8         "Plug Ugly"]   The Plug Uglies were a nativist Baltimore street
gang of the 1850s.

304.4         Wide-Awake gatherings]   See note 27.36.

306.11        Mayor of Baltimore]   George William Brown (1812–1890) was
mayor of Baltimore from November 1860 to September 1861, when he was arrested by the Union army on suspicion of disloyalty. He was held without
charge until November 1862, when he was released shortly after the expira-
tion of his mayoral term.

306.14–17     the mayor's patience . . . with a revolver.]   In his memoir
*Baltimore and the Nineteenth of April, 1861* (1887), George Brown quoted
from Colonel Jones's report, and then wrote: "The statement that I begged
Captain Follansbee not to let the men fire is incorrect, although on this occasion I did say, 'Don't shoot.' It then seemed to me that I was in the wrong
place, for my presence did not avail to protect either the soldiers or the citizens, and I stepped out from the column. Just at this moment a boy ran forward and handed to me a discharged musket which had fallen from one of
the soldiers." After relating how he gave the musket to a shopkeeper, Brown
continued: "The statement in Colonel Jones's report that I seized a musket
and killed one of the rioters is entirely incorrect. The smoking musket seen
in my hands was no doubt the foundation for it. There is no foundation for
the other statement that one of the police shot a man with a revolver."

306.30    M. V. M.]    Massachusetts Volunteer Militia.

310.3–4    *Frederick Dent . . . Jesse Root Grant*]    Dent (1786–1873), Grant's father-in-law, owned a farm in St. Louis County, Missouri. Jesse Root Grant (1794–1873) was living in Covington, Kentucky.

311.20    Fred.]    Frederick Tracy Dent (1820–1892), Grant's brother-in-law, was a career army officer who graduated from West Point in 1843. He later served as an aide-de-camp to Grant, 1864–65.

321.3    three . . . citizens]    John Forsyth (1812–1877), editor of the *Mobile Daily Commercial Register*, who had served as U.S. minister to Mexico, 1856–58; Martin Crawford (1820–1883), a Democratic congressman from Georgia, 1855–61; Andre B. Roman (1795–1866), governor of Louisiana, 1831–35 and 1839–43.

321.33–34    an intermediary, . . . character]    John A. Campbell (1811–1889), an associate justice of the U.S. Supreme Court from 1853 until his resignation on April 30, 1861, served as an intermediary between the Confederate commissioners and Secretary of State Seward. Campbell was an assistant secretary of war in the Confederate government, 1862–65, and part of a Southern delegation that unsuccessfully negotiated with Lincoln and Seward at Hampton Roads, Virginia, on February 3, 1865.

322.19    received on the 8th of April a reply]    The memorandum stated the Secretary of State had no authority to recognize the commissioners as diplomatic agents, or to correspond or communicate with them.

325.6    *posse comitatus*]    See note 78.33.

335.5–10    brave fellows . . . State of Maryland.]    Eight runaway slaves sought protection at Fort Pickens on March 12, 1861. They were turned over to the city marshal of Pensacola by Lieutenant Adam J. Slemmer, the commander of the federal garrison at the fort. After receiving false reports of an imminent slave insurrection, Brigadier General Benjamin F. Butler, the Union commander at Annapolis, wrote to Governor Thomas Hicks on April 23, 1861, offering to help suppress any uprising.

339.14–15    your plan for a campaign]    In his letter of April 27, 1861, McClellan proposed forming an army of 80,000 men in Ohio and then advancing either through western Virginia on Richmond, or through Kentucky on Nashville.

339.31–32    Forts Jackson and Saint Philip]    Forts on opposite banks of the Mississippi River southeast of New Orleans.

341.15    the Col.]    Israel B. Richardson (1815–1862), an 1841 graduate of West Point who had retired from the army in 1855. Richardson later served as a brigade and division commander in the Army of the Potomac, and was fatally wounded at Antietam.

344.34–35     studying Hardee] *Rifle and Light Infantry Tactics* (1855) by William J. Hardee (1815–1873), the most widely used training manual of the Civil War era. A veteran of the U.S.-Mexican War and instructor at West Point, Hardee became a Confederate general and served as a corps commander in the western theater.

347.16–17     Mr. Washburn] Congressman Elihu Washburne; see note 147.29.

347.20–21     Governer Yates] Richard Yates (1815–1873) was the Republican governor of Illinois, 1861–65, and served in congress as a Whig, 1851–55, and in the Senate as a Republican, 1865–71.

348.32     *valiant* Pillow] Gideon Pillow (1806–1878), a former law partner of President James Polk, had served as a major general of volunteers in the U.S.-Mexican War. Pillow became a Confederate brigadier general in 1861, but was relieved of duty following his defeat by Grant at Fort Donelson in February 1862.

350.12     Singleton] James W. Singleton (1811–1892) was a Democratic attorney and railroad president in Illinois.

350.17     Browning] Orville Hickman Browning (1806–1881), a longtime friend of Lincoln's who served as a Republican senator from Illinois, June 1861–January 1863, and as secretary of the interior, 1866–69.

350.21     Doolittle] James R. Doolittle (1815–1897) was a Republican senator from Wisconsin, 1857–69.

350.23     Col. Hamilton] James A. Hamilton (1788–1878), a son of Alexander Hamilton, was a New York attorney active in Republican politics.

351.10–11     Ellsworth's Zouave Firemen.] The 11th New York Infantry was made up of volunteer firemen from New York City. Elmer Ellsworth (1837–1861), the regimental commander, had read law in Lincoln's office in Springfield before the war.

351.32–33     the dandy regiment] The 7th New York militia regiment.

352.8     Jeff. Davis' manifesto] Davis's address to the Confederate Congress of April 29, 1861; see pp. 313–32 in this volume.

352.26–32     Saw at breakfast . . . Union they scorn.] This paragraph was crossed out in the manuscript of Hay's diary.

353.3     "Abreuve nos sillons,"] From the "Marseillaise": "Qu'un sang impur / Abreuve nos sillons" ("Let impure blood / soak our fields").

353.5     Dahlgren gun] A muzzle-loading naval gun designed by John A. Dahlgren (1809–1870), a U.S. Navy ordnance officer.

353.21     Carl Schurz] Schurz (1829–1906) was a German émigré who had campaigned for Lincoln among both German- and English-speaking voters. He served as U.S. minister to Spain, 1861–62; as a general in the Union army, 1862–65; as a Republican senator from Missouri, 1869–75; and as secretary of the interior, 1877–81.

354.1–3    Mrs. Whitman . . . young John Brown]    Sarah Helen Whitman (1803–1878) was a poet and social reformer who had become friends with John Hay while he was attending Brown University. Thomas Earle, a friend of Thomas Wentworth Higginson, served with the 25th Massachusetts Regiment. Thomas Wentworth Higginson (1823–1911) was a Massachusetts minister, writer, and abolitionist who had helped finance John Brown's raid on Harpers Ferry. Higginson would later command the 1st South Carolina Volunteers, 1862–64, one of the first black regiments to be officially recognized by the U.S. government. John Brown Jr. (1821–1895), John Brown's eldest child, helped his father with preparations for the Harpers Ferry raid, but did not participate in it.

355.26    "All . . . divine."]    Lord Byron, *The Bride of Abydos* (1813), canto I, stanza I.

358.26–27    Hugh & Charley Ewing & John Hunter]    Hugh Ewing (1826–1905) and Charles Ewing (1835–1883), Sherman's brothers-in-law, were both attorneys. John Hunter was Charles Ewing's law partner.

358.30    Gen. Frost]    Daniel M. Frost (1823–1900) commanded the Missouri militia at Camp Jackson. Frost, a West Point graduate who had served in the U.S.-Mexican War, later became a Confederate general.

358.31    Willy]    William T. Sherman Jr. (1854–1863).

360.5–6    Tom Turner . . . his appointment]    Sherman had sought his brother's help in obtaining an army commission for Thomas Turner, the son of Sherman's army friend and former banking partner Henry S. Turner (1811–1881). Thomas Turner later joined the Confederate army.

361.18    Major Cary]    John B. Cary (1819–1898) had founded the Hampton Military Academy in 1852. He later served as lieutenant colonel of the 32nd Virginia Regiment and was seriously wounded during the Seven Days' Battles in 1862.

365.10    Charleston-Baltimore Convention]    See Chronology, April–June 1860.

365.11–12    Front street . . . Maryland Institute.]    The Northern Democrats who nominated Stephen A. Douglas met at the Front Street Theater in Baltimore, while the Southern Democrats who nominated John C. Breckinridge met at the Maryland Institute. "Hard Shells" were Northern Democrats who gave strong support to proslavery candidates and policies.

367.11–12    "ANDREW and BUTLER correspondence,"]    While serving as a brigadier general of the Massachusetts militia, Benjamin F. Butler offered to suppress a rumored slave insurrection in Maryland (see note 335.5–10). John A. Andrew (1818–1867), the Republican governor of Massachusetts, wrote to Butler on April 25, 1861, criticizing his offer as "unnecessary" and arguing that Union troops should not protect disloyal communities. Butler replied on May 9, defending his action on moral and political grounds and describing the prospect of a slave insurrection as "letting loose four millions of worse than savages upon the homes and hearths of the South."

369.7     My Brother]   William Stone (c. 1840–c. 1882) became a captain in the Confederate army and was wounded twice fighting in the eastern theater.

369.12    Uncle Bo]   Bohanan Ragan, a younger brother of Kate Stone's mother. He joined the Confederate army in 1861 and survived the war.

369.32    Little Sister]   Amanda Stone (c. 1850–1934).

370.9     Mr. Newton]   Albert Newton, who tutored the younger children in the Stone family.

370.31    Richmond]   A town in Madison Parish, Louisiana.

371.8     Ashburn]   Ashburn Ragan, Mrs. Stone's youngest brother, who died of a fever in 1861 at age eighteen.

372.1     "The Jacobite Fiddler,"]   Poem by the English writer George Walter Thornbury (1828–1876).

372.19    Tiger Rifles]   Name originally given to Company B of the 1st Louisiana Special Battalion and later used for the battalion as a whole. The company was mainly recruited from among Irish immigrant dock workers; its commander, Captain Alexander White, had served a prison sentence for pistol-whipping a man.

372.21    Perrit Guards]   The Perrit (or Perret) Guards became Company H of the 5th Louisiana Infantry.

376.11    Wickham Hoffman]   Hoffman (1821–1900), a lawyer in New York City, was an aide-de-camp to Governor Edwin Morgan. He later served as an assistant adjutant general in the Union army, 1862–65, and as a diplomat in France, Britain, Russia, and Denmark.

376.25    (D'Utassy . . . "Garibaldi Guard,"]   The 39th New York Volunteers was recruited in New York City and contained companies made up of Hungarian, German, Swiss, Italian, French, Spanish and Portuguese immigrants. Colonel Frederick George D'Utassy (1827–1892) commanded the regiment until 1863, when he was cashiered and sentenced to one year at hard labor after being court-martialed for fraud and embezzlement.

377.8     General Sandford's parlor]   Charles W. Sandford (1796–1878) served as a major general in the New York state militia throughout the war and commanded troops during the 1863 draft riots in New York City.

377.10　(not James A.'s Aleck, but John C.'s)] James A. Hamilton (see note 350.23) and John C. Hamilton (1792–1882) were both sons of Alexander Hamilton.

377.11　Alexandrian movement] On May 24, 1861, U.S. forces occupied Alexandria, Virginia.

377.15　Schuyler Hamilton] The son of John C. Hamilton, Schuyler Hamilton (1822–1903) graduated from West Point in 1841. He was wounded twice in Mexico and served as an aide-de-camp to General Winfield Scott before resigning from the army in 1855. Hamilton served as Scott's military secretary in 1861 and as a brigadier general in the western theater in 1862 before leaving the army because of poor health.

377.33　President Felton] Cornelius Felton (1807–1862) was president of Harvard, 1860–62.

377.36　Colonel Blenker's Germans] Louis Blenker (1812–1863), a German émigré, organized the 8th New York Infantry Regiment. He later became a brigade and division commander in the Army of the Potomac and served until June 1862, when he was relieved of duty.

377.39　"Brooklyn Zouaves"] The 14th New York militia regiment, also known as the 14th Brooklyn.

378.5　tête-du-pont] Bridgehead.

378.14–15　Colonel Ellsworth] During the Union occupation of Alexandria on May 24, 1861, Colonel Elmer Ellsworth (see note 351.10–11) took down a Confederate flag that was flying from the roof of the Marshall House hotel. On his way down the stairs Ellsworth was confronted by James Jackson, the hotel's proprietor, who killed him with a shotgun. Jackson was then shot and bayoneted by a corporal in Ellsworth's regiment. The incident was widely publicized, and both Ellsworth and Jackson were considered martyrs by their respective sides in the conflict.

379.14–15　Colonel Burnside's] See note 273.40.

379.20　Goddard] Robert Hales Ives Goddard (1837–1916) was a partner in Goddard Brothers, a successful textile manufacturing firm in Rhode Island. He enlisted as a private in the Rhode Island militia in 1861 and later served as an officer on the staff of General Ambrose Burnside.

379.24 25　field-preaching . . . Lauderdale and Claverhouse] Following the restoration of episcopacy in Scotland by Charles II in 1662, Presbyterian Covenanters began holding their services in the open air. John Maitland, Duke of Lauderdale (1616–1682), secretary of state for Scotland, 1660–80, and John Graham of Claverhouse (1648–1689), who commanded royal troops in Scotland from 1678 until his death at the Battle of Killiecrankie in 1689, became notorious for their persecution of Covenanters.

379.36      Wise . . . Edward Everett]   A cousin of the Virginia secessionist
Henry Wise (see Biographical Notes), Lieutenant Henry Wise (1819–1869)
was a naval officer, currently serving in the ordnance bureau, who also wrote
popular travel books and adventure novels under the name "Harry Gringo."
A Unitarian clergyman and professor of Greek at Harvard who served as
president of the college, 1846–49, Everett (1794–1865) was also a congressman from Massachusetts, 1825–35, governor of Massachusetts, 1836–40, U.S.
minister to Great Britain, 1841–45, secretary of state, 1852–53, a senator from
Massachusetts, 1853–54, and the vice presidential candidate on the 1860 Constitutional Union ticket.

379.39      N. P. Willis]   Nathaniel Parker Willis (1806–1867) was a journalist,
poet, and writer of short stories and travel sketches.

380.6      General Mansfield]   Brigadier General Joseph King Fenno
Mansfield (1803–1862) commanded the Washington defenses in the spring of
1861. He later led a division in Virginia and a corps at Antietam, where he was
fatally wounded.

380.7      Bache . . . Trowbridge.]   Alexander Dallas Bache (1806–1867)
was superintendent of the U.S. Coast Survey from 1843 until his death.
William P. Trowbridge (1828–1892) was assistant superintendant of the survey.

380.38–40      Arlington House . . . Colonel Lee]   The house had been
built by George Washington Parke Custis (1781–1857), grandson of Martha
Custis Washington and the adopted son of George Washington. His will gave
a life interest in the property to his only child, Mary Custis Lee (1807/8–
1873), who had married Robert E. Lee in 1831.

388.22–24      the conspiracy . . . suspension of the writ]   On January 22,
1807, President Thomas Jefferson sent a special message to Congress in which
he accused former vice president Aaron Burr of conspiring to foment war
with Spain and detach the western states from the Union. William Branch
Giles, a Democratic-Republican senator from Virginia, immediately introduced a bill in Congress suspending the writ of habeas corpus in cases of treason for three months. It passed the Senate on January 23 with only one
dissenting vote, but was rejected by the House of Representatives, 113–19, on
January 26.

393.2      Blackstone]   William Blackstone (1723–1780), *Commentaries on the
Laws of England* (4 vols., 1765–69).

393.36      statute of 31 Car. II.]   The Habeas Corpus Act of 1679, passed in
the thirty-first year of the reign of Charles II (the beginning of his reign was
dated from the execution of Charles I in 1649).

394.4      the statute of 13 Wm. III.]   The Act of Settlement of 1701.

394.20      Hallam's Constitutional History]   Henry Hallam (1777–1859),
*The Constitutional History of England, from the accession of Henry VII to the
death of George II* (3 vols., 1827).

395.1    'Petition of Right' (3 Car. I.)]   The Petition of Right passed Parliament and received the royal assent in 1628.

397.6–7    Commentaries . . . Story]   *Commentaries on the Constitution of the United States* (3 vols., 1833) by Joseph Story (1779–1845), who served as an associate justice of the U.S. Supreme Court, 1811–45.

397.34    Ex . . . Swartwout]   Erick Bollman and Samuel Swartwout were associates of Aaron Burr who were arrested in the lower Mississippi Valley and brought to Washington, D.C., under military guard. After being committed to trial for treason by the circuit court for the District of Columbia, they applied to the U.S. Supreme Court for writs of habeas corpus. On February 13, 1807, Chief Justice John Marshall ruled that under the 14th section of the judiciary act of 1789, the Supreme Court had the power to issue a writ of habeas corpus. In a second opinion delivered on February 21, Marshall ordered Bollman and Swartwout to be discharged, ruling that the evidence presented failed to support charges of treason.

403.6    "We may be Happy yet."]   Song from the opera *The Daughter of St. Mark* (1844), with music by Michael William Balfe (1808–1870) and words by Alfred Baum (1796–1860).

404.14–15    Judge Jackson]   Henry R. Jackson (1820–1898), an attorney from Savannah who had served as a judge on the Georgia superior court, 1849–53.

405.13–14    Agrarianism in ancient Rome]   The movement for redistributing public land led by the tribunes Tiberius Gracchus (163–133 B.C.E.) and Caius Gracchus (153–121 B.C.E.) resulted in violent political and social conflict, and was seen by some as contributing to the eventual decline and fall of the Roman republic.

407.16    M. E. & Amb. Plen.]   Minister Extraordinaire and Ambassador Plenipoteniary.

408.37–38    the Times . . . my letters]   Henry Adams wrote thirty-one unsigned letters that were printed in *The New York Times*, June 7, 1861–January 21, 1862.

409.15    Lord John]   Lord John Russell (1792–1878) was foreign secretary in the Liberal government led by Lord Palmerston, 1859–65. Russell had held unofficial meetings on May 3 and May 9, 1861, with Confederate diplomatic commissioners William Yancey, Pierre Rost, and Ambrose Mann, but refused to discuss British recognition of the Confederacy with them.

409.22    Lord Lyons]   See note 292.9.

409.35    Clay and Burlingame]   Cassius Clay (1810–1903) was U.S. minister to Russia, 1861–62 and 1863–69. Anson Burlingame (1820–1870) served as a congressman from Massachusetts, 1855–61. He was appointed as U.S. minister to Austria in 1861, but was not accepted by the Austrian government because of his support for Hungarian independence. While traveling to their posts, both Clay and Burlingame made public statements criticizing Britain for granting belligerent rights to the Confederacy.

410.12     the Article on the last Winter]   The article was eventually published as "The Great Secession Winter of 1860–1861" in *Proceedings of the Massachusetts Historical Society,* 1909–10.

410.22–24     Margaret . . . Bridget]   Family servants.

410.24–27     Mary . . . Brooks]   Henry Adams's younger siblings Mary Adams, later Mary Adams Quincy (1846–1928), and Brooks Adams (1848–1927).

410.35–36     despatch . . . Seward]   Charles Francis Adams received a dispatch on June 10 from Secretary of State Seward, dated May 21, 1861, instructing him to break off relations with the British government if it held any further meetings with Confederate envoys and to warn Lord Russell that recognition of the Confederacy would result in Anglo-American war. Adams chose not to convey the full force of his instructions, and was assured by Lord Russell that the British government did not intend to recognize the Confederacy or hold further meetings with the Confederate commissioners.

411.4–5     It . . . blunder.]   The remark "c'est pire qu'un crime, c'est un faute" ("it was worse than a crime, it was a blunder"), made regarding Napoleon's summary execution of the duc d'Enghien in 1804, has been variously attributed to the French diplomat Charles Maurice de Talleyrand (1754–1838), to Napoleon's minister of police Joseph Fouché (1759–1820), and to the French politician Antoine Boulay de la Meurthe (1761–1840).

412.3     *Benjamin McCulloch*]   McCulloch (1811–1862) had fought in the Texas War of Independence, the U.S.-Mexican War, and with the Texas Rangers against the Comanches. He was appointed a brigadier general in the Confederate army in May 1861 and served until March 7, 1862, when he was killed at the Battle of Pea Ridge in Arkansas.

416.10     Convention of Notables]   See note 300.14.

417.14–15     Cushings, and Touceys]   For Caleb Cushing, see note 145.15. Isaac Toucey (1792–1869), a Democrat from Connecticut, served in congress, 1835–39, as governor, 1846–47, as attorney general of the United States, 1848–49, as a senator, 1852–57, and as secretary of the navy, 1857–61.

418.34–35     wonderful ethnologist . . . Review"]   In an article in the February 1861 *De Bow's Review,* George Fitzhugh (1806–1881) wrote: "The Cavaliers, Jacobites, and Huguenots who settled the South, naturally hate, contemn, and despise the Puritans who settled the North. The former are master races, the latter, a slave race, the descendants of the Saxon serfs. The former are Mediterranean races, descendants of the Romans; for Cavaliers and

Jacobites are of Norman descent, and the Normans were of Roman descent, and so were the Huguenots. The Saxons and Angles, the ancestors of the Yankees, came from the cold and marshy regions of the North; where man is little more than a cold-blooded, amphibious biped." A journalist and lawyer from Front Royal, Virginia, Fitzhugh was the author of *Sociology for the South, or the Failure of Free Society* (1854) and *Cannibals All! or, Slaves Without Masters* (1857).

419.2–3     cabinet officer . . . peculation]   Secretary of War John Floyd (see note 187.11). Floyd was accused of treason in the Northern press for transferring 115,000 muskets and rifles from Northern to Southern arsenals in the spring of 1860, and for ordering the shipment of 124 large cannon from Pittsburgh to coastal forts in Mississippi and Texas on December 20, 1860. (The order to transfer the artillery was rescinded by Joseph Holt, Floyd's successor as secretary of war.)

419.10     Jonathan Wild]   A receiver of stolen goods in London, Wild (c. 1682–1725) became notorious for selling stolen merchandise back to its owners under the guise of helping them to recover their property. He also organized a "corporation" of thieves and informed on those who refused to work for him, becoming known as the "Thief-taker General" for his success in apprehending criminals. Wild was eventually convicted of robbery and hanged at Tyburn.

420.28–33     Lord de Roos . . . your pardon!"]   Henry William Fitzgerald de Ros, Baron de Ros (1793–1839) sued John Cumming for libel in 1836 after Cumming accused him of repeatedly cheating at cards. In February 1837 a jury in London determined the accusation to be truthful and delivered a verdict for the defendant. The story of de Ros having his hand pinned with a fork is considered apocryphal.

420.34     Governor Letcher]   See note 297.26.

420.35     disasters . . . Norfolk]   Federal forces burned the arsenal at Harpers Ferry on April 18, 1861, and the navy yard at Norfolk on April 19 before they were occupied by Virginia militia. The Confederates were able to salvage significant amounts of war matériel from both locations.

423.8–9     two regiments . . . engine-house]   John Brown's raid on the Harpers Ferry arsenal ended on October 18, 1859, when a detachment of Marines sent from Washington, D.C., under the command of Lieutenant Colonel Robert E. Lee stormed the fire engine house where Brown and his remaining men were holding several hostages. Twelve companies of Virginia and Maryland militia were at Harpers Ferry by the end of the siege.

423.11     Ancient Pistol]   Pistol, a soldier who serves as an ancient (standard bearer) for Sir John Falstaff, is a character in *2 Henry VI, Henry V,* and *The Merry Wives of Windsor.*

426.2        Garrison . . . Phillips]   William Lloyd Garrison (see note 61.38–39) and Wendell Phillips (1811–1884), a lawyer, orator, and radical abolitionist allied with Garrison.

444.15      the besieged regiment]   Grant had been told that an Illinois regiment was surrounded by rebels along the railroad west of Palmyra, Missouri.

447.12      Great Bethel]   On June 10, 1861, about 4,000 Union troops were repulsed when they attacked a Confederate outpost defended by 1,100 men at Great Bethel, Virginia, between Hampton and Yorktown. Less than a hundred men on both sides were killed or wounded in the engagement, also known as Big Bethel or Bethel Church.

447.16–17     camp at Philippi . . . dispersed.]   Union troops overran the Confederate camp at Philippi in northwestern Virginia (now West Virginia) on June 3, 1861.

448.21      gallant General Garnett]   Confederate Brigadier General Robert S. Garnett (1819–1861) was an 1841 graduate of West Point who fought in the U.S.-Mexican War. Garnet was serving as a major in the U.S. Army when he resigned his commission in April 1861.

452.13–14     "the name . . . fear death,"]   Cf. *Julius Caesar*, I.ii.88–89: "I love / The name of honour more than I fear death."

452.27      my little Edgar]   Edgar Ballou was born in 1856.

453.9        Little Willie]   William Ballou was born in 1859.

455.1–2      my servant, John Scott]   Scott was a free black man who had been an officer's servant in the U.S.-Mexican War.

455.9        made on the 18th.]   Union and Confederate troops had skirmished on July 18, 1861, near Blackburn's Ford.

456.36–37     Colonel Cocke]   Philip St. George Cocke commanded a Confederate brigade during the battle.

457.6        "Washington Artillery"]   A New Orleans artillery battalion organized in 1838. Four of its companies served throughout the war with the Army of Northern Virginia, while a fifth company served with the Army of Tennessee.

457.16–17     "Hampton Legion" . . . Wade Hampton.]   Hampton (1818–1902) was a wealthy South Carolina plantation owner who raised six infantry companies, four cavalry companies, and an artillery battery in early 1861. The Legion was broken up in 1862 as part of a general reorganization of the Army of Northern Virginia, and its elements were reassigned to different infantry, cavalry, and artillery units. Hampton was successively appointed as a brigadier general (1862), major general (1863), and lieutenant general (1865), and later served as governor of South Carolina, 1876–79, and as a senator, 1879–91.

459.11    Sherman's . . . battery]   Company E, 3rd U.S. Artillery, was famous for its role in the American victory at Buena Vista in 1847 while under the command of Thomas W. Sherman (1813–1879). Battery I, 1st U.S. Artillery was commanded at Bull Run by Captain James B. Ricketts (1817–1887), who later became a division commander in the Union army.

460.34    Stuart's regiment]   The 1st Virginia Cavalry commanded by J.E.B. Stuart (1833–1864), who became the cavalry commander of the Army of Northern Virginia in July 1862.

464.23    my friend]   Frederick Warre, an attaché at the British legation in Washington.

464.30    *viaticum*]   Provisions for the journey.

480.35    the nipple]   The part of the gun's firing mechanism onto which the percussion cap was fitted.

481.21    Mr. Raymond]   Henry J. Raymond (1820–1869) was the co-founder and editor of *The New York Times*, 1851–69.

483.14    Cairo]   Russell had visited Cairo, Illinois, in late June 1861.

485.28    Colonel Hunter]   David Hunter (1802–1886) commanded a division at Bull Run and was later appointed a major general of volunteers.

488.33    chaussée]   Causeway, highway.

489.35    Soyer or Careme]   Alexis Benoit Soyer (1809–1858) and Marie-Antoine Carême (1784–1833), noted French chefs and writers on cooking.

496.2    left Congress]   The Provisional Confederate Congress.

496.23    murder of Jackson]   See note 378.14–15.

498.18–20    Patterson's men . . . Genl Jo Johnston]   Robert Patterson (1792–1881), a veteran of the War of 1812 and the U.S.-Mexican War, commanded the Union forces in the Shenandoah Valley. His failure to engage Joseph E. Johnston (1807–1891) allowed Johnston to send most of his troops to Manassas Junction in time for them to fight at Bull Run.

498.24    brother's front fence]   The front fence of Blair House on Pennsylvania Avenue in Washington, D.C.

504.25    Patterson, or Banks]   Robert Patterson was relieved on July 25, 1861, and succeeded as commander of Union forces in the Shenandoah Valley by Major General Nathaniel P. Banks (1816–1894).

506.13–14    "Eugene" . . . en guerre]   During the War of the Spanish Succession, Austrian commander Prince Eugène of Savoy (1663–1736) and John Churchill, Duke of Marlborough (1650–1722) won victories together over the French at Blenheim (1704), Oudenarde (1708), and Malplaquet

(1709). "Malbrough s'en va-t-en guerre" ("Marlborough goes off to war") was a popular French folk song of the eighteenth century.

506.24    Wilson of Massachusetts]   Henry Wilson (1812–1875) was a Republican senator from Massachusetts, 1855–73, and vice president of the United States, 1873–75.

507.2    Senator Harlan.]   James Harlan (1820–1899) served as a Republican senator from Iowa, 1855–65 and 1867–73, and as secretary of the interior, 1865–66.

507.11    Mrs. Davis's drawing room]   Varina Howell Davis (1826–1906), wife of Jefferson Davis.

507.29    Mrs. McLean . . . Joe Davis]   Margaret Sumner McLean (1828–1905) was married to Eugene McLean, a West Point graduate from Maryland who had resigned his commission and joined the Confederate army. Her father, Edwin Sumner (1797–1863), was a Union general, and her brothers Edwin Jr. and Samuel also served as Union officers. Joseph Robert Davis (1825–1896), a nephew of Jefferson Davis, was serving as an aide to his uncle.

508.19–20    Mr. Barnwell . . . Mr. Hunter]   Robert Barnwell (1801–1882) was a congressman from South Carolina, 1829–33, and served in the Senate in 1850. He was a member of the Confederate Provisional Congress, 1861–62, and of the Confederate Senate, 1862–65. Robert M. T. Hunter (1809–1887) was a congressman from Virginia, 1837–43 and 1845–47, and a senator, 1847–61. A member of the Confederate provisional congress in 1861 and of the Confederate Senate, 1862–65, Hunter was appointed as the secretary of state of the Confederacy on July 25, 1861, and served until February 1862.

508.29    Kirby Smith . . . turnpike]   Edmund Kirby Smith (1824–1893) commanded a brigade that arrived at Manassas Junction by train from the Shenandoah Valley at midday on July 21 and reached the battlefield in the late afternoon. When Smith was wounded, Colonel Arnold Elzey assumed command of the brigade and joined the counterattack that drove the Union army from the field.

509.11–12    Mr. Rives . . . Arnoldus VanderHorst]   William Cabell Rives (1793–1868) served as a congressman from Virginia, 1823–29, as U.S. minister to France, 1829–32 and 1849–53, and as a senator, 1832–34, 1836–39, and 1841–45. Rives was a member of the Confederate Provisional Congress, 1861–62, and the Confederate House of Representatives, 1864–65. James A. Seddon (1815–1880) was a congressman from Virginia, 1845–47 and 1849–51, a member of the Confederate Provisional Congress, 1861–62, and Confederate secretary of war, 1862–65. Arnoldus VanderHorst (1835–1881) was a plantation owner from South Carolina and an officer in the Confederate army.

509.17–18    Hon. Mr. Clingman . . . Brewster]   Thomas Clingman (1812–1897) was a congressman from North Carolina, 1843–45 and 1847–58, and a senator, 1858–61. Clingman later became a brigadier general in the Confederate army. Henry Brewster (1816–1884) was a lawyer from Texas who had practiced in Washington, D.C., before the war, and who later served as a staff officer in the Confederate army.

509.28 Arnold Harris] Harris (c. 1810–1866) was a shipping agent and co-founder of the *States and Union*, an anti-Republican newspaper published in Washington, D.C., from the fall of 1859 until the spring of 1861. On July 22 he left Washington in an attempt to recover the body of Colonel James Cameron, the brother of Secretary of War Simon Cameron, from the Bull Run battlefield, and was arrested the following day by Confederate troops for crossing the lines without a flag of truce. Harris was held in the Richmond county jail until September 30, 1861, when he was released.

510.6 Trescot] William Henry Trescot (1822–1898) was a lawyer from South Carolina who served as secretary of the U.S. legation in London, 1852–54, and as assistant secretary of state, June–December 1860.

510.20 John Waties] A lawyer from Charleston, South Carolina, Waties (1828–1873) fought at Bull Run with Hampton's Legion.

510.26 Mrs. Preston's room.] Caroline and John Preston were friends of the Chesnuts' from Columbia, South Carolina.

510.27 Mr. Venable] Charles Scott Venable (1827–1900), a professor of mathematics and astronomy at South Carolina College, fought at Bull Run as a private in the 2nd South Carolina Infantry. He later served as an aide-de-camp to General Robert E. Lee, 1862–65.

510.35 "It is a far cry to Lochow"] In *The Legend of Montrose* (1819) by Sir Walter Scott, a proverbial expression used by the Campbell clan to express the difficulty of an invading army reaching Loch Awe, their ancestral domain in the Scottish Highlands.

511.6 Mr. Mason] See note 145.8.

512.4 Dr. Gibbes] Robert Wilson Gibbes (1809–1866) was a physician, naturalist, and publisher of the Columbia *Daily South Carolinian*.

513.1 Mr. Hammond] James Henry Hammond (1807–1864) was governor of South Carolina, 1842–44, and a Democratic senator, 1857–60.

513.10 Camden DeLeon . . . surgeon general] David Camden DeLeon (1816–1872) was a surgeon in the U.S. Army, 1838–61. He was appointed as surgeon general of the Confederate army on May 12, 1861, and served until July 30, 1861, when he was succeeded by Samuel Preston Moore (1813–1889), who held the position for the remainder of the war.

513.29–30 Clingman . . . cut his throat] Thomas Clingman (see note 509.17–18) may have attempted suicide in 1834 while suffering from a painful inflammation of the eyes that made him temporarily blind.

515.1 White Sulphur, Roony Lee] White Sulphur Springs, a resort in western Virginia (now West Virginia). William Henry Fitzhugh (Rooney) Lee (1837–1891) was Robert E. Lee's second son and the third of his seven children. He served as a Confederate cavalry officer during the war, rising in rank from captain to major general.

515.30 Smith Lee] Sydney Smith Lee (1802–1869) was an officer in the U.S. Navy, 1820–61. Lee served in the U.S.-Mexican War, commanded Matthew Perry's flagship in the squadron that visited Japan in 1853, and was superintendant of the Philadelphia navy yard before resigning his commission in April 1861. During the Civil War he held a series of shore commands in the Confederate navy.

515.37 Blücher] Field Marshal Gebhard Leberecht von Blücher (1742–1819) led the Prussian army that reached the Waterloo battlefield on the evening of June 18, 1815, as Napoleon was making his final attacks against the Duke of Wellington's positions.

517.7 Havelock's . . . the East] Sir Henry Havelock (1795–1857) led a relief column during the Indian Rebellion that left Allahabad on July 7, 1857, and captured Cawnpore on July 17. His troops fought their way through to the besieged residency at Lucknow on September 25, and reinforced its garrison until the siege was ended by Sir Colin Campbell on November 17. Havelock died of dysentery at Lucknow on November 24, 1857.

518.25 Harriet] Harriet Grant was a niece of Mary Chesnut.

520.2–3 Sans peur, sans reproche] Without peer, without reproach.

520.9 "J'en suis . . . coeur."] I am angry, with all my heart.

520.10–11 "Moi! malheureux . . . malheureux?'] Me! Unhappy! Or is it 'How unhappy I am?'

520.31–33 Mrs. Long . . . or cousin] Mary Sumner Long was the wife of Armistead Long, a Confederate officer, and the sister of Margaret Sumner McLean (see note 507.29). The sisters were distant cousins of Massachusetts Senator Charles Sumner.

520.34 Keitt, Boyce] Lawrence Keitt (1824–1864) was a Democratic congressman from South Carolina, 1853–60, and a member of the Confederate provisional congress, 1861. He became colonel of the 20th South Carolina Regiment in 1862 and was fatally wounded at the Battle of Cold Harbor in 1864. William Boyce (1818–1890) served as a Democrat in congress, 1853–60, and was a member of the Confederate Provisional Congress, 1861–62, and the Confederate House of Representatives, 1862–64.

525.3–4 "thanks of Congress"] McClellan was voted the "thanks of Congress" on July 16, 1861, for his successful campaign in western Virginia.

525.8 fait d'éclat] Glorious deed.

526.19–20    Commander Gen. Tyler] Brigadier General Andrew Tyler (1799–1882) commanded the First Division at Bull Run.

532.29    "Whoso would . . . save it,"] Cf. Matthew 16:25: "whosoever will lose his life for my sake shall find it."

541.37    the Prince] Napoleon Joseph Charles Paul Bonaparte (1822–1891), known as Prince Napoleon, was the first cousin of Napoleon III. He made a private visit to the United States and Canada, July 27–September 26, 1861, and crossed the lines to meet with Beauregard and Joseph Johnston at Manassas, August 8–9.

550.33    "Pelican Ranger."] A member of either Company G or Company D of the 3rd Louisiana Infantry.

551.7–8    stub-and-twist gun] A gun with barrels made from high quality scrap iron.

555.1–2    affair at Crane Creek] On August 2, 1861, Lyon's command skirmished with the Confederate advance guard at Dug Springs, near present-day Clever, Missouri, several miles from Crane Creek. In *With the Light Guns in '61–'65*, Woodruff described the aftermath of the skirmish: "General Rains' unattached Missourians in seeming hordes, came rushing south across the ford at Crane Creek, with any imaginable number and style of vehicles and people, mounted and on foot. Our advance had feigned a retreat on over-taking the enemy, and fallen back in expectation of bringing on an attack at the ford. The disorder was terrifying and had well nigh panicked the unat-tached and unarmed Missourians."

555.34    Exodus 4-4] Possibly a setting error for Exodus 14:24.

555.39    Snead's Fight for Missouri] Thomas Snead (1828–1890), *The Fight for Missouri, from the election of Lincoln to the death of Lyon* (1886). Snead served at Wilson's Creek as an aide to Sterling Price.

556.38    appendix] The appendix to *With the Light Guns in '61–'65* is not printed in this volume.

559.9    Totten] James Totten (c. 1818–1871), a career artillery officer who graduated from West Point in 1841, surrendered the federal arsenal at Little Rock to Arkansas state authorities on February 8, 1861. After serving in the western theater throughout the Civil War, Totten was dismissed from the army in 1870 after a court-martial convicted him of "neglect of duty" and "conduct to the prejudice of good order and military discipline."

559.29–30    President David Walker] Walker (1806–1879) was president of the Arkansas state convention that rejected, and then approved, secession in 1861. He was an associate justice of the Arkansas supreme court, 1848–57 and 1874–78, and served as its chief justice, 1866–68.

559.35–36    one-armed . . . Sweeny] Thomas Sweeny (1820–1892) came to the United States from Ireland in 1832 and lost his right arm at the Battle of Churubusco in 1847 while serving in a New York volunteer regiment during the U.S.-Mexican War. He later commanded a brigade at the Battle of Shiloh and a division during the 1864 Atlanta campaign.

560.13    "dutch"]    German.

566.5–6    Shields Green, . . . Denmark Vesey]    Shields Green (1836?–1859), a fugitive slave from Charleston, South Carolina, met John Brown in 1858 while Brown was staying with Frederick Douglass at his home in Rochester, New York. Green joined Brown's raid on Harpers Ferry and was captured, tried for murder, and hanged on December 16, 1859. Nat Turner (1800–1831) led a slave insurrection in Southampton County, Virginia, August 22–24, 1831, during which more than fifty white men, women, and children were killed. More than one hundred African Americans were killed without trial during the suppression of the revolt, and Turner and twenty others were executed. Denmark Vesey (1767?–1822) was a personal servant to slave-trader Joseph Vesey before winning a lottery in 1800 that allowed him to buy his freedom. In 1821–22 he planned a slave uprising in South Carolina set for July 14, 1822. Charleston authorities learned of the plot, and Vesey was executed along with thirty-four other black men.

569.19    Gen. Anderson]    See note 157.10.

570.8    Sam. Glover]    Samuel T. Glover (1813–1884) was an attorney in St. Louis.

570.10    Hurlbut]    Brigadier General Stephen A. Hurlbut (1815–1882), an attorney active in Illinois Republican politics who was serving under Frémont in Missouri, was accused of habitual drunkenness. Hurlbut did not resign and served in the Union army through the war.

574.3    located in Van Buren]    The U.S. district court for western Arkansas, which also had jurisdiction over Indian Territory, was located in Van Buren, Arkansas. In 1871 the court was moved to nearby Fort Smith.

576.25–26    Caspar's . . . George]    Captain Caspar Crowninshield (1837–1897), an 1860 graduate of Harvard College, commanded Company D of the 20th Massachusetts Infantry. He transferred to the 1st Massachusetts Cavalry in December 1861 and later served with the 2nd Massachusetts Cavalry, becoming its colonel in November 1864. Caspar Crowninshield was a cousin of Benjamin Crowninshield (see note 180.20). First Lieutenant George B. Perry was second-in-command of Company D.

577.6    Riddle . . . arm]    First Sergeant William Riddle had his right arm amputated above the elbow.

577.15–16    Baker's brigade]    Colonel Edward D. Baker (1811–1861) commanded the Third Brigade of Stone's Division. It was composed of four infantry regiments, only one of which, the 71st Pennsylvania (also known as the

1st California), fought at Ball's Bluff. Baker, a longtime friend of Abraham Lincoln, had served as a Whig congressman from Illinois, 1845–47 and 1849–51. He later moved to the Pacific coast and was a Republican senator from Oregon, 1860–61.

577.26    Col. Lee]    Colonel William Raymond Lee (1807–1891), commander of the 20th Massachusetts.

577.27    Gen. Baker]    Edward D. Baker had been appointed as a major general of U.S. volunteers, but had not decided whether he would accept the commission, which would require him to resign from the Senate.

577.19    rough sketch:]    The sketch is not reproduced in this volume. It depicts the deployment of Baker's troops and the 20th Massachusetts in a rectangular-shaped field with woods on either side, with "Rebels / Hill" written at the top and "Wooded banks / River" at the bottom. A note to the right of the sketch reads: "The Rebels had 2 inf & one cavalry regt. how full is not known," and a note to the left reads: "Engaged on our side 3 regs. consisting 700 of 15th Mass 300 of Mass 20th 700 men of Bakers brig."

578.1–2    Tremblet's company]    Captain Henry M. Tremlett (1833–1865) commanded Company A of the 20th Massachusetts. He later became the lieutenant colonel of the 39th Massachusetts Infantry and was fatally wounded at Gravelly Run, Virginia, on March 31, 1865.

578.7    Bartlett]    Captain William Francis Bartlett (1840–1876) was the commander of Company I, in which Henry Livermore Abbott served as second lieutenant. Bartlett lost a leg in the Peninsula Campaign in 1862, but continued to serve and was wounded again at Port Hudson in Louisiana, in the Battle of the Wilderness, and in the Petersburg mine assault, where he was captured. He inspired the poem "The College Colonel" by Herman Melville, published in *Battle-Pieces and Aspects of the War* (1866).

578.14    The general]    Edward D. Baker.

578.17    Frank]    Captain Bartlett.

578.38    adjutant & major]    First Lieutenant Charles Lawrence Peirson (1834–1920) was the adjutant of the 20th Massachusetts. He later served as lieutenant colonel of the 39th Massachusetts Infantry. Major Paul Joseph Revere (1832–1863), a grandson of the Revolutionary War hero, became the commander of the 20th Massachusetts in April 1863 and was fatally wounded at Gettysburg on July 2.

579.13    col., major & adjutant are prisoners]    Lieutenant Peirson was exchanged on January 27, 1862, and Colonel Lee and Major Revere were paroled on February 23 and exchanged on April 30. Lee resumed command of the regiment during the Peninsula Campaign and led it until after the Battle of Antietam, when he suffered a breakdown and resigned his commission.

579.14     Capt. Dreher is nearly dead]   Ferdinand Dreher (c. 1831–1863), a
German émigré who commanded Company C, survived his wound. He returned to the regiment in 1862 and was fatally wounded at Fredericksburg.

579.15     Capt. Putnam's arm is amputated]   John C. Putnam, the commander of Company H, survived his surgery.

579.17     Lieut. Putnam]   Second Lieutenant William Lowell Putnam
(1840–1861), the son of the writer Mary Lowell Putnam (1810–1898) and a
nephew of James Russell Lowell (see Biographical Notes), died on October 22.

579.18     Lieut. Holmes]   Oliver Wendell Holmes Jr. (1841–1935) was later
wounded in the neck at Antietam and in the foot at the Second Battle of
Fredericksburg, and served with the 20th Massachusetts until his three-year
enlistment expired in July 1864. Holmes later served as an associate justice of
the Massachusetts supreme judicial court, 1883–99, as its chief justice, 1899–
1902, and as an associate justice of the U.S. Supreme Court, 1902–32.

579.19     Lieut. Lowell]   First Lieutenant James Jackson Lowell (1837–1862),
a nephew of James Russell Lowell, returned to the regiment in February 1862
and was fatally wounded at the Battle of Glendale on June 30.

579.23–24     Col. Palfrey]   Lieutenant Colonel Francis Winthrop Palfrey
(1831–1889) had remained at Camp Benton. Palfrey served with the 20th
Massachusetts until Antietam, where he was disabled by a severe shoulder
wound.

579.26     Gen. Lander]   Brigadier General Frederick W. Lander (1821–1862)
commanded the Second Brigade of Stone's Division, to which the 20th Massachusetts was assigned.

581.24     Stone]   Brigadier General Charles Stone (1824–1887) commanded
a division in the Army of the Potomac and was Colonel Edward Baker's immediate superior. Stone was later blamed for the defeat at Ball's Bluff by the
congressional Joint Committee on the Conduct of the War and fell under
suspicion of disloyalty. He was arrested on February 9, 1862, and imprisoned
without charge for 189 days. After his release Stone served in various staff and
command assignments before resigning from the army in September 1864.

581.27–28     Cogswell is a prisoner]   Colonel Milton Cogswell (1825–1882),
the commander of the 42nd New York Infantry, crossed the Potomac with a
company of his regiment on the afternoon of October 21, 1861, and assumed
command of the Union forces at Ball's Bluff after Edward Baker was killed.
Cogswell was paroled in March 1862 and exchanged six months later.

582.7     Wade, Trumbull & Chandler]   Benjamin Wade (see Biographical
Notes); Lyman Trumbull (1813–1896) was a Republican senator from Illinois,
1855–73; Zachariah Chandler (1813–1879) was a Republican senator from
Michigan, 1857–75, and secretary of the interior, 1875–77.

582.15    wounded friend Col Kelley]   Benjamin F. Kelley (1807–1891) had been wounded during the Union victory at Philippi in western Virginia on June 3, 1861.

582.17    Romney]   A town on the South Branch of the Potomac River in northern Virginia (now West Virginia).

584.17    the little duke (Chartres)]   Robert Philippe d'Orléans, duc de Chartres (1840–1910), grandson of the deposed French monarch Louis-Philippe, and his brother Louis-Philippe d'Orléans, comte de Paris (1838–1894), served as aides to McClellan from September 1861 to July 1862.

584.22    saying nothing about Halleck.]   Scott had wanted Major General Henry W. Halleck (1815–1872) to replace him as general-in-chief.

585.25    Your historical examples]   In a letter to Charles Francis Adams Jr. dated October 15, 1861, Henry Adams cited the popular support shown for the ministry led by William Pitt the younger (1759–1806) in 1795 despite a series of defeats in the war with revolutionary France, and then wrote: "The English have the true bull-dogs grip, and that is what we must have if we expect to do anything either in victory or in defeat."

585.28    unwilling King the elder Pitt]   William Pitt the elder (1708–1778) became leader of the House of Commons and secretary of state for the southern department in December 1756 despite the opposition of George II. Pitt used his offices to successfully direct British foreign and military policy in the Seven Years' War and presided over a series of victories in Canada, the West Indies, and India before resigning in 1761.

585.29    Holt in the War Department]   Joseph Holt (1807–1894), a leading Kentucky unionist, had served as postmaster general, March 1859–December 1860, and as secretary of war from January 1861 until the end of the Buchanan administration. Holt was appointed judge advocate general of the U.S. Army in September 1862 and held the position until 1875.

585.30–31    Mr. Dana]   Richard Henry Dana (1815–1882), the author of *Two Years Before the Mast* (1840) and a prominent Boston attorney active in Massachusetts Republican politics. Dana, a friend of Charles Francis Adams Sr., served as U.S. attorney for Massachusetts, 1861–66.

586.3    Independents]   *The Independent*, a weekly journal published in New York.

587.17    Van Vliet]   Brigadier General Stewart Van Vliet (1815–1901) was chief quartermaster of the Army of the Potomac, August 1861–July 1862.

588.16    "festina lente"]   Make haste slowly.

588.36    Bayard Smith]   Margaret Bayard Smith (1778–1844), a leading figure in early nineteenth-century Washington society and author of the novels *A Winter in Washington* (1824) and *What Is Gentility?* (1828).

589.6–7    the O & M]  The Ohio and Mississippi Railroad.

591.31–32    Genl. McClernand]  Brigadier General John A. McClernand (1812–1900) had served as a Democratic congressman from Illinois, 1843–51 and 1859–61. In the spring and summer of 1861 McClernand helped rally southern Illinois to the Union cause.

592.21–22    Parrott guns]  Muzzle-loading rifled cannon, named after the New York ordnance manufacturer Robert R. Parrott (1804–1877).

593.11    Gen. Polk]  Major General Leonidas Polk (1806–1864) commanded the Confederate forces at Columbus, Kentucky.

593.18    Col. Scott's regiment]  The 12th Louisiana Infantry, commanded by Thomas L. Scott (1829–1876).

593.27–30    Sixth Iowa . . . Seventh Iowa]  The 7th Iowa Infantry fought at Belmont, the 6th Iowa Infantry did not.

593.36    the Fourth regiment]  The 4th Tennessee Infantry, commanded by Rufus P. Neely (1808–1901).

594.24–27    General Pillow . . . Cheatham]  Gideon Pillow (see note 348.32) and Brigadier General Benjamin F. Cheatham (1820–1886) were Polk's principal subordinate commanders at Belmont.

595.12    poor, gallant Armstrong]  Captain J. Welby Armstrong, a Memphis schoolmaster serving with the 2nd Tennessee Infantry, was killed by artillery fire.

595.14–15    Captain Billy Jackson]  William H. Jackson (1835–1903) later commanded a Confederate cavalry division in the western theater.

595.16–17    Jimmy Walker . . . not recover]  Walker died of his wounds.

596.14–15    steamer, . . . very bad condition]  The *Coatzacoalcos* had been damaged in the gale that scattered the Port Royal expedition on November 1, 1861, three days after it sailed from Hampton Roads, Virginia.

597.34    fine Fresnel lens]  A compound lens used in lighthouses, developed by Augustin-Jean Fresnel (1788–1827).

598.4–5    Mr. *Rhett*'s house . . . General Drayton's headquarters]  Robert Barnwell Rhett (1800–1876) was a leading South Carolina secessionist and publisher of the *Charleston Mercury*. Brigadier General Thomas F. Drayton (1808–1891) commanded the Confederate defenses at Port Royal.

598.6–7    Mons. de Ribaudiere]  Jean Ribault (c. 1520–1565) established a fort at Port Royal in 1562. The fort was abandoned in the spring of 1563 when the garrison built a small boat and sailed for France.

600.11    *San Jacinto* and told of Mason and Slidell being on board!]  The U.S.S. *San Jacinto* intercepted the British mail packet *Trent* off Cuba on

November 8, 1861, and seized Confederate envoys James Mason (see note 145.8) and John Slidell (see note 187.27).

600.31    Ripley]   Brigadier General Roswell S. Ripley (1823–1887) commanded the defenses at Charleston, South Carolina.

600.35–36    the *North American*]   The *Philadelphia North American.*

601.36    a proclamation]   Sherman issued a proclamation addressed to "the People of South Carolina" on November 8, 1861. The proclamation concluded: "The obligation of suppressing armed combinations against the constitutional authorities is paramount to all others. If in the performance of this duty other minor but important obligations should be in any way neglected, it must be attributed to necessities of the case, because rights dependent on the laws of the State must be necessarily subordinate to military exigencies created by insurrection and rebellion."

604.1    He come to Beaufort]   Similar stories of Lincoln visiting the South before the war, often without being recognized, were recorded in the 1920s and 1930s in the oral histories of former slaves from Missouri, Arkansas, Tennessee, Mississippi, and North Carolina.

604.2    Col. Paul Hamilton]   Hamilton (1762–1816) was governor of South Carolina, 1804–6, and secretary of the navy, 1809–12.

607.30    "sum of all villainies."]   John Wesley (1703–1791) described the slave trade as "that execrable sum of all villainies" in a 1772 journal entry. The phrase was later used by American abolitionists to describe slavery in the United States.

607.37–38    horrid scenes of St. Domingo]   See note 172.14–15.

608.36–37    "He knoweth . . . our uprising;"]   Cf. Psalm 139:2.

609.7–8    his blood . . . our children!"]   Matthew 27:25.

609.21–22    We should . . . delight]   From the hymn "How vain are all things here below" by Isaac Watts (1674–1748).

609.28–29    "All things . . . love God,"]   Romans 8:28.

609.30    "rejoices in tribulations, also."]   Romans 5:3.

611.10    "avenge not yourselves!"]   Romans 12:19.

611.17    Samuel . . . witch of Endor.]   See 1 Samuel 28:7–20.

611.36    "whom the Lord . . . chasteneth."]   Hebrews 12:6.

611.36–37    "It is the . . . him good."]   1 Samuel 3:18.

612.3–4    "the wicked which is his sword"]   Psalm 17:13.

612.29    at Leesburg]   Leesburg, Virginia, near the site of the Battle of Ball's Bluff, October 21, 1861.

613.1    Springfield, and Lexington] Springfield was a Confederate name for the Battle of Wilson's Creek, August 10, 1861. Confederate troops commanded by Sterling Price captured Lexington, Missouri, on September 20, 1861.

613.2    Columbus.] The Battle of Belmont, November 7, 1861, was fought across the river from Columbus, Kentucky.

613.18    "Thus far shalt thou go, and no farther."] Cf. Job 38:11.

613.31    "The sword . . . of Gideon!"] Judges 7:20.

614.37–38    "Be still . . . in the earth!"] Psalm 46:10.

615.12    Mr. Memminger] See note 94.9–11.

615.20    ship laden with weapons] The steamer *Fingal* reached Savannah, Georgia, on November 12, 1861, carrying fifteen thousand rifles and two million rounds of ammunition purchased by Confederate agents in Britain.

616.38–39    "his thoughts are very deep,"] Cf. Psalm 92:5.

618.6–7    "though he slay me yet will I trust in him."] Job 13:15.

619.33–37    God is our . . . thereof, Selah!] Psalm 46:1–3.

619.37–38    The Lord . . . refuge, Selah!"] Psalm 46:7.

620.10    love mercy . . . before God] Micah 6:8.

620.18–19    Sihon . . . king of Bashan] See Numbers 21:21–26 and Numbers 21:33–35.

620.27    whole head . . . is faint] Isaiah 1:5.

621.38    The bloodthirsty Jeffreys] George Jeffreys (1648–1689), lord chief justice of England, 1683–85, conducted the notorious "Bloody Assizes" following Monmouth's Rebellion in 1685 that resulted in approximately 200 executions.

622.16–17    "all the Kingdoms . . . glory of them"] Matthew 4:8.

625.40–626.1    "thy people shall all be righteous,"] Isaiah 60:21.

626.11–14    Nation would . . . ploughshares] Isaiah 2:4.

628.18    Bull Run] The Confederate name for the skirmish at Blackburn's Ford, July 18, 1861.

631.11–13    a link of . . . Greensboro] The 48-mile-long Piedmont Railroad linking Danville and Greensboro was completed in late May 1864.

633.3    The distinguished gentlemen] James Mason and John Slidell.

633.24    Mr. Faulkner] Charles J. Faulkner (1806–1884) was a Whig, and then Democratic, congressman from Virginia, 1851–59. He was appointed

U.S. minister to France in January 1860 by President Buchanan, but was replaced by the Lincoln administration in March 1861. On August 12, 1861, Faulkner was arrested in Washington, D.C., where he had gone to settle his accounts. Although he was never formally charged, press reports alleged that he had purchased arms for the Confederacy while serving in France. Faulkner was exchanged on December 25, 1861, for Alfred Ely (1815–1892), a Republican congressman from upstate New York who had been captured by the Confederates at Bull Run.

634.1–2    "blockades to be . . . at Paris]    The Declaration of Paris on the maritime laws of war was signed on April 16, 1856, by Great Britain, France, Austria, Sardinia, Russia, and Turkey.

639.17    Lagow]    First Lieutenant Clark Lagow (1828–1867), Grant's aide-de-camp.

645.12–13    Earl Russell]    See note 409.15.

645.14    revocation of Mr. Bunch's Exequatur]    The Lincoln administration revoked the exequatur (official recognition of consular credentials) of Robert Bunch, the British consul at Charleston, South Carolina, after learning that he had held diplomatic conversations with Confederate authorities. Bunch remained in Charleston until February 1863, but had his vice-consul assume responsibility for signing official documents.

645.17    last three articles of the Paris Declaration]    The Declaration of Paris (see note 634.1–2) contained four articles. The first article abolished privateering; the second and third articles made both enemy goods carried on neutral ships and neutral goods carried on enemy ships free from capture, unless contraband of war; the fourth article required that to be legally binding, blockades "must be effective; that is to say maintained by a force sufficient really to prevent access to the enemy's coastline."

645.24    Lord Palmerston]    Henry John Temple, third Viscount Palmerston (1784–1865) served as foreign secretary, 1830–34, 1835–41, and 1846–51, as home secretary, 1852–55, and as prime minister, 1855–58 and 1859–65.

646.5    Secretary at War]    A civilian official responsible for managing the finances of the British army. Palmerston held the position from 1809 to 1828.

646.21    Capt. Wilkes]    Charles Wilkes (1798–1877) was commissioned as a midshipman in 1818 and had commanded an expedition that explored Antarctica and the Pacific Northwest, 1838–42.

646.24–25    Eustis, & Macfarlane]    George Eustis (1828–1872), secretary to John Slidell, and James Edward MacFarland (1829–1897), secretary to James Mason.

647.25    Mr. Bright]    A prominent orator and reformer who served in the House of Commons, 1843–88, John Bright (1811–1889) was a leading British supporter of the Union cause.

647.29    Mr. Layard] Sir Austen Layard (1817–1894) was undersecretary for foreign affairs, 1861–66.

647.34    Wilson] Charles L. Wilson (1818–1878), owner of the *Chicago Daily Journal*, was first secretary of the London legation, 1861–64.

648.4–5    orders . . . James Adger] Commander John B. Marchand (1808–1875), the captain of the U.S.S. *James Adger*, sailed from New York on October 16, 1861, with orders to intercept the Confederate warship *Nashville*, which was believed to be carrying Mason and Slidell to England. The British government had received reports that Marchand while drunk had admitted to having been ordered to remove the Confederate envoys from a British mail steamer.

648.16–17    Moncton Milnes] Richard Monckton Milnes (1809–1885), a poet, writer, literary patron, biographer of John Keats, and a member of parliament from 1837 to 1863, when he was made Baron Houghton.

648.28–29    the Nashville] A side-wheel steamer that sailed between New York and Charleston, the *Nashville* was seized by the Confederates and refitted as a commerce raider. She was destroyed by the Union navy in the Ogeechee River, Georgia, in February 1863.

649.3    Horatio Ward's] Ward (1810–1868) was an American banker living in London.

649.8    arrival of the Fingal] See note 615.20.

649.21–22    Chester . . . the Martyr."] *John Rogers: the Compiler of the First Authorised English Bible; the Pioneer of the English Reformation; and Its First Martyr* (1861) by the American genealogist Joseph Lemuel Chester (1821–1882).

650.20    Fancy] Boxing fans.

652.1    Fairfax] Thomas Fairfax (1612–1671) was a commander of parliamentary forces during the English Civil War, 1642–45, and their commander in chief, 1645–50.

659.13–14    Judge McLean his circuit] John McLean (1785–1861) was appointed to the Supreme Court by President Jackson in 1829 and served until his death on April 4, 1861. His circuit included Michigan, Ohio, Indiana, and Illinois.

665.40    *pro tanto*] To that extent.

673.7–8    Caspar Crowninshield's] See note 576.25–26.

673.14–15    Sargent . . . Williams] Horace Binney Sargent (1821–1908) was the lieutenant-colonel, and Robert Williams (1829–1901) the colonel, of the 1st Massachusetts Cavalry.

673.40 Koh-i-noor] "Mountain of light," an Indian diamond weighing 191 carats (later recut to 108 carats) that became part of the British crown jewels after the annexation of Punjab in 1849.

678.3 *George Washington Custis Lee*] Lee (1832–1913) was serving as an aide to Jefferson Davis.

678.33 W H. Mary] White House, the Custis family plantation on the Pamunkey River in New Kent County, Virginia. Mary Custis Lee (1835–1918) was Robert E. Lee's second child and oldest daughter.

680.18 Greenbrier . . . Richmond.] Greenbrier was later renamed Traveller, and became the most famous of Robert E. Lee's wartime horses. Richmond died in the summer of 1862.

681.8 Mr. Eads] James B. Eads (1820–1887) was a leading engineer in St. Louis.

681.18 Mr. Gibson . . . Gov Gamble] Charles Gibson (1825–1899) acted as an agent in Washington, D.C., for the Unionist government of Missouri while serving as solicitor general of the U.S. court of claims, 1861–64. Hamilton Gamble (1798–1864), a former judge of the state supreme court, was elected provisional governor of Missouri by Unionist members of the state convention on July 31, 1861, and served until his death.

681.19 Genl Halleck] Major General Henry W. Halleck assumed command of the Department of Missouri on November 19, 1861.

681.26 chief of staff, Genl Marcey] Brigadier General Randolph Marcy (1812–1887), who was McClellan's father-in-law.

683.17 Assistant Secretary of War] Thomas A. Scott (1823–1881), a vice president of the Pennsylvania Railroad, served as assistant secretary of war, August 1861–June 1862.

683.24–25 Brigadier-General Franklin] William B. Franklin (1823–1903) commanded a division in the Army of the Potomac.

683.26 Secretary of the Treasury] Salmon P. Chase (1808–1873) was a Free Soil senator from Ohio, 1849–55, Republican governor of Ohio, 1856–60, secretary of the treasury, 1861–64, and chief justice of the U.S. Supreme Court, 1864–73.

683.33 General Buell] Brigadier General Don C. Buell (1818–1898) commanded the Army of the Ohio.

686.12 West Point.] West Point, Virginia, at the head of the York River.

686.37–39 General Burnside's expedition . . . Newbern] The expedition commanded by Brigadier General Ambrose Burnside sailed for North Carolina from Hampton Roads, Virginia, on January 11, 1862. Burnside captured Roanoke Island at the northern end of Pamlico Sound on February 8 and New Bern on March 14.

687.1        Beaufort]   Burnside captured Beaufort, North Carolina, on April 26, 1862.

687.27–28        annexed paper, marked (A)]   This paper is not included in this volume.

689.21–22        paper hereto annexed, marked (B)]   This paper is not included in this volume.

690.10        Ship Island]   An island in the Gulf of Mexico near Biloxi, Mississippi, that had been occupied by Union forces on September 17, 1861, and made into a base for future operations against New Orleans.

692.21        Tadd."]   Thomas (Tad) Lincoln (1853–1871), President Lincoln's youngest son.

693.2        *Charles A. Dana*]   Dana (1819–1897) was the managing editor of the *New York Tribune*, 1849–62, and the editor of the *New York Sun*, 1868–97. He served as a special commissioner for the War Department, 1862–63, and as assistant secretary of war, 1864–65.

# Index

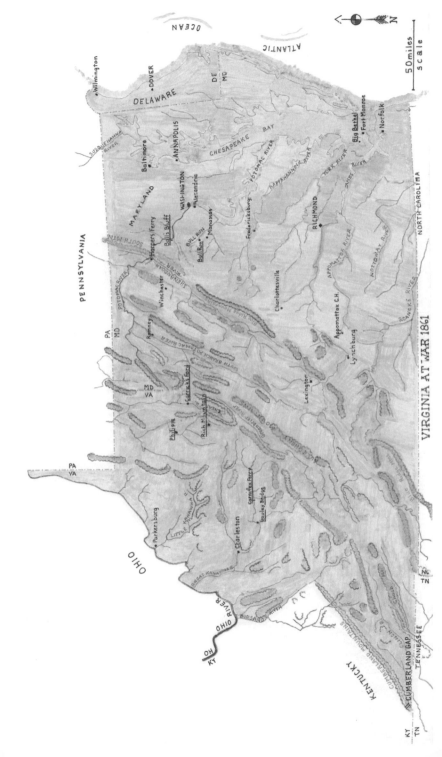

VIRGINIA AT WAR 1861